DOCUMENTARY HISTORY OF THE FIRST FEDERAL CONGRESS OF THE UNITED STATES OF AMERICA

March 4, 1789–March 3, 1791

LINDA GRANT DE PAUW, EDITOR

SPONSORED BY

THE NATIONAL HISTORICAL PUBLICATIONS COMMISSION

AND

THE GEORGE WASHINGTON UNIVERSITY

VOLUME II

SENATE EXECUTIVE JOURNAL AND RELATED DOCUMENTS

LINDA GRANT DE PAUW, Editor

CHARLENE BANGS BICKFORD, Assistant Editor

LAVONNE MARLENE SIEGEL, Assistant Editor

The Johns Hopkins University Press, Baltimore and London

057409

The Johns Hopkins University Press, Baltimore, Maryland 21218
The Johns Hopkins University Press Ltd., London

Library of Congress Catalog Card Number 73-13443
ISBN 0-8018-1572-X

Library of Congress Cataloging in Publication Data

United States. 1st Congress, 1789–1791. Senate.
  Senate executive journal and related documents.

  (Documentary history of the First Federal Congress of the United States of America,
March 4, 1789–March 3, 1791, v. 2)
  Bibliography: p.
  1. United States—Politics and government—1789–1797. I. De Pauw, Linda
Grant, ed. II. Title.
JK1059.D6 vol. 2 [JK1251]   328.73'01   73-13443
ISBN 0-8018-1572-X

CONTENTS

The Constitution of the United States provides that the executive powers of the President shall be shared by the Senate. In making treaties and in appointing officers of the United States, the President must seek the "advice and consent" of the Senate. Ever since the First Federal Congress the Senate, recognizing its special executive powers, has directed the Secretary of the Senate to keep a separate Senate Executive Journal, in which its executive activities are recorded.

This volume documents the executive activities of the First Senate. These include ratification of a consular convention with France and treaties with various Indian nations; unsuccessful attempts to free American prisoners in Algiers; and, most significant, approval of appointments to the entire corps of federal offices, thus establishing the human structure for Constitutional government. The volume is divided into two parts, the Senate Executive Journal proper and the related executive documents. There follows an appendix of brief biographies of the men appointed to federal offices, with a selected list of sources on those individuals.

Part I is based on the clean manuscript copy of the Senate Executive Journal as it was copied in Secretary Samuel A. Otis's office by clerks Benjamin Bankson and Samuel Otis, Jr. The Journal was not printed until 1828, when the Senate ordered all the Executive Journals for earlier years to be printed and then continued to order printing for all successive sessions.

The Journal has been reproduced exactly except that raised letters have been lowered and superfluous punctuation marks have been removed. Beginning or closing quotation marks have been added when these were obviously unintentionally omitted. The spellings of proper names have been regularized to conform to the signatures used by the individuals at the time of the First Congress, or, when these were unavailable, to conform to the most commonly used spellings.

As in Volume I, the Senate Legislative Journal, we have included cross-reference notes to enable the reader to follow action on a particular subject from day to day without consulting the index. All documents referred to in the Journal are identified by a footnote the first time they are mentioned. The note refers the reader to the point in Part II where the document is reproduced in full and also, where appropriate, identifies the document by Evans number[1] for the reader who may wish to consult Readex microcards. Docu-

[1] We use the term "Evans numbers" to apply to the numbers assigned to printed documents in any one of the three related bibliographies of early American imprints: Charles Evans, *American Bibliography*, vols. 7 and 8 (New York: Peter Smith, 1942); Clifford Shipton and James Mooney, *National Index of American Imprints through 1800, The Short-Title Evans* (Worcester: The American Antiquarian Society and Barre Pub-

ments reproduced in the Journal are not reprinted in Part II. If a document as printed in the Journal varies significantly from the original, the variation is described.

All documents forwarded to the Senate for consideration in advising and consenting to treaties and appointments and not printed in the Journal are reproduced in Part II. When a document could not be identified by a reference to the Journal itself, reference was made to executive messages, lists and dispatch books from the Office of Foreign Affairs, and the files of the Continental Congress Papers. As far as possible, the documents reproduced are those actually seen by the Senators. Thus, the French consular convention is reproduced from the signed and sealed original brought from Paris, but the letter of Governor Thomas Carleton to Governor John Hancock dated 21 June 1785 is reproduced from a copy made for the use of the Senate by a clerk in the Department of State. As with the Journal in Part I, we have reproduced the documents exactly except for the lowering of raised letters and the insertion of missing quotation marks. For documents in the Senate Records which were in French we have included contemporary English translations available to the Senators.

The documents in Part II are arranged topically according to the date journalized. Thus, the body of documentation on any topic is printed together according to when Congress first considered that topic. Within the topical category the documents are arranged according to when they were written.

The appendix relates to the Senate's work in filling executive offices. Although we have not attempted to do the work of prosopographers, exhaustively researching all the men nominated to federal offices, we have attempted to collect certain basic factual data on each of them and to list the main sources used in our research. Since most of the original government agents were obscure men, we expect that this data will make the significance of their appointments more apparent. Perhaps they may then be judged more charitably than they were by an anonymous Bostonian who wrote in 1789:

Ye Lucky Fav'rites! dandled—G-d knows why!

In the soft lap of pamper'd luxury;

Who reap the harvest of the lab'rer's toil,

And thankless fatten on unlawful spoil;

Who drain your country of her stinted store,

And wasting thousands—*yawn for thousands more.* . . ."

The editors wish to thank again all those thanked in volume one and to give special recognition to those who have helped on this second volume.

lishers, 1969); Roger Bristol, *Supplement to Charles Evans' American Bibliography* (Charlottesville: University Press of Virginia, 1970). The Readex Microprint Corporation's edition of *Early American Imprints, 1639–1800*, edited by Clifford Shipton, is keyed to these numbers.

We thank Charleston County Library, Connecticut Historical Society, Connecticut State Library, Fairfield Historical Society, Filson Club (Louisville, Kentucky), Historical Society of Delaware, Maine Historical Society, Maine State Library, Nantucket Historical Association, New London County Historical Society, Ohio Historical Society, Old Gaol Museum (York, Maine), State of North Carolina Department of Archives and History, University of Virginia Library, and Valentine Museum (Richmond, Virginia). The staffs of the Adams Papers and the Jefferson Papers were especially considerate of our elaborate requests for information. We are particularly indebted to Dorothy Twohig of the Washington Papers and to Paul Smith and Rosemary Plakas of the Library of Congress.

We are proud of the efforts of our many searchers: Susan Burns, Janet Fichman, Mary Giunta, Roberta Haber, Richard Marmaro, Judith Owens, Gail Ross, and especially Richard Pandich for completing the biographies and Helen Veit for her work on handwriting identification. They in turn appreciate the assistance given them by the staff of the National Archives and the National Historical Publications Commission, particularly James Brown, Roger Bruns, Joyce Eberly, H. B. Fant, Ken Harris, Sara Jackson, Faye Kidd, George Perros, Sandy Rangle, and Fred Shelley.

Finally, we want to thank Roger Davis for his preliminary work on the index for this volume, Mary Sittig for her transcription of the Journal, and Mary Barnes for bearing the heavy load of making document transcriptions and holding up an end of proofreading.

ASP	American State Papers
CC	Continental Congress
DLC	United States Library of Congress, Washington, D.C.
DNA	United States National Archives, Washington, D.C.
E	Evans number (with 5 digits)
M	Microcopy number
MHi	Massachusetts Historical Society, Boston, Massachusetts
RG	Record Group, located in the National Archives, Washington, D.C.

    11   General Records of the United States Government
    46   Records of the United States Senate—SR
    59   General Records of the Department of State
    360 Records of the Continental Congress and the Constitutional Convention—PCC

ILLUSTRATIONS

Bassett, Richard	Delaware
Butler, Pierce	South Carolina
Carroll, Charles	Maryland
Dalton, Tristram	Massachusetts
Dickinson, Philemon	New Jersey

(Took his seat on December 6, 1790, after being elected to fill the vacancy caused by the resignation of William Paterson.)

Ellsworth, Oliver	Connecticut
Elmer, Jonathan	New Jersey
Few, William	Georgia
Foster, Theodore	Rhode Island
Grayson, William	Virginia

(Died March 12, 1790.)

Gunn, James	Georgia
Hawkins, Benjamin	North Carolina
Henry, John	Maryland
Izard, Ralph	South Carolina
Johnson, William Samuel	Connecticut
Johnston, Samuel	North Carolina
King, Rufus	New York
Langdon, John	New Hampshire
Lee, Richard Henry	Virginia
Maclay, William	Pennsylvania
Monroe, James	Virginia

(Took his seat on December 6, 1790, after being elected to fill the vacancy caused by the death of William Grayson.)

Morris, Robert	Pennsylvania
Paterson, William	New Jersey

(Resigned on November 13, 1790, after being elected Governor of New Jersey.)

Read, George	Delaware
Schuyler, Philip	New York
Stanton, Joseph, Jr.	Rhode Island
Strong, Caleb	Massachusetts
Walker, John	Virginia

(Appointed to fill the vacancy caused by the death of William Grayson. Served from March 31 through November 9, 1790.)

Wingate, Paine	New Hampshire

The following is a list of the clerks who transcribed numerous documents printed in Part II.

SENATE SECRETARIES AND CLERKS
  Samuel A. Otis, secretary   (1789–1814)
  Benjamin Bankson   (1789–90)
  Samuel A. Otis, Jr.   (1790–91)

CONTINENTAL CONGRESS SECRETARIES AND CLERKS
  Roger Alden   (1785–89)
  Benjamin Bankson   (1781–89)
  George Bond   (1778–?)
  Charles Thomson   (1774–89)

OFFICE OF FOREIGN AFFAIRS AND DEPARTMENT OF STATE CLERKS
  Jacob Blackwell   (1785–98)
  John Marsden Pintard, French translator   (1785–90)
  Henry Remsen, Jr.   (1784–92)
  Walter Stone   (1783–?)
  George Taylor, Jr.   (1785–98)

WAR OFFICE CLERKS
  William Knox   (1789)
  John Stagg, Jr.   (1786–?)

SECRETARIES TO GEORGE WASHINGTON
  William Jackson   (1789–91)
  Tobias Lear   (1786–93)
  Robert Lewis   (1789–?)
  Thomas Nelson, Jr.   (1789–90)

PART I

SENATE EXECUTIVE JOURNAL

FIRST SESSION

MONDAY, May 25TH, 1789

The Senate being assembled,

General Knox brought the following Message from the President, which he delivered into the hands of the Vice President, and withdrew.

GENTLEMEN of the SENATE,

In pursuance of the Order of the late Congress, treaties between the United States and several Nations of Indians, have been negotiated and signed. These treaties, with sundry Papers respecting them, I now lay before you, for your consideration and advice, by the hands of General Knox, under whose official superintendence the business was transacted, and who will be ready to communicate to you any information on such points as may appear to require it.

New York, May 25th, 1789   GO. WASHINGTON[1]

The Secretary at War having examined the negotiations of the Governor of the Western territory with certain Northern and North western Indians, and the treaties made in consequence thereof at Fort Harmar on the 9th of January 1789, begs leave to

REPORT

That the several treaties of Peace which have been made with the northern tribes of Indians, and those North west of the Ohio, since the conclusion of the late War with Great Britain, are as follows. To wit:

---

[1] The message, in the hand of Tobias Lear and signed by George Washington, and the following report, in the hand of John Stagg, Jr., and signed by Henry Knox, are in President's Messages on Indian Relations, Executive Proceedings, RG 46, Records of the United States Senate (hereinafter RG 46 will be cited as SR), DNA. Annotations on the report refer to a later publication of U.S. Laws. A transcript of the report, in a nineteenth-century hand, probably made by ASP, is in the above location. The related documents are printed in Part II of this volume under the heading Indian Relations—Northern.

1st. The treaty at Fort Stanwix on the 22d day of October 1784, between Oliver Wolcott, Richard Butler and Arthur Lee Commissioners Plenipotentiary from the United States on the one part, and the Sachems and Warriors of the six Nations on the other.

2nd. The treaty entered into by the said Commissioners Plenipotentiary, and the Sachems and Warriors, of the Wyandot, Delaware, Chippawa, and Ottawa Nations of Indians at Fort McIntosh the 21st day of January 1785.

3d. The treaty at the mouth of the great Miami the 31st of January 1786, between Commissioners from the United States and the Chiefs and Warriors of the Shawonoe Nation.

That the treaties of Fort Stanwix and Fort McIntosh were entered on the Journals of the United States in Congress assembled, June 3d 1785, and the treaty of the Miame, on the 17th day of April 1786.

That it may be proper to observe that the Indians are greatly tenacious of their Lands, and generally do not relinquish their right, excepting on the principle of a specific consideration expressly given for the purchase of the same.

That the practice of the late english Colonies and Government in purchasing the indian claims has firmly established the habit in this respect, so that it cannot be violated, but with difficulty and an expence greatly exceeding the value of the Object.

That the treaties of Fort Stanwix and of Fort McIntosh, do not state, that the limits therein defined are by virtue of a purchase from the Indians.

That the said treaties have been opposed and complained of, will appear by the representation to Congress accompanying this Report, marked No. 1.

That in consequence of the said Representation Congress on the 21st day of July 1787, passed the following Resolve:

"RESOLVED, That the Superintendant of Indian affairs for the northern department, inform the five Nations—the Hurons and other Indian Nations who joined in the representation made to Congress dated the 18th day of December 1786, that Congress on the 18th of the present Month July 1787, received their said Representation, and have taken it into their serious consideration and in due time will send them an answer."

That on the 5th of October following Congress,

"RESOLVED, That a general treaty be held with the tribes of Indians within the limits of the United States inhabiting the Country north west of the Ohio, and about Lake Erie as soon after the first of April next, as conveniently may be and at such place and at such particular time as the Governor of the Western Territory shall appoint for the purpose of knowing the causes of uneasiness among the said tribes, and hearing their complaints, of regulating trade and amicably settling all affairs concerning lands and boundaries between them and the United States.

"That the Governor of the Western Territory hold the said Treaty, agreeably to such instructions as shall be given him for that purpose."

That on the 12th of October 1787, Congress Resolved—

"That twenty thousand dollars be and hereby are appropriated for the purpose of Indian treaties whenever the same shall hereafter be judged necessary by a majority of the United States in Congress Assembled, and that the Resolutions for holding a general treaty with the Indians passed the fifth day of the present Month be and they are hereby repealed."

That on the 22d day of October 1787, Congress Resolved—

"That the Governor of the Western territory be and he is hereby empowered to hold a general treaty with the[2] Indian tribes the ensuing Spring if in his Judgment the Public good requires it, and that he be authorised to draw for such sums of Money appropriated by the Resolve of Congress of the 12th instant, as may be necessary to effect this Object not exceeding the[3] sum of fourteen thousand Dollars."

That on the 2nd of July 1788, Congress Resolved—

"That the sum of twenty thousand dollars in addition to the fourteen thousand dollars already appropriated, be appropriated for defraying the expences of the treaties which have been ordered or which may be ordered to be held on the present year, with the several Indian tribes in the northern department and for extinguishing the Indian claims; the whole of the said twenty thousand dollars, together with six thousand dollars of the said fourteen thousand dollars to be applied solely to the purpose of extinguishing Indian claims to the lands they have already ceded to the United States, by obtaining regular Conveyances for the same, and for extending a purchase beyond the limits hitherto fixed by treaty; but that no part of the said sums be applied for any purpose, other than those abovementioned."[4]

---

[2] The rough CC Journal includes the word "adjacent" at this point.
[3] The rough CC Journal includes the words "whole the" at this point.
[4] The preceding resolutions are in RG 360, Papers of the Continental Congress, 1774–1789 (hereinafter RG 360 will be cited as PCC), item 1, M247, roll 14, DNA.

That the instructions to the Governor of the Western territory marked No. 2 will further show the sense of Congress on this subject.

That the treaties of Fort Harmar on the 9th of January 1789, with the Sachems and Warriors of the six Nations, the Mohawks excepted, and with the Sachems and Warriors of the Wyandot, Delaware, Ottawa, Chippawa, Pattiwatima, and Sac nations, inhabiting part of the Country north west of the Ohio, appear to have been negotiated by the Governor of the Western territory, so as to unite the interests of the United States with the justice due the said Indian Nations.

That the reservation in the treaty with the six Nations of six Miles square round the Fort at Oswego, is within the territory of the State of New York and ought to be so explained, as to render it conformable to the Constitution of the United States.

That if this explanation should be made, and the Senate of the United States should concur in their approbation of the said treaties, it might be proper that the same should be ratified, and published with a proclamation enjoining an observance thereof.

All which is humbly submitted to the President of the United States.

H. KNOX

War Office May 23d 1789

ORDERED, That the Message from the President, with the Papers accompanying the same, lie on the Table for consideration.[5]

---

[5] On June 12 a committee was appointed to consider this message and to report.

THURSDAY, JUNE 11TH, 1789

A Message from the President of the United States, was received by Mr. Jay.

GENTLEMEN of the SENATE,

A Convention between His Most Christian Majesty and the United States for the purposes of determining and fixing the functions and prerogatives of their respective Consuls, Vice Consuls, Agents and Commissaries, was signed by their respective Plenipotentiaries on the 29th of July 1784.

It appearing to the late Congress that certain alterations in that Convention ought to be made, they instructed their Minister at the Court of France to endeavour to obtain them. It has accordingly been altered in several respects, and as amended was signed by the Plenipotentiaries of the contracting Powers on the 14th of November 1788.

The sixteenth Article provides, that it shall be in force during the term of twelve years, to be counted from the day of the exchange *of Ratifications, which shall be given in proper form,* and exchanged on both sides within the space of one year, or sooner if possible.

I now lay before you the original, by the hands of Mr. Jay, for your consideration and advice. The Papers relative to this negotiation are in his custody, and he has my orders to communicate to you whatever official Papers and information on the subject, he may possess and you may require.

New York June 11th 1789   GO. WASHINGTON
                               Prest. of the United States[6]

The Message being read, was ordered to lie for consideration.[7]

FRIDAY, JUNE 12TH, 1789

Proceeded to the consideration of the President's Message of 25th Ultimo, respecting the Indian treaties held by Govr. St. Clair, with the Chiefs of the six Nations—and appointed
           Mr. Few
           Mr. Read &

---

[6] The message, in the hand of Tobias Lear and signed by George Washington, is in President's Messages on Foreign Relations, Executive Proceedings, SR, DNA. The related documents are printed in Part II of this volume under the heading Consular Convention with France.

[7] On June 12 John Jay was ordered to furnish the Senate with translations of the Consular Convention.

Mr. Henry, a Committee thereon.[8]

The Message from the President of the 11th of June, was again read—Whereupon,

ORDERED, that Mr. Jay furnish the Senate with an accurate translation of the Consular Conventions between his Most Christian Majesty and the United States, and a Copy thereof for each Member of Senate.

The farther consideration of the President's Message of June 11th, was postponed.[9]

TUESDAY, JUNE 16TH, 1789

A Message from the President, by Mr. Jay—

GENTLEMEN of the SENATE,

Mr. Jefferson the present Minister of the United States at the Court of France, having applied for permission to return home for a few Months, and it appearing to me proper to comply with his request, it becomes necessary that some Person be appointed *to take charge* of our Affairs at that Court during his absence.

For this purpose I nominate WILLIAM SHORT Esquire, and request your advice on the propriety of appointing *him*.

There are in the Office for foreign Affairs Papers which will acquaint you with his Character, and which Mr. Jay has my directions to lay before you at such time as you may think proper to assign.

New York June 15th 1789   GO. WASHINGTON[10]

ORDERED, that Mr. Jay lay before the Senate to morrow at 12 o'Clock, the Papers referred to in the President's Message of this day, relative to the Character of Mr. Short.

ORDERED, that the Message from the President lie for consideration.[11]

---

[8] On August 12 this committee reported, and consideration of the report was postponed.

[9] On June 17 John Jay was ordered to lay all papers relating to the Consular Convention before the Senate.

[10] The message, in the hand of Tobias Lear and signed by George Washington, is in Executive Nominations, first session, Executive Proceedings, SR, DNA. The related documents are printed in Part II of this volume under the heading Nomination of William Short.

[11] On June 17 John Jay brought the requested papers to the Senate, and William Short's nomination was considered.

W E D N E S D A Y, JUNE 17TH, 1789

Agreeably to the Order of yesterday, Mr. Jay brought to the Senate the Papers referred to in the President's Message received the 16th.[12]

ORDERED, that Mr. Jay examine the translation of the Consular Convention and report his opinion as to its fidelity, and that he lay before the Senate all the Papers in his Custody relative to the negotiations and whatever official Papers and information on the subject, he may possess.[13]

Proceeded to consider the Nomination of WILLIAM SHORT Esquire, to take charge of the Affairs of the United States at the Court of Versailles as contained in the President's Message received the 16th.[14]

T H U R S D A Y, JUNE 18TH, 1789

The Senate proceeded in the consideration of the President's Message on the Nomination of WILLIAM SHORT Esquire.

RESOLVED, that the consent of the Senate to the President's Nomination of Officers be given by ballot—The negative being shewn by a blank ballot, and the affirmative by the word "Aye."

The Senate proceeded by ballot to determine upon the nomination of WILLIAM SHORT Esquire, agreeably to the President's Message of the 16th and,

RESOLVED, that the President of the United States be informed, that the Senate advise and consent to his appointment of WILLIAM SHORT Esquire, to take Charge of our Affairs at the Court of France, during the absence of the Minister Plenipotentiary at that Court.

ORDERED, that an authenticated Copy of the above Resolve be transmitted to Mr. Jay for communication.

---

[12] The Daily Journal of the Office of Foreign Affairs notes the document that John Jay brought to the Senate. The journal is in PCC, item 127, vol. II, M247, roll 142, DNA.

[13] On July 21 the Senate ordered John Jay to appear before them on July 22.

[14] On June 18 William Short's nomination was agreed to.

T U E S D A Y, July 21st, 1789

ORDERED, That the Secretary of Foreign Affairs be requested, to attend the Senate to Morrow at 12 O'Clock, and to bring with him such Papers as are requisite to give full information, relative to the Consular Convention between France and the United States.[15]

W E D N E S D A Y, July 22nd, 1789

The Secretary of Foreign Affairs attended, agreeably to the order of yesterday—and made the necessary explanations.[16]

WHEREAS a Convention refered this day to the Senate, bears reference to a Convention pending between the Most Christian King and the United States, previous to the adoption of our present Constitution.

RESOLVED, That the Secretary of foreign Affairs, under the former Congress, be requested to peruse the said Convention, and to give his opinion how far he conceives the faith of the United States to be engaged, either by former agreed Stipulations, or Negotiations, entered into by our Minister at the Court of Versailles to ratify, in its present sense or form, the Convention now referred to the Senate.[17]

M O N D A Y, July 27th, 1789

The Secretary of Foreign Affairs reported his opinion upon the Consular Convention, between France and the United States as follows:

Office for Foreign Affairs 25th July 1789

The Secretary of the United States for the department of Foreign Affairs, under the former Congress, in pursuance of the Resolution of the 22nd of July 1789

REPORTS,

That he has compared the two Conventions of 1784 and 1788.

---

[15] On July 22 John Jay brought these papers to the Senate, and the Senate requested that he give his opinion on the Convention.

[16] The documents which John Jay was directed to bring to the Senate are printed in Part II of this volume under the heading Consular Convention with France. A list from the Daily Journals of the Office of Foreign Affairs, dated July 22, 1789, and located in PCC, item 127, vol. II, M247, roll 142, DNA, records the papers that came into the Senate.

[17] The resolution, in the hand of Pierce Butler, is in Senate Simple Resolutions and Motions, SR, DNA. The word "Versaills" is crossed out, and "Versailles" is written below it in the hand of Samuel Otis. On July 27 John Jay made a report on the Convention.

That the Copies of them, received from Mr. Jefferson, and now before the Senate, are so printed and their Variations so clearly marked, as that he cannot contrast them in a Manner better calculated for an easy and accurate comparison.

That, in his opinion, there exist, in the Convention of 1788, no Variations from the original Scheme sent to Doctor Franklin in 1782; nor from the Convention of 1784, but such as render it less ineligible than either of the other two.

That, although he apprehends that this Convention will prove more inconvenient than beneficial to the United States, yet he thinks that the Circumstances under which it was formed render its being ratified, by them indispensable.

The Circumstances alluded to are these.

The original Scheme of 1782, however exceptionable, was framed and agreed to by Congress.

The Convention of 1784 was modelled by that Scheme, but, in certain Instances, deviated from it; but both of them were to be perpetual in their Duration.

On Account of those Deviations, Congress refused to ratify it, but promised to ratify one corresponding with the Scheme, provided its Duration was limited to eight or ten Years; but they, afterwards extended it to twelve.

By an Instruction to Mr. Jefferson of 3d October 1786, he was, among other things, directed to propose to the King "That the said Convention be so amended as perfectly to correspond with the Scheme in every Part, where a Deviation from the same is not permitted by the said Act (of 1782) And, further, that he represent to his Majesty the Desire of Congress to make the said Convention probationary, by adding a Clause for limiting its Duration to eight or ten Years. That he assure his Majesty of the Determination of Congress to observe, on all occasions, the highest Respect for Candor, and good Faith, in all their Proceedings, and that, on receiving the Convention so amended, and with such a Clause, they will immediately ratify it."

In the Letter which accompanied these Instructions is the following paragraph.

"The original Scheme of the Convention is far from being unexceptionable, but, a former Congress having agreed to it, it would be improper now to recede; and, therefore, Congress are content to ratify a Convention made conformable to that Scheme, and to their Act of 25th January 1782, provided a Clause limiting its Duration be added."

On the 27th July 1787 Congress gave to Mr. Jefferson a Commission, in general Terms, to negotiate and conclude, with his Most Christian Majesty a Convention for regulating the Privileges, &c. of their respective Consuls.

In one of the Letters then written to him, is this Paragraph.

"Congress confide fully in your Talents and Discretion, and they will ratify any Convention that is not liable to more Objections than the one already in Part concluded, provided that an Article, limiting its duration to a Term not exceeding twelve Years, be inserted."

As the Convention in Question is free from several Objections to which the one of 1784 was liable, and is, in every Respect preferable to it, and as it contains a Clause limiting its Duration to twelve Years, it seems to follow as of necessary Consequence, that the United States ought to ratify it.

All which is submitted to the Wisdom of the Senate.

JOHN JAY[18]

WEDNESDAY, JULY 29TH, 1789

The Senate having duly considered the "Convention between his Most Christian Majesty and the United States of America, for the purpose of defining and establishing the Functions and Privileges of their respective Consuls and Vice Consuls" transmitted to the Senate by the President of the United States, thro' the Secretary for Foreign Affairs.

RESOLVED unanimously, That the Senate do consent to the said Convention and advise the President of the United States to Ratify the same.[19]

ORDERED, That the Secretary of the Senate carry an attested copy of the above resolution to the President of the United States.

---

[18] The report, in the hand of George Taylor, Jr., and signed by John Jay, is in President's Messages on Foreign Relations, Executive Proceedings, SR, DNA. The resolution of July 22, 1789, prefaces the report. The name Sam. A. Otis, noted at the end of the resolution, is lined out and the resolution crossed out, probably by an ASP editor. Filed with the report is an extract of Thomas Jefferson's letter dated November 14, 1788, in the hand of John Jay. The related documents, including Jefferson's entire letter, are printed in Part II of this volume under the heading Consular Convention with France. On July 29 the Senate consented to the Consular Convention, and the President was notified.

[19] The resolution, in the hand of Richard Henry Lee, is in Other Records, Executive Proceedings, SR, DNA.

	GEORGIA	
Districts & Ports	Officers	Nominations
2. Sunbury	Collector	Cornelius Collins
3. Brunswick	Collector	James Seagrove
4. St. Mary's	Collector	George Handley

New York
August 3d 1789

GO. WASHINGTON[23]

ON MOTION, to reconsider the Rule adopted the 18th June, relative to the mode of determining upon the Nominations by Ballot.

It Passed in the negative.

A MOTION,

"That a Committee be appointed to wait on the President of the United States, and confer with him on the mode of communication proper to be pursued between him and the Senate in the formation of Treaties and making appointments to Offices" was made

Postponed till to Morrow.[24]

&,

ON MOTION,

To dispense with Balloting upon the present occasion, and to consider the Nomination now before the Senate *viva vôce.*

It Passed in the Negative:

And it was agreed to proceed by Ballot, a Caveat being assented to, that it should not be considered as a precedent.

Agreed to begin with the State of New York, and proceeding to take into consideration the Nominations of Collectors, Naval Officers and Surveyors, contained in the Message from the President of the United States of this date,

[23] In the original document the Districts, Ports, and Officers for each state are in the hand of Tobias Lear, except Suffolk and Smithfield, Virginia, which are in the hand of George Washington. The nominations are in the hand of George Washington, except in the cases of Jonathan Fitch, Eli Elmer, John Scott, and James Gibbons, in which the first names are in the hand of Samuel Otis. These were probably filled in when the document came into the Senate. Gibbons's name is corrected from John, in Washington's hand, to James. Above the name of David Lambert are written the words "by order, Corbin Braxton for," in the hand of Benjamin Bankson. This correction conforms the list to Washington's message of August 5, 1789. Each nomination is marked "Aye" in the hand of Samuel Otis, except that of Benjamin Fishbourn, which is marked "Nay." "Wicassett" is spelled "Wiscassett" in the original list. Although Washington's message lists Rappahannock under Virginia no. 5, Tappahannock is the correct name for the district as set up by the Collection Bill [HR-11]. The Senate corrected the name when voting on the nomination.

[24] On August 6 a committee was appointed to confer with the President on this subject.

the Senate did advise and consent to the appointment of the following Officers of the Revenue,
  To wit:

For the State of NEW YORK

Districts & Ports	Names	Appointments
Sagg Harbour	John Gelston	Collector[25]
New York	John Lamb	Collector
	Benjamin Walker	Naval Officer
	John Lasher	Surveyor
City of Hudson	John C. Ten Broeck	Surveyor
Albany	Jeremiah Lansing	Surveyor[26]

For the State of CONNECTICUT

Districts & Ports	Names	Appointments
New London	Jedediah Huntington	Collector
	Nathaniel Richards	Surveyor
Stonington	Jonathan Palmer	Surveyor
Middletown	Asher Miller	Surveyor[27]
New Haven	Hezekiah Rogers	Surveyor
Fairfield	Samuel Smedley	Collector

For the State of NEW JERSEY

Districts & Ports	Names	Appointments
Perth Amboy	John Halstead	Collector
Burlington	John Ross	Collector

For the State of MASSACHUSETTS

Districts & Ports	Names	Appointments
Newbury Port	Stephen Cross	Collector
	Jonathan Titcomb	Naval Officer
	Michael Hodge	Surveyor
Gloucester	Epes Sargent	Collector
	Samuel Whittemore	Surveyor

---

[25] On May 25, 1790, the Senate was notified that John Gelston had resigned this appointment and Henry Dering had been nominated to replace him.

[26] On March 30, 1790, the Senate was notified that Jeremiah Lansing had resigned this office and Henry Bogart had been nominated to replace him.

[27] On February 9, 1790, the Senate was notified that Asher Miller had resigned this appointment and Comfort Sage had been nominated to replace him.

For the State of MASSACHUSETTS

Districts & Ports	Names	Appointments
Salem	Joseph Hiller	Collector
&	William Pickman	Naval Officer
	Bartholomew Putnam	Surveyor
Beverley	Josiah Batchelder	Surveyor
Ipswich	Jeremiah Staniford	Surveyor
Marblehead	Richard Harris	Collector[28]
Boston &	Benjamin Lincoln	Collector
Charlestown	James Lovell	Naval Officer
	Thomas Melvill	Surveyor
Plymouth	William Watson	Collector
Barnstable	Joseph Otis	Collector
Nantucket &		
Sherbourne	Stephen Hussey	Collector
Edgartown	John Pease	Collector
New Bedford	Edward Pope	Collector
Dighton	Hodijah Baylies	Collector
York	Richard Trevett	Collector
Biddeford &		
Pepperelborough	Jeremiah Hill	Collector
Portland &	Nathaniel F. Fosdick	Collector
Falmouth	James Lunt	Surveyor
Bath	William Webb	Collector
Wiscassett	Francis Cook	Collector
Penobscott	John Lee	Collector
Frenchman's Bay	Melatiah Jordan	Collector
Machias	Stephen Smith	Collector
Passamaquody	Lewis Frek. Delesdernier	Collector

For the State of NEW HAMPSHIRE

Districts & Ports	Names	Appointments
Portsmouth	Joseph Whipple	Collector
	Eleazer Russell	Naval Officer
	Thomas Martin	Surveyor

ORDERED, That the Secretary lay before the President of the United States, an authenticated Copy of the proceedings of Senate upon his Message of this day. Which was accordingly done.

---

[28] On August 2, 1790, the Senate was notified that Richard Harris had died and Samuel Gerry had been nominated to replace him.

TUESDAY, August 4th, 1789

Proceeded to consider the Nominations of Collectors, Naval Officers and Surveyors, contained in the Message from the President of the United States of the 3d of August, and advised and consented to the appointment of the following Persons,

To wit:

For the State of NEW JERSEY

Districts & Ports	Names	Appointments
Bridgetown	Eli Elmer	Collector

For the State of CONNECTICUT

Districts & Ports	Names	Appointments
New Haven	Jonathan Fitch	Collector

For the State of PENSYLVANIA

Districts & Ports	Names	Appointments
Philadelphia	Sharpe Dulany	Collector
	Frederick Phile	Naval Officer
	Samuel Meredith	Surveyor[29]

For the State of DELAWARE

Districts & Ports	Names	Appointments
Wilmington	George Bush	Collector

For the State of MARYLAND

Districts & Ports	Names	Appointments
Baltimore	Otho H. Williams	Collector
	Robert Purviance	Naval Officer
	Robert Ballard	Surveyor
Chester	John Scott	Collector[30]
Oxford	Jeremiah Banning	Collector
Vienna	John Muir	Collector
Snow Hill	John Gunby	Collector
Annapolis	John Davidson	Collector

[29] On September 11 Samuel Meredith was nominated to be Treasurer of the United States, and William McPherson was nominated to replace him as Surveyor.

[30] On December 17, 1790, the Senate was notified that John Scott had died and Jeremiah Nichols had been nominated to replace him.

For the State of MARYLAND

Districts & Ports	Names	Appointments
Nottingham	George Biscoe	Collector
Town Creek	Robert Young	Surveyor[31]
Nanjemoy	John Coates Jones	Collector
St. Mary's	Robert Chesley	Surveyor
George Town	Jas. Maccubbin Lingan	Collector

For the State of VIRGINIA

Districts & Ports	Names	Appointments
Hampton	Jacob Wray	Collector[32]
Norfolk & Portsmouth	William Lindsay	Collector
	Philemon Gatewood	Naval Officer
	Daniel Bedinger	Surveyor
Suffolk	Archibald Richardson	Surveyor[33]
Smithfield	James Wells	Surveyor
Bermuda Hundred or City Point	William Heth	Collector
City Point	Christopher Roane	Surveyor
Petersburg	James Gibbons	Surveyor
York Town	Abraham Archer	Collector
West Point	John Spotswood Moore	Surveyor
Tappahannock	Hudson Muse	Collector
Urbanna	Staige Davis	Surveyor[34]
Port Royal	George Catlett	Surveyor
Fredericksburg	William Lewis	Surveyor
Yeocomico River including Kinsale	Vincent Redman	Collector
Dumfries including Newport	Richd. Marshall Scott	Collector
Alexandria	Charles Lee	Collector
	Samuel Hanson	Surveyor
Cherry Stone	George Savage	Collector[35]

---

[31] On September 11 Charles Chilton was nominated for this position after Robert Young declined.

[32] On April 28, 1790, the Senate was notified that Jacob Wray had resigned this appointment and George Wray had been nominated to replace him.

[33] On May 25, 1790, the Senate was notified that Archibald Richardson had resigned this appointment and Benjamin Bartlett had been nominated to replace him.

[34] On September 11 Peter Kemp was appointed to this position after Staige Davis declined it.

[35] On May 25, 1790, the Senate was notified that George Savage had resigned this appointment and Nathaniel Wilkins had been nominated to replace him.

For the State of VIRGINIA

Districts & Ports	Names	Appointments
South Quay	Thomas Bowne	Collector
Louisville	Peyton Short	Collector[36]

For the State of SOUTH CAROLINA

Districts & Ports	Names	Appointments
George Town	John Cogdell	Collector
Charleston	George Abbott Hall	Collector
	Isaac Motte	Naval Officer
	Edward Weyman	Surveyor

For the State of GEORGIA

Districts & Ports	Names	Appointments
Savannah	John Habersham	Collector
	John Berrien	Surveyor
Sunbury	Cornelius Collins	Collector

State of SOUTH CAROLINA
  Beaufort ——— Agnew Collector
    Postponed for want of his Christian Name.

State of VIRGINIA
  Richmond ——— Surveyor
           Postponed.
  Folly Landing ——— Gibbs Collector
    Postponed for want of his Christian Name.

And the further Consideration of the Nominations for the State of Georgia, was postponed.

WEDNESDAY, AUGUST 5TH, 1789

A MESSAGE from the President of the United States, by Mr. Lear his Secretary

"GENTLEMEN of the SENATE,

---

[36] On February 9, 1790, the Senate was notified that Peyton Short had declined this appointment and Richard Taylor had been nominated to replace him.

"In the list of Nominations which I laid before you on the 3d Instant there was a mistake in giving in the name of David Lambert as Surveyor of the Port of Richmond.

"This mistake I now desire to correct by inserting in place thereof, the name of Corbin Braxton—

"August 5th 1789   "Go. WASHINGTON"[37]

Proceeded to consider the Nominations of Collectors, Naval Officers and Surveyors, contained in the Messages from the President of the United States of the 3d and 5th of August; and the Senate did advise and consent to the appointment of the following Persons—To wit:

	For the State of VIRGINIA	
Richmond	Corbin Braxton	Surveyor[38]

	For the State of GEORGIA	
Brunswick	George Handley	Collector[39]
St. Mary's	James Seagrove	Collector

Proceeded to consider the Nomination of Benjamin Fishbourn Naval Officer for the Port of Savannah, and upon the question to advise and consent to the appointment, it

---

[37] The message, in the hand of Tobias Lear and signed by George Washington, is in Executive Nominations, first session, Executive Proceedings, SR, DNA. The following letter, written by Tobias Lear and dated by Samuel Otis, is filed with the message.

Tobias Lear to Samuel A. Otis

Sir,

Among the nominations which were made by the President of the United States and yesterday laid before the Senate for their advice & consent—was the name of David Lambert for the Surveyor of Richmond in Virginia. The President understood that he had been the Searcher at that place under the State, and *therefore* put him in nomination as Surveyor, but he has this morning been informed that David Lambert has not been in the Office, or discharged the duties of Searcher; he therefore wishes the name of CORBIN BRAXTON to be substituted in the place of David Lambert—and has accordingly directed me to give you this information, that the change may be made before the nominations for Virginia are taken into consideration by the Senate of the United States.

I am Sir,
Your most Obedient
Humble Servant
TOBIAS LEAR

August 4th 1789

[38] On December 17, 1790, the Senate was notified that Corbin Braxton had resigned this appointment and Zachariah Rowland had been nominated to replace him.

[39] On February 9, 1790, the Senate was notified that George Handley had resigned this appointment and Christopher Hillary had been nominated to replace him.

Passed in the Negative.[40]

And the Secretary, according to order, laid a certified Copy of the Proceedings before the President of the United States.

A MOTION

"That it is the opinion of the Senate that their advice, and consent to the appointment of Officers should be given in the presence of the President" was,

Postponed until to morrow.

THURSDAY, AUGUST 6TH, 1789

ORDERED, that Mr. Izard

Mr. King, and

Mr. Carroll, be a Committee to wait on the President of the United States, and confer with him on the mode of communication proper to be pursued between him and the Senate, in the formation of Treaties, and making appointments to Offices.[41]

FRIDAY, AUGUST 7TH, 1789

Mr. Lear, the Secretary to the President of the United States, brought the following Messages to the Senate.

And he withdrew.

GENTLEMEN of the SENATE,

My Nomination of *Benjamin Fishbourn* for the place of Naval Officer of the Port of Savannah not having met with your concurrence, I now nominate *Lachlan McIntosh* to that Office.

Whatever may have been the reasons which induced your dissent, I am persuaded they were such as you deemed sufficient. Permit me to submit to your consideration whether on occasions where the propriety of Nominations appear questionable to you, it would not be expedient to communicate that circumstance to me, and thereby avail yourselves of the information which led me to make them, and which I would with pleasure lay before you. Probably my reasons for nominating Mr. Fishbourn may tend to shew that such a

---

[40] On August 7 the President sent the Senate a message defending his nomination of Benjamin Fishbourn.

[41] On August 10 consideration of the President's message on Benjamin Fishbourn was postponed until the report of this committee.

mode of proceeding in such cases might be useful. I will therefore detail them.

FIRST, While Colonel Fishbourn was an Officer, in actual service and chiefly under my own eye, his conduct appeared to me irreproachable; nor did I ever hear any thing injurious to his reputation as an Officer or a Gentleman. At the storm of Stoney Point his behaviour was represented to have been active and brave, and he was charged by his General to bring the account of that success to the Head Quarters of the Army. SECONDLY, Since his residence in Georgia, he has been repeatedly elected to the Assembly as a Representative of the County of Chatham in which the Port of Savannah is situated, and sometimes of the Counties of Glynn and Cambden—he has been chosen a Member of the Executive Council of the State, and has lately been President of the same; he has been elected by the Officers of the Militia in the County of Chatham, Lieutenant Colonel of the Militia in that District—and on a very recent occasion—to wit: in the month of May last, he has been appointed by the Council (on the suspension of the the late Collector) to an office in the Port of Savannah nearly similar to that for which I nominated him—which Office he actually holds at this time. To these reasons for nominating Mr. Fishbourn, I might add that I received private Letters of recommendation, and oral testimonials in his favour, from some of the most respectable Characters in that State: but as they were secondary considerations with me, I do not think it necessary to communicate them to you.

It appeared therefore to me, that Mr. Fishbourn must have enjoyed the *confidence* of the Militia Officers, in order to have been elevated to a Military Rank; the *confidence* of the Freemen, to have been elected to the Assembly; the *confidence* of the Assembly, to have been selected for the Council; and the *confidence* of the Council, to have been appointed Collector of the Port of Savannah.

New York

August 6th 1789   GO. WASHINGTON[42]

GENTLEMEN of the SENATE,

By the Act for settling the Accounts between the United States and individual States, a Person is to be appointed to fill the vacant Seat at the Board of Commissioners for settling the Accounts between the United States and individual States; I therefore nominate JOHN KEAN, of the State of South

---

[42] A letterbook copy of the message, in the hand of Robert Lewis, is in The George Washington Papers, series 2, vol. 25, roll 9, Manuscript Division, DLC. On August 10 consideration of this message was postponed until the report of the committee on communication with the President.

Carolina, to fill the vacant seat at the said Board of Commissioners.
New York
August 6th 1789   GO. WASHINGTON[43]

Proceeded to consider the Nominations of Collectors, Naval Officers and Surveyors, contained in the Messages from the President of the United States of the 3d and 6th August, and the Senate did advise and consent to the appointment of the following Persons—to wit:

For the State of SOUTH CAROLINA
Beaufort   Andrew Agnew   Collector
                      For the State of GEORGIA
Savannah   Lachlan McIntosh   Naval Officer

Proceeded to consider the Nomination of JOHN KEAN to fill the vacant Seat at the Board of Commissioners for settling the accounts between the United States and individual States, and the Senate did advise and consent to his appointment.

And the Secretary according to order, laid a certified Copy of the proceedings, before the President of the United States.

MONDAY, AUGUST 10TH, 1789

ON MOTION, to commit the Message from the President of the United States relative to the Nomination of Mr. Fishbourn—It was postponed until a Committee appointed on the 6th August "to wait on the President of the United States" should Report.[44]

WEDNESDAY, AUGUST 12TH, 1789

The Committee to whom was referred the Message of the President of the United States of the 25th of May 1789 with the Indian Treaties and Papers accompanying the same—Reported;[45] and the consideration thereof was postponed until the 26th.[46]

---

[43] The message, in the hand of Tobias Lear and signed by George Washington, is in Executive Nominations, first session, Executive Proceedings, SR, DNA.

[44] On August 20 this committee reported.

[45] The report, in the hand of George Read, is in Various Select Committee Reports, SR, DNA.

[46] On August 26 this committee's report was printed.

T U E S D A Y, AUGUST 18TH, 1789

A Message from the President of the United States by Mr. Lear his Secretary, who delivered the following communication to the Vice President. And withdrew.

GENTLEMEN of the SENATE,

In conformity to the Law re-establishing the Government of the Western territory, I nominate

        ARTHUR ST. CLAIR, Governor
        WINTHROP SARGENT, Secretary
        SAMUEL HOLDEN PARSONS ⎫
        JOHN CLEVES SYMMES and ⎬ Judges of the Court
        WILLIAM BARTON ⎭

I also nominate EBENEZER TUCKER, Surveyor of Little Egg Harbour in the State of New Jersey.

New York   ⎫
August 18th 1789 ⎬   GO. WASHINGTON[47]

READ, and the consideration thereof was postponed till to morrow.[48]

T H U R S D A Y, AUGUST 20TH, 1789

A Message from the President of the United States by Mr. Lear his Secretary, Who delivered the following communication to the Vice President— And withdrew.

GENTLEMEN of the SENATE,

In consequence of an act providing for the expenses which may attend negotiations or Treaties with the Indian Tribes, and the appointment of Commissioners for managing the same, I nominate BENJAMIN LINCOLN, as one of three Commissioners whom I shall propose to be employed to negotiate a Treaty with the Southern Indians. My reason for nominating him at this

---

[47] The message, in the hand of Tobias Lear and signed by George Washington, is in Executive Nominations, first session, Executive Proceedings, SR, DNA. The following notation, in the hand of Samuel Otis, appears at the bottom of the message:

                   ⎡ also W Gibb
     "Tomorrow" ⎨ Collector
                   ⎨ Folly Landing
                   ⎣ Virginia."

[48] On August 20 these nominations were agreed to.

early moment, is, that it will not be possible for the Public to avail itself of his services on this occasion unless his appointment can be forwarded to him by the Mail, which will leave this place to morrow Morning.

New York

August 20th 1789   Go. Washington[49]

Proceeded to consider the nominations of Governor &c. of the Western territory as contained in the Message from the President of the United States of the 18th August; and the Senate did advise and consent to the appointment of

> ARTHUR ST. CLAIR, to be Governor of the
> Western territory;
> of WINTHROP SARGENT, to be Secretary; and
> of SAMUEL HOLDEN PARSONS,[50] ⎫
>   JOHN CLEVES SYMMES, and   ⎬ to be Judges.
>   WILLIAM BARTON[51]   ⎭

Proceeded to consider the Nomination

of EBENEZER TUCKER, to be Surveyor of Little Egg Harbour in the State of New Jersey; And of

WILLIAM GIBBS, to be Collector of Folly Landing in the State of Virginia.— ⎰ And, the Senate did advise & consent to their being appointed to ⎱ Office agreeably to the Nominations respectively.

Also, Proceeded to consider the Nomination of

BENJAMIN LINCOLN, as one of the Three Commissioners to be employed to negotiate a Treaty with the Southern Indians;

And the Senate did advise and consent to his appointment accordingly.

Mr. Izard in behalf of the Committee, appointed the 6th of August, "to wait on the President of the United States, and confer with him on the mode of communication" &c. REPORTED,[52]

The consideration of which was postponed till to morrow.[53]

The Secretary laid before the President an attested Copy of the proceedings of Senate on the Nominations made in his Messages of the 3d, 18th & 20th August 1789.

---

[49] The message, in the hand of Tobias Lear and signed by George Washington, is in Executive Nominations, first session, Executive Proceedings, SR, DNA.

[50] On March 30, 1790, the Senate was notified that Samuel Parsons had died and Rufus Putnam had been nominated to replace him.

[51] On September 11 George Turner was nominated in the place of William Barton, who declined.

[52] The report, in the hand of Benjamin Bankson, is in Various Select Committee Reports, SR, DNA. It was extracted in the Journal on August 21, 1789.

[53] On August 21 a system of communication was agreed to, and the President was notified.

FRIDAY, AUGUST 21ST, 1789

The SENATE proceeded to consider the Report of the Committee appointed the 6th August.

The Committee appointed to wait on the President of the United States, and confer with him on the mode of communication proper to be pursued between him, and the Senate in the formation of Treaties, and making appointments to Offices,[54] REPORTED,

Which Report was agreed to, whereupon—

"RESOLVED, That when Nominations shall be made in writing by the President of the United States to the Senate, a future day shall be assigned, unless the Senate unanimously direct otherwise, for taking them into consideration. That when the President of the United States shall meet the Senate in the Senate Chamber, the President of the Senate shall have a Chair on the floor, be considered as at the head of the Senate, and his Chair shall be assigned to the President of the United States. That when the Senate shall be

---

[54] From this point to the resolve beginning "That when nominations . . .," the original report reads:

Report,

That they have waited on the President of the United States, have conferred with him on the subject committed to them, and have collected from him the following sentiments. That the President being vested by the Constitution with the power of making Treaties, and appointing Officers, with the advice and consent of the Senate; when those powers are exercised, the Senate are evidently a Council only to the President, though their concurrence is necessary to his Acts. That it seems incident to this relation between them that not only the time, but the place, and manner of consultation should lie with the President, who may meet the Senate in the Senate Chamber, or convene them to his own house according to circumstances.

That whenever the Government shall have buildings of it's own, an Executive Chamber will no doubt be provided, where the Senate will generally attend the President: the place may depend on the nature of the business.

That the opinions both of the President, and Senate as to the proper manner may be changed by experience. That in some kinds of business, it may be found best for the President to make his propositions in person; in others by written message.

That on some occasions it may be most convenient that the President should attend the deliberations and decisions of the Senate on his propositions; on others that he should not; or that he should not attend the whole of the time. That in other cases, as in Treaties of a complicated nature, it may happen that he send his propositions in writing, and attend the Senate in person, after they shall have had sufficient time for Consultation. That in the appointment of foreign Ministers it may be proper that the President should consult the Senate in person, not only respecting the nomination, but the quality of the Officer to be appointed. That many other varieties as to the mode may be suggested by practice.

The Committee therefore recommend that the Senate should accommodate their Rules to the uncertainty of the particular mode, and place that may be adopted:

And for that purpose submit the following Resolutions to the Senate.

convened by the President of the United States, to any other place, the President of the Senate, and Senators shall attend at the place appointed. The Secretary of the Senate shall also attend, to take the minutes of the Senate.

"That all questions shall be put by the President of the Senate, either in the presence or absence of the President of the United States; and the Senators shall signify their assent or dissent, by answering viva voce ay, or no."

And the Secretary laid before the President of the United States an attested Copy of the proceedings.

A MESSAGE from the President of the United States by Mr. Lear his Secretary, Who delivered the following Communication to the Vice President —And withdrew.

GENTLEMEN of the SENATE,

In addition to the Nomination which I made yesterday, of BENJAMIN LINCOLN, as one of the three Commissioners to be employed to negotiate a Treaty with the Southern Indians, I now nominate CYRUS GRIFFIN and DAVID HUMPHREYS, as the two other Commissioners to be employed to negotiate the before mentioned Treaty.

New York
August 21st 1789   GO. WASHINGTON[55]

PROCEEDED to consider the last recited nominations, and the Senate did advise and consent to the appointments accordingly.

And an attested Copy of the proceedings was laid before the President of the United States.

A MESSAGE from the President of the United States by Mr. Lear his Secretary, who delivered the following communication to the Vice President—And withdrew.

GENTLEMEN of the SENATE,

The President of the United States will meet the Senate in the Senate Chamber, at half past Eleven O'Clock to morrow;[56] to advise with them on the terms of the Treaty to be negotiated with the Southern Indians.

New York
August 21st 1789   GO. WASHINGTON[57]

---

[55] The message, in the hand of Tobias Lear and signed by George Washington, is in Executive Nominations, first session, Executive Proceedings, SR, DNA.

[56] In the original message the word "tomorrow" is underlined.

[57] The message, in the hand of Tobias Lear and signed by George Washington, is in President's Messages on Indian Relations, Executive Proceedings, SR, DNA. On August 22 the President reported to the Senate relative to the Southern Indians and requested advice on several questions.

S A T U R D A Y, August 22D, 1789

The President of the United States came into the Senate Chamber, attended by General Knox, and laid before the Senate the following state of facts with the questions thereto annexed for their advice and consent.

"To conciliate the powerful tribes of Indians in the southern District, amounting probably to fourteen thousand fighting Men, and to attach them firmly to the United States, may be regarded as highly worthy of the serious attention of government.

"The measure includes, not only peace and security to the whole southern frontier, but is calculated to form a barrier against the Colonies of an European power, which in the mutations of Policy, may one day become the enemy of the United States. The fate of the southern States therefore, or the neighbouring Colonies, may principally depend on the present measures of the Union towards the southern Indians.

"By the papers which have been laid before the Senate it will appear that in the latter end of the year 1785, and the beginning of 1786, treaties were formed by the United States with the Cherokees, the Chickasaws and Choctaws. The report of the Commissioners will shew the reasons why a treaty was not formed at the same time with the Creeks.

"It will also appear by the Papers that the States of North Carolina and Georgia, protested against said treaties, as infringing their legislative rights, and being contrary to the Confederation. It will further appear by the said Papers, that the treaty with the Cherokees has been entirely violated by the disorderly white People on the frontiers of North Carolina.

"The opinion of the late Congress respecting the said violation, will sufficiently appear, by the Proclamation which they caused to be issued on the first of September 1788.

"By the public News-Papers it appears that on the 16th of June last, a truce was concluded with the Cherokees by Mr. John Steele on behalf of the State of North Carolina, in which it was stipulated that a treaty should be held as soon as possible, and that in the mean time all hostilities should cease on either side.

"As the Cherokees reside principally within the territory claimed by North Carolina, and as that State is not a Member of the present Union, it may be doubted whether any efficient measures in favor of the Cherokees could be immediately adopted by the general Government.

"The Commissioners for negotiating with the Southern Indians may be instructed to transmit a Message to the Cherokees, stating to them, as far as may be proper, the difficulties arising from the local claims of North Carolina, and to assure them that the United States are not unmindful of the Treaty at Hopewell, and as soon as the difficulties which are at present opposed to the Measure, shall be removed; the Government will do full justice to the Cherokees.

"The distance of the Choctaws and Chickasaws from the frontier settlements seems to have prevented those tribes from being involved in similar difficulties with the Cherokees.

"The Commissioners may be instructed to transmit Messages to the said tribes containing assurances of the continuance of the friendship of the United States; and that measures will soon be taken for extending a trade to them agreeably to the treaties of Hopewell. The Commissioners may also be directed to report a plan for the execution of the said treaties respecting trade.

"But the case of the Creek Nation is of the highest importance and requires an immediate decision. The cause of the hostilities between Georgia and the Creeks is stated to be a difference in judgment concerning three treaties made between the said Parties—To wit—at Augusta in 1783—at Galphinton in 1785—and at Shoulderbone in 1786. The State of Georgia asserts, and the Creeks deny the validity of the said treaties.

"Hence arises the indispensable necessity of having all the circumstances respecting the said treaties critically investigated by Commissioners of the United States, so that the further measures of Government may be formed on a full knowledge of the case.

"In order that the investigation be conducted with the highest impartiality, it will be proper, in addition to the evidence of the documents in the public possession, that Georgia should be represented at this part of the proposed treaty with the Creek Nation.

"It is however to be observed, in any issue of the enquiry, that it would be highly embarrassing to Georgia to relinquish that part of the lands, stated to have been ceded by the Creeks, lying between the Ogeeche and Oconee Rivers; that State having surveyed and divided the same among certain descriptions of its Citizens who settled and planted thereon until dispossessed by the Indians.

"In case therefore, the issue of the investigation should be unfavorable to the claims of Georgia, the Commissioners should be instructed to use their best endeavours to negotiate with the Creeks, a solemn conveyance of the said lands to Georgia.

"By the report of the Commissioners who were appointed under certain acts of the late Congress, by South Carolina and Georgia, it appears that they have agreed to meet the Creeks on the 15th of September ensuing. As it is with great difficulty the Indians are collected together at certain seasons of the Year, it is important that the above occasion should be embraced, if possible, on the part of the present Government, to form a treaty with the Creeks. As the proposed treaty is of great importance to the future tranquility of the

State of Georgia, as well as of the United States, it has been thought proper that it should be conducted on the part of the general Government, by Commissioners whose local situations may free them from the imputation of prejudice on this subject.

"As it is necessary that certain principles should be fixed previously to forming instructions for the Commissioners; the following questions arising out of the foregoing communications, are stated by the President of the United States, and the advice of the Senate requested thereon.

"1st

"In the present state of Affairs between North Carolina, and the United States, will it be proper to take any other measures for redressing the injuries of the Cherokees, than the one herein suggested?

"2nd

"Shall the Commissioners be instructed to pursue any other measures respecting the Chickasaws and Choctaws than those herein suggested?

"3d

"If the Commissioners shall adjudge that the Creek Nation was fully represented at the three treaties with Georgia, and that the cessions of land were obtained with the full understanding and free consent of the acknowledged Proprietors, and that the said treaties ought to be considered as just and equitable:[58] In this case shall the Commissioners be instructed to insist on a formal renewal and confirmation thereof? And in case of a refusal, shall they be instructed to inform the Creeks that the Arms of the Union shall be employed to compel them to acknowledge the Justice[59] of the said Cessions?

"4th

"But if the Commissioners shall adjudge that the said treaties were formed with an inadequate or unauthorised representation of the Creek Nation, or that the treaties were held under circumstances of constraint or unfairness of any sort, so that the United States could not with justice and dignity request or urge a confirmation thereof; In this case shall the Commissioners, considering the importance of the Oconee lands to Georgia, be instructed to use their highest exertions to obtain a cession of said lands? If so shall the Commissioners be instructed, if they cannot obtain the said cessions on better terms, to offer for the same, and for the further great object of attaching the Creeks to the Government of the United States, the following conditions.

"1st. A compensation in money or goods to the amount of ———— Dollars, the said amount to be stipulated to be paid by Georgia, at the period which shall be fixed, or in failure thereof by the United States.

---

[58] At this point in the original message the word "valid" is lined out and "equitable" is written above it in the hand of Samuel Otis.

[59] At this point in the original message the word "validity" is lined out and "Justice" is written above it in the hand of Samuel Otis.

"2nd. A secure[60] Port on the Altamaha or St. Mary's Rivers, or at any other place between the same as may be mutually agreed to by the Commissioners[61] and the Creeks.

"3d. Certain pecuniary considerations to some, and honorary Military distinctions to other influential Chiefs, on their taking oaths of allegiance to the United States.

"4th. A solemn guarrantee by the United States, to the Creeks, of their remaining territory, and to maintain the same if necessary by a line of Military Posts.

"5th

"But if all offers should fail to induce the Creeks to make the desired cessions to Georgia, shall the Commissioners make it an Ultimatum?

"6th

"If the said cessions shall not be made an ultimatum, shall the Commissioners proceed and make a treaty, and include the disputed lands within the limits, which shall be assigned to the Creeks;[62] If not, shall a temporary boundary be marked, making the Oconee the line, and the other parts of the treaty be concluded?

"In this case shall a secure[63] port be stipulated, and the pecuniary, and honorary considerations granted?

"In other general objects, shall the treaties formed at Hopewell, with the Cherokees, Chickasaws and Choctaws, be the basis of a treaty with the Creeks?

"7th

"Shall the sum of twenty thousand dollars appropriated to Indian expenses and treaties, be wholly applied, if necessary, to a treaty with the Creeks? If not, what proportion?"[64]

WHEREUPON the Senate proceeded to give their advice and consent.

The first Question, vizt.: "In the present state of Affairs between North Carolina, and the United States, will it be proper to take any other measures, for redressing the injuries of the Cherokees, than the one herein suggested?"

Was, at the request of the President of the United States, postponed.

---

[60] At this point in the original message the word "free" is lined out and "secure" is written above it in the hand of Samuel Otis.

[61] At this point in the original message the word "Georgia" is lined out and "the Commissioners" is written above it in the hand of Samuel Otis.

[62] At this point in the original message the word "No," written in the hand of Samuel Otis, is crossed out.

[63] At this point in the original message the word "free" is lined out and "secure" is written above it in the hand of Samuel Otis.

[64] The message, in the hand of Tobias Lear, is in President's Messages on Indian Relations, Executive Proceedings, SR, DNA. On the back of the cover sheet is an extraneous note on the Articles of Amendment. The related documents are printed in Part II of this volume under the heading Indian Relations—Southern.

The second Question, viz.: "Shall the Commissioners be instructed to pursue any other measures respecting the Chickasaws and Choctaws, than those herein suggested?" being put,

Was answered in the Negative.

The consideration of the remaining questions was postponed till Monday next.[65]

MONDAY, AUGUST 24TH, 1789

The President of the United States being present in the Senate Chamber, attended by General Knox,

The Senate resumed the consideration of the state of facts and questions thereto annexed, laid before them by the President of the United States, on Saturday last.

And the 1st Question, viz.: "In the present state of Affairs between North Carolina, and the United States, will it be proper to take any other measures, for redressing the injuries of the Cherokees, than the one herein suggested?" being put, Was answered in the negative.

The third Question, viz.: "If the Commissioners shall adjudge that the Creek Nation was fully represented at the three treaties with Georgia, and that the cessions of land were obtained with the full understanding and free consent of the acknowledged Proprietors, and that the said treaties ought to be considered as just and equitable: In this case shall the Commissioners be instructed to insist on a formal renewal and confirmation thereof? And in case of a refusal, shall they be instructed to inform the Creeks that the arms of the Union shall be employed to compel them to acknowledge the justice of the said Cessions."

Was wholly answered in the affirmative.

The fourth Question and its four sub divisions, viz.: "But if the Commissioners shall adjudge that the said treaties were formed with an inadequate or unauthorised representation of the Creek Nation, or that the treaties were held under circumstances of constraint or unfairness of any sort, so that the United States could not with justice and dignity request or urge a confirmation thereof; In this case shall the Commissioners, considering the importance of the Oconee lands to Georgia, be instructed to use their highest exertions to obtain a cession of said lands? If so shall the Commissioners be instructed, if they cannot obtain the said cessions on better terms, to offer for the same, and for the further great object of attaching the Creeks to the Government of the United States, the following Conditions,

---

[65] On August 24 the Senate further considered the President's questions and consented to appropriations for making a treaty.

"1st. A compensation in Money or Goods to the amount of ———- Dollars, the said amount to be stipulated to be paid by Georgia, at the period which shall be fixed, or in failure thereof by the United States.

"2nd. A secure Port on the Altamaha or St. Mary's Rivers, or at any other place between the same as may be mutually agreed to by the Commissioners and the Creeks.

"3d. Certain pecuniary considerations to some, and honorary Military distinctions to other influential Chiefs, on their taking oaths of allegiance to the United States.

"4th. A solemn guarantee by the United States, to the Creeks of their remaining territory, and to maintain the same if necessary by a line of Military Posts."

Was wholly answered in the affirmative. The blank to be filled at the discretion of the President of the United States.

The fifth Question, viz.: "But if all offers should fail to induce the Creeks to make the desired Cessions to Georgia, shall the Commissioners make it an ultimatum?"

Was answered in the negative.

The sixth Question being divided, the first part containing as follows, vizt. "If the said cessions shall not be made an ultimatum, shall the Commissioners proceed and make a treaty, and include the disputed lands within the limits, which shall be assigned to the Creeks;"

Was answered in the Negative.

The remainder, viz.: "If not shall a temporary boundary be marked, making the Oconee the line, and the other parts of the Treaty be concluded?

"In this case shall a secure Port be stipulated, and the pecuniary and honorary considerations granted?

"In other general objects, shall the treaties formed at Hopewell, with the Cherokees, Chickasaws, and Choctaws, be the basis of a treaty with the Creeks?"

Was all answered in the affirmative.

On the seventh Question, viz.: "Shall the sum of twenty thousand dollars appropriated to Indian expenses and treaties, be wholly applied, if necessary, to a Treaty with the Creeks? If not, what proportion?"

It was agreed to advise and consent to appropriate the whole sum if necessary, at the discretion of the President of the United States.[66]

The President of the United States withdrew from the Senate Chamber, and the Vice President put the question of adjournment, to which the Senate agreed.

---

[66] On January 11, 1790, the President sent the Senate a report of the Southern Indian Commissioners as well as a copy of his instructions to them.

WEDNESDAY, AUGUST 26TH, 1789

Proceeded to consider the report of a Committee, appointed June the 10th,[67] on Indian Treaties made at Fort Harmar the 9th day of January 1789. viz.

The Committee to whom was referred the Message of the President of the United States of the 25th of May 1789, with the Indian treaties and Papers accompanying the same,

REPORT,

That the Governor of the Western territory on the 9th day of January 1789—at Fort Harmar entered into two Treaties. One with the[68] Sachems and Warriors, of the Six Nations, the Mohawks excepted; the other with the Sachems and Warriors of the Wyandot, Delaware, Ottawa, Chippawa, Pattawatima and Sac Nations—that those treaties were made in pursuance of the Powers and instructions heretofore given to the said Governor by the late Congress, and are a confirmation of the Treaties of Fort Stanwix in October 1784—and of Fort McIntosh in January 1785[69]—and contain a more formal and regular conveyance to the United States of the Indian Claims to the Lands yielded to these[70] States by the said Treaties of 1784 and 1785.

Your Committee therefore submit the following Resolution, to wit:

"That the Treaties concluded at Fort Harmar on the 9th day of January 1789, between Arthur St. Clair Esqe. Governor of the Western territory on the part of the United States and the Sachems and Warriors of the Six Nations (the Mohawks excepted) and the Sachems and Warriors of the Wyandot, Delaware, Ottawa, Chippawa, Pattawatima and Sac Nations be accepted, and that the President of the United States be advised to execute and enjoin an Observance of the same."

ORDERED that the consideration thereof be postponed.[71]

---

[67] The date should read "June the 12th."

[68] At this point in the original report the words "Warriors and" are crossed out.

[69] At this point in the original report the words "with this that those Treaties of 1789" are crossed out.

[70] At this point in the original report the word "said" is crossed out.

[71] On September 8 the Senate consented to the Treaty at Fort Harmar with the Wyandots, Delawares, Ottawas, etc.

T U E S D A Y, September 8th, 1789

The Senate proceeded to the consideration of the Message from the President of the United States, of the 25th of May 1789, accompanying the Treaties formed at Fort Harmar, by Arthur St. Clair Esqe. on the part of the United States—namely, a Treaty with the Sachems and Warriors of the Six Nations, the Mohawks excepted, and a treaty with the Sachems and Warriors of the Wyandot, Delaware, Ottawa, Chippawa, Pattawatima and Sac Nations —Whereupon,

RESOLVED, That the President of the United States be advised to execute and enjoin an observance of the Treaty concluded at Fort Harmar on the 9th day of January 1789, between Arthur St. Clair, Governor of the Western territory, on the part of the United States, and the Sachems and Warriors of the Wyandot, Delaware, Ottawa, Chippawa, Pattawatima and Sac Nations.

And an attested Copy of the proceedings was laid before the President of the United States.[72]

F R I D A Y, September 11th, 1789

A Message from the President of the United States—Which, Mr. Lear his Secretary delivered to the Vice President, and withdrew.

GENTLEMEN of the SENATE,

I nominate for the Department of the Treasury of the United States—
> ALEXANDER HAMILTON (of New York) Secretary
> NICHOLAS EVELEIGH (of South Carolina) Comptroller
> SAMUEL MEREDITH (of Pensylvania) Treasurer
> OLIVER WOLCOTT Junr. (of Connecticut) Auditor
> JOSEPH NOURSE (in Office) Register.

For the Department of War—
> HENRY KNOX.

For Judge in the Western Territory, in place of WILLIAM BARTON, who declines the appointment—
> GEORGE TURNER.

For Surveyor in the District of Rappahannock, State of Virginia, in place of STAIGE DAVIS who declines the appointment—I nominate
> PETER KEMP.

For Surveyor of Town Creek in the District of Patuxent, State of Maryland, in place of ROBERT YOUNG who declines the appointment—I nominate
> CHARLES CHILTON.

---

[72] On September 17 the President sent another message related to the treaties at Fort Harmar to the Senate. This message was committed.

And, in case the nomination of SAMUEL MEREDITH should meet the advice and consent of the Senate—I nominate as Surveyor of the Port of Philadelphia—

WILLIAM McPHERSON.

New York ⎱
September 11th ⎰ 1789   GO. WASHINGTON[73]

ORDERED, That the rules be so far dispensed with as that the Senate do consider the President's Message at this time—and;

On the question to advise and consent to the appointment of ALEXANDER HAMILTON (of New York) to be Secretary for the Department of the Treasury of the United States,

It passed in the Affirmative.

On the question to advise and consent to the appointment of NICHOLAS EVELEIGH (of South Carolina) to be Comptroller, & of SAMUEL MEREDITH, to be Treasurer,

It passed in the affirmative.

ORDERED, That the further consideration of the Message from the President of the United States be postponed until to Morrow.

ORDERED, That the Secretary lay before the President of the United States a certified Copy of the proceedings.

S A T U R D A Y, SEPTEMBER 12TH, 1789

The Senate proceeded in the consideration of the Message from the President of the United States of the 11th of September—And

On the question to advise and consent to the appointment of OLIVER WOLCOTT Junr. (of Connecticut) to be Auditor, for the Department of the Treasury of the United States,

It passed in the affirmative.

On the question to advise and consent to the appointment of JOSEPH NOURSE, (in Office) Register,

It passed in the affirmative.

On the question to advise and consent to the appointment of HENRY KNOX, Secretary for the Department of War,

It passed in the affirmative.

On the question to advise and consent to the appointment of GEORGE TURNER, for Judge in the Western territory,

It passed in the affirmative.

---

[73] The message, in the hand of Tobias Lear and signed by George Washington, is in Executive Nominations, first session, Executive Proceedings, SR, DNA. The nominations, except for that of William McPherson, are marked with the letter "c," probably indicating Senate concurrence.

On the question to advise and consent to the appointment of PETER KEMP, for Surveyor in the District of Rappahannock, State of Virginia,

It passed in the affirmative.

On the question to advise and consent to the appointment of CHARLES CHILTON, for Surveyor of Town Creek, in the District of Patuxent, State of Maryland,

It passed in the affirmative.

ORDERED, That the further consideration of the Message from the President of the United States, of the 11th of September, be postponed for a few days.

ORDERED, That the Secretary lay before the President of the United States, a certified Copy of the proceedings of the Senate upon his Message of the 11th of September.

WEDNESDAY, SEPTEMBER 16TH, 1789

A Message from the President of the United States, by Mr. Lear his Secretary, which he delivered to the Vice President—and withdrew.

UNITED STATES, September 16th 1789

GENTLEMEN of the SENATE,

I nominate LEMUEL WYATT as Collector for the Port of Rehoboth in the State of Massachusetts.

GEORGE WASHINGTON[74]

The Senate agreed so far to dispense with the rules as to proceed at this time to the consideration of the President's Message, And

Upon the question to advise and consent to the appointment of LEMUEL WYATT as collector for the Port of Rehoboth,

It passed in the Affirmative.

ORDERED, that the Secretary do lay a certified copy of the proceedings of Senate hereupon before the President of the United States.

THURSDAY, SEPTEMBER 17TH, 1789

A Message from the President of the United States, by the Secretary at War, which he delivered to the Vice President—and withdrew.

GENTLEMEN of the SENATE,

It doubtless is important that all treaties and compacts, formed by the

---

[74] The message, in the hand of William Jackson and signed by George Washington, is in Executive Nominations, first session, Executive Proceedings, SR, DNA.

United States with other Nations, whether civilized or not, should be made with caution, and executed with fidelity.

It is said to be the general understanding and practice of Nations, as a check on the mistakes and indiscretions of Ministers or Commissioners, not to consider any treaty, negociated, and signed by such Officers, as final and conclusive until ratified by the sovereign or government from whom they derive their powers: this practice has been adopted by the United States, respecting their treaties with European Nations; and I am inclined to think it would be adviseable to observe it in the conduct of our treaties with the Indians: for tho' such treaties, being on their part, made by their Chiefs or Rulers, need not be ratified by them, yet being formed on our part by the agency of subordinate Officers, it seems to be both prudent and reasonable, that their acts should not be binding on the Nation until approved and ratified by the Government. It strikes me that this point should be well considered and settled, so that our national proceedings in this respect may become uniform, and be directed by fixed, and stable principles.

The treaties with certain Indian Nations, which were laid before you with my Message of the 25th May last, suggested two questions to my mind—vizt. 1st. Whether those Treaties were to be considered as perfected, and consequently as obligatory, without being ratified, if not, then 2ndly. whether both, or either, and which of them ought to be ratified; on these questions, I request your opinion and advice.

You have indeed advised me *"to execute and enjoin an observance of"* the treaty with the Wyandots &c.—You Gentlemen doubtless intended to be clear and explicit, and yet without further explanation, I fear I may misunderstand your meaning—for—If by my executing[75] that treaty, you mean that I should make it (in a more particular, and immediate manner than it now is) the act of Government, then it follows that I am to ratify it. If you mean by my *executing it*, that I am to see that it be carried into effect and operation, then I am led to conclude, either that you consider it as being perfect and obligatory in its present state and therefore to be executed and observed, or that you consider it as to derive its completion and obligation from the silent approbation and ratification which my Proclamation may be construed to imply. Altho I am inclined to think that the latter is your intention, yet it certainly is best that all doubts respecting it be removed.

Permit me to observe that it will be proper for me to be informed of your sentiments relative to the treaty with the six Nations, previous to the departure of the Governor of the Western Territory, and therefore I recommend it to your early consideration.

September 17th 1789   Go. Washington[76]

---

[75] In the original message the word "executing" is underlined.

[76] The message, in the hand of John Stagg, Jr., and signed by George Washington, is in President's Messages on Indian Relations, Executive Proceedings, SR, DNA.

ORDERED, that the President's Message be committed to
> Mr. Carroll,
> Mr. King and
> Mr. Read.[77]

F R I D A Y, SEPTEMBER 18TH, 1789

Mr. Carroll, on behalf of the Committee appointed yesterday upon the President's Message of the 17th of September, Reported as follows,[78]

The Committee to whom was referred a Message from the President of the United States of the 17th September 1789,[79]

REPORT,

That the Signature of treaties with the Indian Nations has ever been considered as a full completion thereof, and that such treaties have never been solemnly ratified by either of the contracting Parties as hath been commonly practised among the civilized Nations of Europe, wherefore the Committee are of opinion that the formal ratification of the Treaty concluded at Fort Harmar on the 9th day of January 1789, between Arthur St. Clair, Governor of the Western territory on the part of the United States, and the Sachems and Warriors of the Wyandot, Delaware, Ottawa, Chippawa, Pattawatima and Sac Nations is not expedient or necessary, and that the Resolve of the Senate of the 8th September 1789 respecting the said treaty, authorises the President of the United States to enjoin[80] a due observance thereof.

That as to the Treaty made at Fort Harmar on the 9th of January 1789, between the said Arthur St. Clair and the Sachems and Warriors of the Six Nations (except the Mohawks) from particular circumstances affecting a part of the ceded lands the Senate did not judge it expedient to pass any act concerning the same.

ORDERED, that the consideration of the Report be postponed until Monday next.[81]

The Senate proceeded to consider the Message from the President of the United States of September the 11th nominating WILLIAM McPHERSON as Surveyor of the Port of Philadelphia—and,

Upon the question to advise and consent to his appointment,

> It passed in the affirmative.

---

[77] On September 18 this committee reported, and the report was printed.

[78] The report, in the hand of Charles Carroll, is in Various Select Committee Reports, SR, DNA.

[79] In the original report, the words "Mr. Carroll from" precede this line and the words "made the following" follow it.

[80] The words "and cause a" are lined out of the original report at this point.

[81] On September 22 the Senate passed a resolution consenting to the treaty with the Wyandots, Delawares, Ottawas, etc., and ordered the treaty with the Six Nations postponed until the next session.

ORDERED, that the Secretary do lay before the President of the United States an attested Copy of the proceedings of Senate hereon.

T U E S D A Y, SEPTEMBER 22ND, 1789

The Senate proceeded to consider the report of the Committee appointed the 17th on the President's Message of that date—and

ON MOTION to postpone the Report and substitute the following, to wit:

"RESOLVED, that the Senate do advise and consent that the President of the United States ratify the Treaty concluded at Fort Harmar on the 9th day of January 1789, between Arthur St. Clair, Governor of the Western Territory on the part of the United States, and the Sachems and Warriors of the Wyandot, Delaware, Ottawa, Chippawa, Pattawatima and Sac Nations."[82]

It passed in the affirmative, And

It being suggested that the Treaty concluded at Fort Harmar on the 9th day of January 1789, between Arthur St. Clair, Governor of the Western Territory on the part of the United States, and the Sachems and Warriors of the six Nations (except the Mohawks) may be construed to prejudice the claims of the States of Massachusetts and New York and of the Grantees under the said States respectively.

ORDERED, that the consideration thereof be postponed until the next session of Senate.[83]

ORDERED, that the Secretary lay before the President of the United States a certified Copy of the proceedings of Senate upon his Message of 17th September.

T H U R S D A Y, SEPTEMBER 24TH, 1789

A Message was received from the President of the United States by Mr. Lear his Secretary, Which he delivered to the Vice President—And he withdrew.

---

[82] The resolve, in the hand of Oliver Ellsworth, is in Other Records, Executive Proceedings, SR, DNA. The letter "a," signifying agreement by the Senate, is noted at this point. Following this resolve is a second one, in the hand of Oliver Ellsworth, which is crossed out. It reads:

"Resolved that the Senate do advise & consent that the President

"And also the Treaty made at fort Harmar the same time & place between the Sd. Arthur St. Clair & the Sachem on the part of the United States & the Sachems & Warriors of the Six Nations (except the Mohawks)."

[83] The order and the preceding statement, in the hand of Rufus King, are filed with the previous resolution in Other Records, Executive Proceedings, SR, DNA.

UNITED STATES, September 24th 1789

GENTLEMEN of the SENATE,

I nominate for the Supreme Court of the United States

JOHN JAY of New York, Chief Justice ⎤
JOHN RUTLEDGE of South Carolina   ⎥
JAMES WILSON of Pennsylvania   ⎥
WILLIAM CUSHING of Massachusetts ⎬ Associate Judges
ROBERT H. HARRISON of Maryland   ⎥
JOHN BLAIR of Virginia   ⎦

I also nominate for district Judges, Attornies and Marshals, the Persons whose names are below and annexed to the districts respectively—Vizt.:

DISTRICTS	JUDGES	ATTORNIES	MARSHALS
Main	David Sewall	William Lithgow	Henry Dearborn
New Hampshire	John Sullivan	Saml. Sherburne Junr.	John Parker
Massachusetts	John Lowell	Christopher Gore	Jonathan Jackson
Connecticut	Richard Law	Pierrepont Edwards	Philip Bradley
Pennsylvania	Francis Hopkinson	William Lewis	Clement Biddle
Delaware	Gunning Bedford	George Read junr.	Allan McLane
Maryland	Thomas Johnson	Richard Potts	Nathal. Ramsay
Virginia	Edmund Pendleton	John Marshall	Edwd. Carrington
South Carolina	Thomas Pinckney	John Julius Pringle	Isaac Huger
Georgia	Nathal. Pendleton	Mathw. McAllister	Robt. Forsyth
Kentucky	Harry Innes	George Nicholas	Saml. McDowell junr.

GO. WASHINGTON[84]

S A T U R D A Y, SEPTEMBER 26TH, 1789

The Senate proceeded to consider the Message from the President of the United States of the 24th instant, And the Nomination of JOHN JAY of New York to be Chief Justice of the Supreme Court of the United States;

And on the Question to advise and consent thereto,

---

[84] The message, in the hand of William Jackson and signed by George Washington, is in Executive Nominations, first session, Executive Proceedings, SR, DNA. Inserted between the names of Richd. Potts and Nathaniel Ramsay are the letters "p" and "c," which indicate passage of, or concurrence in, the nomination. The first names of Richard Law and Robert Forsyth appear to be written by Tobias Lear.

It passed in the affirmative.

The Senate proceeded to consider the nomination of JOHN RUTLEDGE of South Carolina to be one of the associate Judges;

And on the question to advise and consent thereto,

It passed in the affirmative.

The Senate proceeded to consider the nomination of JAMES WILSON of Pennsylvania, to be one of the associate Judges;

And on the question to advise and consent thereto,

It passed in the affirmative.

The Senate proceeded to consider the Nomination of WILLIAM CUSHING of Massachusetts, to be one of the associate Judges;

And on the question to advise and consent thereto,

It passed in the affirmative.

The Senate proceeded to consider the Nomination of ROBERT H. HARRI-SON of Maryland, to be one of the associate Judges;

And on the question to advise and consent thereto,

It passed in the affirmative.[85]

The Senate proceeded to consider the nomination of JOHN BLAIR of Virginia, to be one of the associate Judges;

And on the question to advise and consent thereto,

It passed in the affirmative.

The Senate proceeded to consider the nomination of DAVID SEWALL, to be Judge for the district of Main;

And on the question to advise and consent thereto,

It passed in the affirmative.

The Senate proceeded to consider the nomination of WILLIAM LITHGOW, to be Attorney for the district of Main;

And on the question to advise and consent thereto,

It passed in the affirmative.

The Senate proceeded to consider the nomination of HENRY DEARBORN, to be Marshal for the district of Main;

And on the question to advise and consent thereto,

It passed in the affirmative.

The Senate proceeded to consider the nomination of JOHN SULLIVAN to be Judge for the district of New Hampshire;

And on the question to advise and consent thereto,

It passed in the affirmative.

The Senate proceeded to consider the nomination of SAMUEL SHERBURNE Junr. to be Attorney for the district of New Hampshire;

---

[85] On February 9, 1790, the Senate was notified that Robert Harrison had declined this appointment and James Iredell had been appointed in his place.

And on the question to advise and consent thereto,
It passed in the affirmative.
The Senate proceeded to consider the nomination of JOHN PARKER, to be Marshal for the district of New Hampshire;
And on the question to advise and consent thereto,
It passed in the affirmative.
The Senate proceeded to consider the nomination of JOHN LOWELL, to be Judge for the district of Massachusetts;
And on the question to advise and consent thereto,
It passed in the affirmative.
The Senate proceeded to consider the nomination of CHRISTOPHER GORE, to be Attorney for the district of Massachusetts;
And on the question to advise and consent thereto,
It passed in the affirmative.
The Senate proceeded to consider the nomination of JONATHAN JACKSON, to be Marshal for the district of Massachusetts;
And on the question to advise and consent thereto,
It passed in the affirmative.
The Senate proceeded to consider the nomination of RICHARD LAW, to be Judge for the district of Connecticut;
And on the question to advise and consent thereto,
It passed in the affirmative.
The Senate proceeded to consider the nomination of PIERREPONT EDWARDS, to be Attorney for the district of Connecticut;
And on the question to advise and consent thereto,
It passed in the affirmative.
The Senate proceeded to consider the nomination of PHILIP BRADLEY, to be Marshal for the district of Connecticut;
And on the question to advise and consent thereto,
It passed in the affirmative.
The Senate proceeded to consider the nomination of FRANCIS HOPKINSON, to be Judge for the district of Pennsylvania;
And on the question to advise and consent thereto,
It passed in the affirmative.
The Senate proceeded to consider the nomination of WILLIAM LEWIS, to be Attorney for the district of Pennsylvania;
And on the question to advise and consent thereto,
It passed in the affirmative.
The Senate proceeded to consider the nomination of CLEMENT BIDDLE, to be Marshal for the district of Pennsylvania;
And on the question to advise and consent thereto,
It passed in the affirmative.

The Senate proceeded to consider the nomination of GUNNING BEDFORD, to be Judge for the district of Delaware;

And on the question to advise and consent thereto,

It passed in the affirmative.

The Senate proceeded to consider the nomination of GEORGE READ Junr. to be Attorney for the district of Delaware;

And on the question to advise and consent thereto,

It passed in the affirmative.

The Senate proceeded to consider the nomination of ALLAN MCLANE, to be Marshal for the district of Delaware;

And on the question to advise and consent thereto,

It passed in the affirmative.

The Senate proceeded to consider the nomination of THOMAS JOHNSON, to be Judge for the district of Maryland;

And on the question to advise and consent thereto,

It passed in the affirmative.[86]

The Senate proceeded to consider the nomination of RICHARD POTTS to be Attorney for the district of Maryland;

And on the question to advise and consent thereto,

It passed in the affirmative.

The Senate proceeded to consider the nomination of NATHANIEL RAMSAY, to be Marshal for the district of Maryland;

And on the question to advise and consent thereto,

It passed in the affirmative.

The Senate proceeded to consider the nomination of EDMUND PENDLETON, to be Judge for the district of Virginia;

And on the question to advise and consent thereto,

It passed in the affirmative.[87]

The Senate proceeded to consider the nomination of JOHN MARSHALL, to be Attorney for the district of Virginia;

And on the question to advise and consent thereto,

It passed in the affirmative.[88]

The Senate proceeded to consider the nomination of EDWARD CARRING-TON, to be Marshal for the district of Virginia;

And on the question to advise and consent thereto,

It passed in the affirmative.

---

[86] On February 9, 1790, the Senate was notified that Thomas Johnson had declined this appointment and William Paca had been nominated to replace him.

[87] On February 9, 1790, the Senate was notified that Edmund Pendleton had declined this appointment and Cyrus Griffin had been nominated to replace him.

[88] On February 9, 1790, the Senate was notified that John Marshall had declined this appointment and William Nelson, Jr., had been nominated to replace him.

The Senate proceeded to consider the nomination of THOMAS PINCKNEY, to be Judge for the district of South Carolina;

And on the question to advise and consent thereto,

It passed in the affirmative.[89]

The Senate proceeded to consider the nomination of JOHN JULIUS PRINGLE, to be Attorney for the district of South Carolina;

And on the question to advise and consent thereto,

It passed in the affirmative.

The Senate proceeded to consider the nomination of ISAAC HUGER, to be Marshal for the district of South Carolina;

And on the question to advise and consent thereto,

It passed in the affirmative.

The Senate proceeded to consider the nomination of NATHANIEL PENDLETON, to be Judge for the district of Georgia;

And on the question to advise and consent thereto,

It passed in the affirmative.

The Senate proceeded to consider the nomination of MATTHEW MCALLISTER, to be Attorney for the district of Georgia;

And on the question to advise and consent thereto,

It passed in the affirmative.

The Senate proceeded to consider the nomination of ROBERT FORSYTH, to be Marshal for the district of Georgia;

And on the question to advise and consent thereto,

It passed in the affirmative.

The Senate proceeded to consider the nomination of HARRY INNES, to be Judge for the district of Kentucky;

And on the question to advise and consent thereto,

It passed in the affirmative.

The Senate proceeded to consider the nomination of GEORGE NICHOLAS, to be Attorney for the district of Kentucky;

And on the question to advise and consent thereto,

It passed in the affirmative.[90]

The Senate proceeded to consider the nomination of SAMUEL MCDOWELL junr. to be Marshal for the district of Kentucky;

And on the question to advise and consent thereto,

It passed in the affirmative.

ORDERED, that the Secretary lay before the President of the United States, the proceedings of the Senate upon his Message of 24th September 1789.

A Message from the President of the United States—

---

[89] On February 9, 1790, the Senate was notified that Thomas Pinckney had declined this appointment and William Drayton had been nominated to replace him.

[90] On March 30, 1790, the Senate was notified that George Nicholas had declined this appointment and James Brown had been nominated to replace him.

Mr. Lear his Secretary informed the Vice President that he was commanded to bring the following Nominations to the Senate—
And he withdrew.

UNITED STATES, September 25th 1789

GENTLEMEN of the SENATE,

I nominate, JAMES DUANE, Judge
      WILLIAM S. SMITH, Marshal   for the district
      RICHARD HARRISON, Attorney   of New York

      DAVID BREARLY, Judge
      THOMAS LOWREY, Marshal   for the district
      RICHARD STOCKTON, Attorney   of New Jersey

And, I likewise nominate,

THOMAS JEFFERSON, for Secretary of State;

EDMUND RANDOLPH, for Attorney General;

SAMUEL OSGOOD, for Post Master General.

GO. WASHINGTON[91]

The Senate proceeded to consider the Message from the President of the
United States of the 25th of September, and the nomination of JAMES
DUANE, to be Judge for the district of New York;
   And on the question to advise and consent thereto,
             It passed in the affirmative.

The Senate proceeded to consider the nomination of WILLIAM S. SMITH,
to be Marshal for the district of New York;
   And on the question to advise and consent thereto,
             It passed in the affirmative.

The Senate proceeded to consider the nomination of RICHARD HARRISON,
to be Attorney for the district of New York;
   And on the question to advise and consent thereto,
             It passed in the affirmative.

The Senate proceeded to consider the nomination of DAVID BREARLY, to be
Judge for the district of New Jersey;
   And on the question to advise and consent thereto,
             It passed in the affirmative.[92]

The Senate proceeded to consider the nomination of THOMAS LOWREY, to
be Marshal for the district of New Jersey;
   And on the question to advise and consent thereto,
             It passed in the affirmative.

---

[91] The message, in the hand of William Jackson and signed by George Washington,
is in Executive Nominations, first session, Executive Proceedings, SR, DNA.

[92] On December 17, 1790, the Senate was notified that David Brearly had died and
Robert Morris had been nominated to replace him.

The Senate proceeded to consider the nomination of RICHARD STOCKTON, to be Attorney for the district of New Jersey;

And on the question to advise and consent thereto,

It passed in the affirmative.[93]

The Senate proceeded to consider the nomination of THOMAS JEFFERSON, to be Secretary of State;

And on the question to advise and consent thereto,

It passed in the affirmative.

The Senate proceeded to consider the nomination of EDMUND RANDOLPH, to be Attorney General;

And on the question to advise and consent thereto,

It passed in the affirmative.

The Senate proceeded to consider the nomination of SAMUEL OSGOOD, to be Post Master General;

And on the question to advise and consent thereto,

It passed in the affirmative.

ORDERED, That the Secretary lay before the President of the United States, the proceedings of the Senate on his Message of the 25th September 1789.

T U E S D A Y, SEPTEMBER 29TH, 1789

A Message from the President of the United States—

Mr. Lear his Secretary informed the Vice President, that he was commanded to bring the following nomination to the Senate—And he withdrew.

UNITED STATES of America, Septemr. 29th 1789

GENTLEMEN of the SENATE,

I nominate WILLIAM CARMICHAEL as Charge des Affaires from the United States of America, to the Court of Spain.

GO. WASHINGTON[94]

The Senate proceeded to consider the above Message.

And, upon the question to advise and consent to the appointment of WILLIAM CARMICHAEL, as Charge des Affaires from the United States of America, to the Court of Spain;

It passed in the affirmative.

---

[93] On January 3, 1791, the Senate was notified that Richard Stockton had resigned this position and Abraham Ogden had been nominated to replace him.

[94] The message, in the hand of Tobias Lear and signed by George Washington, is in Executive Nominations, first session, Executive Proceedings, SR, DNA. In the original message the words "of America" do not appear in the heading.

ORDERED, That the Secretary lay before the President of the United States, the proceedings of the Senate on his Message of this day.

A Message from the President of the United States by the Secretary at War; which he delivered to the Vice President—And withdrew.

UNITED STATES, September 29th 1789

GENTLEMEN of the SENATE,

Agreeably to the Act of Congress for adapting the establishment of the Troops in public service to the Constitution of the United States, I nominate the Persons, specified in the enclosed list, to be the commissioned Officers thereof.

This nomination differs from the existing arrangement only in the following cases—to wit:

Lieutenant ERKURIES BEATTY promoted to a vacant Captaincy in the Infantry—Ensign EDWARD SPEAR promoted to a vacant Lieutenancy of Artillery —JACOB MELCHER who has been serving as a volunteer, to be an Ensign, vice BENJAMIN LAWRENCE, who was appointed nearly three years past, and has never been mustered, or joined the Troops.

It is to be observed that the order, in which the Captains and Subalterns are named, is not to affect their relative rank, which has been hitherto but imperfectly settled, owing to the perplexity of promotions in the State-quotas conformably to the late Confederation.

GO. WASHINGTON[95]

OFFICERS of the REGIMENT of INFANTRY

Lieut. Colo. Commandant Josiah Harmar } And a Brigadier General by brevet, he having been appointed such by a Resolve of Congress of the 31st of July 1787.

Majors

John Palsgrave Wyllys
John F. Hamtramck

Captains

Jonathan Heart
David Ziegler
William McCurdy
John Mercer
David Strong
John Smith

---

[95] The message, in the hand of William Jackson and signed by George Washington, is in Executive Nominations, first session, Executive Proceedings, SR, DNA. The list which follows, in the hand of Tobias Lear and signed by George Washington, is filed with the message.

Joseph Ashton
Erkuries Beatty

Lieutenants

John Armstrong
John Pratt
Ebenezer Frothingham
William Kersey
Thomas Doyle
William Peters
Jacob Kingsbury
Ebenezer Denny

Ensigns

Francis Luse
Cornelius Ryrer Sedam
Nathan McDowell
Abner Prior
Robert Thompson
Asa Heartshorn
John Jeffers
Jacob Melcher

Surgeon

Richard Allison

Mates

John Elliot
John Scott
John Carmichael
Joshua Sumner

OFFICERS of the BATTALION ARTILLERY
Major Commandant   John Doughty
Captains

Henry Burbeck
William Ferguson
Joseph Savage
James Bradford

Lieutenants

John Peirce
Moses Porter
William Moore
Dirck Schuyler
Mahlon Ford
Matthew Ernest

Edward Spear
Ebenezer Smith Fowle

Surgeons Mate

Nathan Hayward

United States
September 29th } 1789

GO. WASHINGTON

The Senate proceeded to consider the above Nominations,
And on the question to advise and consent to their appointment
It passed in the affirmative.

ORDERED, that the Secretary lay before the President of the United States,
the proceedings of the Senate upon his Message of this day.[96]

Attest,
SAM. A. OTIS Secretary

---

[96] On June 2, 1790, the President sent another list of military appointments to the Senate.

SECOND SESSION

MONDAY, JANUARY 11TH, 1790

A Message from the President of the United States by the Secretary at War, was read as followeth—

UNITED STATES, January 11th 1790

GENTLEMEN of the SENATE,

Having advised with you upon the terms of a treaty to be offered to the Creek Nation of Indians, I think it proper you should be informed of the result of that business, previous to its coming before you in your legislative capacity.

I have therefore directed the Secretary for the Department of War, to lay before you my Instructions to the Commissioners, and their report in consequence thereof.

The apparently critical state of the southern frontier will render it expedient for me to communicate to both Houses of Congress, with other papers, the whole of the transactions relative to the Creeks, in order that they may be enabled to form a judgement of the measures which the case may require.

(signed)   GO. WASHINGTON[1]

ORDERED, That the Communication from the President of the United States be deferred for consideration.[2]

---

[1] The message, in the hand of Tobias Lear and signed by George Washington, is in President's Messages on Indian Relations, Executive Proceedings, SR, DNA. The related documents are printed in Part II of this volume under the heading Indian Relations—Southern.

[2] On August 4 the President sent the Senate a message relating to a secret article for the Treaty at New York with the Creeks. On the same day the Senate consented to the secret article.

T U E S D A Y, FEBRUARY 9TH, 1790

The following Messages from the President of the United States, were brought to the Senate by his Secretary—

UNITED STATES, February 9th 1790

GENTLEMEN of the SENATE,

You will perceive from the Papers herewith delivered, and which are enumerated in the annexed list,[3] that a difference subsists between Great Britain

---

[3] The list, in the hand of Tobias Lear, reads as follows:

A List of Papers delivered to the Senate with the foregoing Message—in the Bundle Marked—A.

No.   1. Resolve of the Legislature of Massachusetts dated June [July] 6th & 7th. 1784.
    2. Deposition of John Mitchell dated Octr. 9th. 1784.
    3. Report of Generals Lincoln & Knox to the Governor of Massachusetts dated October 19th 1784.
    4. Extract of a letter from the Honorable John Adams to Lieutenant Governor Cushing dated Octr. 25th 1784.
    5. Letter from Governor Hancock to Governor Parr of Nova Scotia—dated November 12th. 1784.
    6. Letter from Governor Parr to Governor Hancock dated December 7th 1784.
    7. Letter from Rufus Putnam to the Committee of Massachusetts dated December 27th. 1784.
    8. Report of the Secretary for foreign Affairs respecting Eastern Boundary dated April 21st 1785.
    9. Deposition of Nathan Jones dated March 17th. 1785.
   10. Copy of a Letter from Governor Carlton to Governor Hancock dated June 21st. 1785.
   11. Letter from James Avery to Governor Bowdoin dated August 23d. 1785.
   12. Advice of the Council of the Commonwealth of Massachusetts to the Governor dated September 9th. 1785.
   13. Letter from Governor Bowdoin to Governor Carlton dated September 9th. 1785.
   14. Report of the Secretary for foreign Affairs dated September 22d. 1785.
   15. Resolution of Congress dated October 13th. 1785.
   16. Copy of a letter from the Honorable John Jay to the Honorable John Adams—dated 1st. Novr. 1785.

A List of Papers delivered to the Senate with the foregoing Message—in the Bundle Marked—B.

No.   1. The Petition of James Boyd to the President, the Senate and the House of Representatives of the United States of America.
    2. Copy of the Proceedings of the Legislature of the Commonwealth of Massachusetts on the Petition of James Boyd, and a letter of instruction to the Delegates of that Commonwealth in Congress dated November 10th. 1786.
    3. Copy of a Declaration of John Mitchell relative to a Survey made by him in the year 1764 to ascertain the River, known by the name of St. Croix.
    4. Copy of a Declaration of Nathan Jones to the same effect as the preceding.

and the United States relative to the boundary line between our Eastern and their Territories. A plan for deciding this difference, was laid before the late Congress; and whether that, or some other Plan of a like kind, would not now be eligible, is submitted to your consideration.

In my opinion it is desireable that all questions between this and other Nations, be speedily and amicably settled; and in this instance I think it advisable to postpone any negotiations on the subject, until I shall be informed of the result of your deliberations, and receive your advice as to the propositions most proper to be offered on the part of the United States.

As I am taking measures for learning the intentions of Great Britain respecting the further detention of our Posts &c. I am the more solicitous that the business now submitted to you, may be prepared for negotiation, as soon as the other important affairs which engage your attention will permit.

GO. WASHINGTON[4]

UNITED STATES, February 9th 1790

GENTLEMEN of the SENATE,

I nominate as Collectors, Naval Officers and Surveyors for the Ports of the several districts in the State of North Carolina, the Persons whose names are respectively annexed to the Offices in the following List.

Districts	Ports	Officers	Nominations
Wilmington	Wilmington	Collector	James Read
		Naval Officer	John Walker
		Surveyor	Thomas Callender
	Swansborough	Surveyor	———
Newbern	Newbern	Collector	John Daves
	Beaufort	Surveyor	John Easton

5. Copy of a plan delivered to Capt. John Mitchell Surveyor, by His Excellency Francis Bernard Esqr. then Governor of the Province of the Massachusetts Bay, for the direction of the said Surveyor.

6. Copy of Remarks drawn up by C. Morris L. General respecting the Western limits of New Brunswick and the property of the Islands in the Bay of Passamaquody.

7. Extract of a letter from His Excellency John Adams Esquire to His Honor Lieutenant Governor Cushing Dated Autewel near Paris October 25th. 1784.

8. Extract from the Journals of Congress May 20th 1785.

9. Extracts from sundry Publications respecting the Boundaries of Nova Scotia.

Annotations on the list probably correspond to marks made by later publishers.

[4] The message, in the hand of Tobias Lear and signed by George Washington, is in President's Messages on Foreign Relations, Executive Proceedings, SR, DNA. The related documents are printed in Part II of this volume under the heading Northeast Boundary Dispute with Great Britain.

Districts	Ports	Officers	Nominations
Washington	Washington	Collector	Nathan Keais
	Edenton	Collector	Thomas Benbury
	Hartford	Surveyor	Joshua Skinner Junr. (Son of William)
Edenton	Murpheysborough	do	Hardy Murfree
	Plymouth	do	Levi Blount
	Winsor	do	————
	Skewarkey	do	Henry Hunter
	Winton	do	William Wynns
	Bennits Creek	do	John Baker
Camden	Plankbridge on Sawyers Creek	Collector	Isaac Gregory
	Nixinton	Surveyor	Hugh Knox
	Indian-town	do	Thomas Williams
	Currituck Inlet	do	————
	Pasquotank River Bridge	do	Edmund Sawyer
	New-biggen Creek	do	Elias Albertson

I likewise nominate SAMUEL SHAW to fill the Office of Consul of the United States of America at Canton in China.

GO. WASHINGTON[5]

UNITED STATES, February 9th 1790

GENTLEMEN of the SENATE,

Among the Persons appointed during your late Session, to Offices under the national Government, there were some who declined serving. Their names and Offices are specified in the first column of the annexed list. I supplied these vacancies, agreeably to the Constitution, by temporary appointments; which you will find mentioned in the second column of the list. These appointments will expire with your present Session, and indeed ought not to endure longer than until others can be regularly made—for that purpose I now nominate to you the Persons named in the third column of the list, as being in my opinion qualified to fill the Offices opposite to their names in the first.

GO. WASHINGTON[6]

---

[5] The message, in the hand of Tobias Lear and signed by George Washington, is in Executive Nominations, second session, Executive Proceedings, SR, DNA. The letter "a," probably indicating Senate agreement, follows each nomination.

[6] The message and the list which follows, in the hand of Tobias Lear and signed by George Washington, are in Executive Nominations, second session, Executive Pro-

A LIST of vacancies and Appointments which have taken place in the national Offices, during the late recess of the Senate, and of Persons nominated for them by the President of the United States on the 8th day of February 1790.

First Column Resignations	Second Column Temporary Appointments	Third Column Nominations
Robert H. Harrison, one of the Associate Judges of the Supreme Court	———	James Iredell, of North Carolina
Thomas Johnson, District Judge of Maryland	William Paca	William Paca
Edmund Pendleton, District Judge of Virginia	Cyrus Griffin	Cyrus Griffin
John Marshall, Attorney for the District of Virginia	William Nelson Junr.	William Nelson Junr.
Thomas Pinckney, District Judge of South Carolina	William Drayton	William Drayton
George Handley, Collector of the Port of Brunswick, in Georgia	———	Christopher Hillary
Peyton Short, Collector of the Port of Louisville in Kentucky	———	Richard Taylor
Asher Miller, Surveyor of the Port of Middletown in Connecticut	———	Comfort Sage

GO. WASHINGTON

ORDERED, that the consideration of the Message from the President of the United States, in respect to the "difference that subsists between Great Britain and the United States relative to the Eastern boundary" be postponed for consideration.[7]

ceedings, SR, DNA. The letter "a," probably indicating Senate agreement, follows each nomination.

[7] On February 10 the Senate committed this message.

ORDERED, That the consideration of the Message from the President of the United States, relative to "certain Persons who declined the acceptance of Offices, and to certain temporary appointments during the recess" be postponed until tomorrow.

ORDERED, that the Rules be so far dispensed with, as to proceed to consider the Message from the President of the United States, and the nominations of Collectors &c. for the State of North Carolina—and

On the question to advise and consent to the appointment of

JAMES READ, to be Collector of the Port of Wilmington—
It passed in the affirmative.

On the question to advise and consent to the appointment of JOHN WALKER, to be Naval Officer of the Port of Wilmington—
It passed in the Affirmative.

On the question to advise and consent to the appointment of THOMAS CALLENDER, to be Surveyor of the Port of Wilmington—
It passed in the Affirmative.

On the question to advise and consent to the appointment of JOHN DAVES, to be Collector of the Port of Newbern—
It passed in the Affirmative.

On the question to advise and consent to the appointment of JOHN EASTON, to be Surveyor of the Port of Beaufort—
It passed in the Affirmative.

On the question to advise and consent to the appointment of NATHAN KEAIS, to be Collector of the Port of Washington—
It passed in the Affirmative.

On the question to advise and consent to the appointment of THOMAS BENBURY, to be Collector of the Port of Edenton—
It passed in the Affirmative.

On the question to advise and consent to the appointment of JOSHUA SKINNER Junr. (Son of William) to be Surveyor of the Port of Hartford—
It passed in the Affirmative.

On the question to advise and consent to the appointment of HARDY MURFREE, to be Surveyor of the Port of Murpheysborough—
It passed in the Affirmative.

On the question to advise and consent to the appointment of LEVI BLOUNT, to be Surveyor of the Port of Plymouth—
It passed in the Affirmative.[8]

On the question to advise and consent to the appointment of HENRY HUNTER, to be Surveyor of the Port of Skewarkey—
It passed in the Affirmative.

---

[8] On May 25, 1790, the Senate was notified that Levi Blount had resigned this appointment and Thomas Freeman had been nominated to replace him.

On the question to advise and consent to the appointment of WILLIAM
WYNNS to be Surveyor of the Port of Winton—
It passed in the Affirmative.
On the question to advise and consent to the appointment of JOHN BAKER,
to be Surveyor of the Port of Bennits Creek—
It passed in the Affirmative.
On the question to advise and consent to the appointment of ISAAC
GREGORY, to be Collector of the Port of Plankbridge on Sawyers Creek—
It passed in the Affirmative.
On the question to advise and consent to the appointment of HUGH KNOX,
to be Surveyor of the Port of Nixinton—
It passed in the Affirmative.
On the question to advise and consent to the appointment of THOMAS
WILLIAMS, to be Surveyor of the Port of Indian-town—
It passed in the Affirmative.
On the question to advise and consent to the appointment of EDMUND
SAWYER, to be Surveyor of the Port of Pasquotank River bridge—
It passed in the Affirmative.
On the question to advise and consent to the appointment of ELIAS
ALBERTSON, to be Surveyor of the Port of New-biggen Creek—
It passed in the Affirmative.
And, a certified Copy as usual, of the advice and consent of the Senate,
was laid before the President of the United States.
ORDERED, that the nomination of Samuel Shaw, to fill the Office of Consul
of the United States of America, at Canton in China, be postponed until
tomorrow.

WEDNESDAY, FEBRUARY 10TH, 1790

The Senate proceeded to consider the Nominations made by the President
of the United States in his Messages of the 9th instant—And,
On the question to advise and consent to the appointment of SAMUEL
SHAW, to fill the Office of Consul of the United States of America, at Canton
in China—
It passed in the Affirmative.
On the question to advise and consent to the appointment of JAMES
IREDELL, to be one of the Associate Judges of the Supreme Court—
It passed in the Affirmative.
On the question to advise and consent to the appointment of WILLIAM
PACA, to be District Judge of Maryland—
It passed in the Affirmative.

On the question to advise and consent to the appointment of CYRUS GRIF-FIN, to be District Judge of Virginia—

It passed in the Affirmative.

On the question to advise and consent to the appointment of WILLIAM NELSON Junr. to be Attorney for the District of Virginia—

It passed in the Affirmative.

On the question to advise and consent to the appointment of WILLIAM DRAYTON, to be District Judge of South Carolina—

It passed in the Affirmative.[9]

On the question to advise and consent to the appointment of CHRISTO-PHER HILLARY, to be Collector of the Port of Brunswick, in Georgia—

It passed in the Affirmative.

On the question to advise and consent to the appointment of RICHARD TAYLOR, to be Collector of the Port of Louisville, in Kentucky—

It passed in the Affirmative.

On the question to advise and consent to the appointment of COMFORT SAGE, to be Surveyor of the port of Middletown, in Connecticut—

It passed in the Affirmative.

And, a certified Copy as usual, of the advice and consent of the Senate, was laid before the President of the United States.

The Senate proceeded to consider the Message from the President of the United States of the 9th instant, in respect to the "difference that subsists between Great Britain and the United States, relative to the Eastern boundary"—And,

ORDERED, that the Message with the papers accompanying the same be committed to

Mr. Strong,
Mr. Butler,
Mr. Paterson,
Mr. Hawkins &
Mr. Johnson, to Report what is proper to be done thereon.[10]

T H U R S D A Y, FEBRUARY 18TH, 1790

A message from the President of the United States, by his Secretary, was read:

---

[9] On June 11, 1790, the Senate was notified that William Drayton had died and Thomas Bee had been appointed to replace him.

[10] On February 18 the President sent further documents relating to the Northeast boundary to the Senate, and these documents were referred to this committee.

UNITED STATES, February 18th 1790

GENTLEMEN of the SENATE,

By the mail of last evening I received a Letter from His Excellency John Hancock, Governor of the Commonwealth of Massachusetts, enclosing a Resolve of the Senate and House of Representatives of that Commonwealth, and sundry Documents relative to the Eastern boundary of the United States.

I have directed a copy of the Letter and Resolve to be laid before you. The documents which accompanied them being but copies of some of the papers which were delivered to you with my communication of the ninth of this month, I have thought it unnecessary to lay them before you at this time. They will be deposited in the Office of the Secretary of State, together with the originals of the above mentioned Letter and Resolve.

G. WASHINGTON[11]

ORDERED, That the message and Papers accompanying the same be committed to the Committee appointed the 10th of February, to take into consideration the Presidents message of a similar nature.[12]

---

[11] The message, in the hand of Tobias Lear and signed by George Washington, is in President's Messages on Foreign Relations, Executive Proceedings, SR, DNA. The related documents are printed in Part II of this volume under the heading Northeast Boundary Dispute with Great Britain.

[12] On March 9 this committee reported.

T U E S D A Y, March 9th, 1790

Mr. Strong reported on behalf of the Committee, to whom were referred the Messages from the President of the United States, of the 9th and 18th of February, respecting the "difference that subsists between Great Britain and the United States relative to the Eastern boundary;" which report was read:[13] And

ORDERED, That it lie until to morrow.[14]

W E D N E S D A Y, March 10th, 1790

Agreeably to the order of the day, the Senate proceeded to consider the report of the Committee, to whom were referred the messages from the President of the United States, of the 9th and 18th of February, respecting the "difference that subsists between Great Britain and the United States, relative to the Eastern Boundary;" Which is as follows:[15]

That in their opinion effectual measures should be taken as soon as conveniently may be, to settle all disputes with the Crown of Great Britain relative to that Line.[16]

That it would be proper to cause[17] a Representation of the case to be made to the Court of Great Britain, and[18] to propose that Commissioners be appointed to hear and finally decide those disputes, in the manner pointed out in the Report of the late Secretary of the United States for the department of Foreign Affairs, of the 21st of April 1785, a copy of which Report accompanied the first of the said Messages.

And, that Measures should be taken to perpetuate the Testimonies of John

---

[13] The report, in the hand of Caleb Strong, is in Various Select Committee Reports, SR, DNA. It was printed in the journal on March 10, 1790. After the report was introduced into the Senate, it was amended—the amendments were written on the original report by Samuel Otis—and it became the Senate resolution of March 24, 1790.

[14] On March 10 this report was printed and considered.

[15] In the original report the above paragraph reads: "The Committee to whom the Presidents Messages of the 9th. & 18th. of February relating to the Differences subsisting between Great Britain & the United States relative to the eastern Boundary of the said States, were committed, beg leave to report. . . ."

[16] At this point in the original report the letter "a" is written, probably indicating Senate agreement to this paragraph.

[17] At this point in the original report the word "present" is lined out and "cause" is written above it. This correction was made before the report was presented.

[18] At this point in the original report the phrase "if the said disputes cannot be otherwise amicably adjusted" is inserted, in the hand of Samuel Otis. This addition is included in the Senate resolve of March 24, 1790.

Mitchell and Nathan Jones, who were appointed by the late Governor Bernard, in 1764, to ascertain the River St. Croix.[19]

ORDERED, That the farther consideration hereof be postponed.[20]

The Senate agreed to advise and consent that the President of the United States should direct the word "Junior," to be annexed to the name of Jonathan Palmer, appointed Surveyor of Stonington in the State of Connecticut, August the 3d 1789.

M O N D A Y, MARCH 15TH, 1790

On motion,

The Senate proceeded to consider the report of the Committee appointed upon the President's messages of the 9th and 18th of February, respecting the "difference that subsists between Great Britain and the United States, relative to the Eastern boundary"—

ORDERED, That the consideration hereof be farther postponed.[21]

W E D N E S D A Y, MARCH 24TH, 1790

The Senate proceeded in the farther consideration of the report of the Committee, to whom was referred the Messages from the President of the United States, of the 9th and 18th of February 1790, respecting the "difference subsisting between Great Britain and the United States, relative to the Eastern boundary"—which being amended was accepted:

Whereupon

RESOLVED, That the Senate do advise that effectual Measures should be taken as soon as conveniently may be to settle all Disputes with the Crown of Great Britain relative to that Line.

That it would be proper to cause a Representation of the Case to be made to the Court of Great Britain, and if the said disputes cannot be otherwise amicably adjusted, to propose that Commissioners be appointed to hear and finally decide those disputes, in the manner pointed out in the report of the late Secretary of the United States for the Department of foreign Affairs of

---

[19] At this point in the original report the phrase "and of any other Persons who may have useful Information on this subject" is inserted, in the hand of Samuel Otis. This addition is included in the Senate resolution of March 24, 1790. Following the insert is the letter "a," probably indicating Senate agreement.

[20] On March 15 this report was considered again.

[21] On March 24 this report was considered again, and a resolution on the Northeast boundary was agreed to.

the 21st of April 1785, a Copy of which Report accompanied the first of the said Messages.

And that Measures should be taken to perpetuate the Testimony of John Mitchell and Nathan Jones, who were appointed by the late Governor Bernard in 1764, to ascertain the River St. Croix, and of any other Persons who may have useful information on this subject.

ORDERED, that a Copy of this Resolve be laid before the President of the United States, and the original Papers returned to the Office of the Secretary of State.

TUESDAY, MARCH 30TH, 1790

A message from the President of the United States, by his Secretary, was read:

UNITED STATES, March 30, 1790

GENTLEMEN of the SENATE,

I nominate the following persons to fill the Offices which are affixed to their respective names, viz.

RUFUS PUTNAM, to be one of the Judges in the Western Territory, in the place of SAMUEL HOLDEN PARSONS, deceased.

JAMES BROWN, to be Attorney for the United States in the District of Kentucky, in the place of GEORGE NICHOLAS, who has declined his appointment.

HENRY BOGART (of Albany), to be Surveyor of the Port Albany, in the place of JEREMIAH LANSING, who has resigned his Office.

GO. WASHINGTON[22]

WEDNESDAY, MARCH 31ST, 1790

The Senate proceeded to the consideration of the Message from the President of the United States, of the 30th of March, nominating

RUFUS PUTNAM, to be one of the Judges in the Western Territory, in the place of SAMUEL HOLDEN PARSONS, deceased.

JAMES BROWN, to be Attorney for the United States in the district of Kentucky, in the place of GEORGE NICHOLAS, who has declined his Appointment—and[23]

---

[22] The message, in the hand of Tobias Lear and signed by George Washington, is in Executive Nominations, second session, Executive Proceedings, SR, DNA. The letter "a," probably indicating Senate agreement, follows each nomination.

[23] On February 25, 1791, the Senate was notified that James Brown had declined this appointment and William Murray had been nominated to replace him.

HENRY BOGART, (of Albany) to be Surveyor of the Port of Albany, in the place of JEREMIAH LANSING, who has resigned his Office.

RESOLVED, That the Senate do advise and consent to their appointment to the Offices to which they are respectively nominated.

And a certified Copy as usual, of the above Resolve was laid before the President of the United States.

WEDNESDAY, APRIL 28TH, 1790

A Message from the President of the United States by Mr. Nelson, was read:

UNITED STATES, April 28th 1790

GENTLEMEN of the SENATE,

I nominate GEORGE WRAY to be Collector of the Port of Hampton in the State of Virginia in the place of JACOB WRAY resigned: Also, JOHN MCCULLOUGH to be Surveyor of the Port of Swansborough in the district of Wilmington, and WILLIAM BENSON to be Surveyor of the Port of Windsor in the district of Edenton, both in the State of North-Carolina.

GO. WASHINGTON[24]

ORDERED, That the Message lie for consideration.

THURSDAY, APRIL 29TH, 1790

The Senate proceeded to the consideration of the Message from the President of the United States, of the 28th of April, nominating,

For the State of Virginia

		for the District of	for the Port of
George Wray	Collector	"	Hampton

For the State of North Carolina

John McCullough,	Surveyor	Wilmington	Swansborough
William Benson,	Surveyor	Edenton	Windsor and,

RESOLVED, That the Senate do advise and consent to their appointment to the Offices, to which they are respectively nominated.

And, a certified copy as usual, of the above Resolve was laid before the President of the United States.

---

[24] The message, in the hand of Thomas Nelson, Jr., and signed by George Washington, is in Executive Nominations, second session, Executive Proceedings, SR, DNA.

T U E S D A Y, MAY 25TH, 1790

A Message from the President of the United States by his Secretary, was read:

UNITED STATES, May 25th 1790

GENTLEMEN of the SENATE,

I nominate the following Persons to fill the Offices affixed to their names, vizt.

SAMUEL JASPER, to be Surveyor of the Port of Currituck Inlet, in the State of North Carolina.

NATHANIEL WILKINS, to be Collector of the Port of Cherry Stone in the State of Virginia, in the place of GEORGE SAVAGE, who has resigned.

HENRY DERING, to be Collector of the Port of Sagg Harbour in the State of New York, in the place of JOHN GELSTON who has resigned.

THOMAS DAVIS FREEMAN, to be Surveyor of the Port of Plymouth in the State of North Carolina, in the place of LEVI BLOUNT who has resigned.

BENJAMIN BARTLETT, to be Surveyor of the Port of Suffolk in the State of Virginia, in the place of ARCHIBALD RICHARDSON, who has resigned.

GO. WASHINGTON[25]

ORDERED, That the message lie for consideration.

W E D N E S D A Y, MAY 26TH, 1790

The Senate proceeded to consider the message from the President of the United States of the 25th of May,   and

RESOLVED, That they do advise and consent to the appointment of

SAMUEL JASPER, to be Surveyor of the Port of Currituck Inlet, State of North Carolina.

HENRY DERING, to be Collector of the Port of Sagg Harbour, State of New York—in the place of JOHN GELSTON, who has resigned.

THOMAS DAVIS FREEMAN, to be Surveyor of the Port of Plymouth, State of North Carolina, in the place of LEVI BLOUNT, who has resigned.

ORDERED, That the nomination of Nathaniel Wilkins and of Benjamin Bartlett, be postponed.

---

[25] The message, in the hand of Tobias Lear and signed by George Washington, is in Executive Nominations, second session, Executive Proceedings, SR, DNA. Following each nomination is the letter "a." In addition, the nominations of Wilkins and Bartlett have the letter "p." The letter "a" probably indicates Senate agreement, while "p" probably indicates temporary postponement during the proceedings.

And, a certified copy as usual, of the above Resolve was laid before the President of the United States.

T H U R S D A Y, MAY 27TH, 1790

The Senate proceeded to consider the message from the President of the United States of the 25th of May,   and
RESOLVED, That they do advise and consent to the appointment of
NATHANIEL WILKINS, to be Collector of the Port of Cherry Stone, State of Virginia, in the place of GEORGE SAVAGE, who has resigned.
BENJAMIN BARTLETT, to be Surveyor of the Port of Suffolk State of Virginia, in the place of ARCHIBALD RICHARDSON, who has resigned.
And, a certified copy as usual, of the above Resolve was laid before the President of the United States.

T U E S D A Y, June 1st, 1790

A Message from the President of the United States, by his Secretary, was read:

UNITED STATES, May 31st 1790

GENTLEMEN of the SENATE,

MR. DE POIREY served in the America Army for several of the last years of the late War, as Secretary to Major General the Marquis de la Fayette, and might probably at that time have obtained the Commission of Captain from Congress upon application to that Body. At present he is an Officer in the French National Guards, and solicits a Brevet Commission from the United States of America. I am authorised to add, that, while the compliance will involve no expense on our part, it will be particularly grateful to that friend of America, the Marquis de la Fayette.

I therefore nominate M. DE POIREY to be a Captain by Brevet.

GO. WASHINGTON[26]

ORDERED, That the message lie for consideration.

W E D N E S D A Y, June 2nd, 1790

The Senate proceeded to consider the Message from the President of the United States of the 31st of May, and the nomination of

M. DE POIREY, to be a Captain by Brevet in the service of the United States, and

RESOLVED, That the Senate do advise and consent to his appointment.

ORDERED, That the Secretary communicate as usual to the President of the United States, the proceedings of Senate hereupon.

A message from the President of the United States, by his Secretary, was read:

UNITED STATES, June 2d 1790

GENTLEMEN of the SENATE,

The Troops at present in service consisting of one regiment of Infantry and one Battalion of Artillery were apportioned by the Acts of the former Congress on the States of Massachusetts, Connecticut, New York, New Jersey and Pennsylvania; and as the Officers of said Troops are in actual service, I

---

[26] The message, in the hand of Tobias Lear and signed by George Washington, is in Executive Nominations, second session, Executive Proceedings, SR, DNA.

nominate them, as in the list hereunto annexed, according to their ranks respectively, for appointments under the act for regulating the military establishment of the United States, passed the 30th of April 1790. And as the said Act requires an additional number of Officers for one battalion of Infantry, I nominate, under the head of *"New Appointments"* in the annexed List, the Officers for the same from Maryland, Virginia, North Carolina and Georgia; it being proposed to raise the said battalion in those States.

Go. Washington[27]

INFANTRY
OFFICERS IN SERVICE

Rank	Names	State
Lieutenant Colonel Commandant	Josiah Harmar	Brigadier General by Brevet 31st July 1787 Pennsylvania
Majors	John Palsgrave Wyllys	Connecticut
	John F. Hamtramck	New York
Captains	1. David Ziegler	Pennsylvania
	2. Jonathan Heart	Connecticut
	3. David Strong	Ditto
	4. William McCurdy	Pennsylvania
	5. John Mercer	New Jersey
	6. John Smith	New York
	7. Joseph Ashton	Pennsylvania
	8. Erkuries Beatty	Ditto
Lieutenants	1. Thomas Doyle	Pennsylvania
	2. John Armstrong	Ditto
	3. Ebenezer Frothingham	Connecticut
	4. John Pratt	Ditto
	5. William Kersey	New Jersey
	6. William Peters	New York
	7. Jacob Kingsbury	Connecticut
	8. Ebenezer Denny	Pennsylvania
Ensigns	1. Cornelius R. Sedam	New Jersey
	2. Nathan McDowell	Pennsylvania
	3. John Jeffers	Connecticut
	4. Abner Prior	New York

[27] The message, in the hand of Tobias Lear and signed by George Washington, is in Executive Nominations, second session, Executive Proceedings, SR, DNA. The list which follows, in the hand of John Stagg, Jr., and signed by George Washington, is filed with the message.

INFANTRY

OFFICERS IN SERVICE

Rank	Names	State
	5. Asa Heartshorn	Connecticut
	6. Robert Thompson	Pennsylvania
	7. Jacob Melcher	Ditto
	8. John Morgan	New Jersey—vice Francis Luse resigned 1 May 1790
Surgeon	Richard Allison	Pensylvania
	John Elliott	New York
	John M. Scott	New Jersey

New Appointments

Rank	Names	State	
Major	Alexander Parker	Virginia	
Captains	1. Alexander Trueman	Maryland	
	2. Joseph Monfort	North Carolina	
	3. Michael Rudolph	Georgia	
	4. Ballard Smith	Virginia	Officers
Lieutenants	1. Thomas Martin	Georgia	who served
	2. Thomas Pasteur	North Carolina	in the
	3. Mark McPherson	Maryland	late War
	4. John Steel	Virginia	
Ensigns	1. Richard Archer	Ditto[28]	
	2. Thomas Seayres	Ditto	
	3. Ezekiel Polk	North Carolina	
	4. James Clay	Georgia	

ARTILLERY

OFFICERS IN SERVICE

Rank	Names	State
Major Commandant	John Doughty	New Jersey
Captains	1. William Ferguson	Pennsylvania
	2. James Bradford	New York
	3. Henry Burbeck	Massachusetts
	4. Joseph Savage	Ditto
Lieutenants	1. Mahlon Ford	New Jersey
	2. Dirck Schuyler	New York
	3. John Peirce	Massachusetts
	4. Moses Porter	Ditto

[28] On December 17, 1790, the Senate was notified that Richard Archer had declined this appointment and John Heth had been nominated to replace him.

ARTILLERY
OFFICERS IN SERVICE

Rank	Names	State
	5. William Moore	Ditto
	6. Mathew Ernest	New York
	7. Ebenezer Smith Fowle	Massachusetts
	8. Edward Spear	Pennsylvania
Surgeons Mate }	Nathan Hayward	Massachusetts
		Go. WASHINGTON

ORDERED, That the Message lie for consideration until to morrow.[29]

THURSDAY, JUNE 3D, 1790

The Senate proceeded to consider the Message from the President of the United States, of the 2d of June, and the nominations therein contained, and

RESOLVED, That the Senate do advise and consent to their appointment.

ORDERED, That the Secretary communicate as usual, to the President of the United States, the proceedings of Senate hereupon.[30]

FRIDAY, JUNE 4TH, 1790

A message from the President of the United States, by Mr. Lear his Secretary was read, as follows:

UNITED STATES, June 4th 1790

GENTLEMEN of the SENATE,

I nominate the following persons to be Consuls and Vice-Consuls of the United States of America for the Ports which are affixed to their Names—Vizt.

Cadiz   RICHARD HARRISON of Virginia to be Consul of the United States of America for the Port of Cadiz in the Kingdom of Spain, and for such parts of the said Kingdom as shall be nearer to the said Port than to the residence of any other Consul or Vice-Consul of the United States in the said Kingdom;

---

[29] On June 3 these nominations were agreed to.

[30] On March 3, 1791, the President sent another list of military appointments to the Senate.

Bilboa	EDWARD CHURCH of Massachusetts to be Consul of the United States of America for the Port of Bilboa in the Kingdom of Spain, and for such parts of the said Kingdom as shall be nearer to the said Port than to the residence of any other Consul or Vice-Consul of the United States in the said Kingdom;
Madeira	JOHN MARSDEN PINTARD of New-York to be Consul of the United States of America for the Island of Madeira, and such other Islands of the allegiance of her most faithful Majesty as are nearer to the same than to the residence of any other Consul or Vice-Consul of the United States within the same allegiance;
Liverpool	JAMES MAURY of Virginia to be Consul of the United States of America for the Port of Liverpool in the Kingdom of Great Britain, and for such parts of the said Kingdom as shall be nearer to the said Port than to the residence of any other Consul or Vice-Consul of the United States in the said Kingdom;
Cowes	THOMAS AULDJO of the Kingdom of Great Britain, to be Vice-Consul of the United States of America for the port of Cowes, and such parts of the same Kingdom as shall be nearer to the said Port than to the residence of any other Consul or Vice-Consul of the United States within the said Kingdom;
Dublin	WILLIAM KNOX of New York to be Consul of the United States of America for the Port of Dublin in the Kingdom of Ireland, and for such parts of the said Kingdom as shall be nearer to the said Port than to the residence of any other Consul or Vice-Consul of the United States in the said Kingdom;
Marseilles	The Sieur ETIENNE CATHALAN the younger of the Kingdom of France, Vice-Consul of the United States of America for the Port of Marseilles and for such parts of the same Kingdom as shall be nearer to the said Port than to the residence of any other Consul or Vice-Consul of the United States within the same Kingdom;
Bordeaux	JAMES FENWICK of Maryland to be Consul of the United States of America for the port of Bordeaux in the Kingdom of France, and for such parts of the same Kingdom as shall be

nearer to the said Port than to the residence of any other Consul or Vice-Consul of the United States in the same Kingdom;

Nantes BURRILL CARNES of Massachusetts to be Consul of the United States of America for the Port of Nantes in the Kingdom of France, and for such parts of the said Kingdom as are nearer to the said Port than to the residence of any other Consul or Vice-Consul of the United States in the same Kingdom;

Havre The Sieur DE LA MOTTE of the Kingdom of France, to be Vice-Consul of the United States of America for the port of Havre de Grace, and such parts of the said Kingdom as shall be nearer to the said Port than to the residence of any other Consul or Vice-Consul of the United States within the same Kingdom;

Rouen NATHANIEL BARRETT of Massachusetts, to be Consul of the United States of America for the Port of Rouen in the Kingdom of France, and for such parts of the said Kingdom as shall be nearer to the said Port than to the residence of any other Consul or Vice-Consul of the United States in the said Kingdom;

Hispaniola SYLVANUS BOURNE of Massachusetts, to be Consul of the United States of America for the Island of Hispaniola, and for such other Islands of the allegiance of his most Christian Majesty, as shall be nearer thereto than to the residence of any other Consul or Vice-Consul of the United States within the same allegiance;

Martinique FULWAR SKIPWITH of Virginia, to be Consul of the United States of America for the Island of Martinique, and for such other Islands and places of the allegiance of his Most Christian Majesty as shall be nearer thereto than to the residence of any other Consul or Vice-Consul of the United States within the same allegiance;

Hamburgh JOHN PARISH, merchant of Hamburgh, to Vice-Consul of the United States of America for Hamburgh.

GO. WASHINGTON[31]

---

[31] The message, in the hand of Tobias Lear and signed by George Washington, is

ORDERED, That the message lie for consideration.

M O N D A Y, JUNE 7TH, 1790

The Senate proceeded to consider the message from the President of the United States of the 4th of June,   and
RESOLVED, That they do advise and consent to the appointment of

Cadiz
    RICHARD HARRISON of Virginia to be Consul of the United States of America for the Port of Cadiz in the Kingdom of Spain, and for such parts of ye said Kingdom as shall be nearer to the said Port than to the residence of any other Consul or Vice-Consul of the United States in the said Kingdom;

Madeira
    JOHN MARSDEN PINTARD of New York, to be Consul of the United States of America, for the Island of Madeira, and such other Islands of the allegiance of her most faithful Majesty as are nearer to the same than to the residence of any other Consul or Vice-Consul of the United States within the same allegiance;

Liverpool
    JAMES MAURY of Virginia to be Consul of the United States of America for the Port of Liverpool in the Kingdom of Great Britain, and for such parts of the said Kingdom as shall be nearer to the said Port than to the residence of any other Consul or Vice-Consul of the United States in the said Kingdom;

Dublin
    WILLIAM KNOX of New York to be Consul of the United States of America for the port of Dublin in the Kingdom of Ireland, and for such parts of the said Kingdom as shall be nearer to the said Port than to the residence of any other Consul or Vice-Consul of the United States in the said Kingdom;

Bordeaux
    JAMES FENWICK[32] of Maryland, to be Consul of the United States of America for the Port of Bordeaux in the Kingdom of France, and for such parts of the same Kingdom as shall be nearer to the said Port than to the residence of any other Consul or Vice-Consul of the United States in the same Kingdom;

---

in Executive Nominations, second session, Executive Proceedings, SR, DNA. The letter "a" is written after each nomination, except those of Pintard, Fenwick, Barrett, and Skipwith.

[32] On June 23 the Senate was notified that Fenwick's Christian name was Joseph.

Nantes   BURRILL CARNES of Massachusetts, to be Consul of the United
              States of America for the Port of Nantes in the Kingdom of
              France, and for such parts of the said Kingdom as are nearer
              to the said Port than to the residence of any other Consul or
              Vice-Consul of the United States in the same Kingdom;

Rouen   NATHANIEL BARRETT of Massachusetts to be Consul of the
              United States of America for the port of Rouen in the King-
              dom of France, and for such parts of the said Kingdom as
              shall be nearer to the said Port than to the residence of any
              other Consul or Vice-Consul of the United States in the said
              Kingdom;

Hispaniola   SYLVANUS BOURNE of Massachusetts, to be Consul of the
              United States of America for the Island of Hispaniola, and
              for such other Islands of the allegiance of his most Christian
              Majesty as shall be nearer thereto than to the residence of any
              other Consul or Vice-Consul of the United States within the
              same allegiance;   and of

Martinique   FULWAR SKIPWITH of Virginia, to be Consul of the United
              States of America for the Island of Martinique, and for such
              other Islands and places of the allegiance of his most Christian
              Majesty as shall be nearer thereto than to the residence of any
              other Consul or Vice-Consul of the United States within the
              same allegiance.

ORDERED, That the nominations of Edward Church, Thomas Auldjo, The
Sieur Etienne Cathalan the younger, The Sieur de La Motte and John Parish
be postponed.

ORDERED, That the Secretary, as usual, lay before the President of the
United States, an attested Copy of the Resolutions of Senate upon his message of the 4th of June 1790.

A message from the President of the United States, by Mr. Lear his Secretary, was read, as follows:

UNITED STATES, June 7th 1790

GENTLEMEN of the SENATE,

In pursuance of the law lately passed for giving effect to an Act, entitled,
"An Act to establish the Judicial Courts of the United States," within the
State of North Carolina—I nominate the following persons to fill the Judicial
Offices in that district—Vizt.

WILLIAM R. DAVIE   to be Judge[33]
JOHN SITGREAVES   to be Attorney—and
JOHN SKINNER   to be Marshall of the district
of North Carolina.

I likewise nominate the following Persons to fill Offices established by Law within the Territory of the United States south of the River Ohio—Vizt.

WILLIAM BLOUNT   to be Governor
DAVID CAMPBELL & }
JOHN MCNAIRY   }   to be Judges—and

DANIEL SMITH, to be Secretary of the Territory of the United States south of the River Ohio.[34]

ORDERED, That the message lie for consideration.

T U E S D A Y, JUNE 8TH, 1790

The Senate proceeded to consider the message from the President of the United States, of the 7th of June, and the nominations therein contained, and RESOLVED, That they do advise and consent to their appointment.

ORDERED, That the Secretary lay before the President of the United States, an attested Copy of the Resolution of Senate upon his message of the 7th of June 1790.

F R I D A Y, JUNE 11TH, 1790

A message from the President of the United States, by Mr. Lear his Secretary was read, as follows:

UNITED STATES, June 11th 1790

GENTLEMEN of the SENATE,

I nominate THOMAS BEE to be Judge of the South Carolina district, in the place of WILLIAM DRAYTON deceased.

GO. WASHINGTON[35]

ORDERED, That the message lie for consideration.

---

[33] On August 2 the Senate was notified that William R. Davie had declined this office and John Stokes had been nominated to replace him.

[34] The message, in the hand of Tobias Lear and signed by George Washington, is in Executive Nominations, second session, Executive Proceedings, SR, DNA. The letter "a," probably indicating Senate agreement, follows each nomination.

[35] The message, in the hand of Tobias Lear and signed by George Washington, is in Executive Nominations, second session, Executive Proceedings, SR, DNA.

MONDAY, JUNE 14TH, 1790

The Senate proceeded to consider the message from the President of the United States, of the 11th of June, and

RESOLVED, That they do advise and consent to the appointment of

THOMAS BEE, to be Judge of the South Carolina district, in the place of WILLIAM DRAYTON, deceased.

ORDERED, That the Secretary lay before the President of the United States, an attested Copy of the Resolution of Senate upon his message of the 11th of June 1790.

A message from the President of the United States by Mr. Lear his Secretary was read, as follows:

UNITED STATES, June 14th 1790

GENTLEMEN of the SENATE,

I nominate the following Persons to be Collectors, Naval Officers and Surveyors of the Ports of New Port and Providence in the State of Rhode Island and Providence Plantations—Vizt.

WILLIAM ELLERY to be Collector,
ROBERT CROOKE to be Naval Officer, } of New-Port
DANIEL LYMAN to be Surveyor
JEREMIAH OLNEY to be Collector,
THEODORE FOSTER to be Naval Officer, } of Providence
WILLIAM BARTON to be Surveyor

GO. WASHINGTON[36]

ORDERED, That the Rules be so far dispensed with as that the Senate proceed to the consideration of the message from the President of the United States of this day,

Whereupon

RESOLVED, That the Senate do advise and consent to the appointment of the persons therein named, to the Offices to which they are respectively nominated.

ORDERED, That the Secretary lay before the President of the United States, the proceedings of Senate upon this message.

THURSDAY, JUNE 17TH, 1790

The Senate resumed the consideration of the Message from the President of the United States, of the 4th of June—

---

[36] The message, in the hand of Tobias Lear and signed by George Washington, is in Executive Nominations, second session, Executive Proceedings, SR, DNA.

And on motion that it be

RESOLVED, that it may be expedient to advise and consent to the appointment of Foreigners to the Offices of Consuls or Vice-Consuls for the United
States.[37]

A motion was made to postpone this to take up the following—

RESOLVED, that in the opinion of[38] Senate the Appointment of Consuls
and Vice-Consuls should be confined to Citizens of the United States, except
in special cases[39] of urgent necessity[40]—

It passed in the Negative.

And on the main question,

It passed in the Affirmative.

RESOLVED, That the Senate do advise and consent to the appointment

Bilboa	Of EDWARD CHURCH of Massachusetts to be Consul of the United States of America for the Port of Bilboa in the Kingdom of Spain, and for such parts of the said Kingdom as shall be nearer to the said Port than to the residence of any other Consul or Vice-Consul of the United States in the said Kingdom;
Cowes	Of THOMAS AULDJO of the Kingdom of Great Britain, to be Vice-Consul of the United States of America for the Port of Cowes, and such parts of the same Kingdom as shall be nearer to the said Port than to the residence of any other Consul or Vice-Consul of the United States within the said Kingdom;[41]
Marseilles	Of The Sieur ETIENNE CATHALAN the younger of the Kingdom of France, to be Vice-Consul of the United States of America for the Port of Marseilles and for such parts of the same Kingdom as shall be nearer to the said Port than to the residence of any other Consul or Vice-Consul of the United States within the same Kingdom; &
Hamburgh	Of JOHN PARISH, merchant of Hamburgh, to be Vice-Consul of the United States of America for Hamburgh.

[37] The resolution, in the hand of Pierce Butler, is in Other Records, Executive Proceedings, SR, DNA. It is endorsed "Executive" at the top by Samuel Otis.

[38] At this point in the original resolution the word "the" is included.

[39] At this point in the original resolution the words "of great necessity" are lined
out.

[40] The resolution, in the hand of Oliver Ellsworth, is in Other Records, Executive
Proceedings, SR, DNA. It is endorsed "Executive" at the top by Samuel Otis. Otis also
wrote "Motion to postpone" at the bottom of the original.

[41] On February 23, 1791, the Senate was notified that Thomas Auldjo's Vice
Consulate should be moved from Cowes to Poole.

ORDERED, That the consideration of the nomination of The Sieur de La Motte be postponed.

ORDERED, That the Secretary lay before the President of the United States, the proceedings of Senate upon his message of the 4th of June 1790.

T U E S D A Y, JUNE 22D, 1790

The Senate resumed the consideration of the Message from the President of the United States, of the 4th of June 1790;   and

RESOLVED, That they do advise and consent to the Appointment of

Havre   The Sieur DE LA MOTTE of the Kingdom of France, to be Vice-Consul of the United States of America for the Port of Havre de Grace, and such parts of the said Kingdom as shall be nearer to the said Port than to the residence of any other Consul or Vice-Consul of the United States, within the same Kingdom.

ORDERED, That the Secretary communicate to the President of the United States, the proceedings of Senate upon his message of the 4th of June 1790.

W E D N E S D A Y, JUNE 23D, 1790

A Message from the President of the United States by Mr. Lear his Secretary, was read as follows:

UNITED STATES, June 23d 1790

GENTLEMEN of the SENATE,

In my nomination of Persons for Consular Appointments, on the 4th of the present month, the name of *James* instead of JOSEPH FENWICK, was, by mistake, laid before you to be Consul for the Port of Bordeaux.

GO. WASHINGTON[42]

ORDERED, That the Secretary do correct the Record agreeably to the message from the President of the United States, so as that it stand Joseph, instead of "James" Fenwick.

And, that this Order be communicated to the President of the United States.

---

[42] A letterbook copy of the message, in the hand of Robert Lewis, is in The George Washington Papers, series 2, vol. 25, roll 9, Manuscript Division, DLC.

F R I D A Y, July 2nd, 1790

A message from the President of the United States, by his private Secretary was read as follows:

UNITED STATES, July 2d 1790

GENTLEMEN of the SENATE,
    I nominate

HENRY MARCHANT to be Judge,
WILLIAM CHANNING to be Attorney, and
WILLIAM PECK to be Marshal of the Judicial Court of the United States, within the district of Rhode Island and Providence Plantations.

I likewise nominate the following Persons to fill Offices in the Revenue Department of the United States, within the State of Rhode Island and Providence Plantations—Vizt.

EBENEZER THOMPSON to be Naval Officer of the Port of Providence, in the place of THEODORE FOSTER, who is appointed a Senator of the United States.

DANIEL ELDRIDGE UPDIKE to be Surveyor of the Port of North-Kingston.

JOB COMSTOCK to be Surveyor of the Port of East Greenwich.

NATHANIEL PHILLIPS to be Surveyor of the Ports of Warren and Barrington.

SAMUEL BOSWORTH to be Surveyor of the Port of Bristol.

GEORGE STILLMAN to be Surveyor of the Port of Pawcatuck River.

JOHN ANTHONY ABORN to be Surveyor of the Port of Patuxet.

G. WASHINGTON[43]

ORDERED, That the message lie for consideration.

S A T U R D A Y, July 3D, 1790

The Senate proceeded to consider the Message from the President of the United States of the 2nd of July 1790, and the nominations therein contained, and

RESOLVED, That they do advise and consent to the appointment of the Persons therein mentioned, to the Offices to which they are respectively nominated, except of Daniel Eldridge Updike, postponed for want of information.

ORDERED, That the Secretary communicate to the President of the United States, the proceedings of Senate upon his message of the 2d of July 1790.

---

[43] The message, in the hand of Tobias Lear and signed by George Washington, is in Executive Nominations, second session, Executive Proceedings, SR, DNA. The letter "a," probably indicating Senate agreement, follows each nomination.

M O N D A Y, August 2nd, 1790

A message from the President of the United States by his private Secretary was read as follows:

United States, August 2d 1790

Gentlemen of the Senate,

I nominate the following persons to fill the Offices affixed to their names— vizt.

In the Judicial Department

William Peery, of the State of Delaware, to be one of the Judges in the Territory of the United States south of the river Ohio.

John Stokes, to be Judge of the North Carolina District, in place of William R. Davie who has declined his appointment.

In the Revenue Department

Samuel Russell Gerry to be Collector of the Port of Marblehead in the State of Massachusetts, in place of Richard Harris, deceased.

Zachariah Rhodes, to be Surveyor of the Port of Patuxet in the State of Rhode-Island, in place of John Anthony Aborn who has declined his appointment.

Thomas Arnold, to be Surveyor of the Port of East Greenwich in the State of Rhode Island, in place of Job Comstock who has declined his appointment.

In the Consulate Department

Joshua Johnson of Maryland, to be Consul of the United States of America for the Port of London in the Kingdom of Great Britain, and for such other parts of the said Kingdom as shall be nearer to the said Port than to the residence of any other Consul or Vice-Consul of the United States in the same Kingdom.

Francisco Sarmento of the Kingdom of Spain, to be Vice-Consul of the United States of America for the Island of Teneriffe and for such other of the Canary Islands as shall be nearer to Teneriffe than to the residence of any other Consul or Vice-Consul of the United States within the same allegiance.

John Street of the Island of Fayal, to be Vice-Consul of the United States of America, for the said Island of Fayal, and for such other of the Azores or Western Islands as shall be nearer to Fayal than to the residence of any other Consul or Vice-Consul of the United States within the same allegiance.

EBENEZER BRUSH of New York, to be Consul of the United States of America for the Port of Surinam and for such other parts of the Colony of Guiana as shall be nearer to the said Port than to the residence of any other Consul or Vice-Consul of the United States within the same allegiance.

GO. WASHINGTON[44]

ORDERED, That the message lie for consideration.

TUESDAY, AUGUST 3D, 1790

The Senate proceeded to consider the message from the President of the United States of the 2d of August 1790—and

RESOLVED, That they do advise and consent to the Appointment of

WILLIAM PEERY of the State of Delaware, to be one of the Judges in the Territory of the United States south of the River Ohio[45]—

JOHN STOKES, to be Judge of the North-Carolina district, in place of WILLIAM R. DAVIE, who has declined his appointment[46]—

SAMUEL RUSSELL GERRY, to be Collector of the Port of Marblehead in the State of Massachusetts, in place of RICHARD HARRIS, deceased—

ZACHARIAH RHODES, to be Surveyor of the Port of Patuxet in the State of Rhode-Island, in place of JOHN ANTHONY ABORN, who has declined his appointment—

THOMAS ARNOLD, to be Surveyor of the Port of East Greenwich in the State of Rhode Island, in place of JOB COMSTOCK, who has declined his appointment—and of

JOSHUA JOHNSON of Maryland, to be Consul of the United States of America for the Port of London in the Kingdom of Great Britain, and for such other parts of the said Kingdom as shall be nearer to the said Port than to the residence of any other Consul or Vice-Consul of the United States in the same Kingdom.

ORDERED, That the Nomination of Francisco Sarmento, John Street, and Ebenezer Brush, be postponed.

---

[44] The message, in the hand of Tobias Lear and signed by George Washington, is in Executive Nominations, second session, Executive Proceedings, SR, DNA. The letter "c," probably indicating Senate concurrence, follows the first six nominations. The letter "p," probably indicating postponement, follows the last three nominations.

[45] On February 25, 1791, the Senate was notified that William Peery had declined this appointment and Joseph Anderson had been nominated to replace him.

[46] On December 17, 1790, the Senate was notified that John Stokes had died and John Sitgreaves had been nominated to replace him.

The Senate resumed the consideration of the message from the President of the United States of the 2d of July 1790, and

RESOLVED, That they do advise and consent to the Appointment of

DANIEL ELDRIDGE UPDIKE, to be Surveyor of the Port of North Kingston, in the State of Rhode Island.

ORDERED, That the Secretary communicate to the President of the United States, the proceedings of Senate, upon his Messages of the 2d of July, and 2d of August 1790.

WEDNESDAY, AUGUST 4TH, 1790

A message from the President of the United States, by his private Secretary was read as follows:

UNITED STATES, August 4th 1790

GENTLEMEN of the SENATE,

In consequence of the general principles agreed to by the Senate in August 1789, the adjustment of the terms of a treaty is far advanced between the United States, and the Chiefs of the Creek Indians now in this City, in behalf of themselves and the whole Creek Nation.

In preparing the Articles of this Treaty, the present arrangements of the trade with the Creeks have caused much embarrassment. It seems to be well ascertained that the said trade is almost exclusively in the hands of a Company of British Merchants, who, by agreement, make their importations of Goods from England into the Spanish Ports.

As the trade of the Indians is a main mean of their political management, it is therefore obvious, that the United States cannot possess any security for the performance of treaties with the Creeks, while their trade is liable to be interrupted or withheld, at the caprice of two foreign Powers.

Hence it becomes an object of real importance to form new channels for the commerce of the Creeks through the United States. But this operation will require time, as the present arrangements cannot be suddenly broken without the greatest violation of faith and morals.

It therefore appears to be important to form a secret article of a treaty similar to the one which accompanies this message.

If the Senate should require any further explanation the Secretary of War will attend them for that purpose.

GO. WASHINGTON[47]

[47] The message, in the hand of Tobias Lear and signed by George Washington, is in President's Messages on Indian Relations, Executive Proceedings, SR, DNA. The

The President of the United States states the following question for the consideration and advice of the Senate.

If it should be found essential to a treaty, for the firm establishment of peace with the Creek Nation of Indians, that an article to the following effect should be inserted therein, will such an article be proper? vizt.

SECRET ARTICLE

The commerce necessary for the Creek nation shall be carried on through the Ports, and by the Citizens of the United States, if substantial and effectual arrangements shall be made for that purpose by the United States, on, or before the first day of August, one thousand seven hundred and ninety two. In the mean time, the said commerce may be carried on through its present channels, and according to its present regulations.

And, whereas the trade of the said Creek Nation is now carried on wholly or principally through the territories of Spain, and obstructions thereto may happen by war, or prohibitions of the Spanish government.

It is therefore agreed between the said parties, that in the event of any such obstructions happening, it shall be lawful for such persons as[48] ——— shall designate, to introduce into and transport through the territories of the United States to the country of the said Creek Nation, any quantity of goods, wares and merchandize, not exceeding in value in any one year Sixty thousand dollars, and that, free from any duties or impositions whatsoever, but subject to such regulations, for guarding against abuse, as the United States shall judge necessary; which privilege shall continue as long as such obstruction shall continue.

United States   }
August 4th 1790   Go. WASHINGTON

The Senate proceeded to consider the message from the President of the United States of this day.

Whereupon

RESOLVED, That the Senate do advise and consent to the execution of the Secret article referred to in the message, and that the blank in the said article be filled with the words "The President of the United States."

ORDERED, that the Secretary, as usual communicate this Resolution to the President of the United States.[49]

---

statement and Secret Article which follow, in the hand of John Stagg, Jr., and signed by George Washington, are filed with the message. In the document the date, in the hand of Tobias Lear, has been crossed out. The related documents are printed in Part II of this volume under the heading Indian Relations—Southern.

[48] At this point in the original message the phrase "The P of the US" is inserted, in the hand of Samuel Otis.

[49] On August 6 the President sent a message to the Senate appointing Henry Knox to treat with the Creeks.

THURSDAY, AUGUST 5TH, 1790

The Senate resumed the consideration of the message from the President of the United States of the 2d of August 1790—and

RESOLVED, That they do advise and consent to the Appointment of

JOHN STREET of the Island of Fayal, to be Vice-Consul of the United States of America for the said Island of Fayal, and for such other of the Azores or Western Islands as shall be nearer to Fayal than to the residence of any other Consul or Vice-Consul of the United States within the same allegiance—and of

EBENEZER BRUSH of New York, to be Consul of the United States of America for the Port of Surinam, and for such other parts of the Colony of Guiana, as shall be nearer to the said Port than to the residence of any other Consul or Vice-Consul of the United States within the same allegiance.

And on the question to advise and consent to the Appointment of

FRANCISCO SARMENTO of the Kingdom of Spain, to be Vice-Consul of the United States of America for the Island of Teneriffe, and for such other of the Canary Islands as shall be nearer to Teneriffe than to the residence of any other Consul or Vice-Consul of the United States within the same allegiance.

It passed in the Negative.

ORDERED, That the Secretary communicate to the President of the United States, the proceedings of Senate of this day, upon his message of 2d August 1790.

FRIDAY, AUGUST 6TH, 1790

A message from the President of the United States by his private Secretary was read as follows:

UNITED STATES, August 6, 1790

GENTLEMEN of the SENATE,

Considering the circumstances which prevented the late Commissioners from concluding a Peace with the Creek Nation of Indians, it appeared to me most prudent that all subsequent measures for disposing them to a Treaty should in the first Instance be informal.

I informed you on the 4th inst. that the adjustment of the Terms of a Treaty with their Chiefs now here, was far advanced—such further Progress has since been made, that I think measures may at present be taken for conducting and concluding that Business in Form. It therefore becomes necessary that a proper Person be appointed and authorized to treat with these Chiefs, and to conclude a treaty with them. For this purpose I nominate to you HENRY KNOX.

G. WASHINGTON[50]

The Senate agreed to dispense with the rule so far as to take into consideration, the above recited message at this time.

RESOLVED, That they do advise and consent to the Appointment of HENRY KNOX, agreeably to the nomination therein contained.

ORDERED, That the Secretary communicate this Resolution of Senate to the President of the United States.[51]

A message from the President of the United States by his private Secretary was read as follows:

UNITED STATES, August 6th 1790

GENTLEMEN of the SENATE,

I nominate the following Persons to be Commissioners of Loans in the States to which their names are respectively affixed—viz.

In the State of New Hampshire	Nathaniel Gilman[52]
Massachusetts	Nathaniel Appleton
Rhode Island	———
Connecticut	William Imlay
New York	John Cochran
New Jersey	James Ewing
Pennsylvania	Thomas Smith
Delaware	James Tilton
Maryland	Thomas Harwood
Virginia	John Hopkins
North Carolina	William Skinner
South Carolina	John Neufville
Georgia	Richard Wylly

GO. WASHINGTON[53]

---

[50] The message, in the hand of Tobias Lear and signed by George Washington, is in President's Messages on Indian Relations, Executive Proceedings, SR, DNA. At the bottom of the message is a note in the hand of Samuel Otis which reads: "Resolved &c."

[51] On August 7 the President sent the treaty that Henry Knox negotiated with the Creeks to the Senate for approval.

[52] On December 24 the Senate was notified that Nathaniel Gilman had declined this appointment and William Gardner has been nominated to replace him.

[53] The message, in the hand of Tobias Lear and signed by George Washington, is in Executive Nominations, second session, Executive Proceedings, SR, DNA. At the bottom of the message is the notation "Ordered to lie," in the hand of Samuel Otis. The letter "c" follows each nomination, probably indicating Senate concurrence.

ORDERED, To lie for consideration.

S A T U R D A Y, AUGUST 7TH, 1790

The Senate proceeded to consider the Message from the President of the United States of the 6th of August, and the Nominations of Commissioners of Loans therein contained—and

RESOLVED, That they do advise and consent to the Appointments, agreeably to the Nominations therein contained.

A written message from the President of the United States, was communicated to the Senate by his Secretary which he delivered to the Vice President.

And he withdrew.

UNITED STATES, August 7th 1790

GENTLEMEN of the SENATE,

I nominate JABEZ BOWEN, to be Commissioner of Loans in the State of Rhode Island and Providence Plantations . . . and

DANIEL BENEZET Junior, to be Collector of the Port of Great Egg Harbour in the State of New Jersey.

GO. WASHINGTON[54]

It was agreed so far to dispense with the rule as to consider the Message from the President of the United States of the 7th of August, at this time—and

RESOLVED, That the Senate do advise and consent to the Appointments, agreeably to the Nominations therein contained.

ORDERED, That the Secretary communicate to the President of the United States, their proceedings on his Messages of the 6th and 7th of August 1790.

A written message from the President of the United States was communicated to the Senate by the Secretary at War, which he delivered to the Vice President.

And he withdrew.

UNITED STATES, August 7th 1790

GENTLEMEN of the SENATE,

I lay before you a Treaty between the United States and the Chiefs of the Creek Nation, now in this City, in behalf of themselves and the whole Creek Nation, subject to the ratification of the President of the United States, with the advice and consent of the Senate.

---

[54] The message, in the hand of Tobias Lear and signed by George Washington, is in Executive Nominations, second session, Executive Proceedings, SR, DNA. The letter "c," probably indicating Senate concurrence, follows both nominations.

While I flatter myself that this Treaty will be productive of present peace and prosperity to our southern frontier, it is to be expected that it will also, in its consequences, be the means of firmly attaching the Creeks and the neighbouring tribes to the interests of the United States.

At the same time it is to be hoped that it will afford solid grounds of satisfaction to the State of Georgia, as it contains a regular, full, and definitive relinquishment, on the part of the Creek Nation, of the Oconee land, in the utmost extent in which it has been claimed by that State, and thus extinguishes the principal cause of those hostilities, from which it has more than once experienced such severe calamities.

But although the most valuable of the disputed land is included, yet there is a certain claim of Georgia, arising out of the Treaty, made by that State at Galphinton in November 1785, of land to the eastward of a new temporary line from the forks of the Oconee and Oukmulge in a southwest direction to the St. Mary's River, which tract of land the Creeks, in this City, absolutely refuse to yield.

This land is reported to be generally barren, sunken, and unfit for cultivation, except in some instances on the margin of the rivers, on which, by improvement, Rice might be cultivated—its chief value depending on the timber fit for the building of ships, with which it is represented as abounding.

While it is thus circumstanced on the one hand, it is stated by the Creeks on the other to be of the highest importance to them, as constituting some of their most valuable winter hunting ground.

I have directed the Commissioner, to whom the charge of adjusting this Treaty has been committed, to lay before you such Papers and documents, and to communicate to you such information relatively to it, as you may require.

Go. Washington[55]

Ordered, That the Message with the Treaties therein referred to be read, and that they lie for consideration.[56]

M O N D A Y, August 9th, 1790

A written Message from the President of the United States was communicated to the Senate by his Secretary, which he delivered to the Vice President—and he withdrew.

United States, August 9th 1790

---

[55] The message, in the hand of William Jackson and signed by George Washington, is in President's Messages on Indian Relations, Executive Proceedings, SR, DNA. The related documents are printed in Part II of this volume under the heading Indian Relations—Southern.

[56] On August 9 the Senate considered this treaty.

GENTLEMEN of the SENATE,

I nominate WILLIAM IRVINE, of the State of Pennsylvania, JOHN TAYLOR GILMAN of the State of New Hampshire,[57] and JOHN KEAN of the State of South Carolina, to be Commissioners for settling the Accounts between the United States and individual States.

GO. WASHINGTON[58]

ORDERED, That this Message lie for consideration.

The Senate resumed the consideration of the Message from the President of United States of the 7th of August 1790, and the Treaty therein mentioned.

ON MOTION to refer this Treaty to a select Committee, the yeas and nays were required by one fifth of the Senators present

Mr. Butler		Yea
Mr. Carroll	Nay	
Mr. Dalton	Nay	
Mr. Ellsworth	Nay	
Mr. Few		Yea
Mr. Foster		Yea
Mr. Gunn		Yea
Mr. Hawkins	Nay	
Mr. Henry		Yea
Mr. Johnston		Yea
Mr. Izard	Nay	
Mr. King	Nay	
Mr. Lee		Yea
Mr. Morris		Yea
Mr. Paterson	Nay	
Mr. Read	Nay	
Mr. Stanton	Nay	
Mr. Wingate	Nay	

Nays—10
Yeas— 8

and

It passed in the Negative.

ON MOTION, "That on the final question when the advice and consent of the Senate is requested, any Member shall have a right to enter his Protest or

[57] On December 23 the Senate was notified that John Gilman had resigned this appointment and Woodbury Langdon had been nominated to replace him.

[58] The message, in the hand of Tobias Lear and signed by George Washington, is in Executive Nominations, second session, Executive Proceedings, SR, DNA. The letter "c," probably indicating Senate concurrence, is written above each nomination.

dissent on the Journal, with reasons in support of such dissent; Provided the same be offered within two days after the determination on such final question"—

The yeas and nays were required by one fifth of the Senators present—

Mr. Butler		Yea
Mr. Carroll	Nay	
Mr. Dalton	Nay	
Mr. Ellsworth	Nay	
Mr. Few	Nay	
Mr. Foster	Nay	
Mr. Gunn		Yea
Mr. Hawkins	Nay	
Mr. Henry	Nay	
Mr. Johnston	Nay	
Mr. Izard		Yea
Mr. King	Nay	
Mr. Lee		Yea
Mr. Morris	Nay	
Mr. Paterson	Nay	
Mr. Read	Nay	
Mr. Schuyler	Nay	
Mr. Stanton	Nay	
Mr. Wingate	Nay	

Nays—15

Yeas— 4

and

It passed in the Negative.

ORDERED, that the further consideration of this Message, and the Treaty entered into with the Chiefs of the Creek Nation, be postponed.[59]

T U E S D A Y, AUGUST 10TH, 1790

The Senate proceeded to consider the Message from the President of the United States, and his nomination of Commissioners to settle the Accounts between the United States and the individual States—and

RESOLVED, That the Senate do advise and consent to the appointments agreeably to the nominations therein contained.

A written Message from the President of the United States was by his Secretary, delivered to the Vice President.

---

[59] On August 11 the President asked the Senate to authorize the execution of the treaties of Hopewell with the other Southern Indian tribes, and the Senate agreed.

And he withdrew.

UNITED STATES, August 10th 1790

GENTLEMEN of the SENATE,

I nominate JOHN C. JONES, the present Collector of the Port of Nanjemoy in the State of Maryland, to be Collector of the District of Cedar Point, when the Act to provide more effectually for the collection of duties &ca. shall take effect.

And

JEREMIAH JORDAN to be Surveyor of the Port of Lewellensburg in the State of Maryland.

GO. WASHINGTON[60]

It was agreed by unanimous consent to proceed to the consideration of the last recited Message and nominations—and

RESOLVED, That the Senate do advise and consent to the appointments agreeably thereto.

ORDERED, That the Secretary communicate to the President of the United States the proceedings on his Message and nominations of the 9th and 10th instant.

W E D N E S D A Y, AUGUST 11TH, 1790

A written Message from the President of the United States was delivered to the Vice President, by his Secretary, and he withdrew.

UNITED STATES, August 11th 1790

GENTLEMEN of the SENATE,

Although the treaty with the Creeks may be regarded as the main foundation of the future peace and prosperity of the South Western frontier of the United States, yet in order fully to effect so desireable an object the treaties which have been entered into with the other tribes in that quarter must be faithfully performed on our parts.

During the last year I laid before the Senate a particular statement of the case of the Cherokees. By a reference to that paper it will appear that the United States formed a treaty with the Cherokees in November 1785—That the said Cherokees thereby placed themselves under the protection of the United States, and had a boundary assigned them.

---

[60] The message, in the hand of Tobias Lear and signed by George Washington, is in Executive Nominations, second session, Executive Proceedings, SR, DNA. The letter "c," probably indicating Senate concurrence, follows both nominations.

That the white people settled on the frontiers had openly violated the said boundary by intruding on the Indian lands.

That the United States in Congress assembled did, on the first day of September 1788, issue their proclamation forbidding all such unwarrantable intrusions and enjoining all those who had settled upon the hunting grounds of the Cherokees to depart with their families and effects without loss of time, as they would answer their disobedience to the injunctions and prohibitions expressed at their peril.

But information has been received, that notwithstanding the said treaty and proclamation, upwards of five hundred families have settled on the Cherokee lands, exclusively of those settled between the fork of French Broad and Holstin Rivers mentioned in the said treaty.

As the obstructions to a proper conduct on this matter have been removed since it was mentioned to the Senate on the 22nd of August 1789, by the accession of North Carolina to the present Union, and the cessions of the land in question, I shall conceive myself bound to exert the powers entrusted to me by the Constitution in order to carry into faithfull execution the treaty of Hopewell, unless it shall be thought proper to attempt to arrange a new boundary with the Cherokees, embracing the settlements, and compensating the Cherokees for the cessions they shall make on the occasion. On this point therefore I state the following questions, and request the advice of the Senate thereon.

1st. Is it the judgment of the Senate that overtures shall be made to the Cherokees to arrange a new boundary so as to embrace the settlements made by the white people since the treaty of Hopewell in November 1785?

2nd. If so—Shall compensation to the amount of ———— dollars annually, or of ———— dollars in gross be made to the Cherokees for the land they shall relinquish, holding the occupiers of the land accountable to the United States for its value?

3rd. Shall the United States stipulate solemnly to guarantee the new boundary which may be arranged?

GO. WASHINGTON[61]

Agreed by unanimous consent to proceed to the consideration of this Message;
Whereupon
RESOLVED, That the Senate do advise and consent that the President of the United States do at his discretion cause the Treaty concluded at Hopewell

[61] The message, in the hand of Tobias Lear and signed by George Washington, is in President's Messages on Indian Relations, Executive Proceedings, SR, DNA. The related documents are printed in Part II of this volume under the heading Indian Relations—Southern.

with the Cherokee Indians to be carried into execution according to the Terms thereof, or to enter into arrangements for such farther Cession of Territory from the said Cherokee Indians as the Tranquility and Interest of the United States may require: provided the sum which may be stipulated to be paid to the said Cherokee Indians do not exceed One thousand Dollars annually; and provided further, that no person who shall have[62] taken possession of any lands within the Territory assigned to the said Cherokee Indians by the said Treaty of Hopewell shall be confirmed in any such[63] possessions but by a compliance with such terms as Congress may hereafter prescribe.[64]

RESOLVED[65] in case a new or other Boundary, than that stipulated by the treaty of Hopewell, shall be concluded[66] with the Cherokee Indians, that the Senate do advise, and consent solemnly to guarantee the same.[67]

ORDERED, That the Secretary communicate to the President of the United States the proceedings of Senate on his Message of this day.[68]

THURSDAY, AUGUST 12TH, 1790

The Senate proceeded to consider the Message from the President of the United States of the 7th of August 1790, communicating a Treaty entered into with the Chiefs of the Creek Nation of Indians.

And on the question to advise and consent to the ratification of the said Treaty made with the Creek Nation and referred to in the Message of the President of the United States of the 7th of August 1790—

The yeas and nays were required by one fifth of the Senators present

Mr. Butler		Nay
Mr. Carroll	Yea	
Mr. Dalton	Yea	
Mr. Ellsworth	Yea	
Mr. Few		Nay
Mr. Foster	Yea	
Mr. Gunn		Nay
Mr. Hawkins	Yea	
Mr. Henry	Yea	

---

[62] At this point in the original resolution the words "located or" are lined out.

[63] At this point in the original resolution the words "locations or" are lined out.

[64] At this point in the original resolution "prescribe" reads "prescribed."

[65] At this point in the original resolution the word "that" is lined out.

[66] At this point in the original resolution the words "between the Creeks be" are lined out.

[67] The resolutions, in the hand of Rufus King, are in Other Records, Executive Proceedings, SR, DNA.

[68] On August 12 the Senate consented to the Treaty of New York with the Creeks.

Mr. Johnson	Yea	
Mr. Johnston	Yea	
Mr. Izard	Yea	
Mr. King	Yea	
Mr. Lee	Yea	
Mr. Paterson	Yea	
Mr. Read	Yea	
Mr. Schuyler	Yea	
Mr. Stanton	Yea	
Mr. Walker		Nay

Yeas—15
Nays— 4

and it was

RESOLVED, (two thirds of the Senators present concurring therein) that the Senate do consent to the aforesaid treaty, and do advise the President of the United States to ratify the same.

ORDERED, that the Secretary communicate to the President of the United States the Resolution of Senate upon the aforementioned treaty.

Attest,

SAM. A. OTIS Secy.

THIRD SESSION

F R I D A Y, December 17th, 1790

A written Message from the President of the United States by Mr. Lear his Secretary was delivered to the Vice President.
And he withdrew.

UNITED STATES, December 17th 1790

GENTLEMEN of the SENATE,

Since your last Session I have appointed ROBERT MORRIS Judge of the District of New Jersey, in place of DAVID BREARLY deceased; and JOHN HETH of Virginia an Ensign in the Troops of the United States, in place of RICHARD ARCHER who has declined his appointment.

As these Appointments expire with your present Session, I nominate

ROBERT MORRIS to be Judge of the District of New Jersey, in place of DAVID BREARLY deceased.   and

JOHN HETH of Virginia to be an Ensign in the Troops of the United States, in place of RICHARD ARCHER who has declined his appointment.

I likewise nominate

JOHN SITGREAVES to be Judge of the District of North Carolina in place of JOHN STOKES deceased.

WILLIAM HILL to be Attorney for the United States in the District of North Carolina, in place of JOHN SITGREAVES, if his nomination as Judge meets your concurrence.

ZACHARIAH ROWLAND to be Surveyor of the Port of Richmond in the State of Virginia, in place of CORBIN BRAXTON who has resigned his Appointment—and

JEREMIAH NICOLS to be Collector of the Port of Chester in the State of Maryland, in place of JOHN SCOTT deceased.

GO. WASHINGTON[1]

---

[1] The message, in the hand of Tobias Lear and signed by George Washington, is in Executive Nominations, third session, Executive Proceedings, SR, DNA. The letter "a," probably indicating Senate agreement, follows each nomination.

ORDERED, That this Message lie for consideration.

M O N D A Y, DECEMBER 20TH, 1790

The Senate proceeded to consider the Message from the President of the United States of the 17th of December 1790 and the Nominations therein contained of

ROBERT MORRIS to be Judge of the District of New Jersey, in place of DAVID BREARLY deceased.

JOHN HETH of Virginia to be an Ensign in the Troops of the United States, in place of RICHARD ARCHER who has declined his appointment.

JOHN SITGREAVES to be Judge of the District of North Carolina in place of JOHN STOKES deceased.

WILLIAM HILL to be Attorney for the United States in the District of North Carolina, in place of JOHN SITGREAVES.

ZACHARIAH ROWLAND to be Surveyor of the Port of Richmond in the State of Virginia, in place of CORBIN BRAXTON who has resigned his Appointment—and

JEREMIAH NICOLS to be Collector of the Port of Chester in the State of Maryland, in place of JOHN SCOTT deceased—and

RESOLVED, That the Senate advise and consent to the appointments respectively.

ORDERED, That the Secretary lay this Resolution before the President of the United States.

T H U R S D A Y, DECEMBER 23RD, 1790

A written Message from the President of the United States by Mr. Lear his Secretary was delivered to the Vice President.

And he withdrew.

UNITED STATES, December 23rd 1790

GENTLEMEN of the SENATE,

I nominate WOODBURY LANGDON of the State of New Hampshire to be one of the Commissioners for settling the Accounts between the United States and individual States, in place of JOHN TAYLOR GILMAN who has resigned his appointment—and

WILLIAM GARDNER to be Commissioner of Loans in the State of New

Hampshire, in place of NATHANIEL GILMAN who has declined his Appointment.

GO. WASHINGTON[2]

ORDERED, That this Message lie for consideration.

F R I D A Y, DECEMBER 24TH, 1790

The Senate proceeded to consider the Message from the President of the United States of the 23rd of December 1790 and the Nominations therein contained of

WOODBURY LANGDON of the State of New Hampshire to be one of the Commissioners for settling the Accounts between the United States and individual States, in place of JOHN TAYLOR GILMAN who has resigned his appointment—and

WILLIAM GARDNER to be Commissioner of Loans in the State of New Hampshire, in place of NATHANIEL GILMAN who has declined his Appointment.

RESOLVED, That the Senate advise and consent to the appointments respectively.

ORDERED, That the Secretary lay this Resolution before the President of the United States.

---

[2] The message, in the hand of Tobias Lear and signed by George Washington, is in Executive Nominations, third session, Executive Proceedings, SR, DNA. The letter "a," noted at the end of the message, may indicate Senate agreement to both nominations.

M O N D A Y, January 3rd, 1791

A written Message from the President of the United States by Mr. Lear his Secretary was delivered to the Vice President.

And he withdrew.

UNITED STATES, January 3rd 1791

GENTLEMEN of the SENATE,

I nominate ABRAHAM OGDEN to be Attorney for the United States in the District of New Jersey, in place of RICHARD STOCKTON who has resigned.

Go. WASHINGTON[3]

ORDERED, That this Message lie for consideration.

T U E S D A Y, January 4th, 1791

The Senate proceeded to the consideration of the Message from the President of the United States and the Nomination of

ABRAHAM OGDEN to be Attorney for the United States in the District of New Jersey, in place of RICHARD STOCKTON who has resigned.

RESOLVED, That the Senate advise and consent to his appointment accordingly.

ORDERED, That the Secretary lay this Resolution before the President of the United States.

M O N D A Y, January 17th, 1791

A Message from the President of the United States by Mr. Lear his Secretary who communicated to the Senate a Letter from His most Christian Majesty to the President and Members of Congress.

And he withdrew.

UNITED STATES, January 17th 1791

GENTLEMEN of the SENATE,

I lay before you a Letter from His most Christian Majesty, addressed to the President and Members of Congress of the United States of America.

Go. WASHINGTON[4]

---

[3] The message, in the hand of Tobias Lear and signed by George Washington, is in Executive Nominations, third session, Executive Proceedings, SR, DNA. At the bottom of the page, in the hand of Samuel Otis, is the notation "Message 30th Decr. in the Legislative Journal."

[4] The message, in the hand of Tobias Lear and signed by George Washington, is in President's Messages on Foreign Relations, Executive Proceedings, SR, DNA.

The Letter referred to in the Message is as follows.

To OUR VERY DEAR FRIENDS AND ALLIES The President and Members of the general Congress of the United States of North America.

VERY DEAR GREAT[5] FRIENDS and ALLIES—We have received the Letter by which you inform us of the new mark of confidence that you have shewn to Mr. Jefferson and which puts a period to his appointment of Minister Plenipotentiary at our Court.

The manner in which he conducted during his residence with us, has merited our esteem and entire approbation and it is with pleasure that we now give him this testimony of it.

It is with the most sincere pleasure that we embrace this opportunity of renewing these assurances of regard and friendship which we feel for the United States in general and for each of them in particular; under their influence we pray God that he will keep you, VERY DEAR FRIENDS AND ALLIES, under his holy and beneficient protection.

Done at Paris this 11th September 1790

Your good friend and Ally
LOUIS
MONTMORIN   (SEAL)

The United States of North America[6]

ORDERED, That the Secretary return this Letter to the President of the United States.

---

[5] The word "great," in the hand of Samuel Otis, has been inserted at this point in the document to conform it to the French copy.

[6] A copy of the letter, in the hand of Tobias Lear, is in President's Messages on Foreign Relations, Executive Proceedings, SR, DNA. Attached to this letter is a French copy in the hand of Tobias Lear. It reads:

TRÈS-CHERS GRANDS AMIS ET ALLIÈS. Nous avons reçu la lettre par la-quelle vous nous avez informès de la nouvelle marque de confiance qui vous avez donnée au Sieur Jefferson et qui met fin aux fonctions de la place de votre Ministre Plenipotentiare auprès de nous. La maniere dont il s'est conduit pendant tout le tems qu'il a résidé à notre Cour, lui a merité notre estime et un entiere approbation de notre part. C'est avec plaisir qui nous lui rendons ce temoinage nous en avons un bien sicere à profiter de cette occasion pour vous renouveller ces assurances de l'affection et de l'amitié que nous portons aux Etats Unis en general et a chacun d'eux en particulier. Sur ce nous prions Dieu qu'il vous ait, Tres chers grand Amis & Alliés, en sa sainte et digne garde. Ecrit à Paris ce 11 Septembre 1790.

Notre Bon Ami et Allié
Louis.
Montmorin   (SEAL)

Aux Etats Unis de l'amerique septentrionale. A nos tres chers grands amis et alliés Les Prèsident et Membres du Congrès général des Etats Unis de l'amérique septentrionale.

WEDNESDAY, JANUARY 19TH, 1791

A written Message from the President of the United States by Mr. Lear his Secretary was delivered to the Vice President.

And he withdrew.

UNITED STATES, January 19th 1791

GENTLEMEN of the SENATE,

I lay before you a representation of the Chargé des Affaires of France, made by order of his Court, on the Acts of Congress of the 20th of July 1789, and 1790, imposing an extra tonnage on foreign Vessels, not excepting those of that Country; together with the Report of the Secretary of State thereon: and I recommend the same to your consideration, that I may be enabled to give to it such answer as may best comport with the justice and the interests of the United States.

GO. WASHINGTON[7]

The papers referred to in the above Message were read as follows.

The Secretary of State having received from the Chargé des Affaires of France a Note on the Tonnage payable by French Vessels in the ports of the United States has had the same under his consideration, and thereupon makes the following REPORT to the President of the United States.

The Chargé des Affaires of France, by a Note of the 13th of December represents, by order of his Court, that they consider so much of the Acts of Congress of July 20th 1789 and 1790 as imposes an extraordinary Tonnage on foreign Vessels, without excepting those of France, to be in contravention of the 5th Article of the Treaty of Amity and Commerce between the two Nations; that this would have authorised on their part a proportional modification in the favours granted to the American Navigation: but that his Sovereign had thought it more conformable to his principles of friendship and attachment to the United States to order him to make representations thereon, and to ask, in favour of French Vessels, a modification of the Acts which impose an extraordinary Tonnage on foreign vessels.

The Secretary of State in giving in this paper to the President of the United States, thinks it his duty to accompany it with the following observations.

The 3rd and 4th Articles of the Treaty of Amity and Commerce between France and the United States, subject the vessels of each nation to pay, in

---

[7] The message, in the hand of Tobias Lear and signed by George Washington, is in President's Messages on Foreign Relations, Executive Proceedings, SR, DNA. A copy of the message, in the hand of Samuel Otis, Jr., and attested by Samuel Otis, is in Various Select Committee Reports, SR, DNA.

the ports of the other, only such duties as are paid by the most favoured Nation: and give them reciprocally all the privileges and exemptions, in navigation and commerce, which are given by either to the most favoured Nations. Had the contracting parties stopped here, they would have been free to raise or lower their Tonnage as they should find it expedient; only taking care to keep the other on the footing of the most favored nation.

The question then is whether the 5th Article, cited in the Note, is any thing more than an application of the principle comprised in the 3d and 4th to a particular object? or whether it is an additional stipulation of something not so comprised?

I. That it is merely an application of a principle comprised in the preceding Articles, is declared by the express words of the article, to wit, *"Dans l'exemption cidessus* est *nommément compris* &c." *"in the above exemption is particularly comprised* the imposition of 100 sois per Ton established in France on foreign Vessels." Here then is at once an express declaration that the exemption from the duty of 100 sols, is *comprised* in the 3d and 4th Articles; that is to say, it was one of the exemptions, enjoyed by the most favoured Nations, and, as such, extended to us by those Articles. If the exemption spoken of in this 1st member of the 5th Article was *comprised* in the 3rd and 4th Articles, as is expressly declared, then the reservation by France out of that exemption (which makes the 2d member of the same article) *was also comprised*: that is to say, if *the whole* was comprised, *the part* was comprised. And if this reservation of France in the 2d member was comprised in the 3d and 4th Articles, then the counter-reservation by the United States (which constitutes the 3d and last member of the same article) was also comprised. Because it is but a corresponding portion of a similar whole on our part, which had been comprised by the same terms with theirs.

In short the whole Article relates to a particular duty of 100 sols laid by some antecedent law of France on the vessels of foreign Nations, relinquished as to the most favoured, and consequently to us. It is not a new and additional stipulation then, but a declared application of the stipulations comprised in the preceding Articles to a particular case, by way of greater caution.

The doctrine laid down generally in the 3d and 4th Articles, and exemplified specially in the 5th amounts to this. "The vessels of the most favoured Nations, coming from foreign ports, are exempted from the duty of 100 Sols: therefore you are exempted from it by the 3d and 4th Articles. The vessels of the most favored nations, coming coastwise, pay that duty: therefore you are to pay it by the 3d and 4th Articles. We shall not think it unfriendly in you to lay a like duty on Coasters, because it will be no more than we have done ourselves. You are free also to lay that or any other duty on Vessels coming from foreign ports: provided they apply to all other nations, even the most favoured. We are free to do the same, under the same restriction. Our exempting you from a duty which the most favoured Nations do not pay, does not exempt you from one which they do pay."

In this view it is evident that the 5th Article neither enlarges, nor abridges the stipulations of the 3rd and 4th. The effect of the Treaty would have been precisely the same had it been omitted altogether; consequently it may be truly said that the reservation by the United States in this Article is completely useless. And it may be added with equal truth that the equivalent reservation by France is completely useless: as well as her previous abandonment of the same duty: and in short the whole Article. Each party then remains free to raise or lower it's Tonnage, provided the change operates on all nations, even the most favoured.

Without undertaking to affirm, we may obviously conjecture, that this Article has been inserted on the part of the United States from an over-caution to guard, *nommement, by name,* against a particular aggrievance, which they thought they could never be too well secured against: and that has happened, which generally happens; doubts have been produced by the too great number of words used to prevent doubt.

II. The Court of France however understands this Article as intended to introduce something to which the preceding articles had not reached; and not merely as an application of them to a particular case. Their opinion seems to be founded on the general rule, in the construction of instruments, to leave no words merely useless, for which any rational meaning can be found. They say that the reservation by the United States of a right to lay a duty equivalent to that of the 100 Sols, reserved by France, would have been completely useless, if they were left free, by the preceding articles, to lay a Tonnage to any extent whatever, consequently that the reservation of a part proves a relinquishment of the residue.

If some meaning, and such a one, is to be given to the last member of the article, some meaning, and a similar one, must be given to the corresponding member. If the reservation by the United States of a right to lay an equivalent duty, implies a relinquishment of their right to lay any other, the reservation by France of a right to continue the specified duty to which it is an equivalent, must imply a relinquishment of the right on her part to lay or continue any other. Equivalent reservations by both, must imply equivalent restrictions on both. The exact reciprocity stipulated in the preceding articles, and which pervades every part of the Treaty, ensures a counter-right to each party for every right ceded to the other.

Let it be further considered that the duty called *tonnage* in the United States is in lieu of the duties for anchorage, for the support of Buoys, Beacons, and Light-Houses, to guide the Mariner into harbour, and along the coast, which are provided and supported at the expence of the United States, and for fees to Measurers, Weighers, Guagers &ca. who are paid by the United States; for which articles, among many others (light-house money excepted) duties are paid by us in the ports of France under their specific names. That Government has hitherto thought these duties consistent with the Treaty; and consequently the same duties under a general, instead of specific names, with us, must be equally consistent with it; it is not the name, but the thing which is essential. If we have renounced the right to lay any port duties, they must be understood to have equally renounced that of either laying new or continuing the old. If we ought to refund the port duties received from their vessels since the date of the Act of Congress, they should refund the port duties they have received from our vessels since the date of the Treaty; for nothing short of this is the reciprocity of the Treaty.

If this construction be adopted then, each party has forever renounced the right of laying any duties on the Vessels of the other coming from any foreign port, or more than 100 Sols on those coming coastwise. Could this relinquishment be confined to the two contracting parties alone, the United States would be the gainers, for it is well known that a much[8] greater number of American than French Vessels are employed in the Commerce between the two Countries: but the exemption, once conceded by the one nation to the other, becomes immediately the property of all others, who are on the footing of the most favoured nations. It is true that those others would be obliged to yield the same compensation, that is to say, to receive our Vessels duty free. Whether we should gain or lose in the exchange of the measure with them, is not easy to say.

Another consequence of this construction will be that the Vessels of the most favoured Nations, paying no duties will be on a better footing than those of natives, which pay a moderate duty, consequently either the duty on these also must be given up, or they will be supplanted by foreign Vessels in our own ports.

The resource then of duty on Vessels for the purposes either of revenue or regulation, will be forever lost to both. It is hardly conceivable that either party, looking forward to all these consequences, would see their interest in them.

III. But if France persists in claiming this exemption, what is to be done? The claim indeed is couched in mild and friendly terms; but the idea leaks out that a refusal would authorize them to modify proportionally the favors

---

[8] At this point in the original report there is an asterisk, and the following note, in the hand of Thomas Jefferson, appears at the bottom of the page:

By an official paper from the Bureau of the balance of Commerce of France, we find that of the Ships which entered the ports of France from the United States in the Year 1789, only 13 amounting to 2105 Tons were French, and 163 making 24,173 Tons were American.

granted, by the same article, to our navigation. Perhaps they may do what we should feel much more severely; they may turn their eyes to the favours granted us by their Arrets of December 29th 1787 and December 7th 1788 which hang on their will alone, unconnected with the Treaty. Those Arrets, among other advantages, admit our whale oils to the exclusion of that of all other foreigners. And this monopoly procures a vent for seven twelfths of the produce of that Fishery, which experience has taught us could find no other market. Near two thirds of the produce of our Cod fisheries too have lately found a free vent in the Colonies of France.[9] This indeed has been an irregularity growing out of the anarchy reigning in those Colonies. Yet the demands of the Colonists, even of the Government party among them, (if an auxiliary disposition can be excited by some marks of friendship and distinction on our part) may perhaps produce a constitutional concession to them to procure their provisions at the cheapest market; that is to say, at ours.

Considering the value of the interests we have at stake, and considering the smallness of difference between foreign and native Tonnage, on french vessels alone, it might perhaps be thought adviseable to make the sacrifice asked; and especially if it can be so done as to give no title to other the most favoured nations to claim it. If the act should put french vessels on the footing of those of Natives, and declare it to be in consideration of the favours granted us by the Arrets of December 29th 1787, and December 7th 1788, (and perhaps this would satisfy them), no Nation could then demand the same favour, without offering an equivalent compensation. It might strengthen too the tenure by which those Arrets are held, which must be precarious, so long as they are gratuitous.

It is desirable, in many instances, to exchange mutual advantages by Legislative Acts rather than by Treaty: because the former, though understood to be in consideration of each other, and therefore greatly respected, yet when they become too inconvenient, can be dropped at the will of either party:

---

[9] At this point in the original report there is an asterisk, and the following, in the hand of Thomas Jefferson, appears at the bottom of the page:

Abstract of the produce of the Fisheries exported from the United States from August 20th 1789 to August 14th 1790, in which is omitted one quarter's exportations from Boston, Plymouth, Dighton, Penobscot, Frenchman's Bay, Machias, and New York, of which the returns are not received.

	Cod fishery	Whale fishery	both fisheries
France and the french West Indies	586,167 dollrs.	131,906 dollrs.	718,073 dollrs.
The rest of the World	307,097 "	101,306 "	408,403 "
Whole produce	893,264 "	233,212 "	1,126,476 "

whereas stipulations by Treaty are forever irrevocable but by joint consent, let a change of circumstances render them ever so burthensome.

On the whole, if it be the opinion that the 1st construction is to be insisted on, as ours, in opposition to the 2d urged by the Court of France, and that no relaxation is to be admitted, an answer shall be given to that Court defending that construction, and explaining in as friendly terms as possible, the difficulties opposed to the exemption they claim.

2. If it be the opinion that it is advantageous for us to close with France in her interpretation of a reciprocal and perpetual exemption from Tonnage; a repeal of so much of the Tonnage law will be the answer.

3. If it be thought better to wave rigorous and nice discussions of right, and to make the modification an act of friendship and of compensation for favours received, the passage of such a bill will then be the answer.

TH. JEFFERSON
Jan. 18, 1791[10]

L. G. Otto to the Secretary of State

(Translation)

Philadelphia Decemr. 13th 1790

Sir,

During the long stay you made in France, you had opportunities of being satisfied of the favorable dispositions of his Majesty to render permanent the ties that united the two Nations, and to give stability to the Treaties of alliance and of commerce, which form the basis of this Union. These treaties were so well maintained by the Congress formed under the ancient Confederation, that they thought it their duty to interpose their authority whenever any laws made by individual States appeared to infringe their stipulations, and particularly in 1785 when the States of New Hampshire and of Massachusetts had imposed an extraordinary tonnage on foreign vessels, without exempting those of the french Nation. The reflections that I have the honor to address to you in the subjoin'd Note, being founded on the same principles, I flatter myself that they will merit on the part of the Government of the United States the most serious attention.

I am with respect
Sir
Your most obt. and
most humble Servt.
(signed)   L. G. OTTO[11]

---

[10] The report, in the hand of Jacob Blackwell and signed by Thomas Jefferson, is in President's Messages on Foreign Relations, Executive Proceedings, SR, DNA. The related documents are printed in Part II of this volume under the heading Tonnage on French Vessels.

[11] The translation, in the hand of Henry Remsen, Jr., is in President's Messages on

L. G. Otto to the Secretary of State

(Translation)

NOTE

The underwritten Chargé des Affaires of France has received the express order of his Court to represent to the United States, that the Act passed by Congress the 20th July 1789 and renewed the 20th July of the present year, which imposes an extraordinary Tonnage on foreign vessels without excepting french vessels, is directly contrary to the spirit and to the object of the Treaty of Commerce, which unites the two Nations, and of which his Majesty has not only scrupulously observed the tenor, but of which he has extended the advantages by many regulations very favorable to the Commerce and Navigation of the United States.

By the 5th article of this Treaty, the Citizens of these States are declared exempt from the tonnage duty imposed in France on foreign vessels, and they are not subject to that duty but in the coasting business. Congress has reserved the privilege of establishing *a duty equivalent to this last*, a stipulation founded on the state in which matters were in America at the time of the signature of the Treaty; there did not exist at that epoch any duty on tonnage in the United States.

It is evident that it was the non-existence of this duty, and the motive of a perfect reciprocity stipulated in the preamble of the Treaty, that had determined the King to grant the exemption contained in the Article 5th; and a proof Congress had no intention to contravene this reciprocity is, that *it only reserves a privilege of establishing on the coasting business, a duty equivalent to that which is levied in France.* This reservation would have been completely useless, if by the words of the Treaty Congress thought themselves at liberty to lay *any* tonnage they should think proper on french vessels.

The undersigned has the honor to observe that this contravention of the 5th article of the Treaty of Commerce, might have authorized his Majesty to modify proportionably the favors granted by the same Article to the American Navigation; but the King always faithful to the principles of friendship and attachment to the United States; and desirous of strengthening more and more the ties which subsist so happily between the French Nation and these States, thinks it more conformable to these views to order the undersigned to make representations on this subject, and to ask in favor of french vessels, a modification of the Act which imposes an extraordinary tonnage on foreign vessels. His Majesty does not doubt but that the United States will acknowlege the justice of this claim, and will be disposed to restore things to the footing on which they were at the signature of the Treaty of the 6th February 1778.

Foreign Relations, Executive Proceedings, SR, DNA. A French copy is printed in Part II of this volume under the heading Tonnage on French Vessels.

Philadelphia December 13th 1790
(signed)   L. G. OTTO[12]

L. G. Otto to the Secretary of State

(Translation)

New York 8th January 1791

Sir,

I have the Honor herewith to send you a Letter from the King to Congress, and one which M. de Montmorin has written to yourself. You will find therein the sincere Sentiments with which you have inspired our Government, and the regret of the Minister in not having a more near relation of correspondence with you. In these every Person who has had the advantage of knowing you in France participates.

At the same time, it gives me pain, Sir, to be obliged to announce to you, that the complaints of our Merchants on the subject of the Tonnage duty increase, and that they have excited not only the attention of the King, but that of several Departments of the Kingdom. I have received new orders to request of the United States a decision on this matter, and to solicit, in favor of the aggrieved Merchants, the restitution of the Duties which have already been paid. I earnestly beg of you Sir, not to lose sight of an object, which, as I have already had the honor to tell you verbally, is of the greatest importance for cementing the future commercial connections between the two Nations.

In more particularly examining this question, you will, perhaps, find that motives of convenience are as powerful as those of Justice to engage the United States to give to his Majesty the satisfaction which he requires. At least twice as many American Vessels enter the Ports of France as do those of France the Ports of America. The exemption of the Tonnage-duty then is evidently less advantageous for the French than for the Navigators of the United States. Be this as it may, I can assure you, Sir, that the delay of a decision in this respect, by augmenting the just complaints of the French Merchants, will only augment the difficulties. I therefore beg of you to enable me, before the sailing of the Packet, which will take place towards the last of this Month, to give to my Court a satisfactory answer.

I have the honor to be,
with a respectful attachment
Sir,
Your most humble
and

[12] The translation, in the hand of Henry Remsen, Jr., is in President's Messages on Foreign Relations, Executive Proceedings, SR, DNA. A French copy is printed in Part II of this volume under the heading Tonnage on French Vessels.

most obedient Servant
L. G. OTTO

His Excelly. M. Jefferson ⎱ 13
     Secy. of State ⎰

ORDERED, That this Message and Papers be committed to
                    Mr. Morris,
                    Mr. King,
                     "   Izard,
                     "   Strong, and
                     "   Ellsworth, to consider and report what is
proper to be done thereon.[14]

---

[13] The translation, in the hand of George Taylor, Jr., is in President's Messages on Foreign Relations, Executive Proceedings, SR, DNA. A French copy is printed in Part II of this volume under the heading Tonnage on French Vessels.

[14] The vote for committee, recorded by Samuel Otis and located in Other Records, Yeas and Nays, SR, DNA, is as follows:

Mr. Bassett	IIII				
" Butler	I				
" Carroll					
" Dalton					
" Dickinson	III				
" Ellsworth	JHH	III			
" Elmer					
" Few	I				
" Foster	I				
" Gunn	I				
" Hawkins	II				
" Henry					
" Johnson	III				
" Johnston	JHH	II			
√ " Izard	III	JHH	JHH		
√ " King	JHH	JHH	JHH		
" Langdon	JHH	I			
" Lee					
" Maclay					
" Monroe	IIII				
√ " Morris	JHH	JHH	JHH	JHH	I
" Read	JHH	II			
" Schuyler	II				
" Stanton					
√ " Strong	JHH	JHH			
" Wingate	I				

On January 27 this committee reported.

T H U R S D A Y, JANUARY 27TH, 1791

Mr. Morris reported from the Committee appointed to take into consideration the Message of the President of the United States of the 19th instant.[15]

ORDERED, That the report lie for consideration.[16]

F R I D A Y, JANUARY 28TH, 1791

The Senate took into consideration the report of the Committee made yesterday on the Message of the President of the United States of the 19th instant, and after debate the farther consideration thereof was postponed.

M O N D A Y, JANUARY 31ST, 1791

The Senate resumed the consideration of the report of the Committee made the 27th instant and after debate it was farther postponed.[17]

---

[15] The report, in the hand of Rufus King, is in Various Select Committee Reports, SR, DNA. It was printed in the journal on February 26, 1791.

[16] On January 28 and 31 this report was considered.

[17] On February 2 a letter from William Short on the subject of tonnage was sent to the Senate. On February 26 the Senate again considered this report and agreed to two resolutions on tonnage.

TUESDAY, FEBRUARY 1ST, 1791

Mr. Langdon reported from the Committee appointed as per Legislative Journal December 15th 1790 on that part of the Speech of the President of the United States which relates to the Commerce of the Mediterranean, together with his Message recorded also on the Legislative Journal of the 30th of December 1790, and on the Letter of the 20th of January from the Secretary of State respecting the American prisoners in captivity at Algiers, with the papers accompanying the same; and the report is that it be[18]

1	"RESOLVED, That the[19] Se-
2	nate[20] advise and consent,
3	that the President of the
4	United States, take such
5	measures as he may think[21] neces-
6	sary for the redemption of the
7	Citizens of the United States
8	now in captivity at Algiers,
9	provided the expense shall
10	not exceed forty thousand dol-
11	lars; and also that measures
12	be taken to confirm the Treaty
13	now existing between the United
14	States and the Emperor of Moroc-
15	co;[22] provided no greater sum
16	than Twenty thousand dollars
17	be expended in that business."[23]

ON MOTION to postpone the first clause of the report to wit: from "RESOLVED" line 1st to "that" line 11th.

It passed in the Negative.

---

[18] In the original report the preceding paragraph reads: "The Committee to whom was Referred that part of the Presidents speech which Relates to the Trade of the Mediterranian also the letter from the Secretary of State dated 20th. Jany. 1791 with the papers Accompanying the same—Report the followg. Resolve."

[19] At this point in the original report the words "President of the United States" are lined out.

[20] At this point in the original report the word "do" is included.

[21] At this point in the original report the word "deem" is lined out and "think" is written above it.

[22] The following phrase is lined out in the original report, conforming it to the Senate amendment of this date. The word "dele" is noted beside the lines.

[23] The report, in the hand of John Langdon, is in Various Select Committee Reports, SR, DNA. The related documents are printed in Part II of this volume under the heading United States Prisoners in Algiers.

And on motion to expunge from the second clause of the report, these words, lines, 15, 16 & 17 "provided no greater sum than twenty thousand dollars be expended in that business."

It passed in the Affirmative.

And the report as amended, was agreed to—Whereupon

RESOLVED, That the Senate do advise and consent that the President of the United States do take such measures as he may think necessary for the redemption of the Citizens of the United States now in captivity at Algiers, provided the expense shall not exceed forty thousand dollars; And also, that measures be taken to confirm the Treaty now existing between the United States and the Emperor of Morocco.

ORDERED, That the Secretary communicate this resolution to the President of the United States.

Mr. Langdon from the Committee appointed the 15th of December 1790, as recorded on the Legislative Journal of that date, REPORTED January the 6th 1791 on the same subject.[24]

"That the Trade of the United States to the Mediterranean can not be protected, but, by a Naval force, and that it will be proper to resort to the same as soon as, the state of the public finances will admit."[25]

ON MOTION,

ORDERED, That this report be re-committed, with an instruction to the Committee to consider the subject and report generally thereon—See Legislative Journal of the 6th and 20th of January for farther instructions to this Committee.[26]

WEDNESDAY, FEBRUARY 2D, 1791

A Letter from the Secretary of State enclosing an extract of one from William Short Chargé des Affaires at the Court of France, was read.[27]

[24] In the original report this paragraph reads: "Mr. Langdon from" (in the hand of Samuel Otis) "The Committee to whom was Referred that part of the Presidents Speech which Relates to the Trade of the Mediterranian, also the Presidents Message of the 30th. December, with the papers Accompaning the Same—Are of Opinion."

[25] The report, in the hand of John Langdon, is in Various Select Committee Reports, SR, DNA. Following the report are two crossed-out orders, in the hand of Samuel Otis. The first states, "Senate of the United States/ Jany. 21st 1791/ Ordered, That this report be recommitted/ Attest/ Sam. A. Otis Secy." and refers to Senate legislative action. The second states, "Feb. 1st 1791/ Ordered, That this report be again recommitted/Attest/Sam. A. Otis Secy." and refers to the recommitment of the above report in Executive session.

[26] On February 22 the President sent the Senate a message about the U.S. Prisoners in Algiers and a treaty with Morocco.

[27] These documents are printed in Part II of this volume under the heading Tonnage on French Vessels.

ORDERED, That the Letter and enclosure lie for consideration.

MONDAY, FEBRUARY 14TH, 1791

A written Message from the President of the United States by Mr. Lear his Secretary was delivered to the Vice President.
And he withdrew.

UNITED STATES, February 14th 1791

GENTLEMEN of the SENATE,

Conceiving that in the possible event of a refusal of Justice on the part of Great Britain, we should stand less committed should it be made to a private rather than to a public person, I employed Mr. Gouverr. Morris, who was on the spot, and without giving him any definite Character, to enter informally into the conferrence before mentioned. For your more particular information, I lay before you the Instructions I gave him, and those parts of his communications wherein the British Ministers appear either in conversation or by Letter. These are, two Letters from the Duke of Leeds to Mr. Morris, and three Letters of Mr. Morris giving an account of two Conferences with the Duke of Leeds, and one with him and Mr. Pitt. The sum of these is, that they declare without scruple they do not mean to fulfill what remains of the Treaty of Peace to be fulfilled on their part (by which we are to understand the delivery of the Posts and payment for property carried off) 'till performance on our part, and compensation where the delay has rendered the performance now impracticable: that on the subject of a treaty of commerce they avoided direct answers, so as to satisfy Mr. Morris they did not mean to enter into one unless it could be extended to a Treaty of Alliance offensive and defensive, or unless in the event of a rupture with Spain.

As to the sending a Minister here, they made excuses at the first conference, seem disposed to it in the second, and in the last express an intention of so doing.

Their views being thus sufficiently ascertained, I have directed Mr. Morris to discontinue his communications with them.

GO. WASHINGTON[28]

ORDERED, That this Message lie for consideration.

---

[28] The message, in the hand of Tobias Lear and signed by George Washington, is in President's Messages on Foreign Relations, Executive Proceedings, SR, DNA. Included with the above document is Washington's message to both houses, which was printed in the Senate Legislative Journal on February 14, 1791. The related documents are printed in Part II of this volume under the heading Commercial Relations with Great Britain.

FRIDAY, FEBRUARY 18TH, 1791

A written Message from the President of the United States by Mr. Lear his Secretary was delivered to the Vice President.
And he withdrew.

UNITED STATES, Feby. 18th 1791

GENTLEMEN of the SENATE,

The aspect of affairs in Europe during the last summer and especially between Spain and England, gave reason to expect a favorable occasion for pressing to accomodation the unsettled matters between them and us. Mr. Carmichael, our Chargé des Affaires at Madrid, having been long absent from his Country, great changes having taken place in our circumstances and sentiments during that interval, it was thought expedient to send some person in a private Character, fully acquainted with the present state of things here to be the bearer of written and confidential instructions to him, and at the same time to possess him in full and frequent conversations, of all those details of facts, and topics of argument, which could not be conveyed in writing, but which would be necessary to enable him to meet the reasonings of that Court with advantage. Colo. David Humphreys was therefore sent for these purposes.

An additional motive for this confidential mission arose in the same quarter. The Court of Lisbon had, on several occasions, made the most amicable advances for cultivating friendship and intercourse with the United States. The exchange of a diplomatic character had been informally, but repeatedly suggested on their part. It was our interest to meet this nation in its friendly dispositions, and to concur in the exchange proposed. But my wish was, at the same time, that the Character to be exchanged should be of the lowest and most economical grade. To this it was known that certain rules, of long standing at that Court, would produce obstacles. Colo. Humphreys was charged with dispatches to the Prime Minister of Portugal, and with instructions to endeavour to arrange this to our views. It happened, however, that, previous to his arrival at Lisbon, the Queen had appointed a Minister *Resident* to the United States. This embarrassment seems to have rendered the difficulty completely insurmountable. The Minister of that Court, in his conferences with Colo. Humphreys, professing every wish to accomodate, yet expresses his regrets that circumstances do not permit them to concur in the grade of Chargé des Affaires; a grade of little privilege or respectability by the rules of their Court, and held in so low estimation with them, that no proper Character would accept it to go abroad. In a Letter to the Secretary of State he expresses the same sentiments, and announces the appointment, on their part, of a Minister *Resident* to the United States, and the pleasure with which the Queen will receive one from us at her Court. A copy of his Letter and also of Colo. Humphreys giving the details of this transaction, will be delivered to you.

On consideration of all circumstances, I have determined to accede to the desire of the Court of Lisbon, in the Article of Grade. I am aware that the consequences will not end here, and that this is not the only instance in which a like change may be pressed. But should it be necessary to yield elsewhere also, I shall think it a less evil, than to disgust a government so friendly, and so interesting to us, as that of Portugal.

I do not mean that the change of grade shall render the mission more expensive.

I have therefore nominated DAVID HUMPHREYS Minister Resident from the United States to her Most faithful Majesty the Queen of Portugal.

GO. WASHINGTON[29]

ORDERED, That this Message lie for consideration.

MONDAY, FEBRUARY 21ST, 1791

The Senate proceeded to the consideration of the Message from the President of the United States of the 18th instant and the nomination therein contained of DAVID HUMPHREYS to be Minister Resident from the United States to her Most faithful Majesty the Queen of Portugal—and—

RESOLVED, That the Senate advise and consent to his appointment accordingly.

ORDERED, That the Secretary communicate this Resolution of Senate to the President of the United States.

TUESDAY, FEBRUARY 22D, 1791

A written Message from the President of the United States by Mr. Lear his Secretary was delivered to the Vice President.

And he withdrew.

UNITED STATES, February 22d 1791

GENTLEMEN of the SENATE,

I will proceed to take measures for the ransom of our citizens in captivity at Algiers, in conformity with your resolution of advice of the first instant,

[29] The message, in the hand of Tobias Lear and signed by George Washington, is in President's Messages on Foreign Relations, Executive Proceedings, SR, DNA. The related documents are printed in Part II of this volume under the heading Diplomatic Exchange with Portugal.

so soon as the monies necessary shall be appropriated by the Legislature, and shall be in readiness.

The recognition of our treaty with the new Emperor of Morocco requires also previous appropriation and provision—the importance of this last to the liberty and property of our citizens induces me to urge it on your earliest attention.

Go. Washington[30]

Ordered, That the Message be committed to the Committee appointed the 15th of December 1790 to consider and report on that part of the Presidents Message relating to the Commerce of the Mediterranean. For this Committee see the Legislative Journal of the 15th of December 1790.[31]

A written Message from the President of the United States by Mr. Lear his Secretary was delivered to the Vice President.

And he withdrew.

United States, February 22d 1791

Gentlemen of the Senate,

I lay before you a Report of the Secretary of War relative to the Appointment of two Brigadier Generals of Militia in the Territory of the United States South of the Ohio. And I nominate

John Sevier to be Brigadier General of the Militia of Washington District—and

James Robertson to be Brigadier General of the Militia of Miro District; both within the said Territory.

Go. Washington[32]

Ordered, That this Message lie for consideration.

WEDNESDAY, February 23D, 1791

The Senate proceeded to the consideration of the Message from the President of the United States of the 22d instant and the nominations therein contained of—

John Sevier to be Brigadier General of the Militia of Washington District—and,

---

[30] The message, in the hand of William Jackson and signed by George Washington, is in President's Messages on Foreign Relations, Executive Proceedings, SR, DNA.

[31] On March 1 this committee reported.

[32] The message, in the hand of Tobias Lear and signed by George Washington, is in Executive Nominations, third session, Executive Proceedings, SR, DNA. The related documents are printed in Part II of this volume under the heading Nominations of Militia Officers for Territory South of the Ohio River.

JAMES ROBERTSON to be Brigadier General of the Militia of Miro District —both within the Territory of the United States South of the Ohio— and

RESOLVED, That they do advise and consent to the Appointments therein mentioned respectively.

ORDERED, That the Secretary communicate this Resolution of Senate to the President of the United States.

A written Message from the President of the United States by Mr. Lear his Secretary was delivered to the Vice President.

And he withdrew.

UNITED STATES, February 23d 1791

GENTLEMEN of the SENATE,

Information having been received from Thomas Auldjo, who was appointed Vice-Consul of the United States at Cowes in Great Britain, that his Commission has not been recognized by that Government, because it is a port at which no foreign Consul has yet been received, and that it has been intimated to him, that his Appointment to the port of Poole and parts nearer to that than to the residence of any other Consul of the United States, would be recognized, and his residence at Cowes not noticed. I have, therefore, thought it expedient to nominate

THOMAS AULDJO to be Vice-Consul for the United States at the Port of Poole, in Great Britain, and such parts within the Allegiance of his Britanic Majesty, as shall be nearer thereto than to the residence of any other Consul, or Vice-Consul of the United States within the same Allegiance.

I also nominate

JAMES YARD, of Pennsylvania, to be Consul for the United States in the Island of Santa Cruz, and such other parts within the Allegiance of his Danish Majesty as shall be nearer thereto than to the residence of any other Consul or Vice-Consul of the United States within the same Allegiance.

GO. WASHINGTON[33]

ORDERED, That this Message lie for consideration.

THURSDAY, FEBRUARY 24TH, 1791

The Senate proceeded to the consideration of the Message from the Presi-

---

[33] The message, in the hand of Tobias Lear and signed by George Washington, is in Executive Nominations, third session, Executive Proceedings, SR, DNA. The letter "a," probably indicating Senate agreement, follows both nominations.

dent of the United States of the 23d instant and the Nominations therein
contained of

THOMAS AULDJO to be Vice-Consul for the United States at the Port of
Poole, in Great Britain, and such parts within the Allegiance of his
Britanic Majesty, as shall be nearer thereto than to the residence of any
other Consul, or Vice-Consul of the United States within the same Allegiance—and

JAMES YARD, of Pennsylvania, to be Consul for the United States in the
Island of Santa Cruz, and such other parts within the Allegiance of his
Danish Majesty as shall be nearer thereto than to the residence of any
other Consul or Vice-Consul of the United States within the same
Allegiance—and

RESOLVED, That they do advise and consent to the Appointments therein
mentioned respectively.

ORDERED, That the Secretary communicate this Resolution of Senate to the
President of the United States.

FRIDAY, FEBRUARY 25TH, 1791

A written Message from the President of the United States by Mr. Lear
his Secretary was delivered to the Vice President.
And he withdrew.

UNITED STATES, February 25th 1791

GENTLEMEN of the SENATE,

I nominate JOSEPH ANDERSON of the State of Delaware, to be one of the
Judges in the Territory of the United States south of the Ohio, in place
of WILLIAM PEERY who has declined his appointment—and

WILLIAM MURRAY, of Kentucky, to be Attorney for the United States in
the District of Kentucky, in place of JAMES BROWN who has declined
his appointment.

GO. WASHINGTON[34]

ORDERED, That this Message lie for consideration.

SATURDAY, FEBRUARY 26TH, 1791[35]

The Senate proceeded to the consideration of the Message from the Presi-

[34] The message, in the hand of Tobias Lear and signed by George Washington, is
in Executive Nominations, third session, Executive Proceedings, SR, DNA. The letter
"a," probably indicating Senate agreement, follows both nominations.
[35] A rough copy of the proceedings for this date, in the hand of Samuel Otis, is in

dent of the United States of the 25th instant and the Nominations therein contained of

> JOSEPH ANDERSON, of the State of Delaware, to be one of the Judges in the Territory of the United States south of the Ohio, in place of WILLIAM PEERY who has declined his appointment—and
>
> WILLIAM MURRAY, of Kentucky, to be Attorney for the United States in the District of Kentucky, in place of JAMES BROWN who has declined his appointment—and

RESOLVED, That they do advise and consent to the Appointments therein mentioned respectively.

ORDERED, That the Secretary communicate this Resolution of Senate to the President of the United States.

The Report of the Committee to whom was referred the Message of the President of the United States of the 19th instant, with the Note of the Chargé des Affaires of France of the 13th of December was taken into consideration and being amended was agreed to.[36]

Whereupon

RESOLVED, as the opinion of the Senate, that the fifth Article of the treaty of amity and commerce between the United States, and his Most Christian Majesty, is merely an illustration of the third and fourth Articles of the same treaty, by an application of the Principles comprized in the[37] last mentioned Articles, to the case stated in the former.[38]

RESOLVED, that the Senate do advise that an answer be given to the Court of France, defending in the most friendly manner, this construction, in opposition to that urged by the said Court.[39]

ORDERED, That the Secretary communicate these Resolutions to the President of the United States.

Various Select Committee Reports, SR, DNA. This is the only surviving page from the Executive rough journal.

[36] In the original report the preceding paragraph reads: "The committee to whom was referred the presidents message of the 19th. instant, with the note of the Chargé des Affaires of France of the 13th. of December submit the following Resolutions."

[37] At this point in the original report the word "latter" is lined out and "last mentioned" is written above it.

[38] In the original report there is a second resolution following this paragraph which has been crossed out. It reads: "Resolved, that the Senate do advise that an answer be given to the Court of France defending this construction in opposition to that urged by the said Court, and at the same time explaining in the most friendly Terms, the Difficulties opposed to the Exemptions they claim—." Inserted above the first line of this resolution is a note from Otis to the copyist which reads: "N B this must not be end."

[39] The following order, in the hand of Samuel Otis, is written on the original report.

T U E S D A Y, MARCH 1ST, 1791

Mr. Langdon reported from the Committee to whom was referred the Message of the President of the United States of the 22d of February last.[40]

ORDERED, that the Report lie until to morrow for consideration.[41]

T H U R S D A Y, MARCH 3D, 1791

The Vice President notified the Senate that it was the request of the President of the United States that they would assemble on the 4th day of March instant to transact some public business of importance.

The Senate took into consideration the report of the Committee on the Message of the President of the United States of the 22d of February Whereupon

It was resolved as follows[42]—

Whereas, since the resolution of the Senate advising the President of the United States[43] to take measures for the ransom of the American captives at Algiers, large Appropriations of money have been made for the protection of the western frontiers.

RESOLVED, That the Senate do advise and consent that the President of the United States[44] suspend any operations under the said Resolution for the ransom of the said captives until the situation of the Treasury shall more clearly authorize appropriations of money for that purpose.[45]

ORDERED, That the Secretary communicate this resolution to the President of the United States.

A written Message from the President of the United States with sundry military nominations annexed was communicated to the Senate by Mr. Lear his Secretary.

And he withdrew.

---

[40] The report, in the hand of Rufus King, is in Various Select Committee Reports, SR, DNA. It was printed in the Journal on March 3, 1791.

[41] On this date the Moroccan Treaty Bill [S-23] was presented in Senate Legislative session. On March 3 this committee report was considered, and a resolution on the U.S. prisoners in Algiers was agreed to.

[42] The following line precedes the original report: "The committee to whom was referred the presidents message of the 22d. feby. submit the following Resolution."

[43] In the original report the words "of the US" are inserted in the hand of Samuel Otis. This insertion is probably a result of Senate action on the report.

[44] In the original report the words "of the UStates" are inserted in the hand of Samuel Otis, probably as the result of Senate action on the report. The word "do" is also included at this point.

[45] The order, which follows the report, is noted at the bottom of the original document by Samuel Otis.

The Message and Nominations were read.

UNITED STATES, 3d March 1791

GENTLEMEN of the SENATE,

Certain vacancies having taken place in the Offices of the Troops established by an Act passed on the 30th of April 1790, I nominate, to fill those vacancies, the persons whose names are in the annexed list under the head of the first Regiment. I likewise nominate the persons to fill the Offices affixed to their Names in the annexed list under the head of the Second Regiment, agreeably to a Law passed this day.

GO. WASHINGTON[46]

ORDERED, That the Message and Nominations lie for consideration.[47]

Attest

SAM. A. OTIS Secretary

---

[46] The message, in the hand of Tobias Lear and signed by George Washington, is in Executive Nominations, third session, Executive Proceedings, SR, DNA. The list, in the hand of John Stagg, Jr., and signed by George Washington, is filed with the message.

[47] On March 4 the list of military nominations was printed.

FOURTH SESSION

F R I D A Y, MARCH 4TH, 1791

The Senate assembled conformably to the Summons from the President of the United States of the first day of March 1791, which was read by the Secretary of the Senate as follows.

The PRESIDENT of the UNITED STATES
    to the PRESIDENT of the SENATE

Certain matters touching the public good requiring that the Senate shall be convened on Friday the 4th instant, I have desired their attendance, as I do yours by these Presents, at the Senate Chamber in Philadelphia on that day, then and there to receive and deliberate on such Communications as shall be made to you on my part.

Philadelphia March 1st 1791   GO. WASHINGTON[1]

---

[1] The message, in the hand of Henry Remsen, Jr., and signed by George Washington, is in Other Records, Executive Proceedings (2nd Congress), SR, DNA. The only Senators who attended the one-day fourth session were those who remained in Philadelphia at the close of the third session. The following note, in the hand of Tobias Lear and located in The George Washington Papers, series 2, vol. 25, roll 9, Manuscript Division, DLC, explains the selection.

Tuesday March 1st. 1791

The President of the United States having thought proper to convene the Senate on the 4th of March, for the dispatch of public business of an Executive Nature, the following Summonses were sent to the President of the Senate, and to each member of that body who were in the City of Philadelphia. A Summons was likewise addressed to every member of the Senate who was absent; but as the business for which they were about to be convened would not probably engage the Senate more than one or two days, it was not thought proper to send them to the States where the absent members resided, the Summonses of this nature were therefore left in the Senate Chamber—when the others were sent to the residence of each individual in the City of Philadelphia.

The following form letter was sent to the Senators.

The President of the United States

125

SENATORS PRESENT

From	New Hampshire	The Hone.	John Langdon
	and	" "	Paine Wingate
"	Rhode Island	" "	Joseph Stanton Junr.
"	Connecticut	" "	W. S. Johnson
"	New York	" "	Rufus King
"	New Jersey	" "	Philemon Dickinson
"	Pennsylvania	" "	Robert Morris
"	Delaware	" "	Richard Bassett
"	Maryland	" "	John Henry
"	Virginia	" "	Richard H. Lee
"	North Carolina	" "	Samuel Johnston
	and	" "	Benjn. Hawkins
"	South Carolina	" "	Pierce Butler
	and	" "	Ralph Izard
"	Georgia	" "	James Gunn

The terms for which the following Senators were at first appointed having expired on the 3d instant, in consequence of the classing, conformably to the Constitution, agreed to on the 15th of May 1789 and 27th June 1790, which classing appears at large on the Journals of the Legislative proceedings of Senate of the last mentioned dates; and they being reappointed by the States respectively annexed to their names,

The Hone. Theodore Foster, from the State of Rhode Island
" "   Oliver Ellsworth, from the State of Connecticut
" "   George Read, from the State of Delaware
" "   Charles Carroll, from the State of Maryland
and
" "   James Monroe, from the State of Virginia
appeared in Senate, were respectively qualified and took their Seats.

The Hone. Mr. Carroll, a Senator from the State of Maryland having omitted to procure certified Credentials, was on his own declaration and the

To ———, Senator for the State of ———

Certain matters touching the public good requiring that the Senate shall be convened on Friday the 4th Instant, you are desired to attend at the Senate Chamber in Philadelphia on that Day, then and there to receive and deliberate on such communications as shall be made on my part.

Philadelphia March 1st 1791.   GO. WASHINGTON

Although the session of March 4, 1791, has been classified as a special session of the Second Congress, the proceedings for that day have been included in this volume for two reasons. First, the Senators who attended the session were members of the First Congress, and some were not members of the Second Congress. Second, the business considered by this session was the unfinished work of the First Congress.

testimony of his Colleague Mr. Henry, qualified, and took his seat, engaging forthwith to return his credentials formally authenticated.

The Secretary of the Senate read the record of the Senate in their Executive capacity of March the 3d 1791.

ORDERED, That the Secretary of the Senate, wait on the President of the United States and acquaint him, that a quorum of the Senate is assembled, agreeably to his summons of the 2d instant, and that they are ready to receive his communications.

The Secretary of the Senate having communicated the Message—

Two written Messages from the President of the United States, were by Mr. Lear his Secretary delivered to the Vice President.

And he withdrew.

The first Message is as follows.

UNITED STATES, MARCH 4th 1791

GENTLEMEN of the SENATE,

The Act for the admission of the State of Vermont into this Union having fixed on this, as the day of its admission, it was thought that this would also be the first day on which any Officer of the Union might legally perform any Act of authority relating to that State. I therefore required your attendance to receive nominations of the several Officers necessary to put the federal Government into motion in that State.

For this purpose I nominate

NATHANIEL CHIPMAN to be Judge of the District of Vermont.

STEPHEN JACOB, to be Attorney for the United States in the District of Vermont.

LEWIS R. MORRIS, to be Marshall of the District of Vermont—and

STEPHEN KEYES to be Collector of the Port of Allburg[2] in the State of Vermont.

GO. WASHINGTON[3]

The other Message is subjoined.

UNITED STATES, 4th March 1791

GENTLEMEN of the SENATE,

Pursuant to the powers vested in me by the Act intitled "An Act repealing

---

[2] In the original message "Allburg" is spelled "Allburgh."

[3] The message, in the hand of Tobias Lear and signed by George Washington, is in Executive Nominations, special session, Executive Proceedings (Second Congress), SR, DNA. The letter "a" follows each nomination except that of Stephen Keyes, which appears to be followed by the letter "c." The letter "a" probably indicates Senate agreement, while the letter "c" probably indicates Senate concurrence.

after the last day of June next the duties heretofore laid upon distilled Spirits imported from abroad and laying others in their stead, and also upon Spirits distilled within the United States, and for appropriating the same," I have thought fit to divide the United States into the following Districts—namely—

The District of New Hampshire, to consist of the State of New Hampshire.

The District of Massachusetts, to consist of the State of Massachusetts.

The District of Rhode Island and Providence Plantations, to consist of the State of Rhode Island and Providence Plantations.

The District of Connecticut, to consist of the State of Connecticut.

The District of Vermont, to consist of the State of Vermont.

The District of New York, to consist of the State of New York.

The District of New Jersey, to consist of the State of New Jersey.

The District of Pennsylvania, to consist of the State of Pennsylvania.

The District of Delaware, to consist of the State of Delaware.

The District of Maryland, to consist of the State of Maryland.

The District of Virginia, to consist of the State of Virginia.

The District of North Carolina, to consist of the State of North Carolina.

The District of South Carolina, to consist of the State of South Carolina.

The District of Georgia, to consist of the State of Georgia.

And I hereby nominate as Supervisors of the said Districts respectively the following persons—viz.—

For the District of	
New Hampshire	JOSHUA WENTWORTH
For the District of Massachusetts	NATHANIEL GORHAM
For the District of Rhode Island and Providence Plantations	JOHN S. DEXTER
For the District of Connecticut	JOHN CHESTER
For the District of Vermont	NOAH SMITH
For the District of New York	WILLIAM S. SMITH
For the District of New Jersey	AARON DUNHAM
For the District of Pennsylvania	GEORGE CLYMER
For the District of Delaware	HENRY LATIMER
For the District of Maryland	GEORGE GALE

For the District of Virginia	} EDWARD CARRINGTON
For the District of North Carolina	} WILLIAM POLK
For the District of South Carolina	} DANIEL STEVENS
For the District of Georgia	} JOHN MATHEWS

GO. WASHINGTON[4]

ORDERED, That the Rule be so far dispensed with, as that the Senate proceed at this time, to the consideration of the Message of the President of the United States, and the nominations therein contained, of

NATHANIEL CHIPMAN to be Judge of the District of Vermont.

STEPHEN JACOB to be Attorney for the United States in the District of Vermont.

LEWIS R. MORRIS to be Marshall of the District of Vermont—and

STEPHEN KEYES to be Collector of the Port of Allburgh in the State of Vermont.

Whereupon

RESOLVED, that the Senate do advise and consent to these appointments agreeably to the respective nominations.

ORDERED, that the Secretary communicate this Resolution to the President of the United States.

ORDERED, that the rule be so far dispensed with as that the Senate proceed at this time, to the consideration of the Message of the President of the United States and the nominations therein contained, of Supervisors of the several Districts within the United States, as divided, conformably to the powers, by law, vested in the President of the United States to wit:

For the District of New Hampshire	} JOSHUA WENTWORTH
For the District of Massachusetts	} NATHANIEL GORHAM
For the District of Rhode Island and Providence Plantations	} JOHN S. DEXTER
For the District of Connecticut	} JOHN CHESTER

---

[4] The message, in the hand of Tobias Lear and signed by George Washington, is in Executive Nominations, special session, Executive Proceedings (Second Congress), SR, DNA. The letter "a," probably indicating Senate agreement, follows each nomination except that of John Mathews. The letter "d" follows his nomination.

For the District of Vermont	NOAH SMITH
For the District of New York	WILLIAM S. SMITH
For the District of New Jersey	AARON DUNHAM
For the District of Pennsylvania	GEORGE CLYMER
For the District of Delaware	HENRY LATIMER
For the District of Maryland	GEORGE GALE
For the District of Virginia	EDWARD CARRINGTON
For the District of North Carolina	WILLIAM POLK
For the District of South Carolina	DANIEL STEVENS
For the District of Georgia	JOHN MATHEWS

Whereupon

RESOLVED, that the Senate do advise and consent to these appointments agreeably to the respective nominations.

ORDERED, that the Secretary communicate this Resolution to the President of the United States.

A written Message from the President of the United States was delivered to the Vice President by Mr. Lear his Secretary.

And he withdrew.

UNITED STATES, 4th March 1791

GENTLEMEN of the SENATE,

In pursuance of an Act intitled "An Act for raising and adding another Regiment to the military establishment of the United States, and making further provision for the protection of the frontiers"—I nominate for the following Offices therein mentioned.

Major General   Arthur St. Clair
Quarter Master   Samuel Hodgdon
Chaplain   John Hurt

GO. WASHINGTON[5]

[5]The message, in the hand of Tobias Lear and signed by George Washington, is in Executive Nominations, special session, Executive Proceedings (Second Congress), SR, DNA. The letter "a," probably indicating Senate agreement, follows each nomination.

ORDERED, that the rule be so far dispensed with, as that the Senate proceed at the present time, to the consideration of the Message of the President of the United States of this date and the nominations therein contained

Of ARTHUR ST. CLAIR to be a Major General

Of SAMUEL HODGDON to be Quarter Master

and of JOHN HURT to be Chaplain, in pursuance of the Act abovementioned in the Message of the President of the United States.   and

RESOLVED, that the Senate do advise and consent to these appointments agreeably to the respective nominations.

ORDERED, that the Secretary communicate this Resolution to the President of the United States.

ORDERED, that the Secretary of the Senate obtain from the Secretary of War, a list of the Officers of the Army of the United States, now in Commission.

The List above mentioned was laid before the Senate.

The Senate proceeded to consider the Military Nominations made in pursuance of the Law referred to in the Message of the President of the United States of the 3d instant, and thereto annexed, of

NOMINATIONS for
PROMOTIONS and
APPOINTMENTS

FIRST REGIMENT

Major David Ziegler   —   vice Wyllys killed
Major Richard Call   —   vice Parker declined Virginia

CAPTAINS

Thomas Doyle	vice Ziegler promoted
John Armstrong	vice Mercer resigned
John Pratt	vice Heart promoted

LIEUTENANTS

Cornelius Sedam	vice Doyle promoted
John Jeffers	vice Frothingham killed
Abner Prior	vice Armstrong promoted
Asa Heartshorn	vice Heart promoted
Thomas Seayres	vice Steel declined

ENSIGNS
APPOINTMENTS

| Daniel Britt | Pensylvania |
| Hamilton Armstrong | ditto |

Ensigns
Appointments

Bartholomew Shomburg	promoted from *Serjeant Major*
Bernard Gaines	Virginia
John Wade	Pennsylvania
Ross Bird	ditto

Second Regiment
Appointments

Lieut. Colol. Commandt.	John Doughty	New Jersey
1. Major	Lemuel Trescott	Massachusetts
2. Major	John Burnham	Ditto
3. Major	Jonathan Heart	Connecticut

Captains

1.	Robert Kirkwood	Delaware
2.	Thomas Hunt	Massachusetts
3.	John Mills	ditto
4.	John Pray	ditto
5.	Richard Brooke Roberts	South Carolina
6.	John H. Buell	Connecticut
7.	David Sayles	Rhode Island
8.	Jonathan Cass	New Hampshire
9.	Constant Freeman	Massachusetts
10.	Patrick Phelon	ditto
11.	Thomas H. Cushing	Massachusetts
12.	Joseph Shaylor	Connecticut

Lieutenants

1.	Samuel Newman	Massachusetts
2.	Bezalael Howe	New Hampshire
3.	Henry Sherman Junr.	Rhode Island
4.	Daniel Bradley	Connecticut
5.	John Platt	Delaware
6.	William Rickard	Massachusetts
7.	Richard Surcomb Howe	ditto
8.	Richard Humphrey Greaton	ditto
9.	John Higginson	ditto
10.	Winslow Warren	ditto
11.	Russell Bissell	Connecticut
12.	Francis Huger	South Carolina

ENSIGNS

1. Martin Brimmer Sohier — Massachusetts
2. Richard Edwards — Massachusetts
3. Edward Miller — Connecticut
4. John Thomson — ditto
5. George Tillinghast — Rhode Island
6. Joseph Smith Gilman — New Hampshire
7. Joseph Peirce Junr. — ditto
8. David Cobb Junr. — Massachusetts
9. Joseph Dickinson — South Carolina
10. Thomas Duff — Delaware
11. Edward Turner — Massachusetts
12. Theodore Sedgwick 3d — ditto

Surgeon	William Eustis	Massachusetts
Surgeons Mate	Joshua Sumner	Connecticut
Surgeons Mate	John F. Carmichael	New Jersey

THE BATTALION OF ARTILLERY

MAJOR COMMANDANT
William Ferguson — vice Doughty promoted

CAPTAIN
Mahlon Ford — vice Ferguson promoted

LIEUTENANTS
Daniel McLane — vice Moore dead
Abimael Youngs Nicholl — vice Fowle dead
George Ingersoll — vice Ford promoted[6]

[March 3d. 1791]   [GO. WASHINGTON]

RESOLVED, that the Senate advise and consent to the Appointments agreeably to the respective nominations annexed to the said Message.

ORDERED, that the Secretary communicate this Resolution to the President of the United States.

A Letter was read from the Hone. Sam. W. Johnson resigning his Seat in the Senate of the United States.[7]

---

[6] Following each nomination is the letter "a", probably indicating Senate agreement. The first name of Richard Brooke Roberts and the entire nomination of Ross Bird are in the hand of Tobias Lear. The nomination of John Wade and the names of Joseph Dickinson and George Ingersoll are in the hand of George Washington, as is the word "Virginia" following the nomination of Richard Call.

[7] The letter is printed in Part II of this volume under the heading Resignation of William S. Johnson.

ORDERED, that the *Vice President* be requested to acquaint the Governor of the State of Connecticut that *William Samuel Johnson*, a Senator of the United States from that State, has resigned his Seat in the Senate.[8]

ORDERED, that the Secretary of the Senate wait on the President of the United States and acquaint him, that the Senate, having finished the business before them, are ready to adjourn.

The President of the United States directed the Secretary of the Senate to acquaint them that he had no farther communications to make at this time.

Whereupon—
The Senate adjourned without day.

Attest,

SAM. A. OTIS Secretary

---

[8] This letter has not been located. A letter from Samuel Huntington to John Adams dated March 21, 1791, indicates that Adams did send a letter and a copy of the resignation to Huntington on March 4, 1791. This letter is in the Adams Papers, MHi.

PART II

RELATED DOCUMENTS

Indian Relations—Northern

Treaty at Fort Stanwix

ARTICLES of a TREATY concluded at Fort Stanwix, on the twenty second day of October One thousand seven hundred and Eighty four BETWEEN Oliver Wolcott Richard Butler & Arthur Lee Commissioners Plenipotentiary, from the United States in Congress Assembled on the one Part AND the Sachems & Warriors of the Six Nations on the other.

THE UNITED STATES of AMERICA give peace to the Senecas Mohawks Onondagas & Cayugas, and receive them into their protection upon the following Conditions.

ARTICLE 1ST. Six Hostages shall be immediately delivered to the Commissioners by the said Nations to remain in possession of the United States till all the prisoners White & Black which were taken by the said Senecas Mohawks, Onondagas & Cayugas, or by any of them, in the late War from among the people of the United States shall be delivered up.

ART. 2ND. The Oneida and Tuscarora Nations shall be secured in the possession of the Lands on which they are settled.

ART. 3D. A Line shall be drawn BEGINING at the Mouth of a Creek about

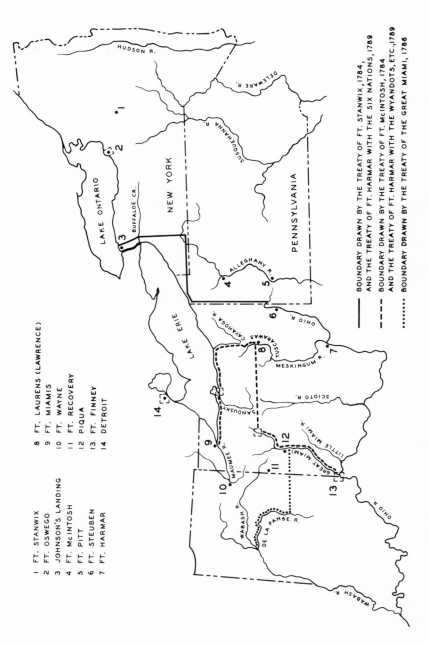

1 FT. STANWIX
2 FT. OSWEGO
3 JOHNSON'S LANDING
4 FT. McINTOSH
5 FT. PITT
6 FT. STEUBEN
7 FT. HARMAR

8 FT. LAURENS (LAWRENCE)
9 FT. MIAMIS
10 FT. WAYNE
11 FT. RECOVERY
12 PIQUA
13 FT. FINNEY
14 DETROIT

—— BOUNDARY DRAWN BY THE TREATY OF FT. STANWIX, 1784, AND THE TREATY OF FT. HARMAR WITH THE SIX NATIONS, 1789
– – – BOUNDARY DRAWN BY THE TREATY OF FT. McINTOSH, 1784 AND THE TREATY OF FT. HARMAR WITH THE WYANDOTS, ETC., 1789
········ BOUNDARY DRAWN BY THE TREATY OF THE GREAT MIAMI, 1786

Boundaries between the United States and the Northern Indians, 1789. (Map by John Spurbeck.)

four Miles East of Niagara called Oyonwayea or Johnston's Landing a place upon the Lake named by the Indians Oswego & by us Ontario, from thence Southerly in a direction always four miles East of the carrying path between Lake Erie & Ontario to the Mouth of Tehoseroron or Buffaloe Creek on Lake Erie thence South to the North Boundary of the State of Pennsylvania, thence West to the end of the said North Boundary thence South along the West Boundary of the said State to the River Ohio, The said Line from the Mouth of the Oyonwayea to the Ohio shall be the Western boundary of the Lands of the Six Nations, so that the Six Nations shall and do yield to the United States all claims to the Country West of the said boundary and then they shall be secured in the peaceful possession of the Lands they inhabit East & North of the same reserving only Six Miles square around the Fort of Oswego to the United States for the support of the same.

ART. 4TH. The Commissioners of the United States in consideration of the present circumstances of the Six Nations and in execution of the humane and Liberal views of the United States, upon the signing of the above Articles will order Goods to be delivered to the said Six Nations for their use and comfort.

{ Mohawks {	ONOGWENDAHONJI	his X mark	[Seal]	OLIVER WOLCOTT	[Seal]
	TOUIGHNATOGON	his X mark	[Seal]		
{ Onondagas {	OHEADARIGHTON	his X mark	[Seal]		
	KENDARINDGON	his X mark	[Seal]		
{ Sennecas {	TAYAGONENDAGIGHTI	his X mark	[Seal]	RICHARD BUTLER	[Seal]
	TEHONWAEAGHRIYAGI	his X mark	[Seal]		
{ Oneidas {	OTYADONENGHTI	his X mark	[Seal]		
	DAGAHEARI	his X mark	[Seal]		

		his		
Cayuga {	ORAGHGOANENDAGEN	X mark	[Seal]	ARTHUR LEE [Seal]

		his	
Tuscarora {	ONONGHSAWENGHTI	X mark	[Seal]
	THARONDAWAGON	X mark	[Seal]

		his	
Senneca {	KAYENTHOGHKE	X mark	[Seal]

WITNESSES

SAML. JA. ATLEE ⎫
WM. MACLAY ⎬ Penna. Commrs.
FRANS. JOHNSTON ⎭
AARON HILL
ALEXANDER CAMPBELL
SAML. KIRKLAND MISSY.
JAMES DEAN
SAML. MONTGOMERY
DARICK LANE Capt.
JOHN MERCER Lieut.
WILLIAM PENNINGTON Lieut.
MAHLON FORD Ensign
HUGH PEEBLES[1]

[1] The treaty, in the hand of Alexander Campbell, is Indian Treaty no. 9, RG 11, General Records of the United States Government (hereinafter RG 11, General Records of the United States Government will be cited as RG 11), M668, roll 2, DNA. E-18817. It is related to Henry Knox's report journalized May 25, 1789.

Treaty at Fort McIntosh

ARTICLES of a TREATY concluded at Fort McIntosh the 21st day of January 1785 BETWEEN the Commissioners Plenipotentiary of the UNITED STATES of AMERICA of the one part and the SACHEMS and WARRIORS of the WIANDOT DELAWARE CHIPPAWA and OTTAWA nations of the other.

THE COMMISSIONERS plenipotentiary of the UNITED STATES in CONGRESS assembled give peace to the WIANDOT DELAWARE CHIPPAWA and OTTAWA Nations of Indians in the following Conditions.

Article 1st. Three Chiefs One from among the Wiandot and two from among the Delaware Nations shall be delivered up to the Commissioners of the United States to be by them retained, till all the Prisoners white and black taken by the said Nations or any of them shall be restored.

Article 2nd. The said Indian Nations do acknowledge themselves and all their tribes to be under the protection of the United States and of no Other Sovereign whatsoever.

Article 3d. The boundary line Between the United States and the Wiandot and Delaware Nations shall begin at the mouth of the River Cayahoga, and run thence up the said river to the portage between that and the Tuscarawas branch of Meskingum—then down the said branch to the forks at the crossing place above Fort Lawrence—then Westerly to the portage of the Big-Miame which runs into the Ohio at the mouth of which branch the Fort stood which was taken by the French in 1752—then along the said portage to the Great Miame or Ome river—and down the south-east side of the same to its mouth thence along the South shore of Lake Erie to the mouth of Cayahoga where it began.

Article 4th. The United States allot all the Lands contained within the said lines to the Wiandot and Delaware Nations to live and to hunt on—and to such of the Ottawa nation as now live thereon—saving and reserving for the establishment of trading posts, six miles square at the mouth of Miame or Ome river—and the same at the portage on that branch of the big Miame—which runs into the Ohio—and the same on the Lake of Sanduske where the Fort formerly stood—and also two miles square on each side of the lower rapids of Sanduske river—which posts and the lands annexed to them shall be to the use and under the government of the United States.

Article 5th. If any Citizen of the United States or other person not being an Indian shall attempt to settle on any of the land alloted to the Wiandot and Delaware Nations, in this Treaty except on the lands reserved to the United States in the preceding Article, such person shall forfeit the protection of the United States and the Indians may punish him as they please.

Article 6th. The Indians who sign this Treaty as well in behalf of all their Tribes as of themselves do acknowledge the Lands East South and West of the lines described in the third Article so far as the said Indians formerly claimed the same to belong to the United States and none of their Tribes shall presume to settle upon the same or any part of it.

Article 7th. The post of Detroit with a district begining at the mouth of the river Rosine on the West end of Lake Erie and running west six Miles up the southern bank of the said river—thence northerly and always six miles west of the strait till it strikes the Lake St. Clair, shall be also reserved to the sole use of the United States.

Article 8th. In the same manner the post of Michellinchenac with it's dependences and 12 miles square about the same shall be reserved to the use of the United States.

Article 9th. If any Indian or Indians shall commit a robbery or murder on any Citizen of the United States the tribe to which such offenders may belong shall be bound to deliver them up at the nearest post, to be punished according to the Ordinances of the United States.

ARTICLE 10TH. The Commissioners of the UNITED STATES in pursuance of the humane and liberal views of Congress upon this Treaty's being signed will direct goods to be distributed among the different tribes for their use and comfort.

SEPARATE ARTICLE—It is agreed that the Delaware chiefs Kelelamand or Lt. Col. Henry, Hengue-pushees, or the Big-cat, Wicocalind, or Capt. White eyes—who took up the hatchet for the United States, and their families shall be received into the Delaware nation, in the same situation and rank, as before the war—and enjoy their due portions of the lands given to the Wiandot and Delaware nations in this treaty, as fully as if they had not taken part with America, or as any other person or persons in the said nations.

DAUNGHQUAT	his X mark	[Seal]	G. CLARK	[Seal]
ABRAHAM KUHN	his X mark	[Seal]		
OTTAWERRERI	his X mark	[Seal]		
HOBOCAN	his X mark	[Seal]		
WALINDIGHTUN	his X mark	[Seal]	RICHARD BUTLER	[Seal]
TALAPOXIC	his X mark	[Seal]		
WINGENUM	his X mark	[Seal]		
PACKELANT	his X mark	[Seal]		
GINGEWANNO	his X mark	[Seal]	ARTHUR LEE	[Seal]

WAANOOS	his X mark	[Seal]
KONALAWASSEE SHAWNAQUM	their X X mark	[Seal] [Seal]
QUECOOKKIA	his X mark	[Seal]

WITNESSES

SAML. J. ATLEE ⎫
FRAS. JOHNSTON ⎬ P. Commrs.
                            ⎭
ALEX CAMPBELL
JOS. HARMAR Lt. Col. Com.
ALEXDR. LOWREY
JOSEPH NICHOLAS inte[rprete]r
[J.] BRADFORD
GEORGE SLAUGHTER
VAN SWEARIGEN
JOHN BOGGS
G. EVANS
D. LUCKETT[1]

---

[1] The treaty, in the hand of Josiah Harmar, is Indian Treaty no. 10, RG 11, M668, roll 2, DNA. E-19278. It is related to Henry Knox's report journalized May 25, 1789. The Separate Article is in the hand of Alexander Campbell.

Treaty of the Great Miami

ARTICLES of a TREATY concluded at the Mouth of the Great Miami on the North-western bank of the Ohio the Thirty first day of January one thousand seven hundred and Eighty six BETWEEN the Commissioners plenipotentiary of the UNITED STATES of America of the one part, and the Chiefs and Warriors of the Shawanoe nation of the other part.

ARTICLE I. Three Hostages shall be immediately delivered to the Commissioners to remain in the possession of the United States untill all the Prisoners white and black taken in the late war from among the Citizens of the United States by the Shawanoe nation, or by any other Indian or Indians residing in their Towns shall be restored.

ARTICLE II. The Shawanoe nation do acknowledge the United States to be the sole and absolute Sovereigns of all the territory ceded to them by a Treaty of peace made between them and the King of Great Britain the fourteenth day of January one thousand seven hundred and eighty four.

ARTICLE III.   If any Indian or Indians of the Shawanoe nation, or any other Indian or Indians residing in their Town, shall commit murder or robbery on, or do any injury to the Citizens of the UNITED STATES or any of them, that NATION shall deliver such Offender, or Offenders to the Officer commanding the nearest Post of the UNITED STATES to be punished according to the ordinances of Congress; and in like manner any Citizen of the UNITED STATES who shall do an injury to any Indian of the Shawanoe nation, or to any other Indian or Indians residing in their Towns and under their protection shall be punished according to the laws of the UNITED STATES.

ARTICLE IIIITH.   The Shawanoe nation having knowledge of the intention of any nation or body of Indians to make war on the Citizens of the UNITED STATES, or of their counselling together for that purpose, and neglecting to give information thereof to the Commanding Officer of the nearest Post of the United States, shall be considered as parties in such war, and be punished accordingly; and the United States shall in like manner inform the Shawanoes of any injury designed against them.

ARTICLE VTH.   The United States do grant peace to the SHAWANOE nation, and do receive them into their friendship and protection.

ARTICLE VI.   The United States do allot to the SHAWANOE nation lands within their territory to live and hunt upon beginning at the South line of the lands allotted to the WIANDOTS and Delaware nations, at the place where the main branch of the great Miami which falls into the Ohio intersects said line— then down the river Miami to the fork of that river next below the old Fort which was taken by the French in 1752, thence due west to the river de la Panse—then down that river to the river WABASH—beyond which lines none of the citizens of the United States shall settle, nor disturb the Shawanoes in their settlement and possessions; and the Shawanoes do relinquish to the UNITED STATES, all title, or pretence of title they ever had to the Lands east, west, and south, of the east west and south lines before described.

ARTICLE VIITH.   If any Citizen or Citizens of the UNITED STATES shall presume to settle upon the lands allotted to the SHAWANOES by this Treaty he or they shall be put out of the protection of the UNITED STATES.

IN TESTIMONY whereof the parties hereunto have affixed their hands and seals the day and year first above mentioned.
Attest.   ALEXANDER CAMPBELL
        Secy. Commissioners

AWEECONY	his X mark	[Seal]		
KAKAWIPALATHY	his X mark	[Seal]		
MALUNTHY	his X mark	[Seal]	G. CLARK	[Seal]

MUSQUAUCONOCAH	his X mark	[Seal]	RICHD. BUTLER	[Seal]
MEANYMSECAH	his X mark	[Seal]	SAML. H. PARSONS	[Seal]
WAUPAUCOWELA	his X mark	[Seal]		
NIHIPEEWA	his X mark	[Seal]		
NIHINESSICOE	his X mark	[Seal]		

[WITNESSES]

JOHN BOGGS

SAM. MONTGOMERY

DANIEL ELLIOT

JAMES RINKER

NATHL. SMITH

JOSEPH SUFFARIN	his X mark	& KEMEPEMO SHAWNO
ISAAC ZANE	his X mark	WIANDOT
THE HALF KING OF THE WIANDOTS THE CRANE OF YE WIANDOTS	their X mark	
CAPT. PIPE OF THE DELAWARES	his X mark	
CAPT. BOHONGEHELAS	his X mark	

	his	
TETEBOCKSHICKA	X	
	mark	
	his	
THE BIG CAT OF YE DELAWARES	X	
	mark	
	his	
PIERRE DROULLAR	X	
	mark	

W. FINNEY Majr. B.B.

THOS. DOYLE Capt. B.B.

NATHAN MCDOWELL Ens.

JOHN TASSINGOR

HENRY GOVY

	his	
KAGY	X	CALLOWAY[1]
	mark	

[1] The treaty, in the hand of Alexander Campbell, is Indian Treaty no. 14, RG 11, M668, roll 2, DNA. E-20041, E-45004. It is related to Henry Knox's report journalized May 25, 1789.

Speech of the United Indian Nations to the Continental Congress

SPEECH of the UNITED INDIAN NATIONS, at their confederate Council held near the mouth of the Detroit River, the 28th November & 18th Decr. 1786.
PRESENT.
The five Nations, the Hurons, Delawares, Shawanese, Ottawas, Chippewas, Powtewattimies, Twichtwees, Cherokees, and the Wabash Confederates.

To the Congress of the United States of America

BRETHREN OF THE UNITED STATES OF AMERICA.

It is now more than three years since peace was made between the King of Great Britain and you, but we the Indians were disappointed finding ourselves not included in that peace according to our expectations, for we thought that its conclusion would have promoted a friendship between the United States and Indians, and that we might enjoy that happiness that formerly subsisted between us and our elder brethren. We have received two very agreeable messages from the Thirteen United States—we also received a message from the King, whose war we were engaged in, desiring us to remain quiet; which we accordingly complied with. During the time of this tranquility, we were deliberating the best method we could to form a lasting reconciliation with the Thirteen United States. Pleased at the same time, we thought we were entering upon a reconciliation and friendship with a set of people born on the same continent with ourselves, certain that the quarrel between us was not of our own making. In the course of our councils we imagined we hit upon an expedient that would promote a lasting peace between us.

Brothers—We still are of the same opinion as to the means which may tend to reconcile us to each other; and we are sorry to find, altho' we had the best thoughts in our minds, during the before-mentioned period, mischief has nevertheless happened between you and us. We are still anxious of putting our plan of accommodation into execution, and we shall briefly inform you of the means that seem most probable to us of effecting a firm and lasting peace and reconciliation. The first step towards which should, in our opinion, be, that all treaties carried on with the United States, on our part, should be with the general voice of the whole confederacy, and carried on in the most open manner, without any restraint on either side. And especially as landed matters are often the subject of our councils with you, a matter of the greatest importance and of general concern to us, in this case we hold it indispensably necessary that any cession of our lands should be made in the most public manner, and by the united voice of the Confederacy—Holding all partial treaties as void and of no effect.

Brothers—We think it is owing to you that the tranquility which since the peace between us has not lasted, and that that essential good has been followed by mischief, and confusion, having managed every thing respecting your own way. You kindled your council fires where you thought proper without consulting us, at which you held seperate treaties, and have entirely neglected our plan of having a general conference with the different nations of the confederacy. Had this happened we have reason to believe every thing would now have been settled between us in a most friendly manner. We did every thing in our power at the treaty of Fort Stanwix, to induce you to follow this plan, as our real intentions were at that very time to promote peace and concord between us, and that we might look upon each other as friends having given you no cause or provocation to be otherwise.

Brothers—Notwithstanding the mischief that has happened, we are still sincere in our wishes to have peace and tranquility established between us, earnestly hoping to find the same inclination in you. We wish therefore you would take it into serious consideration, and let us speak to you in the manner we proposed— Let us have a treaty with you early in the spring—let us pursue reasonable steps —let us meet half ways for our mutual convenience—we shall then bring in oblivion the misfortunes that have happened, and meet each other on a footing of friendship.

Brothers—We say let us meet half way and let us pursue such steps as become upright and honest men. We beg that you will prevent your Surveyors, and other people from coming upon our side the Ohio River. We have told you before, we wished to pursue just steps, and we are determined they shall appear just and reasonable, in the eyes of the world. This is the determination of all the chiefs of our confederacy now assembled here, notwithstanding the accidents that have happened in our villages, even when in council, where several innocent chiefs were killed when absolutely engaged in promoting a peace with you—the Thirteen United States.

Although then interrupted, the chiefs here present still wish to meet you in the Spring, for the before-mentioned good purpose, when we hope to speak to each other without either haughtiness or menaces.

Brothers—We again request of you in the most earnest manner, to order your Surveyors and others that mark out lands, to cease from crossing the Ohio, until we shall have spoken to you because the mischief that has recently happened has originated in that quarter; we shall likewise prevent our people from going over until that time.

Brothers—It shall not be our faults, if the plans which we have suggested to you, should not be carried into execution; in that case the event will be very precarious, and if fresh ruptures ensue, we hope to be able to exculpate ourselves, and shall most assuredly with our united force, be obliged to defend those rights and privileges which have been transmitted to us by our Ancestors. And if we should be thereby reduced to misfortunes, the world will pity us when they think of the amicable proposals we now make to prevent the unnecessary effusion of blood. These are our thoughts, and firm resolves, and we earnestly desire that you will transmit to us, as soon as possible your answer, be it what it may.

Done at our Confederated Council Fire, at the Huron Village, near the mouth of the Detroit River, December 18th 1786

> (Signed)   The Five Nations
>   Hurons
>   Shawanese
>   Delewares
>   Ottawaas
>   Chippewas
>   Powtewatimies
>   Twichtwees
>   Cherokees
>   The Wabash Confederates[1]

[1] A copy of the speech, in the hand of John Stagg, Jr., and attested by Henry Knox, is in President's Messages on Indian Relations, Executive Proceedings, SR, DNA. It is related to Henry Knox's report journalized May 25, 1789. A transcript in a nineteenth-century hand, probably made by ASP, is in the above location.

Instructions to the Governor of the Northwest Territory

October 26th. 1787

Sir,

You are carefully to examine into the real temper of the Indian tribes inhabiting the northern Indian department of the United States—if you find it hostile and that the welfare of the frontiers, and the settlements forming in that country demand a treaty, you will then in conjunction with the Super Intendant of Indian affairs for the northern department unless the attendance of the said Super Intendant shall be prevented by any unforeseen event, hold as general a one as you can with all the tribes.

The primary objects of the treaty are, the removing all causes of controversy so that peace and harmony may continue between the United States and the Indian tribes, the regulating trade, and settling boundaries. For these purposes you will do every thing that is right & proper.

The treaties which have been made may be examined but must not be departed from, unless a change of boundary beneficial to the United States can be obtained.

Altho the purchase of the Indian right of Soil is not a primary object of holding this treaty. Yet you will not neglect any opportunity that may offer of extinguishing the Indian rights to the westward as far as the river Mississippi.

You may stipulate that the East & West Line ordered to be seen by the ordinance of the 20th of May 1785 shall be the boundary between the United States and the Indian tribes: provided they stipulate that it shall run throughout unto the River Mississippi. And you may stipulate that any white persons going over the said boundary without a licence from the proper officer of the United States may be treated in such manner as the Indians shall think proper.

You will use every possible endeavor to ascertain who are the real Headmen & Warriors of the several tribes, and who have the greatest influence among them; these Men you will attach to the United States by every means in your power.

Every exertion must be made to defeat all confederations and combinations among the tribes, and to conciliate the white people inhabiting the frontiers towards them.

CHAS. THOMSON Secy.[1]

[1] A copy of the instructions, in the hand of Roger Alden and signed by Charles Thomson, is in President's Messages on Indian Relations, Executive Proceedings, SR, DNA. It is related to Henry Knox's report journalized May 25, 1789. A transcript in a nineteenth-century hand, probably made by ASP, is in the above location.

Additional Instructions to the Governor of the Northwest Territory

July 2. 1788

SIR,

An additional Sum of twenty thousand dollars has been appropriated for the purposes of procuring a permanent peace with the Indian tribes, with which you are authorised to hold a treaty. This sum of six thousand dollars out of the fourteen thousand heretofore appropriated for holding the said treaty are particularly directed to be applied solely to the purpose of obtaining a boundary advantageous to the United States, between them and the said Indian tribes, and for further extinguishing by purchase Indian titles in case it can be done on terms beneficial to the Union.

But it is not expected that any further purchases of lands will be made unless on terms evidently advantageous to the United States, or that any part of the said additional sum will be expended, but in cases apparently necessary.

In fixing a boundary between the United States and the Indian tribes, instead of the East & West Line mentioned in your Instructions you will endeavor to establish an East & West Line as far North as the completion of the forty first degree of North Latitude.

In your negotiations with the Indians you will make immediate payments so far as you shall have monies in hand, but in case you shall find it necessary to engage any considerable part of the said additional sum you are to stipulate that the payments thereof be made in two or three equal annual instalments, the first to be as late in the year 1789 as can be obtained.

CHAS. THOMSON Secy.[1]

[1] A copy of the instructions, in the hand of Roger Alden and signed by Charles Thomson, is in President's Messages on Indian Relations, Executive Proceedings, SR, DNA. It is related to Henry Knox's report journalized May 25, 1789. A transcript in a nineteenth-century hand, probably made by ASP, is in the above location.

Arthur St. Clair to the President

New York May 2d. 1788[1]

SIR,

I have the honor to lay before you the Treaties concluded, in pursuance of the Instructions received from Congress on the twenty sixth of October 1787 and second of July 1788, with several of the Indian Nations in January last. That they were not presented at an earlier period was owing, in part, to my own Indisposition—to the severity of the Winter which rendered the Communication by the Ohio, for a long time impracticable—and to the Circumstance that the last Congress did not assemble after it was in my power to have sent them forward.

With the Treaties I beg leave to submit the Minutes of the proceedings at the different Meetings after Nations were assembled, and I have added to them by way of appendix, all the Letters and Messages that passed between them and me prior to their assembling. These were communicated to the Secretary at War from time to time, and tho' they will, not doubt, be submitted by him to your Consideration. I thought it best, as they form a considerable part of the transactions, to connect them in that way, that the whole might be seen together.

By the Instruction of July the second, I was directed to endeavour at extending the northern Boundary, as far north as the Completion of the forty first Degree of North Lattitude. Besides that it would have been extremely difficult to have made the Indians comprehend how that was to be ascertained. I found that any Attempt to extend the limits at that time would be very ill received, if not defeat entirely the settling a Peace with them; it was therefore not proposed and the Boundaries remain as settled at the former Treaties except the rectifying an Error about the Portage at the Miami Village.

The Negociation was both tedious and troublesome, and for a long time had an unpromising Aspect, but it came at last to as favorable an Issue as could have been expected and I trust will be attended with Consequences freindly to the frontier parts of the united States. There are however several Nations on the Wabash, and the Rivers which empty themsevelves into it, that are ill disposed; and from whom there is reason to expect that a part of the Frontier of Virginia, with and the settlement forming on the Miami, will meet annoyances—indeed that they have not been disturbed during the Winter was not expected, either by me or the Chiefs of the Nations who met me at Fort Harmar. The Wyandots did appoint Persons to go to them and inform them of the Results of the Treaty, and insist upon their desisting from farther hostilities, which may have had some effect in pioducing the late Tranquillity.

The claim of the Wyandot Nation to the Lands reserved to the Shawanese was strongly insisted upon by them and to be made an article of the Treaty: to that I could not consent: but to satisfy them, and that it might be kept in Remembrance, it is inserted at the Bottom of it, by way of Memorandum. It seems this is a Claim that has always been held up, and the Reason it was so much insisted on at this time, they said was, that they were sure that the Shawanese, and Cherokees incorporated with them would combine to give us trouble that it could not be expected to be borne with, much longer—that they would be driven out of the Country, and then it would be claimed and held by the united States by right of Conquest—they farther added that, if the Shawanese continued their depredations, they would, themselves drive them off. They also proposed that a Post should be taken, by the united States at the Miami Village as the surest Means to overaw the Nations on the Wabash. It is certainly well situated for that purpose, and would command the greatest part of the Indian Trade. As it was very uncertain whether Congress might approve of such a Measure; as a Post so far in Land would with difficulty be supported, and were in no readiness to carry it into Execution if it should be approved, I desired them to consider well whether it could be done without a contest with the Indians who live there—and whether, in that Case, there was not Danger of they themselves being involved thro' the ungovernableness of their young Men. They acknowledge they thought there was danger of both, but promised to send some of their principal Men to the Miamies and prepare them for receiving a garrison peaceably, and are to give me Notice in the Spring.

The Reason why the Treaties were made separately with the six Nations and the Wyandots & more westerly Tribes was a Jealousy that subsisted between them which I was not willing to lessen by appearing to consider them as one People—they do not so consider themselves, and I am persuaded their general Confederacy is entirely broken—indeed it would not be very difficult, if Circumstances required it to set them at deadly variance.

The great length of time that elapsed between the appointed period for the Meeting, and that at which the Indians assembled, during which Numbers of them were constantly going and coming, has encreased the Expense in the Article of Provisions considerably; the utmost possible Economy however was used thro the whole of the Business, and in transacting it, I flatter myself with meeting the approbation of Congress.

With the utmost Respect I have the honor to be

Sir
Your most obedient
and
most humble Servant
AR. ST. CLAIR[2]

[1] The letter is incorrectly dated. It should read, "New York May 2d. 1789."
[2] The letter, in the hand of Arthur St. Clair, is in President's Messages on Indian Relations, Executive Proceedings, SR, DNA. It is related to Henry Knox's report journalized May 25, 1789. A transcript in a nineteenth-century hand, probably made by ASP, is in the above location.

Treaty of Fort Harmar with the Wyandots, etc.

ARTICLES of a TREATY made at FORT HARMAR, between ARTHUR ST. CLAIR, GOVERNOR of The Territory of the United States, North West of the River Ohio and Commissioner, Plenipotentiary of the United States of America; for removing all causes of controversy; regulating Trade, and settling boundaries, with the Indian Nations, in the Northern Department; of the One part. AND the SACHEMS & WARRIORS, of the Wyandot, Delaware, Ottawa, Chippewa, Pattawatima and Sac Nations, on the other part.
ARTICLE 1ST.

WHEREAS, the United States in Congress assembled, did by their Commissioners, George Rogers Clark, Richard Butler, and Arthur Lee Esquires, duly appointed for that purpose; at a Treaty holden with the Wyandot, Delaware, Ottawa, & Chippewa Nations at Fort McIntosh on the Twenty first day of January, in the year of our Lord one thousand seven hundred and Eighty five; conclude a peace with the Wyandots, Delawares, Ottawas & Chippewas and take them into their friendship and protection. AND WHEREAS, at the said Treaty it was stipulated that all prisoners that had been made by those Nations, or either of them, should be delivered up to the United States. AND WHEREAS, the said Nations have now agreed to and with the aforesaid Arthur St. Clair, to renew and confirm all the engagements they had made with the United States of America, at the beforementioned Treaty, except so far as are altered by these presents. and there are now in the possession of some individuals of these Nations, certain prisoners; who have been taken by others, not in peace with the said United States, or in Violation of the Treaties subsisting between the United States and them. The said Nations agree to deliver up all the prisoners now in their hands (by what means soever they may have come into their possession) to the said Governor St. Clair at Fort Harmar, or, in his absence to the Officer commanding there; as soon as conveniently may be. and for the true performance of this agreement they do now agree to deliver into his hands, Two persons of the Wyandot Nation to be retained in the hands of the United States, as hostages, until the said prisoners are restored; after which they shall be sent back to their Nation.

ARTICLE 2ND.

AND WHEREAS, at the beforementioned Treaty, it was agreed between the United States and said Nations, That a boundary line should be fixed, between the Lands of those Nations, and the Territory of the United States, which boundary is as follows—VIZ. BEGINNING at the mouth of Cayahoga River, and running thence up the said river to the portage between that, and the Tuscarawa Branch of Muskingum, then down the said Branch to the forks at the crossing place above Fort Laurence; thence westerly to the portage on that Branch of the Big Miami river which Runs into the Ohio, at the mouth of which branch the Fort Stood, which was taken by the French in the year of our Lord, One thousand seven hundred and Fifty Two; then along the said portage to the Great Miami or Omie River, and down the South East side of the same to its mouth, thence along the Southern Shore of Lake Erie, to the mouth of Cayahaga, where it began. and the said Wyandot, Delaware, Ottawa & Chippewa Nations for, and in Consideration of the peace then granted to them by the said United States, and the presents, they then Received; as well, as of a quantity of goods to the Value of Six Thousand dollars, now delivered to them by the Said Arthur St. Clair; the receipt whereof they do hereby acknowledge. do by these PRESENTS, renew and Confirm the said boundary Line; to the end that the Same may remain as a division Line, between the Lands of the United States of America, and the Lands of Said Nations for ever. and the Undersigned Indians do hereby in their own Names, and the names of their Respective Nations and tribes, their heirs and descendants; for the consideration above mentioned, Release, Quit-claim, Relinquish and Cede to the said United States, all the Land, East, South and West, of the Line above described, so far as the said Indians formerly claimed the Same; for them the said United States, to have and to hold the same in True and absolute propriety for ever.

ARTICLE 3RD.

THE UNITED STATES OF AMERICA do by these PRESENTS, relinquish and quit claim to the said Nations, respectively, all the Lands lying between the Limits above described for them the said Indians to live and hunt upon, and otherwise to occupy as they Shall See fit. BUT the said Nations or either of them shall not be at Liberty to sell or dispose of the same, or any part thereof to any Sovereign power, except the United States nor to the Subjects or Citizens of any other Sovereign power, nor to the Subjects or Citizens of the United States.

ARTICLE 4TH.

IT IS AGREED between the said United States and the said Nations; that the individuals of said Nations Shall be at Liberty to hunt within the Territory ceded to the United States, without hindrance or molestation So long as they

Articles of a Treaty made at Fort Harmar, between Arthur St. Clair, Governor of the Territory of the United States, North West of the River Ohio, and Commissioner, Plenipotentiary of the United States of America; for removing all causes of controversy; regulating trade, and settling boundaries, on the Indian Nations, in the Northern Department, of the one part. And the Sachems & Warriors of the Wyandot Delaware, Ottawa, Chippewa, Pottawatima and &c Nations, on the other part.

Article, 1st.

Whereas, The United States in Congress assembled, did by their Commissioners, George Rogers Richard Butler, and Arthur Lee Esquires, duly appointed for that purpose; at a Treaty holden with the Delaware, Ottawa, & Chippewa Nations at Fort McIntosh on the twenty first day of January, in the year of our one thousand seven hundred and Eighty five; concluded a peace with the Wyandots, Delawares, Ottawas Chippewas and take them into their friendship and protection. And whereas, at the said Treaty it was stipulated that prisoners that had been made by those Nations, or either of them, should be delivered up to the United States. And Whereas, the said Nations have now agreed with the aforesaid Arthur St. Clair, to renew and confirm all engagements they had made with the United States of America, at the beforementioned Treaty, except so far as are by these presents. and there are now in the possession of some individuals of their Nations, certain prisoners; been taken by others, not in peace with the said United States, or in violation of the Treaties subsisting between the States and them. The said Nations agree to deliver up all the prisoners now in their hands they may have come into their possession to the said Governor St. Clair at Fort Harmar, or in his absence Officer commanding there; so soon as conveniently can be. and for the true performance of this agreement they now agree to deliver into his hands, two persons of the Wyandot Nation to be retained in the hands of the States, as hostages, until the said prisoners are restored; after which they shall be sent back to their Nation

Article 2nd.

And whereas, at the beforementioned Treaty, it was agreed between the United States and said that a boundary line should be fixed, between the lands of these Nations, and the Territory of the United States boundary is as follows — Viz. Beginning at the mouth of Cuyahoga River, and running thence up said river to the portage between that, and the Tus- carawa Branch of the Muskingum, then down the said

to the forks at the crossing place above Fort Laurence thence westerly to the portage on that Branch of the Big Miami river which runs into the Ohio, at the mouth of which branch the Fort Stood, which was taken by the in the year of our Lord One thousand seven hundred and fifty two; thence along the said portage to the Great or Omie River, and down the south East side of the same to its mouth; thence along the southern shore of Lake Erie, to the mouth of Cuyahoga, where it began and the said Wyandots & Delaware, Ottawa &Chippewa for, and in consideration of the peace then granted to them by the said United States, and the presents received; as well, as of a quantity of goods to the value of Six Thousand dollars now delivered to them by the said Arthur St. Clair; the receipt whereof they do hereby acknowledge. do by these Presents, renew and Confirm the said boundary Line, to the one that the same may remain as a division Line between the Lands of United States of America, and the Lands of said Nations for ever. and the Undersigned Indians do in their own Names, and the names of their respective Nations and tribes, their heirs and descendants, for the -deration abovementioned, release, Quit Claim relinquish and cede to the said United States, all the Land, East and West, of the Lines above described, so far as the said Indians formerly claimed the same; for them United States, to have and to hold the same in time and absolute property for ever.

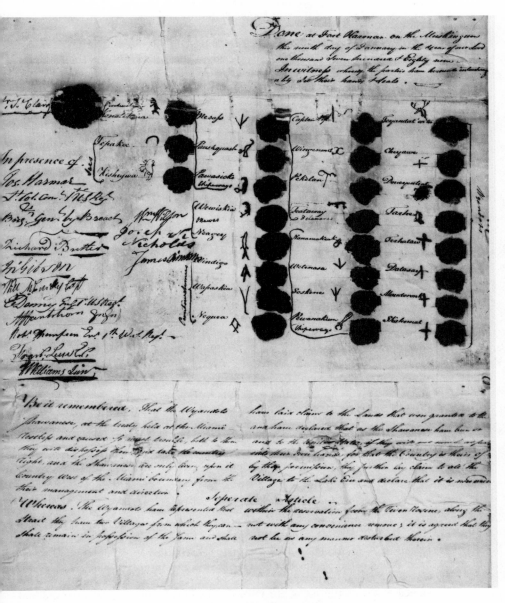

Treaty of Fort Harmar with the Wyandots, etc., 1789. The seals next to the signatures of the participants are of red-orange wax, and light blue ribbon is threaded through the parchment under the seals. (Courtesy of the National Archives, Washington, D.C.)

demean themselves peaceably, and offer no Injury or annoyance to any of the Subjects or Citizens of the said United States.

ARTICLE 5TH.

IT IS AGREED That if any Indian or Indians of the Nations beforementioned shall commit a murder, or robbery, on any of the Citizens of the United States: The nation or tribe to which the Offender belong On complaint being made, shall deliver up the person or persons complained of, at the nearest post of the United States; to the end that he or they may be tried: and if found guilty punished according to the Laws established in the Territory of the United States, North west of the River Ohio, for the punishment of Such offenses, if the Same Shall have been committed within the said Territory, or according to the Laws of the State where the offence may have been committed, if the Same has happened in any of the United States. In like manner if any Subject or Citizen of the United States Shall commit murder or Robbery on any Indian or Indians of the Said Nations; upon complaint being made thereof, he or they Shall be arrested, tried, and punished, agreeable to the Laws of the State, or of the Territory, wherein the offence was committed That nothing may interrupt the peace & harmony, now established between the United States and said Nations.

ARTICLE 6TH.

AND WHEREAS, The practice of Stealing horses has prevailed very much, to the great disquiet of the Citizens of the United States, and if persisted in cannot fail to involve, both the United States of America and the Indians in endless animosity, it is agreed that it Shall be put an entire Stop to on both sides. Nevertheless should some individuals in defiance of this agreement, and of the laws provided against such offences continue to make depredations of that nature; the person convicted thereof shall be punished with the utmost severity the Laws of the Respective States, or Territory of the United States, North West of the Ohio, where the offences may have been committed, will admit of. and all horses so Stolen, either by the Indians from the Citizens or Subjects of the United States; or by the citizens or Subjects of the United States from any of the Indian Nations; may be reclaimed, into whose possession soever they may have passed and upon due proof shall be restored; any Sales in Market Ouvert; notwithstanding. And the Civil Magistrates in the United States respectively, and in the Territory of the United States, Northwest of the Ohio, Shall give all necessary aid & protection to Indians claiming Such Stolen horses.

ARTICLE 7TH.

TRADE, shall be opened with the Said Nations, and they do hereby respectively engage to afford protection to the persons & property of such as may be duly licensed to reside among them for the purposes of Trade, and to their Agents, Factors & Servants. But no person shall be permitted to reside at their towns or at their hunting camps as a Trader, who is not furnished with a License for that purpose, under the hand and Seal of the Governor of the Territory of the United States Northwest of the Ohio for the time being or under the hand and Seal of one of his deputies for the management of Indian affairs, to the end that they may not be imposed upon in their traffick, and if any person or persons shall intrude themselves without such Licence they promise to apprehend him or them, and to bring them to the said Governor, or one of his deputies for the purpose beforementioned to be dealt with according to Law, and that they may be defended against persons who might attempt to Forge such licences; they further engage to give Information to the said Governor, or one of his deputies of the Names of all Traders, residing among them from time to time; and at least once in every Year.

ARTICLE 8TH.

SHOULD any NATION of Indians meditate a war against the United States, or either of them and the same shall come to the Knowledge of the before-mentioned Nations or either of them, they do hereby engage to give immediate notice thereof to the Governor, or in his absence to the officer commanding the Troops of the United States at the Nearest Post. And should any Nation with hostile intentions against the United States or either of them, attempt to pass thro' their Country, they will endeavour to prevent the Same, and in like manner give information of such attempt to the said Governor, or commanding Officer as soon as possible, that all causes of mistrust and Suspicion, may be avoided between them and the United States. In like manner the United States shall give notice to the said Indian Nations of any harm that may be meditated against them, or either of them, that shall come to their Knowledge, and do all in their power to hinder and prevent the same, that the Friendship between them may be uninterrupted.

ARTICLE 9TH.

IF ANY PERSON or persons, citizens, or Subjects of the United States, or any other person not being an Indian, shall presume to settle upon the Lands confirmed to the said Nations, he and they shall be out of the protection of the United States, and the said nations may punish him or them, in such manner as they see fit.

ARTICLE 10TH.

THE UNITED STATES renew the Resolutions heretofore made in the before-mentioned Treaty at Fort McIntosh for the establishment of Trading posts in manner and form following; that is to Say, Six Miles square at the mouth of the Miami or Omie River. Six miles square at the portage upon that Branch of the Miami which Runs into the Ohio. Six miles square upon the Lake Sandusky where the Fort, formerly stood and Two miles Square upon each side the Lower Rapids on Sandusky river, which posts and the Lands annexed to them shall be for the use and under the Government of the United States.

ARTICLE 11TH.

THE POST at DETROIT, with a district of Land, beginning at the mouth of the River Rosine at the West end of Lake Erie, and running up the Southern Bank of said river Six miles; thence Northerly and always Six Miles West of the Strait, until it Strikes the Lake St. Clair, shall be reserved for the use of the United States.

ARTICLE 12TH.

IN LIKE MANNER, the post at Michilimackinac, with its dependecies and Twelve miles Square about the same shall be Reserved to the sole use of the United States.

ARTICLE 13TH.

THE UNITED STATES of AMERICA Do hereby Renew and confirm the peace

& Friendship entered into with the said Nations at the Treaty beforementioned held at Fort McIntosh, and the said Nations again acknowledge themselves, and all their Tribes to be under the protection of the Said United States, and no other power whatever.

ARTICLE 14TH.

THE UNITED STATES of AMERICA Do also receive into their Friendship and protection the Nations of the Pattiwatimas, and Sacs, and do hereby establish a League of Peace and Amity between them respectively and all the Articles of this treaty so far as they apply to these Nations, are to be considered as made and concluded in all, and every part expressly, with them and each of them.

ARTICLE 15TH.

AND WHEREAS, in describing the boundary beforementioned, the words if strictly, constructed would carry it from the portage on that Branch of the Miami which runs into the Ohio, over to the River Au Glaize which was neither the Intention of the Indians, nor of the Commissioners. It is hereby declared, that the Line shall Run from the said Portage directly to the first fork of the Miami River which is to the Southward & Eastward of the Miami Village, Thence down the Main Branch of the Miami River to the said Village, and thence down that River to Lake Erie and along the Margin of the Lake to the place of Beginning.

DONE at FORT HARMAR on the Muskingum this ninth day of January in the Year of our Lord one thousand Seven hundred & Eighty nine. IN WITNESS whereof the parties have hereunto interchangeably Set their hands & Seals.

AR. ST. CLAIR [Seal]

Peoutewatamies:
KONATIKINA [his] X [mark] [Seal]
WINDIGO [his] X [mark] [Seal]
WAPASKEA [his] X [mark] [Seal]
NEQUEA [his] X [mark] [Seal]

Sacs:
TEPAKEE [his] X [mark] [Seal]
KESHEYWA [his] X [mark] [Seal]

Ottawas:
WEWISKIA [his] X [mark] [Seal]
NEAGEY [his] X [mark] [Seal]

Delawares:
CAPTAIN PIPE [his] X [mark] [Seal]
WINGENOND [his] X [mark] [Seal]
PEKELAN [his] X [mark] [Seal]
TEATAWAY [his] X [mark] [Seal]

Chipeways				Wyandots			
MESASS	[his] X [mark]	[Seal]		TEYANDAT 'ON' TEC	[his] X [mark]	[Seal]
PAUSHQUASH	[his] X [mark]	[Seal]		CHEYAWE	[his] X [mark]	[Seal]
PAWASICKO	[his] X [mark]	[Seal]		DOUEYENTEAT	[his] X [mark]	[Seal]
NANAMAKEAK	[his] X [mark]	[Seal]		TARHE	[his] X [mark]	[Seal]
WETENASA	[his] X [mark]	[Seal]		TERHATAW	[his] X [mark]	[Seal]
SOSKENE	[his] X [mark]	[Seal]		DATASAY	[his] X [mark]	[Seal]
PEWANAKUM	[his] X [mark]	[Seal]		MAUDORONK	[his] X [mark]	[Seal]
				SKAHOMAT	[his] X [mark]	[Seal]

IN PRESENCE OF

JOS. HARMAR
Lt. Col. Comt.
1st. U.S. Regt.
Brigr. Genl. by Brevet

RICHARD BUTLER
JNO. GIBSON
WILL. MCCURDY Capt.
E. DENNY Ens. 1st. U.S. Regt.
A. HARTSHORN Ensn.
ROBT. THOMPSON Ens. 1th. U.S. Regt.

FRANS. LUSE Ens.
I. WILLIAMS JUNR.
WM. WILSON
JOSEP NICHOLAS
JAMES RINKER

BE IT REMEMBERED, That the Wyandots have laid claim to the Lands that were granted to the shawanese, at the treaty held at the Miami and have declared that as the Shawanese have been so Restless and caused so much trouble, both to them and to the United States, if they will not now be at peace they will dispossess them, and take the country into their own hands, for that the Country is theirs of Right, and the Shawanese are only living upon it by their permission, they further lay claim to all The Country West of the Miami boundary from the Village to the Lake Erie and declare that it is now under their management and direction.

SEPERATE ARTICLE

WHEREAS, The Wyandots have Represented that within the reservation from the River Rosine, along the Strait they have two Villages from which they cannot with any convenience remove; it is agreed that they shall remain in possession of the same and shall not be in any manner disturbed therein.

The following are the Names of the Hostages left at Fort Harmar agreeably to the first Article.

Wyandots	CHEWAYE DATASY TEHAMENDAYE TAYANOQUAY HOMEHONEATOO
Chipewa	AQUAYWESASS[1]

[1] The treaty, in the hand of Josiah Harmar, is Indian Treaty no. 15, RG 11, M668, roll 2, DNA. It is related to Henry Knox's report journalized May 25, 1789. A copy, in the hand of Benjamin Bankson, is in Transcribed Treaties and Conventions, 1789–1801, Records of the Secretary, SR, DNA.

Treaty of Fort Harmar with the Six Nations

ARTICLES of a TREATY made at FORT HARMER the ninth day of January in the Year of our Lord one thousand seven hundred and eighty nine between Arthur St. Clair Esquire Governor of the Territory of the united States of America north west of the River Ohio, and Commissioner plenipotentiary of the said united States for removing all Causes of Controversy, regulating Trade and settling Boundaries between the Indian Nations in the northern Department and the said united States of the One Part, and the Sachems and Warriors of the six Nations of the other Part. viz.

ARTICLE FIRST.

Where as the united States in Congress assembled did by their Commissioners Oliver Woolcut, Richard Butler and Arthur Lee Esquires duly appointed for the purpose, at a Treaty held with the said six Nations viz. with the Mohawks Oneidas, Onondagas Tuscororas Cuyugas and Senecas, at Fort Stanwix on the twenty second day of October, one thousand seven hundred and eighty four, give Peace to the said Nations, and receive them into their Friendship and

Protection. And whereas the said Nations have now agreed to and with the said Arthur St. Clair to renew and confirm all the Engagements and Stipulations [blotted out] entered into at the before mentioned Treaty at Fort Stanwix: And whereas it was then and there agreed between the united States of America and the said six Nations that a Boundary Line should be fixed between the Lands of the said six Nations and the Territory of the said United States, which Boundary Line is as follows viz. "Beginning at the mouth of a Creek about four Miles east of Niagara called Ononwayea or Johnsons landing place upon the Lake named by the Indians Oswego, and by Us Ontario, from thence southerly in a direction always four Miles east of the carrying place between Lake Erie and Lake Ontario to the mouth of Tehoseroton or Buffaloe Creek upon Lake Erie; thence south to the northern Boundary of the State of Pennsylvania; thence west to the end of the said north Boundary; thence south along the west Boundary of the said State to the River Ohio. The said Line from the mouth of Ononwayea to the Ohio shall be the western Boundary of the Lands of the six Nations, so that the six Nations shall and do yield to the united States all Claim to the Country west of the said Boundary, and then they shall be secured in the possession of the Lands they inhabit east north and south of the same, reserving only six Miles square round the Fort of Oswego for the support of the same." The said six Nations except the Mohawks none of whom have attended at this time for and in consideration of the Peace then granted to them, the Presents they then received, as well as in consideration of a Quantity of Goods, to the value of three thousand Dollars now delivered to them by the said Arthur St. Clair the receipt whereof they do hereby acknowledge, do hereby renew and confirm the said Boundary Line in the words before mentioned to the end that it may be and remain as a [blotted out] Division Line between the [blotted out] Lands of the said six Nations and the Territory of the united States forever. And the under signed Indians as well in their own Names as in the Name of their respective Tribes and Nations their Heirs and Descendants, for the Considerations before mentioned do release, quit Claim, relinquish and Cede to the United States of America all the Lands west of the said Boundary or division Line between the said Line and the Strait from the mouth of Ononawayea and Buffaloe Creek, for them the said united States of America to have and to hold the same in true and absolute Propriety for ever.

ARTICLE SECOND.

The United States of America confirm to the six Nations all the Lands which they inhabit lying East and North of the before mentioned Boundary Line, and relinquish and quit Claim to the same and every part thereof excepting only six Miles square round the Fort of Oswego, which six Miles square round said Fort is again reserved to the United States by these Presents.

ARTICLE THIRD.

The Oneida and Tuscorora Nations are also again secured and confirmed in the possession of their respective Lands.

ARTICLE FOURTH.

The united States of America renew and confirm the Peace and Friendship entered into with the six Nations, (except the Mohawks) at the Treaty before mentioned held at Fort Stanwix declaring the same to be perpetual. And if the Mohawks shall within six Months declare their assent to the same they shall be considered as included.

Done at Fort Harmar on the Muskingham the day and Year first above written. In witness whereof the Parties have hereunto inter changeably set their Hands and Seals.

AR. ST. CLAIR   [Seal]

CAGEAGA or dogs round the fire	[Seal]	GYANTWAIA or Cornplanter	[his] X [Seal] [mark]
SAWEDOWA or The Blast	[Seal]	GYASOTA or Big Cross	[his] X [Seal] [mark]
KIONDUSHOWA or Swiming Fish	[Seal]	KANASSEE or New arrow	[Seal]
ONCAHYE or Dancing Feather	[Seal]	ACHIOUT or Half Town	[Seal]
SOHAEAS or Falling mountain	[Seal]	ANACHOUT or The Wasp	[his] X [Seal] [mark]
OTACHSAKA or Broken Tomahawk	[his] X [Seal] [mark]	CHISHEKOA or Wood Bug	[his] X [Seal] [mark]
TEKAHIAS or Long Tree	[his] X [Seal] [mark]	SESSEWA or Big bale of a Kettle	[Seal]
ONECHSETEE or Loaded man	[his] X [Seal] [mark]	SCIAHOWA or Council Keeper	[Seal]
KIAHTULAHO or Snake	[Seal]	TEWANIAS or Broken Twig	[Seal]
AQUEIA or Bandy Legs	[Seal]	SONACHSHOWA or Full moon	[Seal]
KIANDOGEWA or Big Tree	[his] X [Seal] [mark]	CACHUNWASSE or Twenty canoes	[Seal]

OWENEWA	[his]		HICHONQUASH	
or	X	[Seal]	or	[Seal]
Thrown in the water	[mark]		Tearing asunder	

IN PRESENCE OF

JOS. HARMAR
Lt. Colo. Comt. 1st. U.S. Regt.
Brigr. General by Brevets
RICHARD BUTLER
JNO. GIBSON
WILL. McCURDY Capt.
E. DENNY Engn. 1st. U.S. Regt.
A. HARTSHORN Engn.
ROBT. THOMPSON Ens. 1 U.S. Regt.
FRANS. LUSE Ens.
JOSEPH NICHOLAS

SEPARATE ARTICLE

Should a Robbery or Murder be committed by an Indian or Indians of the said Nations upon the Citizens or Subjects of the united States or any of them or by the Citizens or Subjects of the united States or any of them upon any Indian or Indians of the said Nations the Parties accused of the same shall be tried, and if found guilty be punished according to the Laws of the State, or of the Territory of the united States as the case may be, where the same was committed. And should any Horses be stolen either by the Indians of the said Nations from the Citizens or Subjects of the united States or any of them, or by any of the said Citizens and Subjects from any of the said Indians they may be reclaimed into whose Possession soever they may have come, and upon due proof shall be restored any Sales in open Market notwithstanding and the Parties convicted shall be punished with the utmost Severity the Laws will admit. And the said Nations engage to deliver the Parties that may be accused of their Nations, of either of the before mentioned Crimes at the nearest Post of the united States if the Crime was committed within the Territory of the united States, or to the Civil Authority of the State, if it shall have happened within any of the united States.

AR. ST. CLAIR[1]

[1] The treaty with the separate article, in the hand of Arthur St. Clair, is Indian Treaty no. 16, RG 11, M668, roll 2, DNA. It is related to Henry Knox's report journalized May 25, 1789. A copy, in the hand of Benjamin Bankson, is in Transcribed Treaties and Conventions, 1789–1801, Records of the Secretary, SR, DNA.

Indian Relations—Southern

Treaty of Augusta

GEORGIA.

Articles of convention held at Augusta, in the county of Richmond, and state afore said, this first day of November, in the year of our Lord one thousand seven hundred and eighty-three, and in the eighth year of the independence of the said state, between John Twiggs, Elijah Clark, Edward Telfair, Andrew Burns and William Glascock, commissioners appointed by the authority of the same, on the one part, and the Tallesee King, Tallesee Warrior, the Fat King, Mad Fish, Topwar King, Alachago, Hitcheto Warrior, Okoney, Okolege, Cuse King, Second Man, Inomatwhata, Inomatawtusnigua, Head Warrior, Gugahacho, head men, warriors and chiefs of the hordes or tribes of Creek Indians, in behalf of the said nation, on the other part, as follows:

WHEREAS a good understanding and union between the inhabitants of the said state and the Indians aforesaid, is reciprocally necessary and convenient, as well on account of a friendly intercourse and trade as for the purposes of peace and humanity: It is therefore agreed and covenanted:

I.   That all differences between the said parties heretofore subsisting, shall cease and be forgotten.

II.   That all just debts due by any of the said Indians to any of the merchants or traders of the said state, shall be fairly and fully paid; and all negroes, horses, cattle or other property taken during the late war, shall be restored.

III.   That a new line shall be drawn without delay, between the present settlements in the said state and the hunting grounds of the said Indians; to begin on Savannah River, where the present line strikes it, thence up the said river to a place on the most northern branch of the same, commonly called Keowee, where a northeast line, to be drawn from the top of the Ocunna mountain, shall intersect; thence along the said line in a southwest direction to the said mountain; thence in the same direction to Tugalo River: thence to the top of the Currohee mountain; thence to the head or source of the most southern branch of the Oconee River, including all the waters of the same; thence down the said river to the old line.

IV.   In consideration of the friendship which the people and government of the said state bear to the Indians aforesaid, and of their good will evinced by their present attendance, the commissioners aforesaid have made presents to them to a considerable amount, which they hereby acknowledge to have received.

V.   That a trade shall be carried on by the traders and merchants of the said state to the towns of the said Indians; in which the traders who shall reside among them and the pack-horsemen in going and coming shall be protected; the trade to be subject to future regulations of government.

VI.   And lastly, they the said head men, warriors and chiefs, whose hands and seals are hereunto affixed, do hereby for themselves and for the nation they are empowered and do effectually represent, recognize, declare and acknowledge, that all the lands, waters, woods and game, lying and being in the state eastward of the line herein before particularly mentioned and described, is, are and do belong, and of right appertain to the people and government of the state of Georgia; and they the said Indians aforesaid, as well for themselves as the said nation, do give up, release, alien, relinquish, and forever quit claim to the same and every part thereof.

Done and executed at Augusta aforesaid, the day and year above mentioned, in the presence of those whose names are subscribed.

JOHN TWIGGS	(L.S.)	TALLESEE KING	X (L.S.)
ELIJAH CLARK	(L.S.)	TALLESEE WARRIOR	X (L.S.)
EDWARD TELFAIR	(L.S.)	FAT KING	X (L.S.)
ANDREW BURNS	(L.S.)	MAD FISH	X (L.S.)
WILLIAM GLASCOCK	(L.S.)	TOPWAR KING	X (L.S.)
		ALACHAGO	X (L.S.)

HITCHETO WARRIOR	X (L.S.)
OKOLEGE	X (L.S.)
COWETAW	X (L.S.)
CUSE KING	X (L.S.)
SECOND MAN	X (L.S.)
INOMATUHATA	X (L.S.)
INOMATAWTUSNIGUA	X (L.S.)
SUGAHACHO	X (L.S.)

Signed, sealed and delivered in presence of Cornelius Dysart, Richard Henson, John Lamar.[1]

[1] Horatio Marbury and William H. Crawford, *Digest of the Laws of the State of Georgia* (Savannah: Seymour, Woolhopter and Stebbins, 1802), pp. 605-6. The original has not been located. The treaty is related to George Washington's message journalized August 22, 1789.

Treaty of Galphinton

Articles of a treaty concluded at Galphinton, on the twelfth day of November, one thousand seven hundred and eighty-five, between the underwritten commissioners, in behalf of the state of Georgia, of the one part; and the kings, head men and warriors in behalf of themselves, and all the Indians in the Creek nation of the other in the following conditions.

ARTICLE I.

THE said Indians for themselves and all the tribes or towns within their respective nations, within the limits of the state of Georgia, have been and now are members of the same, since the day and date of the constitution of the said state of Georgia.

II. If any citizen of this state or other person or persons shall attempt to settle or run any of the lands reserved to the Indians for their hunting grounds, such person or persons may be detained until the governor shall demand him or them, and then it shall be lawful for any of the tribes near such offenders to come and see the punishment, according to such laws as now are or hereafter shall be enacted by the said state for trying such offences.

III. It shall in no case be understood, that the punishment of the innocent, under the idea of retaliation shall be practised on either side.

IV. If any citizen of this state or other white person or persons shall commit a robbery or murder or other capital crime on any Indian, such offenders shall be delivered up to justice, and shall be tried according to the laws of the state, and due notice of such intended punishment shall be sent to some one of the tribes.

V. If any Indian shall commit a robbery or murder or other capital crime on any white person, such offenders shall receive a punishment adequate to such offence, and due notice of such intended punishment shall be given to his honor the governor.

VI.   In case of any design being formed in any neighboring tribes, against the peace or safety of the state, which they shall know or suspect, they shall make known the same to his honor the governor.

VII.   All white person or persons shall be at liberty and conducted in safety into the settled parts of the state, when they shall require it, except such persons as shall come under the restrictions pointed out in the second article.

VIII.   The said Indians shall restore all the negroes, horses or other property that are or may be among them, belonging to any citizen of this state or any other person or persons whatever, to such person as the governor shall direct.

IX.   That the trade with the said Indians shall be carried on as heretofore.

X.   All horses belonging to any Indian that shall be found in the said state, such horses shall be restored to such person as the head men or the tribe where such Indian may reside shall direct.

XI.   The present temporary line reserved to the Indians for their hunting ground, shall be agreeable to the treaty held at Augusta in the year one thousand seven hundred and eighty-three; and that a new temporary line shall begin at the forks of the Oconee and Oakmulgee Rivers, thence in a southwest direction, until it shall intersect the most southern part of the stream called St. Mary's River, including all the islands and waters of the said stream, thence down the said river to the old line. And all the ground without the said new temporary lines, when run and completed, shall be reserved to the Indians for their hunting grounds as aforesaid.

In witness whereof the parties have hereunto affixed their hands and seals the day and year above written.

On the part of the state

JOHN TWIGGS	(L.S.)	} Commissioners
ELIJAH CLARK	(L.S.)	

On the part of the Indians

WARRIOR KING	X	(L.S.)
O'KEMULGEY TUSKONUCKY	X	(L.S.)
TUSKIA MICKO	X	(L.S.)
CUSRATER MICKO	X	(L.S.)
ENCHALUCKO	X	(L.S.)
POHILLKE OAKFUSKIES	X	(L.S.)
INNEHANA UFOLLIES	X	(L.S.)
ABICO TUSKANUCKY	X	(L.S.)
INNEHA MICKO	X	(L.S.)
YAHOLO MICKO	X	(L.S.)
COSO MICKO	X	(L.S.)
OPOHELTHE MICKO	X	(L.S.)
CUSO MICKO	X	(L.S.)

Dickson Tallicus	X	(*L.S.*)
Upalahajoe	X	(*L.S.*)
Opoyhajoe	X	(*L.S.*)
Wartucko Micko	X	(*L.S.*)

Signed, sealed and delivered in presence of Thomas Glascock, John King, J. Clements, Jared Irwin, James Darouzeaux, I.P.T. for the state of Georgia, Philip Scott, *his* X *mark*, William Moore.[1]

[1] Marbury and Crawford, *Digest of the Laws of the State of Georgia*, pp. 607–8. The original has not been located. The treaty is related to George Washington's message journalized August 22, 1789.

Treaty of Hopewell with the Cherokees

Articles of a Treaty,

Concluded at Hopewell, on the Keowee, between Benjamin Hawkins, Andrew Pickens, Joseph Martin and Lacklan McIntosh, Commissioners Plenipotentiary of the United States of America, of the one Part, and the Head-Men and Warriors of all the Cherokees of the other.

The Commissioners Plenipotentiary of the United States in Congress assembled, give peace to all the Cherokees, and receive them into the favor and protection of the United States of America, on the following conditions.

Art. 1.   The Head-Men and Warriors of all the Cherokees, shall restore all the prisoners, citizens of the United States, or subjects of their allies, to their intire liberty: They shall also restore all the negroes, and all other property taken during the late war from the citizens, to such person, and at such time and place, as the commissioners shall appoint.

Art. 2.   The Commissioners of the United States in Congress assembled, shall restore all the prisoners taken from the Indians, during the late war, to the Head-Men and Warriors of the Cherokees, as early as is practicable.

Art. 3.   The said Indians for themselves, and their respective tribes and towns, do acknowledge all the Cherokees to be under the protection of the United States of America, and of no other sovereign whosoever.

Art. 4.   The boundary allotted to the Cherokees for their hunting grounds, between the said Indians and the citizens of the United States, within the limits of the United States of America, is, and shall be the following, viz. beginning at the mouth of Duck river on the Tenessee; thence running north-east, to the ridge dividing the waters running into Cumberland from those running into the Tenessee; thence eastwardly along the said ridge to a north-east line to be run, which shall strike the river Cumberland forty miles above Nashville; thence along the said line to the river; thence up the said river to the ford where the Kentucky road crosses the river, thence to Campbells line, near Cumberland gap; thence to the mouth of Clauds creek on Holstein; thence to the Chimmey Top mountain; thence to Camp creek, near the mouth of Big Limestone, on

Nolichuckey; thence a southerly course six miles to a mountain; thence south to the North-Carolina line; thence to the South-Carolina Indian boundary, and along the same south-west over the top of the Oconee mountain till it shall strike Tugalo river; thence a direct line to the top of the Currohee mountain; thence to the head of the South fork of Oconee river.

ART. 5. If any citizen of the United States, or other person not being an Indian, shall attempt to settle on any of the lands westward or southward of the said boundary which are hereby allotted to the Indians for their hunting grounds, or having already settled and will not remove from the same within six months after the ratification of this treaty, such person shall forfeit the protection of the United States, and the Indians may punish him or not as they please—provided nevertheless, that this article shall not extend to the people settled between the fork of French Broad, and Holstein rivers, whose particular situation shall be transmitted to the United States in Congress assembled for their decision thereon, which the Indians agree to abide by.

ART. 6. If any Indian or Indians, or person residing among them, or who shall take refuge in their nation, shall commit a robbery, or murder or other capital crime on any citizen of the United States, or person under their protection, the nation, or the tribe to which such offender or offenders may belong, shall be bound to deliver him or them up to be punished according to the ordinances of the United States; provided that the punishment shall not be greater than if the robbery or murder, or other capital crime, had been committed by a citizen on a citizen.

ART. 7. If any citizen of the United States, or person under their protection, shall commit a robbery or murder or other capital crime, on any Indian, such offender or offenders shall be punished in the same manner as if the murder or robbery or other capital crime, had been committed on a citizen of the United States; and the punishment shall be in presence of some of the Cherokees, if any shall attend at the time and place, and that they may have an opportunity so to do, due notice of the time of such intended punishment shall be sent to some one of the tribes.

ART. 8. It is understood that the punishment of the innocent under the idea of retaliation, is unjust, and shall not be practised on either side, except where there is a manifest violation of this treaty: and then it shall be preceded, first by a demand of justice, and if refused, then by a declaration of hostilities.

ART. 9. For the benefit and comfort of the Indians, and for the prevention of injuries or oppressions on the part of the citizens or Indians; the United States in Congress assembled shall have the sole and exclusive right of regulating the trade with the Indians, and managing all their affairs in such manner as they think proper.

ART. 10. Until the pleasure of Congress be known, respecting the ninth article, all traders, citizens of the United States, shall have liberty to go to any of the tribes or towns of the Cherokees to trade with them, and they shall be protected in their persons and property, and kindly treated.

ART. 11. The said Indians shall give notice to the citizens of the United States, of any designs which they may know or suspect to be formed in any neighbouring tribe, or by any person whosoever, against the peace, trade or interest of the United States.

ART. 12. That the Indians may have full confidence in the justice of the United States respecting their interests, they shall have the right to send a deputy of their choice, whenever they think fit, to Congress.

ART. 13. The hatchet shall be forever buried, and the peace given by the United States, and friendship re-established between the said states on the one part, and all the Cherokees on the other, shall be universal; and the contracting parties shall use their utmost endeavours to maintain the peace given as afore-said, and friendship re-established.

IN WITNESS of all, and every thing herein determined, between the United States of America, and all the Cherokees—We their underwriten commissioners, by virtue of our full powers have signed this definitive treaty, and have caused our seals to be hereunto affixed. DONE at Hopewell, on the Keowee, this twenty-eighth of November, in the year of our Lord one thousand seven hundred and eighty-five.

(Signed)	BENJAMIN HAWKINS,	(L.S.)
	ANDW. PICKENS,	(L.S.)
	JOS. MARTIN,	(L.S.)
	LACHN. MCINTOSH,	(L.S.)

KOATOHEE, or Corn Tassell of Toquo,
his X mark

SCHOLAUETTA, or Hanging Man of Chota,
his X mark

TUSKEGATAHU, or Long Fellow of Chistohoe,
his X mark

OOSKWHA, or Abraham of Chilkowa,
his X mark

KOLAKUSTA, or Prince of North,
his X mark

NEWOTA, or the Gritz of Chicamaga,
his X mark

KONATOTA, or the Rising Fawn of Highwassay,
his X mark

TUCKASEE, or Young Tarrapin of Allajoy,
his X mark

Toostaka, or the waker of Oostanawa,
his
X
mark

Untoola, or Gun rod of Seteco,
his
X
mark

Unsuokanail, Buffalo White Calf New Cussee,
his
X
mark

Kostayeak, or Sharp Fellow Wataga,
his
X
mark

Chonosta, of Cowe,
his
X
mark

Chescoonwha, Bird in Close of Tomotlug,
his
X
mark

Tuckasee, or Tarrapin of Hightowa,
his
X
mark

Chesetoa, or the Rabit of Tlacoa,
his
X
mark

Chesecotetona, or Yellow Bird of the Pine Log,
his
X
mark

Sketaloska, Second Man of Tillico,
his
X
mark

Chokasatahe, Chickasaw Killer Tasonta,
his
X
mark

Onanoota, of Koosoatee,
his
X
mark

Ookoseta, or Sower Mush of Kooloque,
his
X
mark

Umatooetha, the Water Hunter, Choikamawgee,
his
X
mark

Wyuka, of Lookout Mountain,
his
X
mark

TULCO, or Tom of Chatuga,	his X mark
WILL, of Akoha,	his X mark
NECATEE, of Sawta,	his X mark
AMOKONTAKONA, Kutcloa,	his X mark
KOWETATAHEE, in Frog-Town,	his X mark
KEUKUCH, Talkoa,	his X mark
TULATISKA, of Chaway,	his X mark
WOOALUKA, the way layer, Chota,	his X mark
TATLIUSTA, or Porpus of Tilassi,	his X mark
JOHN, of Little Tallico,	his X mark
SKELELAK,	his X mark
AKONOLUCHTA, the Cabbin,	his X mark
CHEANOKA, of Kawetakac,	his X mark
YELLOW BIRD,	his X mark

(Witnesses) WM. BLOUNT,
SAM. TAYLOR, major,
JOHN OWEN,

JESS WALTON,
JOHN COWAN, capt. commandant,
THOS. GEGG,
W. HAZZARD,
JAMES MADISON, } Sworn Interpreters.[1]
ARTHUR COODEY, }

[1] A printed copy of the treaty is Indian Treaty no. 11, RG 11, M668, roll 2, DNA. E-19279. The original has not been located. The treaty is related to George Washington's messages journalized August 22, 1789, and August 11, 1790.

Treaty of Hopewell with the Choctaws

Articles of a Treaty concluded at Hopewell on the Keowee near Seneca old town between Benjamin Hawkins, Andrew Pickens and Joseph Martin, Commissioners plenipotentiary of the United States of America of the one part, And Yockonahoma, great Medal chief of Soonacoha, Yockahoopoie leading chief of Bugtoogoloo, Minghoopoie, leading chief of Haskooqua, Tobocoh great Medal Chief of Congetoo, Pooshemastubie Gorget captain of Senayazo, and Thirteen Small Medal Cheifs of the first class, Twelve Medal and gorgot captains, Commissioners plenipotentiary of all the Choctaw Nation of the other part.

The Commissioners plenipotentiary of the United States of America give peace to all the Choctaw Nation, and receive them into the favour and protection of the United States of America on the following conditions:

ARTICLE THE 1ST.

The Commissioners plenipotentiary of all the Choctaw Nation shall restore all the prisoners citizens of the United States or subjects of their Allies to their entire liberty if any there be in the Choctaw Nation. They shall also restore all the Negros and all other property taken during the late war from the citizens to such person and at such time and place as the Commissioners of the United States of America shall appoint: If any there be in the Choctaw Nation.

ARTICLE 2ND.

The Commissioners plenipotentiary of all the Choctaw Nation do hereby acknowledge the tribes and towns of the said Nation and the lands within the boundary allotted to the said Indians to live and hunt on as mentioned in the third article to be under the protection of the United States of America and of no other Sovereign whosoever.

ARTICLE THE 3RD.

The boundary of the lands, hereby allotted to the Choctaw Nation to live and hunt on, within the limits of the United States of America is and shall be the following Vizt. Beginning at a point on the thirty first degree of North latitude where the Eastern boundary of the Natches district shall touch the same, Thence East along the said 31st. degree of North latitude, being the Southern boundary of the United States of America, untill it shall strike the Eastern boundary of the lands on which the Indians of the said Nation did live and hunt, on the twenty

Ninth of November one thousand seven hundred and eightly two while they were under the protection of the King of Great Britain—Thence Northerly along the said Eastern boundary untill it shall meet the Northern boundary of the said lands—Thence Westerly along the said Northern boundary untill it shall meet the western boundary thereof—Thence Southerly along the same to the beginning Saving and reserving for the establishment of trading posts, Three tracts or parcels of land of six miles square each, at such places as the United [States] in Congress assembled shall think proper, which posts and the lands annexed to them, shall be to the use and under the government of the United States of America.

ARTICLE THE 4TH.

If any citizen of the United States or other person not being an Indian shall attempt to settle on any of the lands hereby allotted to the Indians to live and hunt on, such person shall forfeit the protection of the United States of America, and the Indians may punish him or not as they please.

ARTICLE THE 5TH.

If any Indian or Indians or persons residing among them, or who shall take refuge in their Nation, shall commit a robbery or murder or other capital crime on any citizen of the United States of America or person under their protection, The tribe to which such offender may belong or the Nation shall be bound to deliver him or them up to be punished according to the Ordinances of the United States in Congress assembled: Provided that the punishment shall not be greater than if the robbery or murder or other capital crime had been committed by a citizen on a citizen.

ARTICLE THE 6TH.

If any citizen of the United States of America or person under their protection shall commit a robbery or murder, or other capital crime on any Indian such offender or offenders shall be punished in the same manner as if the robbery or murder or other capital crime had been committed on a citizen of the United States of America: And the punishment shall be in presence of some of the Choctaws if any will attend at the time and place: And that they may have an opportunity so to do, due notice if practicable of the time of such intended punishment shall be sent to some one of the tribes.

ARTICLE THE 7TH.

It is understood that the punishment of the innocent under the Idea of retaliation is unjust and shall not be practiced on either side, except, where there is a manifest violation of this treaty: And then it shall be preceded first by a demand of Justice and if refused then by a declaration of hostilities.

ARTICLE THE 8TH.

For the benefiet and comfort of the Indians and for the prevention of injuries or oppressions on the part of the Citizens or Indians The United States in Congress assembled shall have the sole and exclusive right of regulating the Trade with the Indians and managing all their affairs in such manner as they think proper.

ARTICLE THE 9TH.

Untill the pleasure of Congress be known respecting the eighth article, all Traders citizens of the United States of America shall have liberty to go to any of the tribes or towns of the Choctaws to trade with them, and they shall be protected in their persons and property and kindly treated.

ARTICLE THE 10TH.

The said Indians shall give notice to the citizens of the United States of America of any designs which they may know or suspect to be formed in any neighbouring tribe or by any person whosoever against the peace, Trade or interest of the United States of America.

ARTICLE THE 11TH.

The Hatchet shall be forever buried and the peace given by the United States of America and friendship re-established between the said States on the one part, and all the Choctaw Nation on the other part, shall be universal: And the Contracting parties shall use their utmost endeavours to maintain the peace given as aforesaid and friendship reestablished.

IN WITNESS of all and every thing herein determined between the United States of America and all the Choctaws, We their underwritten commissioners by virtue of our full powers have signed this definitive Treaty, and have caused our seals to be hereunto affixed.

DONE at Hopewell on the Keowee this 3rd. day of January in the year of our lord One thousand seven hundred and eighty six.

BENJAMIN HAWKINS		[Seal]		his	
ANDW. PICKENS		[Seal]	TUSHKAHOOMOCH	X	[Seal]
JOS. MARTIN		[Seal]		mark	
	his			his	
YOCKENAHOMA	X	[Seal]	YOOSHENOCHHA	X	[Seal]
	mark			mark	
	his			his	
YOCKEHOOPOIE	X	[Seal]	TOOTEHOOMA	X	[Seal]
	mark			mark	
	his			his	
MINGOHOOPOIE	X	[Seal]	TOOBENOHOOMOCH	X	[Seal]
	mark			mark	
	his			his	
TOBOCOH	X	[Seal]	CSHECOOPOOHOOMOCH	X	[Seal]
	mark			mark	
	his			his	
POOSHEMASTUBY	X	[Seal]	STONAKOOHOOPOIE	X	[Seal]
	mark			mark	
	his			his	
POOSHAHOOMA	X	[Seal]	TUSHKEHEEGAHBA	X	[Seal]
	mark			mark	
	his			his	
TUSCOONOOHOOPOIE	X	[Seal]	TESHUHANOCHLOCH	X	[Seal]
	mark			mark	
	his			his	
SHINSHEMASTUBY	X	[Seal]	POOSHONALTLA	X	[Seal]
	mark			mark	

YOOPAKOOMA	his X mark	[Seal]	OKANCONNOOBA	his X mark	[Seal]
STOONOKOOHOOPOIE	his X mark	[Seal]	AUTOONACHUBA	his X mark	[Seal]
TEHAKUHBAY	his X mark	[Seal]	PANGOKOOLOCH	his X mark	[Seal]
POOSHOMASTUBY	his X mark	[Seal]	STEABEE	his X mark	[Seal]
TUSKKAHOOMOCH	his X mark	[Seal]	TENCTEHENNA	his X mark	[Seal]
			TUSHKEMENTAHOCK	his X mark	[Seal]
			TUSHTALLA	his X mark	[Seal]
			CSHNAANGCHABBA	his X mark	[Seal]
			CUNNOPOIE	his X mark	[Seal]

WITNESS

WM. BLOUNT
JOHN WOODS
SAML. TAYLOR
ROBERT ANDERSON
BENJN. LAURENCE
JOHN PITCHLYNN ⎱ Interpreters[1]
JAMES COLE ⎰

[1] The treaty, in the hand of Benjamin Hawkins, is Indian Treaty no. 12, RG 11, M668, roll 2, DNA. It is related to George Washington's messages journalized August 22, 1789, and August 11, 1790.

Treaty of Hopewell with the Chickasaws

Articles of a treaty concluded at Hopewell on the Keowee near Seneca old town between Benjamin Hawkins, Andrew Pickens and Joseph Martin Commissioners plenipotentiary of the United States of America of the one part, and Piomingo head warrior and first minister of the Chickasaw Nation, Mingatushka one of the leading chiefs, and Latopoia first beloved man of the said Nation & Commissioners plenipotentiary of all the Chickasaws of the other part.

The Commissioners plenipotentiary of the United States of America give peace to the Chickasaw Nation and receive them into the favour and protection of the said States on the following conditions.

ARTICLE THE 1ST.

The Commissioners plenipotentiary of the Chickasaw Nation shall restore all the prisoners citizens of the United States to their entire liberty, if any there be in the chickasaw Nation. They shall also restore all the Negros and all other property taken during the late war from the Citizens, if any there be in the Chickasaw Nation, to such person and at such time and place as the commissioners of the United States of American shall appoint.

ARTICLE THE 2ND.

The Commissioners plenipotentiary of the Chickasaws, do hereby acknowledge the tribes and the towns of the Chickasaw Nation, to be under the protection of the United States of America and of no other sovereign whosoever.

ARTICLE 3RD.

The boundary of the lands hereby allotted to the Chickasaw Nation to live and hunt on within the limits of the United States of America is and shall be the following vizt.

Beginning on the ridge that divides the waters running into the Cumberland from those running into the Tennessee at a point in a line to be run North East which shall strike the Tennessee at the Mouth of Duck river, Thence running westerly along the said ridge till it shall strike the Ohio, thence down the Southern banks thereof to the Mississipi, Thence down the same to the Choctaw line or Natches district, Thence along the said line or the lines of the district Eastwardly as far as the Chickasaws claimed and lived and hunted on, the 29th of November one thousand seven hundred and eighty two. Thence the said boundary eastwardly shall be, the lands allotted to the Choctaws and Cherokees to live and hunt on, and the lands at present in the possession of the Creeks, Saving and reserving for the establishment of a trading post a tract or parcel of land to be laid out at the lower part of the Muscle shoales at the Mouth of Ocochappo, in a circle *whos diamiter*[1] shall be five miles on the river, which post and the lands annexed thereto shall be to the use and under the government of the United States of America.

ARTICLE THE 4TH.

If any citizen of the United States or other person not being an Indian shall attempt to settle on any of the lands hereby allotted to the Chickasaws to live and hunt on, such person shall forfeit the protection of the United States of America and the Chickasaws may punish him or not as they please.

ARTICLE THE 5TH.

If any Indian or Indians or persons residing among them, or who shall take refuge in their Nation, shall commit a robbery or murder or other capital crime on any citizen of the United States or person under their protection, The Tribe to which such offender or offenders may belong or the nation shall be bound to deliver him or them up to be punished according to the Ordinances of the United States in Congress assembled: Provided that the punishment shall not be greater, than if the robbery or murder or other capital crime had been committed by a citizen on a Citizen.

ARTICLE THE 6TH.

If any citizen of the United States of America or person under their protection shall commit a robbery or murder or other capital crime on any Indian, such offender or offenders shall be punished in the same manner as if the robbery or murder or other Capital crime had been committed on a citizen of the United States of America. And the punishment shall be in presence of some of the Chickasaws if any will attend at the time and place, and that they may have an opportunity so to do, due notice if practicable of such intended punishment shall be sent to some one of the Tribes.

ARTICLE THE 7TH.

It is understood that the punishment of the innocent under the Idea of retaliation is unjust and shall not be practised on either side except where there is a manifest violation of this Treaty: And then it shall be preceded first by a demand of justice and if refused then by a declaration of hostilities.

ARTICLE THE 8TH.

For the benefit and comfort of the Indians and for the prevention of injuries or apprissions on the part of the citizens or Indians The United States in Congress assembled, shall have the sole and exclusive right of regulating the Trade with the Indians, and managing all their affairs in such manner as they think proper.

ARTICLE THE 9TH.

Untill the pleasure of Congress be known respecting the eighth article all Traders citizens of the United States shall have liberty to go to any of the Tribes or towns of the Chickasaws to trade with them, and they shall be protected in their persons and property and kindly Treated.

ARTICLE THE 10TH.

The said Indians shall give notice to the citizens of the United States of America, of any designs which they may know or suspect to be formed in any neighbouring Tribe or by any person whosoever against the peace Trade or interest of the United States of America.

ARTICLE THE 11TH.

The Hatchet shall be forever buried, and the peace given by the United States of America and friendship reestablished between the said States on the One part and the Chickasaw Nation on the other part shall be universal: and the Contracting parties shall use their utmost endeavours to maintain the peace given as aforesaid and friendship reestablished.

IN WITNESS of all and every thing herein contained between the said States and Chickasaws We their under written Commissioners by Virtue of our full powers have signed this definitive Treaty and have caused our seals to be heretunto affixed.

DONE at Hopewell on the Keowee this 10th day of January in the year of our lord One thousand seven hundred and eighty six.

BENJAMIN HAWKINS	[Seal]	PIOMINGO	his X mark	[Seal]
ANDW. PICKENS	[Seal]	MINGATUSHKA	his X mark	[Seal]
JOS. MARTIN	[Seal]	LATOPOIA	his X mark	[Seal]

WITNESS
WM. BLOUNT
WM. HAZZARD
SAML. TAYLOR
JAMES COLE } Sworn Interpreter[2]

[1] In the original the words "the diamiter of which" are written above the words "whos diamiter."
[2] The treaty, in the hand of Benjamin Hawkins, is Indian Treaty no. 13, RG 11, M668, roll 2, DNA. E-45003. It is related to George Washington's messages journalized August 22, 1789, and August 11, 1790.

Treaty at Shoulder-Bone

GEORGIA.

Articles of a treaty of peace, amity and commerce, concluded near the mouth of Shoulder-bone Creek, a branch of the Occonee River, the third day of November, in the year of our Lord one thousand seven hundred and eighty-six, and of the independence of the United States of America the eleventh, between the subscribing commissioners, in behalf of the state of Georgia, of the one part, and the underwritten kings, head men and warriors, in behalf of the Creek nation, on the other, on the following conditions, namely:

WHEREAS, since the signing of the last treaty held at Galphinton, and dated the twelfth day of November, one thousand seven hundred and eighty-five, between commissioners appointed by the said state and the kings, head men and warriors of the said Creek nation, acts of hostility have been committed by parties of the Indians on inhabitants of the said state, in violation of the said treaty, whereby the friendship and harmony so essentially necessary to both parties have been greatly disturbed: *And whereas* the said parties are now mutually desirous of renewing a treaty, which may comprehend such articles as will give satisfaction to the party injured, and restore peace, friendship and commerce to both. It is therefore covenanted and agreed:

FIRST, the Indians for themselves and the rest of the kings, head men and warriors of the Creek nation, do promise and engage that six of their people who were of the parties that murdered the same number (say six) of the white inhabitants last spring, shall be put to death in a manner satisfactory to the person or persons whom his honor the governor or the commissioners may send to see it done. And that the white people who were the means of the said murders being committed shall be removed from the nation without delay.

SECOND, All negroes, horses, cattle and other property now in the nation, and which were taken from the inhabitants of Georgia, shall be restored to such person or persons as his honor the governor or the commissioners shall direct. All white or other free people in the nation who are held as prisoners or slaves shall also be delivered up to the aforesaid persons.

THIRD, If any citizen of this state or other person or persons shall attempt to settle or run any of the lands reserved for the Indians for their hunting grounds, such person or persons may be detained until the governor shall be informed thereof, and demand him or them, and then any of the tribes near such offenders, to come and see the punishment according to such laws as now are or hereafter may be enacted by the said state for trying such offenders.

FOURTH, The punishing of innocent persons under the idea of retaliation shall not be practised on either side.

FIFTH, If any citizen of the state or other white person or persons shall commit a robbery or murder or other capital crime on any Indian, such offender shall be delivered up to justice and be tried according to the laws of the state, and due notice of such intended punishment shall be sent to some one of the tribes.

SIXTH, If any Indian shall commit a robbery or murder or other capital crime on any white person, such offender shall receive a punishment adequate to the offence, and due notice of such intended punishment shall be given to his honor the governor.

SEVENTH, If the Indians shall know or suspect of any design of any neighboring tribes against the peace or safety of this state, they shall make the same known in the most expeditious manner to his honor the governor.

EIGHTH, All white persons shall be at liberty, and conducted in safety into the settled parts of the state when they shall require it; except such persons as shall come under the restrictions pointed out in the third article.

NINTH, The trade with the Indians shall be carried on as heretofore. And all just debts due by any of the said Indians to any of the merchants or traders of the said state shall be fairly and fully paid.

TENTH, the present temporary lines reserved to the Indians for their hunting grounds shall be agreeable to the treaties held at Augusta and Galphinton, the former bearing date the first day of November, one thousand seven hundred and eighty-three, and the latter the twelfth day of November, one thousand seven hundred and eighty-five, every part of which is hereby fully confirmed. And the said lines shall be marked as soon as the Indians can possibly make it convenient to come down and see it done, the present being their hunting season. And of their intention of attending for the said purpose they shall notify his honor the governor, at least one month before their departure from the nation.

ELEVENTH, After the aforesaid lines are marked, neither white persons nor Indians shall be allowed to pass them without a special license for that purpose; that for a white person to be from under the hand of his honor the governor, and that for a trader or Indian from under the hand of the agent of the state, or his deputy residing in the nation. Any person of either party who shall be found transgressing this article, shall be detained until the authority to whom such offender belongs shall be informed thereof.

TWELFTH, In proof of their good faith and sincere intentions to perform the beforementioned articles, and for the security of the inhabitants of the said state, the Indians agree to leave in the hands of the commissioners five of their people, namely, Chuuocklie Micko, of the Cowetas; Cuchas, of the Cussetas; Suckawockie, brother to the last named, also of the Cussetas; Emathlocks, second man of the Broken Arrow, and Enautaleche, nephew to the head man of the Swaglos. The said Indians, during their stay among the white people, shall be provided with comfortable diet, lodging and clothing, and be well treated in every respect.

In witness whereof the parties have hereunto affixed their hands and seals the day and year above mentioned.

On the part of the state

JOHN HABERSHAM	(L.S.)
ABRAHAM RAVOT	(L.S.)
J. CLEMENTS	(L.S.)
JAMES MCNEIL	(L.S.)
JOHN KING	(L.S.)
JAMES POWELL	(L.S.)
FERDINAND O'NEIL	(L.S.)
JARED IRWIN	(L.S.)

On the part of the Indians

CUSA MICO	X	(L.S.)
NINNEHOMOHTA TUSTE	X	(L.S.)
NUCKIE MICO	X	(L.S.)
MICO CHEE	X	(L.S.)
HOTHLEPOYA MICO	X	(L.S.)
OPOHETHLE MICO, or Tallisee king	X	(L.S.)
OPAYA LATA	X	(L.S.)
OPAYA HAJO	X	(L.S.)
EUFALA TESLONOKY	X	(L.S.)
OKELLASA HAJO	X	(L.S.)
ENEATHLACO OPAYA	X	(L.S.)
WAWLATA MICO	X	(L.S.)
OPAYA EMATHLA	X	(L.S.)
OCKEHAN HAJO	X	(L.S.)
OLACKTA	X	(L.S.)
TULJISCA MICO	X	(L.S.)
TUSTO NUCKIE	X	(L.S.)
HOTTESY MICO	X	(L.S.)
OSUCHEE MATHTA	X	(L.S.)

Cvssita Mico	X	(L.S.)
Enea Mico	X	(L.S.)
Enea Thlaco	X	(L.S.)
Epha Tusto Nuckie	X	(L.S.)
Espane Tusto Nukis	X	(L.S.)
Goppitchu Tusto Nuckie	X	(L.S.)
Oke Lesa	X	(L.S.)
Cousa Tustomuckie	X	(L.S.)
Yahola Mico	X	(L.S.)
Econehot Hajo	X	(L.S.)
Cusa Mico	X	(L.S.)
Cuchas Mico	X	(L.S.)
Ochunnee Hola	X	(L.S.)
Fousachee Mico	X	(L.S.)
Holau Hajo	X	(L.S.)
Tusikia Mico	X	(L.S.)
Ausunuck Tustonuckie	X	(L.S.)
Tusikia Mico	X	(L.S.)
Jeomy Justo Nuckie	X	(L.S.)
Tolobe Mathla	X	(L.S.)
Hitcheta Mico	X	(L.S.)
Opaye Justo Nuchie	X	(L.S.)
Tusto Nuchie	X	(L.S.)
Aulack Hajo	X	(L.S.)
Enea Thlaco	X	(L.S.)
Hopaye Mico	X	(L.S.)
Othlepoya Mico	X	(L.S.)
Chuwackle Mico	X	(L.S.)
Eneuthlocko	X	(L.S.)
Olacte Emathla	X	(L.S.)
Muojoy	X	(L.S.)
Hallatowegie	X	(L.S.)
Will Jones	X	(L.S.)
Chatossaha	X	(L.S.)
Sokakoway	X	(L.S.)
Cuchas Hajo	X	(L.S.)
Toutkis Hajo	X	(L.S.)
Opayouchee	X	(L.S.)
Tusk Encha	X	(L.S.)
Wakse Hajo	X	(L.S.)

Signed, Sealed and delivered in presence of John Twiggs, Daniel McMurphy, John Graves, James Darouzeaux, Philip Scot, *P.S. his mark*, James M. Stewart.[1]

[1] Marbury and Crawford, *Digest of the Laws of the State of Georgia*, pp. 618–21. The original has not been located. The treaty is related to George Washington's message journalized August 22, 1789.

Proclamation of the Continental Congress

By the United States in Congress
　Assembled,
A Proclamation.
Whereas the United States in Congress assembled, by their Commissioners duly appointed and authorised, did on the Twenty-eighth Day of November, One Thousand Seven Hundred and Eighty-five, at Hopewell, on the Keowee, conclude Articles of a Treaty with all the Cherokees, and among other things stipulated and engaged by Article fourth, "That the Boundary allotted to the Cherokees for their Hunting Grounds, between the said Indians and the Citizens of the United States, within the limits of the United States of America, is and shall be the following, viz. 'Beginning at the mouth of Duck river on the Tenesee; thence running north-east to the ridge dividing the waters running into Cumberland from those running into the Tenesee; thence eastwardly along the said ridge to the north-east line to be run, which shall strike the river Cumberland, forty miles above Nashville; thence along the said line to the river; thence up the said river to the ford where the Kentucky road crosses the river; thence to Campbell's line near to Cumberland Gap; thence to the mouth of Claud's Creek on Holstein; thence to the Chimney-Top Mountain; thence to Camp Creek, near the mouth of Big Lime Stone on Nolichuckey; thence a southerly course six miles to a mountain; thence south to the North-Carolina line; thence to the South-Carolina Indian Boundary, and along the same south-west over the top of the Oconee Mountain, till it shall strike Tugalo river; thence a direct line to the top of the Currohee Mountain; thence to the head of the south fork of the Oconee river.' " And by Article fifth, that "If any Citizen of the United States, or other person not being an Indian, should attempt to settle on any of the lands westward or southward of the said Boundary, which were allotted to the Indians for their Hunting Grounds, or having settled previously to concluding the said Treaty, and not removing from the same within six months after the ratification of the said Treaty, such person should forfeit the protection of the United States, and that the Indians might punish him or not as they please; provided, that the said fifth Article should not extend to the People settled between the fork of French Broad and Holstein rivers, whose particular situation should be transmitted to the United States in Congress assembled for their decision thereon, which the Indians agreed to abide by." And Whereas it has been represented to Congress, that several disorderly Persons settled on the Frontiers of North-Carolina, in the vicinity of Chota, have, in open violation of the said Treaty, made intrusions upon the said Indian Hunting Grounds, and committed many unprovoked outrages upon the said Cherokees, who by the said Treaty have put themselves under the protection of the United States, which proceedings are highly injurious and disrespectful to the authority of the Union, and it being the firm determination of Congress to protect the said Cherokees in their rights, according to the true intent and meaning of the said Treaty; The United States In Congress Assembled, have therefore thought fit to issue, and they Do hereby

issue this their PROCLAMATION, strictly forbidding all such unwarrantable intrusions, and hostile proceedings against the said Cherokees; and enjoining all those who have settled upon the said Hunting Grounds of the said Cherokees, to depart with their Families and Effects without loss of time, as they shall answer their disobedience to the injunctions and prohibitions expressed in this Resolution at their peril: Provided, that this Proclamation shall not be construed as requiring the removal of the People settled between the fork of French Broad and Holstein rivers, referred to in the said Treaty: Provided also, that nothing contained in this Proclamation shall be considered as affecting the Territorial Claims of the State of North-Carolina.

DONE *in Congress, this First Day of* September, *in the Year of our Lord One Thousand Seven Hundred and Eighty-eight, and of our Sovereignty and Independence the Thirteenth.*

CYRUS GRIFFIN, President
CHARLES THOMSON, Secretary[1]

[1] The printed Proclamation is in Broadsides of the Continental Congress, 1775–88, RG 11, M332, roll 9, DNA. E-21517. It is related to George Washington's message journalized August 22, 1789.

Cherokee Nation to the President and the Senate

We the warriors chiefs and representatives of the cherokee Nation Resident and living in the following towns of Chota, Toquoh, Cettico, Little Telliquo Tumotly, Nioh or the Tassells town, Coettee, Chilhowah Tallassee, Great Telliquoh, Big Highwassa, Cheestowa, Eastanora Chatanugah, Chickamaugah, Stickoe, Ottilletaraconahah, Catatogah, Nicojackee, Tuskeegah, and Cheescheehah, our said towns lying and being on the Great rivers of tenasee Telliquo, highwassa Ammoah &c. &c.

We the said warriors representatives And Cheifs being Met at our ancient and beloved town of Chota on Tenasee at our Council fire having Considered the Nature and Circumstance of our Country And Nation, Are sorry to inform our Elder brother General Washington, and the Great Council of the united States That from the bad Conduct of some of our young and Inconsiderate men too much encouraged by bad white men, who too often Frequent our nation under pretentions of doing us good Services and keeping peace Between us and our Elder Brothers the Americans: Have darkened our land with war, and Stained our White Chair of Fre[i]ndship with blood, but to our great Joy the Great Sperit above have removed the Cloud & Permits the Sun to Shine again in friendship upon Each party. tho the darkness have lasted so long that Our Country and towns have been Spoiled, our Selves become Naked, and Suffer much with Hunger.

We now make Known to the great Congress of america, that Our desire and intention is to live in the most perfect & Strict Friendship and Alliance with our

Elder brothers the americans: That we shall for ever listen to and abide by their instructions Advice and determination, placing the Strongest Confidence that the Great Council is composed of such, who have eyes of pitty and hearts of humanity and Compassion, that they will not devest us of our rights and possessions, which our ancient Fathers and predecessors have enjoyed time out of mind.

We still remember and abide by the treaty held with your Commissioners in south Carolina in the year 1785. And tho our hunting grounds and towns north of tenesee and holeson rivers is sold unto white people for to Settle upon without our Consent, we still hope Congress will have mercy Upon us: For if our country is all taken from us we shall not be able to raise our children, neither is there any place left for us to remove too.

We rejoice much to hear that the Great Congress have got new powers And have become Strong. we now Hope that whatever is done hereafter by the Great Council will no more be destroyed and made small by any State:

We shall always be ready to listen with open Ears And Willing hearts to you or any one Joined with you & to no other for protection, & regulating all matters.

We beg leave to Make it Known to your Great And beloved Council, that we have appointed & Constituted Our beloved brother Bennit Ballew, to be our Cheife And Representative, in And over all that part of the Cherokee Nation Comprehending the towns lying on the aforesaid Rivers. Tenasee, highwassa, Telliquo, and ammoah, And all lying North and North West of Said rivers & Towns. that we have Given and Gra[n]ted into the said Benit Ballew full powers and Authorities to transact and Negociate all manner of things in any wise touching Appurtaining or relateing to the aforesaid towns and that part of our Nation, in our behalf and in our name and Stead [blotted out] in the same manner and form as tho We were personally present our selves in as full and Ample Manner to all intents and purposes and in Testimony of which we have sent our great and beloved Warrior and Cheife, the Riseing Faun Sheenuhteetah of Great Highwassa to accompany our beloved Cheife and representative Bennit Ballew to Congress. then and there to Make known to your Great beloved Council the truth and Sincereity of this our Instrument and writing touching the premisses. and to do whatever the said Bennit Ballew may think for the Good, Tranquility and safety of our nation Trusting that the Great Council and Elder brothers Will do us Justice, Quiet us in our possessions. particularly our lands lying north of the rivers Tenesee And Holeson, It is our hunting grounds and we Have no other to get our livings on

Done in Council at Chota the 19th day of May 1789. Singed and Acknowledged before us.

X	HICKOGESKEE
X	AUCOEE
X	OKILLOLEE
X	FOTACHAWEE

X	AOWAYALLOW
X	KEENERTITER
X	CUNESUTTEHIE
X	WOLSCONEE
X	AMMOCHULOLOCA
X	OHALUCA
X	CHENOWEE
X	TETARTELSEA
X	CLAUNUSEE
X	NONTONAKEY
X	SAYOVOTA
X	SQUOLLEEOTTE
X	AMMODANESCA
X	COOSATEHEE
X	AIANOHALEE
X	SUTONIKEI
X	JOHN STEPHENS: h. Breed
X	CULFUTTEHEE
X	UTTANSO
X	CHEUCONESEE[1]

[1] A copy of the speech, in the hand of John Sevier, is in President's Messages on Indian Relations, Executive Proceedings, SR, DNA. It is related to George Washington's message journalized August 22, 1789. A transcript in a nineteenth-century hand, probably made by ASP, is in the above location.

Tickagiska King to the President

At a Great Talk held by the Warriors and Cheifs of the Cherokee Nation Assembled in Council at the Great and beloved town of Chota, the 19th day of May 1789 addressed to his Excellency the President of the United States

Great Brother,

The Grat being above has Directed our hearts to listen to the talks of peace, and Sorry that ever any [base] misunderstanding arose between us & our white brothers our last Troubles have been Occasioned by our rash inconsiderate young Men, who we doubt have been too Much encouraged by white Men in our towns, that pretend you have sent them Among us to do us Justice, & direct Our Nation how to Manage.

There is a great many towns of us that live on Tenase, Highwassee, Telliquo & Amoah, who are near Neighbours to us the white people, and we Wish to live in peace with them,

We hope that Congress has not forgot the Treaty last held at Hopewell So. Carolina; We intend to abide by it. And hope Congress Will do us Justice, as we look up to them for it, and intend to hear there Good talks, and also the Talks of all them that Are Joined with them, but will not listen to any Others.

Brother at our last Treaty held in so. Carolina We Give up to our White brothers all the land we Could any how Spare, and have but little left, to raise our Women & Children Upon and we hope you wont let any people take any more from us Without our Consent: We are Neither Birds nor Fish; we can Neither Fly in the Air, nor live under Water, therfore We hope pitty will be extended towards us: we are made by the same hand and in same Shape With yourselves.

We Send ~~two~~ some of our head men and Warriors to you with talk and to represent [~~our~~] the Case & Circumstance of our Nation; and we hope you will Settle Matters with them to all our Satisfaction, and that they may return home to Our Country with good tidings of peace, & friendship And any thing done by Congress and our representatives will be held safe by us and fast by us.

We hear that Congress have got Strong powers Now and nothing can be Spoiled that you undertake to do, this we ~~Are inform'd~~ hear from Our Elder brother John Sevier which makes us Glad & rejoice at the news.

We wish you to appoint Some good Men to do the buisness between us & our Elder Brothers. let us have a Man, that dont Speak With two Toungues, nor one that will encourage Mischeife or blood to be Spilt. let their be a good Man appointed, & War Will Never happen between us. ~~him~~ Such a one we Will listen to: but Such as has been Sent among us we Shall not hear, as they have already caused our Nation to be ruined And come almost to Nothing.

TICKAGISKA KING[1]

[1] A copy of the speech, in the hand of John Sevier, is in President's Messages on Indian Relations, Executive Proceedings, SR, DNA. It is related to George Washington's message journalized August 22, 1789. A transcript in a nineteenth-century hand, probably made by ASP, is in the above location.

Report of the Commissioners for Southern Indians to George Washington

Georgia Rock Landing on the Oconee River
June 30th. 1789

SIR,

Agreeably to the appointment of the Executive of North Carolina under the Act of Congress of the 27th. of October 1787 we attended at the Upper War ford on French Broad river from the 25th. of last month, to the 7th. instant, in order to meet in Treaty the Chiefs and Head men of the Cherokee Indians, but as they did not attend on or before that day, we found it necessary to repair to this place as the Executive of the State of Georgia had appointed the 20th. of this month for treating with the Creek Indians. A Treaty with the Creeks appearing to us to be of the greatest importance: we sent to the Cherokees a Talk no. 1.—A.

On our way to this place we met several of the Cherokee Head men at Seneca who gave us the fullest assurances that no hostilities or depredations should be committed by any of their people, against the Citizens of the United States: untill a treaty should be held, and we have every reason to confide in their promises.

Some late depredations which were committed by the Creeks on the frontiers of the State, so alarmed their chiefs, that they returned home after having been a few days on their journey to this place. The talks no. 1 and 2 Mr. McGillivrays letter No. 3. Mr. George Galphins letter No. 4 Mr. John Galphins letter No. 5—6. and 7, and Mr. McGillivrays letter No. 8 will explain to your Excellency their reasons.

We have now with us Mr. John Galphin a Chief Speaker of the lower Creeks, the White bird King or the Great King, with sixteen other Indians: they will return to the Nation tomorrow with our general Talk No. 9. and our letter to Mr. McGillivray No. 10.

The great scarcity of Corn for upwards of eighty miles around us was our principal reason for postponing the Creek Treaty so long: by the middle of Septr. we shall be aided with the new crop.

We are happy to inform your Excellency from good authority that the Creeks are very generally disposed for peace. We are well assured that all the Head Men of that nation with upwards of two thousand Indians will attend the Treaty in September, and we have the fairest prospects of establishing a permanent peace with the Creeks on such terms as will be pleasing to the Indians satisfactory to the State of Georgia, and honorable to the union.

In justice to the State of Georgia we cannot conclude this letter without expressing our entire satisfaction in the conduct of her Government, they have chearfully advanced several thousand dollars us enable us to meet so large a body of Indians in a manner suitable to the importance of the occasion.

We have the Honor to be
Your Excellencys
Most Obedient and very
Humble Servants
(Signed)   ANDREW PICKENS
H. OSBORNE

His Excellency
George Washington
President of the United States

No. 1. A.
To the Head Men, Chiefs, and Warriors of the Cherokee Nation

FRIENDS AND BROTHERS,

Agreeable to our appointment with you we met at this place expecting to have the pleasure of meeting you to settle all disputes that have subsisted between you and the white people. We have waited here for you twelve days and we are now obliged to go and meet the Creeks on the Oconee on the 20th. of this month, so that we can stay no longer. We are therefore under the necessity of postponing the Treaty with you 'till some other time that will be appointed and made convenient for both parties.

We are sorry to find that the people of Cumberland have reason to complain, many of those people have been killed by the indians. You all know that the people of cumberland make no encroachments upon your lands—the line was settled at Seneca and the people of Cumberland do not go over it. We hope none of your people are concerned in such mischief, as it would interrupt the good intentions of Congress towards your people. We expect you will put a stop to all such proceedings against any of our people untill we meet you in Treaty, when we have no doubt of settling all matters to your satisfaction. In token of our friendship we send you a string of White Beads.

Signed

Upper War ford on   ANDW. PICKENS
   French Broad river   JOHN STEELE
      7th. June 1789.   H. OSBORNE

No. 1.

A Talk from the Head Men & Chiefs of the lower Creek Nation to the Commissioners of the United States of Indian Affairs in the Southern Department May 23d. 1789

We received your Talk by Mr. George Galphin but at that present time we were not able to give you an answer, in consequence of a great meeting and a Talk being concluded by Mr. McGillivray, and the whole nation in consequence of the encroachments of the Georgians on our hunting grounds. Orders were given out for our Warriors to be in readiness to turn out in respect to their lands. We then first sent runners every where to stop and turn back all parties they could come up with, until we could hear from Mr. McGillivray and have his advice in the matter; there are some people we believe gone on, the consequence of which we cannot be accountable for, as they were gone before your Talk came in; but I hope there will be no blood spilt, your delay in not sending up your Talk sooner is the reason of it—had your Talk come a little sooner, it might have been a great deal better. We have been informed you would send a Talk to us but its not coming we did not know what to do, now we have sent to Mr. McGillivray to know when he will appoint the time for setting off to meet you at the place you appointed. Mr. Galphin is gone to settle this matter with him, he will bring you word when it will be agreed on by the Chiefs of the lower Creek Nation.

No. 2.

A Talk from the Chiefs Head men and Warriors of the lower Creek Nation

1st. June 1789

The day is coming at last that I hope we shall see you our fathers, friends and brothers again as we used in friendship and renew, all our former friendship, it was never our intention to be against any white people. We now come to take you by the hand, with a clear and willing mind and with an intent to remove all things that had shut our path so long, and to renew our former trade in friendship once more.

We have always received your talks friendly and sent you our talks again, letting you know always our grievances and the reasons why this long dispute, but we now hope all will be forgot, and we now come to make our Talks firm again, as we did when we first took white people by the hand, as we were all made by one master of breath, altho' put in different parts of the Earth—he did not make us to be at variance against each other, but it has happened by the bad doings of our mad people on both sides. When we first met the white people at the sea side, we did not meet in arms but with a desire of being further acquainted with each other, untill the great encroachments of our lands raised us which has occasioned the late troubles among us. You are sensible that at our first meeting at the sea side for the benefit of trade, we gave our land as far as the water ebbed and flowed, and by frequent request granted as far as possible reserving our hunting grounds, for what will be the use of goods brought amongst us if our young men have not hunting ground to kill game to purchase the goods brought to us.

We never met together yet to explain our grievances, but we told them to the beloved man Colo. White, who came here to us, and he promised to lay all our talks that we gave him before the Congress and that we should have redress and justice done us—now we rest with hopes that you will do the same by us, as we expect you have the same talks.

We received your invitation and do expect that when we meet all past grievances will be forgot and laid a one side, and then renew our friendship once more, to the satisfaction of all our people. Mr. George Galphin will acquaint you of every particular. This is all we have to say untill we shall take you by the hand as our fathers, friends and brothers.

James Derezeau
    Interpreter.

No. 3.

Little Tallassie 18th. May 1789

D. Sir,

I have this moment received your letter inclosing a Talk of invitation to the Chiefs and Warriors of the nation to meet the Commissioners of Congress the 20th. June next.

I wish that you could have been up while I was in the lower Towns, the great fatigue which I have undergone this Spring prevents my seeing the lower Chiefs on the occasion.

I have received a letter from the Commissioners and Superintendt. last winter in which they declared in the most pointed and unequivocal terms that it was impossible to make the restitution of Territory the basis of a peace between us and Georgia, which we demanded as a first measure to be complied with by them to lead the way to a lasting peace.

At our late Convention I explained the letter to the Chiefs who were much dissatisfied at the declaration and observed that it was in vain to Talk of peace while an Obstacle of such magnitude was suffered to remain in the way of it on the part of the Georgians—and the warlike preparations which you notice in your letter are carrying on to make another tryal to accomplish by force what can't be obtained by peaceable methods. Our excursions hitherto have been made with no other view than to warn the Georgians to desist from their injustice, and to induce them to listen to reason and humanity, it is well known that if any other was our motive that our force and resources are equal to effect their destruction.

On the present occasion the Chiefs having sent for my opinion and advice I have wrote to them to be explained by Mr. Durauzeaux. I have left the matter to their own choice; If they agree to meet I will likewise go tho' I have the best reasons against it. Yet apprehensions for personal security shall not deter me from fulfilling the duty which I owe my Country.

I am Sir
Your Humble Servant

Mr. Geo. Galphin   (Signed)   ALEX. McGILLIVRAY
at Cussetahs

No. 4.

Lower Creeks May 27th. 1789

GENTLEMEN,

I have to acquaint your honors that on my arrival in the Creek Nation I found it in a very bad situation to bring about a Treaty. I at first began to dispair of having it in my power to effect any of the business I came on as the whole Upper and Lower Creeks, down as far as the Siminolies were ready fitted off to go out to War and would have been started if I had been but four days later on the frontiers of Georgia upwards of three thousand would have been out and intended to have drove Ogechee from the mouth to the Head which I fear they would have effected after viewing the frontiers in such an unprepared State and the Indians going on at such a surprize.

I was told by many of the Indians that if any one else had come at such a time but myself they never should have returned back, the cause of their setting out on such a general excursion was by consent of Mr. McGillivray after a general meeting of the Chiefs and Head Men of the whole Upper and Lower Creeks and being informed by him that they were not to have their lands on the Oconees restored to them again, he acquainted them that the Spaniards had provided for them for the purpose of defending their rights to their lands fifteen hundred stand of Arms and forty thousand weight of Ammunition, this he told me was what the Governor or Commandant at Pensacola told him was what they had orders to do by orders from their King—On hearing of this great supply the Indians were much exalted and I believe would have turned out to a man except the Cussetas, who seemed much against it which was happy for me on my business or I could have done nothing.

On my arrival at the Cussetaws I met with Mr. Barnard who had been at Mr. McGillivrays Talk and had been trying all he could to put a stop to their rash proceedings 'till an express was sent down with an offer of peace on any conditions, as any thing that could be done to prolong the time, untill news could have been got down to have warned the frontiers from such a destruction as must have ensued would have been better than to have it gone on. Mr. Barnards offers could not avail as the Indians seemed determined to prosecute what they begun, Mr. Barnard, life and property were immediately threatened, and every exertion possible made use of to prevent his going off or sending down news to Georgia of what was going forward, at my meeting Mr. Barnard at the Cussetaws I handed him his honor the Governors letter, likewise General Twiggs's, and communicated the whole of my business to him, he acquainted me with every matter respecting the present situation of affairs and gave me every advice he thought necessary to effect any business and then left me to my brother John—to compleat it, as he told me he dared not be seen to concern with me at that time at the risk of his life which I found to be the truth.

My brother having a good deal of influence in the Cowetas through our connection there, which was the most strenuous for mischief I set him to work on them, and myself with the Cussetaws, we in two days got them to stop all that were on the move 'till we could write Mr. McGillivray, they agreed to wait till they heared his answer—after finding out the true situation of affairs and according to my instructions from you I wrote a letter acquainting him fully with my business with the Chiefs of the nation and from whom I was sent, and as head of the nation gave him every security if he attended the Treaty, that no molestation would by any means take place, but that every respect would be shewn him, which I hope your honors will take every step to secure, that my promises to him and the rest of the heads may not be violated. After my letter he left the determination of the business on hand to the head of the Cussetaws and Cowetas, who after seeing his answer consented to treat, he at the same time gave them to understand that if they were inclined to a Treaty he would likewise attend, and by what I can plainly see there is no measure to be fallen upon to settle the present cause of dispute without his voice—even if a Treaty could be called without his consent, it could not be a general one, therefore it would only be leaving matters in the same disagreeable situation that they are now in, and leaving the frontiers still open to perpetual violation, his attendance will put the matter effectually out of every kind of jeopardy one way or other.

I am now at Mr. Barnards on flint river forwarding to you this express, I likewise sent my brother off before I left the Town to Mr. McGillivray, to know exactly when he and the rest of the heads would wish to meet, I set off again for the Cussetaws tomorrow, and on the return of my brother, I shall in a few days set out for Augusta, where I hope by the time I get there you will nearly effect every preparation necessary for a Treaty at the Rock landing.

I shall be particular in ascertaining every necessary intelligence, which I hope in a short time to be able to communicate to your Honors in Augusta—till then I remain with due respect

Your honors Most
Obedt. Humble Servt.
(Signed) GEOE. GALPHIN

P.S. I have inclosed Mr. McGillivrays answer to me for your perusal, and likewise a Talk from the whole of the lower Creeks.

(Signed) G. G.

The Honble. Andw. Pickens & Hy. Osborn Esqs.
  Commissioners for Indian Affairs
    in Southern Department at
      Augusta

No. 5.

Cowetas 23d. May 1789

SIR,

I take the liberty of writing to your honor of the situation of this our Country.
When my brother arrived here we had just had a full meeting of all the
Chiefs, and had long waited for talks but never received any. A John Tarvin
arrived from Augusta who we expected we should have some talks by, but had
none; there were a few private letters for Mr. McGillivray, but nothing of
consequence.

The Chiefs then thought it was not the Georgians intention to make a peace,
on which many turned out—and the day my brother arrived, there were not less
than two thousand under arms, I gave him my assistance and stop't all, and
immediately sent to Mr. McGillivray who acted the same. There might be small
parties out that were gone so far that it was out of our power to stop them—
they turned out before your Talks came up to this Country.

I hope that the small damages which may be done by them will be over-
looked, if not perhaps we shall not agree, as it cannot be accounted for, when
they were in the woods before your Talks came to this Country and I hope all
will be looked over. I am sorry it was not more in my power to assist my
brother, owing to a bad state of health I have been in for some time past; but
finding that he must fall through with his business if I did not assist him, tho'
rode about with him in great pain: and yesterday had a meeting of the lower
Towns from which you will see the Talks. I found it necessary to go up to the
upper towns and see Mr. McGillivray, as it was needless to have a treaty with
part of the nation and not the whole. It may perhaps detain the time longer:
but the business will be well done. I have been told that his Honor the Governor
wrote to Mr. Barnard—am surprized that his Honor is not more acquainted with
business of this Country, then to think that Mr. Barnards influence could be of
any service to that Country, I believe him to be a friend of the State of Georgia,
but I must take the liberty to acquaint you that Mr. Barnard cannot do any
thing here more than a trader nor is it in his power. You will get the fullest
information of this Country by my brother George, and a Treaty you may rely
on we will try if possible to be at the time appointed: but if we should not, you
must wait a few days longer, as this is an extensive Country and business cannot
be done in a day or two. It will be necessary that every preparation be made, for
will try to make a lasting peace, and for that intention I will try to bring the
Chiefs of the whole nation, we may be in number that will come down about two
or three thousand, and hope that you will be in readiness for the reception of
that number.

I must now give some small remarks of the usage I have had in the State of
Georgia—when I was only seventeen the Assembly under some pretence robbed
me of better than forty thousand acres of land, a precident not be equalled in
all the annals of history. I then settled Store on the Oconie River and being
alarmed that the indians were likely to do mischief, Capt. Kemp with several of
the neighbours requested I would go to the nation to know the certainty and if

possible to prevent so shocking a scene, on my way up I met and passed them, no sooner out of sight I got round them, and gave the inhabitants timely notice tho' my horse tired and had to travel on foot forty miles a fatigue I was but little accustomed to—they might had they been possessed of one spark of gratitude recon'd that information a temporal salvation, I leave the judicious part, for I think there must be some, to judge their gratitude, when at that very juncture they burned my house, robbed me of better than two Hundred pounds sterling to induce me to believe it was the Indians and repeatedly threatened my life from no motive I know off but of saving them, had the men who made application the smallest idea of justice they would not have suffered me to be treated as I was. Soon after the Commissioners made application to me to bring the indians to a Treaty it was hardly possible for me to be zealous to serve a people who had so unjustly injured me and were continually declaring they would take my life, however to induce me to undertake it and Exhaust the remains of my shattered fortune they seemed to point out steps that would retrieve my lands, and my own foolish credulity once more permitted me to comply with their request.

The inhabitants were still swearing vengeance against me. I then did not think my life safe, I was then obliged to seek refuge in this my own country where I was in some safety, and I have laid out of my own pockets better than eighty pounds sterling in purchasing the Prisoners that were brought here and risque my Life to save theirs. All this I have done to serve the Georgians. I will write you more satisfactory then at present as I am now in a great hurry. You may be in preparation for a Treaty—and have the Honor to be Sir

Your Most Obedt. Servant
(Signed)   JOHN GALPHIN

The Honble. Henry Osborne Esqr.
  Commissioner of Indian Affairs
    Augusta

No. 6.

Cowetas 1st. June 1789

SIR,

In my last letter to you I mentioned where I was going to the Upper Towns in Order to see Mr. McGillivray, and have just arrived and compleated the business that my brother came on which he must have fallen through with had I not assisted him. I have settled every matter for him and will be ready to start from this place with all the lower Towns the 13th. of this month. I expect to be joined with all the upper Creeks and our Chief Speaker Mr. McGillivray the tenth of this month. We shall have all the Chiefs of the whole nation with us. I can just tell your Honor that there will be more Chiefs at this Treaty, than ever was at a treaty yet, in order to settle every dispute—matters may be settled on good terms, but we cannot come upon any terms unless every dispute is settled on a good footing particularly that of mine concerning my lands which was taken from me when I was under age. I shou'd once have thought myself happy of being a Citizen in the State of Georgia; but it was withheld, and I must now look upon myself a Chief in the whole of the lower Towns as they have now given me the honor of settling their business for them; in my last I gave you my reason for leaving the State of Georgia, but I would still wish every matter could be settled on good terms for a peace, for no man has taken more pains than I have.

I make no doubt there have been some people on the frontiers killed lately but we have lost twelve in number, I think that may be upon a balance for what are lost on the frontiers.

I will try to be down by the time appointed, it will be very necessary that all white people, who have no business should be ordered away as they generally give more disturbance than any others, and for no person to come on this side of the river—as the indians are a jealous people, and hope every method will be taken to keep people back that have no business there, if not we shall return; for the people of Georgia always bully than treat with the Indians, but I hope such steps will not be taken now.

I remain Sir
Your Ob'dt. Servt.
(Signed)   JOHN GALPHIN

The Honble. Henry Osborne Esqr.
   Commissioner of Indian Affairs
     Augusta

No. 7.

Rock landing 24th. June 1789

GENTN.,

I arrived here yesterday and meeting Mr. Brian the interpreter this morning he informed me of seeing a Mr. White head on his way from the nation who did not altogether give him a true account of us, but I can assure you that I have it in my power to settle every matter amicably and satisfactorily to both parties.

I shall wait at this place untill I get an answer to return with—as your honors will find by my instructions that I can settle every thing agreeably.
I have the Honor to be

Gentn.
Your Most Obt. Servt.
(Signed)   JOHN GALPHIN

The Honble.
Board Commissioners for Indian Affairs

No. 8.

SIR,

Upon receipt of this letter you are requested by the Chiefs to proceed to the proposed place of meeting at the Rock landing on the Oconee river where if you meet with the Commissioners you are to inform them that the Chiefs have resolved to put off the meeting for the present for the following reasons.

That when the Talk of invitation arrived here the whole body of Warriors were in Arms, owing to the Commissioners letter of last Winter, ready to turn out, but the Chiefs being ever ready to listen to just terms of peace they agreed to meet the Commissioners to treat as they requested—but some partys having early gone out could not be stopped and they having returned within a few days of the appointed time, for the Chiefs setting out for the rock landing and having done mischief in killing several people, the body of the people stop't the Chiefs from proceeding to the Oconee apprehensive that they might sustain injury and insult from the people of that Country.

The Chiefs are willing to Treat at a time when a few months having passed over each others minds will be more cool and can Talk over matters with calmness and temper, mean time they wish to have an answer from the Commissioners upon what grounds they intend to conduct the treaty on. They apprehend that some demands will be made to which they cannot agree, and they dont wish to meet them to quarrel, but rather desire when they do meet to treat of peace, to do it in a peaceable manner and to conclude a peace on terms that may make it a lasting one.

Wishing you a good journey, remain with Esteem and regard.

Your Most Obedt. Servt.

(Signed)   ALEXR. MCGILLIVRAY

Cowetas 16th. June 1789

P.S. Assure the Commissioners that every exertion will be made by the Chiefs to keep things quiet which may be depended on.

Mr. John Galphin in the Cowetas

No. 9.
To the Head Men Chiefs and Warriors of the Creek Nation

BROTHERS,

We came to this place expecting to meet you agreeably to our invitation which we sent to you by Mr. George Galphin. We are sorry any thing should have happened to prevent your coming. We have heared your reasons from your Chief Speaker Mr. McGillivray with which we are satisfied. We have consulted your beloved man Mr. John Galphin and have fixed the time for meeting you all at this place to be the 15th. of September next. We hope you will be punctual in coming that all disputes may be settled and we may again take you by the hand as friends and brothers.

As a mark of your good intentions we shall expect all the prisoners in the Nation both Whites and Blacks will be sent to this place as soon as possible, where one of us will remain to receive them.

We have strictly charged our people not to cross over to your side of the Oconee and we expect your people will not come on this side, except at this place, before the time for holding the Treaty.

We shall expect that all your people will be prohibited from committing any kind of depredations against ours: so that peace may be preserved and all of us meet at the appointed time as friends and brothers.

(Signed)   ANDW. PICKENS
H. OSBORNE

Rock landing on the Oconee
June 29th. 1789

No. 10.

SIR,

We have received your letter to Mr. John Galphin, and are very sorry we could not have the pleasure of seeing you at the time appointed, but as we have fixed a time agreeable to your wish we hope nothing will prevent your being present on the 15th. of September next. It is our wish and desire to make a firm and lasting peace *on liberal terms* with all the Chiefs of the nation. One of us will remain at this place to have every thing prepared for the Treaty and to receive as many of the Prisoners as can be sent down before that period. You will oblige us much by useing your influence on this subject as it will have a very happy effect in this Country, and tend to promote a good understanding between the Indians and our people, We expect all the prisoners that cannot be sent immediately will be brought to the Treaty.

There are few things vexes the people of this Country so much as having their horses stolen—we wish and have no doubt but you will put a stop to that practice in future and that you will order as many of the stolen horses as can be found in the Nation to be sent to us.

Mrs. Girerdeau a widow lady of liberty County was plundered by a party of your Nation in August last and eight Negroes taken off. She has five young children and the Negroes were the bulk of her and their property, feeling for the widow and Orphans, we have granted her eldest son permission to accompany Mr. Galphin to the Nation. We recommend him to your humanity in the strongest terms, and request you to afford him every necessary assistance in regaining the property, he will return by this rout and we shall be happy to have an oppertunity of rendering you a similar service either in a public or private capacity.

We have spoken very freely to Mr. Galphin, he will give you every necessary information and do away any doubts that may have remained on your mind. It would give us great satisfaction to have some private conversation with you and him prior to the public Talks: We doubt not but all matters may be so settled between us, as will make the Treaty both easy and agreeable to all parties.

For your satisfaction we inclose you a resolve of the Executive of this State and an order of the Governor thereon. It is our wish that no people whatever belonging to the United States should be disturbed or injured either in their persons or property till all matters are finally settled between us.

We are Sir
Your Obedient and
very Humble Servts.
(Signed)   ANDW. PICKENS
H. OSBORNE
Commissioners

Rock Landing
  June 30th. 1789 }

To Alexander McGillivray Esqr.
  Chief Speaker in the
    Creek Nation[1]

[1] A copy of the report with enclosures, in the hand of William Knox, is in Transcribed Reports and Communications from Executive Departments, 1789–1814, Records of the Secretary, SR, DNA. It is related to George Washington's message journalized August 22, 1789.

Beverley Randolph to the President

Richmond August 5th. 1789

SIR,

Two Chiefs of the Cherokee nation of Indians arrived here a few days ago accompanied by Mr. Bennet Ballew, who has full powers from a number of Towns to lay before you their Grievances, and to make some proposals, which may eventually preserve harmony between the Citizens of the United States and the Indians, and perhaps be productive of considerable advantages to both parties. It is at the particular request of these unfortunate people, that I introduce them to you. They appear to me to have been much oppressed, should you view them in this light, your well known regard to public as well as private justice will insure to them every exertion of your power in their behalf. I am unacquainted with Mr. Ballew but I think I owe it to him to inform you, that he is strongly recommended to me by the Honorable William Fleming, as an honest, upright, intelligent man.

I have the Honour
    to be with the highest respect
      your obt. Servant,
        BEVERLEY RANDOLPH[1]

[1] The letter, in the hand of an unknown clerk and signed by Beverley Randolph, is in President's Messages on Indian Relations, Executive Proceedings, SR, DNA. It is related to George Washington's message journalized August 22, 1789. A transcript in a nineteenth-century hand, probably made by ASP, is in the above location.

Bennet Ballew to the President

To the president of the united states of America, the memorial of Bennet Ballew, Agent plenipotentiary from the chiefs & Head warriors of Cherokee Nation, resident & living in the towns of Chota, Toquoh, Cettico Little Telliquo Tumotly, Nioh or the Tassel's town, Coettee, Chilhowah Tallassee, Big Tilliquo,

Big Highwassa, Cheestowa, Eastanolee Chatanugah Chickamaugah, Stickoee Ottilletaraconahah, Catatogah, Nicojachee, Tuskeegah and Cheescheehah, lying on & being on the Great rivers Tenasee Tilliquo Highwassa Ammoah &c. respectfully shewith, that your memorialist, sensible of your past exertions and pleased with the thought of your continued efforts for the well fare & happiness of the united states in particular and of mankind in general, and that nothing which concerns them will be thought be ~~low~~ neath your attention; your memorialist is encouraged to lay before you a brief account of the present unhappy & distressed situation of the Cherokee Indians, notwithstanding his want of abilities to do justice to a cause of such difficulty and importance. From his long residence among them, & other Indian Nations on the Southwestern frontiers of the united States, he hath in some measure become acquainted with their language, manners, & politicks; and more particularly with their hardships & sufferings, from the unrighteous & cruel war lately waged against them. Your memorialist being importuned by the distressed Chiefs of the Nation, to lay their grievances before the beloved President of the united states, & solicit redress, being deeply impressed with compassion for their sufferings, and ~~instigated~~ impelled by the apparent advantages that must accrue to the united States should a firm & lasting peace & union be effected, he was from these considerations induced to undertake the arduous though pleasing task; relying chiefly on the providential influence of the supreme ruler of the universe, on the justice & energy of the federal government and on the magnanimity & benevolence of its First Magistrate, for success in his feeble tho' earnest endeavours to rescue a nation from the deepest imaginable distress, and to ~~render~~ make them a prosperous & a happy people.

They thought that they had a well grounded hope that they might ~~have~~ quietly & peaceably have enjoyed all their lands within the boundary lines established by the treaty of HOPEWELL, in the year 1785; but to their great mortification & distress, the white people, chiefly from North Carolina, have made daily incroachments upon them; and there are now upwards of three thousand families settled within those boundary lines. After receiving reiterated insults & injuries from some of those settlers, a few of the young warriors killed a family of white people within those boundaries, & soon after the nation in general experienced the most dreadful calamities that refined cruelty could devise, or the vindictive arm of Vengeance inflict. Their flourishg. fields of corn & pulse were destroyed & laid waste, some of their wives & children were burnt alive in their town houses, with the most unrelenting barbarity; and to fill up the measure of [blotted out] deception and cruelty, some of their chiefs, who ~~had~~ were ever [blotted out] disposed to peace with the white people, were decoyed, unarmed, into their camp by the hoisting a white flag, & by repeated decrations of friendship and kindness and there massacred in cold blood. Among these were the Old Tassel and his son, who were characterised by their kind offices to the white people, & veneration for the American flag, insomuch that for many years, it was constantly flying at their door.

When your memorialist came to French Broad river, in January last, he found that part of the country in great confusion, and the war carried on with all its horrors, between a party of the North Carolinians and the Cherokees, ~~Indians~~ the former, as it would appear, were determined to extirpate the Indians, & to claim the sole property in their lands. Many prisoners being taken on both sides, & an exchange being earnestly wished for by the Carolinians concerned, they [*blotted out*] chose your memorialist as a neutral person, & one who was formerly acquainted with that nation (having lived long among them as a prisoner during part of our war with the British) [*blotted out*] to bring about the exchange. Your memorialist chearfully undertook, & happily effected it, although strongly opposed by messrs. Dromgoole & Martin of North Carolina, whose scheme was apparently to draw the Indians into a treaty, with a view to extort their lands from them, though expressly contrary to a proclamation of Congress.

The Carolinians, to give a colour to the war, allege that the Cherokees broke the treaty of Hopewell in 1785; but this the Cherokees positively deny, and declare that their intention, even since that time, has [*blotted out*] uniformly been to preserve peace & a good understanding with the white people; and which they earnestly wish to have once more restored; and after engaging your memorialist to assist them with his best endeavours, as far as is consistent with his duty as a citizen of the united States, they, in a grand council of the Nation, after long & mature deliberation, came to the following resolutions.

1st. "That we will immediately treat with all nations with whom we are at war, & procure peace & reconciliation, if possible," which has been happily effected.

2d. "That we will petition Congress to obtain a mutual, perfect & strict alliance with the United States, & abide by their Instructions in all matters of peace & war, provided they secure to us the lands of our forefathers, as bounded by the treaty of Hopewell, in the year 1785."

3d. "That the part of the nation lying adjacent to French Broad & Holstein rivers be incorporated with the white people and become subjects of the united States, living under the same laws with them."

These Resolves the Cherokee Nation most ardently wish may be by your memorialist (accompanied by two of their Chiefs, Nontowakee & Kasokanoe) laid before you sir, as Chief magistrate of the united States, & through you, communicated to the Congress; as some acts of the legislature may perhaps be necessary to carry their system into full effect, & compleat their wishes.

If your Memorialist can be, but in a small degree, instrumental in obtaining for those unfortunate people, & their posterity, the inestimable blessings of peace liberty & safety, he will feel himself one of the happiest of Mankind.

BENNET BALLEW

New York 22 Augt. 1789[1]

[1] The memorial, in the hand of Bennet Ballew, is in President's Messages on Indian Relations, Executive Proceedings, SR, DNA. It is related to George Washington's message journaled August 22, 1789. A transcript in a nineteenth-century hand, probably made by ASP, is in the above location.

Instructions to the Commissioners for Southern Indians

To BENJAMIN LINCOLN, CYRUS GRIFFIN and DAVID HUMPHREYS Esquires, Commissioners plenipotentiary, for negociating and concluding treaties of Peace with the independent tribes or Nations of Indians within the limits of the United States, south of the River Ohio.

Gentlemen,

The United States consider it as an object of high national importance not only to be at peace with the powerful tribes or Nations of Indians south of the Ohio but if possible by a just and liberal system of policy to conciliate and attach them to the interests of the Union.

In order therefore that you may be possessed of all the information relative to the southern Indians contained in the public documents, you have herewith delivered to you copies of the following papers.

To wit,

The several statements which have been made on this subject from the War Office, to which are added—Copies of the Treaties which have been made by the United States with the Cherokees, Chickasaws and Choctaws, and the Commissioners report thereon—The proceedings and reports of James White Esquire Superintendant for the Southern District—The reports of Messrs. Winn and Martin temporary Superintendants—The Resolves of Congress under which Commissioners have been appointed by the States of North Carolina, South Carolina and Georgia, and the said Commissioners Reports—And also certain papers transmitted by Georgia against Joseph Martin one of the aforesaid temporary Commissioners.

The first great object of your Commission is to negociate and establish peace between the State of Georgia and the Creek Nation. The whole Nation must be fully represented and solemnly acknowledged to be so by the Creeks themselves.

You will find the ostensible and probably the real cause of hostilities between Georgia and the Creeks to consist in a difference of Judgment of three Treaties stated to have been made between the said parties, to wit: at Augusta in 1783, at Galphinston in 1785, and at Shoulder Bone in 1786—Copies of which you have herewith delivered to you.

It is a circumstance of the highest consequence to investigate thoroughly all the facts under which the said Treaties were made. The official papers will afford you great information on this subject.

On the one side the objections against the Justice of said Treaties are stated in the several communications of Mr. McGillivray and the communications of the lower Creeks to Mr. White the Superintendant.

On the other side the statement made by the Legislature of Georgia, contains the reasons in support of the Treaties.

The opinion of the Commissioners of the United States of the Treaty of Galphinston is contained in their reports, and the communications of James White Esqr. the Superintendant will shew his Judgment on the case.

But in addition to all these written evidences it may be proper in order that the investigation be conducted with the most perfect impartiality to have such viva voce testimony as can be obtained.

For this purpose you will request the Governor, and Legislature of Georgia if in session, to authorize such person or persons to attend the treaty as he or they may think proper, in order to give you such information as you may request from time to time of the transactions relative to said Treaties.

You will also endeavour to ascertain the facts relative to the said Treaties from the Creeks.

And you will further endeavor to obtain information on Oath of the manner in which the said Treaties were held from such unprejudiced respectable private Characters who were present at the said Treaties as you shall be able to find.

The main points to be ascertained are,

1st. Whether all the lands belonging to the upper and lower Creeks are the common property of the whole Nation?

Or

2dly. Were the lands stated to have been ceded to Georgia by the three treaties or either of them acknowledged by the Upper Creeks to be the sole property of the Lower Creeks?

3dly. Were the acknowledged proprietors of the lands, stated to have been ceded to Georgia, present, or fully represented, at the said three Treaties?

4thly. Did the Creeks present at the said treaties, act with a full understanding of the Cessions, they are stated to have made?

5thly. Were the said Treaties and Cession freely made on the part of the Creeks, uninfluenced by any threat or implication of force?

These circumstances and all others connected therewith, must be critically examined into, in order that you may form your judgment on the said treaties with the greatest accuracy.

If the result of your investigation should be, that the said three treaties and the cessions of land therein contained, were made by a full and authorized representation of the Creek Nation—or that the cessions of land was obtained with the full understanding and free consent of the acknowledged proprietors, and that there were no circumstances of unfairness or constraint of any sort, used to induce the Creeks to make the cessions to Georgia, in this case precisely, you are to insist on a formal renewal and confirmation *of the said Cessions to Georgia,* or such parts thereof as you shall find just. If the Creeks after hearing all your arguments for the renewal of the said Treaties so far as the same may respect the confirmation of such parts of the Cessions of land contained therein as you shall have adjudged just and equitable, should obstinately refuse to confirm the same to Georgia, then you are to inform them that the Arms of the Union will be called forth for the protection of Georgia in the peaceable and just protection of the said lands—and in case the Creeks attempt any molestation or injury to Georgia, that they will be deemed the enemies of the United States and punished accordingly.

But if it should result from your enquiries, that the said treaties and cessions were obtained on the part of Georgia, under such circumstances as to preclude the interference of the United States consistently with their justice and dignity, you are not to urge or persuade the Creeks to a renewal or confirmation thereof.

It is however to be observed that Georgia has proceeded on the principle that the Cessions stated to have been made at Augusta in 1783 was fairly obtained—And that the said State has surveyed and divided the Lands between the Ogechee and Oconee among certain descriptions of its Citizens—That the said Citizens have settled and planted on said Lands in great numbers—should therefore the result of your investigation be unfavorable to the claims of Georgia, it would be highly embarrassing to that State to relinquish the said Lands to the Creeks.

Hence it will be an important accommodation to Georgia to obtain from the Creeks a regular conveyance of the said Lands lying between the Ogechee and Oconee. To accomplish this object therefore you are specially required to use your highest exertions with the Creeks. On your success materially depends the internal peace of Georgia, and probably its attachment to the general government of the United States.

If the prejudices of the Creeks against the United States are not too deeply rooted, it is presumed, that such advantages to that Nation can be stipulated, as to induce them, not only to relinquish to Georgia the Lands in question, but to attach them sincerely and permanently to the United States.

The disputed Lands being entirely despoiled of their game by the settlements are therefore no longer valuable to the Creeks as hunting grounds. If they have not been fairly purchased of the real proprietors by Georgia it ought to be done.

In case the Creeks therefore would be willing to make a proper conveyance, for a given sum, you will stipulate that the same shall be paid by Georgia, at a certain period, or in case of failure by the United States.

While negociating the price to be given for the said Land, you will have due regard to the sums which Georgia actually paid at the Treaty of Augusta—to the present value of the Lands as hunting grounds—and to the other considerations hereafter specified.

In this part of the negociation it would be desireable that the persons who may be appointed by the Governor or Legislature of Georgia to attend the Treaty should concur with you as to the sum which in case of purchase, shall be stipulated to be given.

In addition to the purchase Money for the Lands, and for the further great purpose of attaching the Creeks to the United States, provided the same in your mature judgments should be necessary, you are hereby empowered to make the following stipulations.

1st. A secure Port to the Creeks or their Head Men, on the Altamaha, St. Mary's or any place between the said Rivers, into which, or from which, the Creeks may import or export the articles of Merchandize necessary to the Indian commerce on the same terms as the Citizens of the United States—The number of Arms and quantity of Ammunition however to be regulated by the quantity that shall be regarded as necessary for the hunters.

If any apprehensions should be entertained on the part of the Creeks on account of the safety of the Goods which they might so import or export, it may be stipulated that the same should be protected by a Company of the regular troops of the United States.

The trade of the Creeks is said at present to be engrossed by a company of British Merchants stationed at one of the Bahama Islands, who have connected Mr. McGillivray with them as a partner. The Spaniards have permitted some of the Rivers which empty into the Gulph of Mexico to be the channel of this trade for a certain number of years. Some impediments, or impositions of duties appear to have disgusted Mr. McGillivray with the Spaniards, or with the communication, and renders him desirous of a Port in the United States. If these circumstances could be the means of breaking his connection with the Spanish Colonies, it would be wise policy to afford the Creeks a Port and to protect them in every thing relative thereto.

2ly. Gifts in goods or Money to some and if necessary honorary military distinctions to others, of the influential Chiefs.

The Presents will be regulated by your judgment.

The idea of military distinction arises from the information that Mr. McGillivray possesses a Commission of Colonel or Lieutenant Colonel from the King of Spain. If he could be induced to resign that Commission by the offer of one, a grade higher, the offer ought to be made and substantiated, on his taking a solemn Oath of Allegiance to the United States.

Mr. McGillivray is stated to possess great abilities and an unlimited influence over the Creek Nation, and part of the Cherokees. It is an object worthy of considerable exertion to attach him warmly to the United States. The measure could be attempted and urged with great propriety as it respects his fidelity to the Creeks, and the continuance of his own importance in that Nation.

The United States do not want the Creek Lands, they desire only to be the friends and protectors of the Creeks, and to treat them with humanity and justice.

In case you should be satisfied of his compliance with your desires you will deliver him the presents which are particularly designated for him. And also give him assurances of such pecuniary rewards from the United States as you may think reasonable, consequent on the evidence of his future favorable conduct.

3dly. If you should find the measure necessary in order to accomplish the before recited objects you will further stipulate a solemn guarantee of the United States to the Creeks of their remaining territory, to be supported if necessary by a line of military posts.

This measure will most probably be highly satisfactory to the Creeks as it will entirely prevent any attempts to purchase any part of their Lands, and it will at the same time impress them with the moderation and justice of the General Government.

If these offers with all the benefits resulting therefrom, should be insufficient to induce the Creeks to agree voluntarily to relinquish the disputed Lands between the Ogechee and Oconee Rivers you cannot with propriety make a tender of more favorable conditions.

In this event however you may endeavor to conclude a treaty and establish therein a temporary boundary making the Oconee the line—To stipulate the secure port, and the pecuniary and honorary considerations before recited.

You will establish the principle in case of concluding a Treaty that the Creeks who are within the limits of the United States acknowledge themselves to be under the protection of the United States of America, and of no other Sovereign whosoever and also that they are not to hold any treaty with an individual State nor with the individuals of any State.

You will also endeavor without making it an ultimatum to establish such direct trade as the government of the Union shall authorize. This point however is to be managed with the greatest delicacy for the before recited reasons.

In the general objects of the restoration of Prisoners, Negroes &ca., you will conform to the Treaties of Hopewell with the Cherokees, Chickasaws and Choctaws.

You will also endeavour to obtain a stipulation for certain Missionaries to reside in the Nation provided the general government should think proper to adopt the measure—These Men to be precluded from trade or attempting to purchase any Lands but to have a certain reasonable quantity per head allowed for the purpose of cultivation. The object of this establishment would be the happiness of the Indians, teaching them the great duties of Religion and Morality, and to inculcate a friendship and attachment to the United States.

If after you have made your communications to the Creeks, and you are persuaded that you are fully understood by them, they should refuse to treat and conclude a peace on the terms you propose, it may be concluded that they are decided on a continuance of acts of hostility, and that they ought to be guarded against as the determined enemies of the United States.

In this case you will report such plans both for defensive and offensive measures so as best to protect the Citizens of the United States on the frontiers from any acts of injury or hostility of the Creeks.

Although the policy of attaching influential Chiefs by pecuniary or honorary considerations may not be doubted, yet it has been otherwise with respect to making presents to the Commonality among the Indians. In case therefore you find that the Creeks are willing to relinquish the Land between the Ogechee and Oconee on further payments for the same you will endeavour to stipulate that the mass of the goods you have in charge for the Treaty should be received by the Indians as part or the whole of the consideration for the conveyance of the said Lands as you shall judge proper.

Messrs. Osborne and Pickens have in their report of the 30th. of June last stated that they have agreed to hold a general Treaty with the Creeks at the Rock-landing on the Oconee River in the State of Georgia on the 15th. of September next ensuing. You will make every exertion to be there at that time. Immediately on your arrival at Savannah, you will arrange the transportation by Land or Water of the Goods and Provisions under your direction to the place of Treaty or towards the same so as to arrive with all possible expedition. At the same time you will dispatch expresses to the Governor notifying him of your Commission and arrival, and also to Messrs. Osborne and Pickens, and as soon after as possible you will repair to the place affixed for treating. The troops and the goods may follow agreeably to your directions—perhaps you may change the place of Treaty to some place to which your goods might be transported with greater facility than the Rock-Landing on the Oconee River.

But notwithstanding your greatest exertions it may happen that your arrival may be so retarded, that Messrs. Pickens and Osborne may have held a Treaty, and the Indians may have departed to their own Country.

In this case you will carefully enquire whether there were present at the Treaty a full representation of the whole Creek Nation, and particularly Mr. McGillivray, and whether the Treaty was made under such circumstances as to be consistent with the justice of the United States, and conformable to the spirit of these Instructions. If so you will confirm and ratify the same in as full a manner as if you had been actually present. But if an inadequate representation only should have been present, or any circumstances should have been adopted of which the United States could not with justice and dignity approve, in this case you will use your best endeavours to persuade the Creeks to attend a new Treaty at such place and at such time as you may judge proper. You will observe the same conduct to collect the Creeks in case it should appear that they from any circumstance are disinclined to attend generally the Treaty on the 15th. of September, or provided your arrival should be posterior to that period and you shall learn they did not attend agreeably to the invitation of Messrs. Pickens and Osborne.

[During your negociations with the Creeks you will endeavour to ascertain the following points.

1st.   The number of Warriors in the whole Nation including Upper and Lower Creeks and Semanolies.

2d.   Whether they are armed with common or Rifle Muskets, or in any other manner, and how furnished with Ammunition.

3d.   The number of each division—of Upper Creeks—Lower Creeks—and Semanolies.

4th.   The number of Women and Children and Old Men in each district.

5th.   The number of Towns in each District.

6th.   The names, Characters and residence of the most influential Chiefs—and as far as the same may be their grades of influence.

7th.   The kinds of Government (if any) of the Towns, Districts and Nation.

8th.   Whether they are hunters only, or whether they cultivate and possess Cattle—if so the degree of cultivation and number of Cattle.

9th.   The usual hunting grounds of the whole Nation—and their Districts.

10th.   The kinds and value of Furrs taken annually, and how disposed of.

11th.   The amount of the European goods annually consumed.

12th.   Whether Genseng abounds in that Country—if so whether it is gathered in any considerable quantities?

13th.   To ascertain the nature of the Country west from Georgia to the Mississippi—whether mountainous, hilly, level, or abounding with low grounds and Morasses—The nature of the Soil and kinds of growth.

14th.   To ascertain particularly how far northward the waters of the Mobile, Apalachicola, and Altamaha Rivers are navigable for boats—and the nearest land portages from the northern navigable streams of said rivers to the southern navigable waters or streams of the Tennessee River. The accurate knowledge of this subject is of considerable importance, but the enquiries relative thereto should be circuitously conducted.

15th. To ascertain with great precision the nature of the connexion of the Creeks with the Spaniards, and if practicable to obtain copies of any Treaties between them—Whether the predominating prejudices of the Creeks are in favor or against the Spaniards, and particularly the State of Mr. McGillivray's mind on this subject.

16th. You will endeavor as far as your opportunities will admit to ascertain similar facts relative to the Cherokees, Chickasaws and Choctaws as are contained in the before recited requests relative to the Creeks.]

In case of your concluding a treaty with the Creeks and it should be your Judgment, that a line of military posts would be necessary, to the due observance thereof, and also as a security of the peace with the Cherokees you will report a plan for the stations which should be taken, and the number of troops which should occupy each.

The people who are settled on Cumberland River have just cause of complaints against the Creeks who have during the present year murdered several families within that District. The Creeks can have no cause of complaint against that settlement. This circumstance is to be strongly stated to the Creeks and in case of a continuance of their murders the vengeance of the Union is to be denounced against them.

The peculiar case of the Cherokees seems to require the immediate interposition of the justice of the United States. But as that Nation of Indians are principally resident within the territory claimed by North Carolina which is not a Member of the present Union it may be doubted whether any efficient measures in favor of the Cherokees could be adopted immediately.

By the public News-papers it appears that on the 16th. of June last, a truce was concluded with the Cherokees by Mr. John Steele on behalf of the State of North Carolina. In this truce a Treaty was stipulated to be held as soon as possible and in the mean time all hostilities should cease on both sides.

In the event of North Carolina adopting the Constitution of the United States it will be incumbent on the general government to take every wise measure for carrying into effect the substance of the Treaty at Hopewell. In the mean time you will send a Message to the Cherokees stating to them the difficulties arising from the local claims of North Carolina as far as the same may be proper— That when these shall be removed the United States will convince the Cherokees of their justice and friendship.

You will also transmit a Message to the Whites in the neighbourhood of the Cherokees enjoining an observance of the Truce made by Mr. Steele, until a general Treaty shall take place when justice shall be administered to all parties.

The two Cherokees who have lately come to this City with their Conductor Mr. Bennet Ballew, are to go under your direction to the place of treaty. Good policy requires that they should be kindly treated although there are suspicions that the conduct of Bennet Ballew has not been very proper with respect to the Lands of the Cherokees. You will endeavour to ascertain his real Character and designs and make such use of him as you shall think proper. You have delivered to you Copies of the Papers which Mr. Ballew presented from the Cherokees.

The Treaties with the Choctaws and Chickasaws will inform you of the stipulations of the United States to extend trade to those Nations. You will report a plan for carrying into effect the said stipulations, and you will also transmit to the said Nations messages containing assurances of the continuance of the friendship of the United States and of the intentions of the general government of extending the trade to them agreeably to the Treaties of Hopewell.

You will have regular invoices of all Articles delivered to you for the proposed treaty and you will keep fair accounts of all your disbursements, which you will regularly settle at the Treasury of the United States.

And in all cases where the same may be proper, consistently with the secrecy necessary to be observed, the delivery of the goods ought to be attested by the Commissioned Officers of the Troops who should attend the Commissioners.

You will also keep a regular journal of your transactions and report the same.

It is presumed that you will conduct all your disbursements by that proper economy so necessary to be observed in all transactions of the general government.

You will learn by the Papers delivered to you, that certain goods were left by the Commissioners after the Treaty at Hopewell in the commencement of the Year 1786. It is probable that these goods may have been delivered to Messrs. Pickens and Osborne, you will therefore apply to said Gentlemen for regular invoices of all the goods in their possession for the treaty, distinguishing the means by which they became possessed thereof.

You will also request of them an account of the monies or goods they may have received of the States of South Carolina and Georgia in consequence of the Resolves of Congress of the 26th October 1787, and August 14th. 1788.

As the said Messrs. Pickens and Osborne will most probably be at the proposed place of Treaty with the expectation of conducting the same, you will deliver them the Letter containing the reasons of government for appointing new Commissioners. Were there any services at the Treaty, in which you could employ them, it might be proper so to do.

You will endeavour to avail yourselves as far as may be, of any arrangements which may have been taken by Georgia for the supplies of provision during the holding of the Treaty, or for furnishing the means of transportation, for which the said State will have Credit on the before recited requisitions of Congress of the 26th. of October 1787, and the 14th. of August 1788.

You will please to observe that the whole sum that can be constitutionally expended for the proposed Treaty with the Creeks shall not exceed the sum of twenty thousand dollars. The goods and money which have been delivered to you and the expences which will arise by the removal and return of the Troops, and your own pay will amount to ———— —you will therefore see the necessity of economizing your means, and that the same cannot be extended.

It is however to be observed that the sums you shall think proper to stipulate to the Creeks for the Cessions of the Lands between the Ogechee and Oconee is to be considered additional to the said twenty thousand dollars.

You will from time to time communicate your progress to the Secretary of the War Department, and receive such further directions from him as the case may require.

The Company of Artillery commanded by Capt. Burbeck will accompany you to the place of Treaty and be under your orders. As soon as the Treaty shall be finished you will take the proper measures for the return of the Company to this place, as their time of service will soon expire. The Company will receive one Month and an halfs pay and be furnished with three months rations, which you will cause to be transported as the service may require.

These instructions will be the governing principles of your conduct and they are to be regarded as secret.

But many circumstances may arise which may render some degree of modification necessary. In every event however you will please to remember—That the Government of the United States are determined that their administration of Indian Affairs shall be directed entirely by the great principles of Justice and humanity.

As soon as you shall have concluded your Negociations with the Creeks, and forwarded your Messages as herein directed you will return to this place and make a full report of all your transactions to the Secretary of the War Department.

Given under my hand at the City of New York this 29th. day of August 1789.

Go. WASHINGTON

By Command
of the President of the United States,

H. KNOX[1]

[1] An attested copy of the instructions, in the hand of Samuel Otis, Jr., is in Transcribed Treaties and Conventions, 1789–1801, Records of the Secretary, SR, DNA. The document is related to George Washington's message journalized January 11, 1790.

Report of the Commissioners for Southern Indians

New York, 17th November 1789

SIR,

We have kept a regular Journal of our Negotiations with the Creek Nation, and now make a full Report of the Mission to you as Secretary of the War Department.

We are Sir &c.

B. LINCOLN

(signed)   CYRUS GRIFFIN

D. HUMPHREYS

To the Honble.
Henry Knox Esqr.

A REPORT of the Proceedings of the Commissioners of the United States of

America, for restoring and establishing Peace and Amity, between the United States and all Nations of Indians situated within the Limits of the said States, Southward of the River Ohio.

On the thirty first day of August last We sailed from New York, and arrived at Savannah in the night of the 10th. of September,

In conformity to our Instructions, on the 11th. we wrote the following Letters to the Governor of the State of Georgia; and to Messrs. Pickens & Osborne, the Commissioners then at the Rock Landing.

"Savannah 11th. Septr. 1789

"SIR,

"We have been honored by the Supreme Executive of the United States with the Appointment of Commissioners Plenipotentiary for negotiating and concluding a Treaty of Peace with the Independent Tribes or Nations of Indians within the Limits of the United States, South of the River Ohio, and in consequence thereof it becomes our duty by the earliest Opportunity to communicate this information to your Honor. In our Negotiations many Subjects important to the Interests of the State of Georgia will probably be discussed; Your Honor will therefore, if you should think the measure necessary, appoint some Person or Persons the best informed in the Nature of our Business to attend the Commissioners, that they may from time to time receive from them such information as may be necessary on the Subject of their Negotiations. The Commissioners expect to leave this Town on the morrow, and to be at Augusta with all possible dispatch.

"In expectation that a large number of the Natives would be at the Rock Landing, and lest there might not be a full supply of Provisions to be obtained in the Vicinity thereof, a very considerable quantity of salted Provisions and Flour were put on board of our Vessels, the transportation of which we find will be attended with great delay and expence. We shall therefore store a considerable proportion of it here until Your Honor's opinion can be known, whether there are high degrees of probability that fresh Beef and Indian Corn can be had at or convenient to the Rock Landing, sufficient to answer the great demands which it is very certain will be made for those Articles. If such a probability shall not exist which shall fully satisfy your Honor, the Commissioners in that case have to beg that an Express may be immediately forwarded to Major Habersham, requesting him to forward the whole of the Flour in his hands, or such parts as you may think necessary, by water to Augusta.

"As it is important that we should, as soon as possible, know the state of the Supplies on which we are to rely while on the Negotiation, and as we have been taught to expect that we should be aided essentially by this State we must beg that your Honor would order to be made out for our use, an Invoice of such Stores, the Property of Georgia, as will be placed in our Hands.

"We have the Honor to be &c.

B. LINCOLN

                                        (signed)   C. GRIFFIN
"His Honor the Governor)   D. HUMPHREYS
of the State of Georgia")

                                        "Savannah 11th Septemr. 1789
"GENTLEMEN,
    "Having been appointed Commissioners Plenipotentiary by the Supreme
Executive of the United States of America for concluding Treaties of Peace and
Amity with the Indian Nations South of the Ohio, We thought proper to give
you the earliest possible Notice of our Appointment.
    "The Reasons why it was deemed necessary that the Characters employed in
the execution of this business should not belong to any of the States bordering on
those Tribes of Indians, with whom the Treaties are proposed to be formed,
will be fully, and, we trust, satisfactorily explained to you by the Letter from the
Secretary at War, which we shall have the honor of delivering into your hands.
    "We have also to inform you, that we shall set off from this place as early as
we can possibly make the necessary arrangements, and reach you as soon as may
be. In the mean time, we earnestly hope and expect that you will not remit your
endeavours to have every thing in readiness to give dispatch and success to the
Negotiations; and you will please to communicate every necessary information to
the Creek Nation on the subject. We are convinced this will be the case, because
the interest and happiness of the State of Georgia, not less than the dignity and
honor of the United States seem to require it.
    "On our part, you will be assured Gentlemen, that we shall always take a
particular pleasure in doing Justice to your merits, by making the most favorable
Representations of your public services being with the greatest Respect,
"The Honble.   )   "Gentlemen, Your &c.
    Andrew Pickens   )   B. LINCOLN
    H. Osborne Esqrs.)   (signed)   C. GRIFFIN
    Rock Landing   )   D. HUMPHREYS"

    Immediately after writing these Letters we proceeded to make the necessary
arrangements, relative to the transportation of ourselves, and also a part of the
Goods and Provisions under our direction to the Place of Treaty. We then
dispatched the subsequent Communication to the Secretary at War.

                                        "Savannah 12th. September 1789
"SIR,
    "We arrived here the night before last, after an unusually rough Passage. The
Transport with the Troops (all well) had been in Port nearly two days. We
learnt, upon our arrival, that Mr. McGillevray was actually on his way to the
place for holding the Treaty; and, on the second day of this Month, at a short
distance from it. The number of the Indians who attend him, is said to be
between three and four thousands. Our first care was to send an Express to the
Governor and the late Commissioners, announcing our Mission and suggesting
such arrangements as we deemed indispensable. Particularly we gave information

to the Governor, that from the difficulty of procuring the means of transportation, we should leave the greatest part of the Provisions which we had brought with us at this place, unless in his Judgment they should be absolutely necessary for supporting the Indians, during the continuance of the Treaty. In this case he was requested to send back an Express to Major Habersham, that consequent measures might be taken instantaneously.

"We found it impossible to hire Horses, and therefore have been obliged to purchase five to carry us forward. It was with great difficulty that we have obtained a few poor Teams to transport the most essentially necessary Articles with the Troops, who will march by the rout of Augusta to morrow morning. The greater part of the remaining Stores will at the same time proceed by water to that place; for which place also we shall commence our Journey early in the Morning. Mr. Bellew and the Indians with him, having expressed an earnest inclination of returning to their own Country from hence, and as it would save a travel of at least two hundred Miles, we have furnished them with the means of doing it, and have sent friendly Messages to the Chickasaws, Choctaws and Cherokees by them.

"We have likewise sent an Address to the white People of the State of North Carolina bordering on the Country inhabited by the latter.

"The Captains of the two Sloops which came with us to this place, having insisted upon receiving their Money here, we have accordingly paid them.

"We have the honor to be &c.

B. Lincoln

(signed) C. Griffin

D. Humphreys

"The Honble.

The Secretary at

War

New York"

From Savannah we transmitted friendly Talks to the Cherokees, Chicasaws and Choctaws, expressed in the following words.

"A Message to the Cherokee Nation of Indians, from the Commissioners Plenipotentiary for restoring and establishing Peace and Amity between the United States of America and all the Indian Nations situated within the limits of the said States southward of the River Ohio.

"Brothers of the Cherokee Nation!

"We have been made very happy by receiving information from the Public News-Papers, that, on the 16th. of June last, a Truce was concluded with your Nation by the Commissioner of North Carolina, on behalf of that State: and that, in this Truce, a Treaty was stipulated to be held as soon as possible, and in the mean time that all hostilities should cease on both sides.

"Whereupon, We the Commissioners Plenipotentiary aforesaid do think proper to confirm the said Truce and to give the strongest assurances of the friendly dispositions of the United States towards the Cherokee Nation. And we have made the same known to all those whom it might concern and particularly to all the Inhabitants of the Frontiers bordering on the Cherokee Towns and

Settlements; declaring, in consequence of the full powers vested in us by the Supreme Executive of the United States of America, that it is the sincere intention of the said States to cultivate a friendly intercourse between our Citizens and your People: and strictly enjoining an observance of the Truce aforesaid upon the former.

"HEAD MEN & warring CHIEFS of all the CHEROKEES hearken to what we have to say to you!

"Notwithstanding there are some difficulties arising from the local Claims of North Carolina which prevent us at present from writing to you so fully as we could wish, yet we would not omit so good an Opportunity to assure you (by the return of your beloved Man Mr. Bennet Bellew and your beloved Chief Nontowaky) that when those difficulties shall be removed, the general Government of the United States will be desirous to take every wise measure to carry into effect the substance of the Treaty at Hopewell, as well as to convince you of their justice and friendship.

"NOW BROTHERS!

"We have nothing more to add at this time, except that we wish you all the Happiness which we wish to the most dear of our own fellow Citizens; and that we will send to you another Message on the subject of Public Affairs before we shall return to the beloved City of Congress from whence we came.

"DONE at Savannah under our hands and Seals this 13th day of September, in the Year of our Lord 1789, and in the 14th. Year of the Independence of the United States of America.

B. LINCOLN
(signed)   C. GRIFFIN
D. HUMPHREYS

"Attest,
D. S. FRANKS, Secy."

"A MESSAGE to the Chicasaw Nation of Indians from the Commissioners Plenipotentiary for restoring & establishing Peace and Amity between the United States of America and all the Indian Nations situated within the limits of the said States southward of the River Ohio.

"BROTHERS of the CHICASAW NATION!

"We are glad of an Opportunity by the return of your beloved Man, Mr. Bennet Ballew into your Country, to assure you of the continuation of the strong Friendship of the United States of America for your Nation. We hope that the Peace which was established between the Commissioners Plenipotentiary of the United States of America and the Commissioners Plenipotentiary, of all the Chicasaws, at Hopewell on the Keowee, the tenth day of January, in the year of our Lord one thousand seven hundred and Eighty six, will last as long as the Sun shall shine in the Heaven or the Rivers run into the Ocean.

"BROTHERS,

"We rejoice to inform you of many good things which have happened to our Nation since that Treaty. We have been fast recovering from the Wounds that were made upon us by the British, in the late War. Our People are increasing in number every day. The white Men in the other great Continent begin more and more to respect us. We are at Peace with all the World. A new and great Council Fire is kindled at our beloved City of New York; where the old and the wise Men from all our States come to consult and promote the prosperity of all America. Our union is strong. For, Brothers, we think and act as like one Man. Our great Warrior, General Washington, who, you very well know, drove our Enemies all beyond the great Water, is now the Head Man of all our Councils and the Chief of all our Warriors. He, by the advice of his wise Counsellors, has commanded us to tell you, that the United States regard the red Men with the same favorable Eye that they do the white Men: and that Justice shall always be maintained equally between them.

"Now, Head Men and warring Chiefs of all the Chicasaws listen to us! We are the mouth of the Union for you; and say that we are perfectly satisfied with your conduct since the Treaty of Hopewell; and trust we have given you reason to be satisfied with ours. All that remains for both Nations is to continue to act the same open and friendly part. You, Brothers, may rest assured that your interests are always near to our Hearts; and that, in conformity to the true intent and meaning of the eighth Article of the said Treaty, the general Government of the United States will as soon as the circumstances may conveniently admit, take measures for extending more fully to the Chicasaws, the benefits and comforts arising from a well regulated and mutually advantageous Trade.

"BROTHERS, FAREWELL!

"We wish you all the happiness and prosperity which we wish to our fellow Citizens the white men of the United States.

"DONE at Savannah, under our hands and Seals this 13th. day of September, in the Year of our Lord 1789, and in the 14th. Year of the Independence of the United States of America.

"B. LINCOLN
(signed)   C. GRIFFIN
D. HUMPHREYS*

"Attest,
D. S. FRANKS, Secy."

* A similar Message, with the necessary Alterations was sent to the Choctaws.

We also gave to Mr. Ballew a Copy of an Address to the white Inhabitants contiguous to the Cherokee Nation, accompanied by the Letter which follows it.

"To all those whom it may concern,

"The Commissioners of the United States of America, for restoring and establishing Peace and Amity, between the United States and all Nations of Indians situated within the Limits of the said States, southward of the River Ohio, send GREETING,

"For as much as we have been given to understand that a Truce hath lately been concluded at the Warford, between the Commissioner of the State of North Carolina on the one part, and the Head Men of the Cherokees on the other, in expectation that a further negotiation for the purpose of establishing permanent Peace and tranquility, will take place as soon as the circumstances may admit: and whereas we have sent an official Message to the Cherokee

Nation, with full assurances of the continuation of the good dispositions and friendly intentions of the United States towards them.

"Now THEREFORE, WE the Commissioners Plenipotentiary, aforesaid, do think proper to make the same known to all those whom it may concern, and particularly to all the Inhabitants of the Frontiers bordering on the Towns and Settlements of the said Cherokee Nation. And we do declare, in Virtue of the full Power vested in us, by the Supreme Executive of the United States of America, that it is the sincere intention of the said United States to cultivate a friendly intercourse and perpetual harmony between the Citizens of the United States and the Southern Indians on their Frontiers, upon terms of perfect equality and mutual advantage. We therefore enjoin an observance of the Truce aforesaid; and further declare, that any infraction of the tranquility now subsisting between the said contracting Parties, would directly contravene the manifest intention, and highly incur the displeasure of the Supreme Authority of the United States of America.

"DONE at Savannah, under our hands and Seals, this 13th. day of September, in the Year of our Lord 1789; and in the 14th. Year of the Independence of the United States of America.

B. LINCOLN

(signed)　C. GRIFFIN

D. HUMPHREYS

"Attest,

DAVID S. FRANKS, Secy."

"Savannah 13th. September 1789

"SIR,

"We have thought proper to entrust to your care, friendly Messages from us, the Commissioners Plenipotentiary of the United States of America for restoring and establishing Peace & Amity between the United States and all the Indian Nations situated within the limits of the said States southward of the River Ohio, to the Cherokee, Chicasaw and Choctaw Nations of Indians; which you will be pleased to deliver to the great Councils of those several Nations. We have also given to you, for the satisfaction of the Cherokees, a Copy of the Address which we propose to transmit to the white Inhabitants contiguous to the Cherokee Nation. Relying upon your diligence and zeal to execute with dispatch and fidelity the Business, that we have committed to you, we wish you a prosperous Journey, and are with due consideration.

"Sir, Your &c.

B. LINCOLN

(signed)　C. GRIFFIN

D. HUMPHREYS"

"Mr. Bennet Ballew

On the 13th. we left Savannah, and, on the 17th, arrived at Augusta. We announced our arrival to the Governor the same Evening, and the next Morning addressed to him the following Letter.

"Augusta, 18th. September 1789

"SIR,

"We are extremely unhappy to find that your Honor was so much indisposed as to prevent you from receiving Company, at the time of our arrival, last Evening. We did not, therefore, trouble you with the Letters we had in charge for your Honor, until this Morning. We now take the earliest Moment of laying them before you, with our best wishes for the reestablishment of your Health.

"We have the Honor to be &c.

B. LINCOLN

"His Honor   (signed)   C. GRIFFIN

    The Governor of the   D. HUMPHREYS

      State of Georgia"

To which his Honor was pleased to Reply

"Augusta, 18th. September 1789

"SIRS,

"I am happy that you are arrived thus far on the Business with which you are charged. Whilst we had flattering expectations that the proposed treaty would have taken place with the Creeks, we feel an additional consolation in your appointment from the knowledge you will derive, by the incidents of your negotiations, of all the causes of our complaints.

"Not having recently heard from the Rock-Landing, I could not farther act on that part of your dispatch of the 11th. respecting Provisions, than by sending for the State Agent to meet you at this place, whose arrival I expect every moment.

"Upon the other parts of that and the whole of those of this morning, I shall be happy to see you before I go into Council; and as far as lies in my Power, and I may respond for the Executive Council, you may rely on the support of 'ye Government, in the accomplishment of the Objects of your Mission.

"The Honble.   "I have the honor to be Sirs, &c.

    The Commissioners   (signed)   GEO. WALTON

      Plenipo. for negotiating

        with the Indians south of

        the Ohio"

After a free conversation with the Governor on the Objects of the Mission, he wrote us a Note enclosing an Act of Council of the same date.

"Augusta 18th. September 1789

"SIRS,

"I do myself the honor of enclosing to you a proceeding of the Executive Authority of this day.

"Those details which it shall be necessary to go into on the same ground, shall be comunicated to by Express, through,

"The Honble.   "Sirs,

    The Commissioners for   Your &c.

      Indian Affairs   (signed)   GEO. WALTON"

"IN COUNCIL,

"Augusta, 18th. September 1789

"The Letter of the Honorable the Commissioners for negotiating Treaties with the Indians south of the Ohio, of the 11th. instant dated at Savannah being taken up and another Letter of the 18th. announcing their arrival at Augusta, and enclosing a dispatch from the War Office, of the 29th of August, last, being read and considered. IT IS ORDERED, that the said Commissioners be assured, that every assistance in the power of the State, shall be given which may be necessary to give facility and effect to their Negotiations with the Creek Indians.

"Extract from the Minutes
(sign'd)   J. MEREWETHER, Sy. E. C."

An Answer to our Letter of the 11th. to Messeiurs Pickens & Osborne, we receiv'd at this place.

"Rock Landing, 16th. Septr. 1789

"GENTLEMEN,

"We had this day the honor to receive your joint Letter of the 11th. Instant. Every arrangement that was in our Power to make preparative to the Treaty has been compleat for two weeks past, and the Indians have been encamped at the distance directed by the Secretary at War during the same period.

"We have used every exertion to keep the Indians together and in good humour which has hitherto been done with great difficulty. The same Zeal and Industry shall be continued on our part for their continuance, but at the same time it is necessary to give you the earliest information that the Indians will not remain after Friday next unless you arrive here before the expiration of that day, this Mr. McGillevray informed us yesterday tho' it is his wish to remain longer.

"We have the honor to be
Gentlemen &c.
ANDW. PICKENS

"The Honble.   (sign'd)   H. OSBORNE
  B. Lincoln
  C. Griffin &
  D. Humphreys Esqrs."

To which we made the following Reply

"Augusta 18th. September 1789

"GENTLEMEN,

"We have just been honored by the receipt of the Letter which you addressed to us on the 16th. Instant; and are inexpressibly astonished at the information which you have given, as it is so diametrically contrary to the Ideas which his Honor the Governor of this State had a few Moments before, held out to us.

"Trusting, Gentlemen, that you will still continue your utmost exertions to keep the Indians together, and that, *in all events,* you will have the goodness to forward the Letter which accompanies this to Mr. McGillevray, with the utmost dispatch,

"We have the honor to be &c.

B. LINCOLN

(sign'd)   C. GRIFFIN

D. HUMPHREYS

"To Messeiurs
    Pickens & Osborne
        Rock Landing"

By the same Express we wrote to Mr. McGillevray.

"Augusta, 18th. September 1789

"SIR,

"We left New York eighteen days ago, in vested with full Powers from the Supreme Executive of the United States of America, to conclude a Treaty of Peace and Amity with the Creek Nation of Indians. For the accomplishment of an Object of so much importance, we have pressed our Journey with uncommon expedition. We arrived here last Evening, and, after making the necessary arrangement for our Baggage to follow, we propose departing from this Place for the Rock Landing this afternoon.

"Being this moment, greatly astonished by information from Messrs. Pickens & Osborne, that the Indians would certainly disperse, unless we should arrive within three days after the very day which was originally appointed for the meeting, we shall accelerate our Journey as much as possible. We therefore send an Express with this Letter to let you know that we shall be at the Rock Landing the day after to morrow, and to assure you, that, if a lasting Peace & Friendship shall not be established between the United States and the Creeks, it will not be owing to the want of the best dispositions on the part of the former.

"We are Sir, &c.

B. LINCOLN

(signed)   C. GRIFFIN

D. HUMPHREYS

"The Honble.
    Alexr. McGillevray"

On the afternoon of the 18th. we pursued our Journey, and two of the Commissioners reached the Rock Landing on the 20th. at evening, the other being unavoidably detained on the road. The following Note was immediately sent to Mr. McGillevray to which he replied early the next morning.

"The Commissioners present their most respectful Compliments to Mr. Alexr. McGillevray Chief of the Creek Nation, and have the pleasure to announce that the majority of them, a few Moments since, arrived at this place; and that without delay they shall be ready to proceed to Business.

"ALEXR. McGILLEVRAY Esq.   "Rock Landing
Great Chief of all the Creeks &c. &c. &c.   20th. Septr. 1789"

"Alexr. McGillevray and the rest of the Chiefs are very glad to hear of the arrival of the Honble. y[e] Commissioners of the United States of America at the Rock Landing, a few principal Chiefs intend to visit them this forenoon.
"The Honorable   "20th. September 1789
The Commissioners of the United States
of America at the Rock Landing"

About 11 o'Clock the following Note from Mr. McGillevray was received.

"GENTLEMEN,
"Some of the principal Chiefs accompanied by an Interpreter named Derozeau go over to pay you a visit this forenoon. I beg leave to suggest to you that a private conversation between us will be necessary previous to the opening of the Treaty, and this Camp I think to be the most convenient place for the purpose; I could therefore wish to be honored with the Company of one or two of you this Evening. In suggesting this measure I entreat Gentlemen, that you will not consider it as proceeding from a want of the proper attention in me, which is due to the very respectable characters, that compose the present Commission.
                                                "I am very respectfully
"The Honorable   )   gentlemen, &c.
The Commissioners &c. &c. }   (signed)   ALEXR. MCGILLEVRAY"

The Cussitah King, the Tellasee King & the hallowing King attended the Commissioners accordingly, as a deputation from the whole Nation to congratulate them on their arrival. After the customary Ceremony, they all expressed the most ardent wishes to establish a lasting Peace with the United States; and declared their extreme joy that the day was come which afforded a fair opportunity for accomplishing an Object so interesting and desirable to their Nation.
Soon after this Interview the following Talk was sent to the Indian Camp.

"To the Honorable Alexr. McGillevray great Chief, and all the other Head Men and warring Chiefs of the Creek Nation.
"BROTHERS,
"Having been honored with a Commission by the Supreme Executive of the United States of America, to conclude a Treaty of Peace & Amity with your Nation; we think it expedient, in the first instance, to shew you our full Powers. On the other Part we desire to be favored by you with such Evidence, as the nature of the case may admit, of the fullness and authenticity of the representation of the Creek Nation, which is now present.
"These Preliminaries being satisfactorily settled, so that hereafter there may be no complaints of partial or defective Representation, we shall be ready to make our farther Communications, as soon as the Honble. Mr. Griffin our Colleague shall arrive, which will probably be to morrow.

"21st. Septemr. 1789   (signed)   B. LINCOLN
                                                     D. HUMPHREYS"

Much Conversation was had with Mr. McGillevray upon the subjects of our Negotiations, at the Camp of the Indians, on the evening of the 21st; and at the Quarters of the Commissioners the 22d., where Mr. McGillevray and a number of the other Chiefs passed the day.

Early in the morning of the 23d, a Letter was sent to Mr. McGillevray; and the day was employed by the Commissioners in compleating the draught of a Treaty and other Communications to be laid before the great Council of the Nation.

                              "Rock Landing, 23d. September 1789
"SIR,
"We have the pleasure to inform you that the Honorable Mr. Griffin arrived here the last evening. We are now engaged in preparing the Communications we intend to make to your Nation, which, if agreeable to you, will be delivered to morrow morning. General Lincoln and General Pickens will have the pleasure of attending this forenoon at your black drink. We have the honor to be, Sir,
                                        "Your &c.
                              (signed)   B. LINCOLN
                                           D. HUMPHREYS

"Alexr. McGillevray Esqr.   ⎫
Chief of the Creek Nation" ⎬

At the Conference between General Lincoln and Mr. McGillevray, it was agreed that the Creeks should attend the Commissioners the next day at 11 o'Clock, to hear what they had to communicate. However, late in the same evening, it was understood that it would be a matter of convenience for the Indians to receive the Talks on the west side of the Oconee, and the Commissioners accordingly wrote the subsequent Letter.

                              "Rock Landing, 23d. September 1789
"SIR,
"As we are disposed to do every thing in our Power to accomplish the Objects of our Mission, without an undue regard to matters of Form; and as we understand it would be a matter of convenience for your People that we should attend on your Ground for the purpose of making our communications to morrow, we have no objection to passing the River to your Camp upon that occasion. You will therefore be pleased to consider this Letter as designed to take away all cause of Jealousy, and to put it in your option to arrange the time & place of conference in such manner as shall be most satisfactory to the Creeks. We shall expect your answer by the Bearer, & in the mean time we have the honor to be,

"Sir, your &c.

B. LINCOLN

(signed)   C. GRIFFIN

D. HUMPHREYS

"Alexr. McGillevray Esqe.   )
"Chief of the Creek Nation"   }

To which Mr. McGillevray replied the next Morning

"Indian Camp, Oconee River, 24th Septr. 1789

"GENTLEMEN,

"I have this morning received your Letter, which I explained to the Chiefs who appear satisfied to find that you are disposed to make your Communications to them on this side of the River. They therefore desire that they may be favored with your Company this morning at the Ceremony of their Black drink, when that is over, they wish immediately to proceed to Business with you.

"I have the Honor to be,

Gentlemen, Your &c.

(signed)   ALEXR. MCGILLEVRAY

C.C.N.

"The Honorable
The Commissioners of the
United States of America &c. &c.
Rock Landing."

At the time appointed, the Commissioners attended the Ceremony of *Black drink*, and were conducted to the great Square of the encampment by all the Kings, Chiefs & Warriors in solemn pomp, and much apparent Friendship. The Commissioners then proceeded to Business, and having read and explained their Commissions, gave the following Talk.

"KINGS, HEAD-MEN & WARRIORS of the CREEK NATION!

"This parchment which we hold in our hands, and a Copy of which we now deliver has informed you, that we are appointed by the President of the United States of America, with the advice of his old Counsellors, Commissioners Plenipotentiary for restoring & establishing Peace & Amity between the United States and all the Nations of Indians within the limits of the United States southward of the River Ohio.

"BROTHERS of the CREEK NATION ATTEND!

"We trust that the great Master of Breath who formed us all Brothers, whether white Men or red Men, has created this day to be the time for preventing our People and your People from taking away that breath which none but he can give or should take away. We appeal to you and ask, Are not the Pains and Miseries of the human Race naturally severe enough, without their endeavouring by unkindness to encrease the portion of bitterness & sorrow which must of necessity fall to the lot of Man? Let us try to make each other happy, and not wretched. It is in this way that the general Government of the United States of America intend to act with all the world.

"FRIENDS and BROTHERS,

"We will first speak of the present state & policy of our Nation; and we will next speak of the Reasons which ought to induce you to be in Alliance with us rather than any other People whatever.

"Although, Brothers! we cannot entirely forget the Calamities we suffered in the late war with great Britain, yet we have buried all resentment for the part which the Allies of Britain acted in that bloody scene. That War left many of our Cities, Villages & Towns in a ruinous condition; but we obtained Liberty and Independence. Our Country has recovered from desolation. We are at Peace with all the Nations of the World. We are increasing every day in Numbers. We have the means of happiness in our Power & wish to communicate them to you. Our lands are so extensive that they enjoy all seasons and yield all productions. Our great Ships are made to go in every part of the World where Goods & Merchandize can be obtained. Our Union which was a Child is grown up to Manhood, so that it can speak with a louder voice, & strike with a stronger Arm than ever it has done before: For you must know that a happy change has taken place in our National Government. One great Council is established with full Powers to promote the public good. General Washington who led our Armies to conquest wherever he turned his Face, is now the Head Man of all our Councils and Chief of all our Warriors. You know him, and that he never speaks the thing which is not. He has commanded us to tell you, that, while the general Government of confederated America will vindicate the Rights of every Member of the Union, it will also see that Justice shall be done to the Nations of Indians situated within the limits of the United States: And we are authorised to declare and make known that the United States will guarantee and defend to you, all the Lands of your Nation within the Limits aforesaid, and which shall not be clearly ceded to any part of the Union.

"FRIENDS and BROTHERS of the CREEK NATION!

"A few words only are necessary to prove to you, that it will be more natural for you to be allied with us than with any other People. You are under the necessity of being connected with the white Men, because you want their Goods and Merchandize. We can make a reasonable Profit by your Articles of export and afford such imports as you may want, at rates cheaper than they can be obtained in any other Place. A secure Port in our Country will be much more convenient for you than a Port in any other Country. Thus both of us will be gainers by being Friends. The promotion of our mutual interests will promote our mutual Friendship. This will be found the only sure method to make a Peace happy & lasting.

"BROTHERS!

"We have nothing more to say to you at present: but if you like this Talk and are possessed of the same good disposition for us which we entertain in good faith for you, we are ready to propose to you the draught of a Treaty which we think may be the foundation of a permanent Treaty of Peace & Amity."

THE Talk having been received with strong marks of Approbation, the Commissioners then presented to the Representatives of the Nation the Draught of a Treaty as follows:

"ARTICLES of Peace and Amity agreed upon between the President of the United States of America, in behalf of the said States, by the underwritten Commissioners Plenipotentiary on the one Part; and the undersigned Kings, Head Men and Warriors of all the Creeks, in behalf of themselves and the Creek Nation on the other.

"ARTICLE I. There shall be perpetual Peace & Friendship between all the Citizens of the United States of America; and all the Towns, Tribes and Individuals of the upper and lower Creeks.

"ARTICLE 2ND. The boundary between the Citizens of the said United States & the Creeks is and shall be, from where the former Line strikes the River Savannah, thence up the said River to a place on the most Northern branch of the same, commonly call'd the Keowee, where a Northeast Line to be drawn from the Top of the Occunna Mountain shall intersect, thence along the said Line in a South West direction to Tugaloe River, thence to the Top of the Currahee Mountain, thence to the Head of the most southern branch of the Oconee River (that is to say the River Apalachy) including all the Waters of the same, thence down the said River to the confluence of the Okmulgy, thence on a South west direction to the most Southern part of the River Saint Mary, thence down the said River to the old Line.

"ARTICLE 3D. The Supreme Executive of the United States solemnly guaranties to the Creeks all their remaining Territory, against all aggression or unjust usurpation whatever: and will support the said guarantee, if necessary, by a Line of Military Posts.

"ARTICLE 4TH. The said Indian Chiefs, for themselves & their respective Towns and Tribes within the limits of the United States, do acknowledge the Creeks to be under the Protection of the Supreme Authority of the United States and of no other Sovereign whosoever: and also that they are not to hold any Treaty with an Individual State, or with Individuals of any State.

"ARTICLE 5TH. If any Citizen or Citizens of the United States shall presume to settle upon the Lands guarantied to the Creek Nation by this Treaty, he or they shall be put out of the Protection of the United States; and the Creeks may punish him or them, if they shall think proper.

"ARTICLE 6TH. For the mutual advantage of the contracting Parties it is stipulated, that a free Trade and friendly intercourse shall always be maintained between them, and for the particular benefit of the said Creek Nation it is farther stipulated that a secure Port shall be established, at a place known by the name of Beards Bluff, on the River Altamaha, or, if that shall be found inconvenient, at such other place as shall hereafter be agreed upon; into which or from which, the Creeks may import or export all the Articles of Goods and Merchandize necessary to the Indian Commerce, on the same terms as the Citizens of the United States—Provided that the number of Arms & quantity of Ammunition shall not exceed their annual necessary supply for hunting. And if any just apprehensions should be entertained by the Creeks for the safety of the Goods and Merchandize so imported or exported, the Supreme Executive of the United States will take effectual Measures for protecting the same, by stationing a Body of regular Troops at the said Port.

"ARTICLE 7TH. The general Government of the United States, having the sole & exclusive Right of regulating the Trade between their Citizens and the Indians within the limits of their Territories, will, as soon as may be, adopt an equitable system for the prevention of injuries and oppressions on the part of the Citizens or Indians; and in the mean time, all Traders, Citizens of the United States, shall have liberty to go to any Towns or Tribes of the Creeks to trade with them; and they shall be protected in their Persons and property, and kindly treated.

"ARTICLE 8TH. If any Indian or Indians or Persons residing among the Creeks, or who shall take refuge in their Nation, shall commit a Robbery or Murder, or other capital Crime, on any Citizen of the United States of America, or Person under their Protection, the Tribe to which such offender may belong, or the Nation, shall be bound to deliver him or them to be punished according to the Laws of the United States: Provided the punishment shall not be greater than if the robbery or Murder, or other capital Crime, had been committed by a Citizen on a Citizen.

"ARTICLE 9TH. And if any Citizen of the United States of America, or Person under their protection shall commit a Robbery or Murder, or other capital Crime, on any Indian, such offender shall be punished in the same manner as if the Robbery or Murder, or other capital Crime, had been committed on a Citizen of the United States of America; And the punishment shall be in presence of some of the Creeks, if any will attend: And that they may have an opportunity so to do, proper notice, if practicable, of the time and place of such intended punishment shall be sent to some one of the Tribes.

"ARTICLE 10TH. It is understood that the punishment of the Innocent, under the Idea of Retaliation, is unjust, and shall never be practised on either side.

"ARTICLE 11TH. The Kings, Head Men & Warriors of the Creek Nation will restore to their Liberty, all Prisoners Citizens of the United States, now in that Nation: and they will also restore all Negroes & all other Property taken from Citizens of the United States, during the late hostilities, to such Person or Persons as shall be appointed by the Governor of the State of Georgia to receive them.

"ARTICLE 12TH. The Creeks shall give notice to the Citizens of the United States, of any designs which they may know or suspect to be formed in any neighbouring Tribe, or by any Person whosoever, against the Peace, Trade, and Interest of the United States.

"ARTICLE 13TH. All animosities for past grievances shall henceforth cease; and the contracting Parties will carry the foregoing Treaty into full execution with all good Faith and sincerity."

After some conversation with Mr. McGillevray and the other Chiefs upon the Business of the day, the Commissioners returned to their Quarters; and the next morning received the following note, which was immediately answered.

"GENTLEMEN,

"The Chiefs were in Council until very late last night. The result appears to be, that they are not entirely satisfied with all parts of your Talk. They object, principally, to the Boundary, marked out in the Talk, however it was my decision to let the matter stand as it was, for the present, the hunting Season being at hand; the Chiefs should take care to prevent every act of hostility or depredation on the part of the Warriors during the Winter, and until we heard farther from you on the part of the United States. They resolve to break up to depart; it would be proper to give some presents that they may not complain of losing their time &c. &c.

"I have the honor to be Your &c.

"Honble. The Commissioners   (sign'd)   ALEXR. McGILLEVRAY
  of the
   United States of America &c.

"Rock Landing, 25t Septr. 1789

"SIR,

"We have received your note of this Morning informing us, that the Chiefs were in Council until very late last night; that it appeared they were not entirely satisfied with some parts of our Talk; that they principally objected to the boundary Line marked out in it; that, however, it was your decision to let the matter stand as it was, for the present, establishing in the mean time a certain kind of Truce, until you should hear farther from us on the Part of the United States.

"As the Chiefs object to some part of our Propositions, we have to ask, that they will give us in writing, the only terms upon which they will enter into a Treaty with us. We hope and trust that they will not seperate without affording us this satisfaction. Since we are as well prepared for concluding a Treaty now, as we shall be, at any other time, it is by no means probable that the United States will send another Commission to them. We are not authorised to make any Presents whatever, unless a Treaty of Peace shall be concluded.

"We have the honor to be &c.

           B. LINCOLN
"The Honorable
  A. McGillevray,   (sign'd)   C. GRIFFIN
Chief of the Creek Nation   D. HUMPHREYS"

During this Stage of the Business, Mr. McGillevray solemnly promised that he would pass the Oconee, and have a full and free conference with the Commissioners upon the subject of the Negotiations; and, not more than an hour before his abrupt Departure, he repeated the Promise to one of them, that he would state his objections to the Draught of the Treaty, either in Conversation or writing, the same afternoon. Very soon after this, he sent a verbal Message that he was constrained to fall back four or five Miles for the purpose of obtaining better forage for his Horses and that he hoped the Commissioners would not misconstrue his intentions; yet to their astonishment they afterwards found that he had retreated to a greater distance, under the false pretext mentioned in his subsequent Letter from the Okmulgy.

On the 26th the following Letter was written to Mr. McGillevray. The Honorable Mr. Few appointed by the Executive of Georgia to communicate with the Commissioners, Genl. Pickens & Col. Saunders of Georgia, going at the same time to Mr. McGillevray's Encampment, to convince him of his Error and to persuade him to return. The Hollowing King going also on the part of the Indians.

"Rock Landing, 26th September 1789

"SIR,

"We had on the 24, the pleasure of presenting to you the sketch of a Treaty which appeared to us such an one as you could in justice to yourselves, all circumstances considered have subscribed to. In your observations thereon you say that there are some parts of our Talk to which you object, principally to the Boundary marked out in the Talk. In answer to these observations we informed you, that it was our wish you would give us in writing the Terms only upon which you would enter into a Treaty with us; and we requested at the same time that you would not separate without affording us the satisfaction of receiving your final Terms. We waited with anxious expectation during the afternoon of yesterday hoping we should be favored with them, but as they have not come to hand, and we are informed that you have removed your Camp to the distance of fifteen miles without any intention of returning, not remarking on that Conduct of yours which has too much the appearance of a studied neglect of the Commissioners, we go on to observe, that had you given us your objections to the Boundaries, that would have brought into discussion the validity of former Treaties, had it appeared to us upon a full investigation of this interesting matter, that all had not been right, and that full and perfect Justice had not been done to the Indians, we should have been disposed to have adopted such measures as would have removed all reasonable Grounds of complaint. If you should depart without this enquiry and a full discussion of the whole Business, it cannot be considered in any other Point of light than a refusal to establish any terms of Peace whatever.

"We have the honor to be &c.

                                       B. LINCOLN
"The Honble.   (sign'd)   C. GRIFFIN
    Alexr. McGillevray   D. HUMPHREYS
Chief of the Creek Nation"

In the meantime all the other Kings and Head Men, attending at the Quarters of the Commissioners, addressed them through the White Bird King, in the following Talk.

"You are the great Men whom we look upon as our Brothers, and here are the great Men of my Nation who are come to speak to you. We have been here a long time, and we met with you over the River in Friendship; but all our People have got tired; our Horses are strayed and a good many of our People are gone, yet I have persuaded several to stay to have once more a Talk with you.

"All the Men here present are come to take a peaceable leave of you. As our hunting time is coming on very soon, we are come over to hear what you have to say to us.

"Some of our People are gone up the River to hunt in their way home, I have given orders for them to behave themselves well, if they go on this side of the River, not to take off any of the white People's Horses, and I hope the White's will also behave themselves well and not take off our Horses.

"If our People do not observe these Orders, they shall be seized and sent down to the Whites.

"Although nothing should be done at this time about the Treaty, I hope that it may be done hereafter, and that in the mean time Peace & quietness will be kept on both sides.

"When we get home all our Nation will hear the Talks, and they will be peaceable and quiet for that is the wish of them all.

"I have little more to say at present, but that we are not going off affronted, but in Peace & Friendship.

"It was the intention of our People to do something for our Wives and Children, and I think it was also the intention of the White People.

"I have nothing more to say, but that when we part, I hope to shake hands in Peace; and all our young People are come that they may shake hands with you also."

Then the Cussetaw King arose and lighting a Pipe presented it to the Commissioners and said, "I look upon you as Fathers and elder Brothers and wish to smoke a Pipe with you."

To which the Commissioners answered,

"FRIENDS & BROTHERS!

"In answer to your friendly Talk we would say that, having come from a long distance, we expected to smoke the Pipe of Peace & Friendship with you, and to bury the Hatchet of War for ever.

"We hear that your great Chief and beloved Man Mr. McGillevray is gone from his former Camp, for which we are very sorry.

"The other day we made some propositions for a long Peace & Friendship, — If they were not agreeable to you, Why did you not tell us? and then something else might have been proposed.

"FRIENDS & BROTHERS,

"We are sent to make a Peace which shall be good for all Parties. Persuade your great Chief & beloved Man Mr. McGillevray to come back and hear us again, that all things may be explained.

"We thank you for your good Talk, and we hope you will not return to your Nation until we have taken each other by the hand and concluded a lasting Peace with all our People in Friendship & good Faith.

"We have no more to say to you at present."

On the 27th. we received the following answer from Mr. McGillevray: and on the next day we wrote him our last Letter.

"Camp, Okmulgee River 27th Septr. 1789

"GENTLEMEN,

"I am favored with your Letter of yesterday by Weatherford. I beg to assure you that my Retreat from my former Camp on the Oconee was entirely owing to the want of food for our Horses, and at the earnest entreaty of our Chiefs. Col. Humphrey's and myself at different Interviews entered minutely and deeply into the subject of contest between our Nation and the State of Georgia, I observed to him that we expected ample & full Justice should be given us in restoring to us the encroachments we complained of, in which the Oconee Lands are included, but finding that there was no such Intention and that a restitution of territory hunting Grounds, was not to be the Basis of a Treaty of Peace between us, I resolved to return to the Nation, referring the matter in full Peace till next Spring. Many of the Principals having gone hunting, nothing farther can now be done. I am very unwell and cannot return. We sincerely desire a Peace, but we cannot sacrifice much to obtain it. As for a statement of our disputes, The Honorable Congress has long ago been in possession of, and had declared that they would decide on them in principles of Justice & Humanity. 'Tis that we expect.

"The Honble.   "I have the honor to be,
     The Commissioners of   Gentlemen, &c.
          the United States of   (signed)   ALEXR. MCGILLEVRAY
               America"

"Rock Landing, 28th September 1789

"SIR,

"We are extremely sorry that you would neither give us your objections to our Propositions for forming a Treaty; nor propose such terms as would be acceptable to the Creek Nation, if acceded to by us. Col. Humphreys asserts, that he neither told or intimated to you, that we had offered any Articles in our project of a Treaty, as an Ultimatum. All our Proceedings evince the same thing. You could not avoid having understood from our Letter of the 25th (which you received previous to your departure from the Oconee, and which you have not yet answered) that we were desirous of receiving the Terms upon which you & the Chiefs of the Creek Nation would enter into a Treaty with us. You will also be pleased to recollect, that we expressed at the same time an earnest hope and expectation that they would not separate without giving us this satisfaction.

"These Overtures on our part clearly indicated that we were disposed to make a Peace, upon any Conditions, not incompatible with the Dignity & Justice of the United States. Our last Letter to you of the 26th. explained our Ideas & wishes, if possible, still more unequivocally; and informed you, that if you should depart without our having an opportunity of enquiring into the validity of former Treaties, and fully discussing the whole Business, it could not be considered in any other point of light than a refusal to establish Peace upon any terms whatever. Your not having done this, leaves it only in our Power to return and report a state of Facts to the Supreme Executive of the United States. To obtain still farther information, we shall remain until Monday of next week, at Augusta. To which place we invite you to repair, either in Person, or by some Agent or Agents of the Creek Nation, in order to be present at the Time when we shall attempt to procure farther Documents for establishing Facts; as well as to give, on your part, all such Intelligence, relative to past transactions, as shall be deemed expedient. We pledge our public faith & sacred honor for the safe conduct of yourself, or such Agent or Agents as may be employed by your Nation, to and from the proposed place of conference. Should you conclude to come yourself, or to send an Agent or Agents to the conference at Augusta; the Person or Persons under that description will be pleased to apply for a safe guard to the Commanding Officer at Rock Landing, who has our Instructions on the subject. In the mean time we have to inform the Creeks that the People settled on Cumberland River have just cause to complain against them, because some of them have, during the present Year, murdered several families within that District.

"And as the Creeks can have no cause of complaint against that Settlement, we insist that effectual Measures should be taken on your part, to prevent all acts of hostility and plunder in that Quarter.

"With due Consideration we are &c.
B. LINCOLN

"The Honble.   (sign'd)   C. GRIFFIN
  Alexr. McGillivray,   D. HUMPHREYS
Chief of the Creek Nation"

On the 28th. we gave a short account of our Proceedings to the Secretary at War.

"Rock Landing, 28th. September 1789

"SIR,

"We have the Mortification to inform you that the Parties have separated without forming a Treaty. The Terms which were offered by us at the commencement of the Negotiation were not agreeable to Mr. McGillevray; but neither would he come forward with written objections or propose any Conditions of his own. His verbal Communications were inadmissable upon the Spirit or Words of our Instructions.

"We shall have the honor of stating this Business very fully at a future day, and are with the greatest Respect and Esteem

"Your &c.
B. LINCOLN

"The Honble.   (sign'd)   C. GRIFFIN
The Secretary at War   D. HUMPHREYS
  New York"

Having made all the necessary arrangements concerning the Goods & Stores belonging to the public; We departed from the Rock Landing and arrived at Augusta on the 2d. of October. The same Evening and early the next day we wrote the following Letters to the Governor of Georgia.

"Augusta 2d. October 1789

"SIR,

"We make use of the first moment after our arrival to acquaint your Honor, that We have not been able to conclude a Treaty of Peace between the United States and the Creek Nation; However positive & repeated assurances were given to us by Mr. McGillevray and all the Chiefs of the Creeks present, that the tranquility which now prevails shall be inviolably preserved on the part of their People. Being much fatigued with our Journey we cannot have the honor of waiting upon you until tomorrow Morning, when we shall do ourselves the Pleasure of stating such farther particulars as may be interesting to the State over which you preside.

"We have the Honor to be &c.

B. LINCOLN

(signed)   C. GRIFFIN

D. HUMPHREYS

"His Honor
The Governor of Georgia"

"Augusta 3d. October 1789

"SIRS,

"As a variety of Reports have been circulated throughout the United States, relative to the circumstances under which the Treaties of Augusta in 1783, at Galphinton in 1785, and at Shoulder bone in 1786, were formed; and as it is highly important that Facts should be ascertained; We take the liberty of requesting your Honor, that you will be pleased to assist us in obtaining the information necessary for that purpose.

"The principal points to which our attention has been attracted are: Whether all Lands belonging to the upper & lower Creeks are the common Property of the whole Nation?

"Or, whether the Lands stated to have been ceded to Georgia by the three Treaties or either of them were acknowledged by the upper Creeks to be the sole property of the lower Creeks?

"Whether the acknowledged Proprietors of the Lands, stated to have been ceded to Georgia were present or fully represented, at the said three Treaties?

"Whether the Creeks present at the said Treaties, did act with a full understanding of the Cessions, they are stated to have made?

"And whether the said Treaties and Cessions were freely made on the part of the Creeks, uninfluenced by any threats or implication of Force?

"It is also desirable that any other interesting circumstances connected with the objects of these enquiries, should be made known to us; For example, whether the Indians did, for any considerable length of time, acquiesce quietly in the location and settlement of the Lands in Question?

"What Value in Goods has been given at the several Treaties as Presents or Compensation for the Cessions—And, in effect, whatever other Matters may serve to place the Conduct of the State of Georgia on this subject in it's true Point of Light.

"After being possessed of the written and official Documents, we wish to receive oral informations from private Characters who were present at the several Transactions above alluded to.

"We have the honor to be &c.

B. LINCOLN

(signed)   C. GRIFFIN

D. HUMPHREYS

"His Honor

The Governor of Georgia"

To the preceding Letters the Governor was pleased to send the following Answer, also a Return of depredations committed by the Indians and other Documents.

"Augusta October 4th. 1789

"SIRS,

"The Communications which you were pleased to make to me first after your return from the Rock Landing on the 2d. Inst. shall be laid before Council, and made the foundation of a Proclamation, the object of which shall be to meet and reciprocate the assurances of the Chiefs of the Creek Indians for preserving of Peace.

"With respect to the farther particulars stated in your Letter of the 3d. I am sorry that so many Persons, who were privy to the transactions to which they allude are, at this time, engaged in their attendance on the General Election, whose Testimony where they present, would point to the truth of facts through all that variety of Report which originated equally from private speculation and personal disappointment. I have however, directed such Documents, as are immediately within my Power, to be made out for your present information.

"From all the evidences which have or shall be collected, it will be found, that the Lands between the Mountains and the old Ogeechee Line, North of the Oconee, were ever equally claimed by the Cherokees and the Creeks; and that, by a Convention had before the Revolution, the Lands comprehended within the limits afterwards call'd the ceded Lands, and now Wilkes County, were ceded, at the same time, by the Heads of the two Nations. That during the progress of the late War, the State had been alternately attacked by either; and that, at the close of it, they were respectively called upon to make some satisfaction. Accordingly, in the Spring of 1783 the Cherokees, attended by a few Creeks, came down to Augusta, talked the matter over, avowed their Claim to the Lands in question, agreed to and sign'd a Treaty; and in the Autumn of the same year, the Creeks chiefly of the lower Towns also came down, talked their matter over, avowed their Claim, and agreed to and signed a Treaty on their part; whereby the State obtained the relinquishment of the right, or claim of Right, of both Nations, to the Lands therein described and bounded. These Treaties were laid before the Legislature with all that Order of Business and deliberation, required by public and fair proceedings, and the Lands were divided into Counties. The Offices were opened; and the Lands surveyed, granted, felled, settled and cultivated in perfect Peace.

"The Writer was present at both these Conventions. The first he wrote from Principles previously agreed upon, and which were made the foundation of the Propositions to the Creeks in the Fall. At neither were there any Men in Arms, or the smallest coertion used: The conduct of the Indians was voluntary; and while on their part, they were rendering satisfaction, they also received valuable considerations in Presents. When the Treaties were over, it is within his most lively recollection, that the Commissioners, the Chiefs, the Citizens and the Indians, eat, drank, and reciprocated all the usual marks of Friendship, satisfaction & Peace: nor was it until a considerable time afterwards, that any umbrage was taken by the upper Creeks, when a new motive and principle of direction appeared to have sprung up in the Nation, which pretended for the first time, an equal Claim to the hunting Grounds on the Oconee.

"At the Treaty of Galphinton, in the year 1785, it is said, some new Opinions were disseminated; be that as it may, the Treaty, and the testimony respecting the conduct of it, shew plainly the good intentions of the State upon the occasion.

"The Writer can say but little thereupon, as his engagements were then in a different line which left no surplus attention to the other Departments.

"In the Year 1786, he was of the Legislature, when the arrangements took place for the Convention at Shoulder-bone. To doubt the validity of Treaties had become familiar to the Indians, as well as to think triflingly of the Power of the State. To settle a substantial peace, and to remove these impressions formed the Objects of Government. The Commissioners employed were respectable Men, and the Officers attending, were of service and distinction. A sacrifice of their Fame was not to be expected; and it evidently appears that no unworthy use was made of the Force which was sent upon the Ground.

"In the Year 1787, their Attacks were renewed and repeated on almost all our Frontier. These we resisted, and called upon the Union for support. A Superintendant and Commissioners were appointed; and all their endeavours have not been effectual to remove the cause of the untowardness of that Nation, and our Citizens have continued to be killed and plundered in the most cruel and distressing manner until the late efforts for Peace. Even the new Commission, which the States themselves so highly respected, has been treated with an indifference which ought not to have been expected.

"I have the honor to be

"The Honble.

Sirs &c.

B. Lincoln

C. Griffin } Esqr.

D. Humphreys } Commissioners"

(sign'd)   GEO. WALTON

"RETURN of Depredations committed by the Creek Indians since the commencement of Hostilities in the State of Georgia.

Whites killed	Wounded	taken Prisoners	Blacks killed	Blacks taken Prisoners	Horses taken off & their Value.	Horses taken off not Valued	Horned Cattle taken off	Hogs destroyed	Houses burnt	Sundry Household furniture, farming Utensils, wearing Apparel &c. destroyed
72.	29.	30.	10.	110.	184 £3,995.10.	459.	984.	387.	89.	

"Office of Secretary of Council 5th. October 1789

"I do hereby Certify that the above Estimate of Losses sustained by the Indians since the commencement of Hostilities is taken from the Returns made on Oath and filed in this Office.

"(signed)   J. MEREWETHER, Secy. E. E."

From Augusta we sent a second Message by General Pickens to the Cherokees, accompanied by a Duplicate of our first. We also forwarded many printed Copies of the Address to the Inhabitants bordering on the Towns and Settlements of the Cherokee Nation by the same Conveyance.

"HEADMEN & WARRIORS of all the CHEROKEES!

"We sent to you a friendly Talk from Savannah about one moon past. But lest that should not have reached you all, we now repeat it. We farther inform you, that although a formal Treaty of Peace has not been concluded with the Creek Nation, yet we have received positive and repeated assurances from them, that the same tranquility which now prevails shall be faithfully preserved on their part.

"BROTHERS!

"Had not the hunting Season commenced, so as to prevent us from finding you at home, we should have been happy in seeing you personally before we returned to the far distant *white Town* of Congress. As that will now be impossible, we conclude by cautioning you to beware of listening to bad Men, in such manner as to interrupt the Truce concluded between you and the Commissioner of North-Carolina.

"NOW BROTHERS!

"In assuring you that the general Government of the United States will always do you strict justice, we bid you farewell!

"DONE at Augusta this 5th. day of October in the Year of our Lord 1789, and the 14th. Year of Independence of the United States of America.

B. Lincoln
(sign'd) C. Griffin
"Attest,
D. Humphreys
D. S. Franks, Secy."

On the 6th. of October we left Augusta and arrived at Richmond on the 29th. where we had the satisfaction to meet with Piomingo, the second great Chief of the Chickasaws, attended by other Indians. With him we had frequent Talks, at which he gave us the strongest assurances of the good disposition of that Nation towards the United States, and also of the rooted aversion of the Chicasaws to the whole Creek Nation.

By this Chief we sent a duplicate of our Messages to the Chicasaws and to the Choctaws.

On the 10th. of November, we returned to New York.

Thus stating the facts in a Journal of their Transactions.

The Commissioners are decidedly of Opinion, that the failure of a Treaty at this time with the Creek Nation can be attributed only to their principal Chief Mr. Alexr. McGillevray.

1st. From the repeated declarations and apparent good disposition of all the Kings, Head-Men and Warriors to establish a permanent Peace with the United States.

2nd. From the proposed Boundary being offered to the great Council of the Nation only as the Basis of amicable Negotiation.

3d. From the deception and precipitate retreat of Mr. McGillevray without stating his objections to the draught of a Treaty either Verbally or in Writing.

4th. From many enquiries concerning this Man, and from Mr. McGillevray's own declarations, That without obtaining a full equivalent for the sacrifice, he would not renounce the close connexion which he had formed with the Spanish Goverrment in the hour of distress, a connexion honorable and lucrative to himself, and advantageous to the Creek Nation.

5th. From his frequent intimations that no Treaty could be formed with the Commissioners unless a free and exclusive Port should be granted to him upon the Altamaha or River St. Mary. And

6th. From the most positive refusal to acknowledge the Creek Nation to be within the limits or under the protection of the United States; although in express contradiction to a former Letter written by him on the 5th. of September 1785, to General Pickens.

The Commissioners beg leave further to Report.

That after the most accurate investigation in their power to make, after consulting the best Documents, and having recourse to creditable Depositions, they are unable to discover but that the Treaty of Augusta in the Year 1783, the Treaty of Galphinton in the Year 1785, and the Treaty of Shoulder-bone in the Year 1786, were, all of them, conducted with as full and authorised Representation, with as much substantial form and apparent good faith, and understanding of the Business, as Indian Treaties have usually been conducted, or perhaps can be, where one of the contracting Parties is destitute of the benefits of enlightened Society. That the Lands in question did of right belong to the lower Creeks as their hunting Grounds, have been ceded by them to the State of Georgia for a valuable consideration, and were possessed and cultivated for some years without any Claim or molestation by any part of the Creek Nation.

As Mr. McGillevray and all the other Chiefs, Head Men & Warriors, have given strong assurances in their Talks and by writing, that no farther Hostilities or depredations shall be committed on the part of their Nation: and as the Governor of Georgia, by issuing Proclamations and by other effectual measures will prevent the commission of hostilities & depredations upon the Creek Nation on the part of Georgia, The Commissioners in the best of their judgment REPORT,

That all animosities with the Creek Nation should henceforth cease.

That some Person should be dispatched to the said Nation with the ultimate Draught of a Treaty, to establish perpetual Peace and Amity. That when such a Draught of a Treaty shall be properly executed by the leading Men of the Nation, all the Presents intended for the Indians, and now in the State of Georgia should be distributed among them. That if the Indians shall refuse to execute such Draught of a Treaty

The Commissioners humbly submit

That the Arms of the Union should be called forth for the Protection of the People of Georgia, in the peaceable and just possession of their Lands; and in case the Creeks shall commit further hostilities and depredations upon the Citizens of the United States, that the Creek Nation ought to be deemed the Enemies of the United States and punished accordingly.

B. LINCOLN

(signed)   C. GRIFFIN

D. HUMPHREYS

A LETTER from the Commissioners to the Secretary at War.

New York, 20th. November 1789

SIR,

We made our Communications to the Creek Nation, and they have refused to conclude a Treaty of Peace with the United States; and as in this case We are directed by our Instructions to report such Plans both for defensive and offensive Measures as may be thought best to protect the Citizens of the United States on the Frontiers; In obedience to those Instructions we offer the following Particulars to your consideration.

For defensive Measures, a Line of six Posts ought to be established on the Frontiers of Georgia, and two at least to guard the settlements upon the Cumberland River, the Posts to consist of one compleat Company in each, to be covered by works of sufficient strength to resist any sudden impressions of the Indians, and to serve as places of deposit if Magazines should hereafter be formed. To them also the exposed Inhabitants of those Countries might retire upon the alarm of danger; by this experiment we should be satisfied how far a Line of Posts would be adequate to give complete Protection to the Citizens of the United States living on the Frontiers.

The Stations in Georgia should be as follows:

One upon the navigable Waters of St. Mary; One at Beards Bluff upon the Altamaha; One at the junction of the Oconee & Okmulgee, One at the Rock Landing, One at the Middle trading Path, and one at the upper trading Path, the two latter at such Positions as will be found the most convenient to protect the Frontiers.

If the offensive Plan shall become indispensable, in that case, we beg leave to recommend the most vigorous and effectual Operations by carrying the Arms of the Union into the very Heart of the Creek Country. By this Proceeding the Creek Nation will be taught to feel the weight & superiority of the United States, and the measure would be consistent with the honor and dignity of the Republic. The Forces necessary upon this occasion should consist of Five Regiments of Infantry, seven hundred men to each Regiment: One Regiment of Cavalry of five hundred Men, and a Corps of Artillery of two hundred and forty Men, the whole amounting to 4,250—That two Regiments of Infantry be inlisted from the States of Georgia, South-Carolina, and North-Carolina, if that State should accede to the new Constitution, the Cavalry from the States of Virginia and Maryland, and the remainder of the Forces from the other States indiscriminately. We are induced to recommend only two Regiments to be raised from the more Southern States, because such a measure would probably comprehend all that class of Men whose inclinations might lead them into the field against such an Enemy; and because if the Troops should be drawn altogether, or principally from those States and a defeat should unfortunately take place, it might involve that Country for a time in disagreeable consequences: besides great injuries might be experienced by calling forth, in the first instance, a large proportion of that body of Men which from their Local Situation ought to remain as a reserve.

From the best intelligence, and from observation, we think that Augusta in the State of Georgia ought to be the place of Rendezvous. To that Town, the military & Quarter Masters Stores might be transported from Savannah by water in 15 days. A full supply of waggons can be obtained at no great distance from thence, and upon the Road towards the Ogichee, which might bring with them a load of common Flour each. The rout from Augusta to the Creek Nation is a good one, little more than 200 Miles to their first Towns and about 300 Miles to their Western Settlements.

Two other Routs to the Creek Nation present themselves; from Beards Bluff on the Altamaha to Flint River, the distance about 150 miles, and 70 Miles from the Flint River to the Cowetas.

From Bryant's trading House on Saint Mary's River to the Flint River, and from thence to the Cowetas is nearly the like distance as from Beards Bluff.

The Navigation is good from the Oconee to Beards Bluff and to Bryant trading House, from either of them a tolerable good Waggon Road may be had into the Creek Nation; Yet both of these Routs, particularly while the Boats shall be going up the River St. Marys or the Altamaha, would be attended with considerable embarrasment and danger to the Troops from the Enemy; and the difficulties and long distance for the Waggons to reach Beards Bluff or Bryant's trading House would be almost insurmountable.

In addition to the foregoing Reports We were commanded if possible to ascertain the following Points. Those points have been ascertained, from the best information in our ability to procure.

1st. The number of Warriors in the whole Creek Nation do not exceed 4,500.

2. They are armed pretty generally, with good Rifles, they receive their Ammunition in presents and by purchase from the Spaniards.

3. The lower Creeks and Siminolies are about equal to the upper Creeks in number, the lower Creeks rather more numerous than the Siminolies.

4. The number of old Men, Women and Children in the proportion as four to one of the Warriors.

5. The number of Towns in each district could not be ascertained, probably about Eighty in the whole, of which about 45 are in the upper Country; The Towns are very different in magnitude, and a few of what are called the Mother towns, have the principal direction, in National Affairs, that is to say, the War Towns, in War—and the white Towns, in Peace.

6. Mr. McGillevray of the half-breed is the most influential Chief throughout the Nation. Among the upper Creeks the white Lieutenant has the ascendancy and is considered in some respects as the Rival of Mr. McGillevray. The Mad Dog is the next in authority. Among the lower Creeks the Hallowing King and the Cussitah King, the former commanding the War Towns, and the latter commanding the white Towns, Towns unstained with blood, and which are Towns of refuge. Add to these, the Tellassee King, the white Bird King, the fat-King, the King of the Siminolies and the King of the Euchees.

7. Their kinds of Government approach the qualified Monarchy; in the Towns they have head Men, who are much respected and have authority, both in Peace and War in their respective Towns; in the districts they have Kings or Chiefs and Warriors, the former have the influence in time of Peace, and the latter in time of War. Upon all important occasions, they meet in great Council, and deliberate with freedom, particularly once a year, at the Ceremony of the *first Fruits*, called the *busking*, when they punish great Delinquents, regulate internal policy, and form Plans for hunting or War the ensuing Season.

8. They are in a great measure Hunters; however they cultivate some Indian Corn and Potatoes, possess Cattle and Horses, a few Slaves, and lately in some instances have introduced the Plough.

9. Of late years they are not rigidly confined to particular districts for hunting, but are permitted to go in small Parties throughout the whole Nation, yet pretty generally they find it convenient to keep within their respective Divisions.

10. The kinds of Furs are the Beaver, Otter, Mink, Fox, Squirril and some others, together with Deer and other Skins, the whole amounting annually to somewhat more than £10,000 sterling. They are principally sold to the Indian Traders *in* the Nation and exported through the Spanish settlements.

11. The amount of the European goods annually consumed is about £12,000 sterling, furnished principally by the commercial House, of which Mr. McGillevray is a Partner.

12. Gensang abounds in that Country, but is not yet gathered in any considerable quantities.

13. The Country of the lower Creeks and Siminolies is level, sandy & Piny; The Country of the upper Creeks much broken, with a good Soil & growth; farther to the west and even to the Missisippi the lands are rich and rather low and marshy, abounding with good streams of water, and excellent Timber, such as the Oak, hickory, bucks Eye, Elm and large Gum &c. &c.

14. The Waters of the Mobile are navigable for large Boats, the one Branch 270 Miles from the Ocean, to the hickory Settlement, where Mr. McGillevray resides; and the western Branches about 320 Miles into the Choctaw and Chicasaw Country and within fifty Miles of the great Bent of the Tennessee. The Waters of the Apalachicola, particularly the Flint River and Catahuchee, and the waters of the Altamaha particularly the Rivers Oconee and Okmulgee are navigable for Boats some hundred Miles. From the northern navigable Streams of these Rivers to the southern navigable waters of the Tennessee, there are no established Portages, but the Country is level; good Roads might easily be made, and the greatest distances not more than one hundred Miles.

15. We could not ascertain with precision the nature of the Connexion, which the Creeks have formed with the Spaniards; but from intelligence some what to be relied on we believe that Connexion to consist principally in paying less duties upon Indian Goods imported than the Spaniards themselves pay; by a guarantee of all the Creek Possessions; and by military Distinctions and Presents to Mr. McGillevray, and other considerable Chiefs. We could procure no Copy of any Treaty subsisting between them. The predominating Prejudices of the Creeks are certainly adverse to the Spaniards, particularly Mr. McGillevray has often mentioned and declared that a Connexion with the United States would be more natural to the Creek Nation, if they could obtain such Condition of Interest and Friendship as would justify and induce them to *break* with the Spanish Government.

16. We had but little opportunity to ascertain similar Facts with respect to the other Indians; from our small lights upon this Article of Instruction, We think the Cherokee Nation will be found to contain about 600 Gun-men: The Chicasaws about 700—and the Choctaws about 3000. Their Arms are bad, scarcely any Ammunition, and themselves naked. The Cherokees and Chicasaws cultivate the Ground more than other Indians, and possess Cattle proportionally in greater numbers.

The Choctaws hunt only, are a brave & hardy people in the Woods, but indolent to a great degree at home.

In order to preserve the attachment of the several Indian Nations bordering upon the United States, it appears to us expedient that some adequate means of supplying them with Goods and Ammunition at moderate Prices should immediately be adopted.

With our best endeavours to obtain information concerning the internal state of the Choctaws & Chicasaws we have not been able to succeed fully, so as to justify us in giving any positive opinion upon the best mode of effecting this desirable object: however, in conformity with our Instructions we respectfully suggest—That some uniform Plan of granting Permits to those who may be employed in the Indian Commerce, should be established by the Supreme Authority of the United States; This would be part of the Duty imposed upon the Superintendant, Agent or Commissary of Indian Affairs in the Southern Department. The Fees of Office for granting such Permits ought to be moderate, and might be applied towards the payment of Salary.

An expedient of this sort is highly requisite to prevent Persons of bad Character from defrauding the Indians; from making still more unfavorable impressions upon the inimical Tribes; and from alienating the affections of the friendly Tribes from the United States. This Superintendant, Agent or Commissary, by going through the Indian Towns of all the different Nations would be able to collect such information as might be extremely useful in forming definite Plans of Trade with those People: and in case of War with the Creek Nation, he might be of solid advantage, in bringing the Choctaws and Chicasaws to co-operate with the Arms of the United States.

We have rendered to the Treasury of the United States a full account of all our Disbursements. The Books No. 1 & 2 we now deposit in your Office, they contain Invoices of all the Articles delivered to us for the proposed Treaty, and will clearly accout for the whole of them, by ascertaining those Articles which were necessarily expended and those which now remain in the State of Georgia.

While we sincerely regret that our negotiations with the Creek Nation have not terminated in a Treaty of Peace; We hope it will be found that the Commissioners have been as diligent and attentive to the subjects of their Mission, and as economical in the expenditures of the Public Money as the nature of things would permit.

We have the Honor to be, with Sentiments
of Respect, Sir
Your most humble Servants
B. LINCOLN
(signed)   CYRUS GRIFFIN
D. HUMPHREYS

The Honorable
The Secretary at War

N.B.   The Commissioners wrote the following Letter to Messrs. Pickens & Osborne during their stay at the Rock Landing, and received their Answer with sundry Papers enclosed, which they deposit in the War Office.

"Rock Landing 26th. September 1789

"GENTLEMEN,

"We have received the following Articles of Instructions from the President of the United States, which we do ourselves the honor to communicate to you and wish to be favored with an Answer.

"We are with great Respect
Your &c. &c.
B. LINCOLN
(sign'd) C. GRIFFIN
D. HUMPHREYS

"Messrs. Pickens }
and Osborne }

(Extract)

"You will learn by the Papers delivered to you, that certain Goods were left by the Commissioners after the Treaties of Hopewell in the Commencement of the Year 1786. It is probable that these Goods may have been delivered to Messrs. Pickens and Osborne; You will therefore apply to the said Gentlemen for regular Invoices of all the Goods in their possession for the Treaty, distinguishing the means by which they became possessed thereof.

"You will also request of them an Account of the Monies or Goods they may have received of the States of South Carolina and Georgia in consequence of the Resolves of Congress of the 26th. of October 1787, and August the 14th. 1788."

"Rock Landing 26th. September 1789
"GENTLEMEN,

"In answer to your Letter of this date, We do ourselves the Honor to enclose a Copy of our Letter to Mr. Gervis of Charleston, dated 20th. of April, with a Copy of his Answer dated 6th. June last. We do not know of any Goods being left at Hopewell. The Accounts of Monies received from the States of South Carolina and Georgia, together with an Account of the appropriation and expenditures of the same, we have also the honor to enclose, the Vouchers of all which are ready for your Inspection.

"We have the honor to be, Gentlemen,
Your &c.
"Honble. the Commissioners   (signed) ANDW. PICKENS
for treating with the Indians   H. OSBORNE
South of the Ohio"[1]

[1] An attested copy of the report, in the hand of Benjamin Bankson, is in Transcribed Treaties and Conventions, 1789–1801, Records of the Secretary, SR, DNA. It is related to George Washington's message journalized January 11, 1790.

Treaty of New York

GEORGE WASHINGTON PRESIDENT of the UNITED STATES of AMERICA.

TO ALL TO WHOM THESE PRESENTS SHALL COME; GREETING:—WHEREAS a treaty of peace and friendship between the United States of America, and the Creek nation of Indians was made and concluded on the seventh day of the present month of August by HENRY KNOX secretary for the department of war, who was duly authorized thereto by the President of the United States with the

The State of Georgia, c. 1795. (Courtesy of the Map Division, Library of Congress, Washington, D.C.)

advice and consent of the senate, on the one part, and the kings, chiefs and warriors of the said CREEK nation whose names are thereunto signed on the other part; Which treaty is in the form and words following.

A TREATY of peace and friendship made and concluded, between the PRESIDENT of the UNITED STATES of America, on the part and behalf of the said States and the undersigned KINGS, CHIEFS, and WARRIORS of the CREEK nation of Indians, on the part and behalf of the said nation,

THE parties being desirous of establishing permanent peace and friendship between the United States, and the said Creek nation, and the citizens and members thereof, and to remove the causes of war by ascertaining their limits, and making other necessary just and friendly arrangements: THE PRESIDENT of the United States by HENRY KNOX Secretary for the department of War, whom he hath constituted with full powers for these purposes, by and with the advice and consent of the Senate of the United States, and the CREEK nation by the undersigned KINGS, CHIEFS, and WARRIORS, representing the said Nation have agreed to the following articles.

ARTICLE 1ST. THERE shall be perpetual peace and friendship, between all the citizens of the United States of America, and all the individuals, towns, and tribes, of the upper, middle, and lower Creeks and Semanolies, composing the creek nation of Indians.

ARTICLE 2ND. THE undersigned KINGS, CHIEFS, and warriors, for themselves and all parts of the Creek nation within the limits of the United States, do acknowledge themselves, and the said parts of the Creek nation, to be under the protection of the United States of America and of no other sovereign whosoever, and they also Stipulate, that the said Creek nation will not hold any treaty with an individual State, or with individuals of any State.

ARTICLE 3RD. THE CREEK nation shall deliver as soon as practicable, to the commanding officer of the troops of the United States, Stationed at the Rock-landing on the Oconee river all citizens of the United States, white inhabitants or negroes, who are now prisoners in any part of the said nation. And if any such prisoners or negroes Should not be so delivered, on or before the first day of June ensuing, the governor of Georgia may empower three persons to repair to the said nation in order to claim and receive such prisoners and negroes.

ARTICLE 4TH. THE boundary between the citizens of the United States and the creek nation, is and shall be, from where the old line strikes the river Savannah thence up the said river to a place on the most northern branch of the same, commonly called the Keowee, where a North-East line to be drawn from the top of the Occunna Mountain shall intersect—thence along the said line in a southwest direction to Tugelo-river thence to the top of the Currahee mountain—thence to the head or source of the main south branch of the Oconee river called the Appalachee—thence down the middle of the said main south branch and river Oconee, to its confluence with the Oakmulgee, which form the river Altamaha—and thence down the middle of the said Altamaha to the old line on the said river, and thence along the said old line to the river St. Marys.

And in order to preclude forever, all disputes relatively to the head or source of the main south branch of the river Oconee, at the place where it shall be intersected by the line aforesaid from the Currahee mountain, the same shall be ascertained by an able surveyor on the part of the United States, who shall be assisted by three old citizens of Georgia, who may be appointed by the governor, of the said state, and three old Creek Chiefs to be appointed by the said nation, and the said surveyor, Citizens, and Chiefs, shall assemble for this purpose, on the first day of October, One thousand seven hundred and Ninety one, at the rock landing on the said river Oconee, and thence proceed to ascertain the said head or source of the main south branch of the said river, at the place where it shall be intersected by the line aforesaid to be drawn from the currahee mountain. AND in order that the said boundary shall be rendered distinct and well known, it shall be marked by a line of felled trees at least twenty feet wide, and the trees chopped on each side from the said currahee mountain to the head or source of the said main south branch of the Oconee river and thence down the margin of the said main south branch and river Oconee for the distance of twenty miles, or as much farther as may be necessary to mark distinctly the said boundary. And in order to extinguish forever, all claims of the Creek nation or any part thereof, to any of the land lying to the northward and Eastward of the boundary herein described, it is here by agreed in addition to the considerations heretofore made for the said land, that the United States will cause certain valuable indian goods now in the state of Georgia, to be delivered to the said Creek nation, and the said United States will also cause the sum of one thousand and five hundred dollars to be paid annually to the said Creek nation. AND the undersigned Kings, chiefs, and warriors, do hereby for themselves, and the whole Creek nation their heirs, and descendants, for the considerations above mentioned, release, quit-claim, relinquish, and cede all the land to the northward and Eastward of the boundary herein described.

ARTICLE 5TH. THE United States solemnly guarantee to the Creek nation all their lands within the limits of the United States, to the Westward and southward of the boundary described in the preceding article.

ARTICLE 6TH. IF any citizen of the United States or other person not being an indian, shall attempt to settle on any of the creeks lands, such person shall forfeit the protection of the United States, and the Creeks may punish him or not, as they please.

ARTICLE 7TH. NO citizen or inhabitant of the United States shall attempt to hunt or destroy the game on the creek lands. Nor shall any such citizen or inhabitant go into the creek country without a passport first obtained from the governor of Some one of the United States or the officer of the troops of the United States, commanding at the nearest military post on the frontiers, or such other person as the President of the United States may from time to time authorize to grant the same.

ARTICLE 8TH. IF any Creek indian or indians or person residing among them, or who shall take refuge in their nation, shall commit a robbery or murder or other capital crime, on any of the citizens or inhabitants of the United States, the Creek nation, or town or tribe, to which such offender or offenders may belong, shall be bound to deliver him or them up, to be punished according to the laws of the United States.

ARTICLE 9TH. IF any citizen or inhabitant of the United States or of either of the territorial districts of the United States, shall go into any town settlement, or territory belonging to the Creek nation of indians, and shall there commit any crime upon or trespass against the person or property of any peaceable and friendly indian or indians, which if committed within the jurisdiction of any state or within the jurisdiction of either of the said districts, against a citizen or white inhabitant thereof would be punishable by the laws of Such state or district, such offender or offenders shall be subject to the same punishment, and shall be proceeded against in the same manner, as if the offence had been committed within the jurisdiction of the state or district to which he or they may belong, against a citizen or white inhabitant thereof.

ARTICLE 10TH. IN cases of violence on the persons or property of the individuals of either party, neither retaliation, nor reprisal shall be committed by the other until satisfaction shall have been demanded of the party of which the agressor is, and shall have been refused.

ARTICLE 11TH. THE Creeks shall give notice to the citizens of the United States of any designs which they may know or suspect to be formed in any neighbouring tribe, or by any person whatever against the peace and interests of the United States.

ARTICLE 12TH. THAT the creek nation may be led to a greater degree of civilization and to become herdsmen, and cultivators instead of remaining in a state of hunters, the United States will from time to time furnish gratuitously the said nation with useful domestic animals and implements of husbandry. And further to assist the said nation in so desirable a pursuit, and at the same time to establish a certain mode of communication, the United States will send such and so many persons to reside in said nation as they may Judge proper, and not exceeding four in number, who shall qualify themselves to act as interpreters. These persons shall have lands assigned them by the creeks for cultivation for themselves and their successors in office, but they shall be precluded exercising any kind of traffic.

ARTICLE 13TH. ALL animosities for past grievances shall henceforth cease, and the contracting parties will carry the foregoing treaty into full execution with all good faith and Sincerity.

ARTICLE 14TH. THIS treaty shall take effect and be obligatory on the contracting parties as soon as the same shall have been ratified by the President of the United States, with the advice and Consent of the senate of the United States.

IN WITNESS of all and every thing herein determined between the United States of America and the whole creek nations, the parties have hereunto set their hands and seals in the city of NEW YORK within the United States, this seventh day of August One Thousand Seven hundred and Ninety.

In behalf of the UNITED STATES
H. KNOX secretary of War and
sole Commissioner for treating   [Seal]
with the Creek nation of
Indians

In behalf of themselves and the whole creek nation of Indians

ALEX. McGILLIVRAY   [Seal]

Cusetahs	FUSKATCHE MICO	his X mark	or Bird Tail King	[Seal]
	NEATHLOCK	his X mark	or second Man	[Seal]
	KILLETEMATTHLE	his X mark	or Blue Giver	[Seal]
little Tallisee	OFSAY MICO	his X mark	or the Singer	[Seal]
	TOTKESHAJOU	his X mark	or Samoniac	[Seal]
Big Tallisee	HOPOTHE MICO	his X mark	or Tallisee King	[Seal]
	OPOTOTUCHE	his X mark	or Long Side	[Seal]
Tuckabatchy	SOHOLESSEE	his X mark	or Young second Man	[Seal]
	OCHEE HAJOU	his X mark	or Aleck Cornel	[Seal]
Natches	CHINABIE	his X mark	or the Great Natches Warrier	[Seal]
	NATSOCUACHEHEE	his X mark	or the Great Natchee Warriors Brother	[Seal]
	THAKATEEHEE	his X mark	or the Mole	[Seal]
	OQUAKABEE	his X mark		[Seal]

Cowetas	Tuskena'ah	his X mark	or Big Lieutent.	[Seal]
	Homatah	his X mark	or Leader	[Seal]
	Chinnabie	his X mark	or Matthews	[Seal]
	Juleetaulematha	his X mark	or dry Pine	[Seal]
of the broken Arrow	Chawockly Mico	his X mark		[Seal]
Coosades	Coosades Hopor	his X mark	or the Measurer	[Seal]
	Muthlee	his X mark	or the Misser	[Seal]
	Stimafutchkee	his X mark	or Good Humour	[Seal]
Alabama Chief	Stilnaleeje	his X mark	or Disputer	[Seal]
Oakfoys	Mumagechee	his X mark	or David Francis	[Seal]
				[Seal]
				[Seal]
				[Seal]
				[Seal]

Done in the presence of
Ri. Morris Chief Justice of the State of New York
Richd. Varick Mayor of the City of New York
Marinus Willett

THOS. LEE SHIPPEN of Pennsylvania
JOHN RUTLEDGE Junior
JOSEPH ALLEN SMITH
HENRY IZARD

his
JOSEPH   X   CORNELL Interpreter
mark

NOW KNOW YE. THAT I having seen and considered the said Treaty do by
and with the advice and consent of the SENATE of the United States accept, ratify
and confirm the same, and every article and clause thereof. IN TESTIMONY
whereof I have caused the seal of the UNITED STATES to be hereunto affixed and
signed the same with my hand.

[Seal]   GIVEN at the city of NEW YORK the THIRTEENTH day of August in
           the year of our LORD, ONE thousand seven hundred and ninety and in
           the fifteenth year of the Sovereignty and Independence of the
           UNITED STATES.

BY Command of the
President of the United
States of America
     H. KNOX   GO. WASHINGTON
Secy. for the department of War   By the President
                                                          TH. JEFFERSON[1]

[1] The treaty, in the hand of John Stagg, Jr., is Indian Treaty no. 17, RG 11, M668,
roll 2, DNA. It is related to George Washington's message journalized August 7,
1790. A copy, by Samuel Otis, Jr., is in Transcribed Treaties and Conventions, 1789–
1801, Records of the Secretary, SR, DNA.

Treaty of New York, Secret Articles

GEORGE WASHINGTON PRESIDENT of the UNITED STATES of AMERICA.

TO ALL TO WHOM THESE PRESENTS SHALL COME, GREETING: WHEREAS
the treaty of peace and friendship, between the United States of America and the
Creek nation of Indians made and concluded on the seventh day of the present
month of August, Contains certain secret articles, which are in the form and
words following.

SECRET ARTICLES of the TREATY of peace and friendship made and concluded
on behalf of the United States of America on the one part, and the Creek nation
of Indians on the other part in the City of New York, on this seventh day of
August, one thousand seven hundred and ninety.

ARTICLE IST.   The commerce necessary for the Creek nation shall be carried on
through the ports, and by the citizens of the United States, if substantial and
effectual arrangements shall be made for that purpose by the United States, on
or before the first day of August one thousand seven hundred and ninety two.

In the mean time, the said commerce may be carried on through its present channels and according to its present regulations.

And whereas the trade of the said Creek nation is now carried on wholly or principally through the territories of Spain and obstructions thereto may happen by war or prohibitions of the Spanish government.

It is therefore agreed between the said parties that in the event of any such obstructions happening it shall be lawful for such persons as the President of the United States shall designate to introduce into and transport through the territories of the United States to the country of the said Creek nation, any quantity of goods wares and merchandize not exceeding in value in any one year Sixty thousand dollars, and that free from any duties or impositions whatsoever, but subject to such regulations for guarding against abuse, as the United States shall judge necessary; which privilege shall continue as long as such obstructions shall continue.

ARTICLE 2ND. The United States also agree to allow to each of the great medal chiefs herein after named, a commission, a great medal with proper ornaments, and each one hundred dollars annually for themselves and the other beloved men of their towns respectively—to wit—

Of the Upper Creeks—	The Chiefs the Oakfuskees, Tuckabatchees, and the present Talissee King of the half-way house:
Of the lower Creeks—	The Chiefs of the Cusitahs and Cowetas— And—
Of the Semanolees—	The Chief of Micasukee.

ARTICLE 3RD. In order to effect a consolidation of the interests of the United States and the Creek nation, it is hereby stipulated that Alexander McGillivray the beloved Chief of the said nation shall also be constituted the Agent of the United States in the said nation with the rank of Brigadier General and the pay of one thousand two hundred dollars per annum, on his taking the usual oaths required by law.

ARTICLE 4TH. And the said Alexander McGillivray hereby stipulates to use his highest exertions to endeavor to cultivate the firmest friendship between the United States and the said Creek nation.

ARTICLE 5TH. The United States agree to educate and clothe such of the Creek youth as shall be agreed upon, not exceeding four in number at any one time.

ARTICLE 6TH. These secret articles shall take effect and be obligatory on the contracting parties as soon as the same shall have been ratified by the President of the United States, with the advice and consent of the Senate of the United States.

IN WITNESS of all and every thing herein determined between the United States of America and Alexander McGillivray in behalf of himself and the Creek nation, the parties have hereunto set their hands and seals, at the place and on the day and year above written.

In behalf of the United States.   In behalf of himself and the Creek
  H. KNOX secy. of   [Seal]   Nation.
  War and sole commissioner   ALEX. McGILLIVRAY [Seal]
  for treaty with the Creek nation.
  DONE in the presence of
        RID. MORRIS Chief Justice of the State New York
        RICHD. VARICK Mayor of the City of New York
        MARINUS WILLETT
        JOSEPH ALLEN SMITH
        HENRY IZARD

NOW KNOW YE, THAT I having seen and considered the said secret articles of the said treaty, do by and with the advice and consent of the United States accept, ratify, and confirm the same, and every article and clause thereof; In Testimony whereof I have caused the seal of the United States to be hereunto affixed, and signed the same with my hand.

[Seal]   Given at the city of New York the Thirteenth day of August, in the year of our lord, One Thousand seven hundred and ninety, and in the fifteenth year of the sovereignty and independence of the United States.
BY Command of the
President of the United
States of America.
    H. KNOX
    Secretary for the   GO. WASHINGTON
    department of War   By the President
                                  TH. JEFFERSON[1]

[1] The secret articles, in the hand of John Stagg, Jr., are filed with Indian Treaty no. 17, RG 11, M668, roll 2, DNA. They are related to George Washington's message journalized August 7, 1790. A copy, by Samuel Otis, Jr., is in Transcribed Treaties and Conventions, 1789–1801, Records of the Secretary, SR, DNA.

Consular Convention with France

Instructions and Plan from the Continental Congress to Benjamin Franklin

Jany. 25th 1782

The plan of a Convention respecting Consular powers being reconsidered & amended was read over, together with Instructions to the minister plenipotentiary of these United States respecting it, and the same were agreed to by nine States.

RESOLVED

That the minister plenipotentiary of the United States at the Court of Versailles be & he is hereby authorised & Instructed to enter into a Convention with his most Christian Majesty on the part of the United States for the establishment of Consular powers & privileges, according to the scheme hereto subjoined, unless it shall be deemed by his most Christian Majesty more expedient that the same should be executed in the United States.

That the said minister plenipotentiary use his discretion as to the words or arrangement of the Convention, confining himself to the matter thereof in all respects, except as to so much of the sixth article as relates to the erection of a Chappel, taking care that reciprocal provision be made for the recognition of the Consuls & Vice Consuls of the United States and for the admission of persons attached to the Consulate to the privileges stipulated in the 5th Article, in a manner most conducive to expedition & freest from difficulty.

The Draught of a Convention between his most Christian Majesty and the United States of North America, for defining and regulating the functions and privileges of Consuls Vice Consuls, Agents & Commissaries.

The most Christian King and the United States of North America, having by the 29th article of the treaty of Amity & Commerce concluded between them, granted mutually the liberty of having each in the ports of the other, Consuls, Vice Consuls, Agents & Commissaries, & being willing in consequence thereof to determine & fix in a reciprocal & permanent manner the functions & prerogatives of the said Consuls, Vice Consuls, Agents & Commissaries respectively have agreed as follows.

ARTICLE 1. It shall be the duty of the Consuls, of his most Christian Majesty to present their Commissions in the first instance to the United States in Congress assembled, by whom an Act shall be made recognizing them as such. This Act shall be delivered by the Consuls to the supreme Executive power of the State or States to which they may be sent. Two copies of the exequatur, that is a public notification of the quality of the Consuls shall thereupon issue from the supreme Executive power without fees or perquisites of Office; One to be retained by the Consuls, the other to be published in one or more Gazzettes. This being done, the pre-eminences, authority & privileges stipulated in this Convention, shall be allowed to them in all places, before all tribunals & by all persons.

ART. 2. The Consuls of his most Christian Majesty and of the United States, may appoint any number of Vice Consuls within their respective departments.

Upon the notification of their appointment by the Consuls to the supreme

Executive power of the State to which they may be sent the Exequatur shall be applied for & delivered by the several States to them in the same manner as to the Consuls, and thereupon the pre-eminences, authority & privileges stipulated in this Convention in favor of Vice Consuls shall be allowed in all places before all tribunals & by all persons.

ART. 3.   Consuls & Vice Consuls shall be subjects or Citizens of the power appointing them and interdicted from all traffic or Commerce for their own, or another's benefit.

ART. 4.   Consuls may also appoint any number of Agents within their departments, who may be of their own nation or not at pleasure. They shall receive a Commission from the Consul appointing. They shall not assume any pre-eminence, authority or privilege herein granted to Consuls or Vice Consuls, nor exact any fees or reward under any pretence whatever. But they shall confine themselves wholly to the assisting of merchants, mariners and vessels and giving information respecting them to the nearest Consul or Vice Consul.

ART. 5.   There may be attached to the Consulate at the will of the Consuls within their departments any number of persons. Neither the papers nor houses of Consuls or Vice Consuls shall be searched. Consuls & Vice Consuls shall enjoy full & entire immunities for their persons, and be exempt from personal service, public offices, finding quarters for Soldiers, militia duty, watch, ward, guardian-ship, attorney-ship, Committee-ship, and from all duties, taxes & imposts whatsoever on moveable property; but shall be liable in respect of real & landed property in the same manner as the Subjects or Citizens of the Country. The arms of his most Christian Majesty or of the United States as the case may be shall be placed upon the outward door of their house, and being so placed shall entitle the house to the exemptions aforesaid: But no asylum shall be thereby obtained for malefactors or Criminals, who shall be delivered up immediately on demand. The same privileges & immunities as those granted in this fifth article to Consuls and Vice Consuls shall be granted to persons attached to the Consulate and living under the same roof with the Consuls or Vice Consuls, provided approbation shall be given of their number & appointment by the supreme Executive power of the State to which they may belong.

ART. 6.   Consuls, and Vice Consuls in places where there are no Consuls, may have a Chappel in their houses for the celebration of divine service according to their religious profession. And his Most Christian Majesty and the United States shall cause particular care to be taken, that no obstacle or hindrance be thrown in the way of the funeral Obsequies or Ceremonies observed towards the deceased of either nation.

ART. 7.   In all cases in which it may be necessary that the Consuls or Vice Consuls should perform any juridical or Official Act, the public bodies or the persons in public authority, who shall require such Act, shall either inform them thereof in writing or send a military or civil Officer with a verbal message respecting it: And the Consuls or Vice Consuls shall on their part readily and bona fide do whatsoever may be demanded of them on these occasions.

ART. 8.   The Consuls & Vice Consuls respectively may establish a Chancery, as a depository of the Consular Acts & deliberations, of effects left by the dead

Convention entre le Roi très-Chrétien et les Etats-Unis de l'Amérique à l'effet de déterminer et fixer les fonctions et prérogatives des Consuls et Vice-Consuls respectifs.

Sa Majesté le Roi très-Chrétien et les Etats-Unis de l'Amérique s'étant accordés mutuellement par l'Art. XXIX du Traité d'amitié et de Commerce conclu entr'eux, la liberté de tenir dans leurs Etats, ports respectifs, des Consuls et Vice-Consuls, agens et commissaires et voulans en conséquence déterminer et fixer d'une manière réciproque et permanente les fonctions et prérogatives des Consuls et Vice-Consuls qu'ils ont jugé convenable d'établir de préférence, Sa Majesté très-chrétienne a nommé le Sieur Comte de Montmorin de S.t Herent, Maréchal de ses Camps et armées, Chevalier de ses ordres et de la Toison-d'Or, son Conseiller en tous ses Conseils, Ministre et Sécrétaire d'Etat et de ses Commandemens et finances ayant le Département des Affaires Etrangères; et les Etats-Unis ont nommé le Sieur Thomas Jefferson, ~~~~, Citoyen des Etats-Unis de l'Amérique ~~~~ et leur Ministre Plénipotentiaire auprès du Roi, lesquels, après s'être communiqué leurs pleinpouvoirs respectifs sont convenus de ce qui suit :

de douze ans, à-compter du jour de l'échange des Ratifications, lesquelles seront données en bonne forme et échangées de part et d'autre dans l'espace d'un an ou plustôt si faire se peut.

En foi de quoi, Nous Ministres Plénipotentiaires, avons signé la présente Convention, et y avons fait apposer le cachet de nos armes.

Fait à Versailles le 14 Novembre mil Sept cent quatre-vingt-huit.

L.C. De Montmorin   Th. Jefferson

Consular Convention of 1788 (see pp. 346–51). The seals under the signatures of Thomas Jefferson and L. C. Montmorin are of red-orange wax, and medium-blue ribbon is threaded through the parchment under the seals. (Courtesy of the National Archives, Washington, D.C.)

or saved from Shipwreck, of testaments, obligations, contracts, and all other Acts & things done by or between people of their nation. They may appoint the Officers of the Chancery, administer to them an Oath of Office, intrust to them the keeping of the seal, and the right of affixing the same to Commissions, judgments and other Consular Acts and empower them to discharge the functions of Notaries and Registers.

ART. 9. The Consuls & Vice Consuls respectively shall have the exclusive right of receiving in their Chancery, or on board of Vessels of their nation all the declarations, and other Acts which the Captains, masters, Seamen, passengers & merchants of their nation shall think proper to make or lodge therein; and last wills & testaments & copies of any Act duly authenticated by the Consuls or Vice Consuls, and under the seal of their Consulate shall receive full faith & credit in all Courts of Justice as well in France as in the United States. They shall also have the exclusive right of inventorying the effects of those of their nation, who may die within their Consulate, liquidating their accounts & selling their moveable property. They shall call to their assistance in this business two merchants of their own nation and of their own choice, and cause to be deposited in the Chancery the effects & papers of the deceased of their own nation, without being interrupted therein by any Officer military, judiciary, or of the police. But neither the Consuls nor Vice Consuls shall deliver the Effects of the deceased, or the produce of their sales over to the heir or lawful successor or his representative or attorney until all the debts which the deceased shall have contracted by judgment, Act or bill shall be discharged, the signature or hand writing & genuineness thereof being first certified by two merchants of the same nation with the deceased, and of reputation. In all other cases payment of no debt shall be made unless the creditor shall first enter into a bond with one sufficient surety at least, who is resident on the spot, for the return of all monies unduly received as well the principal as interest and costs. The surety shall not be bound beyond one year in time of peace & two years in time of war. If however within those terms the Creditor shall call upon the lawful representative or successor to the property of the deceased by a proper legal process, & prove his title to the money so received, the surety shall stand discharged.

ART. 10. The Consuls & Vice Consuls respectively shall receive the declarations, Consulats or other Consular Acts of all captains & masters of their respective nations for damages received at sea by leakage, or the throwing of goods overboard. And all Consulats or other Consular Acts made by them in foreign ports for accidents during the Voyage shall be lodged in the Chancery aforesaid. If a subject of France & a Citizen of the United States be jointly interested in the cargo, the damage shall be settled by the tribunals of the Country, not by the Consuls or Vice Consuls. But where subjects or citizens of their own nation are alone interested the Consul or Vice Consul shall then chuse experienced persons of their respective nations to settle the same.

ART. 11. In every case of a wreck, the nearest Consul or Vice Consul may exercise his discretion in saving the vessel wrecked with her Cargo & appurtenances & in storing & securing what is saved, & may also take an inventory thereof. In this business no Officers of the Customs, of Justice, of the police or naval Officer, shall interfere, but upon application made to them for their assistance, in which case they shall exert themselves in the most effectual manner. To prevent all Clashing of jurisdictions in case of Ship-wreck, it is agreed, that where there shall be no Consul or Vice Consul, or they may be more distant from the place of the accident than a judge of the Country having authority, in such cases, this judge shall immediately proceed to the exercise of his authority according to law, but shall retire upon the coming of a Consul or Vice Consul, into whose hands he shall put the whole business, rendering an account of his transactions and receiving from the Consul or Vice Consul reimbursement for all expences. Whatsoever is saved shall be lodged in the nearest Custom house or naval Office; or where there is no Custom house or naval Office, in the nearest place of security with an inventory prepared by the Consul, Vice Consul, or in their absence by the Judge of the Country as aforesaid. Upon the order of the nearest Consul or Vice Consul & without any fees or perquisites for storage, when lodged in public stores, the owner may reclaim the property so saved in person or by attorney, and may either reexport the same free from all duties of exportation or sell it in the Country, if goods of such a quality be not prohibited. In this latter case, of a sale of unprohibited goods there shall be an abatement of the duties on importation in proportion to the damages sustained by the Shipwreck to be determined by the account taken by the Consul, Vice Consul or judge of the Country or any other competent Officer at the time of the accident.

ART. 12. The Consuls & Vice Consuls shall have on board of the vessels of their respective nations, all power & jurisdiction in matters of a civil nature. They shall have the power of causing the laws regulations & ordinances of their respective nations concerning navigation to be observed on board of their said vessels. For this purpose they shall freely & without any molestation or hindrance from any Officer or other person, visit the said vessels. They may cause to be arrested and sequestered every vessel carrying the flag of their respective nations, & even send them back to France or the United States, as the case may be, as well as arrest any captain, Master, seaman or passenger of their respective nations. They may cause to be arrested & Detained in the Country, sailors & deserters of their respective nations, or cause them to be transported therefrom. It shall be sufficient evidence of the Sailors and deserters belonging to their respective nations, if their names appear in the registers of the vessels or the roll of their crew. Proof being thus made concerning Sailors & deserters, all tribunals, judges, and Officers whatsoever shall be interdicted & disabled from taking cognizance in any manner of complaints exhibited by such Sailors or Deserters. But they shall be delivered up to an order signed by the Consuls or Vice Consuls, without being detained, engaged or withdrawn in any manner. That these powers vested in Consuls & Vice Consuls, may be completely executed, all persons in authority shall assist them, and upon a simple requisition made by the Consuls or Vice Consuls in writing shall cause to be kept in prison at the disposal and cost of the Consuls or Vice Consuls the Sailors and Deserters so arrested until an opportunity shall be presented of sending them out of the country.

ART. 13. All offences committed in France by a citizen of the United States, against a subject of his most Christian Majesty, shall be enquired into & punished, according to the laws of France, and those committed in any one of the United States by a subject of his most Christian Majesty against a citizen of the United States shall be enquired into & punished according to the laws of such State. But offences committed in France by a citizen of the United States against a citizen of the United States, or committed in any one of the United States by a subject of his most Christian Majesty against a Subject of his most Christian Majesty shall be subject to the jurisdiction of the Consuls & Vice Consuls of France, or of the United States as the case may be.

ART. 14. All differences & disputes between the subjects of his most Christian Majesty in the United States, or between the citizens of the United States in France, and all differences and disputes concerning commerce, between the Subjects of his most Christian Majesty, one party being resident in France or Elsewhere & another in the United States; or between the citizens of the United States, one party being resident in the United States or elsewhere & another in France shall be heard, tried & decided on by the Consuls or Vice Consuls of their respective nations either by referring the same to arbitration or by makeing a decree summarily & without costs. No Officers civil or military shall intermeddle or interpose herein in any respect. Appeals shall be carried to such Courts as have been or may be appointed by his most Christian Majesty and the United States respectively. No disputes or differences between a subject of his most Christian Majesty, and a Citizen of the United States, shall be determined or taken up in any manner by the Consuls or Vice Consuls, but shall be decided by the Courts of the Country in which the defendant shall be found.

ART. 15. The advantages to Commerce having caused the erection of certain tribunals in France & particular forms for the speedy determination of commercial matters, the merchants of the United States, shall enjoy the benefits of these establishments in france, and the United States in Congress assembled will recommend to the Legislatures of the several States to establish equal advantages in the speedy decision of causes in favor of french merchants in matters of the same nature.

ART. 16. The Subjects of his most Christian Majesty & the citizens of the United States shall be exempt from all personal services in the place of their residence either in France or the United States as the case may be. Whensoever any person in France or the United States as the case may be, shall claim any privilege or exemption as a subject of his most Christian Majesty or of the United States, before any judge, tribunal, or Officer whatsoever, a certificate of the Consul or Vice Consul of the district, containing his name, surname & the place of his residence, and the affidavit of the person claiming such privilege or exemption, that he is a subject of his most Christian Majesty or of the United States as the case may be, shall be sufficient evidence thereof, unless the contrary shall manifestly appear.

ART. 17. Conformably to the third & fourth Articles of the treaty of Amity & Commerce between his most Christian Majesty & the United States, if any other nation by virtue of any convention whatsoever shall receive greater indulgence either in France or in the United States with regard to Consular powers, privileges or authority, the Consuls, Vice Consuls, Agents & Commissaries of France & of the United States, as the case may be, shall participate therein.[1]

[1] The instructions and draft of a convention, in the hand of George Bond, are in PCC, item 4, M247, roll 18, DNA. The Senate received these documents on July 22, 1789. They are related to John Jay's report of July 27, 1789.

Act of the Continental Congress

December 14 1784

On motion of Mr. Jay seconded by Mr. Gerry

RESOLVED, unanimously. Eight States only being represented, that his Excellency the president inform the minister plenipotentiary of The United States at the Court of France that it is the desire of Congress, in case the Convention proposed for regulating and ascertaining the powers and privileges of Consuls should not be already signed, that he delay signing it until he shall receive further Instructions on the subject from Congress.[1]

[1] The resolution, in the hand of Benjamin Bankson, is in PCC, item 5, vol. II, M247, roll 19, DNA. The Senate received the resolution on July 22, 1789. It is related to John Jay's report of July 27, 1789.

Benjamin Franklin to the President of the Continental Congress

Passy February 8th. 1785

SIR,

I received, by the Marquis de la Fayette, the two Letters you did me the Honor of writing to me the 11th. and 14th. of December; the one enclosing a Letter from Congress to the King; the other a Resolve of Congress respecting the Convention for establishing Consuls. The letter was immediately delivered, and well received. The Resolve came too late to suspend signing the Convention, it having been done in July last; and a Copy sent so long since that we now expected the Ratification. As that Copy seems to have miscarried, I now send another. I am not informed what Objection has arisen in Congress to the Plan sent me. Mr. Jefferson thinks it may have been to the Part which restrained the Consuls from all Concern in Commerce. That Article was omitted, being thought unnecessary to be stipulated, since either Party would always have the Power of imposing such Restraints on its own Officers, whenever it should think fit. I am, however, of Opinion that this, or any other reasonable article, or alteration may be obtained at the Desire of Congress, and established by a Supplement.

Permit me, Sir, to congratulate you on your being called to the high Honor of presiding in our national Councils, and to wish you every Felicity, being with the most perfect Esteem, &c.

[signed]   B. FRANKLIN[1]

[1] A copy of the letter, in the hand of George Taylor, Jr., is in PCC, item 100, M247, roll 127, DNA. Filed with the letter are English and French copies of the Convention of 1784, in the hand of George Taylor, Jr. The letter was received by the Senate on July 22, 1789. It is related to John Jay's report of July 27, 1789.

Report of John Jay to the Continental Congress

Office for foreign Affairs July 4th. 1785

The Secretary of the United States for the Department of foreign Affairs to whom was referred a Copy of the Convention respecting french and american Consuls

REPORTS—

That the Convention, of which the abovementioned is a Copy, having been formally executed by french and american Plenipotentiaries, nothing is wanting to perfect that Compact, but the Ratifications specified in the 16th. Article.

The only Question therefore that remains to be decided is, whether Congress ought to ratify this Convention.

To decide this Question properly, it appears necessary (1st.) to recur to the Powers and Instructions given to their Minister on this Subject; and enquire whether he has pursued them essentially, and (2d.) whether in Case of Deviations, they are of such a Nature as to justify a Refusal to ratify.

It is to be observed that on the 25th. January 1782 Congress.

"RESOLVED that the Minister Plenipotentiary of the United States at the Court of Versailles, be and is hereby authorised and *instructed*, to enter into a Convention with His Most Christian Majesty, on the Part of the United States for the Establishment of consular Powers and Priviledges ACCORDING to the Scheme hereunto subjoined; unless it shall be deemed by his Most Christian Majesty more expedient that the same should be executed in the United States.

"That the said Minister Plenipotentiary use *his Discretion* as to the *Words or Arrangement* of the Convention; CONFINING himself to the *Matter* thereof in ALL RESPECTS, except as to so much of the SIXTH Article, as relates to the Erection of a Chapel, taking Care that reciprocal Provision be made for the Recognition of the Consuls and Vice Consuls of the United States, & for the Admission of Persons attached to the Consulate to the Priviledges stipulated in the 5th. Article, in a Manner most conducive to Expedition and free'st from Difficulty."

This is the only Instruction as well as the only Authority given on the Subject, to the American Minister, that your Secretary finds.

SCHEME
Title

Convention between his Most Christian Majesty and *the United States of North America* for defining and regulating the Functions and Priviledges of Consuls, Vice Consuls, Agents and Commissaries.

CONVENTION
Title

Convention between his Most Christian Majesty and the *thirteen United States of North America* for the Purpose of determining and fixing the Functions & Prerogatives of their respective Consuls, Vice-Consuls, Agents & Commissaries.

The Stile of the Confederacy being "the United States of America," the Scheme and the Convention are both erroneous so far as they both add the Word *North*.

But the Title of the Convention departs essentially from that of the Scheme, inasmuch as it limits the Compact to the *thirteen* United States of America, and consequently *excludes* from it all such other States as might before the Ratification of it or in future be created by, or become Parties to, the Confederacy; Whereas the Words in the Title of the Scheme *United States of North America* would if used, have comprehended them all.

SCHEME
1st. Article

It shall be the Duty of the Consuls of his Most Christian Majesty *to present their Commissions in the first Instance to the United States in Congress Assembled* by whom an Act shall be made recognizing them as such. This Act shall be delivered by the Consuls to the Supreme Executive Power of the State or States to which they may be sent. Two Copies of the *Exequatur,* that is, a public Notification of the Quality of the Consuls, shall thereupon issue from the Supreme Executive Power without Fees or Perquisites of Office, one to be retained by the Consuls, the other to be published in one or more Gazettes. This being done the Pre-eminences &c. shall be allowed to them &c.

CONVENTION
1st. Article

The Consuls and Vice Consuls nominated by his Most Christian Majesty and the United States, shall be bound *to present their Commissions on their Arrival in the respective States according to the Form which shall be there established.* There shall be delivered to them, without any Charges, the *Exequatur* necessary for the Exercise of their Functions; and on the Exhibition they shall make of the said *Exequatur* the Governors &ca. having Authority in the Ports and Places of their Consulates shall cause them to enjoy as soon as possible and without Difficulty the Pre-eminences &c.

The Scheme expressly directs that their Commissions shall in the first Instance *be presented to Congress,* but the Convention by omitting this, seems to intend something else—it indeed directs that they shall *present their Commission on their Arrival in the respective States according to the Form "qui s'y trouvera etablis" which shall be there found established*; but whether established by the *State* or by *Congress* is undecided.

The 2d. Articles in both appear to be alike in Substance.

<table>
<tr><td>SCHEME</td><td>CONVENTION</td></tr>
</table>

SCHEME

3d. Article

Consuls and Vice Consuls shall be Subjects or Citizens of the Power appointing them and interdicted from all Traffic or Commerce for their own or anothers Benefit.

CONVENTION

This Article is wholly omitted in the Convention, and that omission is an *Essential*, though perhaps not *in itself* a very important Deviation from the Scheme.

The 4th. Article in the Scheme and the 3d. in the Convention respecting Agents, differ essentially only in this, that the former has these Words *"nor exact any Fees or Reward under any Pretence whatever"* whereas the latter seems to limit that Prohibition, by these Words *"and without Power to exact from the said Merchants any Duty or Emolument whatever under any Pretext whatsoever."*

The 5th. Article in the Scheme and the 4th. in the Convention have no material Difference.

SCHEME

6th. Article

Consuls and Vice Consuls, in Places where there are no Consuls, may have a Chapel in their Houses, for the Celebration of divine Service, according to their religious Profession. And his Most Christian Majesty & the United States shall cause particular Care to be taken that no Obstacle or Hindrance be thrown in the Way of the funeral Obsequies or Ceremonies observed towards the deceased of either Nation.

CONVENTION

This Article is omitted in the Convention. By the Instruction given to the Minister, that Matter seems to have been left to his Discretion. The Omission however appears important to your Secretary from this Consideration, that although the Catholic Religion may be freely and publicly professed and exercised in the United States, yet the Protestant Religion has no legal Toleration in France. This omission therefore is a Departure from the Line of Reciprocity.

The 7th. Article in the Scheme and the 5th. in the Convention are much alike.

The 8th. Article in the Scheme and the 6th. in the Convention are similar.

The 9th. Article in the Scheme and the 7th. in the Convention also correspond.

SCHEME	CONVENTION
Extract from 10th. Article *on Average*	Extract from 8th. Article *on Average*
"If a Subject of France and a Citizen of the United States be jointly interested in the Cargo, the Damage shall be settled by the Tribunals of the Country, not by the Consuls or Vice Consuls. But where Subjects, Citizens of their own Nation are alone interested, the Consul or Vice Consul shall then chuse experienced Persons of their respective Nations to settle the same."	"If a Subject of his Most Christian Majesty and a Citizen of the United States are interested in the said Cargo, the Average shall be fixed by the Tribunals of the Country, and not by the Consuls or Vice Consuls; *and the Tribunals shall admit the Acts and Declarations, if any should have been passed before the said Consuls and Vice Consuls.* But when only the Subjects of their own Nation *or Foreigners* shall be interested, the respective Consuls or Vice Consuls, *and in Case of their Absence or Distance, their Agents furnished with their Commission,* shall officially nominate skilful Persons of their said Nation to regulate the Damages and Averages."

The Convention here appears to differ materially from the Scheme in *three* Respects—(1) As it provides for the Admission in Evidence by our Tribunals of Acts and Declarations passed before Consuls and Vice Consuls respecting the Matter in Controversy, and consequently opens a Door to *exparte* Affidavits. (2) The Scheme confines the Jurisdiction of Consuls and Vice Consuls to Cases where none but their own People are concerned; WHEREAS the Convention extends it to *Foreigners.* (3) The Scheme authorises none but Consuls and Vice Consuls to appoint Persons to settle the Damages in Question; but the Convention makes an ulterior Provision and authorises their Agents ex officio to do it in certain Cases.

The 11th. Article in the Scheme and the 9th. in the Convention are not materially different.

SCHEME	CONVENTION
Extract from 12th. Article	Extract from 10th. Article
"They" (Consuls and Vice Consuls) "may cause to be arrested & sequestred every Vessel carrying the Flag of their respective Nations. They may cause to be arrested and detained in the Country, Sailors and Deserters of their respective Nations, or cause them to be transported therefrom."	"They may cause to be arrested every Vessel carrying the Flag of their respective Nation. They may sequester them, *and even send them back* respectively, from the United States to France or from France to the United States. They may cause to be arrested without Difficulty every *Captain, Master,* Sailor or *Passenger* of their

said respective Nation. They may cause to be arrested and detained in the Country the Sailors and Deserters of their respective Nations, or send them back or transport them out of the Country."

These Articles differ in these Respects. The Scheme does not authorise the Consuls *to send Vessels back* but the Convention does. The Scheme does not authorise them to arrest *Captains and Masters* of Vessels, but the Convention does. The Scheme does not authorise them to arrest *Passengers*, but the Convention does.

SCHEME	CONVENTION
13th. Article	11th. Article
All Offences committed in France by a Citizen of the United States against a Subject of his Most Christian Majesty shall be enquired into and punished according to the Laws of France, those committed in any one of the United States by a Subject of his Most Christian Majesty against a Citizen of the United States, shall be enquired into and punished according to the Laws of such State. But Offences committed in France by a Citizen of the United States against a Citizen of the United States, or committed in any one of the United States by a Subject of his Most Christian Majesty against a Subject of his Most Christian Majesty shall be subject to the Jurisdiction of the Consuls and Vice Consuls of France or the United States as the Case may be.	In Cases where the respective Subjects shall have committed any Crime, they shall be amenable to the Judges of the Country.

These two Articles differ in this, that the one in the Scheme gives Cognizance of certain Offences to Consuls and Vice Consuls, but the one in the Convention gives that Cognizance to the Judges of the Country.

The 14th. Article in the Scheme and the 12th. in the Convention differ only in this, that the former refers certain *Offences*, Disputes and Differences to the Jurisdiction of the Consuls and Vice Consuls, whereas the latter is silent as to *Offences*, and omits making any mention of them.

The 15th. Article in the Scheme, and the 13th. in the Convention are alike.

SCHEME
16th. Article

The Subjects of his Most Christian Majesty and the Citizens of the United States shall be exempt from all personal Services in the Place of their Residence, either in France or the United States as the Case may be. Whensoever any Person in France or the United States as the Case may be, shall claim any Priviledge or Exemption of a Subject of his Most Christian Majesty or of the United States, before any Judge, Tribunal or Officer whatsoever, a Certificate of the Consul or Vice Consul of the District, containing his Name, Surname, and the Place of his Residence, and the Affidavit of the Person claiming such Priviledge or Exemption, that he is a Subject of his Most Christian Majesty or of the United States, as the Case may be, shall be sufficient Evidence thereof, unless the contrary shall manifestly appear.

CONVENTION
14th. Article

The Subjects of his Most Christian Majesty and those of the United States who shall prove that they belong to the Body of their respective Nations, by the Certificate of the Consul or Vice Consul of the District, mentioning their Names, Surnames and Place of their Settlement, as inscribed in the Registers of the Consulate, shall not lose, *for any Cause whatever*, in the respective Domains and States, *the Quality of Subjects of the Country of which they originally were,* conformably to the 11th. Article of the Treaty of Amity and Commerce, of the 6th. February 1778, *of which the present Article shall serve as an Interpretation* in Case of Necessity, And the said Subjects respectively shall enjoy in Consequence, Exemption from all personal Service in the Place of their Settlement.

These two Articles vary from each other essentially—*first,* in that the Certificate of the Consul is by the Convention made the *sole* and *conclusive* Proof of Nationality, whereas the Scheme requires also the Affidavit of the Party, and makes that joint Evidence conclusive only in Cases where *the contrary shall not manifestly appear*—*secondly,* in that the Convention declares that Persons having such Certificates *shall not lose for any Cause whatever the Quality of Subjects of the Country of which they originally were,* whereas the Scheme by not giving such Operation to those Certificates, leaves such Persons within the Reach of *Naturalization. Thirdly,* in that the Convention makes this Article Auxiliary to the 6th. Article of the Treaty by declaring that it shall serve as an Interpretation in Case of Necessity—whereas the Scheme does not constitute any Connection between this Article and the Treaty.

There is no Difference between the 17th. Article in the Scheme and the 15th. in the Convention except that the former refers only to the 3d. and 4th. Articles of the Treaty, whereas the latter refers to the 2nd. 3d. and 4th.

The Convention contains an Article vizt. the 16th., which provides for the Exchange of Ratifications, but there is no such Article in the Scheme.

It appeared proper to your Secretary thus particularly to state the principal Variances between the Scheme and the Convention, that Congress may the more easily judge how far they correspond. The Deviations in Question tho' different in Degrees of Importance, yet seem to be alike in this, that they depart from the *Matter* of the Scheme, and not merely from the Verbage or Arrangement of it.

As Sovereigns treat and act with each other by their Ministers, it becomes essential that the Acts of those Ministers should not be obligatory, until after they are ratified; it being reasonable that the Sovereigns should have an Opportunity of judging, whether their Powers have not been exceeded, and whether their Instructions have been pursued. A Refusal to ratify can therefore be warranted only by one or other of these Principles, Vizt. either that their Ministers have exceeded the Powers delegated by their Commission, or departed from the Instructions given them to limit and regulate the Exercise and Use of those Powers, which are commonly expressed in very general Terms.

Hence it becomes important that the Sovereign refusing to ratify, should be in Capacity to shew clearly what the Powers and Instructions given were, and also that the Treaty or Convention in Question is not conformable thereto.

In the present Case there can be no Difficulty, because all the Power and Authority delegated to the American Minister rest entirely on the Resolution of the 25th. of January 1782; which in a few Words, so blends his Authority and his Instructions that he could not communicate to the french Minister, the one without the other.

Where an open and general Commission is given, accompanied by private and particular Instructions, the one may be shewn and the other reserved. And though a Departure from such Instructions is good Cause to refuse a Ratification; yet more Difficulties attend such Cases than the present, because the other Party being ignorant of the Instructions, and relying on the full Powers, treat in full Confidence and Expectation that the Proceedings will be ratified.

But as the french Ministers in this Instance knew exactly how far the American Minister could go, and saw plainly that he was not to depart from the *Matter* of the Scheme which accompanied, & was referred to in, his Powers and Instructions; they could in Case of essential Deviations, only expect a Ratification *de Gratua*, and not *de Jure*; and consequently can have no Reason to be dissatisfied in Case it should be declined.

Thus much appeared necessary to observe, in order to shew that Congress have a Right to refuse the Ratification in Question—but whether it would be politic and expedient to do it, are Questions which must be entirely referred to the Wisdom of Congress. Your Secretary however in Order fully to comply with what he conceived to have been the Intention of Congress in referring the Convention to him, will now proceed to state the several Objections to which in his Opinion it is liable.

The Convention appears well calculated to answer several Purposes; but the most important of them are such, as America has no Interest in promoting. They are these

1st. To provide against Infractions of the french & american Laws of Trade.

2nd. To prevent the People of one Country from migrating to the other.

3d. To establish in each other's Country an influencial Corps of Officers, under one Chief, to promote mercantile and political Views.

The *first* of these Objects is clearly evinced, by the 10th. Article.

The *second* of these Objects though less explicitly, is still sufficiently evident from the 14th. Article.

The *third* of these Objects as it respects *mercantile* Views is apparent from the general Tenor of the Convention; and it appears plain to your Secretary, that a Minister near Congress, Consuls so placed as to include every Part of the Country in one Consulate or other, Vice Consuls in the principal Ports, and Agents in the less important ones, constitute a Corps, so coherent, so capable of acting jointly and secretly, and so ready to obey the Orders of their Chief, that it cannot fail of being influencial in two very important political Respects; *first* in acquiring & communicating Intelligence, and *secondly* in disseminating, and impressing such Advices, Sentiments and Opinions, of Men or Measures, as it may be deemed expedient to diffuse and encourage.

These being the *three* great Purposes which the Convention is calculated to answer; the next Question which naturally occurs is, whether the United States have any such Purposes to answer by establishing such a Corps in France.

As to the 1st.—We have no Laws for the Regulation of our Commerce with France, or any of her Dominions, and consequently we want no Provisions or Guards against the Infraction of such Laws.

As to the 2nd.—We have not the most distant Reason to apprehend or fear that our People will leave us and migrate either to the Kingdom of France or to any of its Territories, and consequently every Restriction or Guard against it must be superfluous and useless.

As to the 3d.—France being a Country in whose Government the People do not participate, where nothing can be printed without previous Licence, or said without being known, and if disliked followed with Inconveniences, such a Corps would there be very inefficient for political Purposes. Where the People are perfectly unimportant, every Measure to influence their Opinions must be equally so—For *political Purposes* therefore we do not want any such Corps in France.

As to assisting our Merchants, and such other Matters as properly belong to Consuls, they would answer all those Purposes just as well, without these extraordinary Powers, as with them.

Hence it is clear to your Secretary that the *three* great Purposes which the Convention is calculated to answer, are such as the United States have no Interest in promoting. Whether France has any such Purposes to answer in the United States, and how far this Convention may facilitate the Pursuit of them, are Questions which the Discernment of Congress renders it unnecessary for your Secretary to discuss.

Your Secretary also considers this Convention as greatly deficient in Reciprocity, inasmuch as by it we are to admit french Consuls into all our Ports and Places without Exception, whereas no Provision is made for the Admission of ours into any of the Ports, Places and Dominions of his Most Christian Majesty except the Kingdom of France only. He also thinks that the Omission of the Article securing to Consuls the Right of worshipping in their own Way in

Chapels in their Houses, is a Deviation from Reciprocity, especially as that Liberty is not only permitted but established here.

But independent of these *general* Circumstances and Considerations your Secretary thinks the Convention is liable to several strong and *particular* Objections.

When these States assumed a Place among the Nations of the Earth they agreed upon and published to the World the Stile and Title by which they were to be known and called, and your Secretary does not conceive that other Nations are more at Liberty to alter that Stile, than the United States are to alter the Title of his Most Christian, Most Catholic, or any other Majesty in Europe. He therefore thinks that no Act should be ratified by Congress until every Error of this Kind is corrected. Though these Matters are very unimportant in themselves, yet they become so as Precedents; one little Liberty unchecked, often smoothing the Way for a greater.

The Convention directs the Consuls on their Arrival in the respective States to present their Commissions according to the Forms which shall be there found established. Although the *Word respective* here used, relates to the two Countries, and not to the individual States of which our Confederacy is composed, yet it still is doubtful whether the Form alluded to is to be established by Congress or the State to which they may be sent and at which they may arrive. The like Remarks apply to the Case of Vice Consuls mentioned in the 2nd. Article.

In Countries where the Laws alone govern, it should in the Opinion of your Secretary, be an invariable Maxim not to permit any civil Power to be exercised in it but by the Citizens of the Country legally and constitutionally authorised thereto; and that as few Persons as possible, should live exempt, in any Respect, from the Jurisdiction of the Laws. In his Opinion therefore none but the immediate Representatives of Sovereigns ought to have such Exemptions. A Consul is not of that Description. According to the Law of Nations Embassadors must be received—but that Law does not extend to Consuls and therefore, every Nation may admit them on their own Terms. It is not, easy to assign a good Reason for granting them a full and entire Immunity for their Persons, Papers, Houses & Servants, other than such as the free Citizens of the Country enjoy— as they are protected by the Laws, they should be subject to them.

But the Convention goes much further. It grants this Immunity not only to Consuls and also to Vice Consuls, but also to all their different Officers, and in general to all Persons attached to the Consulate. Various Abuses, difficult to detect, and still more difficult to correct, would naturally attend such extensive Exemptions from the Process and Jurisdiction of our Laws; which can only proceed in one open plain direct Path, without the Aid of those Detours and Expedients well known and daily practised in absolute Governments.

The 5th. Article, respecting calling upon them for Evidence, seems to be an unnecessary Departure from our Laws. Why should Consuls and Vice Consuls, be called upon to give Evidence in a Manner less formal and less coercive than the first and highest Officers of our Government are.

The 6th. and 7th. Articles establishing consular and vice *consular Chanceries* create an *Imperium in Imperio*, which in several Respects must clash with the internal Policy of these States, and with which it is not clear that Congress can authorise any Persons to interfere—such as

(1) Their Officers shall discharge the Functions of Notaries. If by Notaries be intended such as are known in this Country—they are public Officers who can only be appointed in the manner prescribed by the Governments of the different States.

(2) All Effects left by deceased Persons (of their Nation) are to be deposited there, and they are to have the *exclusive* Right to inventory, liquidate and sell the moveable Effects &c. so left—so that with Respect to these Matters, not only the Executors of the deceased are to be excluded, but our Judge of Probates is to lose his Jurisdiction. And yet consular Copies of such Wills and Acts though unknown to our Laws, are to be admitted as Evidence in our Courts.

(3) If a french Merchant having many Goods in Possession and many Debts to pay, should die; his Creditors according to this System, are to have no other Dependence for Payment but the Integrity of the Consul or Vice Consul who alone can take Possession of his Goods. No Action can be brought against these Officers nor any Process touch any Thing in their Houses—so that our Courts are so far to lose their Jurisdiction, and american Creditors in effect their Right of Action.

(4) Notes given by french Men dying here are put on another Footing from Notes given by our Citizens, with Respect to Evidence. For the Convention demands that the *writing and signing* of them shall be known and certified by *two principal Merchants of his Nation*; which very materially alters our Law on that Subject.

From these and other Circumstances it appears that this Convention will make a strong Line of Separation between french and american Inhabitants in this Country.

The 10th. Article needs no Comment. It gives to Consuls as complete Jurisdiction over french Vessels in our Harbours, as any of the King's Officers could exercise over them in the Harbours of France. One Circumstance however is very striking and merits much Attention Viz. their Power to *arrest Passengers*, which doubtless will be the Case whenever Passengers attempt to come here in a Manner and for Purposes not consistant with the Ordinances against Emigration. And the Power to arrest also the Captains and Masters, is doubtless intended to punish Neglects of those Ordinances, and to render them very circumspect in their Conduct relative to Passengers and Cargoes.

How far the Power of arresting and reexporting Sailors and Deserters may operate on Emigrants is not difficult to foresee; as the Consuls are to be the only Judges, and our Courts are excluded from hearing the Complaints of any Persons whom the Consuls may describe by those Appellations.

The 14th. Article makes the Certificate of a Consul conclusive Proof of a Man's being a Frenchman and declares that he who shall make *such Proof* shall not lose *for any Cause whatever* the Quality of Subject.

That the Manifestation of so important a Fact should depend wholly on such a Certificate; that no counter Proof should be offered and prevail; is really to make the consular Chancery a Court of Record (and that not only for Judicial Acts, but also for Facts) against whose Records and even the Copies of them there can be no averment. This does not comport with the Genius and Spirit either of our Constitutions or our Laws, both of which secure to every Inhabitant and Citizen the inestimable Priviledge of offering in our Tribunals every Species of legal Evidence that may tend to elucidate the Merits of the Cause before them.

But this is not the only Objection to which this Article is liable—one much more interesting is obvious.

Where such Certificates appear the Person named in them is not to lose *for any Cause whatever* the Quality of Subject so that even legal Naturalization is not to operate as a Cause.

That this is the true Construction of that Clause is evident from its expressly referring to the 11th. Article of the Treaty, and declaring that it shall serve as *an Interpretation* thereof. Let us recur to that Article.

After stating the Priviledges which Persons of the two Nations shall enjoy in each others Country, it thus proceeds "But it is at the same Time agreed that its Contents shall not affect the Laws made or *that may be made hereafter in France* against Emigrations, which shall remain in all their Force and Vigour. And the United States on their Part, or any of them, shall be at Liberty to enact such Laws relative to that Matter, as to them shall seem proper."

Now let us collect into one point of View the different Parts of the System, from their dispersed Situation in the Treaty and in the Articles of this Convention, and see how it will operate.

The King has a Right to make what Laws he may think proper respecting Navigation and Emigration.

Suppose a Law directing that every Passenger shall on his Arrival in America immediately report himself to the Consul or Vice Consul nearest the Place of his Arrival, to the End that his Name & Description be entered in the Consular Registers.

The 10th. Article of the Convention declares that they shall cause to be executed the respective Laws, Ordinances and Rules concerning Navigation, on board the said Vessels—and that they may cause every Passenger to be arrested.

Hence it will happen that every Passenger will be noted and described in their Books before such Passenger can obtain Naturalization—and if he should afterwards obtain it, the 14th. Article renders it avoidable by ordaining that "they who shall prove that they belong to the Body of their respective Nations by the Certificate of the Consul or Vice Consul of the District, mentioning their Names, Surnames and Place of their Settlement *as inscribed in the Registers of the Consulate*, shall not lose, *for any Cause whatever* in the respective States and Domains *the Quality of Subjects of the Country of which they originally were*"—and the same Article proceeds to declare, what is really not the Fact, that this is conformable to the 11th. Article of the Treaty; and as if conscious that the said Article does not admit of such Construction, it adds that it shall serve as an Interpretation of it—that is, that it shall be so construed in future. That 11th. Article does no more than declare the Right of the King to make what Laws he pleases against Emigration, but there is nothing in it which says or seems to say, that his Subjects producing the beforementioned Certificates *shall not for any Cause whatever lose that Quality* in our Country.

Although the true Policy of America does not require, but on the contrary militates against such Conventions; and although your Secretary is of Opinion, that the Convention as it now stands ought not to be ratified, Yet as Congress have proceeded so far in the present Instance, he thinks that Instructions should be sent to their Minister at Versailles to state their Objections to the present Form, and to assure the King of the Readiness of Congress to ratify a Convention made agreeable to the Scheme beforementioned provided an Article be added to limit its Duration to eight or ten Years, in order that Practice and Experience may enable them to judge more accurately of its Merits, than can ever be done of mere theoretical Establishments however apparently expedient.

All which is submitted to the Wisdom of Congress,

JOHN JAY[1]

---

[1] The report, in the hand of Henry Remsen, Jr., and signed by John Jay, is in PCC, item 81, vol. 1, M247, roll 107, DNA, E-19319. The Senate received this report on July 22, 1789. It is related to John Jay's report of July 27, 1789.

Act of the Continental Congress Instructing Thomas Jefferson

Octr. 3. 1786

On a report of The Secretary to the United States for the department of foreign affairs to whom was referred back his report of the 4 July 1785 on the Consular Convention between France and the United States ~~having reported.~~ Resolved

That ~~in his Opinion~~ a copy of that report ~~should~~ be transmitted to the minister plenipotentiary of the United States at Paris in order that he may thereby become fully informed of the Objections to which the Convention is liable.

That a certified copy of the Act of Congress of the 25 day of January 1782 authorizing & directing the honble. Doct. Franklin to conclude a consular Convention be also sent to him.

That a certified copy of the Scheme of such Convention referred to in the above act of Congress be also sent to him.

That he be instructed to communicate the said act of Congress, and the said scheme to his Most Christian Majesty and to point out to him the instances in which the convention deviates from the said scheme.

That he be also instructed to propose to his Majesty that the said Convention be so amended as perfectly to correspond with the scheme in every part where a deviation from the same is not permitted by the said act. And further that he represent to his Majesty the desire of Congress to make the said Convention *probationary* by adding a clause for limiting its duration to eight, or ten years. That he assure his Majesty of the determination of Congress to observe on All occasions the highest respect for candor and good faith in all their proceedings & that on receiving the Convention so amended & with such a clause they will immediately ratify it. Resolved That the honorable Thomas Jefferson esq. the Minister plenipotentiary of the United States at the Court of Versailles be and he is hereby authorised and directed to conclude and sign on the part of the United States with the Minister of his most Christian Majesty having equal powers a Convention for the regulation of their respective Consuls conformably to the scheme above mentioned in every respect except where deviations from it are permitted by the said Act of Congress of the 25 day of January 1782, and with a clause limiting the duration of the said convention to any term of years not exceeding ten.

Ordered That the secretary for foreign Affairs write the following letter to Mr. Jefferson.

Sir, I have the honor of transmitting to you herewith enclosed the following papers, viz.,

N. 1. A copy of the Consular Convention signed by the french and American plenipotentiaries.

N. 2. A copy of the act of Congress under which the American plenipotentiary signed the same

N. 3. A copy of the scheme of a convention mentioned and referred to in the said Act.

N. 4. A copy of a report on the said Convention

N. 5. A copy of an Act of Congress containing instructions & giving authorities to you on the subject of the said Convention.

These papers will possess you fully of the whole business. I am persuaded that it will appear to you as it does to Congress to be a delicate one and to require delicate Management.

The original scheme of the Convention is far from being unexceptionable, but a former Congress having agreed to it, it would be improper now to recede, and therefore Congress are content to ratify a convention made conformable to that scheme and to their act of the 25th day of January 1782 provided a clause limiting its duration be added. It will be proper therefore to press on the Court *only* such objections to the Convention as arise from its departure from the scheme. On making an accurate comparison, such departure will appear manifest to his Majesty; and there is reason to expect from his candor, that he will readily consent to remove the objections occasioned by it.

As it certainly is wise to try the merits of institutions entirely new, by actual experience, before Nations adopt them for ever, the propriety of rendering this Convention probationary in the first instance is unquestionable. Congress cannot therefore presume that his Most Christian Majesty will object to a clause for limiting its duration. The design of this Convention being for mutual and reciprocal benefit and convenience it would be doing injustice to his Majesty to suppose that he would wish to provide for its existing longer than it should prove useful and satisfactory. If after the experience of a few years it should be found to answer the purposes intended by it, both parties will have sufficient inducements to renew it, either in its present form, or with such alterations and amendments as time experience & other circumstances may indicate.[1]

[1] The instructions, in the hand of Charles Thomson, are in PCC, item 5, vol. III, M247, roll 19, DNA. The Senate received the resolutions on July 22, 1789. They are related to John Jay's report of July 27, 1789.

John Jay to the President of the Continental Congress

Office for foreign Affairs 9th. October 1786

SIR,

I take the earliest Opportunity of informing your Excellency that Mr. Remsen, on reading the printed Scheme of a consular Convention, observed that it did not exactly correspond with the Copy in this Office. This Circumstance led him to compare it with the original Scheme in the Secretary's Office, and on making that Comparison, he discovered important Omissions in the 12th. Article of the Copy belonging to this Office. As the Discovery of this Omission rescues the 10th. Article of the Convention from the Charge of essential Deviations from the 12th. in the Scheme, and as it shews the latter to be equally liable with the former to the Objections made against it in my Report, I think it my Duty to enclose a Note of this Variation between the original Scheme and the Copy in this Office, that Congress may have an Opportunity of making any further Order that they may think proper on the Subject.

I confess that the *Scheme* now appears to me more ineligible than I before thought it, though I am still of Opinion that the only prudent way of getting over this unpleasant Business, is to conclude a Convention similar even to the Scheme as it *now* appears to be, and renders its Inconveniences temporary by an Article limiting its Duration.

With great Respect and Esteem I have the Honor to be

P.S. The french Packet will ⎱
sail the 15th. Instant ⎰

Your Excellency's
Most obt. & hble. Servt.
JOHN JAY

NOTE

of the Difference between the 12th. Article of the Scheme of the Convention, entered in the Year 1782 on the Journal belonging to the Office for foreign Affairs, and the said Article in the original Scheme, recorded in the secret Journal in the Secretary's Office.

12 Article	12 Article
"They" (Consuls and Vice Consuls) "may cause to be arrested and sequestered, every Vessel carrying the Flag	"They" (Consuls & Vice Consuls) "may cause to be arrested and sequestered, every Vessel carrying the Flag

of their respective Nations, <u>and even send them back to France or the United States as the case may be, as well as arrest any Captain, Master, Seaman or Passenger of their respective Nations.</u> They may cause to be arrested and detained in the Country, Sailors and Deserters of their respective Nations, or cause them to be transported therefrom."

of their respective Nations. They may cause to be arrested and detained in the Country, Sailors and Deserters of their respective Nations, or cause them to be transported therefrom."

The <u>scored</u> Lines shew where the Copy which Mr. Jay used when he made his Report on the consular Convention deviates from the Original.
N.B. There were in that Copy several other Variations from the Original, to the Number of twenty in the whole—all of which are now corrected—but as none of them except the above mentioned materially affect Mr. Jay's Report, it is not thought necessary to enumerate them in this Note.[1]

[1] The letter, in the hand of Henry Remsen, Jr., and signed by John Jay, is in PCC, item 80, vol. III, M247, roll 106, DNA. The Senate received the letter on July 22, 1789. It is related to John Jay's report of July 27, 1789.

Report of John Jay to the Continental Congress

Office for foreign Affairs 10th. May 1787
The Secretary of the United States for the Department of foreign Affairs, to whom was referred that Part of Mr. Jefferson's Letter of the 9th. January last which relates to the Consular Convention, Vizt. "I will certainly do the best I can for the Reformation of the Consular Convention, being persuaded that our States would be very unwilling to conform their Laws either to the Convention or to the Scheme, but it is too difficult and too delicate to form sanguine Hopes; however, that there may be Room to reduce the Convention as much as Circumstances will admit, will it not be expedient for Congress to give me Powers in which there shall be no Reference to the Scheme? The Powers sent me oblige me to produce that Scheme, and certainly the Moment it is produced, they will not abate a Tittle from it. If they recollect the Scheme and insist on it, we can but conclude it, but if they have forgotten it, (which may be) and are willing to reconsider the whole Subject, perhaps we may get rid of something the more of it. As the Delay is not injurious to us, because the Convention whenever and however made is to put us in a worse State than we are in now, I shall venture to defer saying a Word on the Subject 'till I can hear from you in Answer to this. The full Powers may be sufficiently guarded by private Instructions to me not to go beyond the former Scheme. This Delay may be well enough ascribed (whenever I shall have received new Powers) to a Journey I had before apprized

the Minister that I should be obliged to take to some mineral Waters in the South of France, to see if by their Aid I may recover the Use of my right Hand, of which a Dislocation about four Months ago threatens to deprive me in a great Measure—the Surgeons have long insisted on this Measure. I shall return by Bourdeaux, Nantes and L'Orient to get the necessary Information for finishing our Commercial Regulations here. Permit me however to ask as immediately as possible, an Answer either affirmative or negative as Congress shall think best, and to ascribe the Delay on which I venture to my Desire to do what is for the best."

REPORTS,

That in his Opinion the Court of France regard the Consular Convention in its present Form as an interesting Object and that no Article or Provision in it will escape their Recollection. He nevertheless thinks that the Policy of yielding to such Circumstances as cannot without Risque and Hazard be neglected or controuled, will induce them at least to consent to the proposed Article for limiting the Duration of the Convention.

As he perceives no Inconvenience likely to result from giving Mr. Jefferson a Commission, authorizing him in general Terms to negociate and conclude a Convention with his Most Christian Majesty, for ascertaining the Authority and Powers of french and american Consuls, your Secretary thinks it will be adviseable to send him such a Commission, that he may thereby have an Opportunity of endeavoring to realize the Advantages he expects from it, and which under a new Administration (perhaps not well advised of what has passed) may be attainable.

In the Opinion of your Secretary it will therefore be expedient to send Mr. Jefferson a Commission of the following Tenor, Vizt.

WE the United States of America in Congress assembled at the City of New York. To our well beloved Thomas Jefferson Esquire our Minister Plenipotentiary at the Court of his Most Christian Majesty &c. &c. SEND GREETING. Being desirous to promote and facilitate the Commerce between our States and the Dominions of his said Majesty, and for that Purpose to conclude with him a Convention for regulating the Privileges, Powers and Duties of our respective Consuls, Vice Consuls, Agents and Commissaries; and having full Confidence in your Abilities and Integrity, WE do by these Presents authorize and empower you the said Thomas Jefferson in our Name and Behalf, to treat with any Person having equal Powers, from his most Christian Majesty of and concerning such a Convention, and the same in our Name and Behalf to conclude sign and seal; AND WE do promise to ratify & confirm whatever Convention shall in Virtue of this Commission be by you so concluded, provided the Duration of the same be limited to any Term not exceeding twelve Years. WITNESS our Seal and the Signature of his Excellency Arthur St. Clair our President this ——— Day of ——— in the Year of our Lord one thousand seven hundred and eighty seven and the eleventh of our Independence.

Your Secretary thinks it would be proper to write the two following Letters to Mr. Jefferson, the *first* of which he might communicate to the Court.

Sir

Congress being desirous that the Commerce between the United States and France may be promoted by every reciprocal Regulation conducive to that End, wish that no Time may be lost in ascertaining the Privileges, Powers and Duties of their respective Consuls, Vice Consuls and commercial Agents and Commissaries.

They regret the Circumstance which calls you to the South of France, but are perfectly satisfied that you should make that or any other Journey which your Health may require. It is their Wish and Instruction that on your Return to the Court, your Attention may be immediately directed to the above mentioned Subject. Considering that Convention of this Nature however apparently useful in Theory may from some Defects or unforeseen Circumstances be attended with Inconveniences in Practice, they think it best that they should be probationary at least in the first Instance, and therefore that the Term to be assigned for the Duration of the one in Question should not exceed ———— Years. They also think it adviseable, in Order to obviate any Difficulties that might arise from your not having been more formally authorized to complete this Business, to give you an express and special Commission for the Purpose, which I have now the Honor to enclose.

Sir

You will herewith receive another Letter from me of this Date, together with the Commission mentioned in it—both of them are in pursuance of the Ideas suggested in your Letter of the 9th. January last. If the whole Subject should be reconsidered, and a new Convention to be formed, it is the Pleasure of Congress that the Duties, Powers and Privileges of Consuls, Vice Consuls, Agents and Commissaries be accurately delineated, and that they be as much circumscribed and limited as the proper Objects of their Appointment will admit and the Court of France consent to. How far it may be in your Power to obtain a Convention perfectly unexceptionable, must depend on several Circumstances not yet decided. Congress confide fully in your Talents and Discretion, and they will ratify any Convention that is not liable to more Objections than the one already in part concluded, provided an Article limiting its Duration to a Term not exceeding ———— Years be inserted.

All which is submitted to the wisdom of Congress

JOHN JAY[1]

---

[1] The report, in the hand of Henry Remsen, Jr., and signed by John Jay, is in PCC, item 81, vol. III, M247, roll 107, DNA. The Senate received the report on July 22, 1789. It is related to John Jay's report of July 27, 1789.

Thomas Jefferson to John Jay

Paris Nov. 14. 1788

SIR,

In my letter of Dec. 21. 1787. I had the honour of acknoleging the receipt of your two favours of July 27. 1787. which had come to my hands Dec. 19. &

brought with them my full powers for treating on the subject of the Consular convention. being then much engaged in getting forward the Arret which came out the 29th. of Dec. & willing to leave some interval between that act, & the sollicitation of a reconsideration of our Consular convention, I had declined mentioning it for some time, & was just about to bring it on the carpet, when it became necessary for me to go to Amsterdam. immediately after my return, which was about the last of April, I introduced the subject to the Count de Montmorin, & have followed it unremittingly from that time. the office of Marine, as well as that of foreign affairs, being to be consulted in all the stages of the negociation, has protracted it's conclusion till this time. it is at length signed this day, & I have now the honour to inclose the original for the ratification of Congress. the principal changes effected are the following:

The clauses of the Convention of 1784, cloathing Consuls withe the privileges of the law of Nations, are struck out, & they are expressly subjected, in their persons & property, to the laws of the land.

That giving the right of Sanctuary to their houses is reduced to a protection of their Chancery room & it's papers.

Their coercive powers over passengers are taken away: and over those whom they might have termed deserters of their nation, are restrained to deserted seamen only.

The clause allowing them to arrest & send back vessels is struck out, & instead of it they are allowed to exercise a police over the ships of their nation generally.

So is that which declared the indelibility of the character of subject, & the explanation & extension of the 11th. article of the treaty of Amity.

The innovations in the Laws of evidence are done away.

And the Convention is limited to 12. years duration.

Convinced that the fewer examples, the better, of either persons or causes inamenable to the laws of the land, I could have wished still more had been done. but more could not be done with good humor. The extensions of authority given by the Convention of 1784. were so homogeneous with the spirit of this government, that they were prized here. Monsieur de Rayneval has had the principal charge of arranging this instrument with me: &, in justice to him, I must say I could not have desired more reasonable & friendly dispositions than he demonstrated through the whole of it.

I inclose herewith the several schemes successively proposed between us, together with copies of the written observations given in with them, & which served as texts of discussion in our personal conferences. they may serve as a commentary on any passage which may need it, either now or hereafter, and as a history how any particular passage comes to stand as it does. No. 1. is the Convention of 1784. No. 2. is my first scheme. No. 3. theirs in answer to it. No. 4. my next, which brought us so near together, that, in a conference on that, we arranged it in the form in which it has been signed. I add No. 5. the copy of a translation which I have put into their hands, with a request that, if they find any passages in which the sense of the original is not faithfully rendered they will point them out to me. otherwise we may consider it as having their approbation. this, and the Convention of 1784. (marked No. 1.) are placed side by side so as to present to the eye, with less trouble, the changes made; and I inclose a number of printed copies of them for the use of the members who will have to decide on the ratification. it is desireable that the ratification should be sent here for exchange as soon as possible.

With respect to the Consular appointments, it is a duty on me to add some observations which my situation here has enabled me to make. I think it was in the Spring of 1784. that Congress (harrassed by multiplied applications from foreigners, of whom nothing was known but on their own information, or on that of others as unknown as themselves) came to a resolution that the interest of America would not permit the naming any person, not a citizen, to the office of Consul, viceconsul, agent, or commissary. this was intended as a general answer to that swarm of foreign pretenders. it appears to me that it will be best still to preserve a part of this regulation. *Native* citizens, on several valuable accounts, are preferable to Aliens, & to citizens alien-born. they possess our language, know our laws, customs, & commerce, have generally acquaintance in the U.S. give better satisfaction, and are more to be relied on in point of fidelity. their disadvantages are, an imperfect acquaintance with the language of this country, & an ignorance of the organisation of it's judicial & executive powers, & consequent awkwardness whenever application to either of these is necessary, as it frequently is. but it happens that in some of the principal ports of France there is not a single American (as in Marseilles, Lorient, & Havre) in others but one (as in Nantes & Rouen) and in Bordeaux only are there two or three. fortunately for the present moment, most of these are worthy of appointments. but we should look forward to future times when there may happen to be no native citizens in a port but such as, being bankrupt have taken asylum in France from their creditors, or young, ephemeral adventurers in commerce without substance or conduct, or other descriptions which might disgrace the consular office, without protecting our commerce. to avail ourselves of our good *native citizens*. when we have one in a port, &, when there are none, to have yet some person to attend to our affairs, it appears to me adviseable to declare, by a standing law, that no person but a native citizen shall be capable of the office of *Consul*; & that the Consul's presence in his port should suspend for the time the functions of the Viceconsul. this is the rule of 1784. restrained to the office of *Consul* and to *native* citizens. the establishing this by a standing law will guard against the effect of particular applications, & will shut the door against such applications, which will otherwise be numerous. this done, the office of Viceconsul may be given to the best subject in the port whether citizen or alien and that of Consul be kept open for any native citizen of superior qualifications, who might come afterwards to establish themselves in the port. the functions of the Viceconsul would become dormant during the presence of his principal, come into activity again on his departure, & thus spare us & them the painful operation of revoking & reviving their commissions perpetually. add to this that during the presence of the Consul, the Viceconsul would not be merely useless, but would be a valuable counsellor to his principal, new in the office the language laws & customs of the country. every Consul & viceconsul should be restrained in his jurisdiction to the port for which he is named and the territory nearer to that than to any other Consular or Viceconsular port, and no idea permitted to arise that the grade of consul gives a right to any authority whatever over a viceconsul, or draws on any dependance.

To these general facts & observations I will add some local, and of the present moment.

Marseilles. there is no native. Stephen Cathalan, the father has had the Agency, by appointment either of Doctr. Franklin or Mr. Barclay. but his son, of the same name, has solely done the duties, & is best capable of them. he speaks our language perfectly, is familiar with our customs, as having lived in a counting house in London, is sensible, active, & solid in his circumstances. both the port & person merit a Viceconsulate.

Bordeaux. Mr. John Bondfeild, a native citizen, has hitherto acted by appointment from Doctr. Franklin. he is well known in America; is of a [*blotted out*] higher degree of information than is usually to be found, and unexceptionable in every point of view. his circumstances, indeed, have, at one time, been perplexed; but I suppose them to be otherwise now. he is likely to remain long at Bordeaux, and is so much respected that we cannot expect a better subject there. I think him proper for a *Consular* commission.

Nantes. we have but one native citizen there, Mr. Burrell Carnes, who has acted by appointment from Mr. Barclay, and acted well as far as I am able to judge. he is young, & beginning business only, would be proper for the vice-consulate at present, & for the Consulate when time shall have added experience & firm establishment to his present qualifications.

Lorient. no citizen at all. Mr. Loreilhé, a Frenchman and very worthy man, acted for some time: but failing in his affairs he removed to the neighborhood of Bordeaux. after that, I wrote occasionally to Wilt & Delmestre: but they too are become bankrupt. there is lately gone there from Paris a Monsieur Vernés, an uncommonly sensible well informed man, speaking our language well, connected in commerce with the wealthy house of Berard & co. & particularly engaged in the American commerce. I suppose him proper for a Vice-consulate.

Havre. there is no native. Mr. André Limosin has acted by appointment of Doctr. Franklin. he is a very solid merchant, speaks & writes our language, is sensible, experienced, & very zealous. his services hitherto have been so assiduous as to entitle him to the viceconsulate in preference to any other person of that port.

Rouen. there is but one citizen there, Mr. Thomas Appleton, son of Nathaniel Appleton of Boston. he is young, & just beginning business. he is sensible, active, & fit for the viceconsulate, with a view to the Consulate at some future day, as in the case of Mr. Carnes.

The preceding are the only ports worthy of either Consular or Viceconsular establishment. to multiply, would be to degrade them, and excite jealousy in the government. at the following I should suppose Agents sufficient.

Dunkirk. Francis Coffyn. an American & good man appointed by Doctr. Franklyn.

Dieppe. Mr. Cavalier, a Frenchman appointed by Mr. Barclay.

Bayonne. Louis Alexander has meddled for us of his own accord. I know neither good nor harm of him. he writes a broken English, but I do not know whether he speaks the language. tho' a free-port there had entered there but one or two ships from the peace to the autumn of 1787. I have no account since.

Cette. Nicholas Guirrard, named by Dr. Franklin he is of the mercantile house of Guirrard & Portas. I saw one of the partners when at Cette, who spoke English well, is familiar with English usages in commerce, is sensible, & has the appearance of being a good man. but I do not recollect whether the person I describe was Guirrard or Portas. the other partner does not speak English. Mr. Barclay can probably fix this incertainty, as well as give fuller information on all the other persons named. this one whichever he be, is fittest for the Agency.

Besides these I would take the liberty of recommending the appointment of Agents at Toulon, Rochefort, Brest, & Cherburg, merely for the purposes of intelligence. they are king's ports & it is in them that the symptoms of a maritime war will always first shew themselves. such a correspondence therefore will be always proper for your minister here, and in general the consuls & vice consuls should be instructed to correspond with him for his information. it does not appear to me proper that he should have any power of naming or removing them it might lead to abuse.

It is now proper I should give some account of the state of our dispute with Schweighauser & Dobrée. in the conversation I had with Dobrée at Nantes, he appeared to think so rationally on this subject, that I thought there would be no difficulty in accommodating it with him, and I wished rather to settle it by accommodation than to apply to the minister. I afterwards had it intimated to him through the medium of Mr. Carnes, that I had it in idea to propose a reference to arbitrators. he expressed a chearful concurrence in it. I thereupon made the proposition to him formally by letter mentioning particularly that we would chuse our arbitrators of some neutral nation & of preference from among the Dutch refugees here. I was surprized to receive an answer from him wherein, after expressing his own readiness to accede to this proposition, he added that on consulting Mr. Puchelbourg, he had declined it: nevertheless he wished a fuller explanation from me as to the subjects to be submitted to arbitration. I gave him that explanation, & he answered finally that Mr. Puchelbourg refused all accomodation & insisted that the matter should be decided by the tribunals of the country. accomodation being at an end, I wrote to Monsieur de Montmorin, & insisted on the usage of nations, which does not permit the effects of one sovereign to be seised in the territories of another, & subjected to judiciary decision there. I am promised that the stores shall be delivered: but the necessary formalities will occasion some delay. the king being authorized to call all causes before himself, ours will be evoked from the tribunal where it is, and will be ended by an order to deliver up the stores arrested, leaving it to the justice of Congress to do afterwards what is right as to the demand of Schweighauser & Dobrée. I wish I could receive instructions what to do with the stores when delivered. the arms had certainly better be sent to America, as they are good, & yet will sell here for little or nothing. the gun stocks & old iron had better be sold here. but what should be done with the anchors? being thoroughly persuaded that Congress wish that substantial justice should be done to Schweighause & Dobrée, I shall, after the stores are secured, repeat my proposition of arbitration to them. if they then refuse it, I shall return all the papers to America and consider my powers for settling this matter as at an end.

I have received no answer yet from Denmark on the subject of the prizes: nor do I know whether to ascribe this silence to an intention to evade the demand, or to the multitude of affairs they have had on their hands lately. patience seems to be prudence in this case; to indispose them would do no good, & might do harm. I shall write again soon, if no answer be received in the mean time.

I have the honour to be with sentiments of the most perfect esteem & respect, Sir,

Your most obedient
& most humble servant
TH. JEFFERSON[1]

[1] The letter and the enclosures which follow are in PCC, item 87, vol. II, M247, roll 115, DNA. The letter is in the hand of Thomas Jefferson. The Senate received the letter on July 22, 1789. It is related to John Jay's report journalized July 27, 1789. An extract of the letter, in the hand of John Jay, is in President's Messages on Foreign Relations, Executive Proceedings, SR, DNA.

(1)

Thomas Jefferson to Montmorin

Paris June 20. 1788

SIR,

Having had the honor of mentioning to Your Excellency, the wish of Congress that certain changes should be made in the articles for a Consular convention which had been sent to them. I have now that, conformably to the desire you expressed, of giving a general idea of the alternations to be proposed.

The IVth. article gives to Consuls the immunities of the Law of nations. it has been understood however that the laws of France do not admit of this: & that it might be desirable to expunge this article. in this we are ready to concur, as in every other case where an article might call for changes in the established laws either inconvenient or disagreeable.

After establishing in favor of Consuls the general immunities of the law of nations, one consequence of which would have been that they could not have been called upon to give testimony in courts of justice, the Vth. article requires that, after the observance of certain formalities which imply very high respect, they shall make a declaration, but, *in their own houses* [chez eux], as may be pretended, if not justly inferred, from the expressions in the article. but our laws require indispensably a personal examination of witnesses in the presence of the parties, of their counsel, the jury & judges, each of whom has a right to ask of them all questions pertinent to the fact. the first & highest officers of our government are obliged to appear personally to the order of a court to give evidence. the court takes care that they are treated with respect. it is proposed therefore to omit this article for these particular reasons as well as for the general one that, the IVth. being expunged, this, which was but an exception to that, falls of course.

The VIIth. VIIIth. Xth. & XIVth. articles extend their pre-eminences far beyond those which the laws of nations would have given. these articles require that declarations made in the presence of consuls, & certified by them shall be received in evidence in all courts whatever: & in some instances give to their certificates a credibility which excludes all other testimony. the cases are rare in which our laws admit written evidence of facts; & such evidence when admitted, must have been given in the presence of both parties, & must contain the answers to all the pertinent questions which they may have desired to ask of the witness. & to no evidence of whatever nature, written or oral, do our laws give so high credit as to exclude all counter-proof.

These principles are of such antient foundation in our system of jurisprudence, & are so much valued & venerated by our citizens, that perhaps it would be impossible to execute articles which should contravene them. nor is it imagined that these stipulations can be so interesting to this country as to balance the inconvenience & hazard of such an innovation with us. perhaps it might be found that the laws of both countries require a modification of this article, as it is inconcievable that the certificate of an American consul in France could be permitted by one of its courts to establish a fact the falsehood of which should be notorious to the court itself.

The VIIIth. article gives to the consuls of either nation a jurisdiction in certain cases over foreigners of any other. on a dispute arising in France between an American & a Spaniard or an Englishman, it would not be fair to abandon the Spaniard or Englishman to an American consul. on the contrary the territorial judge, as neutral, would seem to be the most impartial. probably therefore it will be thought convenient for both parties to correct this stipulation.

A dispute arising between two subjects of France, the one being in France & the other in the United States, the regular tribunals of France would seem entitled to a preference of jurisdiction yet the XIIth. article gives it to their consul in America, & to the Consul of the United States in France in a like case between their citizens.

The power given by the Xth. article of arresting & sending back a vessel its captain & crew, is a very great one indeed, & in our opinion more safely lodged with the territorial judge. we would ourselves trust the tribunals of France to decide when there is just cause for so high-handed an act of authority over the persons & property of so many of our citizens, to all of whom these tribunals will stand in a neutral & impartial relation, rather than any single person whom we may appoint as consul, who will seldom be learned in the laws, & often susceptible of influence from private interest & personal pique. With us, applications for the arrest of vessels & of their masters, are made to the Admiralty-courts. these are composed of the most learned & virtuous characters in the several states, & the maritime laws common to all nations, are the rule of their proceeding. the exercise of foreign jurisdiction within the pale of their own laws, in a very high case, in a case wherein those laws have made honorable provision, would be a phaenomenon never yet seen in our country, & which would be seen with great jealousy & uneasiness. on the contrary to leave this power with the territorial judge, will inspire confidence & friendship & be really at the same time more secure against abuse.

The power of arresting deserted seamen seems necessary for the purposes of navigation & commerce & will be more attentively & effectually exercised by the consul than by the territorial judge. to this part of the Xth. article therefore, as well as to that which requires the territorial judge to assist the consul in the exercise of this function, we can accede but the extension of the like power to passengers seems not necessary for the purposes either of navigation or commerce, it does not come therefore within the functions of the consul whose institution is for these two objects only, nor within the powers of a commissioner authorized to treat & conclude a convention solely for regulating the powers, privileges & duties of Consuls. the arrest & detention of passengers moreover would often be in contradiction to our bills of rights, which being fundamental, cannot be obstructed in their operation by any law or convention whatever.

Consular institutions being entirely new with us, Congress think it wise to make their first convention probationary & not perpetual. they propose therefore a clause for limiting its duration to a certain term of years. if after the experience of a few years it should be found to answer the purposes intended by it, both parties will have sufficient inducements to renew it, either in its present form, or with such alterations & amendments as time, experience & other circumstances may indicate.

The convention as expressed in the French language will fully answer our purposes in France, because it will there be understood. but it will not equally answer the purposes of France in America, because it will not there be understood. in very few of the courts wherein it may be presented, will there be found a single judge or advocate capable of translating it at all, much less of giving to all its terms, legal & technical, their exact equivalent in the laws & language of that country. should any translation which Congress should undertake to publish for the use of our courts, be conceived on any occasion not to render fully the idea of the French original, it might be imputed as an indirect attempt to abridge or extend the terms of a contract at the will of one party only. at no place are these better helps than here for establishing an English text equivalent to the French in all its phrases: no persons can be supposed to know what is meant by these phrases better than those who form them & no time more proper to ascertain their meaning in both languages than that at which they are formed. I have therefore the honour to propose that the Convention shall be faithfully expressed in English as well as in French, in two columns side by side, that these columns be declared each of them to be text & to be equally original & authentic in all courts of justice.

This, Sir, is a general sketch of the alterations which our laws & our manner of thinking render necessary in this convention, before the faith of our country is engaged for its execution. some of its articles, in their present form, could not be executed at all, & others would produce embarassments & ill humour to which it would not be prudent for our government to commit itself. inexact execution on the one part would naturally beget dissatisfaction & complaints on the other, & an instrument intended to strengthen our connexion might thus become the means of loosening it. fewer articles better observed, will better promote our common interests. as to ourselves we do not find the institution of consuls very necessary. it's history commences in times of barbarism & might well have ended with them. during these they were perhaps useful & may be still be so in countries not yet emerged from that condition. but all civilized nations at this day understand so well the advantages of commerce, that they provide protection & encouragement for merchant strangers & vessels coming among them. so extensive too are commercial connexions now become, that every mercantile house has correspondents in almost every port, they address their vessels to these correspondents, who are found to take better care of their interests, & to obtain more effectually the protection of the laws of the country for them than the consul of their nation can. he is generally a foreigner; unpossessed of the little details of knowledge of greatest use to them. he makes national questions of all the difficulties which arise; the correspondent prevents them. we carry on commerce with good success in all ports of the world: yet we have not a consul in a single port, nor a complaint for the want of one, except from the persons who wish to be consuls themselves, tho' these considerations may not be strong enough to establish the absolute inutility of Consuls, they may make us less anxious to extend their privileges & jurisdictions so as to render them objects of jealousy & irritation in the places of their residence. that This government thinks them useful, is sufficient reason for us to give them all the functions & facilities which our circumstances will admit. instead therefore of declining every article w[hi]ch will be useless to us, we accede to every one which will not be too inconvenient. had this nation been alone concerned, our desire to gratify them might have tempted us to press still harder on the laws & opinions of our country. but Your Excellency knows that we stand engaged in treaties with some nations which will give them occasion to claim whatever privileges we yield to any other. this renders circumspection more necessary. permit me to add one other observation. the English allow to foreign Consuls scarcely any functions within their ports. this proceeds in a great measure from the character of their laws, which eye with peculiar jealousy every exemption from their controul. ours are the same in their general character & rendered still more unpliant by our having thirteen Parliaments to relax instead of one. Upon the whole I hope Your Excellency will see the causes of the delay which this convention has met with, in the difficulties it presents, & our desire to surmount them: & will be sensible that the alterations proposed are dictated to us by the necessity of our circumstances, & by a caution, which cannot be disapproved, to commit ourselves to no engagements which we foresee we might not be able to fulfill.

These alterations with some other smaller ones which may be offered on the sole principle of joint convenience, shall be the subject of more particular explanation whenever your Excellency shall honour me with a conference thereon.

I shall then also point out the verbal changes which appear to me necessary to accomodate the instrument to the views before expressed. In the mean time I have the honour to be with sentiments of the most perfect respect & attachment &c.

/signed/
TH. JEFFERSON[1]

[1] This attested enclosure is in the hand of William Short.

(2)

No. 2.   First Form Proposed on the Part of the United States

Convention entre le roi tres-chretien et les (1) etats-unis de l'Amerique, (2) á l'effet de determiner et fixer les fonctions et prerogatives des consuls, viceconsuls agents et commissaires respectifs.

[Note. (1) omit "treize" & "Septentrionale." (2) the Confederation fixes the title of the Confederacy to be "the United States of America."]

Sa majesté le roi tres chretien et les etats unis de l'Amerique s'etant accordés mutuellement par l'article 29. du traité d'amitié et de commerce conclu entre eux la liberté de tenir dans leurs etats et ports respectifs, des consuls, viceconsuls, agens et commissaires, et voulant en consequence determiner et fixer d'une maniere reciproque et permanente les fonctions et prerogatives des dits consuls, viceconsuls, agens et commissaires, sa M.T.C. a nommé le sieur ———— et les etats unis ont nommé ———— lesquels, après s'etre communiqués leurs pleinpouvoirs respectifs, sont convenus de ce qui suit.

ART. 1.   Les consuls et viceconsuls, (3) *agens et Commissaires* nommés par le R.T.C. et les E.U. (4) *ou de leur autorité,* seront tenus de presenter leurs provisions selon la forme qui se trouvera etablie (5) *par le roi dans ses etats, et par le Congres dans les etats unis.* on leur delivrera, sans aucuns frais l'Exequatur necessaire á l'exercice de leurs fonctions, et sur l'exhibition qu'ils feront du dit Exequatur, les gouverneurs, commandans, chefs de justice, les corps, tribunaux ou autres officiers ayant autorité dans les ports et lieux de leurs consulats, les y feront jouir aussitôt et sans difficulté des preeminences, autorités et privileges accordés reciproquement, sans qu'ils puissent exiger des dits consuls viceconsuls, agents, et commissaires aucun droit sous aucun pretexte quelconque. (6)

[Note. (3) it may be desireable perhaps that the sovereign name the viceconsuls, agents & commissairies himself. therefore the words "agents et commissaires" are proposed to be inserted. if he chuses they should be named by the Consuls. (4) the insertion of the words "ou de leur autorité" enables him to delegate that power to any other. (5) "par le roi T.C. dans ses etats, et par le Congres dans les E.U." this is to preclude the state governments from pretensions which they might set up of establishing the form of recognising Consular commissions.

(6) The amendment of the 1st. article renders the 2d. and first part of the 3d. unnecessary. the latter part of the 3d. article is transferred into the 12th. where the duties & powers of all these officers are defined.]

ART. 4. Les consuls et viceconsuls seront exempts de tout service personnel et offices publics, logement de gens de guerre, milice, guet, garde, tutelle, curatelle, ainsi que de touts droits, taxes, impositions, charges quelconques, fors les biens (7) *meubles et immeubles,* dont ils seront proprietaires (8) *ou possesseurs,* lesquels seront assujettis aux taxes imposées sur les biens de tous autres particuliers. et *à tous autres egards ils seront sujets aux loix du pays, quant à leurs personnes leurs proprietés et leur possessions tout comme le sont les autres etrangers de leur nation.*

[Notes. see letter of June 20. why those passages should be altered which give to Consuls the rights of the law of nations.

(7) "meubles et immeubles." in France the taxes are borne principally by the "biens fonds." but in America they are equally borne by the "biens meubles." (8) "ou possesseurs." in France the proprietor pays the tax; therefore houses occupied by American Consuls in France will pay taxes. in America the possessor pays the tax. without the insertion of these words then, "ou possesseurs," houses occupied by French consuls in America will escape taxes.]

Ils placeront sur la porte exterieur de leur maison les armes de leur souverain, sans cependant que cette marque distinctive puisse donner á la dite maison le droit d'asyle *soit pour des personnes, soit pour des effets quelconques.*

[Note. omit art. 5. see letter of June 20. as to the manner of giving evidence in the U.S.]

ART. 6. Les consuls et viceconsuls respectifs pourront etablir une chancellerie ou seront deposés les actes et deliberations consulaires, tous les effets delaissés par defunts, ou sauvés des naufrages, ainsi que les testamens, obligations, contrats, et generalement tous les actes et procedures faits entre leurs nationaux. (9)

Ils pourront en consequence commettre à l'exercise de la dite chancellerie des personnes capables, les recevoir, leur faire preter serment, leur donner la garde du sceau, et le droit de sceller les commissions, jugemens, et autres actes du consulat ainsi que d'y remplir les fonctions des notaires et grefiers (10) *dans les cas qui n'interesseront que des sujets ou citoyens de leur propre nation.*

[Note. (9) omit "ou par leurs nationaux." and (10) insert "dans les cas qui n'interesseront que des sujets ou citoyens de leur propre nation." every country possesses within it's own limits all the sovereign powers legislative, executive, & judiciary. through complaisance or friendship it sometimes retires from the exercise of it's own judiciary so far as to permit the individuals of another nation, happening to be with them, to have a judge of their own, appointed by their own government, & judging between them according to their own laws. but they should not permit that foreign judicatory, nor those foreign laws to be extended in any instance over their own people, nor over those of any other foreign nation. acts, therefore, done by, or before, those foreign judges should have authority only among their own countrymen.]

ART. 7. Les consuls et viceconsuls respectifs auront le droit exclusif de recevoir dans leur chancellerie, ou abord des batimens, les declarations et tous les autres actes que les capitaines, patrons, equipages, passagers et negocians de leur nation voudront y passer, meme leur testament et autres dispositions de derniere volunté: et les expeditions des dits acts dument legalisés par les dits consuls ou viceconsuls, et munis du sceau de leur consulat, feront foi en justice *comme le feroient les originaux* dans tous les tribunaux des (11) *etats du R.T.C.* et des etats unis, *et dans tous les cas qui n'interesseront que leurs nationaux.*

[Note. (11) "des etats du R.T.C." the present convention is an execution of the 29th. article of the treaty of amity & commerce. that gives to each party "la liberté de tenir dans *leurs etats et ports* respectifs, des consuls &c." not confining them to France alone.]

Ils auront aussi et exclusivement, (12) *en cas d'absence d'executeur testamentaire, curateur ou heritiers legitimes,* le droit de faire l'inventaire la liquidation, & de proceder á la vente des effets mobiliers de la succession des sujets, *ou citoyens* de leur nation qui viendront á mourir dans l'etendue de leurs consulats, ils y procederont avec l'assistance de deux negocians de leur dite nation, (13) *ou de toute autre* á leur choix et feront deposer dans leur chancellerie les effets et papiers des dites successions, sans qu'aucuns officiers militaires, de justice, ou de police du pays, puissent les y troubler, ni y intervenir de quelque maniere que ce soit, mais les dits consuls ne pourront faire la delivrance des successions et de leur produit aux heritiers legitimes, ou á leurs mandataires qu'aprés avoir fait acquitter toutes les dettes que les defunts auront pû avoir contractés dans le pais (14) *á l'effet de quoi les creanciers auront droit de saisir les dits effets dans leurs mains, de meme que dans celles de tout autre individu quelconque, et en poursuivre la vente jusqu'au paiment de ce qui leur sera justement dû lorsque les dettes n'auront eté contracteés par jugement, par acte, ou par billet dont la (15) signature sera reconnu le paiment* ne pourra en etre ordonné qu'en fournissant par le creancier caution suffisante et domiciliée de rendre les sommes indument perçues, principal, interêt et frais; lesquelles cautions cependant demeureront duement dechargées apres une année en tems de paix et deux en tems de guerre, si la demande en decharge ne peut etre formée avant ces delais, contre les heritiers qui se presenteront. (16) *et afin de ne pas faire injustement attendre aux heritiers les effets du defunt, les consuls et viceconsuls feront annoncer sa mort sur quelqu'une des gazettes qui se publient dans l'etendue de leur consulat, et qu'ils retiendront les dits effets sous leurs mains pendant —— mois pour reponde á toutes les justes demandes qui se presenteront: et ils seront tenus aprés ce delai de delivrer aux heritiers l'excedent du montant des demandes qui auront eté formées.*

[Note. (12) "en cas d'absence d'executeur &c." it is presumed that where the decedent has himself preferred another person, & named him his executor, his will ought to be followed. so if his representative be on the spot, the interest becoming his, should not be taken out of his own hands & committed to the consul.

(13) "de tout autre." perhaps there may not be two merchants of his own nation in that port.

(14) "á l'effet de quoi les creanciers &c." the consul standing in the place of

the testamentary executor, should, like him, be obliged to pay debts with the effects: & these should in his hands be open to the creditors, as they would be in the hands of the executor. (15) "dont *l'ecriture et* la signature &c." it should suffice if the signature be proved, tho the body of the instrument be, as it often is, written by another hand. "certifiées par deux notables negocians." it is proposed to omit these words. all legal proof should be received. (16) "et afin de ne pas faire attendre &c." the justice & necessity of this is obvious; otherwise consuls might keep the effects in their own hands, for their own convenience, under pretext that there might be still debts to pay.]

Art. 8. Les consuls et viceconsuls respectifs recevront les declarations, consulats et autre actes consulaires de tous capitaines et patrons de leur nation respective par raison d'avaries essuyées à la mer par des voies d'eau ou de jet de marchandises, et ces capitaines et patrons remettront dans la chancellerie des dits consuls et viceconsuls les consulats et autres actes consulaires qu'ils auront faits dans d'autres ports pour les accidents qui leur seront arrivés pendant leur voyage. si un sujet du roi trés chretien et un habitant des E.U. sont interessés dans la dite cargaison l'avarie sera reglée par les tribunaux du pays, et non par les consuls ou viceconsuls (17); mais lorsqu'il n'y aura d'interessés que les sujets *ou citoyens* de leur propre nation, les consuls ou les viceconsuls respectifs nommeront des experts pour regler les dommages et avaries.
[Note (17) omit "et les dits tribunaux admettront les actes &c. des dits consuls." see Note on Art. 6.]

Art. 9. Dans les cas ou par tempete ou autre accident des vaisseaux ou batiments François echoueront sur les cotes des E.U. et des vaisseaux et batiments des E.U. echoueront sur les cotes des etats du R.T.C. le consul ou le viceconsul le plus proche du lieu du naufrage pourra faire tout ce qu'il jugera convenable, tant pour sauver le dit vaisseau ou batiment, son chargement et apartenances, que pour le magazinage et la sureté des effets sauvés et marchandises il pourra en faire l'inventaire, sans qu'aucuns officiers militaires, des douanes, de justice ou de police du païs puissent s'y immiscer, autrement que pour faciliter aux consuls et viceconsuls capitaine et equipage du vaisseau naufragé ou echoué, tous les secours et faveurs qu'ils leur demanderont, soit pour la celerité et la sureté du sauvetage et des effets sauvés, soit pour eviter tous desordres.

Pour prevenir meme toute espece de conflit et de discussion dans les dits cas de naufrage, il a eté convenu que lorsqu'il ne se trouvera pas de Consul or viceconsul pour faire travailler au sauvetage, ou que la residence du dit consul ou viceconsul qui ne se trouvera pas sur le lieu du naufrage sera plus eloignée du dit lieu que celle du juge territorial competent, ce dernier y fera proceder sur le champ avec toute la celerité, la sureté, et les precautions prescrites par les loix respectives, sauf au dit juge territorial á se retirer le consul ou viceconsul survenant, et a lui remettre les procedures par lui faites, dont le consul ou viceconsul lui fera rembourser les frais.

Les marchandises et effets sauvés devront etre deposés á la Douane ou autre lieu de sureté le plus prochain avec l'inventaire qui en aura eté dressé par le consul ou viceconsul, ou, en leur absence par le juge qui en aura connu, pour les dits effets et marchandises etre ensuite delivrés, après le prelevement des frais et sans forme de proces, aux proprietaires, qui, munis de la main levée du Consul ou viceconsul le plus proche, les reclameront par euxmemes, ou par leurs mandataires, soit pour re-exporter les marchandises; et dans ce cas elles ne payeront aucune espece de droits de sortie, soit pour les vendre dans le pays si elles n'y sont pas prohibées, et dans ce dernier cas, les dites marchandises, se trouvant avariées on leur accordera une moderation les droits d'entrée propor- tionée au dommage souffert, lequel sera constaté par le procés verbal dressé lors du naufrage ou de l'echouement.

ART. 10. Les consuls et viceconsuls (18) pourront faire arreter dans le païs les matelots (19) deserteurs de leurs nations respectives et les renvoyer et faire transporter hors du païs.

(20) *Les registres de vaisseaux, ou roles d'equipage seront reçus en temoignage pour prouver que les personnes arretées comme matelots deserteurs appartiennent á leurs nations respectives; mais n'exclueront point les autres preuves legales relatives au meme fait.*

Dés qu'il y aura des preuves suffisantes que ce sont des matelots deserteurs de telle nation, aucuns tribunaux, juges et officiers quelconques ne pourront en quelque maniere que ce soit, connoitre des plaintes que les dits matelots deserteurs pourroient former; mais ils seront au contraire delivrés sur un ordre signe par le consul ou viceconsul, sans qu'on puisse aucunment, les detenir, engager, ou soustraire et pour parvenir á l'entiere execution des dispositions contenues dans cet article, toutes personnes, ayant autorité seront tenus d'assister les dits consuls ou viceconsuls, et sur un simple requisitoire signé d'eux ils feront detenir et garder dans les prisons, à la disposition, et aux frais des dits consuls et viceconsuls les dits matelots deserteurs jusqu'a ce qu'ils aient occasion de les faire sortir du païs. (21) *mais s'ils ne sont envoyés hors du pays dans un mois du jour de leur arret, ils seront elargis, et ne pourront plus etre arretés pour la meme cause.*

[Note. (18) omit "auront abord des batiments de leur nation &c." see note on Art. 6. and letter of June 20. on the 10th. article.

(19) "matelots *et* deserteurs." omit "*et*." see letter of June 20. on Article 10.

(20) "il suffira pour prouver &c." omit this, & see letter of June 20. on Articles 5. 7. 8. 10. & 14.

(21) "mais s'ils ne sont envoyés hors du pays" &c. this addition is necessary, as neither country would chuse to be converted by the other into a perpetual prison.]

ART. 11. Dans le cas ou les sujets *ou citoyens* respectifs auront commis quelque crime, (22) *ou infraction de la tranquillité publique*, ils seront justi- ciables des juges du païs.

[Note. (22) "ou infraction de la tranquillité &c." the word "crime" is some- times understood with us as meaning *capital crime* only. our laws therefore generally add the expression "or breaches of the peace" to include smaller offences against the peace.]

Art. 12. Tous les differends et procés entre les sujets du roi trés chretien dans les etats unis, ou entre les citoyens des E.U. *dans les etats du R.T.C.* (23) seront terminés par les consuls respectifs, *si l'un des parties le demande* soit par un renvoi pardevant des arbitres, soit par un jugement sommaire et sans frais. [Note (23). omit "et tous les differends et procés &c." see letter June 20. on Art. 12.]

Aucun officier civil ou militaire ne pourra intervenir ou prendre une part quelconque á l'affaire. les appels seront portés devant les tribunaux de France ou des etats unis qui devront en connoitre (24).

[Note (24) "les consuls ou viceconsuls ne pourront connoitre des disputes" &c. this is judged to be unnecessary & even to imply a doubt (which ought not to exist) Whether the exercise of authority here described might not belong to the Consul were he not excluded? whereas it is a fundamental truth that all power is in the state, & that the Consul will have none but what they give him by this convention.]

(25) Les agents respectifs se renfermeront à rendre aux commerçants navigateurs et batiments respectifs tous les services possibles, et á informer le consul ou viceconsul le plus proche des besoins des dits commerçants, navigateurs et batiments sans que les dits agens puissent autrement participer aux immunités, droits et privileges attribués aux Consuls et viceconsuls, et sans pouvoir, sous quelque pretexte que ce soit, exiger aucun droit ou emolument quelconque. [Note (25) "Les agents respectifs &c." this is the part of the 3d. article which is retained & transposed here.]

Art. 13. L'utilité general du commerce ayant fait etablir *dans les etats du R.T.C.* des tribunaux, et des formes particulieres pour accelerer la decision des affaires de commerce, les negocians des E.U. jouiront du benefice de ces etablissements. et le Congrés des E.U. *pourvoira de la maniere la plus conforme á ses loix á l'etablissement.* des avantages equivalents en faveur des negocians François pour la prompte expedition et decision des affaires de la meme nature.

Art. 14. Les sujets du R.T.C. et *les citoyens* des E.U. que justifieront *authentiquement* etre du corps de la nation respective, (26) jouiront en consequence de l'exemption de tout service personel dans le lieu de leur etablissement. [Note (26) "par le certificat du Consul &c." see letter June 20. on Article 10.]

Art. 15. Si quelque autre nation acquiert en vertu d'une convention quelconque un traitement plus favorable relativement aux pre-eminences, pouvoirs, autorité et privileges consulaires, les consuls, viceconsuls et agens du R.T.C. ou des E.U. reciproquement y participeront aux termes stipulées par les articles 2. 3. et 4. du traité d'Amitié et de commerce conclu entre le R.T.C. et les E.U.

Art. 16. *La presente convention aura son plein effet pendant l'espace de douze ans, a compter du jour de l'exchange des ratifications les quelles* seront données en bonne forme, et changées de part et d'autre dans l'espace d'un an, ou plutôt si faire se peut.

En foi de quoi nous soussignés &c.[1]

---

[1] The proposal is in the hand of Thomas Jefferson.

(3)

English Translation

No. 2. First form Proposed on the part of the U. States
Translation

Convention between His Most Christian Majesty & the U. States of America for the purpose of determining & fixing the functions & prerogatives of their respective Consuls, Vice consuls, Agents & Commissaries.

His majesty the Most Christian King & the U. States of America, having by the 29th. Article of the Treaty of Amity & Commerce concluded between them, mutually granted the liberty of having in their respective states & ports, Consuls, viceconsuls, Agents & Commissaries, and being willing in consequence thereof to determine & fix in a reciprocal & permanent manner the Functions & prerogatives of the said Consuls, Viceconsuls agents & Commissaries, His M.C.M. has nominated the Sieur ———— & the U. States of America have nominated ———— who after having communicated to each other their respective full powers, agreed upon what follows.

ARTICLE 1. The Consuls & Vice Consuls *Agents & Commissaries* nominated by His M.C.M. & the U.S. *or by their Authority* shall be bound to present their commissions according to the forms which shall be established *by the King within his dominions & by the Congress within the U.S.* There shall be delivered to them without any charges the Exequatur necessary for the exercise of their functions & on the exhibition which they shall make of the said exequatur, the Governors Commander, Heads of justice, public bodies, tribunals & other officers having authority in the ports and places of their consulate, shall cause them to enjoy as soon as possible & without difficulty, the pre-eminencies authority & privileges reciprocally granted without exacting from the said Consuls Viceconsuls Agents & Commissaries any duty, under any pretence whatever.

ART. 4. The Consuls & Viceconsuls shall be exempt from all personal service & public offices, from soldiers billets, militia, watch, guard guardianship & trusteeship as well as from all duties taxes, impositions & charges whatever except on the estate *real & personal* of which they may be the proprietors or possessors, which shall be subject to the taxes imposed on the estates of all other individuals. *and in all other instances they shall be subject to the laws of the land with respect to their persons their property & possessions in the same manner as other foreigners of their nation are.*

They shall place over the outward door of their House, the arms of their Sovereign without however this mark of distinction giving to the said House the right of asylum *for any person or property whatever.*

ART. 6. The Consuls & Vice Consuls respectively may establish a Chancery where shall be deposited the Consular acts & deliberations all effects left by deceased persons or saved from shipwreck, as well as testaments, obligations, contracts & in general all the acts & proceedings done between persons of their nation.

They may in consequence appoint for the business of the said Chancery capable persons, receive them administer an oath to them, give to them the keeping of the seal & the right of sealing commissions, judgments & other acts of the consulate as well as there to discharge the functions of notaries & registers in cases which shall concern the subjects or citizens of their own nation.

ART. 7. The Consuls & Vice consuls respectively shall have the exclusive right of receiving in their Chancery or on board of vessels the declarations & all the other acts which the captains masters seamens passengers & merchants of their nation would make there even their testaments & other dispositions of last will; & the copies of the said acts duly authenticated by the said consuls or viceconsuls under the seal of their consulate shall receive faith in law *equally as their originals* would, in all the tribunals of the *dominions of the M.C.K.* & of the U. States, & *in all cases which only concern persons of their nations.*

They shall also have & exclusively, *in case of the absence of the Testamentary executor, guardian or lawful representative,* the right to inventory liquidate & proceed to the sale of the personal estate left by subjects or citizens of their nation, who shall die within the extent of their consulate; they shall proceed therein with the assistance of two merchants of their said nation, *or of any other* of their choice, & shall cause to be deposited in their chancery the effects & papers of their said estates, & no officer military judiciary, or of the police of the country shall disturb them or interfere therein in any manner whatsoever: but the said Consuls shall not deliver up the said effects nor the proceeds thereof to the lawful representatives or to their order, till they shall have caused to be paid all debts which the deceased shall have contracted in the country; *for which purpose the creditor shall have a right to attach the said effects in their hands as they might in those of any other individual whatever, and proceed to obtain sale of them till payment of what shall be lawfully due to them. When the debts shall not have been contracted by judgment, deed or note, the signature whereof shall be known payment* shall not be ordered but on the creditors giving sufficient surety resident in the country, to refund the sum he shall have unduly received, principal, interest & costs: which surety shall stand never the less duly discharged after the term of one year in time of peace, & of two in time of war if the discharge cannot be formed before the end of this term against the representatives who shall present themselves. *And in order that the representatives may not be unjustly kept out of the effects of the deceased the Consuls & Viceconsuls shall notify his death in some one of the Gazettes published within their Consulate, & that they shall retain the said effects in their hands ——— months to answer all just demands which shall be presented: and they shall be bound after this delay to deliver to the persons succeeding thereto what shall be more than sufficient for the demands which shall have been formed.*

ART. 8. The respective Consuls & Vice Consuls shall receive the declarations, Consulates & other Consular acts from all Captains & masters of their respective nation on account of average losses sustained at Sea by leakage or throwing merchandize overboard & these Captains & masters shall leave in the chancery of the said Consuls & Vice Consuls the Consulates & other consular acts which they may have made in other ports, on account of the accidents which may have happened to them on their voyage. If a subject of His M.C.M. & a citizen of the U.S. are interested in the said cargo the average shall be fixed by the Tribunals of the Country & not by the Consuls or viceconsuls but when only the subjects or citizens of their own nation shall be interested the respective Consuls & Viceconsuls shall appoint skilful persons to settle the damage & average.

ART. 9. In cases when by tempest or other accident, French ships or vessels shall be stranded on the coast of the U.S. & ships or vessels of the U.S. shall be stranded on the coast of the dominions of the M.C.K. the Consul or Vice Consul nearest to the place of shipwreck shall do whatever he may judge proper, as well for the purpose of saving [*blotted out*] the said ship or vessel, its cargo & appurtenances as for the storing & the security of the effects & merchandize saved. He may take an inventory of them without the intermeddling of any officer of the military, of the customs, of justice, or of the police of the country, otherwise than to give to the Consuls, viceconsuls, captain & Crew of the vessel shipwrecked or stranded all the succour & favour which they shall ask of them either for the expedition & security of the saving & of the effects saved as to prevent all disturbance.

And in order to prevent all kind of dispute & discussion in the said cases of shipwreck, it is agreed that when there shall be no consul or viceconsul to attend to the saving of the wreck or that the residence of the said Consul or viceconsul (he not being at the place of the wreck) shall be more distant from the said place than that of the competent Judge of the country, the latter shall immediately proceed therein, with all the dispatch, certainty & precautions prescribed by the respective laws; but the said territorial Judge shall retire on the arrival of the Consul or Vice Consul & shall deliver over to him the report of his proceedings, the expences of which the Consul or Vice Consul shall cause to be reimbursed to him.

The merchandize & effects saved shall be deposited in the custom House or other nearest place of safety with the inventory of them which shall be made by the Consul or vice consul or in their absence, by the Judge who shall have cognizance thereof, & the said merchandises & effects shall be afterwards delivered after levying therefrom the costs, & without form of process to the proprietors, who, being furnished with a replevy from the nearest Consul or Viceconsul, shall reclaim them by themselves or by their attornies, either for the purpose of reexporting the merchandizes & in that case they shall pay no kind of duties of exportation, or for the purpose of selling them in the country if they are not prohibited, & in this latter case, the said merchandizes being averaged, there shall be granted them an abatement of the entrance duties proportioned to the damage sustained, which shall be ascertained by the verbal process formed at the time of shipwreck or of the vessels running ashore.

ART. 10TH. The Consuls & Vice Consuls may cause to be arrested in the Country the Sailors deserters of their respective nations & send them back and transport them out of the country.

The registers of the vessels or rolls of the crew shall be received in testimony to prove that the persons arrested as deserting sailors belong to their respective nations; but shall not exclude the other legal proofs relative to the same fact.

As soon as there shall be sufficient proofs that they are deserting sailors of such nations, no Tribunals judges & officers whatsoever shall in any manner whatever take cognisance of the complaints which the said Sailors & deserters may make, but they shall on the contrary be delivered up on an order signed by the Consul or Viceconsul without its being in any ones power in any manner to detain engage or withdraw them. And to attain to the complete execution of the arrangements contained in this article all persons having authority shall be bound to assist the said Consuls or Vice Consuls, and on a simple requisition signed by them, they shall cause to be detained & guarded in prison at the disposal & expence of the said Consuls & vice consuls, the said sailors & deserters untill they shall have an opportunity to send them out of the country. *But if they be not sent out of the country in one month from the day of their arrest they shall be set at liberty, & shall be no more arrested for the same cause.*

ART. 11.   In cases where the respective subjects *or citizens* shall have committed any crime *or breach of the peace* they shall be amenable to the Judges of the Country.

ART. 12.   All differences & suits between the subjects of the M.C.K. in the U.S. or between the citizens of the U.S. *in the dominions of the M.C.K.* shall be determined by the respective Consuls, if *one of the parties demands it,* either by a reference to arbitration or by a summary judgment & without costs.

No officer civil or military, shall interfere or take any part whatever in the affair; appeals shall be carried before the tribunals of France or the U.S. to whom it may appertain to take cognizance thereof. The respective Agents shall be bound to render to their respective merchants navigators & vessels all possible service, and to inform the nearest Consul or Vice Consul of the wants of the said merchants, navigators & vessels, without the said Agents otherwise participating in the immunities rights & privileges attributed to the Consuls & viceconsuls, & without power to exact from the said merchants any duty or emolument whatever, under any pretence whatsoever.

ART. 13.   The general utility of commerce having caused to be established *within the dominions of the M.C.K.* particular tribunals and forms for expediting the decision of commercial affairs, the merchants of the U.S. shall enjoy the benefit of those establishments; and the Congress of the U.S. *will provide in the manner the most conformable to its laws* equivalent advantages in favor of the French merchants for the prompt dispatch & decision of affairs of the same nature.

ART. 14.   The subjects of the M.C.K. and the *citizens* of the U.S. who shall prove by legal evidence that they are of the said nations respectively shall in consequence enjoy an exemption from all personal service in the place of their settlement.

ART. 15.   If any other nation acquires by virtue of any convention whatever, a treatment more favorable with respect to the consular pre-eminencies, powers, authority & privileges, the Consuls and viceconsuls of the M.C.K. or of the U.S.

reciprocally shall participate therein agreable to the terms stipulated by the 2d. 3th. & 4th. articles of the treaty of Amity and Commerce, concluded between the M.C.K. and the U.S.

ART. 16. The present Convention shall be in full force during the term of twelve years to be counted from the day of the exchange of ratifications, which shall be given in proper form, and exchanged on both sides within the space of one year, or sooner if possible.

In faith whereof &ca.[1]

[1] The translation is in the hand of John Pintard. The word "Translation" is in the hand of Henry Remsen.

(4)

No. 3.   First Counterproposition on the Part of France, with Notes by Rayneval

Notes

On propose la suppression des mots Agens & Commissaires. Dans le traité on s'etoit reservé le droit d'etablir des Agens ou des Commissaires ou des Consuls. mais puisque c'est la derniere denomination qu'on choisit, il paroit inutile de rappeler les autres.

Il semble convenable d'enoncer precisement que ces officiers publics seront sous le titre de Consuls & Vice-consuls afin d'eviter qu'il ne soit respectivement envoyé ensuite des personnes sous des titres differents d'ou il resulteroit des difficultes de forme. on propose de supprimer la denomination d'agens & de Commissaires partout ou elle est enoncée dans les articles suivants.

No. 3. First Counterproposition on the part of France

Convention entre le Roy trés Chrêtien & les Etats-Unis de l'Amerique a l'effet de determiner & fixer les fonctions & prérogatives des Consuls & Vice-consuls respectifs.

Sa Majesté Le Roi trés Chrêtien & les Etats-Unis de l'Amérique s'etant accordés mutuellement par l'article 29. du traité d'amitié & de commerce conclu entre eux, la liberté de tenir dans leurs Etats & ports respectifs des Consuls, Vice-consuls, Agens & Commissaires & voulant en consèquence determiner & fixer d'une manière reciproque & permanente les fonctions & prerogatives des Consuls & Vice-consuls qu'ils ont jugé convenable d'etablir de preference. Sa Majesté trés Chretienne a nommé le Sr. ———— & les Etats-Unis ont nommé ———— lesquels après s'etre communiqué leurs pleinspouvoirs respectifs sont convenus de ce qui suit.

Quoique Mr. Jefferson paroit desirer que tous les Consuls & Vice-consuls respectifs soient nommés par le Souverain, on n'y voit aucun inconvénient pour nous tous ceux qui sont etablis actuellement en Amérique ont commission du Roi, & on se propose de continuer de même à l'avenir. il est même trés avantageux que cela soit ainsi pour prevenir la trop grande multiplication des Vice-consuls d'Amerique en France. ainsi on supprime les mots *ou de leur autorité* & l'art. 2. de l'ancien projet en totalité, mais il paroit nécéssaire de conserver aux Consuls & Vice-consuls le droit de se nommer des agens dans les ports de leurs districts pour correspondre avec eux, sans que les dits agens ayent aucun caractere public ni exequatur. on propose de laisser subsister l'art. 3. en supprimant l'addition faite à l'art. 12.

ART. 1

Les Consuls & Vice-consuls nommes par le Roi trés Chrêtien & les Etats Unis seront tenus de presenter leurs provisions selon la forme qui se trouvera etablie respectivement par le Roi trés Chrêtien dans ses Etats & par le Congrés dans les Etats-Unis. On leur delivrera sans aucuns frais l'exequatur nécessaire à l'exercice de leurs fonctions, & sur l'exhibition qu'ils feront du dit exequatur, les Gouverneurs, Commandants, Chefs de justice, les corps, tribunaux, ou autres officiers ayant autorité dans les ports & lieux de leurs consulats les y feront jouir aussitôt & sans difficulté, des preeminences, autorités & privileges accordés reciproquement, sans qu'ils puissent exiger des dits Consuls & Vice-consuls aucun droit sous aucun pretexte quelconque.

on propose quelques legers changements à cet article. il paroit nécéssaire d'accorder aux Consuls quelques immunités, mais elles ne sont pas dangereuses dès qu'on excepte les cas de crimes & de dettes. Quant aux papiers de la Chancelerie, il n'est pas possible qu'aucune nation refuse la plus entiere immunité. on a ajouté la soumission à toutes les taxes pour ceux qui feroient le commerce. On observe quant à la saisie pour dettes que les loix civiles de France donnent une plus grande sureté personelle que les loix civiles Anglaises ou Americaines, la contrainte par corps n'ayant lieu généralement que pour les dettes commerciales & d'ailleurs aucun homme ne peut être arrêté en France

ART. 2. Les Consuls, Vice-consuls & toutes les personnes attachées aux fonctions Consulaires jouiront respectivement de l'immunité personelle, sauf les cas de crimes ou de dettes jouiront pareillement d'une pleine & entiere immunité pour leur Chancelerie & les papiers qui y seront renfermés. Ils seront exempts de tout service personel, logement de gens de guerre, milice guet, garde, tutelle curatelle ainsi que de tous droits taxes impositions & charges quelconques, a l'exception seulement des biens, meubles & immeubles dont ils seroient proprietaires ou possesseurs lesquels seront assujettis aux taxes imposées sur ceux de tous autres particuliers. & à tous autres

pour dettes avant d'etre entendû ou du moins cité en justice à un delai suffisant pour la defense. il sembleroit convenable que le Congrès prït quelques mesures pour mettre les Consuls & Vice-consuls à l'abri des inconveniens que les formes etablies dans les Etats-Unis peuvent avoir pour les etrangers. à cet egard ils doivent être considerés comme étant toujours sous la protection immediate de la legislature du pays & n'avoir pas besoin de cautions particulieres.

egards ils demeureront sujets aux loix du Pays comme les nationaux.

Ceux des dits consuls & vice-consuls qui feront le commerce seront respectivement assujettis à toutes les taxes, charges & impositions etablies sur les autres négocians.

Ils placeront sur la porte exterieure de leurs maisons les armes de leur souverain sans que cette marque distinctive puisse donner aux dites maisons le droit d'azile soit pour des personnes soit pour des effets quelconques.

ART. 3. Les Consuls & vice-consuls respectifs pourront etablir des agens dans les differents ports & lieux de leurs departements ou le besoin l'éxigera: ces agens pourront être choisis parmi les negocians nationaux ou etrangers & munis de la commission de l'un des dits consuls. ils se renfermeront respectivement à rendre aux commerçans, navigateurs & batimens respectifs tous les services possibles, & à informer le Consul le plus proche des besoins des dits commerçants navigateurs & batimens, sans que les dits agens puissent autrement participer aux immunités, droits, & privileges attribués aux Consuls & vice-consuls, & sans pouvoir sous quelque pretexte que ce soit, exiger aucun droit ou emolument quelconque des dits commerçants.

On a seulement changé quelques mots & interverti l'ordre des phrases, pour eclaircir cet article & faire cesser les doutes de Mr. Jefferson.

ART. 4. Les Consuls & Vice-consuls respectifs pourront etablir une chancelerie ou seront deposés les deliberations, actes & procedures Consulaires, ainsi que les testamens, obligations contracts & autres actes faits par les nationaux ou entr'eux & les effets delaissés par mort ou sauvés des naufrages.

Ils pourront en consequence commettre à l'exercice de la dite Chancelerie des personnes capables, les recevoir, leur faire prêter serment, leur donner la garde du sceau & le droit de sceller les commissions, jugemens & autres actes consulaires, ainsi que d'y remplir les fonctions de notaires & greffiers du consulat.

On propose de supprimer l'addition des mots dans tous les cas qui n'interessent que les nationaux. cela est egalement avantageux aux deux parties. Un acte fait dans un consulat peut servir même à des habitans du pays pour constater un fait, & comme preuve si ce n'est comme pièce obligatoire.

ART. 5. Les Consuls & Vice-consuls respectifs auront le droit exclusif de recevoir dans leur chancelerie, ou abord des batimens, les declarations & tous les autres actes que les Capitaines, patrons, equipages, passagers & negociants de leur nation voudront y passer, même leur testament & autres dispositions de derniere volonté & les expeditions des dits actes duëment legalises par les dits Consuls ou Vice-consuls & munis du sceau de leur consulat, feront foi en justice & auront la même force que les originaux dans tous les tribunaux des Etats du Roi très Chrêtien & des Etats-Unis.

Ils auront aussi & exclusivement en cas d'absence d'executeur testamentaire, curateur, ou heritiers legitimes, le droit de faire l'inventaire, la liquidation & de proceder à la vente des effets mobiliers de la succession des sujets ou [*blotted out*] citoyens de leur nation qui viendront à mourir dans l'etenduë de leurs consulats. ils y procederont avec l'assistance de deux negocians de leur dite nation, ou à leur defaut de toute autre à leur choix, & feront deposer dans leur chancelerie les effets & papiers des dites successions, sans qu'aucuns officiers militaires, de justice ou de police du pays, puissent les y troubler ni y intervenir de quelque maniere que ce soit, mais les dits Consuls & Vice-consuls ne pourront faire la delivrance des successions & de leur produit aux heritiers legitimes, ou à

corrigez *"n'auront"*

leurs mandataires qu'aprés avoir fait acquitter toutes les dettes que les defunts auront pu avoir contractées dans le pays, à l'effet de quoi les creanciers auront droit de saisir les dits effets dans leurs mains de même que dans celles de tout autre individu quelconque & en poursuivre la vente jusqu'au payement de ce qui leur sera legitimement dû; lorsque les dettes auront été contractées par jugement, par acte, ou par billet dont la signature sera reconnuë, le payement ne pourra en être ordonné qu'en fournissant par le creancier caution suffisante & domiciliée de rendre les sommes induëment percuës, principal, interêts & frais; lesquelles cautions cependant demeureront duëment dechargées après une année en tems de paix & deux en tems de guerre, si la demande en décharge ne peut être formée avant ces delais contre les heritiers qui se presenteront. & afin de ne pas faire injustement attendre aux heritiers les effets du defunt, les Consuls & Vice-consuls feront annoncer sa mort dans quelqu'une des gazettes qui se publient dans l'etendue de leur consulat & qu'ils retiendront les dits effets sous leurs mains pendant quatre mois pour repondre à toutes les justes demandes qui se présenteront: et ils seront tenus aprés ce délai de delivrer aux heritiers l'excedent du montant des demandes qui auront été formées.

ART. 6. Les consuls & vice-consuls respectifs recevront les declarations protestations & rapports de tous Capitaines & Patrons de leur nation respective pour raison d'avaries essuyées à la mer; & ces Capitaines & patrons remettront dans la chancellerie de dits Consuls & Vice-consuls les actes qu'ils auront faits dans d'autres ports pour les accidents qui leur seront arrivés pendant leur voyage. Si un sujet du Roi trés Chretien & un habitant des Etats-Unis ou un etranger sont inté-réssés dans la dite cargaison, l'avarie sera reglée par les tribunaux du pays & non par les consuls & vice-consuls, mais lorsqu'il n'y aura d'interessés que les sujets ou citoyens de leur propre nation, les Consuls ou les Vice-consuls respectifs nommeront des experts pour regler les dommages & avaries.

Art. 7. Dans le cas ou par tempête ou autre accident des vaisseaux ou batimens Francois échoueront sur les côtes des Etats-Unis; & des vaisseaux & batimens des Etats-Unis échoueront sur les côtes des Etats du Roi très Chrêtien le Consul ou le Vice-consul le plus proche du lieu du naufrage pourra faire tout ce qu'il jugera con-venable tant pour sauver le dit vais-seau ou batiment, son chargement & apartenances, que pour le magazinage & la sureté des effets sauvés & mar-chandises. il pourra en faire l'inven-taire sans qu'aucuns officiers militaires, des douanes, de justice, ou de police du pays puissent s'y immiscer autrement que pour faciliter aux Consuls & Vice-consuls, Capitaine & Equipage du vais-seau naufragé ou echoué tous les se-cours & faveurs qu'ils leur deman-deront, soit pour la celerité et la sureté du sauvetage & des effets sauvés, soit pour eviter tous desordres.

Pour prévénir même toute espece de conflit & de discussion dans les dits cas de naufrage, il a été convenu que lorsqu'il ne se trouvera pas de Consul ou Vice-consul pour faire travailler au sauvetage, ou que la residence du dit Consul ou Vice-consul qui ne se trou-vera pas sur le lieu du naufrage sera plus eloignée du dit lieu que celle du juge territorial competent, ce dernier y fera proceder sur le champ avec toute la celerité, la sureté & les precaution prescrites par les loix respectives, sauf au dit juge territorial à se retirer, le Consul ou Vice-consul survenant, & a lui remettre l'expédition des procedures par lui faites, dont le Consul ou Vice-consul lui fera rembourser les frais, ainsi que ceux du sauvetage.

Les marchandises & effets sauvés devront être déposés a la doüane ou autre lieu de sureté le plus prochain avec l'inventaire qui en aura été dressé par le Consul ou Vice-consul, ou en leur absence par le juge qui en aura connû, pour les dits effets & marchandises être ensuite delivrés, aprés le prélevement des frais & sans forme de procès aux proprietaires, qui, munis de la main levée du Consul ou Vice-consul le plus proche, les reclameront par eux-mêmes ou par leurs mandataires, soit pour ré-exporter les marchandises & dans ce cas, elles ne payeront aucune espece de droits de sortie, soit pour les vendre dans le pays si elles n'y sont pas prohibées, & dans ce dernier cas les dites marchandises, se trouvant avariées, on leur accordera une moderation sur les droits d'entrée, proportionée au dommage souffert, lequel sera constaté par le procés verbal dressé lors du naufrage ou de l'echoüement.

On propose de s'etablir cet article qu'on a redigé a peu de chose près comme il l'avoit été dans le premier projet. il est absolument impossible de refuser au Consul la jurisdiction civile abord des batiments de sa nation & entre les equipages. cela seroit d'autant plus deraisonnable que par les articles subsequents, on lui accorde cette même jurisdiction civile sur les nationaux

ART. 8. Les Consuls & Vice-consuls exerceront la police sur tous les batiments de leurs nations respectives & auront àbord des dits batiments tout pouvoir & jurisdiction en matiere civile dans toutes les discussions qui pourront y survenir. ils auront une entiere inspection sur les dits batiments, leurs equipages & les changements & remplacements à y faire & y feront residents à terre, & a plus forte raison il doit la conserver sur ceux qui demeurent sous le pavillon de la nation. l'exercice de la police maritime sur les batiments nationaux est la principale fonction des consuls.

executer les loix, ordonnances & reglements respectifs relatifs à la navigation, auquel effet ils pourront se transporter abord des dits batiments toutes les fois qu'ils le jugeront necessaire, sans qu'aucun officier ou autres personnes puissent les en empêcher.

Cet article relatif à l'extradition des matelots deserteurs paroit devoir être detaché du precedent. on a taché de le rediger d'une manière simple & d'y prévénir toute difficulté en reglant le recours des Consuls aux magistrats territoriaux.

On n'a fait aucune mention des passagers parce qu'il ne paroit pas convenable d'insister sur cet objet. On n'a pas distingué les deserteurs des vaisseaux du Roi de ceux des batiments marchands. les Consuls peuvent reclamer les uns & les autres dans les mêmes formes. on a entierement omis tout ce qui concerne le renvoy des navires.

ART. 9. Les Consuls & Vice-consuls pourront faire arrêter les Capitaines, officiers mariniers matelots & autres personnes des equipages des bâtiments de leurs nations respectives qui auroient deserté des dits batiments pour les renvoyer & faire transporter hors du pays. auquel effet les dits Consuls & Vice-consuls s'adresseront aux tribunaux, juges & officiers competents & leur feront par ecrit la demande des dits deserteurs en justifiant par l'exhibition des registres du batiment ou role d'equipage que ces hommes faisoient partie des susdits equipages. & sur cette demande ainsi justifiée l'extradition ne pourra être refusée, & il sera donné toute aide & assistance aux dits consuls & vice-consuls pour la recherche, saisie & arrestation des susdits deserteurs, lesquels seront même détenus & gardés dans les prisons du pays, à leur requisition & à leurs frais, jusques à ce qu'ils ayant trouvé occasion de les renvoyer. mais s'ils n'etoient renvoyés dans le delai de trois mois à compter du jour de leur arrêt ils seront elargis & ne pourront plus être arrêtés pour la même cause.

Il paroit qu'on pourroit laisser la redaction de Mr. Jefferson. L'expression infraction de la tranquillité publique étant la traduction litterale de l'expression Anglaise convenable à cet article.

ART. 10. Dans le cas ou les sujets ou citoyens respectifs auront commis quelque crime ou infraction de la tranquillité publique ils seront justiciable des juges du pays.

On propose d'ajouter cet article afin de prévénir les inconveniens qui pour-

ART. 11. Lorsque les dits coupables feront partie de l'equipage de l'un des

roient resulter de la liberté qu'auroient les magistrats territoriaux de faire arrêter les gens des equipages des batiments marchands, de retenir ainsi arbitrairement les navires dans le port, & de suspendre de cette maniere toute l'activité du commerce & de la navigation. l'avis donné au Consul ou Viceconsul pour que tous ces actes d'autorité ne soient faits qu'en sa presence, ne suspend pas le cours de la justice puisqu'il ne pourra s'y opposer, mais il sera en mesure de faire des reclamations qui empecheront l'effet des surprises & qu'on pourroit tenter de faire aux magistrats locaux, en leur demandant des decrets ou warrants dont on leur laisseroit ignorer les facheuses consequences. les Consuls & Viceconsuls duëment avertis pourront agir legalement suivant les circonstances pour les interêts generaux du commerce & ceux de leurs nationaux en particulier.

La derniere partie de l'article est important. il ne paroit pas qu'il puisse y avoir de difficulté à remettre au Consul ou au Vice-consul les hommes arrêtés sous la banniere de leur nation, lorsqu'il n'y aura plus le motif pour les detenir dans les prisons territoriales que par consequent la justice du pays n'aura plus aucun droit sur eux. la précaution prise dans cet article est necessaire pour prevenir la desertion. sans cela un matelot qui voudra deserter s'entendra avec un homme du pays, se fera arrêter pour une dette supposée, restera en prison jusques au depart du navire & se fera mettre ensuite en liberté. cette maneouvre reprehensible dejá été pratiquée.

Il est contre tous les principes du droit des gens que les magistrats civils & militaires d'un pays exercent quelque

batiments de leur nation & se seront retirés abord de leurs dits navires, ils pourront y être saisis & arretés, mais l'extradition en sera d'abord demandée par les magistrats territoriaux au Consul de leur nation lequel ne pourra la refuser, & lorsqu'il sera jugé necessaire de faire des perquisitions & recherches abord des dits navires marchands, elle ne pourront être faites qu'en présence des dits consuls & Vice-consuls ou aprés qu'ils en auront été prevenus & invités à s'y rendre. Dans tous les cas aucune personne ne pourra être saisie & arretée soit pour crimes dettes ou autres causes quelconques abord des dits batiments qu'en présence des dits consuls ou vice-consuls ou aprés qu'ils auront été duëment avertis. les dites personnes ainsi saisies & arretées ne pourront ensuite etre mises en liberté qu'apres que le Consul ou Vice-consul en aura été prévénue, & elles lui seront remises s'il le requiert pour être reconduites sur les batiments ou elles auroient été arretées ou autres de leur nation & être renvoyées hors du pays.

ART. 12. Il ne pourra être fait dans aucun cas de perquisitions abord des batiments de guerre respectifs; mais si

acte d'autorité que ce puisse être abord des batiments de guerre d'une nation amie. cet article est conforme à ce qui est reglé avec les autres nations, notamment à ce qui a ete arrêté dans le projet de Convention avec la republique de Genes.

Cet article est le 9me. du projet de Mr. Jefferson. on y a seulement ajouté quelques mots pour designer particulierement les affaires entre les equipages des batiments nationaux qui appartiennent specialement à la juridiction consulaire. on propose de retrancher les mots *si l'une des parties le demande* parceque le recours à des tribunaux etrangers en pareil cas est absolument illegal pour des François.

on a lieu de soupçonner que des coupables s'y sont refugiés, l'extradition en sera demandée par les magistrats ou officiers territoriaux au Consul ou au Vice-consul de la nation ou aux Commandants des dits batiments. dans les ports ou il n'y aura pas de Consul ou vice-consul les dits commandants ne pourront refuser de rendre ces coupables & les enverront à terre pour être remis entre les mains des dits magistrats ou officiers. Dans le cas ou les commandants des susdits batiments de guerre declareroient que ces coupables ne sont pas à leur bord, ils en seront crus sur leur parole sans qu'il puisse être fait aucune recherche ulterieure.

Art. 13. Tout differend & proces entre les sujets du Roi très Chrêtien dans les Etats-Unis, ou entre les citoyens des Etats-Unis dans les Etats du Roi tres Chrêtien & notamment toutes les discussions relatives aux salaires & conditions des engagements des equipages des batiments respectifs & tous differends de quelque nature qu'ils soient qui pourroient s'elever entre les hommes des dits equipages ou entre quelques uns d'eux & leurs Capitaines, ou entre les Capitaines de divers batiments nationaux seront terminés par les Consuls & Vice-consuls respectifs soit par un renvoi par devant des arbitres, soit par un jugement sommaire & sans frais. aucun officier territorial, civil ou militaire ne pourra y intervenir ou prendre une part quelconque à l'affaire; & les appels des dits jugement consulaires seront portés devant les tribunaux de France ou des Etats-Unis qui doivent en connoitre.

Art. 14. L'utilité générale du commerce ayant fait etablir dans les Etats du Roi tres Chrêtien des tribunaux &

des formes particulieres pour accélerer la decision des affaires de commerce, les negociants des Etats-Unis jouiront du benefice de cet etablissement, & le Congrès des Etats-Unis pourvoira de la maniere la plus conforme à ses loix à l'etablissement des avantages equivalents en faveur des negociants François pour la prompte expedition & decision des affaires de la même nature.

ART. 15. Les sujets du Roi très Chrêtien & les Citoyens des Etats-Unis qui justifieront authentiquement être du corps de la nation respective jouiront en consequence de l'exemption de tout service personnel dans le lieu de leur etablissement.

ART. 16. Si quelque autre nation acquiert en vertu d'une convention quelconque un traitement plus favorable relativement aux pre-eminences, pouvoirs, autorité & priviléges consulaires, les Consuls & Vice-consuls du Roi très Chretien ou des Etats-Unis reciproquement y participeront aux termes stipulé par les articles 2. 3. & 4. du traité d'amitié & de commerce conclu entre le Roi & les Etats-Unis.

ART. 17. La presente convention aura son plein effet pendant l'espace de douze ans, à compter du jour de l'echange des ratifications qui seront données en bonne forme et echangées de part et d'autre dans l'espace d'un an, ou plutôt si faire se peut.
En foi de quoi &ca.[1]

---

[1] The copy of the counterproposition and the notes are in the hand of William Short. The heading "No. 3. First Counterproposition on the part of France" is in the hand of Thomas Jefferson.

(5)

English Translation

Translation

Notes

It is proposed to leave out the words Agents & Commissaries. In the Treaty, the right of establishing agents or commissaries or Consuls is reserved. But since the last denomination is chosen, it appears useless to repeat the others.

It appears proper to announce presisely, that these public officers shall be under the title of Consuls & V. consuls in order to prevent any persons being respectively sent hereafter under different titles from whence might result difficulties in point of form. It is proposed to suppress the denomination of agents & Commissaries wherever they are announced in the following articles.

No. 3. First Counterproposition on the part of France

Convention between His most Christian Majesty & the United States of America for the purpose of determining & fixing the functions & prerogatives of their respective Consuls & Vice Consuls.

His Majesty the most Christian King & the U.States of America having by the 29th. Article of the Treaty of Amity & Commerce concluded between them, mutually granted the liberty of having in their respective states & ports Consuls and Vice Consuls ~~which~~ Agents & Commissaries and being willing in ~~they have judged it inconvenient~~ consequence thereof to define and ~~to establish preference. His M.C.~~ establish in a reciprocal & permanent manner the functions & prerogatives of Consuls & Vice Consuls which they have judged it convenient to establish of preference. His M.C. Majesty has nominated the Sieur ——— & the U. States have nominated ——— who after having communicated to each other their respective full powers have agreed on what follows.

Art. 1.

The Consuls & Vice consuls named by the M.C.K. and the U.S. shall be bound to present their commissions according to the forms which shall be established respectively by the M.C.K. within his dominions & by the Congress within the U.S. There shall be delivered to them without any charges, the Exequatur necessary for the exer-

Altho Mr. Jefferson appears desirous that all the respective Consuls & Vice Consuls should be named by the Sovereign, no inconvenience appears to us on this head. all those who are actually established in America, have the Kings commission. it is also very advantageous that this should be the case to prevent the too great multiplication of American

Vice Consuls in France. Therefore the words *or by their authority* are suppressed & the 2d. Art. of the old project totally. But it appears necessary to reserve to Consuls & Vice consuls the right of naming agents in the ports of their districts to correspond with them, without the said Agents having any public character or exequatur.

It is proposed to let the 3d. Art. subsist, by suppressing the addition made to the 12th. Art.

It is proposed to make some slight alterations in this article. It appears necessary to grant Consuls some immunities, but these are not dangerous, when the cases of crimes or debts are excepted. As to the papers of the Chancery, it is impossible for any nation to refuse the fullest immunity. submission to all taxes has been added with respect to those who shall exercise commerce. It is remarked on the subject of seizure for debts that the civil laws of France extend greater personal security than the Civil laws of England or America bodily restraint not generally taking place but for commercial debts, & moreover no person can be arrested in France for debt before being heard, or at least cited judicially with sufficient delay for his defence. It seems proper that Congress take some measures to protect Consuls & V. consuls from the inconveniences which may happen to Foreigners from the forms established in the U. States. For this purpose they ought to be considered as being always under the immediate protection of the legislature of the country, & not in want of any particular security.

cise of their functions and on exhibiting the said exequatur, the Governors Commanders, Heads of justice, bodies corporate, Tribunals & other officers having authority in the ports & places of their Consulates shall cause them to enjoy immediately, and without difficulty, the preeminences, authority & privileges reciprocally granted without exacting from the said Consuls & vice-consuls any duty, under any pretext whatever.

ART. 2. The Consuls & Vice Consuls & all persons attached to the Consular functions shall respectively enjoy personal immunity, excepting in cases of crimes or debts. they shall also enjoy a full & entire immunity for their Chancery & the papers which shall be therein contained: they shall be exempt from all personal service, from soldiers billets, militia, watch, guards, guardianship, trusteeship as well as from all duties taxes impositions & charges whatsoever except on the real & personal estate of which they may be the proprietors or possessors which shall be subject to the taxes imposed on the estates of all other individuals; and in all other instances they shall be subject to the laws of the land as the natives are.

Those of the said Consuls, & Vice-consuls who shall exercise commerce shall be respectively subject to all taxes, charges & impositions established on other merchants.

They shall place over the outward door of their House the arms of their Sovereigns: but this mark of indication shall not give to the said house any privilege of asylum for any person or property whatsoever.

ART. 3. The respective Consuls & V.

Consuls may establish Agents in the different ports & places of their departments where necessity shall require. These Agents may be chosen among the merchants either national or foreign & furnished with a Commission from one of the said Consuls: they shall confine themselves respectively to the rendering to their respective merchants, navigators, and vessels all possible service, and to inform the nearest Consul of the wants of the said merchants, navigators & vessels, without the said Agents otherwise participating in the immunities, rights & privileges attributed to Consuls & viceconsuls & without power under any pretext whatever to exact from the said merchants any duty or emolument whatsoever.

A few words only have been altered & the order of some phrases been changed, to explain this article & remove Mr. Jeffersons doubts.

ART. 4. The Consuls & V. consuls respectively may establish a chancery where shall be deposited the Consular determinations, acts & proceedings as also testaments, obligations, contracts and other acts done by or between persons of their nation, & effects left by death or saved from shipwreck.

They may in consequence appoint for the business of the said Chancery capable persons, receive them, administer an oath to them, give to them the keeping of the seal, & the right of sealing commissions, judgments & other acts of the consulate, as well as there to discharge the functions of notaries & registers of the consulate.

It is proposed to suppress the addition of the words, *in all cases which only concern persons of the same nation*. This being advantageous alike to both parties. An Act done in the Consulate may also answer the purpose of the inhabitants of the country to ~~prove~~ validate a fact, & serve as a proof if not as an obligatory peice.

ART. 5. The Consuls & V. Consuls respectively shall have the exclusive right of receiving in their chancery or on board the vessels, the declarations & all the other acts, which the captains, masters, crews, passengers & merchants of their nation may chuse to make there, even their testaments & other disposals by last will: and the Copies of the said Acts, duly authenticated by the said Consuls or Viceconsuls, under the seal of their consulate shall receive faith in law, equally as their originals would in all the tribunals of the dominions of the M.C. King & the United States.

They shall also have & exclusively in case of the absence of the testamentary executor, guardians or lawful representative the right to inventory liquidate & proceed to the sale of the personal estate left by subjects who shall die within the extent of their consulate; they shall proceed therein with the assistance of two merchants of their said nation, for want of them, of any other of their choice, & shall cause to be deposited in their chancery the effects & papers of the said estates: & no officer military judiciary or of the police of the country shall disturb them or interfere therein in any manner whatsoever but the said Consuls & V. consuls shall not deliver up the said effects, nor the proceeds thereof to the lawful representatives or to their order, till they shall have caused to be paid all debts which the deceased shall have contracted in the country; for which purpose the creditor shall have a right to attach the said effects in their hands as they might in those of any other individual whatever & proceed to obtain sale of them till payment of what shall be lawfully due to them. when the debts *shall not have been contracted by judgment deed or note the signature whereof shall be known payment shall not be ordered but on the creditors giving sufficient surety resident in the country, to refund the sums he shall have unduly received principal interest & costs: which surety nevertheless shall stand duly discharged after a year in time of peace, & two years in time of war, if the

correct *shall not have been.

demand in discharge cannot be formed before these delays against the heirs which shall present themselves. And in order that the representatives may not unjustly be kept out of the effects of the deceased the Consuls & V. consuls shall notify his death in some one of the gazettes published within their consulate, and that they shall retain the said effects in their hands four months to answer all just demands which shall be presented: and they shall be bound after this delay to deliver to the persons succeeding thereto what shall be more than sufficient for the demands which shall have been formed.

ART. 6. The consuls & V. consuls respectively shall receive the declarations protests & Reports of all Captains & Masters of their respective nations on account of average losses sustained at sea; & these captains & masters shall lodge in the Chancery of the said Consuls & V. Consuls the acts which they may have made in other ports on account of the accidents which may have happened to them on their voyage. If a subject of the Most Christian King and a Citizen of the United States or a Foreigner are interested in the said Cargo the average shall be settled by the tribunals of the country and not by the Consuls or Vice consuls; but when only the subjects or citizens of their own nation shall be interested, the respective Consuls or V. Consuls shall appoint skilful persons to regulate the damages & averages.

ART. 7. In cases where by tempest or other accident, French ships or Vessels shall be stranded on the coasts of the U.S. & ships or vessels of the U.S.

shall be stranded on the coasts of the dominions of the M.C. King the Consul or V. Consul nearest to the place of shipwreck shall do whatever he may judge proper, as well for the purpose of saving the said ship or vessel, its cargo & appurtenances, as for the storing & the security of the effects & merchandise saved. He may take an inventory of them, without the intermeddling of any officers of the military, of the customs, of justice or of the police of the country otherwise than to give to the Consuls, V. Consuls captains & crew of the vessels shipwrecked or stranded all the succour & favor which they shall ask of them, either for the expedition & security of the saving & of the effects saved, as to prevent all disturbance.

And in order to prevent any kind of dispute & discussion in the said cases of shipwreck, it has been agreed, that where no Consul or vice Consul shall be found to attend to the salvage, or that the residence of the said Consul or vice Consul (he not being at the place of ship wreck) shall be further distant from the said place than that of the competent territorial Judge, the later shall immediately there proceed therein with all the celerity, safety and precautions prescribed by the respective laws; but the said territorial Judge shall retire on the arrival of the Consul or Vice Consul, and shall deliver over to him the report of his proceedings, the expenses of which the Consul or Vice Consul shall cause to be reimbursed to him as well as those of salvage.

The merchandise & effects saved shall be deposited in the Custom House or other nearest place of safety with the inventory of them which shall have been made by the Consul or V.

Consul, or by the Judge who shall have proceeded in their absence that the said effects & merchandise may be afterwards delivered after levying therefrom the costs & without form of process to the owners, who being furnished with a replevy from the nearest Consul or Vice Consul shall reclaim them by themselves or by their attornies, either for the purpose of reexporting the merchandizes, and in that case they shall pay no duties of exportation, or for the purpose of selling them in the country if they are not prohibited, & in this latter case, the said merchandises being averaged, there shall be granted them an abatement of the entrance duties proportioned to the damage sustained, which shall be ascertained by the verbal process formed at the time of the ship wreck or of the vessels running ashore.

It is proposed to restore this Article, which is nearly reduced as it was in the first project. it is absolutely impossible to refuse the Consul civil jurisdiction aboard the vessels belonging to his nation & over the crew. This would be the more unreasonable as by the following articles this same civil jurisdiction is granted to him over [*blotted out*] residents a shore belonging to his nation, & it is much more reasonable that he ought to preserve it over such as remain under the national Flag. The exercise of maritime police over national vessels is the principal function of Consuls.

ART. 8. The Consuls & V. Consuls shall exercise police over all the vessels of their respective Nations & shall have on board the said vessels all power & jurisdiction in civil matters, in all the disputes which may there arise. They shall have an entire inspection over the said vessels, their crews & the changes & substitutions there to be made & shall there cause to be executed the respective laws, Ordinances & rules concerning Navigation, for which purpose they shall go on board the said vessels whenever they may judge it necessary without interruption from any Officer or other person whatsoever.

This article relating to the delivery of the Sailors deserters appears as tho' it ought to be detached from the preceding one. it has been endeavoured to reduce it to a simple form & to pre-

ART. 9. The Consuls & Vice Consuls may cause to be arrested, the Captains Officers, mariners, sailors & all other persons being part of the crews of the vessels of their respective nations who

vent all difficulty by regulating the recourse of the Consuls to the territorial magistrates.

No mention has been made of the passengers, as it appeared not proper to insist on this matter. The deserters from the Kings ships are not distinguished from those belonging to merchant vessels. The Consuls can claim both in the same manner. The part which concerned sending back the vessels has been totally omitted.

shall have deserted from the said vessels in order to send them back & transport them out of the country. For which purpose the said Consuls & Vice consuls shall address themselves to the courts, Judges & Officers competent & shall demand the said deserters in writing, proving by an exhibition of the registers of the vessels or ships roll that those men were part of the said crews & on this demand thus proved, the delivery shall not be refused, & there shall be given all aid & assistance to the said Consuls & Vice consuls for the search seizure & arrest of the said deserters, who shall even be detained & kept in the prisons of the country, at their request & expence untill they shall have found an opportunity of sending them back. But if they be not sent back within three months, to be counted from the day of arrest they shall be set at liberty & shall no more be arrested for the same cause.

This explanation of Mr. Jeffersons may be left. The expression breach of the peace being the literal translation of the English expression suitable to this article.

ART. 10. In cases where the respective subjects or citizens shall have committed any crime, or breach of the peace, they shall be amenable to the Judges of the country.

It is proposed to add this article in order to prevent the inconveniencies that might result from the liberty which the territorial magistrates might have to arrest the crews of merchant vessels, & then arbitrarily detain the vessels in the port & by that means suspend all activity in commerce & navigation. The advice given to the Consul or Vice Consuls that all these acts of authority be done only in their presence, by no means suspends the course of Justice, seeing he cannot oppose it, but he will be in a situation to make claims which will prevent the

ART. 11. When the said offenders shall be a part of the crew of a vessel of their nation & shall have withdrawn themselves on board ~~them~~ their said vessels, they may be there seized & arrested but ~~order of~~ the delivery shall be first demanded by the territorial magistrates from the Consul of their nation who shall not refuse it, & whenever it shall be judged necessary to make enquiry & search on board the said merchant vessels, such cannot be made but in presence of the said Consuls & Vice Consuls or until after they shall have been informed & invited to

effect of surprizes & which might be attempted on the local Magistrates, by demanding from them decrees & warrants, the fatal consequences of which they might be left in ignorance of. The Consuls & Vice Consuls duly notified might legally proceed according to circumstances for the general interests of Commerce & those of their nation in particular.

The last part of this article is important, it does not appear that there can be any difficulty, in delivering to the Consul or Vice Consul the persons arrested ~~or bound~~ under the Flag of their nation, when there shall be no longer any occasion to detain them in the territorial prisons, & consequently the justice of the country shall have no further right over them. The precaution taken in this article is necessary to prevent desertion. Without ~~that~~ which a sailor who wished to desert might concert measures with a person of the country, to be arrested for a supposed debt, remain in the prison until the sailing of the vessel & afterwards be set at liberty. This reprehensible manoeuvre has been practiced already.

It is contrary to all the principles of the right of nations, that the Civil & military Magistrates exercise any authority whatever on board the Vessels of War belonging to a friendly nation & this article is conformable to regulations with other nations, particularly with what has been agreed to in the project of a Convention with the Republic of Genoa.

repair on board. But at any rate no person can be seized or arrested either on account of crimes, debts or for any other cause whatsoever on board the said vessels but in presence of the said Consuls or V. consuls ~~on board the~~ or until after they shall have been duly notified. The said persons thus seized & arrested shall not afterwards be set at liberty untill the Consul or Vice Consul shall have been notified thereof & they shall be delivered to him, if he requires it, to be put again on board the vessels on which they were arrested or others of their nation to be sent out of the country.

ART. 12. No search shall in any wise be made on board of the respective ships of war. But if there is reason to suppose that offenders have taken refuge on board them, the delivery shall be demanded ~~from~~ by the magistrates or territorial officers from the Consul or Vice Consul of the nation or from the Commanders of the said Vessels. In the ports where there shall be no Consul or Vice Consul the said Commanders shall not refuse to deliver up the offenders & send them ashore to be put into the hands of the magistrates or officers. In case the Commanders of the aforesaid vessels of war should declare that the offenders are not on board their vessels, they shall be believed on their words, without any further search being made.

This Article is the 9th. of Mr. Jeffersons project, some words have only been added to designate in a more particular manner the affairs between the crews of vessels belonging to the same nation which appertain in a special manner to the consular jurisdiction. it is proposed to retrench the words, *If one of the parties demand it* because the recourse to foreign tribunals in such cases is absolutely illegal for Frenchmen.

ART. 13. All differences and suits between the subjects of the M.C.K. in the U.S. or between the citizens of the United States within the dominions of the M.C.K. & particularly all disputes relative to the wages and terms of engagement of the crews of the respective vessels, and all differences of whatever nature they be, which may arise between the privates of the said Crews, or between any of them & their Captains, or between the Captains of different vessels of their nation, shall be determined by the respective Consuls and Vice Consuls either by a referrence to arbitrators, or by a summary judgment & without costs. No officer of the country civil or military shall interfere therein or take any part whatever in the matter, and the appeals from the said Consular sentences shall be carried before the tribunals of France or of the U.S. to whom it may appertain to take cognizance thereof.

ART. 14. The general utility of commerce having caused to be established within the dominions of the M.C.K. particular tribunals and forms for expediting the decision of commercial affairs, the Merchants of the U.S. shall enjoy the benefit of these establishments; and the Congress of the U.S. will provide in the manner the most conformable to its laws equivalent advantages in favor of the French merchants, for the prompt dispatch & decision of affairs of the same nature.

ART. 15. The subjects of the M.C.K. and citizens of the U.S. who shall prove by legal evidence that they are of the said nations respectively shall in consequence enjoy an exemption from all personal service in the place of their settlement.

ART. 16. If any other nation acquires by virtue of any convention whatever, a treatment more favorable with respect to the Consular pre-eminencies, powers, authority & privileges, the Consuls & Vice Consuls of the M.C.K. or of the U.S. reciprocally shall participate therein agreable to the terms stipulated by the 2d. 3d. & 4th. Articles of the treaty of Amity and Commerce concluded between the M.C.K. and the U.S.

ART. 17. The present Convention shall be in full force during the term of twelve years to be counted from the day of the exchange of the ratifications which shall be in proper form and exchanged on both sides within the space of one year or sooner if possible.
In faith where of. &c.[1]

[1] The translation is in the hand of John Pintard. The word "Translation" is in the hand of Henry Remsen, Jr.

(6)

Thomas Jefferson's Observations on the Counterproposition

ARTICLE I. Agreed.

ART. II. The words "jouiront respectivement de l'immunité personnelle, sauf les cas de crimes ou de dettes." are omitted. two descriptions of persons are well known to the laws of both countries. 1. those subject to the laws of the land; and 2. those subject only to the laws of Nations. the obligations & the privileges of each of these are so well settled, that few or no disputes can arise about them. but a middle character between the two would be new and unknown, & would introduce endless questions and discussions. If it be thought that the words "sauf les cas de crimes ou de dettes" replace them fully under the law of the land, then the whole passage is useless. if the exception be as broad as the rule, both may be omitted. but in truth the exception as to "crimes and debts" would not replace them fully under the laws of the land. for 1. they would not be obliged to give testimony in a court of justice. 2. these are cases of trespass, of trust, & of special contract not included in a strict & legal acceptation of the terms "crimes & debts," and in which therefore they would be exempted from the justice of the country.

It is proposed also to omit the words "toutes les personnes attachées aux fonctions consulaires" to prevent the abuses which would inevitably arise from an extension of the Consular immunities to an indefinite number of persons. the subordinate characters really attached to the Consulate, will be compleatly protected against avocation from their duties, or molestation in the exercise of them by the XVth. article "exempting them from all personal services," which is all that can be desired if they be foreigners, & which ought not to be desired if they be natives. for no native should have it in his power to withdraw himself from an obedience to the laws of his country while he remains in it.

ART. III.   Agreed.

ART. IV.   Agreed.

ART. V.   Agreed, only reestablishing the words "comme le feroient" instead of "et auront la meme force que."

ART. VI.   Agreed.

ART. VII.   Agreed.

ART. VIII.   This Article proposes to give to Consuls 1st. civil jurisdiction on board their vessels. 2. a power to execute the ordinances relative to navigation. 3. a right to go on board for these purposes at all times without hindrance. the 1st. and 3d. of these admit of no difficulty: but the 2d. could not be agreed to, because it establishes a whole code at once, the contents of which are unknown to the party within whose territory it is to be executed. when each concedes to the other a civil jurisdiction within it's ports, it knows the extent of it's concession; but, when it permits the enforcement of all the Navigation laws of the other, in the lump, it does not know what it concedes. they may include a criminal jurisdiction; they may be contrary to bills of rights; or if not so at present, they may be hereafter. it is surely prudent and honorable for us both to stipulate to each other only what we know we can execute. but we do not know that we can execute, if we do not know what we stipulate.

ART. IX.   Agreed with two alterations. 1. omitting the words "et autres personnes" because the others "capitaines, officiers, mariniers, et matelots" are supposed to comprehend the whole crew, if they do not, it will be better to add other specifications, rather than words so indefinite as "autres personnes." 2. omitting "par l'exhibition des registres du batiment ou role d'equipage." I suppose that the legal construction of these words must be weaker under the laws of France, than of the United states: otherwise they would not be proposed. their effect in the United states would be to make the ship's roll so conclusive that no contrary evidence could be opposed to it. a master of a ship for instance, inserting in his roll the name of a citizen of the United states, who had never seen his ship, that citizen must be delivered to him, if these words were to remain. it is not probable indeed that the master of a ship would be so indiscreet; but neither is it proper to rest personal liberty on the discretion of a master of a ship. Without these words, the clause will stand "en justifiant que ces hommes faisoient partie des susdits èquipages." his claim may then be supported & contested, as all other claims may be, by every species of legal evidence. he will stand on the same footing with Native officers reclaiming their deserted sailors.

ART. X.   Agreed.

ART. XI.   This article proposes 1. that there shall be no arrest for crimes or debts but in presence of the Consul or Viceconsul. 2. that no ship shall be searched but in his presence. these propositions are new. the principle on which we have proceeded hitherto has been that in all cases where the Nation or any member of it is concerned, the National jurisdiction shall have free & unrestrained course. but this article proposes to clog it with applications to the foreign Consul, and that it shall await his attendance, if he chuses to attend. how quickly he may attend will depend on his being readily found, on his being disengaged, on his distance from the ship, on his personal activity & good faith. some, or all of these circumstances, will generally give full time for the criminal or debtor to escape or for the Contraband goods to be withdrawn.

That part of this article which is intended to prevent a collusive desertion of sailors, not being liable to the same objections, is agreed to as follows. "Lorsque les dits coupables [*blotted out*] feront partie de l'equipage de l'un des batiments de leur nation, [*blotted out*] ils ne pourront etre ensuite mis en liberté qu'aprés que le Consul ou Vice Consul en aura eté prevenu, et [*blotted out*] ils lui seront remis, s'il le requiert, pour etre reconduits sur les batiments ou [*blotted out*] ils auroient eté arretés, ou autres de leur nation, et etre renvoyés hors du pays."

ART. XII.   This article is new also, and liable to the same objections with the preceding, and in a higher degree, as rendering the ports of the two nations still more completely extra-territorial. the clause which would make the captain's word conclusive evidence that the criminal who is seen standing on his deck, is not there, comes under all the objections which were made in a former paper to whatever should controul a fair & full investigation of a fact. our laws permit every species of proof to be opposed by counter-proof. the [*blotted out*] Convention of the Neutral powers in the late war, made the Captain's word conclusive evidence that no contraband goods were on board the vessels under his convoy. but this in cases arising on the high seas. the sea belongs to no nation. no nation therefore has a natural right to search the ship of another on the high seas. the contrary practice has been an abuse, & the abandonment of it is a reformation of that abuse, a re-establishment of natural right. but the Ports of a nation are a part of it's territory. they are often within the body of a town, and an immunity from the restraint of law granted to strangers within the port, would be as productive of disorder, as if granted to those in the town, or in the country. All judges civil & criminal, derive their authority from the sovereign of the country wherein they act. for the encouragement of commerce it is become usual to permit, by Convention, foreign merchants of the same country to refer their disputes to a judge of their own. but in criminal cases, in cases which interest members of their own or any other state, or the state itself, it is apprehended not to be the practice for the nation to part with it's authority, and that neither order nor justice would be promoted by it. particularly to leave to the discretion of a Captain, whether his ship shall be an asylum for fugitive debtors, whether the disorders or crimes committed by his sailors, or by others taking refuge in his ship, should be punished, or not, cannot be a means of encouraging the commerce between the two nations nor promote the interest or honor of either. nor has this impunity any relation to the functions of a Consul, which are the sole object of the present Convention.

ART. XIII. XIV. XV. XVI. and XVII. agreed.[1]

[1] The observations are in the hand of Thomas Jefferson.

(7)

No. 4. Second Form Proposed on the Part of the United States

Convention entre le R.T.C. et les E.U. de l'Amerique à l'effet de determiner et fixer les fonctions et prerogatives des consuls et viceconsuls respectifs.

Sa majesté le R.T.C. et les E.U. de l'Amerique s'etant accordés mutuellement par l'article 29. du traité d'Amitié et de commerce conclu entre'eux, la liberté de tenir dans leurs etats et ports respectifs des consuls, viceconsuls, agens et commissaires, et voulant en consequence determiner et fixer d'une maniere reciproque et permanente les fonctions et prerogatives des consuls et viceconsuls qu'ils ont jugé convenable d'etablir de preference, S.M.T.C. à nommé le Sieur ——— et les E.U. ont nommé ——— lesquels aprés s'etre communiqués leurs pleinspouvoirs respectifs, sont convenus de ce qui suit.

ART. I. Les consuls et viceconsuls nommés par le R.T.C. et les E.U. seront tenus de presenter leurs provisions selon la forme qui se trouvera etablie respectivement par le R.T.C. dans ses etats, et par le Congrés dans les E.U. on leur delivrera sans aucuns frais l'Exequatur necessaire à l'exercise de leurs fonctions, et sur l'exhibition qu'ils feront du dit Exequatur, les gouverneurs, commandants, chefs de justice, les corps tribunaux, ou autres officiers ayant autorité dans les ports et lieux de leurs consulats les y feront jouir aussitot et sans difficulté des preeminences, autorités et privileges accordés reciproquement, sans qu'ils puissent exiger des dits consuls et viceconsuls aucun droit sous aucun pretexte quelconque.

ART. II. Les consuls et viceconsuls jouiront d'une pleine et entiere immunité pour leur chancellerie, et les papiers qui y seront renfermés. ils seront exempts de tout service personnel, logement de gens de guerre, milice, guet, garde, tutelle, curatelle, ainsi que de tous droits, taxes, impositions, et charges quelconques, à l'exception seulement des biens meubles, et immeubles dont ils seroient proprietaires ou possesseurs, lesquels seront assujettis aux taxes imposées sur ceux de tous autres particuliers, et a tous autres egards ils demeureront sujets aux loix du pays comme les nationaux.

Ceux des dit Consuls et viceconsuls qui feront le commerce, seront respectivement assujettis à toutes les taxes, charges et impositions etablies sur les autres negociants.

Ils placeront sur la porte exterieure de leurs maisons les armes de leur souverain, sans que cette marque distinctive puisse donner aux dites maisons le droit d'azile, soit pour des personnes, soit pour des effets quelconques.

Art. III. Les consuls et viceconsuls respectifs pourront etablir des Agens dans les differents ports et lieux de leurs departements, ou le besoin l'exigera: ces Agents pourront etre choisis parmi les negociants nationaux ou etrangers, et munis de la commission de l'un des dits consuls. ils se renfermeront respectivement á rendre aux commerçants, navigateurs et batiments respectifs, tous les services possibles, & à informer le consul le plus proche des besoins des dits commerçants, navigateurs et batiments, sans que les dits agents puissent autrement participer aux immunités attribuées aux consuls, et viceconsuls, et sans pouvoir sous quelque pretexte que ce soit, exiger aucun droit ou emolument quelconque des dits commerçants.

Art. IV. Les consuls et viceconsuls respectifs pourront etablir une chancellerie ou seront deposés les deliberations, actes & procedures consulaires, ainsi que les testaments, obligations, contrats, et autres actes faits par les nationaux ou entr'eux, et les effets delaissés par mort ou sauvés des naufrages.

Ils pourront en consequence commettre á l'exercise de la dite chancellerie des personnes capables, les recevoir, leur faire preter serment, leur donner la garde du sceau, & le droit de sceller les commissions, jugemens & autres actes consulaires, ainsi que d'y remplir les fonctions de Notaires et Greffiers du Consulat.

Art. V. Les consuls et viceconsuls respectifs auront le droit exclusif de recevoir dans leur chancellerie, ou abord des batimens, les declarations & tous les autres actes que les capitaines, patrons, equipages, passagers & negociants de leur nation voudront y passer, meme leur testament & autres dispositions de derniere volonté et les expeditions des dits actes duement legalisés par les dits consuls ou viceconsuls, & munis du sceau de leur consulat feront foi en justice comme le feroient les originaux dans tous les tribunaux des etats du R.T.C. et des E.U.

Ils auront aussi et exclusivement, en cas d'absence d'executeur testamentaire, curateur, ou heritiers legitimes, le droit de faire l'inventaire la liquidation, & de proceder à la vente des effets mobiliers de la succession des sujets ou citoyens de leur nation, qui viendront à mourir dans l'etendue de leur consulat: ils y procederont avec l'assistance de deux negociants de leur dite nation, ou, à leur defaut, de toute autre á leur choix, & feront deposer dans leur chancellerie les effets et papiers des dites successions, sans qu'aucuns officiers militaires, de justice ou de police du pays puissent les y troubler, ni y intervenir de quelque maniere que ce soit; mais les dits consuls & viceconsuls ne pourront faire la delivrance des successions, et de leur produit aux heritiers legitimes, ou à leurs mandataires, qu'après avoir fait acquitter toutes les dettes que les defunts auront pû avoir contractées dans le pays, á l'effet de quoi les creanciers auront droit de saisir les dits effets dans leurs mains de meme que dans celles de tout autre individu quelconque, & en poursuivre la vente jusqu'au paiement de ce qui leur sera legitimement dû. lorsqu'les dettes n'auront eté contractées par jugement, par acte, ou par billet dont la signature sera reconnue, le paiement ne pourra en etre ordonné, qu'en fournissant par le creancier caution suffisante domicilié de rendre les sommes induement perçues, principal interets et frais: lesquelles cautions cependant demeureront duement dechargées aprés une année en tems de paix, & deux en tems de guerre, si la demande en decharge ne peut etre formée avant ces delais contre les heritiers qui se presenteront. et afin de ne pas faire injustement attendre aux heritiers les effets du defunt, les consuls et vicsconsuls feront annoncer sa mort dans quelqu'une des gazettes qui se publient dans l'etendue de leur consulat, & qu'ils retiendront les dits effets sous leurs mains pendant quatre mois pour repondre á toutes les justes demandes qui se presenteront: & ils seront tenus, après ce delai, de delivrer aux heritiers, l'excedent du montant des demandes qui auront eté formées.

ART. VI. Les consuls et vicsconsuls respectifs recevront les declarations, protestations et rapports de tous capitaines et patrons de leur nation respective pour raison d'avaries essuyées à la mer, & ces capitaines & patrons remettront dans la chancellerie des dits consuls et vicsconsuls les actes qu'ils auront fait dans d'autres ports, pour les accidents qui leur seront arrivés pendant leur voyage. si un sujet du R.T.C. et un habitant des E.U. ou un etranger sont interessés dans la dite cargaison, l'avarie sera reglée par les tribunaux du pays, & non par les consuls ou vicsconsuls: mais lorsqu'il n'y aura d'interessés que les sujets ou citoyens de leur propre nation les consuls ou les vicsconsuls respectifs nommeront des experts pour regler les dommages & avaries.

ART. VII. Dans les cas ou par tempetes, ou autres accidents, des vaisseaux ou batimens François echoueront sur les cotes des E.U. et des vaisseaux et batiments des E.U. echoueront sur les cotes des etats du R.T.C. le consul ou le viceconsul le plus proche du lieu du naufrage pourra faire tout ce qu'il jugera convenable tant pour sauver le dit vaisseau ou batiment, son chargement et appartenances, que pour le magazinage et la sureté des effets sauvés & marchandises. il pourra en faire l'inventaire sans qu'aucuns officiers militaires, des douanes, de justice, ou de police du pays puissent s'y immiscer autrement que pour faciliter aux consuls & vicsconsuls, capitaine et equipage du vaisseau naufragé ou echoué tous les secours et faveurs qu'ils leur demanderont, soit pour la celerité et la sureté du sauvetage, et des effets sauvés, soit pour eviter tous desordres.

Pour prevenir meme toute espece de conflit & de discussion dans les dits cas de naufrage, il a eté convenu que lorsqu'il ne se trouvera pas de consul ou viceconsul pour faire travailler au sauvetage, ou que la residence du dit consul ou viceconsul, qui ne se trouvera pas sur le lieu du naufrage, sera plus eloignée du dit lieu que celle du juge territorial competent, ce dernier fera proceder sur le champ avec toute la celerité, la sureté et les precautions prescrites par les loix respectives; sauf au dit juge territorial á se retirer, le consul ou viceconsul survenant, & à leur remettre l'expedition des procedures par lui faites: dont le consul ou viceconsul lui fera rembourser les fraix, ainsi que ceux du sauvetage.

Les marchandises et effets sauvés devront etre deposés à la douane ou autre lieu de sureté, le plus prochain, avec l'inventaire qui en aura eté dressé par le consul ou viceconsul, ou en leur absence par le juge qui en aura connû, pour les dits effets et marchandises etre en suite delivrés, apres le prelevement des frais, & sans forme de procés aux proprietaires, qui munis de la main levee du consul ou viceconsul le plus proche, les reclameront par euxmemes ou par leurs mandataires, soit pour reexporter les marchandises, & dans ce cas, elles ne paieront aucune espece de droit de sortie, soit pour les vendre dans le pays, si elles n'y sont pas prohibées, & dans ce dernier cas, les dites marchandises se trouvant avariées on leur accordera une moderation sur les droits d'entrée, proportionée au dommage souffert, lequel sera constatée par le procés verbal dressé lors du naufrage ou de l'echouement.

ART. VIII.   Les consuls & viceconsuls auront, abord des batimens de leur nation respective, tout pouvoir et jurisdiction en matiere civile: & á cet effet ils pourront s'y transporter sans qu'aucun officier ou autres personnes, puissent les en empecher.

ART. IX.   Les consuls et viceconsuls pourront faire arreter les capitaines, officiers, mariniers, matelots, des equipages des batimens de leurs nations respectives qui auroient deserté des dits batimens, pour les renvoyer, & faire transporter hors du pays. auquel effet les dits consuls et viceconsuls s'adresseront aux tribunaux, juges et officiers competents, et leur feront par ecrit la demande des dits deserteurs, en justifiant que ces hommes faisoient partie des susdits equipages. et sur cette demande ainsi justifiée l'extradiction ne pourra etre refusée; & il sera donné toute aide & assistance aux dits consuls & viceconsuls pour la recherche, saisie et arrestation des susdits deserteurs, lesquels seront meme detenus, & gardés dans les prisons du pays, á leur requisition & á leurs frais, jusques á ce qu'ils ayent trouvé occasion de les renvoyer. mais s'ils n'etoient renvoyés dans le delai de trois mois á compter du jour de leur arrêt, ils seront elargés & ne pourront plus etre arretés pour la meme cause.

ART. X.   Dans le cas ou les sujets ou citoyens respectifs auront commis quelque crime ou infraction de la tranquillité publique, ils seront justiciables des juges du pays.

ART. XI.   Lorsque les dits coupables feront partie de l'equipage de l'un des batimens de leur nation, ils ne pourront ensuite etre mis en liberté qu'aprés que le consul ou viceconsul en aura eté prevenu, et ils lui seront remis, s'il le requiert, pour etre reconduits sur les batimens ou ils auroient eté arretés, ou autres de leur nation, & etre renvoyés hors du pays.

ART. XII.   (to be omitted altogether.)

ART. XIII.   Tous differends et procés entre les sujets du R.T.C. dans les E.U. ou entre les citoyens des E.U. dans les etats du R.T.C. et notamment toutes les discussions relatives aux salaires & conditions des engagemens des equipages des batimens respectifs, et tous differends de quelque nature qu'ils soient qui pourroient s'elever entre les hommes des dits equipages, ou entre quelques uns d'eux & leurs capitaines, ou entre les capitaines de divers batimens nationaux, seront terminés par les consuls & viceconsuls respectifs, soit par un renvoi par devant des arbitres, soit par un jugement sommaire & sans frais.

aucun officier territorial, civil ou militaire ne pourra y intervenir, ou prendre un part quelconque á l'affaire; & les appels des dits jugemens consulaires seront portés devant les tribunaux de France, ou des E.U. qui doivent en connoitre.

Art. XIV. L'utilité generale du commerce ayant fait etablir dans les etats du R.T.C. des tribunaux et des formes particulieres pour accelerer la decision des affaires de commerce, les negocians des E.U. jouiront du benefice des ces etablissemens, & le Congrés des E.U. pourvoira de la maniere la plus conforme á ses loix á l'etablissement des avantages equivalents en faveur des negocians François pour la prompte expedition & decision des affairs de la meme nature.

Art. XV. Les sujets du R.T.C. et les citoyens des E.U. qui justifieront authentiquement etre du corps de la nation respective, jouiront en consequence de l'exemption de tout service personnel dans le lieu de leur etablissement.

Art. XVI. Si quelque autre nation acquiert en vertu d'une convention quelconque un traitement plus favorable relativement aux pre-eminences, pouvoirs, autorité et privileges consulaires, les consuls et viceconsuls du roi T.C. ou des E.U. reciproquement, y participeront aux termes stipulés par les articles 2. 3. & 4. du traité d'amitié & de commerce conclu entre le R.T.C. et les E.U.

Art. XVII. La presente convention aura son plein effet pendant l'espace de douze ans, á compter du jour de l'echange des ratifications, lesquelles seront données en bonne forme, et echangées de part et d'autre dans l'espace d'un an, ou plutot si faire se peut.

En foi de quoi &c.[1]

---

[1] The second proposal is in the hand of Thomas Jefferson.

(8)
English Translation

No. 4. Second form proposed on the part of the U. States.

Convention between His M.C.M. & the U.S. of America for the purpose of defining and establishing the functions & privileges of their respective Consuls & Vice Consuls.

His Majesty the Most C. King & the U.S. of America having by the 29th. Article of the Treaty of Amity & Commerce concluded between them; mutually granted the liberty of having, in their respective states & ports, Consuls, Vice Consuls, Agents & Commissaries, and being willing in consequence thereof to define & establish in a reciprocal & permanent manner the functions & prerogatives of Consuls & Vice Consuls which they have judged it convenient to establish of preference. His M.C. Majesty has nominated the Sieur ——— and the U.S. have nominated ——— who after having communicated to each other their respective full powers, have agreed on what follows.

Art. I. The Consuls & V. Consuls named by the M.C.K. & the U.S. shall be

bound to present their Commissions, according to the forms which shall be
established respectively by the M.C.K. within his dominions, and by the Congress
within the U.S. there shall be delivered to them without any charges the
Exequatur necessary for the exercise of their functions; and on exhibiting the
said exequatur the Governors, Commanders, Heads of justice, bodies corporate,
Tribunals or other Officers having authority in the ports & places of their
Consulates, shall cause them to enjoy immediately, & without difficulty the pre-
eminencies, authority & privileges reciprocally granted, without exacting from
the said Consuls & Vice Consuls any fee under any pretext whatever.

ART. II.   The Consuls & Vice Consuls shall enjoy a full & entire immunity
for their Chancery & the papers which shall be there in contained. they shall be
exempt from all personal service from soldier's billets militia, watch, guard,
guardian ship, trustee ship, as well as from all duties, taxes, impositions &
charges whatsover, except on the estate real & personal of which they may be
the proprietors or possessors which shall be subject to the taxes imposed on the
estates of all other individuals; and in all other instances they shall be subject
to the laws of the land as the natives are.

Those of the said Consuls & Vice Consuls who shall exercise Commerce shall
be respectively subject to all taxes charges & impositions established on other
merchants.

The[y] shall place over the outward door of their Houses, the arms of their
Sovereign without that this mark of distinction shall give to the said House the
right of azylum, for any persons or property whatsoever.

ART. III.   The respective Consuls & V. Consuls may establish Agents in the
different ports & places of their departments where necessity shall require.
These Agents may be chosen Among the Merchants either national or Foreign,
& furnished with a Commission from one of the said Consuls: they shall confine
themselves respectively to the rendering to their respective Merchants, navigators
& vessels all possible service, and to inform the nearest Consul of the wants of
the said merchants, navigators & vessels without the said Agents otherwise participating in the immunities attributed to Consuls & Vice Consuls & with out
power under any pretext whatever to exact from the said merchants any duty or
emolument whatever.

ART. IV.   The respective Consuls & Vice Consuls may establish a Chancery
where shall be ~~established~~ deposited the Consular deliberations, acts & proceedings as also testaments obligations contracts & other acts done by or between
persons of their nations and effects left by deceased or saved from shipwreck.

They may consequently appoint for the business of the said chancery capable
persons, receive them, administer an oath to them, give to them the keeping of
the seal & the right of sealing commissions, judgments & other consular acts as
well as there to discharge the functions of Notaries & Registers of the consulate.

ART. V.   The respective Consuls & Vice Consuls shall have the exclusive right
of receiving in their chancery or on board of vessels, the declarations and all the
other acts which the captains, masters, seamen passengers, and merchants of
their nation would make there, even their testaments & other dispositions of last

will and the copies of the said acts duly authenticated by the said Consuls or Vice Consuls, under the seal of their Consulate shall receive faith in law equally as their originals would, in all the tribunals of the dominions of the M.C. King & of the United States.

They shall also have, and exclusively in case of the absence of the testamentary executor guardian or lawful heirs, the right to inventory, liquidate & proceed to the sale of the personal estate left by subjects or citizens of their nation, who shall die within the extent of their consulate; they shall proceed therein with the assistance of two merchants of their said nation, or, for want of them of any other at their choice, & shall cause to be deposited in their chancery, the effects & papers of the said estates, & no officer military judiciary or of the police of the country shall disturb them or interfere therein in any manner whatsoever; but the said Consuls & Vice Consuls shall not deliver up the said effects nor the proceeds thereof to the lawful representatives or to their order, till they shall have caused to be paid all debts which the deceased shall have contracted in the country; for which purpose the creditor shall have a right to ~~contract~~ attach the said effects in their hands as they might in those of any other individual whatever & proceed to obtain sale of them 'till payment of what shall be lawfully due to them. When the debts shall not have been contracted by judgment, deed or note, the signature whereof shall be known, payments shall not be ordered but on the creditors giving sufficient surety resident in the country, to refund the sums he shall have unduly received, principal, interest & cost, which surety shall nevertheless [*blotted out*] duly discharged after a year in time of peace, & two years in time of war, if the demand in discharge cannot be formed before these delays against the heirs which shall present themselves.

And in order that the representatives may not be unjustly kept out of the effects of the deceased the Consuls & Vice Consuls shall notify his death in some one of the Gazettes published within their Consulate, and that they shall retain the said effects in their hands four months to answer all just demands which shall be presented, and they shall be bound after this delay to deliver to the persons succeeding there to what shall be more sufficient than for the demands which shall have been formed.

ART. VI. The respective Consuls & Vice Consuls shall receive the declarations, protests & reports of all captains & masters of their respective nation on account of average losses sustained at sea: & these captains & masters shall lodge in the chancery of the said Consuls & Vice Consuls the acts which they may have made happened to them on their voyage if a subject of the M.C.K. and a citizen of the U.S. or a foreigner are interested in the said Cargo, the average shall be settled by the tribunals of the Country & not by the Consuls or Vice Consuls: but when only the subjects or citizens of their own nation shall be interested, the respective Consuls or Vice Consuls shall appoint skilful persons to settle the damage and average.

ART. VII. In cases where by tempests or other accidents, French ships or vessels shall be stranded on the coasts of the U.S. & ships or vessels of the U.S. shall be stranded on the coast of the dominions of the M.C.K. The Consul or Vice Consul nearest to the place of shipwreck shall do whatever he may judge proper, as well for the purpose of saving the said ship or vessel its Cargo & appurtenances, as for the storing & security of the effects & merchandise saved. He may take an inventory of them, without the intermeddling of any officers of the military, of the customs of justice or of the police of the country, otherwise than to give the Consuls Vice Consuls, captains & crew of the vessel shipwrecked or stranded all the succour & favor which they shall ask of them either for the expedition & security of the saving & of the effects saved, as to prevent all disturbance.

To prevent even any kind of dispute & discussion in the said cases of shipwreck, it has been agreed, that where no Consul or Vice Consul shall be found to attend to the salvage, or that the residence of the said Consul or Vice Consul (he not being at the place of shipwreck) shall be further distant from the said place than that of the competent territorial Judge the latter shall immediately there proceed therein with all the celerity safety & precautions prescribed by the respective laws; but the said territorial Judge shall retire on the coming of the Consul or V. Consul & shall resign to him the procedures by him done the expenses of which the Consul or V. Consul shall cause to be reimbursed to him, as well as those of saving the wreck.

The merchandize & effects saved shall be deposited in the Custom House or other nearest place of safety with the inventory there of which shall have been made by the Consul or V. Consul or in their absence by the Judge who shall have had cognisance there of that the said effects & merchandize may be afterwards delivered, after levying therefrom the costs, & without form of process, to the proprietors, who being furnished with a replevy from the nearest Consul or V. Consul shall reclaim them by themselves, or by their attornies, either for the purpose of re-exporting the merchandizes, & in that case they shall pay no kind of duties of exportation; or for the purpose of selling them in the Country, if they are not prohibited, & in this latter case, the said merchandize being averaged, there shall be granted them an abatement of the entrance duties proportioned to the damage sustained, which shall be ascertained by the verbal process formed at the time of the shipwreck or of the vessels running ashore.

ART. 8.   The Consuls & V. consuls shall have on board of the vessels of their respective nations all power & jurisdiction in Civil matters, and for this purpose they may go there or without being interrupted by any officer or other person whatsoever.

ART. IX.   The Consuls & V. Consuls may cause to be arrested the Captains, officers, mariners, sailors of the crews of the vessels of their respective nations who shall have deserted from the said vessels, in order to send them back & transport them out of the country. For which purpose the said Consuls & V. Consuls shall address themselves to the competent tribunals Judges & officers & shall demand from them the said deserters in writing, proving that those men made a part of the said crews, & on this demand so proved the delivery shall not be refused, & there shall be given all aid & assistance to the said Consuls & V. Consuls for the search seizure & arrest of the said deserters, who shall even be detained & kept in the prisons of the Country at their request & expence untill they shall have found an opportunity of sending them back. But if they be not sent back within three months, to be counted from the day of their arrest they shall be set at liberty, & shall be no more arrested for the same cause.

ART. X. In cases where the respective subjects or citizens shall have committed any crime, or breach of peace, they shall be amenable to the ~~laws~~ Judges of the country.

ART. XI. When the said offenders shall be a part of a crew of a vessel of their nation, they shall not afterwards be set at liberty untill the Consul or Vice Consul shall have been notified, thereof, & they shall be delivered to him if he requires it, to be put again on board of the vessel on which they were arrested, or of others of their nation, & to be sent out of the country.

ART. XIII. All differences & suits between the subjects of the M.C.K. in the U.S. or between the citizens of the U. States within the dominions of the M.C.K. & particularly all disputes relative to the wages & terms of engagement of the crews of the respective vessels, and all differences of whatever nature they be, which may arise between the privates of the said crews or between any of them & their captains or between the captains of different vessels of their nation shall be determined by the respective Consuls and Vice Consuls either by a reference to arbitration or by a summary judgment & without costs. No officer of the country, civil or military shall interfere therein or take any part whatever in the matter; and the appeals from the said Consular sentences shall be carried before the tribunals of France or of the U. States to whom it may appertain to take cognizance thereof.

ART. XIV. The general utility of Commerce having caused to be established within the dominions of the M.C.K. particular tribunals & forms for expediting the decisions of Commercial affairs, the Merchants of the U.S. shall enjoy the benefit of these establishments; & the Congress of the U.S. will provide in the manner the most conformable to its laws equivalent advantages in favor of the French merchants, for the prompt dispatch & decision of affairs of the same nature.

ART. XV. The subjects of the M.C.K. & the Citizens of the U.S. who shall prove by legal evidence that they are of the said nation respectively shall in consequence enjoy an exemption from all personal service in the place of their settlement.

ART. XVI. If any other nation acquires by virtue of any convention whatever, a treatment more favorable with respect to the consular preeminences, powers authority & privileges; the Consuls & Vice Consuls of the M.C.K. or of the U.S. reciprocally shall participate therein, agreable to the terms stipulated by the 2d. 3d. & 4th. Articles of the treaty of Amity & Commerce, concluded between the M.C.K. & the U.S.

ART. XVII. The present Convention shall be in force during the term of twelve years to be counted from the day of the exchange of ratifications which shall be given in proper form & exchanged on both sides within the space of one year or sooner if possible.

In faith whereof &c.[1]

---

[1] The translation is in the hand of John Pintard.

(9)

Nos. 1 and 5.   Consular Conventions of 1784 and 1788, in English

[*Note*. The passages of the Convention of 1784, which are not in that of 1788, are printed in italics: those of 1788 which were not in that of 1784, are in a small character.] *

1784	**1788**[1]
No. 1.	No. 5.
CONVENTION between His most Christian Majesty and the *thirteen* United States of *North* America, for the purpose of determining and fixing the functions and prerogatives of their respective Consuls, vice-Consuls, *Agents and Commissaries.*	CONVENTION between His most Christian Majesty and the United States of America, for the purpose of defining and establishing the functions and privileges of their respective Consuls and vice-Consuls.
His Majesty the most Christian King and the *thirteen* United States of *North* America, having by the 29th article of the Treaty of amity and commerce concluded between them, mutually granted the liberty of having in their respective States and Ports, Consuls, vice-Consuls, *Agents and Commissaries* and being willing in consequence thereof, to determine and fix in a reciprocal and permanent manner the functions and prerogatives of the said Consuls, vice-Consuls, Agents and Commissaries, His M.C. Majesty has nominated the Sieur Charles Gravier, Count of Vergennes, Baron of Welferding &c., Counsellor of the King in all his Councils, Commander of his Orders, Counsellor of the State of the Sword, Minister and Secretary of State, and of his Commands and Finances; and the United States the Sieur Benjamin	His Majesty the most Christian King and the United States of America having by the 29th article of the Treaty of amity and commerce concluded between them, mutually granted the liberty of having, in their respective States and Ports, Consuls, vice-Consuls, Agents and Commissaries, and being willing in consequence thereof to define and establish in a reciprocal and permanent manner the functions and privileges of Consuls and vice-Consuls, **which they have judged it convenient to establish of preference**, His M.C. Majesty has nominated the Sieur Count of Montmorin of St. Herent, Marechal of his Camps and Armies, Knight of his Orders and of the Golden Fleece, his Counsellor in all his Councils, Minister and Secretary of State and of his Commandments and Finances, having the Department of foreign affairs, and the

---

* Boldface type has been substituted here for what was in small characters in the original document.

Franklin, their Minister Plenipotentiary to His most Christian Majesty, who after having communicated to each other their respective full powers, agreed upon what follows:

United States have nominated[2] Thomas Jefferson, Citizen of the United States of America and their Minister Plenipotentiary near the King, who after having communicated to each other their respective full powers, have agreed on what follows:

ART. 1. The Consuls and vice-Consuls nominated by H.M.C.M. and the U.S. shall be bound to present their commissions *on their arrival in the respective States, according to the form which shall be there established.* There shall be delivered to them without any charges the Exequatur necessary for the exercise of their functions; and on the exhibition they shall make of the said Exequatur, the Governors, Commanders, Heads of justice, public bodies, Tribunals and other Officers having authority in the ports and places of their consulates, shall cause them to enjoy as soon as possible, and without difficulty, the preeminencies, authority and privileges reciprocally granted, without exacting from the said Consuls and vice-Consuls any duty, under any pretext whatever.

ART. 1. The Consuls and vice-Consuls named by the M.C.K. and the U.S. shall be bound to present their commissions **according to the forms which shall be established respectively by the M.C.K. within his dominions, and by the Congress within the U.S.** there shall be delivered to them, without any charges, the Exequatur necessary for the exercise of their functions; and on exhibiting the said Exequatur, the Governors, Commanders, Heads of justice, bodies corporate, Tribunals and other Officers having authority in the ports and places of their consulates, shall cause them to enjoy immediately, and without difficulty, the preeminencies, authority and privileges, reciprocally granted, without exacting from the said Consuls and vice-Consuls any fee, under any pretext whatever.

ART. 4. The Consuls and vice-Consuls, *the Officers of the consulate and in general all* persons attached to the Consular functions, shall enjoy respectively a full and entire immunity for *their persons* their papers, *and their houses. The list of the said persons shall be approved and inspected by the executive power of the place of their residence.* They shall be exempt from all personal service *and public officers,* from soldiers billets, militia, watch, guard, guardianship and trustee-ship, as well as from all duties, taxes, impositions and charges whatsoever, except the real estates of which

ART. II. The Consuls and vice-Consuls and persons attached to their functions **that is to say, their Chancellors and Secretaries,** shall enjoy a full and entire immunity for their **Chancery and the papers which shall be therein contained:** they shall be exempt from all personal service, from soldiers billets, militia, watch, guard, guardianship, trustee-ship, as well as from all duties, taxes, impositions, and charges whatsoever, except on the estate real **and personal** of which they may be the proprietors **or possessors,** which shall be subject to the taxes imposed on the estates of all other individuals: **and in**

they may be proprietors, which shall be subject to the taxes imposed on the estates of all other individuals.

all other instances they shall be subject to the laws of the land as the natives are.

Those of the said Consuls and vice-Consuls who shall exercise commerce shall be respectively subject to all taxes, charges and impositions established on other merchants.

They shall place, over the outward door of their house, the arms of their Sovereign, without that this mark of distinction shall give to the said house the right of asylum *for any malefactor or criminal, so that in case it should happen that any malefactor or criminal takes refuge there, he shall be instantly delivered up, on the first requisition, and without difficulty.*

They shall place over the outward door of their house the arms of their Sovereign: but this mark of indication shall not give to the said house any privilege of asylum **for any person or property whatsoever.**

ART. 2. *The respective Consuls shall have power to establish vice-Consuls in the different ports and places of their departments where necessity shall require. There shall be delivered to them likewise the Exequatur necessary to the exercise of their functions in the form pointed out by the preceding article (1) and, on the exhibition which they shall make of the said Exequatur, they shall be admitted and acknowledged, in the terms and according to the powers, authority and privileges stipulated by the 1st. 4th. and 5th. articles of the present Convention.*

ART. 3. The respective Consuls and vice-Consuls may establish Agents in the different ports and places of their departments where necessity shall require. These Agents may be chosen among the merchants, either national or foreign, and furnished with a commission from one of the said Consuls: it shall be their business respectively to render to their respective merchants,

ART. III. The respective Consuls and vice-Consuls may establish Agents in the different ports and places of their departments where necessity shall require. These Agents may be chosen among the merchants either national or foreign, and furnished with a commission from one of the said Consuls: they shall confine themselves respectively to the rendering to their re-

navigators and vessels all possible service, and to inform the nearest Consul *or vice-Consul* of the wants of the said merchants, navigators and vessels, without the said Agents otherwise participating in the immunities, rights and privileges attributed to the Consuls and vice-Consuls, and without power to exact from the said merchants any duty or emolument whatsoever, under any pretext whatsoever.

ART. 5. *Generally in all cases whatever, which concern the police or administration of justice, where it may be necessary to have a juridical declaration from the said Consuls and vice-Consuls respectively, the Governors, Commandants, chief Justice, public bodies, tribunals or other Officers whatever of their respective residence there having authority, shall be bound to inform them of it, by writing to them, or sending to them a military or civil Officer to let them know, either the object which is proposed, or the necessity there is for going to them to demand from them this declaration, and the said Consuls and vice-Consuls shall be bound on their part to comply faithfully with what shall be desired of them on these occasions.*

ART. 6. The Consuls and vice-Consuls respectively may establish a chancery where shall be deposited the Consular acts and deliberations, all effects left by deceased persons, or saved from shipwreck, as well as testaments, obligations, contracts and in general all the acts and proceedings done between, or by persons of their nation.

They may in consequence appoint for the business of the said chancery

spective merchants, navigators, and vessels all possible service, and to inform the nearest Consul of the wants of the said merchants, navigators and vessels, without the said Agents otherwise particpating in the immunities, rights and privileges attributed to Consuls and vice-Consuls, and without power under any pretext whatever to exact from the said merchants any duty or emolument whatsoever.

ART. IV. The Consuls and vice-Consuls respectively may establish a chancery, where shall be deposited the Consular determinations, acts and proceedings as also testaments, obligations, contracts, and other acts done by, or between persons of their nation, and effects left by decedents,[3] or saved from shipwreck.

They may consequently appoint fit persons to act in the said chancery, capable persons, receive them, administer an oath to them, give to them the keeping of the seal, and the right of sealing commissions, judgments and other acts of the consulate, as well as there to discharge the functions of notaries and registers.

qualify[4] and swear them in, commit to them the custody of the seal, and authority to seal commissions, sentences and other consular acts, and also to discharge the functions of notaries and registers **of their Consulate.**

ART. 7. The Consuls and vice-Consuls respectively shall have the exclusive right of receiving in their chancery, or on board of vessels, the declarations and all the other acts, which the captains, masters, seamen, passengers, and merchants of their nation would make there, even their testaments and other dispositions of last will; and the copies of the said acts, duly authenticated by the said Consuls or vice-Consuls, and under the seal of their consulate, shall receive faith in law in all the tribunals of *France* and the United States.

ART. V. The Consuls and vice-Consuls respectively shall have the exclusive right of receiving in their[5] chancery, or on board their vessels, the declarations and all other acts, which the captains, masters, crews, passengers, and merchants of their nation may chuse to make there, even their testaments and other disposals by last will: and the copies of the said acts, duly authenticated by the said Consuls or vice-Consuls, under the seal of their consulate shall receive faith in law, **equally as their originals would,** in all the tribunals of **the dominions of the M.C. King** and of the United States.

They shall have also, and exclusively

They shall also have, and exclusively, **in case of the absence of the testamentary executor, guardian or lawful representative,**[6] the right to inventory, liquidate and proceed to the sale of the personal estate left by subjects **or citizens** of their nation, who shall die within the extent of their consulate: they shall proceed therein with the assistance of two merchants of their said nation, **or, for want of them, of any other** at their choice, and shall cause to be deposited in their chancery, the effects and papers of the said estates; and no officer military, judiciary, or of the police of the country shall disturb them or interfere therein, in any manner whatsoever: but the said Consuls and vice-Consuls shall not deliver up the said effects, nor the proceeds thereof to the lawful

the right to inventory, liquidate, and proceed to the sale of the moveable effects of the estates left by subjects of their nation, who shall die within the extent of their consulate: they shall proceed therein with the assistance of two merchants of their said nation, of their own chusing, and shall deposit in their chancery the effects and papers of the said estates; and no officer military or civil, or of the police of the country, shall trouble them or interfere therein, in any manner whatsoever: but the said Consuls and vice-Consuls shall not deliver up the same and their product to the lawful heirs or their attornies, until they shall have discharged all the debts which the deceased shall have contracted in the country *by judgment, by acts or by notes, the writing and signing of which shall be known and certified by two principal merchants of the nation of the said deceased: and in all other cases*

the payment of debts cannot be ordered but on the creditors giving sufficient and local security to repay the sums unduly received, principal, interest and costs; which securities however shall remain duly discharged after a year in time of peace, and two years in time of war, if the demand in discharge cannot be formed before these delays against the heirs which shall present themselves.

representatives[7] or to their order, till they shall have caused to be paid all debts which the deceased shall have contracted in the country; **for which purpose the creditor shall have a right to attach the said effects in their hands as they might in those of any other individuals whatever, and proceed to obtain sale of them till payment of what shall be lawfully due to them. When the debts shall not have been contracted by judgment, deed or note, the signature whereof shall be known,** payment shall not be ordered but on the creditor's giving sufficient surety resident in the country, to refund the sums he shall have unduly received, principal, interest and costs: which surety nevertheless shall stand duly discharged after the term of one year in time of peace, and of two in time of war, if the[8] discharge cannot be formed before the end of this term against the representatives[9] who shall present themselves.

And in order that the representatives[10] may not be unjustly kept out of the effects of the deceased the Consuls and vice-Consuls shall notify his death in some one of the gazettes published within their consulate, and that they shall retain the said effects in their hands four months to answer all just[11] demands which shall be presented: and they shall be bound after this delay to deliver to the persons succeeding thereto what shall be more than sufficient for the demands which shall have been formed.

Art. 8.   The respective Consuls and vice-Consuls shall receive the declarations, consulates and other consular acts from all Captains and masters of their respective nation on account of average losses sustained at sea *by*

Art. VI.   The Consuls and vice-Consuls respectively shall receive the declarations, protests and reports of all captains and masters of their respective nation on account of average losses sustained at sea: & these cap-

leakage or throwing merchandise over board and these Captains and masters shall leave in the chancery of the said Consuls and vice Consuls the consulates and other consular acts which they may have had made in other ports, on account of the accidents which may have happened to them on their voyage. If a subject of his M.C.M. and a citizen of the U.S. are interested in the said cargo, the average shall be fixed by the Tribunals of the country, and not by the Consuls or Vice-Consuls: *and the Tribunals shall admit the acts and declarations, if any should have been passed before the said Consuls and Vice-Consuls*: but when only the subjects of their own nation, *or foreigners* shall be interested, the respective Consuls or vice-Consuls *and in case of their absence or distance their agents furnished with their commission* shall officially nominate skilful persons *of their said nation* to regulate the damages and averages.

tains and masters shall lodge in the chancery of the said Consuls and vice-Consuls, the acts which they may have made in other ports on account of the accidents which may have happened to them on their voyage. If a subject of the M.C.K. and a citizen of the U.S. **or a foreigner** are interested in the said cargo, the average shall be settled by the tribunals of the country and not by the Consuls or vice-Consuls; but when

only the subjects **or citizens** of their own nation shall be interested, the respective Consuls or vice-Consuls shall appoint skilful persons to settle the damages and average.

ART. 9. In case by storms or other accidents, French ships or vessels shall run ashore on the coasts of the U.S. and the ships and vessels of the U.S. shall run a shore on the coasts of France, the Consul or vice-Consul nearest to the place of shipwreck, shall do whatever he may judge proper, as well for the purpose of saving the said ship or vessel, its cargo and appurtunances, as for the storing and security of the effects and merchandise saved. He may take an inventory, without any officers military, of the custom house, justices or the police of the country interfering, otherwise than to facilitate to the Consuls, vice-Consuls, captain, and crew of the vessel shipwrecked or run a shore, all the assistance and favour which they shall ask, either for

ART. VII. In cases where by tempest, or other accident, French ships or vessels shall be stranded on the coasts of the U.S. and ships or vessels of the U.S. shall be stranded on the coasts of **the dominions of the M.C.K.** the Consul or vice-Consul nearest to the place of shipwreck shall do whatever he may judge proper, as well for the purpose of saving the said ship or vessel, its cargo and appurtenances, as for the storing and the security of the effects and merchandise saved. He may take an inventory of them, without the intermedling of any officers of the military, of the customs, of justice, or of the police of the country, otherwise than to give to the Consuls, vice-Consuls, captain and crew of the vessel shipwrecked or stranded all the

the celerity and security of the salvage and effects saved, or to prevent all disturbances.

To prevent even any kind of dispute and discussion in the said cases of shipwreck, it has been agreed, that where no Consul or vice-Consul shall be found to attend to the salvage, or that the residence of the said Consul or vice-Consul (he not being at the place of shipwreck) shall be further distant from the said place than that of the competent territorial Judge, the latter shall immediately there proceed therein with all the celerity, safety and precautions prescribed by the respective laws; but the said territorial Judge shall retire on the coming of the Consul or vice-Consul and shall resign to him the procedures by him done, the expences of which the Consul or vice-Consul shall cause to be reimbursed to him.

The merchandise and effects saved shall be deposited in the custom house, or other nearest place of safety, with the inventory of them, which shall be made by the Consul or vice-Consul, or, in their absence, by the Judge who shall have had cognisance thereof, and the said merchandises and effects shall be afterwards delivered, after levying therefrom the costs, and without form of process, to the proprietors, who, being furnished with a replevy from the nearest Consul or vice-Consul, shall reclaim them by themselves, or by their attornies, either for the purpose of reexporting the merchandises, and in that case they shall pay no kind of duties of exportation; or for the purpose of selling them in the Country, if they are not prohibited, and in this

succour and favour which they shall ask of them, either for the expedition and security of the saving and of the effects saved, as to prevent all disturbance.

And in order to prevent all kind of dispute and discussion in the said cases of shipwreck, it is agreed that when there shall be no Consul or vice-Consul to attend to the saving of the wreck, or that the residence of the said Consul or vice-Consul (he not being at the place of the wreck) shall be more distant from the said place than that of the competent Judge of the Country, the latter shall immediately proceed therein, with all the despatch, certainty and precautions prescribed by the respective laws; but the said territorial Judge shall retire, on the arrival of the Consul or vice-Consul, and shall deliver over to him the report of his proceedings, the expences of which the Consul or vice-Consul shall cause to be reimbursed to him, **as well as those of saving the wreck.**

The merchandise and effects saved shall be deposited in the nearest custom house, or other place of safety, with the inventory thereof which shall have been made by the Consul or vice Consul, or by the Judge who shall have proceeded in their absence, that the said effects and merchandise may be afterwards delivered (after levying therefrom the costs) and without form of process, to the owners, who being furnished with an order for delivery from the nearest Consul or vice-Consul, shall reclaim them by themselves, or by their order, either for the purpose of reexporting such merchandise, in which case they shall pay no kind of duty of exportation, or for that of selling them in the Country, if they be not prohibited there, and in latter case, the said merchandises being averaged, there shall be granted them an abatement of the entrance duties proportioned to the damage sustained, which shall be ascertained by the verbal process formed at the time of the shipwreck, or of the vessels running ashore.

ART. 10. The Consuls and vice-Consuls shall have on board of the vessels of their respective Nations, full power and Jurisdiction in Matters, Civil.
They shall cause to be executed the respective laws, Ordinances and rules concerning Navigation, on board the said vessels,
And for this purpose they shall go there without being interrupted by any Officer or other person whatsoever.

They may cause to be arrested every vessel carrying the flag of their respective Nation; they may sequester them and even send them back respectively from the U.S. to France, or from France to the U.S. They may cause to be arrested, without difficulty, every Captain, Master, Sailor *or passenger*
of their respective Nation, they *may cause to be arrested, or detained in the Country, the Sailors and deserters of their respective Nations,* or send them back or transport them out of the Country.
It shall be sufficient proof that the

this last case, the said merchandise, if they be damaged, shall be allowed an abatement of entrance duties proportioned to the damage they have sustained, which shall be ascertained by the affidavits taken at the time the vessel was wrecked or struck.

ART. VIII. The Consuls and[12] vice-Consuls **shall exercise Police over all the vessels of their respective Nations and** shall have on board the said vessels all power and Jurisdiction in Civil Matters, **in all the disputes which may there arise they shall have an entire inspection over the said vessels, their crew and the changes and substitutions there to be made.** For which purpose they may go on board the said vessels whenever they may judge it necessary. **Well understood that the functions hereby allowed shall be confined to the interior of the vessels, and that they shall not take place in any case which shall have any interference with the Police of the ports where the said vessels shall be.**

ART. IX.

The Consuls and vice-Consuls may cause to be arrested the Captains, Officers, Mariners, Sailors, **and all other persons being part of the crews of the vessels** of their respective Nation **who shall have deserted from the said vessels** in order to send them back and transport them out of the Country. **For which purpose the said Consuls and vice-Consuls shall address themselves to the courts, Judges and Officers**

Sailors and deserters belong to one of the respective Nations, that their names be written in the ship's register, or inserted in the roll of the crew.

One and the other of these proofs concerning Sailors and deserters being thus given *no Tribunals, Judges, or Officers whatsoever, shall in any manner whatever take cognisance of the complaints which the said Sailors and deserters may make, but* they shall on the contrary be delivered *up on an order signed by the Consul or vice-Consul, without its being in any one's power in any manner to detain, engage, or withdraw them. And to attain to the complete execution of the arrangements contained in this article all* persons having authority shall be bound to assist the said Consuls or vice-Consuls, and on a simple requisition signed by them, they shall cause to be detained and guarded in prison at the disposal and expence of the said Consuls and vice-Consuls, the said Sailors and deserters until they shall have an opportunity to send them out of the Country.

Art. 11. In cases where the respective subjects shall have committed any crime, they shall be amenable to the Judges of the Country.

competent, and shall demand the said deserters in writing, proving by an exhibition of the registers of the vessel or ship's roll that those men were parts of the said crews: and on this demand so proved (saving however where the contrary is proved) the delivery shall

not be refused; and there shall be given all

aid and assistance to the said Consuls and vice-Consuls for the search, seizure and arrest of the said deserters, who shall even be detained and kept in the prisons of the Country, at their request and expence until they shall have found an opportunity of sending them back. But if they be not sent back within three months, to be counted from the day of their arrest they shall be set at liberty, and shall be no more arrested for the same cause.

Art. X. In cases where the respective subjects or citizens shall have committed any crime, or breach of the peace, they shall be amenable to the Judges of the Country.

Art. XI. When the said offenders shall be a part of the crew of a vessel of their Nation, and shall have withdrawn themselves on board the said vessel they may be there seized and arrested by order of the Judges of the Country: these shall give notice thereof to the Consul or vice-Consul, who may repair on board if he thinks proper: but this notification shall not in any case delay execution of the order in question. The persons arrested shall not afterwards be set at liberty until the Consul or vice-Consul shall have been notified thereof; and they shall be delivered to him, if he requires it to be put again on board of the vessel on which they were arrested, or of others of their Nation, and to be sent out of the Country.

ART. 12. All differences and suits between the subjects of His M.C.M. settled in the U.S. or between the citizens *and subjects* of the U.S. settled in *France, and all differences and suits concerning Commerce, between the subjects of his M.C.M. and one of the parties residing in France or else where, and the other in the U.S. or between the citizens and subjects of the U.S. one of the parties residing in the U.S. or elswhere, and the other in France*

shall be determined by the respective Consuls, either by a reference to arbitration, or by a summary judgment and without costs.

No Officer Civil or Military, shall interfere or take any part whatever in the affair: appeals shall be carried before the Tribunals of France or the U.S. to whom it may appertain to take cognisance thereof. *The Consuls or Vice-Consuls shall not take cognisance of disputes or differences, which shall arise betwixt a subject of His M.C.M. and a citizen of the U.S. but the said disputes shall be brought before the Tribunals to which the defendant shall be amenable.*

ART. XII. All differences and suits between the subjects of the M.C.K. in the U.S. or between the citizens of the United States within **the dominions of the M.C.K.** **and particularly all disputes relative to the wages and terms of engagement of the crews of the respective vessels, and all differences of whatever nature they be, which may arise between the privates of the said crews, or between any of them and their captains, or between the captains of different vessels of their nation,** shall be determined by the respective Consuls **and vice-Consuls,** either by a reference to arbitrations, or by a summary judgment and without costs.

No Officer of the country, civil or military, shall interfere therein or take any part whatever in the matter: and the appeals from the said consular sentences shall be carried before the tribunals of France or of the U.S. to whom it may appertain to take cognizance thereof.

ART. 13. The general utility of

ART. XIII. The general utility of

Commerce having caused to be established *in France* Tribunals & particular forms to accelerate the decision of commercial affairs, the Merchants of the U.S. shall enjoy the benefit of these establishments *in France* and the Congress of the U.S. shall *recommend to the Legislatures of the different States to provide* equivalent advantages in favour of the French Merchants, for the prompt dispatch and decision of affairs of the same nature.

ART. 14. The subjects of his M.C.M. and *those* of the U.S. who shall prove that they belong to the body of their respective Nations *by the certificate of the Consul or vice-Consul of the District, mentioning their names, surnames and place of their settlement, as inscribed in the registers of the consulate, shall not lose, for any cause whatever, in the respective Domains and States, the quality of subjects of the Country of which they originally were, conformably to the 11th. article of the treaty of amity and commerce of the 6th. of February 1778, of which the present article shall serve as an interpretation in case of necessity, and the said subjects respectively* shall enjoy in consequence exemption from all personal service in the place of their settlement.

ART. 15. If any other Nation acquires, by virtue of any convention whatever *either in France or in the U.S.* a treatment more favourable with respect to the consular pre-eminencies, powers, authority and privileges, the Consuls, vice-Consuls *and Agents* of His M.C.M. or the U.S. reciprocally shall participate therein, agreeable to the terms stipulated by the 2d. 3d.

commerce having caused to be established **within the dominions of the M.C.K.** particular tribunals and forms for expediting the decision of commercial affairs the merchants of the U.S. shall enjoy the benefit of these establishments; and the Congress of the U.S. will **provide in the manner the most conformable to its laws**[13] equivalent advantages in favour of the French merchants, for the prompt dispatch and decision of affairs of the same nature.

ART. XIV. The subjects of the M.C.K. and **citizens** of the U.S. who shall prove **by legal evidence** that they are of the said nations respectively

shall in consequence enjoy an exemption from all personal service in the place of their settlement.

ART. XV. If any other nation acquires by virtue of any convention whatever, a treatment more favourable with respect to the consular pre-eminencies, powers, authority and privileges, the Consuls and vice-Consuls of the M.C.K. or of the U.S. reciprocally shall participate therein, agreeable to the terms stipulated by the 2d. 3d. and 4th. articles of the

and 4th. articles of the treaty of amity and commerce, concluded between His M.C.M. and the U.S.

treaty of amity and commerce, concluded between the M.C.K. and the U.S.

ART. 16.

ART. XVI. **The present Convention shall be in full force during the term of twelve years to be counted from the day of the exchange of ratifications,** which shall be given in proper form, and exchanged on both sides within the space of one year, or sooner if possible.

The ratification of the present convention shall be given in proper form, and exchange on both sides within the space of six months, or sooner if possible.

In faith whereof we the underwritten Ministers plenipotentiaries of his most Christian Majesty and the United States of North America have signed the present convention and have thereto affixed the seal of our arms.

In faith whereof we Ministers Plenipotentiary have signed the present Convention, and have thereto set the seal of our arms.

Done at Versailles, the 29th. July one Thousand seven hundred and eighty four.

Done at Versailles the 14th. of November one thousand seven hundred and eighty eight.

GRAVIER DE VERGENNES. { Signed } B. FRANKLIN.   L. C. DE MONTMORIN. { Signed } TH. JEFFERSON.

L.S.   L.S.   L.S.   L.S.[14]

[1] The textual notes which follow reflect the changes made by the Senate between July 27 and July 29, 1789. These changes, in the hand of George Taylor, Jr., conform the treaty to the original French text.
[2] At this point the words "the Sieur" are inserted.
[3] At this point the word "decedents" is lined out and "deceased persons" inserted.
[4] At this point the word "qualify" is lined out and "received" inserted.
[5] At this point the word "their" is lined out and "of" inserted.
[6] At this point the words "guardian or lawful representative" are lined out and "administrator or legal heir" inserted.
[7] At this point the word "representatives" is lined out and "heirs" inserted.
[8] At this point the words "demand in" are inserted.
[9] At this point the word "representatives" is lined out and "heirs" inserted.
[10] At this point the word "representatives" is lined out and "heirs" inserted.
[11] At this point the word "just" is lined out.
[12] At this point the word "and" is lined out and "or" inserted.
[13] At this point the words "for the establishment of" are inserted.
[14] An annotated printed copy of the conventions, which is in PCC, item 47, M247, roll 61, DNA, E-21525, was used to discern the changes made by the Senate. The document is also related to George Washington's message journalized June 11, 1789. A copy of the conventions is in Transcribed Treaties and Conventions, 1789–1801, Records of the Secretary, SR, DNA.

Consular Convention of 1784

CONVENTION entre le Roi Très Chrétien et les treize Etats-Unis de L'Amérique Septentrionale à l'effet de déterminer et fixer les fonctions et prérogatives des Consuls, Vice-Consuls, Agents et Commissaires respectifs.

Sa Majesté le Roi Très Chrétien et les treize-Etats-Unis de l'Amérique septentrionale s'étant accordés mutuellement, par l'Article XXIX du Traité d'amitié et de Commerce conclu entre eux, la liberté de tenir dans leurs Etats et ports respectifs, des Consuls, Vice-Consuls, Agens et Commissaires, et voulant en conséquence déterminer et fixer d'une manière réciproque et permanente les fonctions et prérogatives desdits Consuls, Vice-Consuls, Agens et Commissaires, Sa Majesté Très-Chrétienne a nommé le Sieur Charles Gravier, Comte de Vergennes, Baron de Welferding &c., Conseiller du Roi en tous ses Conseils, Commandeur de ses Ordres, Chef du Conseil-royal des finances, Conseiller d'Etat d'épée, Ministre et Sécrétaire d'Etat et de ses commandemens et finances; et les Etats-Unis le Sieur Benjamin Franklin, leur Ministre Plénipotentiaire près Sa Majesté très-Chrétienne, lesquels, après s'être communiqués leurs pleinpouvoirs respectifs, sont convenus de ce qui suit:

ART. I.

Les Consuls et Vice-Consuls nommés par le Roi très-Chrétien et les Etats-Unis, seront tenus de présenter leurs provisions à leur arrivée dans les Etats-respectifs, selon la forme qui s'y trouvera établie. On leur délivrera sans aucuns frais *l'Exequatur* nécessaire à l'éxercice de leurs fonctions, et sur l'exhibition qu'ils feront dudit *Exequatur,* les Gouverneurs Commandans, Chefs de justice, les Corps, Tribunaux ou autres officiers ayant autorité dans les ports et lieux de leurs Consulats, les y feront jouir aussitôt et sans difficulté, des prééminences, autorité et privilèges accordés réciproquement, sans qu'ils puissent éxiger desdits Consuls et Vice-Consuls aucun droit sous aucun prétexte quelconque.

ART. II.

Les Consuls respectifs auront la faculté d'établir des Vice-Consuls dans les différents ports et lieux de leurs Départemens où le besoin l'éxigera: on leur délivrera également *l'Exequatur* nécessaire à l'éxercice de leurs fonctions dans la forme indiquée par l'Article précédent, et, sur l'exhibition qu'ils feront dudit *Exequatur,* ils seront admis et reconnus dans les termes et selon les pouvoirs, autorité & privilèges stipulés par les Articles I, IV et V de la présente Convention.

ART. III.

Les Consuls et Vice-Consuls respectifs pourront établir des Agens dans les differents ports et lieux de leurs départemens où le besoin l'éxigera; ces agens pourront être choisis parmi les négociants nationaux ou étrangers et munis de la Commission de l'un desdits Consuls, ils se renfermeront respectivement à rendre aux Commerçans, navigateurs et Batimens respectifs, tous les Services possibles, et à informer le Consul ou Vice-Consul le plus proche, des besoins desdits Commerçans, Navigateurs et batimens, sans que lesdits Agens puissent autrement participer aux immunités, droits, et privilèges attribués aux Consuls et Vice-Consuls, et sans pouvoir sous quelque prétexte que ce soit éxiger aucun droit ou émolument quelconque desdits Commercants.

Art. IV.

Les Consuls et Vice-Consuls, les officiers du Consulat et généralement toutes les personnes attachées aux fonctions consulaires, jouiront respectivement d'une pleine et entière immunité pour leur personne, leurs papiers et leurs Maisons. La liste desdites personnes sera aprouvée et visée par le pouvoir éxécutif du lieu de leur résidence.

Ils seront exemts de tout service personnel et offices publics, logement de gens de guerre, milice, guet, garde, tutelle, Curatelle, ainsi que de tous droits, taxes impositions, charges quelconques, fors les biens-fonds dont ils seront propriétaires, lesquels seront assujetis aux taxes imposées sur les biens de tous autres particuliers.

Ils placeront sur la porte extérieure de leur Maison les armes de leur Souverain, sans cependant que cette marque distinctive puisse donner à la dite Maison le droit d'asîle pour aucun malfaiteur ou Criminel, de manière que le cas arrivant où aucun malfaiteur ou Criminel s'y réfugie, il sera rendu sur le champ à la première réquisition, et sans difficulté.

Art. V.

Dans tous les cas généralement quelconques, intéressant la police ou l'administration de la Justice où il sera nécessaire d'avoir une Déclaration juridique desdits Consuls et Vice-Consuls respectifs, les Gouverneur, Commandant, Chef de la Justice, les Corps, Tribunaux ou autres officiers quelconques de leur résidence respective y ayant autorité, seront tenus de les en prévenir, en leur écrivant, ou en leur envoyant un officier militaire ou civil, pour leur faire connaître, soit l'objet que l'on se propose, soit la nécessité dans laquelle on se trouve d'aller chez eux pour leur demander cette déclaration, et lesdits Consuls et Vice-Consuls seront tenus, de leur Côté, de se prêter loyalement à ce qu'on désirera d'eux dans ces occasions.

Art. VI.

Les Consuls et Vice-Consuls respectifs pourront établir une Chancellerie où seront déposés les Actes et délibérations consulaires, tous les effets délaissés par défunts, ou sauvés des naufrages, ainsi que les testaments, obligations, contrats et généralement tous les actes et procédures faits entre leurs Nationaux ou par leurs Nationaux.

Ils pourront en conséquence, commettre à l'éxercice de ladite Chancellerie des personnes capables, les recevoir, leur faire prêter serment, leur donner la garde du sceau et le droit de sceller les Commissions, Jugemens et autres Actes du Consulat, ainsi que d'y remplir les fonctions de Notaires et Grefiers.

Art. VII.

Les Consuls et Vice-Consuls respectifs auront le droit exclusif de recevoir dans leur Chancellerie ou à bord des batimens, les déclarations, et tous les autres actes que les Capitaines, Patrons, Equipages, passagers et Négociants de leur Nation voudront y passer, même leur testament, et autres dispositions de dernière volonté; et les expeditions desdits actes dûment légalisés par les dits Consuls ou Vice-Consuls et munis du sceau de leur Consulat feront foi en justice dans tous les tribunaux de france et des États-Unis.

Ils auront aussi et exclusivement le droit de faire l'Inventaire, la liquidation, et de procéder à la vente des effets mobiliers de la succession des sujets de leur Nation qui viendront à mourir dans l'étenduë de leurs Consulats, ils y procéderont avec l'assistance de deux Négocians de leur dite Nation, à leur choix, et feront deposer dans leur Chancellerie, les effets et papiers desdites successions sans qu'aucuns officiers militaires, de Justice ou de police du Païs, puissent les y troubler ni y intervenir de quelque manière que ce soit, mais lesdits Consuls et Vice-Consuls ne pourront faire la délivrance des successions et de leur produit aux héretiers légitimes, ou à leurs Mandataires, qu'après avoir fait acquiter toutes les dettes que les deffunts auront pû avoir contractées dans le Païs par jugement, par actes ou par billets dont l'écriture et la signature seront reconnuës et certifiées par deux Notables Négocians de la nation desdits défunts, et dans tous autres cas le payement des dettes ne pourra être ordonné, qu'en fournissant par le créancier, caution suffisante et domiciliée de rendre les sommes induement perçuës, principal, intérêt et fraïs; lesquelles cautions cependant demeureront duëment déchargées, après une année en tems de paix, et deux en tems de guerre, si la demande en décharge ne peut être formée avant ces délais, contre les héritiers que se présenteront.

Art. VIII.

Les Consuls et Vice-Consuls respectifs recevront les Déclarations, Consulats ou autres Actes consulaires de tous Capitaines et Patrons de leur Nation respective pour raison d'avaries essuyées à la Mer par des voïes d'eau ou de jet de marchandises, et ces Capitaines et Patrons remettront dans la Chancellerie desdits Consuls et Vice-Consuls, les Consulats et autres actes consulaires qu'ils auront faits dans d'autres ports pour les accidens qui leur seront arrivés pendant leur voyage. Si un sujet du Roi très-Chrétien et un habitant des Etats-Unis sont intéressés dans ladite cargaison, l'avarie sera règlée par les tribunaux du Païs et non par les Consuls ou Vice-Consuls; et lesdits tribunaux admettront les Actes et Déclarations, s'il y en a eû de passés par devant les dits Consuls et Vice-Consuls; mais lorsqu'il n'y aura d'intéressés que les sujets de leur propre nation ou des Etrangers, les Consuls ou les Vice-Consuls respectifs, et en cas d'absence ou d'éloignement, leurs agens, munis de leur Commission, nommeront d'office des experts de leur dite Nation, pour régler les dommages et avaries.

Art. IX.

Dans le cas ou par tempête ou autre accident, des vaisseaux ou batimens français échouëront sur les Côtes des Etats-Unis, et des vaisseaux et batimens des Etats-Unis échouëront sur les côtes de france, le Consul ou le Vice-Consul le plus proche du lieu du naufrage pourra faire tout ce qu'il jugera convenable, tant pour sauver ledit vaisseau ou batiment, son chargement et apartenances, que pour le magazinage et la sûreté des effets sauvés et marchandises. Il pourra en faire l'inventaire sans qu'aucuns officiers militaires, des Douannes, de Justice ou de police du Païs puissent s'y immiscer autrement, que pour faciliter aux Consuls et Vice Consuls Capitaine et Équipage du vaisseau naufragé ou échoué, tous les secours et faveur qu'ils leur demanderont, soit pour la célérité et la sûreté du sauvetage et des effets sauvés, soit pour éviter tous désordres.

Pour prévenir même tout espèce de conflit et de discussions dans lesdits cas de naufrage, il a été convenu que lorsqu'il ne se trouvera pas de Consul ou Vice Consul pour faire travailler au sauvetage, ou que la résidence dudit Consul ou Vice-Consul qui ne se trouvera pas sur le lieu de naufrage, sera plus eloignée dudit lieu que celle du Juge territorial compétent, ce dernier y fera procéder sur le champ avec toute la célérité, la sûreté et les précautions prescrites par les loix respectives, sauf au dit juge territorial à se retirer, le Consul ou Vice-Consul survenant, et à lui remettre les procédures par lui faites, dont le Consul ou Vice-Consul lui fera rembourser les fraîs.

Les marchandises et effets sauvés devront être déposés à la Douane ou autre lieu de sûreté le plus prochain, avec l'inventaire qui en aura été dressé par le Consul ou Vice-Consul, ou, en leur absence, par le Juge qui en aura connu, pour, les dits effets et marchandises, être ensuite délivrés, après le prélevement des fraîs, et sans forme des procès, aux propriétaires, qui, munis de la main-levée du Consul ou Vice-Consul le plus proche, les réclameront par eux-mêmes ou par leurs Mandataires, soit pour réexporter les marchandises; et dans ce cas, elles ne payeront aucune espèce de droits de sortie, soit pour les vendre dans le Païs, si elles n'y sont pas prohibées, et dans ce dernier cas, lesdites Marchandises se trouvant avariées, on leur accordera une modération sur les droits d'entrée proportionnée au dommage souffert, lequel sera constaté par le procès verbal dressé lors du naufrage ou de l'échouëment.

Art. X.

Les Consuls et Vice-Consuls auront à-bord des batimens de leurs Nations respectives tout pouvoir et jurisdiction en matière civile. Ils feront éxécuter les loix, ordonnances et Règlemens respectifs concernant la navigation à bord desdits batimens, et à cet effet ils pourront s'y transporter sans qu'aucun officier ou autres personnes puissent les en empêcher.

Ils pourront faire arrêter tout batiment portant pavillon de leur Nation respective, le faire séquestrer et même le renvoyer respectivement des Etats-Unis en france ou de france dans les Etats-Unis, et faire arrêter sans difficulté, tout Capitaine, patron, matelot ou passager de leur dite Nation respective.

Ils pourront faire arrêter ou détenir dans le Païs les Matelots et Déserteurs de leurs Nations respectives, ou les renvoyer et faire transporter hors du Païs.

Il suffira pour prouver que les Matelots et Déserteurs apartiennent à l'une des Nations respectives, que leurs noms soient inscrits sur les Régistres du vaisseau ou portés sur le rôle d'équipage.

L'une ou l'autre de ces preuves étant ainsi administrée, concernant les matelots et déserteurs, aucuns tribunaux, Juges et officiers quelconques ne pourront, en quelque manière que ce soit, connaître des plaintes que lesdits matelots et Déserteurs pourroient former. Mais ils seront au-contraire délivrés sur un ordre signé par le Consul ou Vice-Consul, sans qu'on puisse aucunement les détenir, engager ou soustraire.

Et pour parvenir à l'entière éxécution des dispositions contenues dans cet article, toutes personnes, ayant autorité, seront tenues d'assister lesdites Consuls ou Vice-Consuls, et sur un simple réquisitoire signé d'eux, ils feront détenir et garder dans les prisons à la Disposition et aux fraîs desdits Consuls et Vice-Consuls les dits matelots et déserteurs jusqu'à ce qu'ils aient occasion de les faire sortir du Païs.

Art. XI.

Dans le cas où les sujets respectifs auront commis quelque crime, ils seront justiciables des Juges du païs.

Art. XII.

Tous les différends et procès entre les sujets du Roi très-Chrétien établis dans les Etats-Unis, ou entre les Citoyens et sujets des Etats-Unis établis en france et tous les différends et procès concernant le Commerce entre les sujets du Roi très-Chrétien et une des parties residente en france, ou ailleurs, et l'autre dans les Etats-Unis ou entre les Citoyens et sujets des Etats-Unis, l'une des parties faisant sa residence dans les Etats-Unis, ou ailleurs, et l'autre en france, seront terminés par les Consuls respectifs, soit par un renvoi par devant des arbitres, soit par un jugement sommaire et sans fraîs.

Aucun officier civile ou militaire ne pourra intervenir ou prendre une part quelconque à l'affaire. Les apels seront portés devant les tribunaux de france ou des Etats-Unis qui devront en connaître. Les Consuls ou Vice-Consuls ne pourront connaître des disputes ou différends qui s'éleveront entre un sujet du Roi très-Chrétien et un Citoyen des Etats-Unis, mais lesdites disputes et différends seront portés devant les tribunaux dont le deffendeur sera justiciable.

Art. XIII.

L'utilité générale du Commerce ayant fait établir en France des tribunaux et des formes particulières pour accélérer la décision des affaires de Commerce, les Négocians des Etats-Unis jouiront du bénéfice de ces Etablissemens en france, et le Congrès des Etats-Unis recommandera aux Législatures des différents Etats de procurer des avantages équivalents en faveur des Négociants français pour la prompte expédition et décision des affaires de la même nature.

Art. XIV.

Les sujets du Roi très-Chrétien et ceux des Etats-Unis qui justifieront être du Corps de la Nation respective, par le Certificat du Consul ou du Vice-Consul du District faisant mention de leurs noms, surnoms et du lieu de leur établissement, comme inscrits dans les Régistres du Consulat, ne pourront perdre, pour telle cause que ce soit, dans les Domaines et Etats-respectifs, la qualité de sujets du Païs dont ils sont originaires, conformément à l'Article XI. du Traité d'Amitié et de Commerce du 6. février 1778 dont le présent article servira d'interprétation en cas de besoin, et lesdits sujets respectifs jouiront en consequence de l'éxemption de tout service personnel dans le lieu de leur Etablissement.

ART. XV.

Si quelqu'autre Nation acquiert en vertu d'une Convention quelconque, soit en france, soit dans les Etats-Unis, un traitement plus favorable relativement aux prééminences, pouvoirs, autorité et privileges consulaires, les Consuls Vice-Consuls et Agens du Roi très-Chrétien ou des Etats-Unis réciproquement, y participeront aux termes stipulés par les Articles II. III. et IV. du Traité d'Amitié et de Commerce conclu entre le Roi très-Chrétien et les Etats-Unis.

ART. XVI.

Les ratifications de la présente Convention seront données en bonne forme et échangées de part et d'autre dans l'espace de six mois ou plustôt si faire se peut.

En foi de quoi, nous soussignés, Ministres Plénipotentiaires de sa Majesté très-Chrétienne et des Etats-Unis de l'Amérique Septentrionale, avons signé la présente Convention et y avons fait apposer le cachet de nos armes.

Fait à Versailles le 29. Juillet mil sept-cent quatre-vingt ~~trois~~ quatre.

GRAVIER DE VERGENNES   B. FRANKLIN[1]
        [Seal]   [Seal]

---

[1] The signed convention, in the hand of an unknown French clerk, is unperfected Treaty p6, RG 11, located in PCC, item 47, M247, roll 61, DNA. It is related to George Washington's message journalized June 11, 1789.

Consular Convention of 1788

CONVENTION entre le Roi très-Chrétien et les Etats-Unis de l'Amérique à l'effet de déterminer et fixer les fonctions et prérogatives des Consuls et Vice-Consuls respectifs.

Sa Majesté le Roi très-chrétien et les Etats-Unis de l'Amérique, s'étant accordés mutuellement par l'Art. XXIX du Traité d'Amitié et de Commerce conclu entr'eux, la liberté de tenir dans leurs Etats et ports respectifs, des Consuls et Vice-Consuls, agens et commissaires, et voulant en conséquence déterminer et fixer d'une manière réciproque et permanente les fonctions et prérogatives des Consuls et Vice-Consuls qu'ils ont jugé convenable d'établir de préférence, Sa Majesté très-chrétienne a nommé le Sieur Comte de Montmorin de St. Herent, Maréchal de ses Camps et armées, chevalier de ses ordres et de la Toison-d'Or, son Conseiller en tous ses Conseils, Ministre et Sécrétaire d'Etat et de ses Commandements et finances aïant le Département des Affaires

Etrangères; et les Etats-Unis ont nommé le Sieur Thomas Jefferson, Citoyen des Etats-Unis de l'Amérique et leur Ministre Plénipotentiaire auprès du Roi, lesquels, après s'être communiqué leurs pleinpouvoirs respectifs sont convenus de ce qui suit:

ARTICLE 1er.

Les Consuls et Vice-Consuls nommés par le Roi très-chrétien et les Etats-Unis seront tenus de présenter leurs provisions selon la forme qui se trouvera établie respectivement par le Roi très-chrétien dans ses Etats, et par le Congrès dans les Etats-Unis. On leur delivrera sans aucuns fraîx l'*Exequatur* nécessaire à l'éxercice de leurs fonctions, et sur l'exhibition qu'ils feront dudit *Exequatur*, les Gouverneurs, Commandants, chefs de justice, les Corps, Tribunaux ou autres officiers aïant autorité dans les ports et lieux de leurs Consulats, les y feront jouir aussitôt et sans difficulté des prééminences, autorité et privilèges accordés réciproquement, sans qu'ils puissent éxiger desdits Consuls et Vice-Consuls aucun droit sous aucun prétexte quelconque.

ART. 2 ond.

Les Consuls et Vice-Consuls et les personnes attacheés à leurs fonctions, savoir leurs Chanceliers et Sécrétaires, jouiront d'une pleine et entière immunité pour leur Chancellerie et les papiers qui y seront renfermés. Ils seront éxemts de tout service personel, logement des gens de guerre, milice, guet, garde, tutelle, curatelle, ainsi que de tous droits, taxes, impositions et charges quelconques, à l'éxception seulement des biens meubles et immeubles dont ils seroient propriétaires ou possesseurs, lesquels seront assujettis aux taxes imposées sur ceux de tous autres particuliers, et à tous égards ils demeureront sujets aux loix du païs comme les nationaux.

Ceux desdits Consuls et Vice-Consuls qui feront le Commerce seront respectivement assujettis à toutes les taxes, charges et impositions établies sur les autres négociants.

Ils placeront sur la porte extérieure de leurs Maisons les armes de leur souverain, sans que cette marque distinctive puisse donner auxdites Maisons le droit d'asîle, soit pour des personnes, soit pour des effets quelconques.

ART. 3.

Les Consuls et Vice-Consuls respectifs pourront établir des agens dans les différens ports et lieux de leurs Départments ou le besoin l'éxigera; ces agens pourront être choisis parmi les Négociants nationaux ou étrangers et munis de la Commission de l'un desdits Consuls. Ils se renfermeront respectivement à rendre aux Commercants, navigateurs et batiments respectifs, tous les services possibles, et à informer le Consul le plus proche des besoins desdits Commerçants, navigateurs et batiments, sans que lesdits agens puissent autrement participer aux immunités, droits et privilèges attribués aux Consuls et Vice-Consuls, et sans pouvoir sous aucun prétexte que ce soit, éxiger aucun droit ou émolument quelconque desdits Commerçants.

Art. 4.

Les Consuls et Vice-Consuls respectifs pourront établir une Chancellerie où seront déposés les délibérations, actes et procédures consulaires, ainsi que les testaments, obligations, Contrats et autres Actes faits par les nationaux ou entr'eux, et les effets délaissés par mort ou sauvés des naufrages.

Ils pourront en conséquence commettre à l'éxercice de ladite Chancellerie des personnes capables, les recevoir, leur faire prêter serment, leur donner la garde du sceau et le droit de sceller les Commissions, jugements et autres actes consulaires ainsi que d'y remplir les fonctions de notaire et greffiers du Consulat.

Art. 5.

Les Consuls et Vice-Consuls respectifs auront le droit exclusif de recevoir dans leur Chancellerie, ou à bord des batiments les déclarations et tous les autres actes que les Capitaines, patrons, Equipages, passagers et négociants de leur Nation voudront y passer, même leur testament et autre dispositions de d[erni]ere volunté et les dispositions desdits actes duëment legalisés par lesdits Consuls ou Vice-Consuls, et munis du sceau de leurs Consulat feront foi en justice comme le feroient les originaux dans tous les Tribunaux des Etats du Roi très-Chrétien et des Etats-Unis.

Ils auront aussi, et exclusivement, en cas d'absence d'Éxécuteur testamentaire, Curateur ou héritiers légitimes, le droit de faire l'Inventaire, la liquidation et de procéder à la vente des effets mobiliers de la succession des sujets ou citoyens de leur nation qui viendront à mourir dans l'étenduë de leur Consulat. Ils y procéderont avec l'assistance de deux négocians de leur dite Nation, ou à leur défaut de tout autre à leur choix, et feront déposer dans leur chancellerie les effets et papiers desdites successions, sans qu'aucuns officiers militaires, de justice ou de police du païs, puissent les y troubler, ni y intervenir de quelque manière que ce soit, mais lesdits Consuls et Vice-Consuls ne pourront faire la délivrance des successions et de leur produit aux héritiers légitimes, ou à leurs Mandataires, qu'après avoir fait aquitter toutes les dettes que les défunts auront pû avoir contractées dans le païs, à l'effet de quoi les créanciers auront droit de saisir lesdits effets dans leurs mains, de même que dans celles de tout autre individu quelconque, et en poursuivre la vente jusqu'au païement de ce qui leur sera légitimement dû; lorsque les dettes n'auront été contractées par jugement, par acte ou par billet dont la signature sera reconnuë, le païement ne pourra en être ordonné, qu'en fournissant par le créancier caution suffisante et domiciliée de rendre Les sommes induëment perçües, principal, interêts et fraîx; lesquelles cautions cependant demeureront duëment déchargées après une année en tems de paix, et deux en tems de guerre, si la demande en décharge ne peut être formée avant ces délais contre les héritiers qui se présenteront. Et afin de ne pas faire injustement attendre aux héritiers les effets du défunt, les Consuls et Vice-Consuls feront annoncer sa mort dans quelqu'une des gazettes qui se publient dans l'étenduë de leur Consulat, et qu'ils retiendront lesdits effets sous leurs mains pendant quatre mois pour répondre à toutes les demandes qui se présenteront: et ils seront tenus après ce délai, de délivrer aux héritiers l'éxédent du montant des demandes qui auront été formées.

Art. 6.

Les Consuls et Vice-Consuls respectifs recevront les déclarations, protestations et raports de tous Captaines et patrons de leur Nation respective pour raison d'avaries essuyées à la mer, et ces Capitaines et patrons remettront dans la Chancellerie desdits Consuls et Vice-Consuls les actes qu'ils auront faits dans d'autres ports pour les accidents qui leur seront arrivés pendant leur voyage. Si un sujet du Roi très-Chrétien et un habitant des Etats-Unis ou un Etranger sont intéressés dans ladite cargaison, l'avarie sera règleé par les tribunaux des païs et non par les Consuls et Vice-Consuls; mais lorsqu'il n'y aura d'intéressés que les sujets ou citoyens de leur propre nation, les Consuls ou les Vice-Consuls respectifs nommeront des experts pour régler les dommages et avaries.

Art. 7.

Dans le cas où par tempête ou autres accidents, des vaisseaux ou batiments français échoüeront sur les Côtes des Etats-Unis, et des vaisseaux et batiments des Etats-Unis échoüeront sur les Côtes des Etats de Sa Majesté très-chrétienne, le Consul ou le Vice-Consul le plus proche du lieu du naufrage pourra faire tout ce qu'il jugera convenable, tant pour sauver ledit vaisseau ou batiment, son chargement et apartenances, que pour le Magazinage et la sûreté des effets sauvés et marchandises. Il pourra en faire l'inventaire sans qu'aucuns officiers militaires, des Doüanes de justice ou de police du païs, puissent s'y immiscer autrement que pour faciliter aux Consuls et Vice-Consuls, Capitaine et Equipage du vaisseau naufragé ou échoüé, tous les secours et faveurs qu'ils leur demanderont, soit pour la célérité et la sûreté du sauvetage et des effets sauvés, soit pour éviter tous désordres.

Pour prévenir même toute espèce de conflit et de discution dans lesdits cas de naufrage, il a été convenu que lorsqu'il ne se trouvera pas de Consul ou Vice-Consul pour faire travailler au sauvetage, ou que la résidence dudit Consul ou Vice-Consul, qui ne se trouvera pas sur le lieu du naufrage, sera plus éloignée dudit lieu que celle du Juge territorial compétent, ce dernier fera procéder sur le champ avec toute la célérité, la sûreté et les précautions prescrites par les loix respectives, sauf audit Juge territorial à se retirer, le Consul ou Vice-Consul survenant, et à lui remettre l'expédition des procédures par lui faites dont le Consul ou Vice-Consul lui fera rembourser les fraîx ainsi que ceux du sauvetage.

Les marchandises et effets sauvés devront être déposés à la Doüane ou autre lieu de sûreté le plus prochain, avec l'Inventaire qui en aura été dressé par le Consul ou Vice-Consul, ou en leur absence par le Juge qui en aura connu, pour lesdits effets et marchandises être ensuite délivrés, après le prélevement des fraix et sans forme de procès, aux propriétaires qui, munis de la main-levée du Consul ou Vice-Consul le plus proche, les réclameront par eux-mêmes ou par leurs mandataires, soit pour réexporter les marchandises, et dans ce cas, elles ne païeront aucune espèce de droits de sortie, soit pour les vendre dans le païs, si elles n'y sont pas prohibées, et dans ce d[erni]er cas lesd[i]tes marchandises se trouvant avariées, on leur accordera une modération sur les droits d'entrée, proportionné au dommage souffert, lequel sera constaté par le procès verbal dressé lors du naufrage ou l'échoüement.

Art. 8.

Les Consuls ou Vice-Consuls éxerceront la police sur tous les batimens de leurs Nations respectives, et auront à bord desdits batimens tout pouvoir et jurisdiction en matière civile dans toutes les discutions qui pourront y survenir; ils auront une entière inspection sur lesdits batimens, leurs équipages et les changements et remplacements à y faire; pour quel effet ils pourront se transporter à bord desdits batimens toutes les fois qu'ils le jugeront nécessaire; bien entendu que les fonctions ci-dessus énoncées seront concentrées dans l'intérieur des batimens et quels ne pourront avoir lieu dans aucun cas qui aura quelque raport avec la police des ports où lesdits batimens se trouveront.

Art. 9.

Les Consuls et Vice-Consuls pourront faire arrêter les Capitaines Officiers-mariniers, matelots et toutes autres personnes faisant partie des Equipages des batimens de leurs Nations respectives qui auroient déserté desdits batimens pour les renvoyer et faire transporter hors du païs. Auquel effet lesdits Consuls et Vice-Consuls s'addresseront aux tribunaux, juges et officiers compétents, et leur feront par écrit la demande desdits déserteurs, en justifiant, par l'exhibition des Registres du Batiment ou Rôle d'Equipage, que ces hommes faisoient partie des susdits Equipages. Et sur cette demande ainsi justifiée, sauf toutefois la preuve contraire, l'extradition ne pourra être refusée, et il sera donné toute aide et assistance auxdits Consuls et Vice-Consuls pour la recherche, saisie et arrestation des susdits déserters, lesquels seront même détenus et gardés dans les prisons du païs, à leur réquisition et à leurs fraîx, jusqu'à ce qu'ils aïent trouvé occasion de les renvoyer. Mais s'ils n'étoient renvoyés dans le délai de trois mois à compter du jour de leur Arrêt, ils seront élargis et ne pourront plus être arrêtés pour la même cause.

Art. 10.

Dans le cas où les sujets ou citoyens respectifs auront commis quelque crime ou infraction de la tranquillité publique, ils seront justiciables des Juges du païs.

Art. 11.

Lorsque lesdits coupables feront partie de l'Equipage de l'un des batimens de leur nation, et se seront retirés à bord desdits navires, ils pourront y être saisis et arrêtés par l'ordre des Juges territoriaux: ceux-ci en préviendront le Consul ou Vice-Consul, lequel pourra se rendre à bord s'il le juge à propos: mais cette prévenant ne pourra en aucun cas retarder l'éxécution de l'ordre dont il est question. Les personnes arrêtées ne pourront ensuite être mises en liberté qu'après que le Consul ou Vice-Consul en aura été prévenu; et elles lui seront remises, s'il le requiert, pour être reconduites sur les batimens où elles auront été arrêteés, ou autres de leur Nation, et être renvoyées hors du païs.

Art. 12.

Tous différends et procès entre les sujets du Roi très-chrétien dans les Etats-Unis ou entre les citoyens des Etats-unis dans les Etats du Roi très-chrétien, et

notamment toutes les discutions relatives aux salaires et conditions des engagements des Equipages des batiments respectifs, et tous différends de quelque
nature qu'ils soient qui pourroient s'élever entre les hommes desdits Equipages
ou entre quelques uns d'eux et leurs Capitaines, ou entre les Captaines de divers
batiments nationaux, seront terminés par les Consuls et Vice-Consuls respectifs,
soit par un renvoi par devant des arbitres, soit par un jugement sommaire et
sans fraîx. Aucun officier territorial civil ou militaire ne pourra y intervenir ou
prendre une part quelconque à l'affaire, et les appels desdits jugements consulaires seront portés devant les tribunaux de france ou des Etats-Unis qui
doivent en connaître.

Art. 13.

L'utilité générale du Commerce aïant fait établir dans les Etats du Roi très-
chrétien des tribunaux et des formes particulières pour accélerer la décision des
affairs de Commerce, les négocians des Etats-Unis jouiront du bénéfice de ces
Etablissements, et le Congrès des Etats-Unis pourvoira de la manière la plus
conforme à ses loix, à l'établissement des avantages équivalents en faveur des
négociants français pour la prompte expédition et décision des affaires de la
même nature.

Art. 14.

Les sujets du Roi très-chrétien et les citoyens des Etats-Unis qui justifieront
authentiquement être du Corps de la Nation respective jouiront en consequence
de l'éxemption de tout service personnel dans le lieu de leur établissement.

Art. 15.

Si quelqu'autre Nation aquiert en vertu d'une Convention quelconque un
traitement plus favorable relativement aux prééminences, pouvoirs, autorité et
privilèges consulaires, les Consuls et Vice-Consuls du Roi très-chrétien ou des
Etats-Unis réciproquement y participeront aux termes stipulés par les Articles
deux, trois et quatre du Traité d'amitié et de Commerce conclu entre le Roi
très-chrétien et les Etats-Unis.

Art. 16.

La présente Convention aura son plein effet pendant l'espace de douze ans,
à-compter du jour de l'échange des Ratifications, lesquelles seront données en
bonne formes et échangeés de part et d'autre dans l'espace d'un an ou plustôt si
faire se peut.

ENFOI de quoi, Nous Ministres Plénipotentiaires, avons signé la présente
Convention, et y avons fait apposer le cachet de nos armes.

FAIT à Versailles le 14 Novembre mil sept cent quatre-vingt-huit.

L. C. DE MONTMORIN   TH. JEFFERSON[1]
    [Seal]   [Seal]

---

[1] The signed convention, in the hand of an unknown French clerk, is Treaty Series 84,
RG 11, DNA. It is related to George Washington's message journalized June 11,
1789.

Nomination of William Short

Thomas Jefferson to John Jay

Paris. Nov. 19. 1788

SIR,

Since my letter of Sep. 5. wherein I acknoleged Mr. Remsen favor of July 25. I have written those of Sep. 24. and of the 14th. inst. this last will accompany the present; both going by the way of London for want of a direct opportunity but they go by a private hand.

No late event worth notice has taken place between the Turks & Austrians. the former continue in the territories of the latter with all the appearances of superiority. on the side of the Russians, the war wears an equal face, except that the Turks are still masters of the Black sea. Oczakow is not yet taken. Denmark furnished to Russia it's stipulated quota of troops with so much alacrity, and was making such other warlike preparations, that it was believed they meant to become principals in the war against Sweden. Prussia and England hereupon interposed efficaciously. their ministers appointed to mediate gave notice to the court of Copenhagen that they would declare war against them in the name of their two sovereigns, if they did not immediately withdraw their troops from the Swedish territories. the court of London has once said that their minister (Elliott) went further in this than he was authorized. however the Danish troops are retiring. Poland is augmenting it's army from 20. to an hundred thousand men. nevertheless it seems as if England & Prussia meant in earnest to stop the war in that quarter, contented to leave the two empires in the hands of the Turks. France, desired by Sweden to join the courts of London & Berlin in their mediation between Sweden & Russia, has declined it. we may be assured she will meddle in nothing external before the meeting of her States general. her temporary annihilation in the political scale of Europe, leaves to England & Prussia the splendid roll of giving the law without meeting the shadow of opposition. the internal tranquillity of this country is perfect. their stocks however continue low; and the difficulty of getting money to face current expences, very great. in the contest between the king & parliament, the latter, fearing the power of the former, pressed the convoking the states general. the government found itself obliged by other difficulties also, to recur to the same expedient. the parliament, after it's recall, shewed that it was now become apprehensive of the states general; and discovered a determination to cavil at their form, so as to have a right to deny their legality if that body should undertake to abridge

353

their powers. the court hereupon very adroitly determined to call the same
Notables who had approved by the nation the last year, to decide on the form
of convoking the etats generaux: thus withdrawing itself from the disputes
which the parliament might excite, & committing them with the nation. the
Notables are now in session. The government had manifestly discovered a disposition that the tiers-etat, or Commons, should have as many representatives in
the States general, as the Nobility and clergy together. but five bureaux of the
notables have voted by very great majorities that they should have only an equal
number with each of the other orders singly. one bureau, by a majority of a
single voice, had agreed to give the Commons the double number of representatives. this is the first symptom of a decided combination between the nobility &
clergy, and will necessarily throw the people into the scale of the king. it is
doubted whether the States can be collected so early as January, tho' the government, urged by the want of money, is for pressing their convocation. it is still
more uncertain what the states will do when they meet. there are three objects
which they may attain, probably without opposition from the court. 1. a periodi-
cal meeting of the States. 2. their exclusive right of taxation. 3. the right of
enregistering laws, and proposing amendments to them as now exercised by the
parliaments. this would lead, as it did in England, to the right of originating laws.
the parliament would by the last measure be reduced to a mere judiciary body,
and would probably oppose it. but against the king & nation their opposition
could not succeed. if the States stop here for the present moment, all will
probably end well, and they may in future sessions obtain a suppression of
letters de cachet, free press, a civil list, and other valuable mollifications of their
government. but it is to be feared that an impatience to rectify every thing at
once, which prevails in some minds, may terrify the court, and lead them to
appeal to force, & to depend on that alone.

Before this can reach you, you will probably have heard of an Arret passed
the 28th of Sep. for prohibiting the introduction of foreign whale oils, without
exception. the English had glutted the markets of this country with their oils.
it was proposed to exclude them, and an Arret was drawn, with an exception
for us. in the last stage of this Arret, the exception was struck out, without my
having any warning or even suspicion of this. I suspect this stroke came from
the Count de la Luzerne, minister of marine; but I cannot affirm it positively. as
soon as I was apprized of this, which was several days after it passed (because
it was kept secret till published in their seaports) I wrote to the count de
Montmorin a letter, of which the enclosed is a copy, and had conferences on
the subject from time to time with him and the other ministers. I found them
possessed by the partial information of their Dunkirk fishermen: and therefore
thought it necessary to give them a view of the whole subject in writing, which
I did in the piece, of which I enclose you a printed copy. I therein entered into
more details than the question between us seemed rigorously to require. I was
led to them by other objects. the most important was to disgust Mr. Neckar, as
an economist, of against their new fishery, by letting him foresee it's expence.
the particular manufactures suggested to them were in consequence of repeated

applications from the shippers of rice & tobacco. other details which do not appear immediately pertinent, were occasioned by circumstances which had arisen in conversation, or an apparent necessity of giving information on the whole matter. at a conference in the presence of M. Lambert on the 16th (where I was ably aided by the Marquis de la Fayette, as I have been through the whole business) it was agreed to except us from the prohibition. but they will require rigorous assurance that the oils coming under our name, are really of our fishery. they fear we shall cover the introduction of the English oils from Halifax. the arret for excepting us was communicated to me, but the formalities of proving the oils to be American were not yet inserted. I suppose they will require every vessel to bring a certificate from their consul or vice consul residing in the state from which it comes. more difficult proofs were sometimes talked of. I supposed I might surely affirm to them that our government would do whatever it could to prevent this fraud, because it is as much our interest as theirs to keep the market for the French & American oils only. I am told Massachusets has prohibited the introduction of foreign fish oils into her ports. this law, if well executed will be an effectual guard against fraud; & a similar one in the other states interested in the fishery would much encourage this government to continue her indulgence to us. tho the Arret then for the re-admission of our oils is not yet passed, I think I may assure you it will be so in a few days, and of course that this branch of commerce, after so threatening an appearance, will be on a better footing than ever, as enjoying jointly with the French oil, a monopoly of their markets. the continuance of this will depend on the growth of their fishery. whenever they become able to supply their own wants it is very possible they may refuse to take our oils. but I do not believe it possible for them to raise their fishery to that, unless they can continue to draw off our fishermen from us. their 17. ships this year had 150. of our sailors on board. I do not know what numbers the English have got into their service. you will readily perceive that these are particulars in these printed observations which it would not be proper to suffer to become public. they were printed merely that a copy might be given to each minister & care has been taken to let them go into no other hands.

I must now trouble Congress with a petition on my own behalf. when I left my own house in Octob. 1783. it was to attend Congress as a member, & in expectation of returning in five or six months. in the month of May following however I was desired to come to Europe, as member of a commission which was to continue two years only. I came off immediately without going home to make any other arrangements in my affairs, thinking they would not suffer greatly before I should return to them. before the close of the two years, Doctor Franklin retiring from his charge here, Congress were pleased to name me to it. so that I have been led on by events to an absence of five years instead of five months. in the mean time matters of great moment to others as well as myself, & which can be arranged by nobody but myself, will await no longer. another motive of still more powerful cogency on my mind is the necessity of carrying my family back to their friends and country. I must therefore ask of Congress a leave of short absence. allowing three months on the sea, going & coming and two months at my own house, which will suffice for my affairs, I need not be from Paris but between five & six months. I do not foresee any thing which can suffer during my absence. the Consular convention is finished except as to the exchange of ratifications, which will be the affair of a day only. the difference with Schweighauser & Dobree relative to our arms will be finished. that of Denmark, if ever finished will probably be long spun out. the ransom of the Algerine captives is the only matter likely to be on hand. that cannot be set on foot till the money is raised in Holland, & an order received for it's application. probably these will take place so that I may set it into motion before my departure. if not, I can still leave it on such a footing as to be put into motion the moment the money can be paid. and even, when the leave of Congress shall be received, I will not make use of it, if there is any thing of consequence which may suffer; but would postpone my departure till circumstances will admit it. but should these be as I expect they will, it will be vastly desirable to me to receive the permission immediately, so that I may go out as soon as the Vernal equinox is over, and be sure of my return in good time & season in the fall. Mr. Short, who had had thoughts of returning to America will postpone that return till I come back. his talents and character allow me to say with confidence that nothing will suffer in his hands. the friendly dispositions of Monsr. de Montmorin would induce him readily to communicate with Mr. Short in his present character, but should any of his applications be necessary to be laid before the council, they might suffer difficulty: nor could he attend the Diplomatic societies, which are the most certain sources of good intelligence. would Congress think it expedient to remove the difficulties by naming him Secretary of legation, so that he would act of course as Chargé des affaires during my absence? it would be just that the difference between the Salary of a secretary, & a secretary of legation should cease as soon as he should cease to be charged with the affairs of the U.S. that is to say, on my return: and he would expect that. so that this difference for 5. or 6. months would be an affair of about 170. guineas only, which would be not more than equal to the additional expences that would be brought on him necessarily by the change of character. I mention these particulars that Congress may see the end as well as beginning of the proposition, and have only to add "their will be done." leave for me being obtained, I will ask it, Sir, of your friendship to avail yourself of various occasions to the ports of France & England to convey me immediate notice of it, & relieve me as soon as possible from the anxiety of expectation, and the incertainty in which I shall be. we have been in daily expectation of hearing of the death of the King of England. our latest news are of the 11th. he had then been despaired of for 3. or 4. days. but as my letter is to pass through England, you will have later accounts of him than that can give you. I send you the newspapers to this date, & have the honour to be with the greatest esteem & respect, Sir, your most obedient humble servt.

TH. JEFFERSON

P.S. the last crop of corn in France has been so short that they apprehend want. Mr. Neckar desires me to make known this scarcity to our merchants, in hopes they would send supplies. I promised him I would. if it could be done without naming him, it would be agreable to him & probably advantageous to the adventurers.[1]

[1] The letter, in the hand of Thomas Jefferson, is in PCC, item 87, vol. II, M247, roll 115, DNA. It is related to George Washington's message journalized June 16, 1789.

Area of the Northeast Boundary Dispute, 1794. (Courtesy of the Map Division, Library of Congress, Washington, D.C.)

Northeast Boundary Dispute with Great Britain

PETITION OF JAMES BOYD, 27 NOVEMBER 1789
OBSERVATIONS BY C. MORRIS F. GENERAL, c. 1789
JOHN HANCOCK TO GEORGE WASHINGTON, 10 FEBRUARY 1790, AND
      RESOLUTION OF THE COMMONWEALTH OF MASSACHUSETTS, 1
      FEBRUARY 1790

A Plan for A Survey[1]

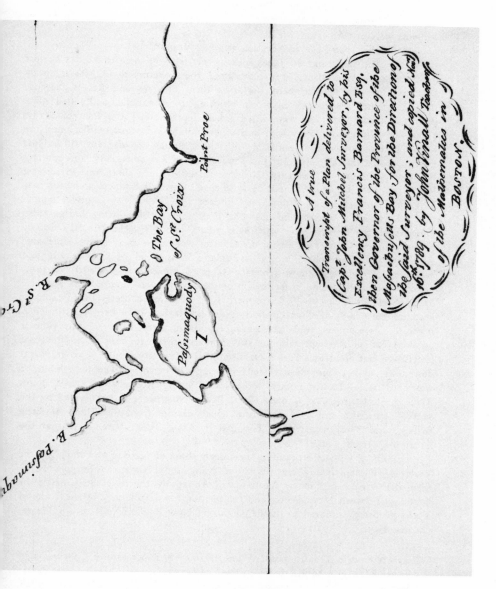

A true Transcript of a Plan delivered to Capt. John Mitchel Surveyor, by his Excellency Francis Barnard Esq. then Governor of the Province of the Massachusetts Bay for the Directions of the said Surveyor; and copied Nov.r 16.r 1769. by John Vinall Teacher of the Mathematics in BOSTON.

The Bay of St Croix

Point Proe

Passimaquody I

R.r St Cr

R. Passimaqu

[1] The Plan is taken from Miscellaneous Manuscripts, entry 820, box 5, E1039, RG 59, DNA.

Extracts Relative to the Boundary Dispute

An Extract from Douglass Summary, Historical & Political of the first planting, progressive Improvements, and present state of the British Settlements in North America.

London Printed 1760 Page 320. Section 7th. first Volume.

As the Cape Sable and St. Jones Indians, persisted in their Hostilities against the Subjects of Great Britain, in Nov. 1744, the Government of Massachusetts Bay declares war against them, declaring them Enemies and Rebels; because they had joined the French enemy in blocking up Annapolis; had killed some British Subjects, and had committed other depredations; the Passamaquady, Penobscot, Noridgwog, Pigwockit and other Indians westward of St. Jones, are forbid to have any correspondence with those Indian Rebels: for all Indians Eastward of a line Beginning at three miles east of Passamaquady, and running North to St. Laurence River, the Government settles for a short time Premiums, Vizt. £100. new Tenor for a male of 12 Æt, and upwards Scalped, and £105 new Tenor if Captivated; for Women & Children £50 Scalps, £55 Captives. Sometime afterwards it was found that the Penobscot & Noridgwog Indians also joined with the french: Page 330. Sect. 7th. When Massachusetts Bay Colony obtained a new Charter (their former Charter was taken away at the same time with many Corporation Charters in England in the end of Charles 2d., and beginning of the like or more arbitrary Reign of James 2d.) 7 of October 1691, Nova Scotia at that time in possession of the French, was annexed (as was also Sagadahock, or Duke of Yorks property) to the Massachusetts Jurisdiction, to keep up the Claim of Great Britain; Nova-Scotia has since been constituted a separate Government; and has continued about forty years to this time a nominal British Province without any British Settlement, only an insignificant preventive, but precarious Fort & Garrison as this Country is rude, a geographical description of it cannot be expected: it is a large extent of Territory, bounded westward by the Bay of Fundy, and a Line running Northward from St. Jones River to St. Laurence or Canada Great River, Northward it is bounded by the said St. Laurence and Gut of Canso, which divides from the Island of Cape Britain; and Southeasterly it is bounded by Cape Sable shore—settled at the Treaty of Utrecht 1713.

P. 332. Sect. 7. Upon the opposite or westerly shore of the Bay of Fundy, are the Rivers of Passamaquady and St. Croix, being about seventeen Leagues N.W. from the Gut or entrance of the bason of Annapolis; the River St. Croix is the boundary between Nova Scotia and the territory of Sagadahock or the Duke of Yorks property: annexed to the neighbouring New England province of Massachusetts Bay.

Extracts from a Treatise entitled The Beginning, Progress and Conclusion of the late War, printed in London in the Year 1770.

"France having, by the Treaty concluded at Aix la Chapelle in Octo. 1748, obtained restitution of Cape Breton her Ministers soon formed and began to execute a design to divide and impair the British American empire, and to enable her farther to distress their trade and fishery, by extending her territories from the River Canada through ~~to~~ the main land to the Atlantic Ocean, westward as far as the River Kenebeck, and eastward so as to include all the main land of Nova Scotia, leaving to the English only part of the Peninsula; for the illustration whereof, with other matters, a Map is hereto annexed: and although Nova Scotia has so often passed from Nation to Nation; the pretensions of France amounted to this, that Great Britain was to hold by the last Cession made to her only a small part of the same Country which had passed to France by former Cessions. Having already observed that all Nova Scotia or Acadia with its ancient boundaries, was ceded by the Utrecht treaty to Great Britain, let us here add that when this Country was first named Nova Scotia the following boundaries were given to it in the grant to Sir William Alexander, to wit, all and singular the lands of the Continent, and the Islands in America within Cape Sable, lying in forty three degrees north Latitude, or thereabouts; thence along the Coast to St. Mary's Bay, and thence passing Northward by a right line across the Gulph or Bay now called Funda to the River St. Croix, and to the remotest western spring head of the same; whence by an imaginary line conceived to run through the land northward to the next road of Ships, river, or Spring discharging itself into the Great River of Canada and proceeding thence eastward along the shores of the Sea of the said River of Canada to the road, haven, or shore, commonly called Gaspie and thence South eastward (versus euronotum) to the Islands called Baccalaos or Cape Breton, leaving the said Islands on the right, and the gulph of said great River of Canada, and the lands of Newfoundland, with the Islands to those lands pertaining, on the left; and thence to the promontory of Cape Breton aforesaid, lying near or about the latitude of 45 degrees, & from the sd. promontory of Cape Breton towards the South & west to the aforesaid Cape Sable, where the Perambulation began."[1]

[1] A copy of each of the above extracts, both in the hand of Benjamin Bankson, is in President's Messages on Foreign Relations, Executive Proceedings, SR, DNA. They are related to George Washington's message journalized February 9, 1790. A second copy of each, also by Benjamin Bankson, is in Transcribed Treaties and Conventions, 1789–1801, Records of the Secretary, SR, DNA.

Resolves of the Massachusetts Legislature

Commonwealth of Massachusetts

In the House of Representatives
July 6 1784

WHEREAS the United States in Congress assembled on the twenty ~~sixth~~ ninth day of January last past, recommended to the Governor of this Commonwealth, to cause enquiry to be made, whether encroachments had actually been made, on the territories of this State, by the subjects of his Britannic Majesty, from the Government of Nova Scotia and it appearing that great encroachments have been made on the said territories. RESOLVED that three Gentlemen be appointed by the General Court whose duty and business it shall be, to repair to the eastern part of this State and there inform themselves what encroachments have been made by his said Britannic Majesty's Subjects on the territories of the Commonwealth, and if they find such have been made, that they make representation thereof to the Governor of Nova Scotia and request him in a friendly manner and as a proof of that disposition for peace and harmony, which should subsist between neighbouring States to recall from off the said territory the said subjects of his Britannic Majesty so found to have encroached thereon; that they receive any communications on the said subject which may be made by the said Governor of Nova Scotia and make report of their proceedings herein to the General Court.

RESOLVED that his Excellency the Governor make a Commission under the seal of the Commonwealth to the Agents to be appointed as aforesaid to transact the said business, and transmit to the said Governor of Nova Scotia a copy of these Resolves. Resolved that Benjamin Lincoln, Henry Knox and George Partridge Esqrs. be and hereby are appointed Agents for the business mentioned in the foregoing resolves. sent up for concurrence

SAMUEL A. OTIS spkr.

In Senate July 7. 1784
  Read & Concurred
    SAMUEL ADAMS President
Approv'd
  JOHN HANCOCK[1]

[1] A copy of the resolution, in the hand of Jacob Blackwell, is in PCC, item 124, vol. I, M247, roll 141, DNA. It is related to George Washington's message journalized February 9, 1790.

Deposition of John Mitchell

I the subscriber an Inhabitant of Chester in the State of New Hampshire, voluntarily make the following declaration—To wit, That I was employed by His Excy. Francis Bernard Esq. Governor of the Province of Mass. Bay in April 1764, as a Surveyor, in company with Mr. Israel Jones, as my deputy, Mr. Nathan Jones, as Commanding Officer, of a party of Troops, & Captain Fletcher as indian Interpreter, to repair to the Bay of Passamaquoddi, to assemble the Indians usually residing there, and from them, to ascertain the River, known by the name of the St. Croix. We accordingly assembled upwards of forty of the principal Indians, upon an Island then called L'Atereel, in the said Bay of Passamaquoddi. After having fully, and freely conversed ~~them~~ with them, upon the subject of our mission, the Chief, commissioned three Indians to shew us the said River St. Croix which is situated nearly six miles North, and about three ~~leagues~~ degrees east of Harbour L'Tete, and East north east, of the Bay or River

Scudac, and distant from it, about nine miles upon a right line. The aforesaid three Indians after having shewn us the River, and being duly informed of the nature and importance of an Oath, did in a solemn manner depose to the truth of their information respecting the identity of the said River St. Croix, and that it was the antient and only River known amongst them by that name. We proceeded conformably to this information in our surveys, and in August following I delivered to Governor Bernard, three plans of the said River St. Croix and the said Bay of Passamaquoddi.

JOHN MITCHEL surveyor

Suffolk ss.

Boston Octo. 9. 1784. The above named John Mitchel personally appeared, and on solemn Oath declared that the above by him subscribed is true.

Before me EZEKL. PRICE Jus. Peace[1]

[1] A copy of the deposition, in the hand of Benjamin Bankson, is in President's Messages on Foreign Relations, Executive Proceedings, SR, DNA. It is related to George Washington's message journalized February 9, 1790. A second copy, by Benjamin Bankson, is in Transcribed Treaties and Conventions, 1789–1801, Records of the Secretary, SR, DNA.

Report of Benjamin Lincoln and Henry Knox to the Governor of Massachusetts

Boston October 19th. 1784

SIR,

In obedience to your Excellency's Commission bearing date July 12. 1784 the subscribers two of the Commissioners named therein proceeded the latter end of August to the Bay of Passamaquoddi and there endeavored to inform themselves of what encroachments had been made by the Subjects of his Britannic Majesty on the territories of this Commonwealth.

They beg leave to inform your Excellency that a very considerable number of British Subjects are settled at a place called St. Andrews on the Eastern Bank of the River Schudac which in the opinion of your Commissioners is clearly within the limits of this State.

By your Excellency's leave they will recite a short state of facts on which this opinion was formed.

There are three very considerable Rivers which empty themselves into the Bay of Passamaquoddi which is from five to seven leagues wide. The eastern River falls into the Bay about a league from the head of it and perpendicular to the Eastern side. The middle River falls into the Bay far on the Westerly side of the head of it and in a direction parallel therewith, The Western River falls into the Bay about Six leagues from the head of it on the Westerly side and nearly perpendicular to it all of which in late British Maps are called St. Croix. The first is by the Indians called Mackadavia, the second Schudac and the third Cobbescook.

From every information the Subscribers could obtain on an enquiry of the Indians and others the Eastern River was the original St. Croix. This is about three leagues East of St. Andrews where the British inhabitants have made a Settlement.

Soon after the Subscribers received their Commission they wrote to Mr. Jay requesting him to give them information whether the Commissioners for negociating the Peace confined themselves in tracing the boundaries of the United States to any particular map and if any one to what. Since their return they received his answer mentioning that Mitchel's Map was the only one that the Commissioners used and on that they traced the boundaries agreed to. This in the opinion of the Subscribers is a fact which must facilitate an equitable decision of the matter, though Mitchel's Map is not accurate at least in the description of the Eastern part of this State. He has described but two instead of three Rivers which empty themselves into the Bay of Passamaquoddi. The Eastern of those he has placed at the head of the Bay near the centre of it and calls it St. Croix. The Western River he has called by the name of Passamaquoddi. Hence it is plain that though the map is inaccurate yet the Eastern River which empties itself into the Bay is in the opinion of Mitchel the St. Croix. This opinion is further supported by the deposition of Mr. Mitchel accompanying this report. The Subscribers are informed that the Mr. Jones mentioned in the deposition is soon expected in this Town who will depose the same facts.

The Subscribers further represent that they find in the maps of a Quarto Volume published in Paris in 1744 from Charlevoies voyages to North America made in 1604 two rivers delineated at the head of the Bay of Passamaquoddi the western of which is called Passamaquoddi, the Eastern St. Croix.

Although the mouth of the River St. Croix is but little more than three leagues east of the banks of the Schudac on which the British Subjects are settled yet from the different courses of the two Rivers the source of the Western branch of the Schudac is nearly an hundred miles from the source of the St. Croix.

From a view of the rapid improvements made by the British Subjects on the banks of the Schudac the Subscribers could not but suppose that the idea of their removal would always embarrass a settlement of the line agreably to the Treaty of Peace. They therefore have thought it their duty to suggest the propriety of quieting such British settlers in their possessions who are desirious of becoming inhabitants of the United States. That the General Court might have time to take this matter into their consideration. They have deferred writing to the Governor of Nova Scotia, though they could not have done this until within a few days past from the necessary delays which have attended the procuring the evidence relative to the ancient St. Croix.

Want of health prevented the attendance of Mr. Partridge

We have the Honor to be &c.

(Signed)   B. LINCOLN

H. KNOX[1]

[1] A copy of the letter, in the hand of Jacob Blackwell, is in PCC, item 124, vol. I, M247, roll 141, DNA. It is related to George Washington's message journalized February 9, 1790.

Extract of a Letter from John Adams to Lt. Governor Thomas Cushing*

Auteuil near Paris Octr. 25th. 1784

In writing upon the subject of the line between Massachusetts & Nova Scotia he observes as follows.

"We had before us, through the whole negociation a variety of Maps, but it was Mitchell's Map upon which was marked out the whole of the Boundary lines of the United States, and the River St. Croix which we fixed on, was upon that Map the nearest River to St. Johns, so that in all Equity good conscience & honor, the River next to St. Johns should be the boundary. I am glad the General Court are taking early measures & hope they will pursue them steadily, until the point is settled, which it may be now, amicably, if neglected long it may be more difficult."[1]

---

[1] A copy of the extract, in the hand of Walter Stone, is in President's Messages on Foreign Relations, Executive Proceedings, SR, DNA. It is related to George Washington's message journalized February 9, 1790. A second copy, by Benjamin Bankson, is in Transcribed Treaties and Conventions, 1789–1801, Records of the Secretary, SR, DNA.

Governor John Hancock to Governor John Parr†

Boston Novemr. 12th. 1784

SIR,

I have the Honor to enclose to your Excellency a Resolution and Proclamation of Congress respecting the boundary Line at the Eastern part of this Common-wealth, and am to inform you that agreeably to the said Resolution an enquiry has been made by a Respectable Committee appointed by this Government for that purpose, who have reported, that upon a most careful examination of the evidence respecting the ancient boundary between Nova Scotia and this State, they found the most Easterly of the three Rivers which empty themselves into the Bay of Passamaquody to be the ancient Line, and now the boundary established by the late Treaty so happily concluded between the Crown of Great Britain and these States. The Committee also report that the Subjects of his Britannic Majesty have made encroachments upon the Territory of this Commonwealth, a large number of whom are now possessing themselves of Lands on the Western side of the said River.

The Government of this State, Sir, is no less desirous than the United States in Congress Assembled of cultivating that Peace and Harmony which I hope will ever subsist between the Citizens of the States and the subjects of his Majesty. Wherefore in pursuance of the Resolution of Congress I am to request your

---

* Lieutenant Governor of Massachusetts
† Governor of Nova Scotia

Excellency will be pleased to recall from off the said Territory those Subjects of his Majesty who have removed themselves from His Dominions and planted themselves within this Commonwealth.

I shall be always ready to give immediate Attention to such Communications as your Excellency shall be pleased to make upon this or any other subject.

I have the Honor to be &c.

(Signed)   JOHN HANCOCK

I had the honor of a verbal Message from your Excellency by Mr. Gregory Townsend, respecting the Probate Papers in the hands of Mr. Hutchinson at Hallifax, that they were packing up and would be sent by the first Opportunity, I have since received no tidings of them; I take the Liberty to request your Excellencys kind interposition, that they may be forwarded before the bad season comes on, more especially as they are Papers of great consequence and are much wanted.[1]

---

[1] A copy of the letter, in the hand of Jacob Blackwell, is in PCC, item 124, vol. I, M247, roll 141, DNA. It is related to George Washington's message journalized February 9, 1790.

Governor John Parr to Governor John Hancock

Hallifax 7 December 1784

SIR,

I had the honor of your Letter dated the 12th November enclosing a Copy of a Resolution of Congress 29th January last, with a Proclamation dated 14th of the same Month. All which I have forwarded to the Governor of New Brunswick within whose Government are the Lands in dispute; and I have transmitted Copies of them to Lord Sydney one of His Majestys principal Secretaries of State.

I have the Honor to be &c.

J. PARR[1]

---

[1] A copy of the letter, in the hand of Jacob Blackwell, is in PCC, item 124, vol. I, M247, roll 141, DNA. It is related to George Washington's message journalized February 9, 1790.

Rufus Putnam to the Committee of Massachusetts*

Rutland Decr. 27. 1784

GENTLEMEN,

As the plan I furnished you on my return from the eastern country, was much more extensive, than what was barely necessary for the delineation of the

---

* Phillips, Wells, and Dane

lands which I surveyed for government comprehending so much of the Passa-maquoddy country as I thought sufficient to give a pretty clear idea of the grounds in dispute between this Commonwealth & Nova Scotia, respecting our eastern boundary: if it is not my duty as a servant of the public, I ask their indulgence as a citizen to mention several matters by way of information and explanation of my plan, & also to make a few observations on the respective claims of the two nations in that quarter.

From Mr. Jones, who is the principal Surveyor employed by the British in that quarter since the peace took place, I learned that they consider the Schoodic as the St. Croix intended in the Treaty—that they fix the mouth of that river at the devil's head, which you will see marked in Township No. V in my plan and the bays of Schoodic, Saint Andrews, Cobbescook &c. &c. formerly com-prehended under the general name of Passamaquoddy, they consider as arms of the sea or parts of the bay of Fundy—here then say they, that is at the devils head, the following description in the Treaty begins vizt. "bounded East by a line to be drawn along the middle of the River St. Croix from its mouth in the Bay of Fundy to its source."

Again, a line drawn from the mouth of St. Croix at devils head, to the mouth of St. Marys river between Georgia & East Florida, they consider as a boundary, to the eastward of which we have no claim on the main land or among the islands, nor yet to the islands westward of such a line, except they ly within 20 leagues of the Sea coast or main land & have not been granted by the Government of Nova Scotia—again in consequence of their claiming the Schoodic river for the St. Croix—all the lands to the eastward of it ase as high as the first falls above mile island, marked in my plan, are surveyed and granted to the Refugees & others, after a judgment of escheat being passed on them for they were formerly granted to others as may be seen in the copy of the Halifax plan.

A straight line, says Mr. Jones drawn from the devils head to the mouth of St. Marys river as above mentioned will fall on the Sea coast or north shore of the bay of fundy, about the mouth of little Machias river, the direction of this line across my plan is marked on the southern edge of it, & in consequence of their claiming such a line, not only all the islands in the bay of Passa-maquoddy whether granted before the peace or since they claim as theirs but the Island of Grand Mannana has been granted by the Governor of Nova Scotia to certain proprietors—& on the same principles a few days before I left the country Mr. Jones began the survey of Sowards Neck.

Their settlements keep pretty equal pace with their Surveys the Island of Grand Mannana has several settlers on it already as well as a number of smaller Islands in the eastern part of Passamaquoddy Bay. The Town of St. Andrews has between two & three hundred houses & a town at present called Schudic, near the head of Navigation, has near one hundred houses, besides which there is a Township at the head of Oak bay granted to a Company of associates, at the head of which is a Mr. Norwood from Cape Ann, another Township west of this is surveyed for a Company from Connecticut, & these Companies obtain the same supplies of provision as the refugees do.

The reason why they have made no surveys on the main land between the devils head & pleasant point or on Moose Island. I presume, is because they consider those lands as the property of Sir Francis Bernard and his associates & that no judgment of escheat respecting them has yet taken place.

Upon supposition that the Maggacadava river, or eastern St. Croix, from the falls makes a north course up to its source & the river Schoodic does the same from the upper pond marked in my plan, then the tract of land between the two rivers in dispute, will be in extent east & west nearly thirty six miles, & by a London Map published immediately after the peace, at least 120 Miles north & south, so that the two rivers in all probability makes a difference of 120 Townships of 6 miles square, within which there is no doubt a great quantity of good lands.

Again to draw a line as they propose from the devils head will cut off at least a quantity of land equal to four or five Townships of 6 Miles square, besides the Island of Grand Mannana & the small islands of on the southern side of it which are equal to three or four such Townships, together with Moose island & some others whose quantities are marked in my plan or report— but besides the value of the lands cut off by this proposed line, it is well to consider that the remainder of the lands bordering on the Schoodic & Cobescook rivers will be of little value to their owners, if they have no communication with the Sea but what depends on the courtesy of their british neighbours. The Bay of Passamaquoddy at present affords great plenty of fish, but if we are to possess no islands in that Bay for curing them, it must prove very injurious to the subjects of America who are or may be employed in taking fish in that quarter. The island of Grand Mannana has a good harbour towards the south east part of it & its southern shore is lined with a number of small islands, among which & in the vicinity of them great plenty of fish are taken & the quality of the lands in Grand Mannana & some of these smaller islands it is said are not inferior to these in the Bay of Passamaquoddy; so that in respect of both farming & fishing these islands are of no small consequence.

But where the Gentlemen of Nova Scotia have got the idea that the United States are bounded by a line drawn through the Atlantic Ocean, from the mouth of St. Marys river to the Mouth of the St. Croix, is hard to conceive, for my own part I cannot find a single hint of such a boundary in all the Treaty. yet as absurd as this Idea appears to be not only Mr. Jones & other Refugees are fallen into the mistake but Governor Parr, must have done so too, or otherwise he would not have patented the island of Grand Mannana for as Mr. Jones told me it had never been granted to before, it cannot now possibly belong to Nova Scotia, on any other principle, but the establishment of such a line.

With respect to the islands the words of the Treaty are these "comprehending all islands within 20 leagues of any part of the Shores of the United States & lying between lines to be drawn due east from the *points* where the aforesaid boundary between Nova on the one part, & east Florida on the other, shall respectively touch the bay of Fundy & the Atlantic Ocean excepting such islands & c.c." Now whenever we can find that point vizt. the middle of the mouth of St. Croix river in the bay of Fundy, we are to draw a line due east from that spot and all Islands lying to the south of such line (and to the *north* of a line drawn due east from the middle of the mouth of St. Marys river) and within 20 leagues of the shore or main lands of the United States, are by the Treaty ceded to *them* "except such islands as now are or heretofore have been with the limits of said province of Nova Scotia." Now altho at present it may be uncertain where to fix this point, vizt. the middle of the mouth of the River St. Croix in the Bay of fundy, yet if we attend to the bearing of Grand Mannana from west passage as marked in my plan, it is certain that if you fix it any where about the bay of Passamaquoddy, a line drawn due east from thence will leave the whole island of Grand Mannana to the south, & this Island lying within much less than 20 leagues of the shore or main land of course belongs to the United States, therefore Governor Parr could never grant this island on any other principle but the one I have mentioned. The survey then made on sowards neck may be of a much more serious nature than was at first apprehended—if the scoodic be the St. Croix intended in the Treaty I agree with the Nova Scotia Gentlemen, that the *real* mouth of that river is at the devils head—but I by no means admit this to be the mouth intended by the Commissioners who formed the Treaty, for to draw a line due east from thence not only crosses over a tract of ~~country~~ main land before it touches the bay of fundy, *proper* & would give every island in the Bay of Passamaquoddy to the United States, but also all the islands along the shore to the eastward of Passamaquoddy for several leagues which I can by no means suppose to be intended, & if we fix this point in the real mouth of the Maggacadava or eastern St. Croix, we shall be involved in the same difficulties as before—so that which ever be the St. Croix intended the point mentioned in the Treaty must be in some other place than either of these I have mentioned—and the most probable opinion I have been able to form of the matter is that the Commissioners considered the whole Bay of Passamaquoddy as the mouth of the river St. Croix and that their real intention was, that a line beginning in the middle of this mouth, at a point where it joins the Bay of fundy, that is on a line drawn from the west to the east cape or head land that forms the bay of Passamaquoddy & from thence drawn through the middle of this bay or mouth & along the middle of the St. Croix ~~river~~ to its source & ca. &c. should be our eastern boundary—my reasons for this opinion are these—from this point wherever it is a line is to be drawn due east, in order to determine what islands belong to the United States and what not, now to draw such line from any point within the eastern Cape or headland, must cross over a tract of main land before it can touch the bay of Fundy proper & involve us in all these difficulties respecting the islands near the eastern shore & beyond Passamaquoddy which I have before mentioned—again the Bay of Passamaquoddy is not mentioned in all the Treaty, altho noticed in Mitchells map and all the maps of that Country in the American Atlas—wherefore the Commissioners I conceive must consider it as a part of the Bay of fundy; or as the mouth of the St. Croix, we have already observed the absurdities of considering it as part of the Bay of fundy & fixing the mouth of the St. Croix at the devils head or any where else within the eastern cape—therefore they must consider it as the mouth of the St. Croix or they could have no respect to it whatever. But if we carefully inspect Mitchells Map, & those in the American Atlass, & compare these drafts with the whole description of our eastern boundary, my hypothesis appears to me the only intelligible and consistent one that can take place—for instance—if we consult Mitchells map a line drawn from the eastern & western capes & bisected in the middle, strikes me as the identical point intended by the Commissioners—from hence a line drawn due east escapes the eastern cape & determines to whom the islands belong in a rational & consistent manner—from hence also a line drawn thro' the middle of the bay & up the St. Croix, will make a pretty equal division of the Bay of Passamaquoddy & the islands therein which it is natural to suppose was intended, & if we inspect the several maps in the American Atlass, the same ideas naturally arise, & upon this principle most if not all Campobello & a great part of Deer Island belongs to us, for the exceptions are respecting these islands only which are situate between lines drawn due east from certain points mentioned in the Treaty.

With respect to the river intended by the Commissioners as the boundary between us & Nova Scotia, I think they alone must determine—for as they are entirely silent with respect to any description but the bare name of St. Croix, & as the Passamaquoddy & Maggacadava have both obtained that name I think it impossible to determine which is the river intended by the description they have given us—it may however be well to observe, that the river Schoodic, or a river by the name of Schoodic, is not to be found in Mitchells Map, the American Atlass, or any other draft that I have seen. Mitchell at the head of his St. Croix has a lake which he calls Koneaki, this is evidently an indian name, but is not the name of either of the lakes or ponds on the schoodic that I have heard of. Mr. Jeffers author of the American atlass in one of his Maps, which he tells us is a new one, made from various surveys and corrected from divers Astronomical observations, has given us two rivers by the name of St. Croix, the eastern one he has contended as the dividing line between us & Nova Scotia—& is undoubtedly the Maggacadava—the western river he calls Passamaquoddy or St. Croix—you will please to observe that in my plan just above the last fall I have marked the mouth of a river coming in on the right near as large as the schoodic called by the natives Passamaquoddy—now if the Treaty should be explained to intend the western St. Croix, yet the boundary line cannot follow the river now known by the name of the Schoodic to its source, but must be confined to the Passama- quoddy or eastern branch of the western St. Croix for with what propriety they should claim beyond this & follow the Schoodic (a river not known in any map) above the forks I cannot conceive, & I think it highly probable that the name of Schoodic was by the Natives originally confined to the western branch & that the name of Passamaquoddy extended from the forks quite down to the Bay of the same name, for otherwise there is no connection between the river & bay which bear the same name, & which probably were derived the one from the other, which is commonly if not always the case. I am Gentlemen. your most respectful

Humble Servant

RUFUS PUTNAM[1]

---

[1] A copy of the letter, in the hand of Walter Stone, is in President's Messages on Foreign Relations, Executive Proceedings, SR, DNA. It is related to George Wash-

ington's message journalized February 9, 1790. A second copy, by Benjamin Bankson, is in Transcribed Treaties and Conventions, 1789–1801, Records of the Secretary, SR, DNA.

Deposition of Nathan Jones

I Nathan Jones of Goldsborough in the County of Lincoln & Commonwealth of Massachusetts Esqr. testify & say, that in the year 1764 I was employed by Sir Francis Bernard then Governor of the Province of Massachusetts Bay as commander of a party ~~to~~ employed to explore the woods & view the rivers & bays particularly that of Passamaquoddi in the eastern parts of said Province & to ascertain the river St. Croix dividing the said Province from the Government of Nova Scotia & to perform a survey there of—accordingly we proceeded & assembled upwards of forty of the indians on an island called La tete & after having fully & freely conversed with them upon the subject of our mission, the Chief commissioned three indians to shew us the said river St. Croix which is situated nearly six miles north, & about three degrees east of the harbour La tete & east north east of the bay or river Scudac & distant from it about nine miles upon a right line—the aforesaid three indians after having shewn us the said river & being duly informed of the nature & importance of an oath did make solemn oath to the truth of their information respecting the identity of the said river St. Croix, & that it was the river known amongst them by that name, which river is the eastern river in the bay of Passamaquoddi, & now known by the name of the Maggacadava we proceeded according to this information in our surveys and agreeable thereto in August following made return of our doings to the said Governor Bernard

NATHAN JONES

Suffolk ss Boston March 17th. 1785. The abovenamed Nathan Jones personally appeared & on Oath declared that the above by him subscribed is true.

Before me EZEKL. PRICE Just. Peace[1]

[1] A copy of the deposition, in the hand of Walter Stone, is in President's Messages on Foreign Relations, Executive Proceedings, SR, DNA. It is related to George Washington's message journalized February 9, 1790. A second copy, by Benjamin Bankson, is in Transcribed Treaties and Conventions, 1789–1801, Records of the Secretary, SR, DNA.

Report of John Jay to the Continental Congress

Office for Foreign Affairs 21st. April 1785

The Secretary of the United States, for the Depart. of Foreign Affairs; to whom was referred the Papers herewith enclosed respecting the Eastern boundary Line of said States—

Reports,

That, in his Opinion, effectual Measures should be immediately taken to settle all Disputes with the Crown of Great Britain, relative to that Line.

He thinks that Copies of the said Papers should be transmitted to the Minister Plenipotentiary of the United States at that Court, with Instructions to present a proper Representation of the Case, and to propose that Commissioners be appointed to hear, and finally decide those Disputes.

If this Measure should appear expedient to Congress, your Secretary would suggest the following Hints on the subject. Vizt.

That the number of Commissioners should be six, or eight, or ten, or twelve, at the Election of his Britannic Majesty, the exact number not being important.

That two Commissions of the like Tenor, to be agreed upon between our and their Ministers, be issued to the whole number Vizt. one by the United States and the other by his Britannic Majesty.

That each party shall name the one half of the whole Number.

That they shall all be Foreigners, or all be Persons of the two Nations, at the Election of his Britannic Majesty; it not being important.

If he should prefer having them of the two Nations, then that he shall name the one Half of them, being Inhabitants of any of his Dominions, except those which are situated in and to the West and South of the Gulph of St. Laurence, and that the United States shall name the other Half, from any of their Countries, except Massachusetts.

That the Commissioners, if of the two Countries shall sit in North-America, but, if Foreigners, in Europe, at any Place which may be agreed upon by our and their Ministers—That, previous to their proceeding to Business, they shall respectively take an Oath, fairly, impartially, and justly, without Fear, Favor, or Affection to hear and decide the said Matters in Difference according to the best of their ~~best~~ Skill and Understanding, agreeable to the Directions, true Intent, and Meaning of the said Commissions.

That in Case of the Death, or Refusal to act of any of the said Commissioners, previous to their opening and proceeding to execute the said Commission (but not afterwards) the Place of such, so dying, or refusing, shall be supplied by the Party who named him, and that a Certificate there of under the Seal of Great Britain, or of the United States, as the case may be, directed to the said Commissioners, by the Style of, The Commissioners for settling the Boundary Line between his Britannic Majesty and the United States, on the easterly side of the latter, shall be full Evidence of [blotted out] such appointment.

That a Majority of the whole Number shall be a Quorum for every Purpose committed to them expressly or necessarily implied in their Commissions—such as choosing their Chairman, appointing Secretaries, and Surveyors, adjourning from Day to Day, or, for a longer Term, which should not exceed ten Days, deciding on Matters of Evidence; and, finally, determining the Matters in Difference &c.

That they keep regular Minutes of their Proceedings—That all Evidence whether oral or written be entered at large in them—That Copies of all Maps and Surveys admitted as Evidence be made and kept with their Papers.

That their Chairman for the Time being, shall have Power to administer Oaths—That Contempts offered to the Board while convened, and sitting on the

Business of the Commission, shall be punishable as Contempts committed in a Court of Justice; and that a Certificate by the Chairman of such Contempt, delivered to any civil Magistrate shall make it the Duty of such Magistrate to apprehend and committed the Offender to Prison, there to remain until thence delivered in due Course of Law.

That both Parties shall have free access to the public Offices & Records of the other, and be supplied with Copies, or Exemplifications of any Parts thereof, on paying the accustomed Fees.

That both Parties shall produce to the Board whatever they may have to offer within three Months after the Opening of the said Commission by a Quorum of the Commissioners, at the Place to be appointed, who shall sit and be ready to do Business during the whole of that Term, unless the Parties shall, by writing under the Hands of their Agent or Agents, sooner declare that they have nothing further to offer.

That, on receiving such Declarations, from both the Parties, if within the said three Months, or from, and immediately after the Expiration of that Term, whichsoever of those Events shall first happen, the Commissioners shall, within two Days thereafter deliver their Judgment in writing under their Hands and Seals, or the Hands and Seals of a Majority of them to the Agents of both Parties, vizt. one Copy for each Party, and that the said Judgment shall be absolute, final and conclusive, between the said Parties.

That, on having given Judgment as aforesaid, or as soon as may be within two Months thereafter, they shall annex Transcripts of all their Minutes, Proceedings, and Maps, or Surveys above mentioned to each of the said Commissions, and under their Hands and Seals, or the Hands and Seals of a Majority of them, shall return the same, the one issued by his Britannic Majesty, to his Britannic Majesty, and the one by the United States, to the United States in Congress assembled, and that the Delivery of the same to their respective Agents shall be deemed and adjudged to be a good & sufficient Return.

That the Allowance to be made the said Commissioners for Service and Expenses be fixed by our and their Minister, and that each Party pay the one Half thereof.

That it be expressly stipulated that his Britannic Majesty shall, within six Months after the Day on which the Judgment shall be delivered to the Agents as aforesaid, cause the United States to be put in full possession of all the Territories, Lands, and Islands, which, by the said Judgment may be adjudged to the said States, and then being in the Possession of his Majesty; and, on the other Hand, that the United States shall, within six Months after the Day on which the Judgment shall be delivered as aforesaid, cause his Britannic Majesty to be put in full Possession of all the Territories, Lands, and Islands, which, by the said Judgment may be adjudged to him, and then being in the Possession of the United States.

All which is humbly submitted to the Wisdom of Congress.

(signed) JOHN JAY[1]

---

[1] A copy of the report, in the hand of Benjamin Bankson, is in President's Messages on Foreign Relations, Executive Proceedings, SR, DNA, E-19323. It is related to

George Washington's message journalized February 9, 1790. A second copy, by Benjamin Bankson, is in Transcribed Treaties and Conventions, 1789–1801, Records of the Secretary, SR, DNA.

Extract from the Journal of the Continental Congress

And be it further Ordained, That three Townships adjacent to Lake Erie be reserved, to be hereafter disposed of by Congress, for the use of the officers, men, and others, refugees from Canada, & the refugees from Nova Scotia, who are or may be entituled to grants of Lands under the resolutions of Congress now existing, or which may hereafter be made respecting them, and for Such-other purposes as Congress may hereafter direct.

May 20 1785[1]

[1] The extract, in the hand of Charles Thomson, is in Miscellaneous Manuscripts, entry 820, box 5, E-1039, RG 59, General Records of the Department of State (hereinafter referred to as RG 59), DNA. It is related to George Washington's message journalized February 9, 1790.

Governor Thomas Carleton* to Governor John Hancock and Proceedings of the Massachusetts Legislature

St. John New Brunswic June 21st
1785

SIR,

In consequence of a letter from your Excellency to the Governor of Nova Scotia which has been transmitted to his Majesty's Ministers, respecting the boundary between this Province & the State of Massachusetts Bay, I have it in charge to inform your Excellency that the Great St. Croix called Schoodiac by the Indians was not only considered by the Court of Great Britain as the River intended & agreed upon by the Treaty to form a part of that boundary but a numerous body of the loyal refugees immediately after the peace built the Town of St. Andrews on the eastern branch bank thereof. And in fact it is the only river on that side of the Province of either such magnitude or extent as could have led to the idea of preparing it as a limit between two large & spacious countries.

In making this communication concerning a point of great public importance, I cannot entertain a doubt, Sir, your Excellency's concurrence with me in contributing to the compleat observance of the Treaty, subsisting between Great

* Governor of New Brunswick

Britain & the United States of America, as far as may in any instance immediately respect the State of Massachusetts & the Province of New Brunswic, & I hope, & am persuaded, that if any further question on this subject should arise, between us it will be considered on both sides with a temper & attention essential for the preservation of national peace and harmony.

> I have the honor to be,
> Your Excellency's
> most obedient & most humble servant
> THOS. CARLETON

In the House of Representatives July 1st. 1785
   Read & sent up

> NATHANIEL GORHAM spkr.

Commonwealth of Massachusetts

In Senate July 1st. 1785.

Resolved that his Excellency the governor be desired to transmit a Copy of the foregoing Letter to the Delegates of this State in Congress to be by them communicated to the United States in Congress assembled.

sent down for concurrence

> SAML. PHILLIPS JR. Presidt.

In the House of Representatives July 1st. 1785.

> Read & Concurred
> NATHL. GORHAM Spkr.

Approved JAMES BOWDOIN[1]

---

[1] A copy of the letter, with the resolution, in the hand of Walter Stone, is in President's Messages on Foreign Relations, Executive Proceedings, SR, DNA. It is related to George Washington's message journalized February 9, 1790. Copies of the letter and the resolution, by Benjamin Bankson, are in Transcribed Treaties and Conventions, 1789–1801, Records of the Secretary, SR, DNA.

James Avery to Governor James Bowdoin*

Passamaquady 23 Augt. 1785

SIR,

Being at this place on some private business of my own, I was informed that the Government of New Brunswick had asserted their claims to Moose Island, Dudley and Fred Isle, all laying to the Westward of Schooduck River, these Islands were surveyed last season by General Putnam, by order of the Committee on Eastern Lands, and the two last mentioned sold by them to Colonel Allan, who has with Mr. De le Derniers settled thereon built Houses and Stores, and

---

* Governor of Massachusetts

cleared up the lands at a great expence, Moose Island is large and well situated for Trade and has a number of worthy Inhabitants settled on it. a few Days ago Mr. Wyer high Sherrif for Charlotte County posted up advertisements on Moose Island directing the Inhabitants to attend the Courts at St. Andrews as Jurymen, this alarmed the Inhabitants as they were threatened in case of refusal to be deprived of their Estates, some weak and designing minds were for complying, others determined not at all events. application was made to me by Col. Allan, the naval officer, Colonel Crane, Major Trescott, with a number of other principal Gentlemen to do something to counteract the proceedings of Mr. Wyer, as it would be very detrimental to the claims of our Government in settling the boundary in regard to the Islands for the Inhabitants to obey and acknowledge the Jurisdiction of Great Britain. therefore I went on to the Island, and warned them (as a Justice of the Peace), that, as they were subjects of this Commonwealth not to obey the orders of any other power whatever, this I conceived my Duty to do, more particularly as it is part of my District as Collector of Excise, and I have a Deputy on the same Island. this matter is of the utmost consequence to our Government, for should the British take in these Islands, we should be entirely cut off from going up the River Scooduck, and likewise these Islands having been Surveyed by order of the Commonwealth, and two of them sold to Gentlemen who have laid out as much as £500 or £600 in Buildings and improvements, our Government must in Honour protect them or repay what damages they may suffer. since this matter has taken place, I was up to St. Andrews on some Business of my own and had a long conversation with Mr. Wyer the high Sherriff, Mr. Pagan, and other principal Persons; they say they acted by advice and directions of Judge Ludlow, who is of opinion that all the Islands in the Bay of Passamaquady belong to New Brunswick, and are determined to support their claim and should the inhabitants refuse to obey their Summons, they may depend on being punished. they also let me see a long Letter from Lord Sidney, wherein he informs, that notwithstanding the opinion of the Massachusetts, and the Report of Generals Knox and Lincoln (which was then before him) his Majesty's Servants were fully clear that Schooduck was the boundary, and his Majesty's Subjects settled between that and the Madecadawie (or what we call St. Croix) might fully rely on their protection. Mr. Wyer made use of many Arguments to shew the propriety of their claims to all the Islands, among others he said, before the War the Inhabitants on all of them, in any of their disputes applied to Magistrates belonging to Nova Scotia for redress and acknowledged them themselves subjects of that Province, and the Massachusetts not asserting any right over them was tacitly acknowledging it to be so.

I hope your Excellency will not think I have been too forward I acted from a principle of public good. agreeable to the principles they advance (as well as Lord Sheffields Ideas in his publications) if the Inhabitants should acknowledge the Jurisdiction of that Government, it would more fully support their claims which I hope now will not be the case. The time was so short it would not admit of the Inhabitants receiving any orders from your Excellency on the subject before the time they were directed to attend I shall continue to keep a deputy

Collector of Excise on moose Island to regulate that business, until I receive orders from your Excellency to the Contrary.

I have the Honor to be &c.

(Signed) JAS. AVERY[1]

[1] A copy of the letter, in the hand of Jacob Blackwell, is in PCC, item 124, vol. I, M247, roll 141, DNA. It is related to George Washington's message journalized February 9, 1790.

Proceedings of the Council of Massachusetts

Commonwealth of Massachusetts

In Council 9 Septemr. 1785

His Excellency the Governor laid before the Council a Letter from James Avery Esqr. relative to the Government of New Brunswick asserting their claims to Moose Island, Dudley and Fred Island all laying to the westward of Schoodic river and requested their advice upon the Subject.

Thereupon Advised that his Excellency the Governor acquaint James Avery Esqr. that the Governor and Council, highly approve of his vigilant attention to the important Interest of the Commonwealth, and that the said James Avery be directed to inform the Inhabitants of the said Islands, that the said Islands are within the Jurisdiction of this Commonwealth, and that this Government confiding in their fidelity expect and require the Inhabitants of the same to conduct themselves in every respect as becomes true and faithful Subjects of this Commonwealth.

That a Letter be wrote by his Excellency the Governor, to the Governor of New Brunswick upon the subject of these encroachments, and that a copy of the Letter from James Avery be sent to our Delegates at Congress with the proceedings of the Governor and Council upon this Business, to be laid before Congress.[1]

[1] A copy of the Council minutes, in the hand of Jacob Blackwell, is in PCC, item 124, vol. I, M247, roll 141, DNA. It is related to George Washington's message journalized February 9, 1790.

Governor James Bowdoin to Governor Thomas Carleton

Commonwealth of Massachusetts

Boston 9th. Septr. 1785

SIR,

I am informed by a Gentleman, who is an Inhabitant in the Eastern part of this Commonwealth that the Government of New Brunswick hath *asserted* a Claim to, Moose Island Dudley and Fred Island; but I flatter myself he has extended his Ideas beyond the real Fact. For he mentions only the Conduct of the Sheriff of your County of Charlotte (Mr. Wyer) grounded on the advice and direction of Judge Ludlow in advertising and directing the Inhabitants of Moose Island to attend the Courts at St. Andrews as Jurymen upon pain, in case of refusal, of forfeiting their Estates.

As I am not informed, that your Excellency has interposed your Authority, I am inclined to believe, that my Informant had been premature in forming an opinion that the Government of New Brunswick had given its Sanction to a measure altogether unexpected and insupportable. I have however given your Excellency this Information, assuring myself, that your Excellency will take order effectually to prevent the above mentioned and every other encroachment on the territorial Rights, and Sovereignty of this Commonwealth and of the United States.

With regard to the Lands lying to the Eastward of the River Schoodic and between that and the River St. Croix, or as the Indians call it Maggacadava, relative to which some of the Subjects of Great Britain under your immediate Government appear to have adopted an improper opinion, it is a matter before Congress who I am assured, will give Instructions to their Minister at the Court of London to assert and maintain their just Claims as set forth in the Treaty agreed to between the two Nations.

I have the Honor to be &c.

(Signed)   JAMES BOWDOIN[1]

---

[1] A copy of the letter, in the hand of Jacob Blackwell, is in PCC, item 124, vol. I, M247, roll 141, DNA. It is related to George Washington's message journalized February 9, 1790.

Report of John Jay to the Continental Congress

Office for Foreign Affairs
22d September 1785

The Secretary of the United States for the Department of Foreign Affairs, to whom were referred certain official Papers delivered to Congress by the Delegates of Massachusetts on the 19 Inst. relative to attempts of the Province of New Brunswick to extend their Jurisdiction to Moose Island &c.—REPORTS.

That in his Opinion the Advice given by the Council to his Excellency the Governor of Massachusetts on the 9 Instant, was proper, and that as one unopposed Encroachment always paves the way for another, the Commonwealth of Massachusetts be advised by Congress to proceed without Voise or Delay to garrison such Places in their actual Possessions as may be most exposed.

Your Secretary proposes by these Garrisons to support the Inhabitants in their Allegiance and to over awe New Brunswick peace Officers, whom Impunity might tempt to be insolent and troublesome. He thinks these Garrisons should not be so large as to give alarm—that they should be under select and discreet

Officers—that they should be formed by immediate Detachments from the Militia of some of the other Counties, be at continental Charge and be, as soon as may be relieved by Detachments from the continental Troops raised *or to be raised* for the *Frontiers*. That they should be ordered never to pass our Limits, and to act only on the Defensive, or when called upon to support the civil Authority. However delicate this Measure may appear, it may in the Opinion of your Secretary be safely confided to the Prudence of the Governor & Council of Massachusetts.

Nothing should be done to provoke Hostilities on the one Hand, and on the other it must be remembered, that too great and manifest Reluctance to assert our Rights by Arms, usually invites Insult and Offence.

Your Secretary is very apprehensive that to permit these Disputes to remain unsettled will be to risque mutual Acts of Violence, which may embroil the two Nations in a War. He therefore takes the Liberty of calling the Attention of Congress to a Report he had the Honor of making to Congress on this Subject the 21 of April last.

Your Secretary thinks that no Nation can consistent with the Experience of all Ages, expect to enjoy Peace and Security any longer than they may continue prepared for War; and he cannot forbear expressing his Fears that the United States are not at present in that desirable Situation.

As the 11 Article of the Treaty of Alliance between his most Christian Majesty and the United States contains an explicit and permanentpetual Guarantee of all the Possessions of the latter, your Secretary thinks it would be adviseable to apprize the Court of France of the Disputes in question, that his Majesty may cooperate with the United States in Measures proper to bring about a Settlement of them. In his Opinion these Measures should be formed and pursued in Concert with France, and in such a manner as that she may have no just Cause to be dissatisfied; or to say that as we acted without her concurrence, we alone are to be responsible for the Consequences.

All which is submitted to the Wisdom of Congress

JOHN JAY[1]

[1] A copy of the report, in the hand of Benjamin Bankson, is in President's Messages on Foreign Relations, Executive Proceedings, SR, DNA. It is related to George Washington's message journalized February 9, 1790. A second copy, by Benjamin Bankson, is in Transcribed Treaties and Conventions, 1789–1801, Records of the Secretary, SR, DNA.

Resolutions of the Continental Congress

United States in Congress Assembled

October 13 1785

RESOLVED, That Copies of the Papers and Documents, received from the Governor of the State of Massachusetts, respecting the Encroachment made by certain Subjects of his Britannic Majesty upon the Territories of that State, and within the Boundaries of the United States, be transmitted to the Minister Plenipotentiary of the United States at the Court of London, to the End that effectual Measures should be immediately taken to settle all Disputes with the Crown of Great Britain relative to that Line.

RESOLVED, That the said Minister Plenipotentiary be and hereby is instructed to present a proper Representation of this Case, and if any Adjustment consistent with the true meaning of the Definitive Articles of Peace and Friendship between the United States and his Britannic Majesty cannot, by such Representation, be obtained in the ordinary mode of Negotiation, that he propose a Settlement and final Decision of the said Dispute by Commissionerssaries mutually appointed for that Purpose, for the Appointment of whom, and for all Purposes incident to the final Determination of the said Dispute by Commissaries conformable to the Laws of Nations, the said Minister Plenipotentiary is hereby vested with full Powers on Behalf of the United States of America.[1]

[1] Copies of the resolutions, in the hand of Benjamin Bankson, are in President's Messages on Foreign Relations, Executive Proceedings, SR, DNA. They are related to George Washington's message journalized February 9, 1790. Second copies, in the hand of Benjamin Bankson, are in Transcribed Treaties and Conventions, 1789–1801, Records of the Secretary, SR, DNA.

John Jay to John Adams

New York 1st. November 1785

DR. SIR,

I have the Honor of transmitting to you herewith enclosed an Act of Congress of the 13th. Ult. respecting british Claims and Encroachments on our Eastern Boundaries, and instructing and authorizing you to take proper Measures for amicably settling the Disputes thence arising. You will also find herewith enclosed the several Papers and Documents referred to in that Act, and of which a List is hereto subjoined.

It also appears to me expedient to send you Copies of two Reports which I have made to Congress respecting these Matters, not for your Direction, but that you may thereby be fully informed of my Sentiments on this interesting Subject.

With great and sincere Regard I am &ca.

(signed)   JOHN JAY[1]

[1] A copy of the letter, in the hand of Henry Remsen, Jr., is in Foreign Letters of the Continental Congress and the Department of State, 1785–90, RG 59, DNA. It is related to George Washington's message journalized February 9, 1790. The list referred to in this letter contains the same documents as bundle A, items 1–15 of the list printed with George Washington's message journalized February 9, 1790. The letter itself is item 16 on Washington's list.

Proceedings of the Legislature of Massachusetts on the Petition of James Boyd

Commonwealth of Massachusetts

In Senate January 20th 1785
Read and thereupon ordered that Samuel Phillips junr. and Charles Turner Esqrs. with such as the honble. house may join be a committee to take the same into consideration and report what is proper to be done thereon.

sent down for concurrence.

SAMUEL ADAMS President

In the House of Representatives January 20th 1785.
Read and concurred and Mr. Swan Mr. Hosmer & Mr. Dane are joined.

SAMUEL A. OTIS Speaker

In Senate June 22 1786. Read and committed to Samuel Adams Esqr. with such as the Honble. house may join to consider and report.

sent down for concurrence.

SAMUEL PHILLIPS JUNR. President

In the House of Representatives June 22nd 1786. Read and concurred, and Mr. Noyes and Mr. Jernigan are joined

ARTEMAS WARD Speaker

On the petition of James Boyd Esquire
A Letter of instruction to the delegates of this Commonwealth at Congress.

It having been represented to this Court by James Boyd Esquire, now resident in Boston that he obtained from the British Government in the year 1767 a grant of fifty thousand acres of land, lying on the banks of the River Schoodick, and that the said Boyd went on and possessed the said lands, introducing at his own charge, a large number of families and that he was at great expence for cattle and farming utensils of all sorts, as well as in the erecting of necessary mills and water works; but in the beginning of the late war between Great Britain and these States he took such an active and decided part in favor of the latter that he soon became very obnoxious to the resentment of the British, and was obliged to leave all his property and possessions, and flee to the protection of the United States, that he has resided in Boston until the present time, in hopes that his aforementioned lands would fall within the bounds of this state, and that he should be reinstated in them, that the whole of his lands are on the Western side of that river, which we suppose to be the St. Croix mentioned in the treaty, and the boundary line between Nova Scotia and these States, but that as the British subjects are at present in the possession of those lands, the said Boyd is unjustly prevented from returning there to occupy and improve them; as we esteem him to have been a good friend to this country and still to remain such, and one who is at present deprived of the possession of a large interest in consequence of his attachment to it. We instruct you to recommend him to the attention and favor of Congress, and to move that honble. body to afford him such relief as they may think proper.

In Senate November 9th 1786. Read and ordered that the aforegoing letter be transcribed that his Excellency the Governor be requested to sign and transmit the same to the delegates from this Commonwealth in Congress.

Sent down for concurrence.

SAMUEL PHILLIPS JUNR. President

In the House of Representatives Novemr. 10th 1786.

read and concurred.

ARTEMAS WARD Speaker

Approved.

JAMES BOWDOIN[1]

[1] An attested copy of the proceedings is in Miscellaneous Manuscripts, entry 820, box 5, E-1039, RG 59, DNA. It is related to George Washington's message journalized February 9, 1790.

Petition of James Boyd

To The President
The Senate and House of Representatives
of the
United States of America
in
Congress assembled.

The PETITION of James Boyd of Boston in the County of Suffolk and COMMONWEALTH of MASSACHUSETTS Esquire, Humbly sheweth

That your Petitioner was possessed from the Year 1767 till the Beginning of our Contest with Great Britain of very large Property in Lands situated on the Eastern Bank of the River Schoodick, granted him by the British Government of Nova-Scotia, and that during said Period he introduced many Families on the same Lands at his own Charge, and expended much Property in getting the same under considerable Improvement and Cultivation; But feeling himself attached to the Cause of America, he took such an active Part in their Favour that the resentment of the British Subjects in that Province compelled him to leave the Country, and flee to the Protection of the United States; & that in Consequence thereof he has suffered Poverty and Distress from that Day to the present Time, that the said Lands which your Petitioner held, are on the western Side of the River St. Croix, and within the Dominions of the United States, but unjustly now held in Possession by British Subjects—That the Facts aforesaid and your Petitioner's Situation have been particularly set forth to Congress by the Legislature of this Commonwealth, in a Letter of Instruction to their Delegates in the Year 1786, signed and transmited by the then Governor Bowdoin, and which is now on the Files of Congress, accompanied wth. a Number of Letters from Governor Bowdoin, the present Governor Hancock and others upon the Subject, to which your Excellency and Honours will please to be refered: that your Petitioner by his thus quitting the British and joining the American Interest has been subjected to peculiar Hardships and Difficulties, which with a large Family he has with great Anxiety sustained: But confiding in the Power and Disposition of the present Congress of the United States to do him compleat Justice he requests them to put him in Possession of his Lands aforesaid now held by British Subjects, tho' on this Side the Line between the two Dominions, or otherwise recompence your Petitioner who has lost the whole of his Property and Means of procuring a comfortable Subsistence in Consequence of his Attachment as aforesaid.

Your Petitioner begs Leave to add that he is possessed of Papers, and that John Mitchel Esq. of the State of Newhampshire (now an old Man about 76 Years of Age) is also possessed of Papers, that may be useful in determing the real Situation of the River St. Croix, entended by the late Treaty of Peace to be the dividing Line between the Dominions of the United States & Great Britain, as will appear by a Plan taken in the Year 1764 by the said Mitchel, and another taken by the Surveyor General of Nova Scotia the Year following, and now in the Possession of your Petitioner, who,

As in Dutybound, will ever pray &c.

JAMES BOYD

Boston, Novr. 27, 1789[1]

[1] The petition, signed by James Boyd, is in Miscellaneous Manuscripts, entry 820, box 5, E-1039, RG 59, DNA. It is related to George Washington's message journalized February 9, 1790.

Observations by C. Morris F. General

Observations on the western limits of that part of Nova Scotia which is now called New Brunswick &c.

Mr. Barnard Governor of Massachusetts bay in the year 1764 caused a survey of the Bay of Passamaquoddy to be made; and proposed to the Governor of Nova Scotia the making of grants of land as being within the Massachusetts Government. The next year Mr. Wilucot the Governor of N. S. sent his Chf. land surveyor to make a survey of that bay also, and upon full inquiry it was found, that there were three rivers emptying into the bay which were called St. Croix that the river called by the Indians Copscook was anciently called by the French St. Croix, & on examining into the original grants of Nova Scotia it evidently appeared that the grant made by King Charles the 2d to his brother the Duke of York in 1663 (called the Duke of York's territory) was bounded by the river St. Croix eastward and by the river Kennebec to the westward that on the 12th of August, the same year Sir William Alexander obtained a grant of Nova Scotia to wit, bounded westerly as far as the river St. Croix and to the furthermost source or spring of that river which comes from the west to mingle its waters with those of the river St. Croix and from thence running towards the north &c.—all the islands in Passamaquoddy bay are included in this grant and have ever since been deemed to belong to N.S.—Upon Governor Wilucot's transmitting to Governor Bernard the plans and reports made by the survey of N.S. in 1765 Governor Bernard the same year applied to and obtained a grant from Governor Wilucot of one hundred thousand acres including Moose island for himself and associates to wit Thomas Pownal, John Mitchel, Thomas Thornton and Richard Jackson between Copscook and Scoodick rivers on the western side Passamaquoddy bay, and the remainder of the principal islands in that bay were the same year granted to sundry other Grantees by the Governor of N.S. so that the whole of Passamaquoddy bay together with Grand Manan and all the Islands in the bay have ever been deemed to be within Nova Scotia untill the seperation of New Brunswick from it.

By the definitive treaty of Peace signed at Paris 3d September 1783 the eastern limits or boundaries of the United States are thus described, east by a line to be drawn a long the middle of the river St. Croix from its mouth in the bay of Fundy to its source, and from its source north to the high lands, comprehending all Islands within twenty leagues of any part of the shores of the United States and laying between lines to be drawn due east from the points where the afd. boundaries between Nova Scotia on the one part, and east Florida on the other part shall respectively touch the bay of Fundy and the Atlantic ocean, excepting such Islands as now are or heretofore have been deemed within the limits of Nova Scotia, This makes it clearly evident that Grand Manan, Passamaquoddy great Island, now called Campo Bello, Deer Island, Moose Island, and indeed all the islands laying in that bay whether on the southern or northern side the line drawn due east from St. Croix should as formerly they did belong to Nova Scotia.

Whether Scoodick or whether Copscook is the river the treaty fixes upon for the boundary I will not presume to say, but from the manner in which those boundaries are expressed I should imagine that river to be the river St. Croix intended, whose source should be found furtherst into the Country, westward and northward towards the high lands mentioned in the treaty being conformable to the old grants of Nova Scotia; and if my conjecture is well founded the St. Croix mentioned in the treaty cannot be effectually & properly ascertained untill accurate surveys are made & proper Commissioners appointed to determine thereupon.

[Nova Scotia, 1789][1]

[1] A copy of the observations is in Miscellaneous Manuscripts, entry 820, box 5, E-1039, RG 59, DNA. It is related to George Washington's message journalized February 9, 1790.

John Hancock to George Washington

Boston February 10th. 1790

SIR,

At the request of the Senate and House of Representatives of this Commonwealth, I have the honor to enclose you some papers evidential of the encroachments made by the Subjects of the King of England upon the Eastern frontier of this Commonwealth.

If the papers transmitted do not give satisfactory proof upon this point, I wish that Congress would direct a mode in which a proper and speedy enquiry may be made.

A speedy investigation of this dispute may have a tendency to prevent a disagreeable contention which is likely to take place between the people on the frontiers of the two nations.

> I have the honor to be
> With sentiments of Esteem
> Sir
> Your most obedient hble. Servant
> (signed)   JOHN HANCOCK

Resolution of the Commonwealth of Massachusetts

Commonwealth of ⎱
Massachusetts   ⎰ In Senate February 1st. 1790

RESOLVED that his Excellency the Governor be and he is here by requested to write to the President of the United States, in behalf of this Commonwealth, informing him that the subjects of his Britannick Majesty have made and still continue to make encroachments on the eastern boundary of this Commonwealth, in the opinion of the Legislature, contrary to the treaty of peace; and that his Excellency be further requested to forward such documents as may be necessary to substantiate the facts.

> Sent down for concurrence
> (signed)   THOMAS DAWES President pro-tem

In the House of Representatives February 1st. 1790.

> Read and concurred
> (signed)   DAVID COBB. Speaker[1]

---

[1] Copies of the letter and the resolution, in the hand of Thomas Nelson, Jr., and certified by Tobias Lear, are in President's Messages on Foreign Relations, Executive Proceedings, SR, DNA. They are related to George Washington's message journalized February 18, 1790.

Tonnage on French Vessels

Traité d'Amitié et de Commerce

Le Roi Très chretien et les treize Etats-unis de l'Amérique septentrionale, savoir, Newhampshire La Baye de Massachusset, Rhode-Island, Connecticut, New York, New Jersey, Pensylvanie, Les Comtés de Newcastle de Kent et de Sussex sur la Delaware, Maryland, Virginie, Caroline septentrionale, Caroline Méridionale et Georgie voulant établir d'une maniere équitable et permanente les règles qui devront être suivies relativement à la Correspondance et au Commerce que les deux parties désirent d'établir entre leurs Païs, Etats et sujets respectifs, Sa Majesté Très chretienne et les dits Etats-unis ont jugé ne pouvoir mieux atteindre à ce but qu'en prenant pour base de leur arrangement l'égalité et la réciprocité la plus parfaite, et en observant d'éviter toutes les préférences onéreuses, source de discussions, d'embarras et de mecontentemens, de laisser à chaque partie la liberté de faire relativement au Commerce et à la Navigation les réglemens intérieurs que seront à sa convenance, de ne fonder les avantages du Commerce que sur son utilité reciproque et sur les loix d'une juste concurrence, et de conserver ainsi de part et d'autre la liberté de faire participer, chacun selon son gré, les autres Nations aux mêmes avantages. C'est dans cet esprit et pour remplir ces vües que Sa de. Majesté ayant nommé et constitué pour son

Plénipotentiaire le S. Conrad-Alexandre Gerard, Sindic Roïal de la Ville de Strasbourg, Secretaire du Conseil d'Etat de Sa Majesté, et les Etats unis aïant, de leur coté, munis de leurs pleins pouvoirs les Srs. Benjamin Franklin Député au Congrès général de la part de l'Etat de Pensylvanie et Président de la Convention du de. Etat Silas Deane ci-devant Député de l'Etat de Connecticut et Arthur Lee *Conseiller ès loix* Les ds. Plénipotentiaires respectifs après l'échange de leurs pouvoirs et après mure déliberation ont conclu et arrêté les points et articles suivans.

ART. IER.

Il y aura une paix ferme, inviolable et universelle et une amitié vraie et sincère entre le Roi Très chrétien, ses heritiers et successeurs, et entre les Etats unis de l'Amérique ainsi qu'entre les sujets de Sa Majesté Très chretienne et ceux des dits Etats, comme aussi entre les peuples Isles, Villes et places situés sous la Jurisdiction du Roi Très chretien et des dits Etats unis, et entre leurs peuples et habitans de toutes les classes, sans aucune exception de personnes et de lieux; Les conditions mentionnées au present Traité seront perpetuelles et permanentes entre le Roi Très Chretien, ses héritiers et successeurs et les dits Etats unis.

ART. 2.

Le Roi Très chretien et les Etats unis s'engagent mutuellement à n'accorder aucune faveur particulière à d'autres Nations en fait de Commerce et de Navigation qui ne devienne aussitôt commune à l'autre partie, et celle ci jouira de cette faveur gratuitement, si la concession est gratuite, ou en accordant la même compensation si la concession est conditionnelle.

ART. 3.

Les sujets du Roi Très chretien ne païeront dans les Ports, havres, rades Contrées, Isles, Cités et lieux des Etats unis ou d'aucun d'entr'eux d'autres ni plus grands droits ou impôts, de quelque nature qu'ils puissent être, et quelque nom qu'ils puissent avoir que ceux que les Nations les plus favorisées sont, ou seront tenües de païer; Et ils jouiront de tous les droits, libertés, priviléges immunités et exemtions en fait de négoce, navigation et commerce, soit en passant d'un Port des dits Etats à un autre, soit en y allant ou en revenant de quelque partie ou pour quelque partie du Monde que ce soit, dont les des. Nations jouissent ou jouiront.

ART. 4.

Les sujets peuples et habitans des d. Etats-unis et de chacun d'iceux ne païeront dans les Ports, havres, rades, Isles Villes et places de la Domination de Sa Majesté Très chretienne en Europe d'autres ni plus grands droits ou impots de quelque nature qu'ils puissent être et quelque nom qu'ils puissent avoir que les Nations les plus favorisées sont ou seront tenües de païer, et ils jouiront de tous les droits, libertés priviléges immunités et exemtions en fait de négoce, navigation et commerce soit en passant d'un port à un autre des ds. Etats du Roi Très chretien en Europe, soit en y allant ou en revenant de quelque partie ou pour quelque partie du monde que ce soit dont les Nations susdes. jouissent ou jouiront.

Art. 5.

Dans l'exemtion ci dessus est nommément compris l'imposition de Cent sous par Tonneau établie en France sur les Navires étrangers, si ce n'est lorsque les Navires des Etats-unis chargeront des marchandises de France dans un port de France pour un autre port de la même Domination auquel cas les ds. navires des ds. Etats-unis acquiteront le droit dont il s'agit aussi longtems que les autres nations les plus favorisées seront obligées de l'acquiter. Bien entendu qu'il sera libre aux dits Etats unis ou à aucun d'iceux d'établir, quand ils le jugeront à propos, un droit equivalent à celui dont il est question pour le même cas pour lequel il est etabli dans les Ports de Sa Majeste Très chretienne.

Art. 6.

Le Roi Très Chretien fera usage de tous les moïens qui sont en son pouvoir pour protéger et défendre tous les Vaisseaux et effets apartenants aux sujets, peuples et habitans des dits Etats-unis et de chacun d'iceux qui seront dans ses ports, havres ou rades ou dans les Mers près de ses Pays Contrées, Isles, Villes et places, et fera tous ses efforts pour recouvrer et faire restituer aux propriétaires légitimes leurs agens ou Mandataires, tous les vaisseaux et effets qui leur seront pris dans l'étendüe de sa jurisdiction; Et les Vaisseaux de guerre de Sa Majesté Très chretienne ou les convois quelconques faisant voile sous son autorité, prendront en toute occasion, sous leur protection tous les Vaisseaux apartenants aux sujets peuples et habitans des ds. Etats unis ou d'aucun d'iceux les quels tiendront le meme cours et feront la même route, et ils défendront les dits Vaisseaux aussi longtems qu'ils tiendront le même cours et suivront la meme route, contre toute attaque force ou violence de la même manière qu'ils sont tenus de défendre et de protéger les Vaisseaux appartenans aux sujets de Sa Majesté Très chretienne.

Art. 7.

Pareillement les dits Etats unis et leurs Vaisseaux de guerre faisant voile sous leur autorité protégeront et défendront conformement au contenu de l'arte. précédent, tous les Vaisseaux et effets apartenants aux sujets du Roi Très Chretien et feront tous leurs efforts pour recouvrer et faire restitüer les dits Vaisseaux et effets qui auront été pris dans l'étendüe de la Jurisdiction des dits Etats et de chacun d'iceux.

Art. 8.

Le Roi Très chretien emploïera ses bons offices et son entremise auprès des Roi ou Empereur de Maroc ou Fez, des Regences d'Alger, Tunis et Tripoli ou auprès aucune d'entr'Elles ainsi qu'auprès de tout autre Prince Etat ou Puissance des côtes de Barbarie en Affrique et des sujets des ds. Roi Empereur, Etats et Puissance et de chacun d'iceux à l'effet de pourvoir aussi pleinement et aussi efficacement qu'il sera possible, à l'avantage, commodité et sûreté des dits Etats-unis et de chacun d'iceux, ainsi que de leurs sujets, peuples et habitans, leurs Vaisseaux et effets contre toute violence, insulte, attaque ou déprédations de la part des ds. Princes et Etats Barbaresques ou de leurs sujets.

Art. 9.

Les sujets habitans, marchands, Commandans des Navires, Maitres et gens de Mer des Etats, Provinces et Domaines des deux parties s'abstiendront et éviteront reciproquement, de pêcher dans toutes les places possédées ou qui seront possedées par l'autre partie. Les sujets de Sa Majesté Très Chretienne ne pêcheront pas dans les havres, Bayes, Criques, rades, côtes et places que les dits Etats-unis possédent ou posséderont à l'avenir, et de la même manière les sujets peuples et habitans des ds. Etats unis ne pêcheront pas dans les havres, Bayes, Criques, rades, Côtes et places que Sa Majesté Très chretienne posséde actuellement ou possédera à l'avenir, et si quelque navire ou Batiment étoit surpris pêchant en violation du presente Traité, le dit navire ou Batiment et sa Cargaison seront confisqués, après que la preuve en aura été faite düement. Bien entendu que l'exclusion stipulée dans le present article n'aura lieu qu'autant et si longtems que le Roi et les Etats-unis n'auront point accordé à cet egard d'exception à quelque Nation que ce puisse être.

ART. 10.

Les Etats unis, leurs Citoïens et habitans ne troubleront jamais les sujets du Roi Très chretien dans la jouissance et exercice du droit de pêche sur les bancs de Terre neuve, non plus que dans la jouissance indefinie et exclusive qui leur apartient sur la partie des Côtes de cette Isle designée dans le Traite d'Utrecht ni dans les droits relatifs à toutes et chacune des Isles qui appartiennent à Sa Majesté très Chretienne. Le tout conformement au véritable sens des Traités d'Utrecht et de Paris.

ART. 11.[1]

Il est convenue et arrêté qu'il ne sera jamais imposé aucun droit sur l'exportation des Melasses qui pourront être tirées par les sujets d'aucun des Etats-unis des Isles d'Amérique qui appartiennent ou pourront apartenir à Sa Majesté très Chretienne.

ART. 12.

En compensation de l'exemtion stipulée par l'article précédent, il est convenu et arrêté qu'il ne sera jamais imposé aucun droit sur l'exportation d'aucune espèce de denrées et marchandises que les sujets de Sa Majesté Très Chretienne pourront tirer des Pays ou possessions actuelles ou futures d'aucun des Treize Etats-unis pour l'usage des Isles qui fournissent les melasses.

ART. 13.

Les sujets et habitans des dits Etats-unis ou de l'un d'eux ne seront point reputés Aubains en France et conséquemment seront exempts du droit d'Aubaine ou autre droit semblable quelque nom qu'il puisse avoir; pourront disposer par Testament, Donation ou autrement de leurs biens meubles et immeubles en faveur de telles personnes que bon leur semblera; Et leurs heritiers sujets des dits Etats-unis, residans soit en France soit ailleurs pourront leur succéder *ab intestat*, sans qu'ils aïent besoin d'obtenir des lettres de naturalité, et sans que l'effet de cette concession leur puisse être contesté ou empêché sous pretexte de quelques droits ou prérogatives des Provinces, Villes, ou personnes privées. Et seront les dits héritiers, soit à titre particulier, soit *ab intestat* exempts de tout droit de detraction ou autre droit de ce genre, sauf néanmoins les droits locaux, tant et si longtems qu'il n'en sera point etabli de pareils par les dits Etats-unis ou aucun d'iceux. Les sujets du Roi Très chretien jouiront de leur côté, dans tous les Domaines des dits Etats d'une entière et parfaite reciprocité relativement aux stipulations renfermées dans le present Article.

Mais il est convenue en même tems que son contems ne portera aucune atteinte aux loix promulguées en France contre les émigrations, ou qui pourront être promulguées dans la suite, les quelles demeureront dans toute leur force et vigueur. Les Etats-unis de leur côté ou aucun d'entr'eux, seront libres de statüer sur cette matière telle loi qu'ils jugeront à propos.

Art. 14.

Les Navires Marchands des deux parties qui seront destinés pour des Ports appartenans à une Puissance ennemie de l'autre Allié, et dont le voïage ou la nature des marchandises dont ils seront chargés donneroit de justes soupçons, seront tenus d'éxhiber, soit en haute Mer, soit dans les Ports et havres non-seulement leurs passeports, mais encore les Certificats qui constateront expressement que leur chargement n'est pas de la qualité de ceux qui sont prohibés comme contrebande.

Art. 15.

Si l'exhibition des dits Certificats conduit à découvrir que le Navire porte des merchandises prohibées et reputées contrebande consignées pour un Port ennemi, il ne sera pas permis de briser les écoutilles des dits Navires, ni d'ouvrir aucune Caisse, Coffre, Malle, Ballots, Tonneaux, et autres Caisses qui s'y trouveront, ou d'en déplacer et détourner la moindre partie des marchandises, soit que le Navire apartienne aux sujets du Roi Très Chretien ou aux habitans des Etats unis jusqu'a ce que la Cargaison ait été mise à terre en presence des Officiers des Cours d'Amirauté, et que l'Inventaire en ait ete fait; mais on ne permettra pas de vendre, échanger ou aliéner les navires ou leur Cargaison en manière quelconque avant que le procès ait été fait et parfait legalement pour déclarer la contrebande, et que les Cours d'Amirauté auront prononcé leur confiscation par Jugement sans préjudice néanmoins des Navires ainsi que des marchandises, qui, en vertu du Traité doivent être censées libres. Il ne sera pas permis de retenir ces marchandises sous pretexte qu'elles ont été entachées par les marchandises de Contrebande, et bien moins encore de les confisquer comme des prises légales. Dans le cas où une partie seulement en non la totalité du chargement consisteroit en marchandises de Contrebande, et que le Commandant du Vaisseau consente à les délivrer au Corsaire qui les aura découverts, àlors le Capitaine qui aura fait la prise après avoir reçu ces marchandises doit incontinent relâcher le Navire et ne doit l'empêcher, en aucune manière, de continuer son voïage. Mais dans le cas où les marchandises de contrebande ne pourroient pas être toutes chargées sur le Vaisseau capteur, àlors le Capitaine du de. Vaisseau sera le maitre, malgré l'offre de remettre la contrebande, de conduire le patron dans le plus prochain port, conformement à ce qui est préscrit plus haut.

Art. 16.

On est convenu au contraire que tout ce qui se trouvera chargé par les sujets respectifs sur des Navires apartenans aux ennemis de l'autre partie, ou à leurs sujets sera confisqué sans distinction des marchandises prohibées ou non prohibées, ainsi et de même que si elles apartenoient à l'ennemi, à l'exception toute fois des effets et marchandises qui auront été mis à bord des dits navires avant la déclaration de guerre, ou même après la de. déclaration, si au moment du chargement on a pu l'ignorer, de manière que les marchandises des sujets des deux parties, soit qu'elles se trouvent du nombre de celles de contrebande ou autrement, les quelles comme il vient d'être dit auront été mises àbord, d'un Vaisseau apartenant à l'ennemi avant la guerre ou même après la de. déclaration, lorsqu'on l'ignoroit ne seront, en aucune manière, sujetes à confiscation, mais seront fidèlement et de bonne foi rendües sans delai à leurs propriétaires qui les reclameront; bien entendu néanmoins qu'il ne soit pas permis de porter dans les Ports ennemis les marchandises qui seront de contrebande. Les deux parties contractantes conviennent que le terme de deux mois passés depuis la déclaration de guerre, leurs sujets respectifs, de quelque partie du monde qu'ils viennent ne pourront plus alléguer l'ignorance dont il est question dans le present article.

ART. 17.

Et afin de pourvoir plus efficacement à la sûreté des sujets des deux parties contractantes, pour qu'il ne leur soit fait aucun prejudice par les Vaisseaux de guerre de l'autre partie ou par des Armateurs particuliers, il sera fait défense à tous Capitaines des Vaisseaux de Sa Majesté très Chretienne et des dits Etats-unis, et à tous leurs sujets de faire aucun dommage ou insulte à ceux de l'autre partie, et au cas où ils y contreviendroient ils en seront punis et de plus ils seront tenus et obligés en leurs personnes et en leurs biens de reparer tous les dommages et intérêts.

ART. 18.

Tous Vaisseaux et marchandises de quelque nature que ce puisse être, lorsqu'ils auront été enlevés des mains de quelques Pirates en pleine Mer, seront amenés dans quelque Port de l'un des deux Etats, et seront remis à la garde des Officiers du de. Port, àfin d'être rendus, en entier, a leur veritable propriétaire, aussitôt qu'il aura düement et sufisament fait conster de sa propriété.

ART. 19.

Les vaisseaux de guerre de Sa Majesté Très Chretienne et ceux des Etats-unis, de même que ceux que leurs sujets auront armés en guerre, pourront, en toute liberté; conduire où bon leur semblera les prises qu'ils auront faites sur leurs ennemis, sans être obligés à aucuns droits, soit des Sieurs Amiraux ou de l'Amirauté, ou d'aucuns autres, sans qu'aussi les dits Vaisseaux ou les des. prises, entrant dans les havres ou Ports de Sa Majesté Très Chretienne ou des dits Etats-unis puissent être arrêtés ou saisis, ni que les Officiers des lieux puissent prendre connoissance de la validité des des. prises, les quelles pourront sortir et être conduites franchement et en toute liberté aux lieux portés par les Commissions dont les Capitaines des dits Vaisseaux seront obligés de faire aparoir. Et au contraire ne sera donné asile ni retraite dans leurs ports ou havres à ceux qui auront fait des prises sur les sujets de Sa Majesté ou des dits Etats unis; Et s'ils sont forcés d'y entrer par tempête ou peril de la Mer, ou les fera sortir le plustôt qu'il sera possible.

ART. 20.

Dans le cas où un vaisseau apartenant à l'un des deux Etats ou à leurs sujets, aura échoué, fait naufrage ou souffert quelqu'autre dommage sur les Côtes ou sous la Domination de l'une des deux parties, il sera donné toute aide et assistance amiable aux personnes naufragées ou qui se trouvent en danger, et il leur sera accordé des sauf conduits pour assûrer leur passage et leur retour dans leur patrie.

ART. 21.

Lorsque les sujets et habitans de l'une des deux parties avec leurs Vaisseaux soit publics et de guerre, soit particuliers et marchands, seront forcés par une tempête, par la poursuite des Pirates et des ennemis, ou par quelqu'autre nécessité urgente de chercher refuge et un abri, de se retirer et entre dans quelqu'une des Rivières, Bayes, rades au Ports de l'une des deux parties, ils seront reçus et traités avec humanité, et jouiront de toute amitié protection et assistance, et il leur sera permis de se pourvoir de rafraichissemens, de vivres et de toutes choses nécessaires pour leur subsistance, pour la reparation de leurs Vaisseaux, et pour continüer leur voïage, le tout moïennant un prix raisonable, et ils ne seront retenus, en aucune manière ni empêchés de sortir des dits ports ou rades, mais pourront se retirer et partir quand, et comme il leur plaira sans aucun obstacle ni empêchement.

ART. 22.

Afin de promouvoir d'autant mieux le Commerce de deux Côtés, il est convenu que dans le cas où la guerre surviendroit entre les deux Nations susdites, il sera accordé, six mois après le déclaration de guerre, aux marchands dans les Villes et Cités qu'ils habitent, pour rassembler et transporter les marchandises, et s'il en est enlevé quelque chose, ou s'il leur a été fait quelqu'injure durant le terme préscrit ci-dessus, par l'une des deux parties, leurs peuples ou sujets, il leur sera donné à cet égard pleine et entière satisfaction.

ART. 23.

Aucun sujet du Roi Très Chretien ne prendra de commission ou de lettres de marque pour armer quelque Vaisseau ou Vaisseaux à l'effet d'agir comme Corsaires contre les dits Etats-unis ou quelques uns d'entr'eux, ou contre les sujets, peuples ou habitans d'iceux, ou contre leur propriété ou celle des habitans d'aucun d'entr'eux, de quelque Prince que ce soit avec lequel les dits Etats-unis seront en guerre. De même aucun Citoïen, sujet ou habitant des susdits Etats-unis et de quelqu'un d'entr'eux ne demandera ni n'acceptera aucune commission ou lettres de marque pour armer quelque Vaisseau, ou Vaisseaux pour courre sus aux sujets de Sa Majesté Très chretienne ou quelques uns d'entre eux ou leur propriété de quelque Prince ou Etat que ce soit avec qui Sa de. Majesté se trouvera en guerre, et si quelqu'un de l'une ou de l'autre Nation prenoit de pareilles commissions ou lettres de marque il sera puni comme Pirate.

ART. 24.

Il ne sera permis à aucun Corsaire étranger non apartenant à quelque sujet de Sa Majesté Très chretienne ou à un Citoïen des dits Etats-unis, lequel aura une commission de la part d'un Prince ou d'une Puissance en guerre avec l'une des deux Nations, d'armer leurs Vaisseaux dans les Ports de l'une des deux parties, ni d'y vendre les prises qu'il aura faites, ni décharger en autre manière quelconque les Vaisseaux, marchandises ou aucune partie de leur Cargaison; Il ne sera même pas permis d'acheter d'autres vivres que ceux qui lui seront nécessaires pour se rendre dans le Port le plus voisin du Prince ou de l'Etat dont il tient sa commission.

ART. 25.

Il sera permis à tous et un chacun des sujets du Roi Très chretien et aux Citoïens, peuple et habitans des susdits Etats-unis de naviguer avec leurs Batimens avec toute liberté et sûreté, sans qu'il puisse être fait d'exception à cet égard, à raison des propriétaires des marchandises chargées sur les dits Batimens venant de quelque Port que ce soit, et destinés pour quelque place d'une Puissance actuellement ennemie ou qui pourra l'être dans la suite de Sa Majesté Très Chretienne ou des Etats-unis. Il sera permis également aux sujets et habitans susmentionnés de naviguer avec leurs Vaisseaux et marchandises, et de fréquenter avec la même liberté et sûreté les Places; Ports et havres des Puissances ennemies des deux parties contractantes ou d'une d'entre Elles, sans opposition ni trouble et de faire le Commerce nonseulement directement des Ports de l'ennemi susdit à un port neutre, mais aussi d'un Port ennemi à un autre Port ennemi, soit qu'il se trouve sous sa jurisdiction ou sous celle de plusieurs; Et il est stipulé par le present Traité que les Batimens libres assûreront également la liberté des marchandises, et qu'on jugera libres toutes les choses qui se trouveront àbord des Navires apartenants aux sujets d'une des parties contractantes, quand même le chargement ou partie d'icelui apartiendroit aux ennemis de l'une des deux, bien entendu néanmoins que la contrebande sera toujours exceptée. Il est également convenu que cette même liberté s'étendroit aux personnes qui pourroient se trouver àbord du Batiment libre, quand même Elles seroient ennemies de l'une des deux parties contractantes, et Elles ne pourront être enlevées des dits Navires, àmoins qu'Elles ne soient militaires, et actuellement au service de l'Ennemi.

ART. 26.

Cette liberté de navigation et de Commerce doit s'étendre sur toutes sortes de marchandises, à l'exception seulement de celles qui sont designées sous le nom de contrebande. Sous ce nom de contrebande ou de marchandises prohibées doivent être compris les armes, Canons, bombes avec leurs fusées et autres choses y relatives, boulets, poudre à tirer, méches, piques, epées, lances, dards, hallebardes, mortiers, petards, grenades, salpêtre, fusils, Balles, Boucliers Casques, Cuirasses, Cote de mailles et autres armes de cette espèce propres à armer les soldats, porte-mousqueton, baudriers, chevaux avec leurs Equipages, et tous autres instrumens de guerre quelconques. Les marchandises dénommées ci-après ne seront pas comprises parmi la contrebande ou choses prohibées, savoir toutes sortes de draps et toutes autres étoffes de laine, lin, soye, cotton ou d'autres matieres quelconques; Toutes sortes de vétemens avec les étoffes dont on a coutume de les faire, l'or et l'argent monnoïé ou non, l'étain, le fer, laiton cuivre, airain, charbons, de même que le froment et l'orge et toute autre sorte de bleds et legumes; Le tabac et toutes les sortes d'épiceries, la viande salée et fumée, poisson sallé, fromage et beurre, bierre, huiles, vins, sucres et toute espece de sel, et en général toutes provisions servant pour la nourriture de l'homme et pour le soutien de la vie; De plus toutes sortes de coton, de chanvre, lin, goudron, poix, cordes, cables, voiles, toiles à voiles, ancres, parties d'ancres,

mats, planches, madriers, et bois de toute espèce et toutes autres choses propres
à la construction et reparation des Vaisseaux et autres matieres quelconques qui
n'ont pas la forme d'un instrument préparé pour la guerre par terre comme par
Mer, ne seront pas reputées contrebande, et encore moins celles qui sont déja
preparées pour quelqu'autre usage: Toutes les choses denommées ci-dessus
doivent être comprises parmi les marchandises libres de même que toutes les
autres marchandises et effets qui ne sont pas compris et particulièrement nommés
dans l'enumeration des marchandises de Contrebande; De manière qu'elles pourront être transportées et conduites de la manière la plus libre par les sujets des
deux parties contractantes dans des places ennemies, à l'exception néanmoins de
celles qui se trouveroient actuellement assiégées bloquées ou investies.
    ART. 27.
    Afin d'écarter et de prévenir de part et d'autre toutes discussions et querelles,
il a été convenu que dans le cas ou l'une des deux parties se trouveroit engagée
dans une guerre, les Vaisseaux et Batimens apartenans aux sujets ou Peuple
de l'autre Allié devront être pourvus de lettres de Mer, ou passeports, les quels
exprimeront le nom, la propriété et le port du Navire, ainsi que le nom et la
demeure du maitre ou Commandant du de. Vaisseau àfin qu'il aparoisse par là
que le même vaisseau apartient réellement et véritablement aux sujets de l'une
des deux parties contractantes, le quel passeport devra être expédié selon le
modèle annexé au present Traité. Ces passeports devront également être
renouvellés chaque année dans le cas ou le Vaisseau retourne chez lui dans
l'espace d'une année. Il a été convenu également que les Vaisseaux susmentionnés, dans le cas où ils seroient chargés devront être pourvus nonseulement
de passeports, mais aussi de Certificats contenant le détail de la Cargaison, le
lieu d'ou le Vaisseau est parti et la déclaration des marchandises de Contrebande
qui pourroient se trouver àbord; Les quels Certificats devront être expédiés dans
la forme accoutumée par les officiers du lieu d'où le Vaisseau aura fait voile,
Et s'il étoit jugé utile ou prudent d'exprimer dans les dits passeports la personne
à la quelle les marchandises apartiennent, on pourra le faire librement.
    ART. 28.
    Dans le cas ou les Vaisseaux des sujets et habitans de l'une des deux parties
contractantes aprocheroient des côtes de l'autre, sans cependant avoir le dessein
d'entrer dans le port, ou après être entré, sans avoir le dessein de décharger la
Cargaison ou rempre leur charge, on se conduira à leur égard suivant les
réglemens généraux préscrits ou à prescrire relativement à l'objet dont il est
question.
    ART. 29.
    Lorsqu'un Batiment apartenant aux dits sujets, peuple et habitans de l'une
des deux parties, sera recontre navigant le long des Côtes ou en pleine Mer par
un vaisseau de guerre de l'autre, ou par un Armateur, le dit Vaisseau de guerre
ou Armateur, afin d'éviter tout désordre, se tiendra hors de la portée du Canon,
et pourra envoïer sa Chaloupe àbord du Batiment marchand et y faire entrer
deux ou trois hommes auxquels le Maitre ou Commandant du Batiment mon-
trera son passeport, lequel devra être conforme à la formule annexée au present

Traité, et constatera la propriété du Batiment, et après que le dit Batiment aura exhibé un pareil passeport, il lui sera libre de continüer son voïage, et il ne sera pas permis de le molester ni de chercher, en aucune manière, de lui donner la chasse ou de le forcer de quiter la Course qu'ils s'etoit proposée.

ART. 30.

Il est convenu que lorsque les marchandises auront été chargées sur les Vaisseaux ou Batimens de l'une des deux parties contractantes, elles ne pourront plus être assujeties à aucune visite; Toute visite et recherche devant être faite avant le chargement, et les marchandises prohibées devant être arrêtées et saisies sur la plage avant de pouvoir être embarquées à moins qu'on n'ait des indices manifestes ou des preuves de versemens frauduleux. De même aucun des Sujets de Sa Majesté Très Chretienne ou des Etats-unis, ni leurs marchandises ne pourront être arrêtés ni molestés pour cette cause par aucune espèce d'embargo; Et les seuls sujets de l'Etat, auxquels les des. marchandises auront été prohibées, et qui se seront emancipés à vendre et aliener de pareilles marchandises, seront düement punis pour cette contravention.

ART. 31.

Les deux parties contractantes se sont accordées mutuellement la faculté de tenir dans leurs ports respectifs des Consuls, Vice-Consuls, Agents et Commissaires, dont les fonctions seront reglées par une Convention particulière.

ART. 32.

Pour d'autant plus favoriser et faciliter le Commerce que les sujets des Etats-unis feront avec la France, le Roi Très Chretien leur accordera en Europe un ou plusieurs ports francs dans les quels ils pourront amener et débiter toutes les denrées et marchandises provenant des treize Etats-unis; Sa Majesté conservera d'un autre côté aux sujets des dits Etats les ports francs qui ont été et sont ouverts dans les Isles françoises de l'Amerique. De tous les quels Ports francs les dits sujets des Etats-unis jouiront conformement aux règlemens qui en déterminent l'usage.

ART. 33.

Le present Traité sera ratifié de part et d'autre et les ratifications seront echangées dans l'espace de six mois ou plustôt si faire se peut.

EN FOI de quoi les Plenipotentiaires respectifs ont signé les articles ci-dessus tant en langue françoise qu'en langue Angloise; Déclarant néanmoins que le present Traité a eté originairement redigé et arrêté en langue françoise; Et Ils y ont apposé le cachet de leurs armes.

FAIT à Paris le sixième jour du mois de fevrier mil sept cent soixante dix huit.

C. A. GERARD   B. FRANKLIN   SILAS DEANE   ARTHUR LEE[2]
   [Seal]   [Seal]   [Seal]   [Seal]

---

[1] At this point and following the words "Art. 12." the symbol "X" appears; and there is a note in the margin, probably meant for a later copyist, which reads: "to be omitted, & the subsequent numbers changed accordingly." This refers to an agreement of September 1, 1778, between France and the United States eliminating Articles 11 and 12 from the Treaty. See PCC, item 85, M247, roll 114, DNA.

[2] The treaty, in the hand of an unknown French clerk, is Treaty Series 83, RG 11, DNA. It is related to Thomas Jefferson's report journalized January 19, 1791.

(English Translation)

The most Christian King, and the thirteen United States of North America, to wit, New-Hampshire, Massachusetts Bay, Rhodeisland, Connecticut, New York, New-Jersey, Pennsylvania, Delaware, Maryland, Virginia, North-Carolina, South Carolina, & Georgia, willing to fix in an equitable and permanent manner the Rules which ought to be followed relative to the Correspondence & Commerce which the two Parties desire to establish between their respective Countries, States, and Subjects, his most Christian Majesty and the said United States have judged that the said End could not be better obtained than by taking for the Basis of their Agreement the most perfect Equality and Reciprocity, and by carefully avoiding all those burthensome Preferences, which are usually Sources of Debate, Embarrasment and Discontent; by leaving also each Party at Liberty to make, respecting Commerce and Navigation, those interior Regulations which it shall find most convenient to itself; and by founding the Advantage of Commerce solely upon reciprocal Utility, and the just Rules of free Intercourse; reserving withal to each Party the Liberty of admitting at its pleasure other Nations to a Participation of the same Advantages. It is in the Spirit of this Intention, and to fulfil these Views, that his said Majesty having named and appointed for his Plenipotentiary Conrad Alexander Gerard, Royal *Sindic* of the City of Strasbourg, Secretary of his Majesty's Council of State, and the United States on their Part, having fully impower'd Benjamin Franklin Deputy from the State of Pennsylvania to the general Congress, and President of the Convention of said State, Silas Deane late Deputy from the State of Connecticut to the said Congress, and Arthur Lee Councellor at Law; The said respective Plenipotentiaries after exchanging their Powers, and after mature Deliberation, have concluded and agreed upon the following Articles.

ARTICLE. 1ST.

There shall be a firm, inviolable and universal Peace, and a true and sincere Friendship between the most Christian King, his Heirs and Successors, and the United States of America; and the Subjects of the most Christian King and of the said States; and between the Countries, Islands, Cities, and Towns, situate under the Jurisdiction of the most Christian King, and of the said United States, and the People and Inhabitants of every Degree; without exception of Persons or Places; & the Terms herein after mentioned shall be perpetual between the most Christian King his Heirs and Successors and the said United States.

ART. 2ND.

The most Christian King, and the United States engage mutually not to grant any particular Favour to other Nations in respect of Commerce and Navigation, which shall not immediately become common to the other Party, who shall enjoy the same Favour, freely, if the Concession was freely made, or on allowing the same Compensation, if the Concession was Conditional.

ART. 3D.

The Subjects of the most Christian King shall pay in the Ports, Havens, Roads, Countries Islands, Cities or Towns, of the United States or any of them, no other or greater Duties or Imposts, of what Nature soever they may be, or by what Name soever called, than those which the Nations most favoured are or shall be obliged to pay; and they shall enjoy all the Rights, Liberties, Privileges, Immunities and Exemptions in Trade, Navigation and Commerce, whether in passing from one Port in the said States to another, or in going to and from the same, from and to any Part of the World, which the said Nations do or shall enjoy.

ART. 4.

The Subjects, People and Inhabitants of the said United States, and each of them, shall not pay in the Ports, Havens Roads, Isles, Cities & Places under the Domination of his most Christian Majesty in Europe, any other or greater Duties or Imposts, of what Nature soever, they may be, or by what Name soever called, than those which the most favour'd Nations are or shall be obliged to pay; & they shall enjoy all the Rights, Liberties, Privileges, Immunities & Exemptions, in Trade, Navigation and Commerce, whether in passing from one Port in the said Dominions in Europe to another, or in going to and from the same, from and to any Part of the World, which the said Nations do or shall enjoy.

ART. 5.

In the above Exemption is particularly comprised the Imposition of 100 Sols ℗ Ton, established in France on foreign Ships; unless when the Ships of the United States shall load with the Merchandize of France for another Port of the same Dominion, in which Case the said Ships shall pay the Duty above-mentioned so long as other Nations the most favour'd shall be obliged to pay it. But it is understood that the said United States or any of them are at Liberty when they shall judge it proper, to establish a Duty equivalent in the same Case.

ART. 6.

The most Christian King shall endeavour by all the means in his Power to protect and defend all Vessels and the Effects belonging to the Subjects, People or Inhabitants of the said United States, or any of them, being in his Ports, Havens or Roads or on the Seas near to his Countries, Islands, Cities or Towns and to recover and restore to the right owners, their agents or Attornies all such Vessels & Effects, which shall be taken within his Jurisdiction; and the Ships of War of his most Christian Majesty or any Convoys sailing under his authority shall upon all Occasions take under their Protection all Vessels belonging to the Subjects, People or Inhabitants of the said United States, or any of them & holding the same Course or going the same Way, and shall defend such Vessels, as long as they hold the same Course or go the same way, against all Attacks, Force and Violence in the same manner, as they ought to protect and defend the Vessels belonging to the Subjects of the most Christian King.

ART. 7.

In like manner the said United States and their Ships of War sailing under their Authority shall protect and defend, conformable to the Tenor of the preceeding Article, all the Vessels and Effects belonging to the Subjects of the most Christian King; and use all their Endeavours to recover & cause to be restored the said Vessels & Effects, that shall have been taken within the Jurisdiction of the said United States or any of them.

ART. 8.

The most Christian King will employ his good Offices and Interposition with the King or Emperor of Morocco or Fez, the Regencies of Algier, Tunis and Tripoli, or with any of them, and also with every other Prince, State or Power of the Coast of Barbary in Africa, and the Subjects of the said King Emperor, States and Powers, and each of them; in order to provide as fully and efficaciously as possible for the Benefit, Conveniency and Safety of the said United States, and each of them, their Subjects, People, and Inhabitants, and their Vessels and Effects, against all Violence, Insult, Attacks, or Depredations on the Part of the said Princes and States of Barbary, or their Subjects.

ART. 9.

The Subjects, Inhabitants, Merchants, Commanders of Ships, Masters and Mariners of the States, Provinces and Dominions of each Party respectively shall abstain and forbear to fish in all Places possessed or which shall be possessed by the other Party: The most Christian Kings Subjects shall not fish in the Havens, Bays, Creeks, Roads Coasts or Places, which the said united States hold or shall hereafter hold; and in like manner the Subjects, People and Inhabitants of the said United States shall not fish in the Havens Bays, Creeks, Roads, Coasts or Places, which the most Christian King possesses or shall hereafter possess; and if any Ship or Vessel shall be found fishing contrary to the Tenor of this Treaty, the said Ship or Vessel with its lading, proof being made thereof, shall be confiscated. It is however understood, that the Exclusion stipulated in the present Article shall take place only so long, and so far as the most Christian King or the United States shall not in this respect have granted an Exemption to some other Nation.

ART. 10.

The United States their Citizens and Inhabitants shall never disturb the Subjects, of the most Christian King in the Enjoyment and Exercise of the Right of Fishing on the Banks of Newfoundland; nor in the indefinite and exclusive Right which belongs to them on that Part of the Coast of that Island which is designed by the Treaty of Utrecht; nor in the Rights relative to all and each of the Isles which belong to his most Christian Majesty; the whole conformable to the true Sense of the Treaties of Utrecht and Paris.

ART. 11.[1]

It is agreed and concluded that there shall never be any Duty imposed on the Exportation of the Mellasses that may be taken by the Subjects of any of the United States from the Islands of America which belong or may hereafter appertain to his most Christian Majesty.

ART. 12.

In compensation of the Exemption stipulated by the preceeding Article, it is agreed and concluded that there shall never be any Duties imposed on the Exportation of any kind of Merchandize which the Subjects of his most Christian Majesty may take from the Countries and Possessions present or future of any of the thirteen United States, for the Use of the Islands which shall furnish Mellasses.

ART. 13.

The Subjects and Inhabitants of the said United States, or any one of them, shall not be reputed Aubains in France, & consequently shall be exempted from the *Droit d'Aubaine* or other similar Duty under what name soever. They may by Testament, Donation, or otherwise dispose of their Goods moveable and immoveable in favour of such Persons as to them shall seem good; and their Heirs, Subjects of the said United States, residing whether in France or else where, may succeed them *ab intestat,* without being obliged to obtain Letters of Naturalization, and without having the Effect of this Concession contested or impeded under Pretext of any Rights or Prerogatives of Provinces, Cities, or Private Persons. And the said Heirs, whether such by particular Title, or *ab intestat,* shall be exempt from all Duty called *Droit de Detraction,* or other Duty of the same kind; saving nevertheless, the local Rights or Duties as much and as long as similar ones are not established by the United States or any of them. The Subjects of the most Christian King shall enjoy on their Part, in all the Dominions of the sd. States, an entire and perfect Reciprocity relative to the Stipulations contained in the present Article.

But it is at the same Time agreed that its Contents shall not affect the Laws made or that may be made hereafter in France against Emigrations, which shall remain in all their Force and Vigour; and the United States on their Part, or any of them, shall be at Liberty to enact such Laws relative to that Matter, as to them shall seem proper.

ART. 14.

The merchant Ships of either of the Parties, which shall be making into a Port belonging to the Enemy of the other Ally and concerning whose Voyage & the Species of Goods on board her there shall be just Grounds of Suspicion shall be obliged to exhibit as well upon the high Seas as in the Ports and Havens not only her Passports, but likewise Certificates expressly shewing that her Goods are not of the Number of those, which have been prohibited as contraband.

ART. 15.

If by the exhibiting of the above said Certificates, the other Party discover there are any of those Sorts of Goods, which are prohibited and declared contraband and consigned for a Port under the Obedience of his Enemies, it shall not be Lawful to break up the Hatches of such Ship, or to open any Chest, Coffers, Packs, Casks, or any other Vessels found therein, or to remove the smallest Parcels of her Goods, whether such Ship belongs to the Subjects of France or the Inhabitants of the said United States, unless the lading be brought on Shore in the presence of the Officers of the Court of Admiralty and an Inventory thereof made; but there shall be no allowance to sell, exchange, or alienate the same in any manner, untill after that due and lawful Process shall have been had against such prohibited Goods, and the Court of Admiralty shall, by a Sentence pronounced, have confiscated the same: saving always as well the Ship itself as any other Goods found therein, which by this Treaty are to be esteemed free: neither may they be detained on pretence of their being as it were infected by the prohibited Goods, much less shall they be confiscated as lawful Prize: But if not the whole Cargo, but only part thereof shall consist of prohibited or contraband Goods and the Commander of the Ship shall be ready and willing to deliver them to the Captor, who has discovered them, in such Case the Captor having received those Goods shall forthwith discharge the Ship and not hinder her by any means freely to prosecute the Voyage, on which she was bound. But in Case the Contraband Merchandises, cannot be all receiv'd on board the Vessel of the Captor, then the Captor may, notwithstanding the Offer of delivering him the Contraband Goods, carry the Vessel into the nearest Port agreable to what is above directed.

ART. 16.

On the contrary it is agreed, that whatever shall be found to be laden by the Subjects, and Inhabitants of either Party on any Ship belonging to the Enemy's of the other or to their Subjects, the whole although it be not of the Sort of prohibited Goods may be confiscated in the same manner, as if it belonged to the Enemy, except such Goods and Merchandizes as were put on board such Ship before the Declaration of War, or even after such Declaration, if so be it were done without knowledge of such Declaration. So that the Goods of the Subjects and People of either Party, whether they be of the Nature of such as are prohibited or otherwise, which, as is aforesaid were put on board any Ship belonging to an Enemy before the War, or after the Declaration of the same, without the Knowledge of it, shall no ways be liable to confiscation, but shall well and truely be restored without Delay to the proprietors demanding the same; but so as that, if the said Merchandizes be contraband, it shall not be any Ways lawful to carry them afterwards to any Ports belonging to the Enemy. The two contracting Parties agree, that the Term of two Months being passed after the Declaration of War, their respective Subjects, from whatever Part of the World they come, shall not plead the Ignorance mentioned in this Article.

ART. 17.

And that more effectual Care may be taken for the Security of the Subjects and Inhabitants of both Parties, that they suffer no injury by the men of War or Privateers of the other Party, all the Commanders of the Ships of his most Christian Majesty & of the said United States and all their Subjects and Inhabitants shall be forbid doing any Injury or Damage to the other Side; and if they act to the contrary, they shall be punished and shall moreover be bound to make Satisfaction for all Matter of Damage, and the Interest thereof, by reparation, under the Pain and obligation of their Person and Goods.

ART. 18.

All Ships and Merchandizes of what Nature soever which shall be rescued out of the Hands of any Pirates or Robbers on the high Seas, shall be brought into some Port of either State and shall be delivered to the Custody of the Officers of that Port, in order to be restored entire to the true Proprietor as soon as due and sufficient Proof shall be made concerning the Property thereof.

ART. 19.

It shall be lawful for the Ships of War of either Party & Privateers freely to carry whithersoever they please the Ships and Goods taken from their Enemies, without being obliged to pay any Duty to the Officers of the Admiralty or any other Judges; nor shall such Prizes be arrested or seized, when they come to and enter the Ports of either Party; nor shall the Searchers or other Officers of those Places search the same or make examination concerning the Lawfulness of such Prizes, but they may hoist Sail at any time and depart and carry their Prizes to the Places express'd in their Commissions, which the Commanders of such Ships of War shall be obliged to shew: On the contrary no Shelter or Refuge shall be given in their Ports to such as shall have made Prize of the Subjects, People or Property of either of the Parties; but if such shall come in, being forced by Stress of Weather or the Danger of the Sea, all proper means shall be vigorously used that they go out and retire from thence as soon as possible.

ART. 20.

If any Ship belonging to either of the Parties their People or Subjects, shall, within the Coasts or Dominions of the other, stick upon the Sands or be wrecked or suffer any other Damage, all friendly Assistance and Relief shall be given to the Persons shipwrecked or such as shall be in danger thereof; and Letters of safe Conduct shall likewise be given to them for their free and quiet Passage from thence, and the return of every one to his own Country.

ART. 21.

In Case the Subjects and Inhabitants of either Party with their shipping whether publick and of War or private and of Merchants, be forced, through Stress of Weather, pursuit of Pirates or Enemies, or any other urgent necessity for seeking of Shelter and Harbour, to retreat and enter into any of the Rivers, Bays, Roads or Ports belonging to the other Party, they shall be received and treated with all humanity and Kindness and enjoy all friendly Protection & Help; and they shall be permitted to refresh and provide themselves at reasonable Rates with victuals and all things needful for the sustenence of their Persons or reparation of their Ships and conveniency of their Voyage; and they shall no Ways be detained or hindred from returning out of the said Ports or Roads but may remove and depart when and whither they please without any let or hindrance.

ART. 22.

For the better promoting of Commerce on both Sides, it is agreed that if a War shall break out between the said two Nations, six Months after the Proclamation of War shall be allowed to the Merchants in the Cities and Towns, where they live, for selling and transporting their Goods and Merchandizes; and if any thing be taken from them, or any Injury be done them within that Term by either Party or the People or Subjects of either, full Satisfaction shall be made for the same.

ART. 23.

No Subjects of the most Christian King shall apply for or take any Commission or Letters of marque for arming any Ship or Ships to act as Privateers against the said United States or any of them or against the Subjects People or Inhabitants of the said United States or any of them or against the Property of any of the Inhabitants of any of them from any Prince or State with which the said United States shall be at War. Nor shall any Citizen Subject or Inhabitant of the said United States or any of them apply for or take any Commission or letters of marque for arming any Ship or Ships to act as Privateers against the Subjects of the most Christian King or any of them or the Property of any of them from any Prince or State with which the said King shall be at War: And if any Person of either Nation shall take such Commissions or Letters of Marque he shall be punished as a Pirate.

ART. 24.

It shall not be lawful for any foreign Privateers, not belonging to Subjects of the most Christian King nor Citizens of the said United States, who have Commissions from any other Prince or State in enmity with either Nation to fit their Ships in the Ports of either the one or the other of the aforesaid Parties, to sell what they have taken or in any other manner whatsoever to exchange their Ships, Merchandizes or any other lading; neither shall they be allowed even to purchase victuals except such as shall be necessary for their going to the next Port of that Prince or State from which they have Commissions.

ART. 25.

It shall be lawful for all and singular the Subjects of the most Christian King and the Citizens People and Inhabitants of the said United States to sail with their Ships with all manner of Liberty and Security; no distinction being made, who are the Proprietors of the Merchandizes laden thereon, from any Port to the places of those who now are or hereafter shall be at Enmity with the most Christian King or the United States. It shall likewise be Lawful for the Subjects and Inhabitants aforesaid to sail with the Ships and Merchandizes afore-mentioned and to trade with the same Liberty and security from the Places, Ports and Havens of those who are Enemies of both or either Party without any Opposition or disturbance whatsoever, not only directly from the Places of the Enemy afore mentioned to neutral Places; but also from one Place belonging to an Enemy to another place belonging to an Enemy, whether they be under the Jurisdiction of the same Prince or under several; And it is hereby stipulated that free Ships shall also give a freedom to Goods, and that every thing shall be deemed to be free and exempt, which shall be found on board the Ships belonging to the Subjects of either of the Confederates, although the whole lading or any Part thereof should appertain to the Enemies of either, contraband Goods being always excepted. It is also agreed in like manner that the same Liberty be extended to Persons, who are on board a free Ship, with this Effect, that although they be Enemies to both or either Party, they are not to be taken out of that free Ship, unless they are Soldiers and in actual Service of the Enemies.

ART. 26.

This Liberty of Navigation and Commerce shall extend to all kinds of Merchandizes, excepting those only which are distinguished by the name of contraband; And under this Name of Contraband or prohibited Goods shall be comprehended, Arms, great Guns, Bombs with the fuzes, and other things belonging to them, Cannon Ball, Gun powder, Match, Pikes, Swords, Lances, Spears, halberds, Mortars, Petards, Granades Salt Petre, Muskets, Musket Ball, Bucklers, Helmets, breast Plates, Coats of Mail and the like kinds of Arms proper for arming Soldiers, Musket rests, belts, Horses with their Furniture, and all other Warlike Instruments whatever. These Merchandizes which follow shall not be reckoned among Contraband or prohibited Goods, that is to say, all sorts of Cloths, and all other Manufactures woven of any wool, Flax, Silk, Cotton or any other Materials whatever; all kinds of wearing Apparel to-gether with the Species, whereof they are used to be made; gold & Silver as well coined as uncoin'd, Tin, Iron, Latten, Copper, Brass Coals, as also Wheat and Barley and any other kind of Corn and pulse; Tobacco and likewise all manner of Spices; salted and smoked Flesh, salted fish, Cheese and Butter, Beer, Oils, Wines, Sugars and all sorts of Salts; & in general all Provisions, which serve for the nourishment of Mankind and the sustenance of Life; further more all kinds of Cotton, hemp, Flax, Tar, Pitch, Ropes, Cables, Sails, Sail Cloths Anchors and any Parts of Anchors, also Ships Masts, Planks, Boards and Beams of what Trees soever; and all other Things proper either for building or repairing Ships, and all other Goods whatever, which have not been worked into the form of any Instrument or thing prepared for War by Land or by Sea, shall not be reputed Contraband, much less such as have been already wrought and made up for any other Use; all which shall be wholly reckoned among free Goods: as likewise all other Merchandizes and things, which are not comprehended and particularly mentioned in the foregoing enumeration of contraband Goods: so that they may be transported and carried in the freest manner by the Subjects of both Confederates even to Places belonging to an Enemy such Towns or Places being only excepted as are at that time beseiged, blocked up or invested.

ART. 27.

To the End that all manner of Dissentions and Quarrels may be avoided and prevented on one Side and the other; it is agreed, that in case either of the Parties hereto should be engaged in War, the Ships and Vessels belonging to the Subjects or People of the other Ally must be furnished with Sea Letters or Passports expressing the name, Property and Bulk of the Ship as also the name and Place of habitation of the Master or Commander of the said Ship, that it may appear thereby, that the Ship really & truely belongs to the Subjects of one of the Parties, which Passport shall be made out and granted according to the Form annexed to this Treaty; they shall likewise be recalled every Year, that is if the Ship happens to return home within the Space of a Year. It is likewise agreed, that such Ships being laden are to be provided not only with Passports as above mentioned, but also with Certificates containing the several Particulars of the Cargo, the Place whence the Ship sailed and or whither she is bound, that so it may be known, whether any forbidden or contraband Goods be on board the same: which Certificates shall be made out by the Officers of the Place, whence the Ship set sail, in the accustomed Form. And if any one shall think it fit or adviseable to express in the said Certificates the Person to whom the Goods on board belong, he may freely do so.

ART. 28.

The Ships of the Subjects and Inhabitants of either of the Parties, coming upon any Coasts belonging to either of the said Allies, but not willing to enter into Port, or being entred into Port and not willing to unload their Cargoes or break Bulk, they shall be treated according to the general Rules prescribed or to be prescribed relative to the Object in Question.

ART. 29.

If the Ships of the said Subjects, People or Inhabitants of either of the Parties shall be met with either sailing along the Coasts or on the high Seas by any Ship of War of the other or by any Privateers, the said Ships of War or Privateers, for the avoiding of any Disorder shall remain out of Cannon Shot, and may send their Boats aboard the Merchant Ship, which they shall so meet with, and may enter her to number of two or three Men only to whom the Master or Commander of such Ship or Vessel shall exhibit his passport concerning the Property of the Ship made out according to the Form inserted in this present Treaty, and the Ship, when she shall have shewed such Passport shall be free and at Liberty to pursue her Voyage, so as it shall not be lawful to molest or search her in any manner or to give her chase, or force her to quit her intended Course.

ART. 30.

It is also agreed that all Goods, when once put on board the Ships or Vessels of either of the two contracting Parties shall be subject to no farther Visitation; but all Visitation or Search shall be made before hand, and all prohibited Goods shall be stopped on the Spot, before the same be put on board, unless there are manifest Tokens or Proofs of fraudulent Practice; nor shall either the Persons or goods of the Subjects of his most Christian Majesty or the United States be put under any arrest or molested by any other kind of Embargo for that Cause; and only the Subject of that State, to whom the said Goods have been or shall be prohibited and who shall presume to sell or alienate such sort of Goods shall be duly punished for the Offence.

ART. 31.

The two contracting Parties grant mutually the Liberty of having each in the Ports of the other, Consuls, Vice Consuls, Agents and Commissaries, whose Functions shall be regulated by a particular Agreement.

ART. 32.

And the more to favour and facilitate the Commerce which the Subjects of the United States may have with France, the most Christian King will grant them in Europe one or more free Ports, where they may bring and dispose of all the Produce and Merchandize of the thirteen United States; and his Majesty will also continue to the Subjects of the said States, the free Ports which have been and are open in the french Islands of America. Of all which free Ports, the said Subjects of the United States shall enjoy the Use, agreable to the Regulations which relate to them.

ART. 33.

The present Treaty shall be ratified on both Sides and the Ratifications shall be exchanged in the Space of Six Months, or sooner if possible.

IN FAITH whereof the respective Plenipotentiaries have signed the above Articles, both in the French and English Languages, declaring nevertheless that the present Treaty was originally composed and concluded in the French Language, and they have thereto affixed their Seals.

DONE AT Paris, this Sixth Day of February, one thousand seven hundred &
seventy eight.

C. A. GERARD   B. FRANKLIN   SILAS DEANE   ARTHUR LEE[2]
[Seal]   [Seal]   [Seal]   [Seal]

[1] On September 1, 1778, an agreement between United States and France eliminated
Articles 11 and 12 from the Treaty. See PCC, item 85, M247, roll 114, DNA.
[2] The treaty, in the hand of William Temple Franklin, is Treaty Series 83, RG 11,
DNA. E-16146, E-16147, E-16643, E-16644, E-43457, E-43585. It is related to
Thomas Jefferson's report journalized January 19, 1791.

M. Lambert à M. Jefferson

LETTRE de M. LAMBERT, Conseiller d'État & au Conseil royal de Finance & de
Commerce, Contrôleur général des finances, à M. Jefferson, Ministre plénipotentiaire des États-Unis d'Amérique près de Sa Majesté Très-Chrétienne.

Versailles, 29 Décembre 1787

J'AI l'honneur, Monsieur, de vous envoyer une copie de l'Arrêt qui vient d'être
rendu au Conseil pour l'encouragement du Commerce des États-unis de l'Amérique en France. Je vous en ferai passer un certain nombre d'exemplaires,
aussitôt qu'il sera imprimé.

Vous y verrez que plusieurs faveurs considérables qui n'avoient point encore
été promises au Commerce Américain, ont été ajoutées à celles que le Roi vous
avoit fait annoncer par la lettre qui vous a été écrite le 22 octobre de l'année
dernière.

Si dans l'intervalle, quelques droits ont été perçus contre les dispositions de
cette lettre, ils seront restitués sur la représentation des acquits.

J'ai donné ordre aussi que l'on vérifiât les faits au sujet desquels on vous a
rapporté que la décision du 24 mai 1786, relativement au commerce du Tabac,
n'avoit pas eu une entière exécution. Vous pouvez être assuré que, s'il est
prouvé qu'on se soit écarté des engagemens pris avec la sanction du Roi, il sera
scrupuleusement pourvu à y satisfaire.

Vous apprendrez encore avec plaisir que les mesures que j'ai prises pour
prévenir l'interruption du commerce des tabacs ont eu un plein succès.

Cette marchandise ne sera point exceptée de celles auxquelles l'entrepôt est
accordé. La Ferme générale ne jouira d'aucune préférence pour l'achat, & les
propriétaires seront complètement les maîtres de leurs spéculations, & d'envoyer
leurs tabacs par mer à l'Étranger.

Il sera seulement pris des mesures pour prévenir les fraudes auxquelles
l'entrepôt pourroit servir de prétexte, & les chambres du commerce des ports
seront consultées pour que les précautions nécessaires ne soient pas incompatibles
avec la liberté dont le Commerce doit jouir dans ses opérations.

Quoique l'approvisionnement actuel de la Ferme générale se monte à environ trois années de sa consommation, j'ai engagé cette Compagnie à continuer d'acheter par année, à compter du 1er. Janvier 1788, jusqu'à la fin de son bail, quatorze mille boucauds de tabac directement apportés dans les ports de France sur bâtimens François ou Américains, & de justifier tous les quartre mois que cet achat sera monté au moins à *quatre mille six cents soixante & six boucauds.*

Quant aux prix, vous avez senti vous-même la necessité de les laisser libres; & cette liberté des prix a été le premier objet des demandes faites par les négocians Américains & François, lors des réclamations qui se sont élevées contre le traité de M. Morris.

La résolution prise alors de forcer les approvisionnemens, quoiqu'à prix onéreux, au point qu'il en résulte que la ferme générale est maintenant approvisionnée pour trois années, montre combien l'intérêt des planteurs & négocians des États-Unis de l'Amérique a toujours été précieux au Roi.

L'arrêt du Conseil joint à cette lettre & les autres dispositions dont j'ai l'honneur de vous faire part, confirment de plus en plus une vérité si propre à resserrer tous les liens qui unissent les deux nations.

J'ai l'honneur d'être avec un très-sincère & inviolable attachement, Monsieur, votre très-humble & très-obéissant serviteur.

Signé LAMBERT

(English Translation)

LETTER from M. LAMBERT, Councellor of State & of the Council royal of Finance and Commerce, Comptroller general of finance to M. Jefferson, Minister plenipotentiary for the United States of America at the Court of Versailles.

Versailles, December 29, 1787

I HAVE the honour, Sir, to send you a copy of an Arret passed in Council, for encouraging the Commerce of the United States of America in France. I shall furnish you with a number of others as soon as they shall be printed.

You will therein see that several considerable favors, not before promised to the American Commerce, have been added to those which the king announced to you, in the letter addressed to you on the 22d. of october of the last year.

If in the mean time any duties have been levied, contrary to the intentions of that letter, they shall be repaid on sight of the vouchers.

I have also ordered a verification of the facts whereon it was represented to you, that the decision of the 24 of may 1786, relative to the Commerce of tobacco, had not been fully executed. Be assured that if it shall appear that engagements have been evaded, which were taken under the sanction of the king, effectual provision shall be made for their scrupulous fulfillment.

You whill learn also with pleasure that the measures I have taken to prevent the interruption of the Commerce of tobacco, have had full success.

This commodity shall not be excepted from among those to which the right of entrepot is given. The farmers general shall have no preference in the purchases, the proprietors shall be perfectly masters of their speculations, and free to export their tobaccoes by sea to foreign countries.

Measures only must be taken to prevent those frauds to which the entrepot might serve as a pretext; and the chambers of commerce for the ports shall be consulted, in order that the precautions necessary for this purpose, may not be in a form incompatible with that liberty which Commerce ought to enjoy in its operations.

Although the present stock of the farmers general amounts to about three years consumption I have engaged that company to continue to purchase yearly from the 1st day of january 1788. to the end of their lease fourteen thousand hogsheads of tobacco brought directly into the ports of France in French or American bottoms, and to shew at the end of every four months that their purchases amount to four thousand six hundred and sixty six hogsheads.

As to the prices, you have been sensible yourself of the necessity of leaving them free; and this freedom of price was the principal object of the applications of the American and French merchants when they complained of the contract of M. Morris.

The determination then taken to force the purchases of tobacco, tho at high prices, insomuch that the farmers general now find themselves possessed of three years provision shews that the interests of the planters and merchants of the United States of America have ever been precious to the King.

The arret of Council herein inclosed, and the other regulations which I have the honour of communicating to you, are a further confirmation of a truth tending somuch to strengthen the bands which unite the two nations.

I have the honour to be with a very sincere and inviolable attachment, Sir, your most humble and most obedient servant.

Signed LAMBERT[1]

[1] The printed letter and the translation are in President's Messages on Foreign Relations, Executive Proceedings, SR, DNA. The letter is related to Thomas Jefferson's report journalized January 19, 1791.

Arrêt du Conseil d'État du Roi

Pour l'encouragement du Commerce de France avec les États-Unis de l'Amérique.
Du 29 Décembre 1787

Extrait des Registres du Conseil d'État.

LE ROI voulant encourager le Commerce de ses Sujets avec les États-Unis de l'Amérique, & faciliter entre les deux Nations des relations réciproquement utiles: Ouï le rapport du sieur Lambert, Conseiller d'État, & ordinaire au Conseil royal des finances & du commerce, Contrôleur général des finances, SA MAJESTÉ ÉTANT EN SON CONSEIL, a ordonné & ordonne ce qui suit:

ARTICLE PREMIER.

LES huiles de baleine, & le spermaceti qui proviendront de la pêche des citoyens & habitans des États-Unis de l'Amérique, & seront apportés en France directement sur Vaisseaux François ou sur Vaisseaux des États-Unis, continueront à n'être soumis qu'à un droit de Sept livres dix sous par barrique du poids de cinq cens vingt livres, & les fanons de baleine ne le seront qu'à un droit de Six livres treize sous quatre deniers par quintal, avec les dix sous pour livre en sus de l'un & l'autre droit, lesquels dix sous pour livre cesseront au dernier décembre mil sept cent quatre-vingt-dix; se réservant, Sa Majesté, d'accorder de plus grandes faveurs aux produits de la pêche de la baleine exercée par les Pêcheurs des États-Unis de l'Amérique, qui seront apportés en France par Vaisseaux François ou des États-Unis, dans le cas où d'après les renseignemens que Sa Majesté fait recueillir, Elle le jugeroit convenable aux intérêts des deux Nations.

II.

LES autres huiles de poisson, & les poissons secs ou salés provenant de même de la pêche des citoyens & habitans des États-Unis, & apportés de même directement en France par leurs Vaisseaux ou par Vaisseaux François, ne payeront autres ni plus forts droits que ceux auxquels sont ou seront soumis, dans le même cas, les huiles & poissons de la même espèce, provenant de la pêche des Villes anséatiques ou des autres Nations les plus favorisées.

III.

LA fabrication des chandelles ou bougies de spermaceti ou blanc de baleine, sera permise en France comme celle des autres chandelles & bougies.

IV.

LES grains, fromens, seigle, riz, pois, fêves, lentilles, graines, les farines, les arbres & arbustes, les potasses, connues sous le nom de *pot-ash* & *pearl-ash*, les peaux & poils de castor, les cuirs en poil, les fourrures & pelleteries, & les bois de construction apportés des États-Unis directement en France sur Vaisseaux François ou des États-Unis, ne seront soumis qu'à un droit d'un Huitième pour cent de la valeur.

V.

TOUT Navire qui ayant été construit dans les Etats-Unis, sera ensuite vendu en France, ou acheté par des François, sera exempt de tous droits, à la charge de justifier que ledit Navire a été construit dans les États-Unis.

VI.

LES thérébentines, brais & goudrons, provenant des États-Unis de l'Amérique, apportés directement en France par Vaisseaux François ou des États-Unis, ne payeront qu'un droit de Deux & demi pour cent de la valeur, & seront les droits mentionnés, tant au présent article qu'en l'article IV, exempts de toute addition de sous pour livre.

VII.

LA sortie des armes de toute espèce & de la poudre à tirer pour les États-Unis de l'Amérique, sera toujours permises sur Vaisseaux François ou des États-Unis, en payant, à l'égard des armes, un droit d'un Huitième pour cent de la valeur, & la poudre, en ce cas, sera exempte de tous droits, en prenant un acquit à caution.

VIII.

LES papiers de toute espèce, même ceux destinés pour tenture & *dominoterie*, les cartons & les livres, seront exempts de tous droits à leur embarquement pour les États-Unis, sur Vaisseaux François ou des États-Unis, & jouiront, en ce cas, de la restitution des droits de fabrication sur les papiers & cartons.

IX.

LES droits d'Amirauté sur les Vaisseaux des États-Unis, entrant ou sortant des ports de France, ne pourront être perçus que conformément à l'Édit du mois de juin dernier, pour les cas qui y sont portés, & aux Lettres-Patentes du 10 janvier 1770, pour les objets auxquels il n'auroit pas été pourvu par ledit Édit; se réservant au surplus Sa Majesté, de faire connoître ses intentions sur la manière dont lesdits droits seront perçus, soit à raison du tonnage des Vaisseaux ou autrement; comme aussi de simplifier lesdits droits d'Amirauté, & de les régler autant qu'il sera possible sur le principe de la réciprocité, aussitôt que les travaux ordonnés par Sa Majesté, aux termes de l'article XXVI dudit Édit du mois de juin dernier, seront achevés.

X.

L'ENTREPÔT de toutes les productions & marchandises des États-Unis, sera permis pour six mois dans tous les ports de France ouverts au Commerce des Colonies; & ne sera ledit entrepôt soumis qu'à un droit d'un Huitième pour cent.

XI.

POUR favoriser l'exportation des armes, des quincailleries, des bijouteries, des bonneteries, de laine & de coton, des gros lainages, des petites draperies & des étoffes de coton de toute espèce, & autres marchandises de fabrique Françoise, qui seront envoyées aux États-Unis de l'Amérique sur Vaisseaux François ou des États-Unis, Sa Majesté se réserve d'accorder des encouragemens, qui seront incessamment réglés en son Conseil, selon la nature de chacune desdites marchandises.

XII.

QUANT aux autres marchandises non dénommées au present arrêt, apportées directement en France des États-Unis, sur leurs Vaisseaux ou sur Vaisseaux François, ou portées de France auxdits États-Unis, sur Vaisseaux François ou des États-Unis, & à l'égard de toutes conventions de Commerce quelconques, veut & ordonne Sa Majesté, que les citoyens des État-Unis jouissent en France des mêmes droits, priviléges & exemptions que les sujets de Sa Majesté, sauf l'exécution des dispositions portées par l'article IX ci-dessus.

XIII.

SA MAJESTÉ accorde aux citoyens & habitans des États-Unis, tous les avantages dont jouissent ou pourront jouir à l'avenir les Nations étrangères les plus favorisées dans ses Colonies de l'Amérique, & de plus Sa Majesté assure auxdits citoyens & habitans des États-Unis, tous les priviléges & avantages dont ses propres sujets de France jouissent ou pourront jouir en Asie & dans les Échelles qui y conduisent, pourvu toutefois que leurs bâtimens ayent été armés & expédiés dans un des ports des États-Unis.

MANDE & ordonne Sa Majesté à Mons. le Duc de Penthièvre, Amiral de France, aux sieurs Intendans & Commissaires départis dans les provinces, au Commissaire départi pour l'observation des Ordonnances dans les Amirautés, aux Officiers des Amirautés, Maîtres des ports, Juges des traites, & tous autres qu'il appartiendra, de tenir la main à l'exécution du présent Règlement, lequel sera enregistré aux Greffes desdites Amirautés, lû, publié & affiché par-tout où besoin sera.

FAIT au Conseil d'État du Roi, Sa Majesté y étant, tenu à Versailles le vingt-neuf décembre mil sept cent quatre-vingt-sept.

Signé   LE CTE. DE LA LUZERNE

(English Translation)

An Act of the King's
Council of State
For the encouragement of the Commerce of France with the United States of America.

December 29, 1787

Extract from the records of the Council of State.

THE KING desirous of encouraging the commerce of his subjects with the United-States of America and of facilitating between the two Nations connections reciprocally useful: Having heard the report of the sieur Lambert, Counsellor of State and of the Royal Council of finance and commerce, Comptroller general of finance, HIS MAJESTY BEING IN HIS COUNCIL, has ordained and does ordain as follows:

ARTICLE FIRST.

WHALE-OILS and spermaceti, the produce of the fisheries of the citizens & inhabitants of the United States of America, which shall be brought into France directly in French vessels or in those of the United-States shall continue to be subjected to a duty only of seven livres ten sols the barrel of five hundred and twenty pounds weight, & whale fins shall be subject to a duty of only six livres thirteen sols four deniers the quintal with the ten sols per livre on each of the said duties; which ten sols per livre shall cease on the last day of December one thousand seven hundred & ninety; His Majesty reserving to himself to grant further favors to the produce of the whale fisheries carried on by the fishermen of the United States of America which shall be brought into France in French vessels or in those of the United States, if, on the information which His Majesty shall cause to be taken thereon, he shall judge it expedient for the interest of the two Nations.

II.

THE other fish-oils and dry or salted fish, the produce in like manner of the fisheries of the citizens & inhabitants of the United States, & brought also directly into France, in their, or in French vessels, shall not pay any other nor greater duties than those to which the oils & fish of the same kind, the produce of the fisheries of the Hanseatic towns, or of other the most favored Nations, are or shall be subject in the same case.

III.

THE manufacture of candles and tapers of spermaceti shall be permitted in France, as that of other candles & tapers.

IV.

CORN, wheat, rye, rice, peas, beans, lentils, flaxseed and other seeds, flour, trees and shrubs, pot-ash and pearl-ash, skins and fur of beaver, raw hides, furs and peltry, and timber brought from the United States directly into France, in French vessels or in those of the United States, shall not be subject but to a duty of one eighth per cent on their value.

V.

VESSELS built in the United States and sold in France, or purchased by French-men shall be exempt from all duties on proof that they were built in the United States.

VI.

TURPENTINE, tar and pitch the produce of the United States of America and brought directly into France in French vessels or in those of the United States shall pay, only a duty of two and a half per cent on their value, and as well the duties mentioned in this as in the fourth article shall be exempt from all addition of sous per livre.

VII.

THE exportation of arms of all sorts, and of gun powder for the United States of America, shall be always permitted in French vessels or in those of the United States, paying for the arms a duty of one eighth per cent on their value: and gunpowder in that case shall be exempt from all duty on giving a cautionary bond.

VIII.

PAPERS of all sorts, even paper hangings and coloured papers, pasteboard and books shall be exempt from all duties on their embarcation for the United States of America, in French vessels or in those of the United States, and shall be entitled in that case to a restitution of the fabrication duties on paper and pasteboard.

IX.

THE Admiralty duties on the vessels of the United-States entering into, or going out of the ports of France, shall not be levied but conformably with the Edict of the month of june last in the cases therein provided for, and with the Letters-patent of the tenth of january one thousand seven hundred and seventy for the objects for which no provision shall have been made by the said Edict: his Majesty reserving to himself moreover to make known his intentions as to the manner in which the said duties shall be levied, whether in proportion to the tonnage of the vessels or otherwise, as also to simplify the said duties of the Admiralty and to regulate them as far as shall be possible on the principle of reciprocity, as soon as the orders shall be completed which were given by his Majesty according to the twenty-sixth article of the said Edict of the month of june last.

X.

THE entrepot (or storing) of all the productions and merchandize of the United States shall be permitted for six months in all the ports of France open to the Commerce of her Colonies; and the said entrepot shall be subject only to a duty of one eighth per cent.

XI.

To favour the exportation of arms, hardware, jewellery bonnetery,[1] of wool and of cotton, coarse woolens, small draperies and stuffs of cotton of all sorts, and other merchandizes of French fabric, which shall be sent to the United States of America, in French vessels or in those of the United States, His Majesty reserves to himself to grant encouragements which shall be immediately regulated in his Council, according to the nature of each of the said merchandizes.

XII.

As to other merchandizes not mentioned in this act, brought directly into France from the United States in their or in French vessels, or carried from France to the said United States in French vessels or in those of the United States, and with respect to all commercial conventions whatsoever His Majesty wills and ordains that the citizens of the United States enjoy in France the same rights, privileges and exemptions with the subjects of His Majesty: saving the execution of what is provided in the ninth article hereof.

XIII.

His Majesty grants to the citizens and in habitants of the United States all the advantages which are enjoyed or which may be here after enjoyed by the most favored nations in his Colonies of America and moreover His Majesty assures to the said citizens and inhabitants of the United States all the privileges and advantages which his own subjects of France enjoy or shall enjoy in Asia and in the scales leading thereto: provided always that their vessels shall have been fitted out and dispatched in some port of the United States.

His Majesty commands and orders M. le duc de Penthievre, Admiral of France, the Intendants and commissaries de parti in the provinces, The commissaries de parti for the observation of the ordinances in the admiralties, the officers of the admiralties masters of the ports, judges des traites, and all others to whom it shall belong to be aiding in the execution of the present regulation which shall be registered in the offices of the said admiralties read published and posted wherever shall be necessary.

Done in the King's council of State, His Majesty present, held at Versailles the twenty ninth of december one thousand seven hundred and eighty seven.

Signed   LE CTE. DE LA LUZERNE[2]

[1] At this point in the original document there is an asterisk, which refers to a note at the bottom of the page, which reads: "This term includes bonnets stockings, socks underwaist coats, drawer gloues and mitaines as sold by the bonnetier."
[2] The printed Arret and the translation are in President's Messages on Foreign Relations, Executive Proceedings, SR, DNA. The Arret is related to Thomas Jefferson's report journalized January 19, 1791. Miscellaneous annotations by an unknown person, probably not contemporary, appear on the document.

Arrêt du Conseil d'État du Roi

Qui excepte de la prohibition portée par l'arrêt du 28 septembre dernier, les Huiles de Baleine & d'autres Poissons, ainsi que les fanons de Baleine, provenant de la pêche des États-unis de l'Amérique.

Du 7 Décembre 1788

Extrait des Registres du Conseil d'État.

LE ROI s'étant fait représenter l'arrêt rendu en son Conseil, le 28 septembre dernier, portant prohibition à l'entrée dans le Royaume, des Huiles de Baleine & de Spermaceti, provenant de pêche étrangère, Sa Majesté auroit reconnu que les Huiles de Veau marin, & celles provenant de poissons & autres animaux vivans dans la mer, n'étant pas comprises dans ledit arrêt, il en pourroit résulter sous le nom desdites Huiles, une introduction frauduleuse d'Huiles de Baleine, & que d'un autre côté, on pourroit induire des dispositions dudit arrêt, une prohibition des Huiles provenant de la pêche des États-unis de l'Amérique; & Sa Majesté voulant faire cesser toute incertitude à cet égard. A quoi voulant pourvoir: Ouï le rapport de sieur Lambert, Conseiller d'État ordinaire & au Conseil des Dépêches, & au Conseil royal des Finances & du Commerce; LE ROI ÉTANT EN SON CONSEIL, a ordonné & ordonne, qu'à compter du 1er. Avril prochain, les Huiles de Veau marin, & celles de poissons & autres animaux vivans dans la mer, provenantes de pêche étrangère, ainsi que les fanons de Baleine, provenant également de ladite pêche étrangère, seront prohibées à l'entrée dans le Royaume, sans toutefois que ladite prohibition puisse s'étendre, tant auxdites Huiles qu'à celles de Baleine & de Spermaceti, ainsi qu'aux fanons de Baleine, provenant de la pêche des États-unis de l'Amérique, & apportés directement en France, sur des bâtimens François, ou appartenant aux Sujets desdits États-unis, lesquelles continueront provisoirement d'être admises conformément aux articles I & III de l'arrêt du 29 décembre dernier; & à la charge en outre par les Capitaines des navires des États-unis, de rapporter des certificats des Consuls de France, résidens dans les ports desdits États-unis; & à leur défaut, des Magistrats des lieux où se feront les embarquemens desdites Huiles, à l'effet de constater que la cargaison desdits navires provient de pêche faite par les Citoyens des États-unis; lesquels certificats seront représentés aux Officiers des Amirautés, ensemble aux Préposés des Fermes, dans les ports de France où se fera le débarquement, pour en être fait mention dans les déclarations d'arrivée. MANDE & ordonne Sa Majesté à Mons. le Duc de Penthièvre, Amiral de France, aux sieurs Intendans & Commissaires départis dans les Provinces, au Commissaire départi pour l'observation des Ordonnances dans les Amirautés, aux Officiers des Amirautés, Maîtres des Ports, Juges des Traites, & à tous autres qu'il appartiendra, de tenir la main à l'exécution du présent arrêt, lequel sera enregistré aux Greffes desdites Amirautés, lû, publié & affiché par-tout où besoin sera.

FAIT au Conseil d'État du Roi, Sa Majesté y étant, tenu à Versailles le sept décembre mil sept cent quatre-vingt-huit.

Signé LA LUZERNE

LE DUC DE PENTHIÈVRE, *Admiral de France.*

VU l'arrêt du Conseil d'État du Roi ci-dessus & des autres parts, à nous adressé: MANDONS à tous ceux sur qui notre pouvoir s'étend, de l'exécuter & faire exécuter, chacun en droit soi, suivant sa forme & teneur: Ordonnons aux Officiers des Amirautés de le faire enregistrer au Greffe de leurs Siéges, lire, publier & afficher par-tout où besoin sera.

FAIT à Vernon le vingt décembre mil sept cent quatre-vingt-huit.

Signé L. J. M. DE BOURBON

Et plus bas, Par Son Altesse Sérénissime.

Signé PERIER[1]

---

[1] The printed Arret is in President's Messages on Foreign Relations, Executive Proceedings, SR, DNA. It is related to Thomas Jefferson's report journalized January 19, 1791. Miscellaneous annotations by an unknown person, probably not contemporary, appear on the document.

Translation

Arrêt of the King's Council of State, Excepting Whale and other Fish Oil, and also Whale Bone, the Product of the Fisheries of the United States of America, from the Prohibition contained in the Arrêt of the 28 September last.

7. December 1788

Extract from the Registers of the Council of State.

The King taking into Consideration the Arrêt pronounced in his Council the 28 December[1] last, prohibiting the Importation of Whale Oil and Spermaceti the produce of foreign Fisheries into the Kingdom, observing, that Oil made from Sea Calves & other Fish and Sea animals not being comprehended in the said Arret, a fraudulent Importation of Whale Oil might take Place under the name of the aforesaid Oils, and that, on the other Hand, it might be inferred from the Tenor of the said Arrêt, that Oils the Produce of the Fisheries of the United States were prohibited; and his Majesty wishing to remove every Doubt on this Head. To provide, therefore, for the same, having heard the Report of the Sieur Lambert, Councellor of State in ordinary & of the Council of Dispatches, and Royal Council of Finances and Commerce; The King being present in his Council has ordained and does ordain, that, reckoning the 1st. Day of April next, Oil made from Sea Calves, and from Fish & other Sea animals produced from foreign Fisheries, as well as Whale-bone produced in like manner from the said Foreign Fisheries shall be prohibited from Importation into the Kingdom, without permitting the said Prohibition, nevertheless, to extend either to the said Kinds of Oils or to the said Whale Oils and Spermaceti or the whale bone produced from the Fisheries of the United States of America, and imported directly into France in French Vessels or those belonging to the Subjects of the said United States, which shall continue to be provisionally admitted agreeable to the 1st. & 3rd. articles of the Arrêt of the 29th. of December last, on condition, however, that the Captains of the said Vessels belonging to the United States bring with them Certificates from the Consuls of France residing in the Ports of the said United States, or, where these cannot be obtained, from the Magistrates of the Places where the Embarkation of the said Oil shall be made, for the Purpose of proving that the Cargo of the said Vessels is the Produce of the Fisheries carried on by the Citizens of the United States, which Certificates shall be presented to the Officers of the Admiralty—also to the Commissioners of the Farms, in the Ports of France, where it shall be landed; to be mentioned in the Report of their arrival. His Majesty commands and orders the Duke de Penthièvre, Admiral of France, the Intendants and Commissaries throughout the Provinces, the Commissaries appointed to observe the Ordinances of the Admiralty, the officers of the Admiralty, Masters of Ports, Judges of Treaties, and all others whom it may concern; to assist in the Execution of the present Arrêt which shall be registered in the offices of the said Admiralties, read, published and posted wherever it may appear necessary.

Done in the King's Council of State, his majesty being present, held at Versailles the 7. of December 1788

(signed)   La Luzerne

The Duke de Penthièvre, Admiral of France.

Having seen the above Arrêt of the King's Council of State and the other Parts addressed to us: we command all those over whom our Power extends, to execute and cause it to be executed, each as his Duty is, agreeable to its Form and Tenor. We order the Officers of the admiralties to register it in the Office of their Jurisdictions, to read, publish and post it wherever it may be necessary. Done at Vernon the 20 of December 1788.

(signed)   L. J. M. DE BOURBON

& beneath by his serene Highness

(signed)   PERIER[2]

[1] The date should be 28 September.
[2] The translation, in the hand of George Taylor, Jr., is in President's Messages on Foreign Relations, Executive Proceedings, SR, DNA. It is related to Thomas Jefferson's report journalized January 19, 1791.

Thomas Jefferson to the President of the Senate

Philadelphia February 2d. 1791

SIR,

As the information contained in the enclosed extracts from a letter of Mr. Short's lately received, has some relation to a subject now before the Senate, I have thought it my duty to communicate them, and have the honor to be with sentiments of the most profound respect and attachment.

Sir

Your most obedient and
most humble servant.
TH. JEFFERSON[1]

[1] The covering letter, in the hand of Jacob Blackwell and signed by Thomas Jefferson, is in President's Messages on Foreign Relations, Executive Proceedings, SR, DNA. It is related to Thomas Jefferson's report journalized January 19, 1791.

Extract of a Letter from William Short to the Secretary of State

Paris   October 21st. 1790

It cannot be dissembled that the National Assembly consider their commerce with the United States of much less importance now than they will do in a short time hence. Some suppose us so much attached to England and to English Manufactures, that every sacrifice which France could make to encourage commercial connections with' us would be lost. They say that the experience of seven years has sufficed to shew this. Others suppose that the commerce with the United States is a losing commerce. They are supported in this opinion by many of their merchants, who tell them there is no instance of a french house having undertaken that commerce, without losing by it. It is easy to answer these arguments so as to satisfy individuals, and a short time will satisfy all; still at present an unfavorable impression remains with many. When they are told that the Americans have continued to trade with England since the peace, because their articles of exportation were either subjected to a monopoly, or to such shackles in France, as prevented their coming here; That losses have been sustained in the American commerce, by the failures which the peace brought on, and by the improper credit given to those who did not deserve it by agents ill chosen or by goods ill assorted; when they are told that the exportations from America to Europe are annually upwards of ninety millions, and of course that they are able to pay for that amount of European manufactures and productions, and that France can furnish the greater part of them, on better or equal terms with England; that the United States furnish raw materials, and receive in return only those which are manufactured; that the transportation of these articles has hitherto benefitted the English, and might now benefit the French marine; they view the subject in a different light, and suppose it well worth attending to: They then come immediately to the necessity of a Treaty of Commerce, as being the only means of securing the advantages to be expected from these connections: They urge that laws, which may be repealed from day to day, cannot be depended on; besides that there is no reciprocity in them: They quote the *Arret du Conseil* for the encouragement of American commerce, and our Act of Congress on impost and tonnage: They complain bitterly on being placed on the same footing with the English, at the first session of the new Congress, the proceedings of the second are not yet known.

The desire of some of the Members of the Committee of Commerce, was to subject our articles imported into France & our Ships, to the same duties and tonnage that we subjected theirs. A desire however not to discourage our commerce entirely; a hope that our system, with respect to them; would be changed; and a wish to have their tariff of duties on importation & exportation, uniform for all, induced them to reject the idea. The report of the Committee of Commerce has been read in the Assembly, and ordered to be printed. You will receive it enclosed. The tariff is under press, and shall be sent also, as soon as it appears. How far it will be adopted I cannot say, but as the Assembly feel the necessity of one being immediately established on the abolition of the internal barriers, it is much more than probable they will adopt it in the lump, to save time, although the Members of the Committee themselves agree that it is very imperfect. They say time and experience alone can shew what alterations should be made. Sacrifices have been mutually made by the different Members of the Committee to each other. In what regards us, those who are Graziers and those who are interested with the Nantucket fishermen, settled in France (of which there are both in the Committee) insist on heavy duties being laid on salted meats & the productions of fisheries. They have succeeded in the Committee, and will probably succeed, for the reasons mentioned above, in the Assembly. The low price of our salted meats alarmed them; they were deaf to the advantages of procuring subsistence, on the best terms possible to the poorer classes; and the preference which should be given to the cultivation of corn above grazing, on account of population. There is little doubt, therefore, that the regulations made by the present Assembly respecting our Commerce, will not be such as we could wish.

The proceedings of a large and tumultuous Assembly are so irregular, that one is obliged to be on a constant watch to prevent the individual members, who are interested, from passing into a Decree, such things as the House do not consider of very great moment, or where there is no other individual particularly interested in it's opposition. The importation of salted provisions and whale oil are in this class. You will see by the tariff enclosed, that the Committee proposes heavy duties on the former, and a prohibition of the latter, without any regard to the Laws formerly made for the encouragement of our Commerce. The Marquis de la Fayette will do whatever he can, to prevent these things passing, and I hope he will succeed. I have spoken to several members on this subject. They all agree on the necessity of putting the American commerce on a different footing; They talk of the propriety of reciprocity insured by a Treaty, and plead that favors hitherto granted to our commerce in France, did not create similar dispositions in America; They say the Nantucket fishermen at L'Orient and Dunkirk, have large quantities of Oil on hand unsold, which proves they are competent to the supplies of the Kingdom, and are buoyed up with the hopes that they will be joined by many others, who will come to settle in France, rather than go to the English possessions.[1]

[1] The extract, in the hand of Henry Remsen, Jr., is in President's Messages on Foreign Relations, Executive Proceedings, SR, DNA. It is related to Thomas Jefferson's report journalized January 19, 1791. A transcript, in a nineteenth-century hand, probably made by ASP, is filed in the same location.

L. G. Otto to the Secretary of State

À Philadelphia le 13e. Dec. 1790

MONSIEUR,

Pendant le long sejour que vous aves fait en France, vous aves eu Lieu de vous convaincre des Dispositions favorables de Sa Majesté pour rendre permanens les Liens qui unissent les deux Nations, et pour donner de la Stabilité aux Traités d'Alliance et de Commerce, qui forment la Base de cette Union. Ces Traités ont été si bien maintenus par le Congrès formé sous l'ancienne Confederation, qu'il a cru devoir interposer son autorité toutes les fois que des Loix faites par des Etats individuels paroissoient en enfreindre les Dispositions, et particulierement lorsqu'en 1785 les Etats du New-Hampshire et du Massachussets avoient imposé des Droits de Tonnage extraordinaires sur les Bâtimens etrangers sans en exempter ceux de la Nation Françoise. Les Reflexions, que j'ai l'Honneur de vous adresser dans la Notte ci-jointe étant fondées sur les mêmes principes, j'ose croire qu'elles meriteront de la Part du Gouvernement des Etats Unis l'attention la plus serieuse.

Je suis avec Respect
Monsr. Votre très humble
et très obéissant Serviteur
L. G. OTTO

Notte.

Le Soussigné Chargé des Affaires de France a reçu l'Ordre exprès de sa Cour de representer aux Etats Unis que l'Acte passé par le Congrès le 20e. Juillet 1789, et renouvelle le 20e. Juillet de l'année courante, qui impose un Droit de Tonnage extraordinaire sur les Bâtimens etrangers sans en excepter les Navires François, est directement contraire à l'Ésprit et au But de Traité de Commerce, que lie les deux Nations, et dont Sa Majesté a non seulement scrupuleusement observé la Teneur, mais dont Elle a etendu les Avantages par plusieurs Réglemens très favorables au Commerce et à la Navigation des Etats Unis.

Par l'Article 5e. de ce Traité les Citoyens de ces Etats sont declarés exempts du Droit de Tonnage imposé en France sur les Bâtimens etrangers, et ils ne sont assujettis à ce Droit que pour le petit cabotage; on a reservé au Congrès la Faculté d'etablir un *Droit equivalent à ce dernier*; Stipulation fondée sur l'Etat ou etoient les Choses en Amérique, lors de la Signature du Traité; il n'existoit à cette Epoque aucun Droit de Tonnage dans les Etats Unis.

Il est evident que c'est la non-existence de ce Droit et le Motif d'une parfaite Reciprocité stipulée dans le Preambule du Traité, qui ont determine le Roi à accorder l'Exemption contenue dans l'Article 5e. et une Preuve que le Congrès n'avoit point L'Intention de porter Atteinte à cette Reciprocité, c'est qu'*il s'est borné à se reserver la Faculté d'etablir sur le petit cabotage un Droit equivalent à celui qui se perçoit en France.* Cette Reserve auroit été completement inutile, si aux Termes du Traité le Congrès s'etoit cru en Liberté de mettre un Droit de Tonnage *quelconque* sur les Bâtimens François.

Le Soussigné à l'Honneur d'observer que cette Atteinte portée à l'Article 5e. du Traité de Commerce auroit pu autoriser Sa Majesté à modifier proportionellement les Faveurs accordées par le même Article à la Navigation Americaine, mais le Roi toujours Fidele à ses principes d'amitié et d'attachement pour les Etats Unis, et voulant confirmer de plus en plus les Liaisons qui subsistent si heureusement entre la Nation Françoise et ces Etats a trouvé plus conforme à ces Vues d'ordonner au Soussigné de faire des Representations à ce Sujet, et de demander en Faveur des Navires François une Modification de l'Acte qui impose un Droit de Tonnage extraordinaire sur les Batimens etrangers. Sa Majesté ne doute pas que les Etats Unis ne reconnoissent la Justice de cette Reclamation et ne soient disposés à remettre les choses sur le Pied ou elles etoient lors de la Signature du Traité du 6e. Fevr. 1778.

A Philadelphie le 13e. Decembre 1790.

L. G. OTTO[1]

---

[1] A copy of the letter and a copy of the note, both in the hand of George Taylor, Jr., are in President's Messages on Foreign Relations, Executive Proceedings, SR, DNA. The English translations were printed in the journal on January 19, 1791.

L. G. Otto to the Secretary of State

À New York le 8. Janv. 1791

MONSIEUR,

J'ai L'honneur de vous adresser ci-joint une Lettre du Roi au Congrès, et une autre que vous ecrit M. de Montmorin. Vous y trouveréz l'Expression sincere des Sentimens, que vous avéz inspirés à notre Gouvernement et des Regrets du Ministre de ne plus être immediatement en Relation avec vous. Ces Sentimens sont partagés par toutes les Personnes qui ont eu l'avantage de vous connoitre en France.

Je suis peine, Monsieur, d'avoir à vous annoncer en même Tems que les Plaintes de nos Négocians au Sujet des Droits de Tonnage se multiplient, et qu'elles ont non seulement fixé l'attention du Roi, mais celle de plusieurs Departemens du Royaume. J'ai reçu de nouveaux Ordres de demander aux Etats Unis une Decision à ce Sujet, et de solliciter en Faveur des Négocians lézés la Restitution des Droits, qui ont dejà été payés. Je vous prie instamment, Monsieur, de ne pas perdre de vue un Objet qui, comme j'ai eu l'Honneur de vous le dire verbalement est de la plus grande Importance pour cimenter les Liaisons futures de Commerce entre les deux Nations.

En examinant plus particulierement cette Question, vous trouveréz peut être que les Motifs de convenance sont aussi puissans que ceux de Justice pour engager les Etats Unis à donder à S.M. la Satisfaction qu'elle demande. Il entre dans les Ports de France au moins deux fois plus de Bâtimens Américaines qu'il ne vient de Batimens François dans les Ports Americains. L'Exemption du Droit de Tonnage est donc evidemment moins avantageuse pour les François que pour les navigateurs des Etats-Unis. Quoiqu'il en soit, je puis vous assurer, Monsieur, que les Delais d'une Decision à cet egard ne pourront que multiplier les Difficultés en augmentant les justes plaintes des Négocians François. Je vous prie en Consequence de me mettre en Etat de donner à ma Cour une Reponse satisfaisante avant l'Expedition du Paque-bot qui partira vers la Fin de ce Mois.

J'ai l'Honneur d'être, avec un respectueux Attachement,

Monsieur,
Votre très humble et
très obeissant Serviteur
L. G. OTTO[1]

[1] A copy of the letter, in the hand of George Taylor, Jr., is in President's Messages on Foreign Relations, Executive Proceedings, SR, DNA. The English translation was printed in the journal on January 19, 1791.

United States Prisoners in Algiers

Report of Thomas Jefferson to the President

The Secretary of State, having had under Consideration the Situation of the Citizens of the United States in Captivity at Algiers, makes the following REPORT thereupon to the President of the United States.

When the House of Representatives, at their late Session, were pleased to refer to the Secretary of State, the Petition of our Citizens in Captivity at Algiers, there still existed some Expectation that certain Measures, which had been employed to effect their Redemption, the Success of which depended on their Secrecy, might prove effectual. Information received during the Recess of Congress, has so far weakened those Expectations as to make it now a Duty to lay before the President of the United States, a full Statement of what has been attempted for the Relief of these our suffering Citizens, as well before, as since he came into Office, that he may be enabled to decide what further is to be done.

On the 25th. of July 1785, the Schooner Maria, Captain Stevens, belonging to a Mr. Foster of Boston, was taken off Cape St. Vincents, by an Algerine Corsair: and five Days afterwards, the Ship Dauphin, Captain Obrian, belonging to Messieurs Irvins, of Philadelphia, was taken by another Algerine, about 50 Leagues Westward of Lisbon. These Vessels, with their Cargoes and Crews, twenty one Persons in Number, were carried into Algiers.

Congress had, some Time before, commissioned Ministers Plenipotentiary for entering into Treaties of Amity and Commerce with the Barbary Powers, and to send to them proper Agents for preparing such Treaties. An Agent was accordingly appointed for Algiers, and his Instructions prepared, when the Ministers Plenipotentiary received Information of these Captures. Though the Ransom of Captives was not among the Objects expressed in their Commissions, because at their Dates the Case did not exist, yet they thought it their Duty to undertake that Ransom, fearing that the Captives might be sold and dispersed through the interior and distant Countries of Africa, if the previous Orders of Congress should be waited for. They, therefore, added a supplementary Instruction, to the Agent, to negociate their Ransom. But while acting thus without Authority, they thought themselves bound to offer a Price so moderate as not to be disapproved. They, therefore, restrained him to Two hundred Dollars a Man; which was something less than had been just before paid for about Three hundred French Captives, by the Mathurins, a religious Order of France, instituted in ancient Times for the Redemption of Christian Captives from the infidel Powers. No. 1. On the Arrival of the Agent at Algiers, the Dey demanded Fifty nine thousand four hundred and ninety six Dollars for the Twenty one Captives, and could not be brought to abate but little from that Demand. The Agent, therefore, returned in 1786, without having effected either Peace or Ransom.

In the Beginning of the next Year, 1787, the Minister Plenipotentiary of the United States, at Paris, procured an Interview with the General of the religious Order of Mathurins, before mentioned, to engage him to lend his Agency, at the Expence of the United States, for the Redemption of their captive Citizens. He proffered, at once, all the Services he could render, with the Liberality and the Zeal, which distinguish his Character. He observed that he had Agents on the Spot, constantly employed in seeking out, and redeeming the Captives of their own Country; that these should act for us, as for themselves; that Nothing could be accepted for their Agency; and that he would only expect that the Price of Redemption should be ready on our Part, so as to cover the Engagement into which he should enter. He added, that, by the Time all Expences were paid, their last Redemption had amounted to near Two thousand five hundred Livres a Man, and that he could by no means flatter us that they could redeem our Captives as cheap as their own: The Pirates would take Advantage of it's being out of their ordinary Line. Still he was in hopes they would not be much higher.

The Proposition was then submitted to Congress, that is to say, in February 1787, and on the 19th. of September, in the same Year, their Minister Plenipotentiary, at Paris, received their Orders to embrace the Offers of the Mathurins. This he immediately notified to the General, observing, however, that he did not desire him to enter into any Engagements till a sufficient Sum to cover them should be actually deposited in Paris. The General wished that the Whole might be kept rigorously secret, as, should the Barbarians suspect him to be acting for the United States, they would demand such Sums as he could never agree to give, even with our Consent, because it would injure his future Purchases from them. He said he had Information from his Agent at Algiers, that our Captives received so liberal a daily Allowance as to evince that it came from a public Source. He recommended that this should be discontinued; engaging that he would have an Allowance administered to them, much short, indeed, of what they had hitherto received, but such as was given to his own Countrymen, quite Sufficient for physical Necessaries, and more likely to prepare the Opinion, that, as they were subsisted by his Charity, they were to be redeemed by it also. These Ideas, suggested to him by the Danger of raising his Market, were approved by the Minister Plenipotentiary, because, this being the first Instance of a Redemption by the United States, it would form a Precedent; because, a high Price given by us, might induce these Pirates to abandon all other Nations, in pursuit of Americans, whereas, the Contrary would take place, could our Price of Redemption be fixed at the lowest Point.

To destroy, therefore, every Expectation of a Redemption by the United States, the Bills of the Spanish Consul at Algiers, who had made the Kind Advances, before spoken of, for the Sustenance of our Captives, were not answered. On the Contrary, a Hint was given that these Advances had better be discontinued, as it was not known that they would be reimbursed. It was necessary even to go further, and to suffer the Captives themselves and their Friends to believe, for a while that no Attention was paid to them, no Notice taken of their Letters. They are still under this Impression. It would have been unsafe to trust them with a Secret, the Disclosure of which might forever prevent their Redemption, by raising the Demands of the Captors to Sums, which a due Regard for our Seamen, still in Freedom, would forbid us to give. This was the most trying of all Circumstances, and drew from them the most afflicting Reproaches.

It was a Twelvemonth afterwards before the Money could be deposited in Paris, and the Negociation be actually put into Train. In the meantime the General had received Information from Algiers of a very considerable change of Prices there. Within the last two or three years the Spaniards, the Neopolitans, and the Russians had redeemed at exorbitant Sums. Slaves were become scarce, and would hardly be sold at any Price. Still he entered on the Business with an Assurance of doing the Best in his power, and he was authorized to offer as far as Three thousand Livres, or Five hundred and fifty five Dollars a Man. He wrote immediately to consult a confidential Agent at Marseilles, on the best Mode of carrying this Business into Effect; from whom he received the Answer No. 2. hereto annexed.

Nothing further was known of his Progress or Prospects when the House of Representatives were pleased, at their last Session, to refer the Petition of our Captives at Algiers, to the Secretary of State. The preceding Narrative shews that no Report could have then been made without risking the Object, of which some Hopes were still entertained. No. 3. Later Advices, however, from the Chargé des Affaires of the United States, at Paris, inform us, that these Measures, though not yet desperate, are not to be counted on. Besides the Exorbitance of Price, before feared, the late Transfer of the Lands and Revenues of the Clergy, in France, to the Public, by withdrawing the Means, seems to have suspended the Proceedings of the Mathurins in the Purposes of their Institution.

It is Time, therefore, to look about for Something more promising, without relinquishing, in the meanwhile, the Chance of Success through them. Endeavours to collect Information, which have been continued a considerable Time, as to the Ransoms which would probably be demanded from us, and those actually paid by other Nations, enable the Secretary of State to lay before the President the following short View, collected from original Papers now in his Possession, or from Information delivered to him personally.

Passing over the Ransoms of the Mathurins, which are kept far below the common Level, by special Circumstances;

No. 4. In 1786, the Day of Algiers demanded from our Agent 59,496 Dollars for 21 Captives, which was 2,833 Dollars a Man. The Agent flattered himself they could be ransomed for 1200 Dollars a piece. No. 5. His Secretary informed us, at the same Time, that Spain had paid 1600 Dollars.

In 1787, the Russians redeemed at 1546 Dollars a Man.

No. 6. In 1788, a well informed Inhabitant of Algiers, assured the Minister Plenipotentiary of the United States at Paris, that no Nation had redeemed, since the Spanish Treaty, at less than from 250 to 300 Pounds sterling, the Medium of which is 1,237 Dollars. Captain Obrian, at the same Date, thinks we must pay 1,800 Dollars, and Mentions a Savoy Captain, just redeemed at 4,074 Dollars.

In 1789, Mr. Logie, the English Consul at Algiers, informed a Person who wished to ransom one of our common Sailors, that he would cost from 450 to 500 Pounds Sterling, the Mean of which is 2,137 Dollars. No. 7. In December of the same Year, Captain Obrian thinks our Men will now cost 2,920 Dollars each, though a Jew Merchant believes he could get them for 2,264 Dollars.

No. 8. In 1790, July 9th. a Mr. Simpson, of Gibraltar, who at some particular Request, had taken Pains to find for what Sum our Captives could be redeemed, finds that the Fourteen will cost 34,792 28/38 Dollars, which is 2,485 Dollars a Man. At the same Date, one of them, a Scotch Boy, a common Mariner, was actually redeemed at 8,000 Livres, equal to 1,481 Dollars, which is within 19 Dollars of the Price Simpson states for common Men: and the Chargé des Affairs of the United States at Paris is informed that the Whole may be redeemed at that Rate, adding Fifty per Cent on the Captains, which would bring it to 1,571 Dollars a Man.

It is found then that the Prices are 1,200, 1,237, 1,481, 1,546, 1,571, 1,600, 1,800, 2,137, 2,264, 2,485, 2,833 and 2,920 Dollars a Man, not noticing that of 4,074 Dollars, because it was for a Captain.

In 1786, there were 2,200 Captives in Algiers, which in 1789 had been reduced by Death or Ransom to 655. Of ours six have died, and one has been ransomed by his Friends.

From these Facts and Opinions some Conjecture may be formed of the Terms on which the Liberty of our Citizens may be obtained.

But should it be thought better to repress Force by Force, another Expedient, for there Liberation, may, perhaps, offer. Captures made on the Enemy, may, perhaps, put us into Possession of some of their Mariners, and Exchange be substituted for Ransom. It is not indeed, a fixed Usage with them to exchange Prisoners. It is rather their Custom to refuse it. However, such Exchanges are sometimes effected, by allowing them more or less of Advantage. They have sometimes accepted of two Moors for a Christian, at others, they have refused five or six for one. Perhaps Turkish captives may be Objects of greater Partiality with them, as their Government is entirely in the Hands of Turks, who are treated in every Instance, as a superior Order of Beings. Exchange too, will be more practicable in our Case, as our Captives have not been sold to private Individuals, but are retained in the Hands of the Government.

The Liberation of our Citizens has an intimate Connection with the Liberation of our Commerce in the Mediterranean, now under the Consideration of Congress. The Distresses of both proceed from the same Cause, and the Measures which shall be adopted for the Relief of the one, may, very probably, involve the Relief of the other.

> TH. JEFFERSON Secretary
> of state
> Dec. 28. 1790[1]

---

[1] The report, in the hand of George Taylor, Jr., and signed by Thomas Jefferson, and the following enclosures are in President's Messages on Foreign Relations, Executive Proceedings, SR, DNA. The numbers identifying each enclosure are also in the hand of Thomas Jefferson. The report and the enclosures are related to the committee report journalized February 1, 1791.

No. 1.
Extract of a letter from Mr. John Lamb,
dated 20th. May 1786

I here give your Excellency an account of the prices of our unfortunate people, and it is as follows vizt.

3 Captains	a 6000	Dollrs. each	pr. head	18000
2 mates	a 4000	do.	do.	8000
2 passengers	a 4000	do.	do.	8000
14 Sailors	a 1400	do.	do.	19600

21 amounts to the enormous sum of 53600

eleven per. Cent to be added according to custom   5896

is spanish milled dollars 59496

so that your Excellency sees how far beyond your expectation the sum amounts, which renders me incapable of acting until further orders. The price the Spaniards are giving for their people is little short of what is charged us, and they have eleven hundred men and some upwards in Algiers; it will cost Spain more than one million and one half of Dollars for their Slaves only. The peace of Spain and their Slaves will amount to more than three million of Dollars.[1]

[1] The extract is in the hand of Jacob Blackwell.

No. 2.
Answer of the Agent of the Mathurins to his General

Aix 19th August 1789

My Lord,

Being at Aix for sometime in order to make use of the baths, I there received the letter which you did me the honor to write me. I find some great difficulties in the way of executing the redemption about which you speak. It does not appear to me possible to give such colour to our proceedings with the Algerines as to make them believe that the United States take no part in the negociation while their subjects only should be redeemed. As to the price of 2500 ₶[1] per. head it will not suffice for the voracity of these covetous people, either because they have more need of Slaves than money, since the general redemption of the French and Spanish Captives, or that, having humiliated Spain and fearing little from France, they have arbitrarily raised the rate of the Slaves; and notwithstanding the tenor of the Treaties with France, the Office at Marseilles was, the last year, obliged to pay for one Slave 4000 ₶. It is true that the number redeemed by France in 1785 did not amount to 100 Louis pr. head, but the King made the agreement in his own name, and in a favourable moment he obtained a piece of politeness from the Dey; a politeness which we cannot flatter ourselves with seeing again renewed, especially at a time when the Regency carries its pretensions so highly against France, as to lead us to fear least some rupture should follow which can perhaps, be avoided only by new sacrifices. Supposing these difficulties, removed you cannot take upon yourselves the said redemption without a permission from the Court, especially if you wish to appear as acting by virtue of the order for the redemption. I am persuaded that the ministry being first informed will not refuse you the said permission.

It will then be necessary to have a confidential person on the spot to act secretly so as not to irritate the french Slaves who might rise against the Nation, and sound the intentions of the Regency with respect to the price. The *Pere Terillo* Governor of the Hospital is a Spaniard and unfit for this negociation. M. Paret, the only french merchant and manager of the House of Messrs. Gimen at Algiers, might execute the Commission but this House will always create a suspicion that the United States are about agreeing for the redemption.

I hardly venture to propose an idea which strikes me, but it is the best I have. Could you not send a religious person, not as a redemptioner, but only as Chaplain of the Hospital of Slaves, for which he might perform the necessary functions? M. Gache appears to me the most proper and best calculated to conduct an affair the success of which I so much desire as well on account of the interest you take in it as for the satisfaction of Mr. Jefferson. I would not wish to put myself in the way on account of my age, though I speak Italian and Spanish which is used at Algiers and especially in the Hospital. However if you should not find a better person, I shall still undertake this voyage in order to give you some marks of my submission and the desire which I have to concur in your zeal for the love of redemption and good of humanity.

The voyage of a religious person would occasion some expence, but it cannot be considerable, because he might lodge in the Hospital, and there would be no commission fees to pay in case of success—not being near enough to confer with M. Gache, I address the present to him that he may transmit it to you with the observations he may make upon it.

(signed)   PERRIN def! gnal.[2]

[1] The symbol ₶ stands for livre tournois.
[2] The Senate copy of the letter is in the hand of Jacob Blackwell.

No. 3.
Extracts of Letters from William Short to the Secretary of State

Extract from a letter of June 4th. 1790 from William Short Esqr. Chargé des Affaires for the United States at the Court of France, to the Secretary of State.

"The affair of our Captives I fear will never be arranged in the present channel. Immediately on the receipt of your letter I wrote to the General of the Mathurins to let him know how much you had this affair at heart, and to beg he would inform me how it stood at present. He was gone into the Country, but I suppose I shall hear from him in a few days."

Extract of a letter from the same to the same dated June 25th. 1790.

"Since my last I have seen the General of the Mathurins, who gives little hopes of any thing being done for our Captives through his channel, although he continues assurances of his zeal in case of any opportunity presenting itself, and I am persuaded he may be counted on as to these assurances. He had begun by transmitting a small sum of money to a person of confidence at Algiers to relieve the more pressing necessities of the Captives. The person who was charged with this Commission found on enquiry that the Captives received a daily allowance, which rendered this relief unnecessary and therefore returned the money. He found also that the opinion at Algiers was, that the allowance of the prisoners was made by the United States—an opinion which would necessarily augment the difficulty of their redemption. The General added that the critical situation in which the religious orders had been for some time had rendered it impossible for him to take any step in this business—that he hoped however some arrangement would be soon made which would enable him to resume those pious occupations, & that he should be always ready to offer his ministry in behalf of the American Captives. The supplies which they have received came certainly from the Spanish Consul. I transmitted some time ago to Mr. Jay an account of them which was sent me by one of the Captives. The General of the Mathurins considered those supplies too considerable, as they would necessarily excite at the same time the suspicions and the avarice of the Algerines. It would have the appearance of cruelty to forbid further supplies from any person whatsoever, and to let the prisoners depend as it were on the charity of the Mathurins, who might be furnished with small sums from time to time for that purpose. But it is perhaps the only means of shortening their captivity. Whoever remains here should be authorized fully to act according to circumstances with respect to the Captives."

Extract of a letter from the same to the same dated July 7, 1790.

"My last letters will have informed you of the present situation of the business relative to the American Captives at Algiers. You will have seen that nothing has been done, or possible to be done, for their redemption; still I will leave nothing untried, and will write you regularly as you desire respecting it.

I omitted mentioning above that the number of our prisoners at Algiers is now reduced to fourteen, a scotch boy who was among them having been redeemed by the intervention of the English Consul. The price was somewhat more than 7000 ₶. but additional and unavoidable expenses raised it on the whole to about 8000 ₶. The person of whom I spoke in the beginning of this letter, told me that he thought the remaining Captives might be redeemed at the same price for the common sailors, and about 12,000 ₶ for each of the Captains.

He added that the Spanish Consul was at present in the greatest favour with the Regency, and would be the most proper person for being charged with such a Commission. The same person told me that he had understood the present Emperor of Morocco had begun his reign by shewing dispositions to observe the treaties made by his predecessor. He thought it probable that ours would be continued. In general however I have understood that we should be obliged to renew it—this is the opinion also of Mr. Carmichael."[1]

[1] The extracts are in the hand of Jacob Blackwell.

No. 4.
Extract of a letter from Mr. John Lamb to the Honble. Thomas Jefferson dated Algiers 29th March 1786

"I am sure by the best information the sum will by no means answer our object if the amount is not greatly augmented. It is my duty to advise to abandon the undertaking as it will be entirely in vain to persevere. It is lost money the expences that arise on the attempt. The last amount that I can give please to let me know. I shall wait at Carthagena for the same. The people will cost for their redemption at least twelve hundred hard dollars pr. head: the number is twenty-one. Your Excellency sees how feeble we are."[1]

[1] The extract is in the hand of Jacob Blackwell.

No. 5.
Extract of a letter from Mr. Paul Randal to the honble. Thomas Jefferson dated Alicant April 2d. 1786

"As the money is paid according to the Treaty, the Dey has set the sum of 3600 dollars on every Spanish Captain 3000 for each mate or Pilot, and 1200 for the private Seamen and Soldiers."[1]

[1] The extract is in the hand of Jacob Blackwell.

No. 6.
Extract of a letter from Richard O'Brian to the Honble. Thomas Jefferson dated Algiers June 2d. 1788

"If any one is redeemed it is at a very exorbitant price. A few days ago an old Savoy Captain of a Merchant vessel was redeemed for the sum of 2150

Algerine Chequins, which is equal to £967.10. Sterling, and even with that price it was with much time the Dey was prevailed on to let him be redeemed; And I think that Sailors will be as high as £400. Sterling as they are very scarce here at present and much wanted to do the duty for the public."[1]

> [1] The extract is in the hand of Jacob Blackwell.

No. 7.
Extract of a Letter from Richard O'Brian, to the Honble. Thos. Jefferson, dated Algiers, December 12th. 1789

		Dollars
"In December 1789, There are in Algiers 2 Masters at the Dey's Price		12,000
2 Mates at 4,000 Dollars each		8,000
11 Mariners @ 1500 Dollrs. each		16,500
	Dollars	36,500
20 pCt. a Duty on Slaves		1,825
Agreeable to the Dey's price in 1786, the whole cost is		38,325

A Mr. Joseph Cowen Bockerie the principal Jew Merchant of Algiers assures me that he will engage, and well knows that he could obtain the Americans Release from Slavery on the following Terms.

		Dollrs.
vizt. for 2 Masters at 2,000 Sequins each		8,000
2 Mates at 3,000 Dollars each		6,000
11 Mariners at 1,300 Dollars each		14,300
	First Cost	28,300
Fees and Duties to the Regency amounts to 20 ℗ Ct.		1,415
	Spanish Dollrs.	29,715

Mr. Bockerie says that at the very furthest he would procure us at 2,000 Dollrs. each, which would be in all 30,000 Dollars, or 6750 pounds sterling—and the Dutch and Spanish Consul are of the same Opinion."[1]

> [1] The extract is in the hand of George Taylor, Jr.

No. 8.
Extract of a Letter from James Simpson, dated Gibraltar August 25th. 1790

"Having lately been desired to inquire by means of my Correspondents at Algiers how many Americans remained there, and the Sum would be demanded for their Ransom, I take the Liberty of enclosing for your Information Copy of the Return made me, and to say that as the Gentleman encharged me to make this Inquiry, wrote in a Stile as if the generous and humane Idea of Ransom flowed from a private Source, I much fear, as the Sum demanded is considerable, I shall not have the Happiness of being encharged by them with Directions for carrying it into Execution."

List of american Prisoners at Algiers 9th. July 1790, with the Sums demanded by the Regency for their Ransom

Crew of the Ship Dolphin captured 30th July 1785.

Richard O Bryan	Captain	Ransom demanded Zs.	2,000
Andrew Montgomery	Mate		1,500
Jacob Tessanior	French passenger		2,000
William Paterson	Seaman (keeps a Tavern)		1,500
Philip Sloan			725
Peleg Lorin			725
John Robertson			725
James Hall			725

Crew of the Schooner Mary taken 25th. July 1785.

Isaac Stephens	Captain	2,000
Alexander Forsyth	Mate	1,500
James Cathcart	Seaman (keeps a Tavern)	900
George Smith	(in the King's House)	725
John Gregory		725
James Hermet		725

Algerine Zequines 16,475

Duty on the above Sum 10 ℔ Ct.   1,647 ½

Sundry Gratifications to Officers of the Dey's Household, and ⎫
Regency, equal to 17 ⅙ Zs. each Person   ⎬   240 ⅓

34792 28/38 Mexican Dollars @ 38 mozunas each, are ⎫
Zequines ⎬   18,362 ⅚ [1]

[1] The extract and enclosed list are in the hand of George Taylor, Jr.

George Washington to the Senate and House of Representatives

United States December 30th 1790

GENTLEMEN OF THE SENATE AND HOUSE OF REPRESENTATIVES,

I lay before you a Report of the Secretary of State on the subject of the Citizens of the United States in captivity at Algiers, that you may provide on their behalf what to you shall seem most expedient.

GO. WASHINGTON[1]

[1] The message, in the hand of Tobias Lear and signed by George Washington, is in President's Messages on Foreign Relations, Executive Proceedings, SR, DNA. It is related to the committee report journalized February 1, 1791.

Thomas Jefferson to the President of the Senate

Philadelphia Jan. 20, 1791

SIR,

I have the honor to inclose you a letter from one of our captive citizens of Algiers, if I may judge from the superscription and from the letters from the same quarter which I have received myself. as these relate to a matter before your house, and contain some information we have not before had, I take the liberty of inclosing you copies of them.

I have the honour to be with sentiments of the most profound respect & attachment   Sir

Your most obedient
& most humble servt.
TH. JEFFERSON[1]

[1] The letter, in the hand of Thomas Jefferson, is in President's Messages on Foreign Relations, Executive Proceedings, SR, DNA. It is related to the committee report journalized February 1, 1791. A transcript of the letter, in a nineteenth-century hand, probably made by ASP, is filed in the same location.

(1)
Richard O'Bryen to William Carmichael*

City of Algiers May the 17th. 1790

ESTEEMED SIR,

I had the Honor of writing you a Letter dated the 11th. Inst. and as Time permits I shall mention other particulars, the Vickelhadge being further sounded relative to a peace with America, says that if the Americans wish to make a Peace with this Regency, why do they not send an Ambassador, or empower some Person to act for them, and I cannot help repeating to you that the Foundation of all Treaties, in this Regency, should be laid by some Person in Algiers, and I am convinced that no Person is more capable than Monsr. Faure. Depend, Sir, you may confide in him, and by empowering Monsr. Faure the Affair would be done with that secrecy which is requisite, considering that America has three powerful Enemies in Algiers Vizt. French and Spaniards, and the most inveterate is the English. But as british Affairs are very unsettled at present, british Influence cannot be very great. And the French have just emerged from having very nearly lost their Peace, and the present Situation of France is such that I believe they cannot afford to give money to this Regency to corrupt the Algerines to the Prejudice of America.

When the English Consul signified to the Dey and Regency, that Spain was arming to support the Grand Duke of Tuscany, the Vickelhadge said that any Nation that took the part of the Russians or Imperialists, that Nation had no

* Ambassador to Spain

longer a Peace with this Regency—so that I assure you that if the Spaniards arm in Favor of the Grand Duke, they are no longer at Peace with Algiers. The spanish Consul said that Spain had armed a small Fleet, as Customary to exercise the Officers of their Marine, and if the Armament was any way extra, it was perhaps on Account of some Disturbance in spanish America—The Vickelhadge said Miramus. So that considering the present Situation of the three Enemies of America in this Quarter, and this Regency in want of Cruisers I cannot perceive that ever a more favorable Opportunity offered for America to make a Peace than the present, and I must observe that those Nations, the Dutch, Danes, Swedes, and Venetians have their Peace on a more solid Basis than the Spanish Peace, for the annual Tribute those Nations pay is the Bait that keeps their Peace, and not any Sentiment of national Honor, or regard to Treaties, but the view of the Tribute annually and for their own Convenience, in being supplied annually with naval and military Stores.

Spain made a very dishonorable and impolitic Peace—what makes the Algerines adhere to it, is owing to the vast Sums of Money and Presents given, which are sufficient to almost tempt these People to adore Lucifer and depend that when the Dey goes to his long Home it will be difficult for the Spaniards to keep their Peace, &c. as they gave a great Sum of money for their Peace, and a second great Sum not to be tributary. These People say at present that they have got all from Spain that they can get, and that it is prejudicial to this Regency to keep the Peace with Spain—but it would be too barefaced for the present Dey & Ministry to break the Peace or Treaty, inasmuch as they themselves made it or agreed thereto.

Indeed America should always be ready to embrace every opportunity of trying for a Peace, and even if refused the second Time, notwithstanding good Policy requires that always some Person should be impowered—for depend it is very prejudicial to America in not having a Peace with the Barbary States, and I compute that the Insurance paid on American Bottoms, and Merchandize amounts annually to upwards of one Million Sterling, which Sum the British Nation gets by insuring American Property on Account of our not being at Peace with the Barbary States.

You will observe that the Spaniards gave the former Vickelhadge thirty two thousand Dollars for bringing the Subject of the spanish Peace before the Dey and Divan, and they gave very valuable Presents, so that considering from the 1st. of June 1785 to May 1790, it is generally said here that the Spanish Peace and Ryalas or Presents & Redemptions have cost Spain full 4½ millions of Dollars. And as I often wrote you, that there is no doing Business with these People without first giving Presents, it being the Custom of this Country, therefore I think that the Vickelhadge's Demand of an American Schooner of 12 Guns was by no means high—for as you will observe that he would promise and engage to be the Friend and Advocate—so that if the Americans did not succeed, the Vickelhadge of course would not expect to get the Schooner—but still, it would be requisite to reward him for his Trouble and good Intentions, so as to keep him the Friend of America on another Occasion. But all in a great Measure depends on the Vickelhadge—the Dey is led by him in every respect, and by liberally rewarding him, the Terms of the Peace would not be very high, for all depends on his Representations to the Dey, and no one dare oppose him.

But to keep the Peace hereafter, much Attention should be paid to the prime Minister—indeed no one can say with any Degree of certainty who may be the Dey's Successor, and a Peace made by one Party in opposition to the Other, cannot be said to be on a firm Basis or lasting; for if the Party in Opposition once gets the Helm of State, they will not consider themselves bound to keep the Peace made by the other Party, and there is a great Party that disapproved of making a Peace with Spain. Many respectable Turks here say that it was nothing but Bribery or a Torrent of Corruption, which the Algerine Ministry could not resist that obtained Spain a Peace. Indeed it was by no means the Voice of the People—Fine. NB., These are the Copies of the Letters I wrote to Mr. Carmichael, which you will please to signify to him if he is in Europe.

Esteemed Sir, &c.

RICHARD O'BRYEN[1]

[1] A copy of the letter, in the hand of George Taylor, Jr., is in President's Messages on Foreign Relations, Executive Proceedings, SR, DNA. It is related to the committee report journalized February 1, 1791. A transcript of the letter, in a nineteenth-century hand, probably made by ASP, is in the same location.

(2)
Richard O'Bryen to William Carmichael

City of Algiers June the 24th. 1790

ESTEEMED SIR,

I have the Honor of informing you that good Fortune and favorable Opportunities offering, the following particulars were communicated to his Excellency the Effendi Vickelhadge General of the Marine and Minister for foreign Affairs for this Regency by two of my Brother Sufferers in the Dey's Palace, viz. George Smith and Philip Sloan—the 1st. is Chamberlain to the Vickelhadge, the 2d. is Capt. aproa of the Dey's palace.

"That the United States of America abounds in Masts, Yards, Spars of all sizes fit for Vessels, and Plank and Scantling, Tar, Pitch, and Turpentine and Iron—That these Articles are cheaper in America than they are in any part of Europe.

"That there is no Nation in the World that builds such fine and fast sailing Cruisers as the Americans—that the Americans never did the Algerines any Injury that they never fitted out Cruisers against them, and always wished to make an honorable Peace with this Regency as the Americans considered the Algerines to be a brave People like themselves.

"That the Americans have but little Money, and that the Currency of the Country, is paper Money, but that America abounds in Maritime Stores—that if the Algerines would make a Peace with America they may be supplied with American Cruisers at a very cheap rate, and also with all the Productions of

America which this Regency may want for their Marine, and as the Americans have no Money to give for a Peace, they would give Masts, Yards, Spars, Plank, Scantling, Tar, Pitch, Turpentine, and Philadelphia Iron, and by being at Peace with America, the Algerines would be supplied with Cruisers and Stores, and need not be at the Trouble and Expense of building Cruisers in Algiers, and of Course would take many Prizes, and could pay all their Attention to their Marine in constructing Gun Boats to protect the City.

"That these Propositions were partly the Instructions of the american Ambassador who came here in 1786 and intended only to ascertain our Ransom, and try to make a Peace on honorable Terms with this Regency, and to see if this Regency would not take for our Ransom and for the Peace in lieu of Money american Masts, Yards, Plank, and Scantling, Tar, Pitch & Turpentine all to be agreed on at a certain fixed Price by Treaty, but that Mr. Lamb could speak Nothing but English and the french Consul and Conde D'Espilly, the Spanish Ambassador would not take the Trouble to explain Mr. Lamb's Propositions, as the Terms of the Peace would be advantageous to the Algerines, and that the french and spaniards advised Mr. Lamb to return to America that the Algerines would not make a Peace with the United States of America.

"That America is one thousand Leagues Distance from Algiers—that the Commerce of America is chiefly to the West India Islands, and from one State to another—that our chief Commerce is our Coasting Trade, and that we have but little Trade to Europe, particularly to the Mediterranean and Ports adjacent—that the American Cargoes are of but little Value, and consist of Wheat, Flour, Salt, Pork and Fish, and a few Cargoes of Naval Stores—that these Vessels are manned with fewer Sailors than those of any other Nation, that they sail faster, and consequently are less liable to be captured, and of course little profit the Algerines can derive by being at War with the Americans who wish to make an honorable Peace with this Regency, and that in Case the Algerines should be at war with the northern Nations of Europe, the algerines may be supplied with maritime Stores by the Americans, and that if the Regency would not find it to their advantage to sell the Americans Passports for the Mediterranean and Ports adjacent, or elsewhere at a certain reasonable Price and on Conditions to be fixed by Treaty which Conditions would exclude and prevent any pretext of Quarrels or Embroylas, and as it would be the Interest of America to encourage her Trade in the Mediterranean so on the Increase of America more passports would be required and the greater the advantage would be to the Algerines. This would open a Channel for this Regency, having a Resource for supplying their marine in Case they should be at war with the Dutch, Danes, or Swedes, the Nations that supply the Algerines at present, and that the Americans will as liberally reward any Person that is their Friend and Advocate in making the Peace as their Circumstances will admit."

These Propositions were explained to his Excellency the Minister for foreign Affairs at sundry Times from the 7th to the 13th of may 1790.

The Vickelhadge asked how these Propositions of the american Ambassador were known to us—he was answered that Captain O'Bryen read Mr. Lamb's

Instructions several Times, and he explained them to us. His Excellency the vickelhadge said that when Mr. Lamb was in Algiers in 1786, that at that Period this Regency was settling the Spanish Peace, and that the american Ambassador was by no means a suitable Person as he spoke Nothing but English, and they knew Nothing of his Propositions—that after the Americans had freed themselves from the British, that the British Nation had demanded as a Favor of this Regency not to make a Peace with the Americans, and that some Time before the American Ambassador came, the French and Conde D'Espilly tried all their Influence against the American's obtaining a Peace. That these three Nations were, and are the Enemies of America, and that he would explain all more particularly to the American Ambassador if he came to make a Peace— but that those Nations had no Influence over the Algerines, and that Nothing should prejudice this Regency against the Americans, if they came to make a Peace.

The Vickelhadge said he believed this Regency would make a Peace with America on as easy Terms as possible, considering the present Times, and as the Americans had no Money to give for a Peace, we must give the productions of America, vizt. Tar, Pitch, Turpentine, Masts, Yards, Spars, Plank & Scantling, and Cruisers american built.

The Vickelhadge said as he intended to be the Friend and Advocate of America in making a Peace with this Regency, he would expect for his Weight, Trouble, and Influence, an American built Schooner of 12 Guns, which of course would not cost much—that he would pave the way with the Dey and Divan, so that America would succeed, and that he would recommend it strongly to the Dey to make a Peace with America, and that he knew the former Vickelhadge was promised by and through Mr. Lamb and Wolf more than the amount of a Schooner, but that he would esteem and do more for getting an American Schooner, than he would for Sacks of money—that he or this Regency did not want Money, they only wanted american Cruisers and Naval Stores for their Marine.

The Vickelhadge said that he wished much to know about getting the Schooner—to this Question I returned for Answer, that it was impossible for us to say positively, but that we would write to the american Divan or to Congress and to the American Ambassador at Madrid. He asked when the American Divan met to do Business, and respecting our Form of Government, and was answered that last March Congress met, and that our Government is founded on Liberty and Justice. The Vickelhadge said that a few Months ago the Portuguese asked for a Peace and that it was refused them—he said he hoped if the Americans sent an Ambassador to Algiers to make the Peace, that they would send a Man that could speak the Spanish or Italian Language—he ridiculed much the sending a Man to make the Peace that no one could under-stand what he had to say, and said that the Conde D'Espilly was a bad and false Man.

Indeed I hope Congress will appoint a proper Person to negociate the Peace, and I should certainly recommend Mr. Faure as a good Assistant; I think you may confide in him. But all I now mention is entirely unknown to any Person in this Country excepting the Vickelhadge and I and my two brother sufferers in the Dey's Palace, and I hope all will be managed with that good Policy and Secrecy that such important Business requires, as no Person here has any Idea that the Americans are thinking of a Peace.

It will be very requisite for you to give an Answer as soon as possible and as fully as your Situation will admit of, writing by two Conveyances, and what you would wish to communicate or say in Answer to the Vickelhadge, write it separate from other Particulars, which you would think proper to communicate to me—as I would wish, (if you think proper) to communicate your Answer, thro' the same channel to the Vickelhadge, directing to me under cover to the Care of Monsieur Faure, to avoid any Suspicions.

I hope Congress will give the Ambassador they sent to Algiers as extensive Powers as possible, and should the Terms of the Peace be too great, that his Instructions will admit him to see on what Terms he could procure 150 Passports of Algiers—for as you will conceive that until you give some Answer and empower some Person to act that it is impossible to know exactly on what Terms america may obtain Peace, or what Heads of the Treaty may be. I think all wears a favorable Aspect.

I have stated the Particulars communicated to the Vickelhadge, and his Answers, and submit all with much Respect to your Consideration—indeed it would have been impossible to have brought the Affair to its present Meridian in any other Manner—for depend the Vickelhadge would not have listened to propositions different from what have been communicated, and I have the Pleasure to add that about a Month ago the Noznagee asked the Capt. Aproa, one of my Crew, why the Americans did not try for a Peace.

I hope no American Vessel will be captured for depend it would be very prejudicial towards obtaining a Peace—it would occasion the Terms to be greater than they would be if none were captured, and would be a Clue for the Enemies of America to persuade the Algerines that much was to be got by being at War with the United States of America.

And I take the Liberty of mentioning that a few Lines from you to the Spanish, would be requisite, as he thinks you are displeased with him respecting the Affair of our Disbursements, so as not to have any Enemies to America in this Quarter—This in a great Measure would lull him and Consul Logie asleep.

You will recollect, Sir, that I wrote you that all Nations pay 1/3 or 1/4 more than they used to pay, or is agreed on by Treaty, owing to the spanish Peace, which has hurt all Nations here except the British—And some Hints from you to Congress would be requisite on this Subject.

I am sorry to hear that you have taken a Tour to France, for you will not receive this Letter as soon as I could wish. I write under Cover to Messrs. Etienne Drouilhoult and Compy. Banquiers at Madrid, and as the Port is to be embargoed in a few Days, and the Vessel a Danish Ship bound to Spain, Time will not permit me to write more particularly or correctly, and I hope you will receive this Letter, as I believe it will be some Time before I shall have another Opportunity of writing to you.

You will observe that the Vickelhadge sways the whole Regency as he thinks proper, and that his Influence is very great—for by his Recommendations to the Bey of Tunis, the present Vickelhadge of Tunis was appointed to that Office; and the Vickelhadge of Algiers has a Brother at present a great Man at Constantinople. Great Care should be taken not to lose the Friendship of the present Noznagee (the Prime Minister) the Head of opposition—for by making these two great Men the Friends of America, any Thing can be done in this Regency. The plain Question is will America give Cruisers and Maritime Stores to this Regency to make a Peace, otherwise the Algerines can get Cruisers (to take Americans) from other Nations. They have Money sufficient to build a large Fleet, but at present all their Cruisers are gone up the Levant except two, and three Gallies—so that this Regency are much in want of Cruisers, and I dare say never a more favorable Opportunity offered, or will offer for America than the present, which bids fair to open an extensive Field of Commerce and Wealth to America.

I would have wrote you concerning the Morocco Affairs, but I suppose you have heard all sometime past. I hope we shall keep our Peace with Morocco, for the Situation of West Barbary is such as to be very detrimental to American Commerce, if we unfortunately should lose the Peace with the new Emperor. I need not mention to you the distressed and suffering Situation of my Brother Sufferers in the Marine.

Esteemed Sir,
Your most obedient
most humble servant
RICHARD O'BRYEN

N.B. The Copy of this Letter I sent to Mr. Carmichael—it was dated May the 15th. 1790, and not being certain where he was, I thought it of sufficient Importance to write to you, so that should Mr. Carmichael be in France, as Report says, you will give him these Letters to read, keeping the same Time Copies, and transmit such Parts thereof to Congress as you think requisite, or to Mr. Jefferson. The same Time acknowledge the Receipt of these Letters as soon as possible, so that I may know you have received them.[1]

[1] A copy of the letter, in the hand of George Taylor, Jr., is in President's Messages on Foreign Relations, Executive Proceedings, SR, DNA. It is related to the committee report journalized February 1, 1791. A transcript of the letter, in a nineteenth-century hand, probably made by ASP, is in the same location.

(3)
Richard O'Bryen to Thomas Jefferson

City of Algiers July 12th. 1790

ESTEEMED SIR,

We the fourteen unfortunate Americans in Algiers, were informed by Mr. Abraham Bushara & Dininio, capital Jew merchants of this City, that they had received orders from America, by way of London and Lisbon,[1] to make application to this Regency, to ascertain & fix the ransom of the American captives, after their surmounting many difficulties, at last on the 7th. instant prevailed on the Dey & Ministry to agree and fix the price of the said fourteen Americans at Seventeen thousand two hundred and twenty five Algerine sequins. I have often explained relative to the purport of Mr. Lamb's audiences when in Algiers; at present I shall only mention to you that Mr. Lamb had five audiences with the Dey and Ministry, and he agreed for the ransom or release of the American captives agreeable to the price then asked. The ransom of the fourteen Americans at present in Algiers, amounted to 17,500 Algerine sequins.

At that period there were nearly 3,000 Slaves in Algiers; but the Spaniards, Neapolitans and other Nations redeeming their people, and the Pest in 1787–88 carrying off 780 slaves (among this number were six Americans) the number of Slaves is reduced to 700. The major part of these are deserters from the Spanish garrison of Oran. Since that period the Dey has raised the price on Slaves, and is but little inclinable to admit of slaves being redeemed, they being much wanted to do the public work, which be assured, Sir, is very laborious. The price asked for the Americans is by no means exorbitant, considering the present want of Slaves, and the terms of release of captives of other Nations.

Mr. Bushara & Dininio having a great knowledge of these people, were thereby very fortunate in prevailing on the Dey and Ministry, to fix the release of the Americans at 17,225 sequins. Our greatest fears were, that the Dey would not permit us to be redeemed on any terms. The Dey asked 27,000 sequins, but was prevailed on by the prime Minister to let our ransom be on the terms mentioned.

The Dey and Ministry signified that the ransom of the Americans was fixed and agreed on with Mr. Lamb, the american Ambassador, in 1786; and that he promised to return with the Money in four months, but that he broke his word and agreement. The Ministry observed, that if the Americans did not keep their word on so small an affair as the sum asked for our release, that there was no dependence to be put in them in Affairs of more importance. Indeed, Sir, I hope for the honor and interests of the United States of America, that the price now fixed for our release will be immediately agreed to: and be assured, Sir, if this opportunity in our behalf is not embraced, that we shall be the most miserable slaves in the World, for we shall be doomed to perpetual Slavery.

After the price was fixed, the prime Minister observed that he could not conceive what ideas the Americans had of the Algerines, by first sending an ambassador, who making a regular bargain or agreement for our release & promising to return in four months, had not kept his word. We said that at that time our country was forming a Government, and that we did not suppose the Ambassador had informed Congress of the agreement he made. The prime Minister said the ambassador did not act right. We answered, that perhaps he did not understand that he made a regular bargain, or that all was badly interpreted. Much passed on this subject. The present Causendal, or Lord chamberlain to the Dey, said he was present when Mr. Lamb agreed for our release.

On the 8th. instant the prime Minister sent privately to me, and desired that when I wrote to mention all he said, and make it known to my Country. Indeed we are much indebted to the prime Minister; for depend, Sir, he is a friend to America. He was so when Mr. Lamb was in Algiers; and even at that period, had matters been well managed, the foundation of a peace might have been laid.

Should any change happen in this Government, we apprehend it would be very prejudicial to our release; or should the Portuguese, Neapolitans or Genoese redeem their people on higher terms, than is at present asked for the Americans, depend upon it, Sir, that to get us clear would be attended with much difficulty.

You will please to consider, Sir, what our sufferings must have been in this country, during the trying period of five years captivity, twice surrounded with the pest and other contagious distempers, far distant from our country, families, friends and connections.

Depend upon it, Sir, that it is prejudicial to any nation that leaves it's subjects in slavery; for in no respect can it answer any public benefit, or be any advantage to the Country they belong to. The longer the time they are in slavery, the greater the difficulty is there in releasing them: and it is well known that the price of the slaves is rising on every application, owing to the decrease of slaves, as the Algerines find they cannot carry on the public work without slaves.

Since our redemption has been ascertained & fixed, several applications have been made to the Dey and Ministry to permit captives of other Nations to be redeemed on the same terms as fixed on for the Americans; but the Dey answered, that he wanted slaves. These applications were for certain persons, but not for any general or national redemption.

On the 7th. of April 1786 Mr. Lamb agreed with the Dey on these terms for the release of the Americans.

For each Master 3,000 Sequins.

For each Mariner 750 Sequins.

For each Mate 2,000 Sequins.

At present there are in Algiers, at the Dey's price with Mr. Lamb,

2 Masters at 3,000 Sequins each, is	6,000
2 Mates at 2,000 Sequins each, is	4,000
10 Mariners at 750 Sequins each, is	7,500
Sequins	17,500

Duties and fees on the ransom of ⎫
slaves, amounting to 15 or 18 per Cent ⎭

On the 7th. July 1790 our ransom was ascertained and fixed by Bushara & Dininio with the Dey and Ministry at, vizt.

2 Masters, O Bryen & Stephens, at 2,000 sequins each, is	4,000
2 Mates, Alexander Forsyth & Andrew Montgomery, at ⎫ 1,500 sequins each, is ⎭	3,000
Jacobus Jysanier a young lad aged 22 years & page to the dey	2,000
William Patterson a smart seaman at	1,500
James Cathcart a young lad understanding navigation	1,500
George Smith a young lad & page to the Dey at	900
Philip Sloan at	700

John Robertson	at	700
Peleg Lorin	at	700
James Harnet	at	700
James Hull	at	700
John Gregory Billings	at	700

First cost	17,100
Extra fees	125
Sequins	17,225

N.B. a sequin is equal to 8s. sterling.

A duty of 15 or 18 per Cent to be added, ⎫
being fees on the redemption of slaves ⎭

Indeed, Sir, there is no alternative. We are at the lowest price that any public slaves will be redeemed whilst the present Government stands; and I am shure our Country will see, by our ransom, the fatal and bad consequence of being at War with the Barbary States, particularly so commercial a Nation as the American is. All other commercial Nations have experienced the bad policy of a War with the Barbary States.

Who could have thought that the haughty spanish Nation would have given such vast sums for making and keeping peace with the Barbary States, and changed their national flag. But the Spaniards saw they were made a sort of political tool by all the other commercial Nations.

The Regency, some time past, wanted three of the young Americans to embrace the Mahometan religion, but they would not. This I suppose may account for the motives of their price being something extra.

Two months past one of my crew, Charles Colvill, was redeemed by charitable contributions raised by his friends. His ransom cost 1,700 dollars. I believe he returns to America. He is capable of giving much information on Barbary affairs.

Three Algerine gallies have taken a polacre with sixteen greeks, with a pass from the deceased Grand Seignior. They are enslaved by the Algerines by their having been under Jerusalem colours. They also took a Neapolitan Brig, the crew of which escaped; and a Genoese vessel, but an armed Tartan of Genoa retook this vessel with 20 moors & turks on board. The Algerine Galley took another Neapolitan Vessel near Toulon—the neapolitan seamen in that port manned their boats, and went out of Toulon and retook the vessel. This is likely to be a serious affair. Depend upon it, Sir, that the Chamber of Commerce of Marseilles must pay all damages.

I have now the pleasure of informing you, that the Court of Portugal has dropped their idea of making a peace with this Regency. I believe all their propositions were rejected by the Algerines. Indeed, Sir, this is very fortunate for the Americans, for if the Algerines were at peace with Portugal, the cruisers of this Regency would meet with no obstruction in their cruising in the Atlantic, which of course would be very prejudicial to the commerce of America.

The Minister for Foreign Affairs being further sounded relative to a peace with America, asked if we had wrote to our Country the purport of what he said on the subject. He was answered, that I had wrote on the subject to the American ambassadors in Europe.

He answered and said that he would do all he had promised, and not deviate or withdraw his word. This answer was about the 4th. of June. Indeed as the present Minister for foreign Affairs has expressed himself so friendly in behalf of America, I hope there will be a lasting friendship between them & him, who, you may depend Sir, is well inclined to serve the Americans.

My brother sufferers & I, Sir, return you our sincere thanks for befriending us so much in the cause of liberty, being convinced that you have done all in your power with the Congress, to redeem this unfortunate and faithful remnant of Americans; and we make not the least doubt, that our Country will immediately see the necessity of agreeing to pay the sum for our release, as has been ascertained. Our dependence is on a generous and humane Country, whom that God may prosper is the sincere wish of, Esteemed Sir

> Your most obt. most h'ble. Servt.
> RICHARD O BRYEN in behalf)
> of myself and brother Captives (

P.S.

We are much indebted to the)
Spanish Consul & other gentle- (
men for many favors, rendered (
in times of impending danger[2])

---

[1] This was probably "Livorno" in the original letter by O'Bryen. See Richard O'Bryen to the Congress of the United States, 12 July 1790.
[2] A copy of the letter, in the hand of Henry Remsen, Jr., is in President's Messages on Foreign Relations, Executive Proceedings, SR, DNA. It is related to the committee report journalized February 1, 1791. A transcript of the letter, in a nineteenth-century hand, probably made by ASP, is filed in the same location.

(4)
Richard O'Bryen to the Congress of the United States

City of Algiers July the 12th. 1790

THE HONOURABLE THE CONGRESS OF THE UNITED STATES OF AMERICA,

We the fourteen unfortunate Americans in Slavery—Being informed by Mr. Abraham Bushara & Dininio, Jew Merchants in Algiers, that He had Received orders to assertain the Ransom of the American Captives. Mr. Bushara & Dininio after Surmounting many Difficulties, at last on the 7th. Inst. prevailed on the Dey & Ministry, to agree, for the price of the Said fourteen Americans, at the Sum of Seventeen thousand two Hundred and twenty five Algerine Sequins —Honoured Sirs, being further Informed by Bushara & Dininio, that their orders came from Congress to London & from thence to Livorn[o] & so to algiers.

I have often Explained Relative to the purport of Mr. Lambs audiences with the Dey & Ministry, But Shall at present Confine myself to that part Relative to his agreeing for the Ransom of the American Captives.

When Mr. Lamb was in Algiers 1786 he had 5 audiences with the Dey & Ministry. The Sum for our Release was agreed on & amounted to 17,500 Sequins or 35,000 Dollars. That is for 14 Americans, of Course I do not include those that Died, but Substract or Deduct their price from the Sum total. at that Period there was nearly three thousand Slaves in Algiers but the pest that Raged in 1787–88 Swept of 780 Slaves, amongst this number were 6 Americans. The Spaniards, Niapolitans, & other Nations Redeeming their people & Causelties that has happened Since has Reduced the Number of Slaves to 700. The Major part of these are Deserters from the Spanish Garrison of Oran.

Since that Great Storm of mortality, the Dey has Raised his price & is but Little Inclineable, to admit of Slaves, Being Redeemed, He Being much wanted to do the public work which be assured Honoured Sirs is Very Laborious.

Honoured Sirs, the price asked for the Americans, is by no means Exorbitant Considering the present want of Slaves, & the Sums of Redemption of Captives of other nations. Mr. Bushara & Dininio, Having a Great knowledge of those people was there by Very fortunate in prevailing on the Dey and ministry to fix the Release of the Americans at 17,225 Sequins our Greatest fears Being that the Dey & Ministry would not permit us to be Redeemed on any Terms & considering that on a 2d. application the Dey Generally Raises his price. The Dey & Ministry Signified that the Ransom of the Americans was fixed and agreed on with Mr. Lamb, the American Ambassador in 1786, and that he promised to Return with the money in 4 Munths, But that he Broke his word or agreement. The Ministry observed that if the Americans did not keep their word on So Small and affaire as the Sum asked for our Release, that there was no Dependence to be put in them in affairs of more importance. Indeed Sirs, I hope for the Honour & interests of the united States of America, that the price now fixed will be immediatly agreed to.

and Be assured Honoured Sirs, that if the Terms is not Complyed with, that we are the Most Wretched & Miserablest Slaves in the world, for we shall be Doomed in perpetual Slavery. The prime minister used his influence in our Behalf, and after the price was fixed on the prime Minister Observed that he Could not Conceive what Ideas the Americans had of the Algerines, first Sending & ambassador, & he Makeing a Regular Bargain or agreement for our Release & promised to Return in 4 Munth with the money for our Release, But that he did not keep his word or agreement.

We said that, at that time our Country was forming their Government, and that we Suposed the ambassador did not inform Congress that he made any agreement. The prime minister Said the ambassador Did not act Right. much passed on this Subject. The prime Minister Desired that we would Make known all he Said to our Country. The present Lord Chamberlain to the Dey Said he was present when Mr. Lamb agreed for our Release.

Honoured Sirs, Should any Change happen in this Government, we your unfortunate Subjects apprehend it would be Very prejudicial towards our Release, or Should the portugeese Niopolitans or other nations Redeem their people on higher Terms than is at present asked for the Americans. Depend Sirs to Get us Clean, would be attended with Much Difficulty.

Honoured Sirs, you will please to Consider what our Sufferings must have been in this Country During the trying Period of 5 years Captivity, twice surrounded with the pest and other Contagious Distempers, far Distant from our Country families friends & Connections.

Depend Honoured Sirs, that it is Very Prejudicial to any Nation that Leaves their Subjects in Slavery—for in no one Respect Can it be any advantage to the Country He Belong to—for the Greater the time He are in Slavery—the Greater Difficulty in Releaseing them & it is well known that the price of Slaves is Riseing on Every application—owing to there Being but 700 Slaves here which is fewer than has been these 100 years—and as all public Duty in the Marine & Sundry other Departments is Done by Slaves the Algerines finds He Cannot Carry on their public work without them. Since our Redemption has been assertained, Several applications has been Made to the Dey and ministry to permit Captives of other nations to be Ransomed on the Same terms as the Americans, But the Dey answered that he wanted Slaves. These applications were Made in Behalf of Certain Captives, But no application has been made for a General Redemption. On the 7th. of April 1786 Mr. L[amb met wi]th the Dey and Regency as Viz. for the Ransom of Americans

2 Masters at 3,000 Sequins [Each] is	6,000	Sequins
2 Mates at 2,000 Sequins Each is	4,000	
10 Mariners at 750 Sequins Each is	7,500	

that is for the 14 Living   Sequins 17,500

Duties & feese on Slaves Being Redeemed amounting to 15 or 18 pr. Ct. to be added. July the 7th 1790, our Ransom was assertained &c. by Bushara & Dininio as Viz.

2 Masters, OBryen & Stephens at 2,000 Sequins Each is	4,000	Sequins
2 Mates, Alexander Forsyth & Andrew Montgomery at 1,500 Sequins Ech.	3,000	
Jacobus Iysanier a young Lad at 2,000 Sequins is	2,000	
William Patterson a Smart Seaman at 1,500 Sequins	1,500	
James Cathcart a young lad understanding Navigation at	1,500	
George Smith a young lad & page to the Dey at	900	
Philip Sloan at 700 Sequins	700	
John Robertson at 700 Sequins	700	
Pelig Lorin at 700 Sequins	700	
James Hull at 700 Sequins	700	
James Harnet at 700 Sequins	700	
John Gregory Billings at 700 Sequins	700	

	Total first Cost	17,100
A Sequin is Equal to 8s. Ster.	New feese Extra	125
	Algerine Sequins	17,225

a Duty of 15 or 18 per Ct. to be added.

Terms of our Release as Exact as I could Learn by the Dey's pallace.

Honoured Sirs, there is no alternative. Depend that we are at the Lowest price that any public Slaves will be Redeemed at, whilst this present Government Stands, and I am Shure our Country will perceive by the Sum asked for our Release the fatal and Bad Consequences of Being at war with the Barbary States particularly So Commercial a Nation as the Americans is trying to Be. all other Commercial nations has Experienced the Bad policy of Being at war with the Barbary States, But Interestial Views for Commerce makes them pay Tributes, & Several of them keeps their peace on Humiliatiing & Dishonourable Terms. who would have thought that the Haughty & Bigotted Spaniard would have Given Such Vast Sums of Money to Make & keep their peace with the Mahomitans & Change their National Flag. But the Spaniards Seen He were made a Tool of by all the other Commercial nations. Those Mariners that is at a high price was often asked by Some men in office to Embrace the Mahomitan Religion, But he would not. Indeed I supose by their not agreeing to Turn moors, their Ransom is Something Extra.

Honoured Sirs, I have wrote William Carmichael [& Wi]lliam Short Esqr. your ambassaders at the Courts of Spain & France, Respecting the propositions I have Dropt to the ministry to all so their answers Respecting a peace with America.

Indeed I believe that the peace May be Made nearly on the Terms I have wrote to the ambassaders and I can only assure you Honoured Sirs, that by the hints Dropt by the Ministry that He are Desireable to have a peace with america.

We hope Honoured Sirs, that we Shall Shortly be finally Extricated from our present Wretched State of Slavery—or Depend we are Doomed to Perpetual Slavery, But our Trust is in the Humanity of our Country.

Honoured Sirs
your Most Obedient
Most Humble Servant
& Petitioner
RICHARD OBRYEN[1]

In behalf of My Self & Brother
Sufferers

---

[1] The letter, in the hand of Richard O'Bryen, is in President's Messages on Foreign Relations, Executive Proceedings, SR, DNA. It is related to the committee report journalized February 1, 1791.

Commercial Relations with Great Britain

GEORGE WASHINGTON TO GOUVERNEUR MORRIS, 13 OCTOBER 1789,
    WITH ENCLOSURE
GOUVERNEUR MORRIS TO GEORGE WASHINGTON, 7 APRIL 1790
DUKE OF LEEDS TO GOUVERNEUR MORRIS, 28 APRIL 1790
GOUVERNEUR MORRIS TO GEORGE WASHINGTON, 29 MAY 1790
GOUVERNEUR MORRIS TO DUKE OF LEEDS, 10 SEPTEMBER 1790
DUKE OF LEEDS TO GOUVERNEUR MORRIS, 10 SEPTEMBER 1790
GOUVERNEUR MORRIS TO GEORGE WASHINGTON, 18 SEPTEMBER 1790

George Washington to Gouverneur Morris

New York October 13th. 1789

SIR,

My letter to you, herewith enclosed, will give you the Credence necessary, to enable you to do the business which it commits to your management, and which I am persuaded you will readily undertake.

Your enquiries will commence by observing, that as the present Constitution of Government, and the Courts established in pursuance of it, remove the objections heretofore made to putting the United States in possession of their frontier Posts, it is natural to expect, from the assurances of his Majesty and the national good Faith, that no unnecessary delays will take place. Proceed then to press a speedy performance of the Treaty, respecting that object.

Remind them of the Article by which it was agreed, that Negroes belonging to our citizens should not be carried away; and of the reasonableness of making compensation for them. Learn with precision, if possible, what they mean to do on this head.

The commerce between the two Countries you well understand. You are apprized of the sentiments and feelings of the United States on the present state of it; and you doubtless have heard, that in the late session of Congress, a very respectable number of both Houses, were inclined to a discrimination of Duties unfavorable to Britain, and that it would have taken place, but for conciliatory considerations, and the probability that the late change in our government and circumstances, would lead to more satisfactory arrangements.

Request to be informed therefore, whether they contemplate a Treaty of Commerce with the United States, and on what principles or terms in general.

In treating this subject, let it be strongly impressed on your mind, that the privilege of carrying our productions in our Vessels to their Islands, and bringing in return, the productions of those Islands to our own ports and markets, is regarded here as of the highest importance; and you will be careful not to countenance any idea, of our dispensing with it in a Treaty. Ascertain, if possible, their views on this point; for it would not be expedient to commence negociations, without previously having good reasons to expect a satisfactory termination of them.

It may also be well for you, to take a proper occasion of remarking, that their omitting to send a Minister here, when the United States sent one to London, did not make an agreeable impression on this Country; and request to know what would be their future conduct, on similar occasions.

It is in my opinion very important, that we avoid errors in our system of policy respecting Great Britain; and this can only be done by forming a right judgment of their disposition and views. Hence you will perceive how interesting it is, that you obtain the information in question, and that the business be so managed, as that it may receive every advantage, which abilities, address and delicacy can promise and afford.

> I am Sir
> Your most obedient
> humble Servant
> (signed)   GEORGE WASHINGTON

(Enclosure)

New York October 13th. 1789

SIR,

It being important to both countries, that the Treaty of Peace between Great Britain and the United States, should be observed and performed with perfect and mutual good Faith; and that a Treaty of Commerce should be concluded by them on principles of reciprocal advantage to both, I wish to be ascertained of the sentiments and intentions of the Court of London on these interesting subjects.

It appears to me most expedient to have these enquiries made informally, by a private Agent; and understanding that you will soon be in London, I desire you in that capacity, and on the authority and credit of this Letter, to converse with his Britannic Majesty's ministers on these points, Vizt. whether there be any, and what objections to now performing those Articles in the Treaty, which remain to be performed on his part; and whether they incline to a Treaty of Commerce with the United States, on any, and what terms.

This communication ought regularly to be made to you by the Secretary of State; but that Office not being at present filled, my desire of avoiding delays, induces me to make it under my own hand. It is my wish to promote harmony and mutual satisfaction between the two Countries, and it would give me great pleasure to find, that the result of your Agency in the business now committed to you, will conduce to that end.

I am Sir

Your most obedient

humble Servant

(signed) GEORGE WASHINGTON[1]

[1] Copies of the letter and the enclosure, both in the hand of Henry Remsen, Jr., are in President's Messages on Foreign Relations, Executive Proceedings, SR, DNA. They are related to George Washington's message journalized February 14, 1791.

Gouverneur Morris to George Washington

London April 7th. 1790

SIR,

I arrived in this City on Saturday evening the twenty eighth of March, and called the next morning on the Duke of Leeds, Minister for foreign affairs. He was not at home. I therefore wrote to him a note, copy whereof is enclosed, as also of his answer received that evening. On Monday the twenty ninth, I waited upon him at Whitehall, and after the usual compliments presented your letter, telling him that it would explain the nature of my business. Having read it, he said with much warmth and gladness in his appearance, "I am very happy Mr. Morris to see this letter, and under the President's own hand. I assure you it is very much my wish, to cultivate a friendly and commercial intercourse between the two countries *and more*, and I can answer for the rest of his Majesty's servants, that they are of the same opinion." "I am happy my Lord to find that such sentiments prevail, for we are too near neighbours not to be either good friends or dangerous enemies." "You are perfectly right Sir, and certainly it is to be desired, as well for our mutual interests, as for the peace and happiness of mankind, that we should be upon *the best footing*." I assured him of our sincere disposition to be upon good terms, and then proceeded to mention those points in the Treaty of Peace which remained to be performed, and first I observed, that by the Constitution of the United States, which he had certainly read, all obstacles to the recovery of british debts are removed, and that if any doubts could have remained, they are now done away by the organization of a federal Court, which has cognizance of causes arising under the treaty. He said he was happy to receive this information: That he had been of opinion, and had written so to Mr. Adams, that the articles ought to be performed, in the order in which they stood in the Treaty. Not chusing to enter into any discussion of his conduct in relation to Mr. Adams, I told his Grace that I had but one rule of or principle both for public and private life, in conformity to which I had always entertained the idea, that it would consist most with the dignity of the United States, first to perform *all their* stipulations, and then to require such performance from others: and that (in effect) if each party were, on mutual covenants, to suspend ~~their~~ his compliance expecting that of the other, all Treaties would be illusory. He agreed in this sentiment, upon which I added that the United States had now placed themselves in the situation just mentioned: and here I took occasion to observe, that the southern states who had been much blamed in this country for obstructing the recovery of british debts, were not liable to all the severity of censure which had been thrown upon them; that their negroes having been taken or seduced away, and the payment for those negroes having been stipulated by treaty, they had formed reliance on such payment for discharge of debts contracted with british merchants, both previously and subsequently to the war; that the suspension of this resource had occasioned a deficiency of means, so that their conduct had been dictated by an overruling necessity. Returning then to the main business, I observed that as we had now fully performed our part, it was proper to mention that two articles remained to be fulfilled by them, vizt. that which related to the posts, and that regarding a compensation for the negroes; unless indeed they had sent out orders respecting the former subsequent to the writing of your letter; and I took the liberty to consider *that* as a very probable circumstance. He now became a little embarrassed, and told me that he could not exactly say how that matter stood. That as to the affair of the negroes, he had long wished to have it brought up and to have something done, but something or other had always interfered. He then changed the conversation, but I brought it back, and he changed it again. Hence it was apparent that he could go no farther than general professions and assurances. I then told him, that there was a little circumstance which had operated very disagreeably upon the feelings of America. Here he interrupted me "I know what you are going to say, our not sending a Minister. I wished to send you one, but then I wished to have a man every way equal to the task, a man of abilities, and one agreable to the people of America, but it was difficult. It is a great way off, and many object on that score." I expressed my persuasion that this country could not want men, well qualified for every office; and he again changed the conversation—therefore, as it was not worth while to discuss the winds and the weather, I observed that he might probably chuse to consider the matter a little, and to read again the Treaty, and compare it with the american Constitution. He said that he should, and wished me to leave your letter, which he would have copied and would return to me. I did so, telling him that I should be very glad to have a speedy answer, and he promised that I should.

Thus, Sir, this matter was begun, but nine days have since elapsed, and I have heard nothing farther from the Duke of Leeds. It is true that Easter holidays have intervened, and that public business is in general suspended for that period. I shall give them sufficient time to shew, whether they are as well disposed as he has declared, and then give him a hint. Before I saw him, I communicated to the French ambassador *in confidence,* that you had directed me to call for a performance of the Treaty. He told me at once, that they would not give up the Posts: Perhaps he may be right. I thought it best to make such communication, because the thing itself cannot remain a secret; and by mentioning it to him, we are enabled to say with truth, that in every step relating to the Treaty of Peace, we have acted confidentially in regard to our Ally.

With perfect respect I have the honor to be

Sir

Your most obt. and h'ble. Servant.
(Signed)   GOUVR. MORRIS[1]

[1] A copy of the letter, in the hand of Henry Remsen, Jr., is in President's Messages on Foreign Relations, Executive Proceedings, SR, DNA. It is related to George Washington's message journalized February 14, 1791.

Duke of Leeds to Gouverneur Morris

Whitehall April 28th. 1790

SIR,

I should not have so long delayed returning an answer to the letter you received from General Washington, which you had the goodness to communicate to me last month, had I not heard you were in Holland. I received some time ago a note from you, which I should sooner have acknowledged, but was at first prevented by a multiplicity of engagements, and since by illness.

The two subjects contained in General Washington's letter, are indisputably of the highest importance; and I can safely assure you, that it has ever been the sincere and earnest wish of this Country, to fulfil her engagements (contracted by the Treaty of Peace) with the United States, in a manner consistent with the most scrupulous fidelity.

We cannot but lament every circumstance, which can have delayed the accomplishment of those engagements (comprized in the Treaty) to which those States were in the most solemn manner bound; and should the delay in fulfilling them have rendered their final completion impracticable, we have no scruple in declaring our object is to retard the fulfilling such subsequent parts of the Treaty, as depend entirely upon Great Britain, until redress is granted to our subjects upon the specific points of the Treaty itself, or a fair and just compensation obtained, for the non-performance of those engagements on the part of the United States.

With respect to a commercial treaty between the two countries, I can only say, that it is the sincere wish of the British government, to cultivate a real and bona fide system of friendly intercourse with the United States; and that every measure which can tend really & reciprocally, to produce that object, will be adopted with the utmost satisfaction by Great Britain.

I am, Sir, your most obedient humble Servant

(signed)   LEEDS[1]

[1] A copy of the letter, in the hand of Henry Remsen, Jr., is in President's Messages on Foreign Relations, Executive Proceedings, SR, DNA. It is related to George Washington's message journalized February 14, 1791.

Gouverneur Morris to George Washington

London May 29th. 1790

SIR,

I do myself the honor to enclose a copy of my letter of the first instant. On the night of the fourth there was a hot press here, which has continued ever since; and the declared object is to compel Spain to atone for an insult offered to Great Britain, by capturing two vessels in Nootka sound. Permit me to observe incidentally, that it would not be amiss for the American captain, who was a witness of the whole transaction, to publish a faithful narrative. The general opinion here, is that Spain will submit, and that Spain only is the object of the armament. But I hold a very different faith. If Spain submits, she may as well give up her American dominions; for the position advanced here is, that Nations have a right to take possession of any territory unoccupied. Now, without noticing the inconsistency between this assertion and those which preceeded the War of 1755, when France built fort Duquesne upon ground unoccupied by british subjects, it cannot escape the most cursory observation, that the British sitting down in the vicinity of the Spanish settlements, will establish such a system of contraband traffic, as must ruin the commerce of Cadiz, and the revenue now derived from it by the Spanish monarch. In former letters I have communicated in some measure my ideas upon the second opinion. I shall not therefore recapitulate them, but only in general notice, that the armament against Spain, should Spain shrink from the contest, will undoubtedly be sent to the Baltic with decisive effect. You will observe also, that the Ministers count upon the nullity of France, of which I shall say a word presently.

In consequence of the orders for impressing of seamen, a number of Americans were taken, and the applications made for their relief, were in some instances ineffectual. On the morning of the twelfth, Mr. Cutting called to inform me, that he was appointed Agent to several of the American masters of Ships. I gave him my advice as to the best mode of proceeding and particularly urged him to authenticate all the facts by affidavits, assuring him that if he was unsuccessful, I would endeavour to obtain the assistance of such persons, as I might be acquainted with. On the seventeenth Mr. Payne called to tell me, that he had conversed on the same subject with Mr. Burke, who had asked him if there was any minister, consul or other agent of the United States, who could properly make application to the Government: To which he had replied in the negative, but said that I was here, who had been a member of Congress, and was therefore the fittest person to step forward. In consequence of what passed thereupon between them, he urged me to take the matter up, which I promised to do. On the eighteenth I wrote to the Duke of Leeds requesting an interview. He desired me to come at three O'Clock of the next day, but his note was delivered after the hour was passed, and very shortly after it came another note giving me an appointment for the twentieth.

Upon entering his closet, he apologized for not answering my letters. I told him that I had in my turn an apology to make, for troubling him with an affair on which I was not authorized to speak. He said I had misunderstood one part of his letter to me; for that he certainly meant to express a willingness to enter into a Treaty of commerce. I replied, that as to my letter I supposed he would answer it at his leisure, and therefore we would wave the discussion; that my present object was to mention the conduct of their Press-gangs, who had taken many American seamen, and had entered American Vessels with as little ceremony, as those belonging to Britain. "I believe my Lord this is the only instance in which we are not treated as Aliens." He acknowledged that it was wrong, and would speak to Lord Chatham on the subject. I told him that many disagreeable circumstances had already happened, and that there was reason to expect many more, in a general impress through the british dominions: That masters of vessels on their return to America would excite much heat, "and *that* my Lord combined with other circumstances may perhaps occasion very disagreeable events; for you know that when a wound is but recently healed 'tis easy to rub off the skin." He then repeated his assurances of goodwill, and exprest an anxious wish to prevent all disagreement, observing at the same time, that there was much difficulty in distinguishing between the seamen of the two countries. I acknowledged the inconveniences to which they might be subjected, by the pretence of british seamen to be Americans, & wished therefore that some plan might be adopted, which founded on good faith, might at the same time prevent the concealment of British sailors, and protect the Americans from insult. As a means of accomplishing that end, I suggested the idea of certificates of citizenship, to be given by the Admiralty Courts of America to our seamen. He seemed much pleased, and willing at once to adopt it; but I desired him to consult first the King's servants in that particular department; and having again reminded him that I spoke without authority, took my leave, but at his request promised to visit him again the next day.

The morning of the twentyfirst I found him sitting with Mr. Pitt, to whom he presented me. The first point we took up was that of the impress. Mr. Pitt expressed his approbation of the plan I had proposed to the Duke, but observed that it was liable to abuse, notwithstanding every precaution which the Admiralty Offices in America could take. I acknowledged that it was, but observed, that even setting aside the great political interests of both countries, it was for the commercial interest of Britain rather to wink at such abuse; for that if they should be involved in a War with the *House of Bourbon*, our commerce with Britain must be in American bottoms, because a War premium of insurance, would give a decided preference to the manufactures of other Countries in our markets: But that no wages would induce our seamen to come within the British dominions, if they were there by liable to be impressed. Mr. Pitt replied to this, that the degree of risque & consequently the rate of insurance must depend upon the *Kind of war*. Not taking any direct notice of this expression, I observed, that notwithstanding the wretched state of the *French government*, there still existed much force in that country, and that the power of commanding human labor must also exist somewhere, so that if the government could not arm their fleets, there would still be many privateers; and that in effect the slenderest naval efforts, must involve merchant vessels in considearble danger. Returning then to the consideration of the principal point, we discussed the

means of carrying the plan into effect, and for that purpose I recommended, that
his Majesty s servants should order all their Marine officers, to admit as evidence
of being an American seaman, the certificate to that effect of the Admiralty in
America, containing in it a proper description of the person &c. but without
excluding however other evidence: and observed that in consequence of the
communication that such orders were given, the Executive authority in America,
without the aid of the Legislature, by directions to the several Admiralties, might
carry the plan into effect, so far as relates to those seamen who should apply
for certificates. I am induced to believe that this measure, if adopted, will not
only answer the desired end, but be productive of other good consequences in
America, which I will not now trouble you with the detail of.

This affair being so far adjusted, we proceeded to new matter, and they both
assured me that I had misapprehended the Duke's letter in regard to a Treaty
of commerce. I answered coolly, that it was easy to rectify the mistake; but it
appeared idle to form a new Treaty, until the parties should be thoroughly
satisfied about that already existing. Mr. Pitt then took up the conversation, and
said that the delay of compliance on our part had rendered that compliance less
effectual, and that cases must certainly exist where great injury had been sustained
by the delay. To this I replied, that delay is always a kind of breach, since as
long as it lasts, it is the non-performance of stipulations. I proceeded then to a
more exact investigation of the question—and first (as I knew them to be
pestered with many applications for redress, by those who had, and those who
pretended to have suffered) I attempted to shew what I verily believe to be the
fact, vizt. that the injury was much smaller than was imagined, because among
the various classes of American debtors, those only should be considered who
had the ability and not the will to pay at the peace, and were now deprived of
the ability. These I supposed to be not numerous, and as to others, I stated
interest as the natural compensation for delay of payment; observing that it was
impossible to go into an examination of all the incidental evils. In the second
place I desired him to consider, that we in turn complained that the British
government had not, as they ought, paid for the slaves which were taken away.
That we felt for the situation they were in of being obliged, either to break
faith with slaves whom they had seduced by the offer of freedom, or to violate
the stipulations they had made with us upon that subject. That we were willing
therefore to wave our literal claims, but had every right to insist on compensation; and that it would not be difficult for the Planters to shew, that they had
sustained an annual loss from the want of men to cultivate their lands, and
thereby produce the means of paying their debts. Mr. Pitt exclaimed at this, as
if it were an exaggerated statement. I at once acknowledged my belief, that in
this, as in all similar cases, there might be some exaggeration on both sides;
"but Sir, what I have said tends to shew that these complaints and enquiries are
excellent, if the parties wish to keep asunder; if they wish to come together, all
such matters should be kept out of sight, and each side perform now, as well as
the actual situation of things will permit." Mr. Pitt then made many professions
of an earnest desire to cultivate the best understanding &c. &c. &c. On the
whole, he thought it might be best to consider the subject generally, and see if

on general ground some compensation could not be made mutually. I immediately replied, "if I understand you Mr. Pitt, you wish to make a new Treaty instead of complying with the old one." He admitted this to be *in some sort* his idea. I said that even on that ground, I did not see what better could be done, than to perform the old one. "As to the compensation for negroes taken away, it is too trifling an object for you to dispute, so that nothing remains but the posts. I suppose therefore that you wish to retain those Posts." "Why perhaps we may." "They are not worth the keeping; for it must cost you a great deal of money and produce no benefit. The only reason you can have to desire them, is to secure the fur trade, and that will center in this country, let who will carry it on in America." I gave him the reasons for this opinion, which I am sure is well founded, but I will not trouble you with them. His answer was well turned. "If you consider these Posts as a trivial object there is the less reason for requiring them." "Pardon me Sir, I only state the retaining them *as useless to you.* But this matter is to be considered in a different point of light. Those who made the peace acted wisely, in separating the possessions of the two countries by so wide a water. It is essential to preserve this Boundary if you wish to live in amity with us. Near neighbours are seldom good ones; for the quarrels among borderers frequently bring on Wars. It is therefore essential to both parties that you should give them up; but as to us it is of particular importance, because our national honor is interested. You hold them with the avowed intention, of forcing us to comply with such conditions as you may impose." "Why Sir, as to the considerations of national honor we can retort the observation, and say our honor is concerned in your delay of performance of the Treaty." "No Sir, your natural and proper course was to comply fully on your part, and if then we had refused a compliance, you might rightfully have issued letters of marque and reprisal, to such of your subjects as were injured by our refusal. But the conduct you have pursued, naturally excites resentment in every American bosom. We do not think it worth while to go to War with you for these posts; *but we know our rights, and will avail ourselves of them when time and circumstances may suit.*" Mr. Pitt asked me if I had powers to treat. I told him I had not, and that we could not appoint any person as minister, they had so much neglected the former appointment. He asked me, whether we would appoint a minister if they would. I told him I could almost promise that we should, but was not authorized to give any positive assurance. The question then was how to communicate on this subject. I suggested, that since much time might be unnecessarily consumed by reason of the distances and uncertainty of communication, it would perhaps be expedient for them to appoint a minister, and delay his departure until you should have made a similar appointment. Mr. Pitt said they might communicate to you their intention to appoint &c:—I told him that his communication might encounter some little difficulty, because you could not properly hear any thing from the british consuls, those being characters unacknowledged in America. His pride was a little touched at this. "I should suppose Mr. Morris, that attention might as well be paid to what they say, as that the Duke of Leeds and I should hold the present conversation with you." "By no means Sir; I never should have thought of asking a conference with his Grace, if I had not possessed a letter from the President of the United States, which you know my Lord I left with you, and which I dare say you have communicated to Mr. Pitt." He had. Mr. Pitt said they could in like manner write a letter to one of their Consuls. "Yes Sir, and the *letter* will be attended to, but not the Consul, who is in no respect different from any other british subject, and this is the circumstance which I wished you to attend to." He said in reply to this, that etiquette ought not to be pushed so far, as to injure business and keep the countries asunder. I assured him that the rulers of America had too much understanding to care for etiquette, but prayed him at the same time to recollect, that they (the british) had hitherto kept us at a distance instead of making advances. That you had gone quite as far as they had any reason to expect, in writing the letter just mentioned; but that from what had passed in consequence of it, and which (as he might naturally suppose) I had transmitted, we could not but consider them as wishing to avoid an intercourse. He took up this point, and exprest again his hope that I would remove such an idea, assuring me that they were disposed to cultivate a connection &c:—To this I replied, that any written communication which his Grace of Leeds might make should be duly transmitted; but I did not like to recite mere conversation, because it might be misconceived, and disagreeable questions afterwards arise, whereas written things remain and speak for themselves. They agreed to the propriety of this sentiment. I observed further, that our disposition towards a good understanding was evidenced, not only by your letter, but also by the decision of a majority of the house of Representatives, against laying extraordinary restrictions on british vessels in our ports. Mr. Pitt said, that instead of restrictions we ought to give them particular privileges in return for those which we enjoy here. I assured him that I knew of none except that of being impressed, a privilege which of all others we least wished to partake of. The Duke of Leeds observed in the same stile of jocularity, that we were at least treated in that respect as the most favoured nation, seeing that we were treated like themselves. But Mr. Pitt said seriously, that they had certainly evidenced good will towards us, by what they had done respecting our commerce. I replied therefore with like seriousness, that their regulations had been dictated by a view to their own interest, and therefore as we felt no favor, we owned no obligation. The subject being now pretty well exhausted, they promised to consult together, and give me the result of their deliberations. This I am yet to receive; but I learn that Mr. Grenville has this day consulted some persons skilled in the fur trade, and that from his conversation it seemed probable that they would give up the Posts. *My information is good.*

I have already said that the Ministers here count upon the nullity of France. They do not however expect that she will violate her treaty with Spain, and therefore they are rather, I believe, in hopes that Spain will submit to such terms as they may impose. How far they may be bound to aid Prussia, seems as yet to be doubtful, but for my own part I believe that a war is inevitable, and I act on that ground. If it does not take place, they will I think desire such things of us in a treaty of commerce, as we shall not be disposed to grant; but if it does happen, then they will give us a good price for our neutrality, and Spain I think will do so too; wherefore this appears to be a favourable moment for treating with that Court about the Missisippi.

Before I close this letter already too long, I must entreat permission to make one or two explanatory observations. It is evident that the conduct of this Government towards us, from the time of my first interview with the Duke of Leeds, has depended on the contingencies of war or peace with the neighbouring powers, and they have kept things in suspense accordingly. When therefore they came a little forward, it proved to me their apprehension of a rupture. I have some reason to think that they are in greater danger than they are themselves aware of, and I have much cause to suspect that they meditate a blow in Flanders, in which it is not improbable that they will be foiled and disappointed. Believing therefore that I knew their motives, it only remained to square my conduct and conversation accordingly. And here you will consider that the characteristic of this nation is pride; whence it follows, that if they are brought to sacrifice a little of their self importance, they will readily add some other sacrifices. I kept therefore a little aloof, and did not as I might have done, obtain an assurance that they would appoint a minister if you would. On the contrary, it now stands on such ground that they must write a letter making the first advance which you of course will be in possession of; and to that effect I warned them against sending a message by one of their Consuls.

With perfect respect I have the honor to be

Sir

Your most obt. and h'ble. Servant

(signed)   GOUVR. MORRIS

P.S. May 30th.

It is utterly impossible for me to copy the letters which I intended to enclose. It is now near One O'Clock in the morning, and Mr. Williams sets off at Eleven.[1]

[1] A copy of the letter, in the hand of Henry Remsen, Jr., is in President's Messages on Foreign Relations, Executive Proceedings, SR, DNA. It is related to George Washington's message journalized February 14, 1791.

Gouverneur Morris to Duke of Leeds

London September 10th. 1790

MY LORD,

At the close of a conversation with your Grace and the right honorable Mr. Pitt on the twenty first of May last, I was told that you would confer together, and transmit a reply to the letter which I had the honor of addressing to your Grace on the thirtieth of April. In expectation of that reply I have patiently waited in this City to the present hour, tho' called by many affairs to the Continent; but my departure cannot be much longer delayed, and therefore it becomes necessary to intrude once more on your Grace's attention.

I was led to believe my Lord, that a friendly connection might have taken place between this Country, and that of which I have the honor to be a citizen. How far it might be useful to Great Britain I presume not to conjecture, being perfectly convinced from the wisdom and extensive information of his Majesty's ministers, that the best rule for private judgment must be derived from their conduct. But my Lord I candidly own, that such connection appears to be of great consequence to America, and therefore the hope of becoming instrumental to the accomplishment of it was most pleasing: nor am I ashamed to avow my concern at the disappointment.

Your Grace will readily recollect the purport of that letter, which you did me the honor to write on the twenty eighth of April, and that mine of the thirtieth entreated a communication of the nature and extent of that redress, which his Majesty's minister's expected upon the specific points of the Treaty of peace, and the kind and measure of compensation they would require, in case (as had been supposed) the specific performance on our part were ~~not~~ now impracticable. Months having elapsed in silence, your Grace will I hope pardon me for observing, that the pointed avowal of a determination to with hold performance unless upon certain conditions, the communication of which is with held, might be construed into unconditional refusal. Your personal integrity and honor my Lord, the acknowledged justice of his majesty, and the pride of british faith, prohibit me from harbouring that idea: But it may perhaps be entertained by my countrymen, and if it should, it may lead to measures which in their consequences shall eventually induce the two nations to seek, rather the means of reciprocal injury, than of mutual advantage. I humbly hope that this may never happen. The sentiment of America has long been conciliatory, and I should feel inexpressible satisfaction, if your Grace would possess me of the means of restoring activity to her friendly dispositions.

With perfect respect I have the honor to be
&c. &c. &c.

(signed)   GOUVR. MORRIS[1]

---

[1] A copy of the letter, in the hand of Henry Remsen, Jr., is in President's Messages on Foreign Relations, Executive Proceedings, SR, DNA. It is related to George Washington's message journalized February 14, 1791.

Duke of Leeds to Gouverneur Morris

Whitehall September 10th. 1790

SIR,

I have just received the honor of your letter of this day's date. I well remember the nature of the conversation you allude to, as well as the particular points upon which the two countries mutually complain of a non-observance of Treaty. Each party may perhaps have reason of complaint. I can assure you, Sir, I sincerely lament it. I am not entering into a ministerial discussion upon the subject of our not being already farther advanced in (what we are both interested in) a real bonafide intercourse of friendship; but am only acknowledging, confidentially, my own private opinion, and what it has not been hitherto in my power to remedy.

I shall, I trust, be enabled very soon to address myself upon a new subject to General Washington, and in the meantime shall be very happy to see you, Sir, before your departure for America.

I have the honor &c. &c.

(signed)   LEEDS[1]

[1] A copy of the letter, in the hand of Henry Remsen, Jr., is in President's Messages on Foreign Relations, Executive Proceedings, SR, DNA. It is related to George Washington's message journalized February 14, 1791.

Gouverneur Morris to George Washington

London September 18th. 1790

SIR,

I had the honor to address you on the sixteenth of August, and stated as nearly as I could the situation of Russia and Sweden. This situation has produced a very natural effect. Sweden being unsupported by her allies, & Russia having nothing to gain by farther fighting, but a part of the Finland desarts not worth fighting for, they have struck a bargain of peace immediately, without the interference of any one else. This leaves the Russian & Turk to pursue their game single handed. The ministers of Britain are by no means well pleased that they were not consulted by the Swede; and I think it probable that if Russia makes peace with the Turks, it will be without the mediation of Prussia or England; for as things are situated, it seems impossible for those powers to do the Empress any mischief before next spring.

The National assembly of France have also adopted as a national compact, the old family compact with Spain; and they are arming as fast as their disjointed condition will admit. At the same time the general opinion of this country seemed to be, that the ministry would obtain very honorable terms from Spain; whereas the ministers themselves were (as I believe) much embarrassed as to the line of conduct which they should pursue. To support the high tone in which they first opened, would probably bring on a bloody war for an empty sound: To recede, would expose them to severe animadversion at home, & a loss of reputation abroad. These circumstances appearing to me favorable, I wrote the letter of which No. 1. is a copy. It is calculated—first, to operate upon an administration which I believed to be divided in regard to America, and a Sovereign who hates the very name, while he prides himself upon his piety and moral fame—secondly, it was intended as a ground of future justification for any measures which Congress might think proper to adopt—and thirdly, it had, I own, a special view to the nature ~~and~~ of this government ~~of this~~ and people, for if they do eventually get engaged in war, and feel a little from our coldness;

and if in addition thereto, the commercial men find any ground of complaint, it will make them so eager to rectify their mistake, as to give us considerable advantages. In answer to this letter, I received that of which No. 2 is a copy. This was written in his own hand writing, and as it is said therein to be not ministerial but confidential, we must so consider it. Consequently it is not a public paper. The inference to be drawn from it is, that the Council could not agree, as yet, upon the answer to be given. Hence I concluded, that those who, pursuing the true interests of Great Britain, wish to be on the best terms with America, are outnumbered by those whose sour prejudices and hot resentments render them averse to every intercourse, except that which may immediately subserve a selfish policy. These then do not yet know America. Perhaps America does not yet know herself. *They* believe that british credit is essential to our commerce. Useful it certainly is at present; but let our *public* credit be well established and supported, and in a very few years our commercial resources will astonish the world. We are yet but in the seeding time of national prosperity, and it will be well not to mortgage the crop before it is gathered. Excuse, I pray Sir, this digression. The matter of it is not wholly inapplicable.

A copy of my answer to the Duke, and of his reply, are in the papers No. 3 & 4. In consequence of the latter I waited upon him the fifteenth instant, and I saw at once by his countenance that he felt himself obliged to act an aukward part. I waited therefore for him to begin the conversation, which he did by saying he understood I was going to America. I told him he had mistaken my Letter, for that by the *continent*, I meant the continent of Europe. After some pause, he said that he hoped soon to fix upon a minister to America; that they had a person in contemplation, who was not however absolutely agreed on. I did not ask who it was. After a farther pause, he said that *in order to save time* & obviate difficulties, the intention was to send over a gentleman with a common letter of recommendation, but having letters of credence in his pocket. I exprest my perfect approbation of this expedient. He told me that he was earnestly desirous of a real bona fide connection, not merely by the words of a treaty, but in reality. I met these by similar professions, but took care to confine them to a commercial intercourse, for mutual benefit, on liberal terms. He told me that as to the two points of the treaty, there were still difficulties. He wished they could be got out of the way. He then hesitated a little, and dropt the conversation. Having waited some time for him to resume it, and being convinced by his silence, that it was intended to hold a conference and say nothing, I determined to try for information in a different way. I began therefore by expressing, with an air of serious concern, my conviction, that their detention of the Western posts would form an insurmountable barrier against a treaty with us. Knowing so well as he did the nature of popular governments, he would not be surprized that some in America should oppose a treaty with Britain from serious doubt as to the policy of the measure, and others from private reasons; and he must see that holding those posts, would form an argument for one, and a pretext for the other. Finding that he felt this, I added that their conduct in this respect, gave serious alarm to reasonable well meaning men. Some believed their design was to deprive us of our share in the fur trade, which they considered as a serious injury; but others were convinced, that holding those posts was attended with great and useless expence to Britain, which the benefits of the fur trade by no means compensated; and even that she would derive those benefits, whether that trade were carried on through the medium of Canada or of the United States. Hence they inferred some other, and consequently some hostile views; so that every murder committed by the indians was attributed to british intrigues: and altho' some men of liberal minds might judge differently, their arguments could have little weight with the many who felt themselves aggrieved. He owned that there was force in these ~~objections~~ reflections. I told him farther, that I did not presume to judge of the great circle of European politics, but according to my limited comprehension, was led to suppose that they could not act with the same decisive energy towards their neighbours, while they doubted of our conduct. He said I was perfectly right, and he said so in a manner which shewed, that this had been urged and felt during the late negociations. I proceeded therefore a little farther (premising that this conversation was merely from one gentleman to another) and prayed him to consider, that in a war between Britain and the house of Bourbon (a thing which must happen at some time or other) we can give the West-India islands to whom we please, without engaging in the war ourselves; and our conduct must be governed by our interest. He acknowledged that this was naturally to be expected; and it seemed from his manner, that the same thing had been represented before, but not in such strong colours. I observed that those preferences which we had a right to give in our own ports, and those restrictions which we had a right to impose, would have a most extensive operation. Assured him of my sincere belief, that their exclusive System, as far as it related to the commerce of their islands, had a tendency to injure that navigation which it was their object to encrease; because if we met them on equal ground of restriction, they would lose more in one way than they gained in another. That they had many large ships employed in carrying the single article of Tobacco; and if we should pass a Navigation Act to meet theirs, they could not bring us a yard of cloth which contained Spanish wool, and so of other things. I thought I could perceive, that considerations like these had already given them some alarm, I therefore said that I supposed his people had transmitted information of the attempts made in Congress to adopt such regulations. He said they had. I observed that not having yet received the laws passed by Congress, I could not say exactly what had been done. That I hoped things were yet open for treaty. *That doubtless there were many persons in this Country, who to gratify the resentment occasioned by losses or disappointments in the American war, would be glad to urge on a state of commercial hostility,* but this would prove perhaps a losing game to both. He really thought it would. Having gone as far in that line as was useful, I took a short turn in my subject, and said I had waited with great patience during the negociations they were carrying on, because I supposed *they would naturally square their conduct towards us by their position in respect to other nations.* I made this observation in a careless manner as a thing of course, but immediately fixing my eye upon him, he shewed that it was exactly the circumstance they had wished to conceal. I added, that finding the

Northern courts were now at peace, *and supposing they had come to their final decisions with respect to the house of Bourbon, I thought it probable that they were prepared to speak definitively to us also.* Here I waited for his answer, which indeed I did not expect to receive. He was pretty sufficiently embarrassed, and from his look and manner I collected quite as much as he was willing to communicate. After some little sayings of no consequence, he asked me what the United States would think of the undefined claim of Spain to America. Having no objection to take that information from his questions, which could not be drawn forth in his answers, I told him that it would make no impression on our minds. That the Spaniards being in fact apprehensive of danger from us, were disposed to make sacrifices for our friendship. That the navigation of the Missisippi, hitherto the bone of contention, was I believed given up by them already, or would soon be so; and as for their claims they never could affect us, and therefore we did not care any thing about them. That their reason for withholding that navigation hitherto was the fear of contraband trade, and for the same reason they must in my opinion sacrifice the last man and last shilling, upon the question about Nootka Sound. He said he had always thought the danger of contraband ought to be considered in dealing on this subject, for that Nations like individuals, ought to treat with candour and honesty. We had a good deal of conversation on that, and other topics in which America was not directly concerned, and then I told him that if they came to any determination in regard to us speedily, I should wish to be apprized of it. He assured me that I should, and offered to make his communications to you through me, and for that purpose to address his letters to me in Paris; but for reasons communicated in a former letter, I thought it best to decline this offer, and therefore observe that his own packets would give him a speedier and more certain means of conveyance. I then took my leave.

I have troubled you, Sir, with the leading features of this conversation, that you might the better judge of the conclusions I draw from it. I think the Cabinent is divided on the question of war or peace. If France appeared strong enough to excuse a *retrogade manoeuvre*, I believe they would discover all at once, that Spain has better reasons to urge than they had been before apprized of, & therefore *on principles of Justice*, and having received the strongest assurances of brotherly love from the Catholic King, the Defender of the Faith would disarm. His ministers will not treat with us at present, unless they could see their way to an offensive and defensive alliance, which we shall be in no hurry to contract. Should war break out, the anti-american party will I believe agree to any terms; for it is more the taste of the medecine which they nauseate, than the size of the dose. Mr. Pitt I believe wishes a continuance of peace. Observe that he is rather the Queen's man than the Kings, and that since his Majesty's illness *She* has been of great consequence. This depends in part on a medical reason. To prevent the relapse of persons who have been mad, they must be kept in constant awe of somebody, and it is said that the Physician of the King gave the matter in charge to his royal consort, who performs that, like every other part of her conjugal duty, with singular zeal and perseverance. He, and all those who are in possession of his entire confidence, wish (it is said) for war, which gives you know great patronage, and by the encrease of taxes and offices encreases the influence and power of the crown. The king *and his friends* are also violently indisposed to America.

Things being so situated, and having business on the continent, I shall leave this city in a few days, and shall perhaps write a farther letter of lamentations to the Duke of Leeds before I go. I intend to write such a letter to you on the whole business as may, in case of need, be laid before the legislature, and consequently before the public.

I long since expressed my opinion to you, Sir, that the appearances of prosperity here were fallacious. In nothing are they more so, than in the affairs of the India company, which are deplorably bad; and they are now engaged in a war with Tippoo Saib, which terminate how it may, must make them worse.

It is time to close this lengthy epistle. Let me therefore entreat you to receive the assurances of that sincere respect and esteem with which I have the honor to be, Sir, your most obedient and humble Servant.

(signed)   GOUVR. MORRIS[1]

---

[1] A copy of the letter, in the hand of Henry Remsen, Jr., is in President's Messages on Foreign Relations, Executive Proceedings, SR, DNA. It is related to George Washington's message journalized February 14, 1791.

Diplomatic Exchange with Portugal

DePinto to Thomas Jefferson

Lisbon 30th. November 1790

SIR,

I have just received the Letter which your Excellency has done me the Honor to write to me, dated the 7th. of August, transmitted to me by Colonel Humphreys. It is with a perfect Satisfaction, Sir, that I observe you at the Head of a Department through which I can have the Advantage of communicating to you with that Confidence which your Virtues have inspired me, and which may in Time become the Basis of reciprocal Connections of Friendship and Interest between the two Nations.

I am fully convinced, Sir, of all the Difficulties which a New Constitution carries with it, and of the Time which it requires to bring it to perfection: I also know, Sir, the advantages of a prudent Economy, and how essential it is for your Constitution, and cannot but applaud it.

It was in Consequence of these Principles that I avoided all Etiquette on the Subject by proposing to her Majesty the Queen only a Resident Minister for the United States of America, without even waiting for a previous Nomination on their part, and the Choice has fallen on Monsr. Freire, Secretary of Legation at the Court of London.

I think, Sir, that this Step will fully answer the strict Views of Economy, by putting it in your Power to transact the public Business with more Dignity, seeing no other Difference between the Title of Resident and that of Chargé d'Affaires, than merely the Name. But notwithstanding the Conviction of this, it is of the last Importance for us, as it was impossible to find any proper person willing to go to America simply in the Character of Chargé d'Affaires; and you will observe, Sir, that we cannot dispense with requiring a Reciprocity of Character in the Representatives of the two Nations.

I flatter myself then, Sir, that your Government in its Wisdom will see that the Title of Resident Minister has nothing which will infringe upon its economical Views, and that by giving more Weight to its Agents in Europe, it cannot but gain in point of Negociation.

From these Principles, you will be persuaded, Sir, of the Pleasure with which the Queen will see at her Court a Resident Minister from the United States, and of the Share which he will always have in her Royal Benevolence.

After having informed you of the true Sentiments of her Majesty, permit me, Sir, to renew to you those of the most sincere Friendship and perfect Consideration, with which I have the Honor to be,

Your Excellency's
Very humble and
obedient Servant
DE PINTO[1]

[1] The translation, in the hand of George Taylor, Jr., is in President's Messages on Foreign Relations, Executive Proceedings, SR, DNA. It is related to George Washington's message journalized February 18, 1791.

David Humphreys to Thomas Jefferson

Lisbon November 30th. 1790

SIR,

As soon as my baggage was landed, I wrote a note to M. de Pinto, advising that I was charged with the delivery of a letter from you to him, and requesting the honor of being informed at what time it would be convenient for his Excellency to receive it. To this he gave an extremely polite answer, and fixed upon the 25th. of this month at his house in Tunqueira. I accordingly waited on him, and though he had been so much indisposed the preceding night as to refuse all other visits that morning, as soon as my name was sent in, he received me in his closet with great goodness. Upon perusing your letter he enquired kindly about your health, expressed himself strongly attached to you personally, and gave the most pointed assurances of his dispositions to promote a friendly intercourse between our two nations; at the same time declaring that he had been much mortified in not having been able to carry your former negociations into effect; but that you knew it was not owing to his fault, and adding that he was very happy to have obtained from the Queen the nomination of the Chr. de Freire as *Minister Resident* in the United States, because Mr. de Freire was so well known to Mr. Adams, yourself & many respectable Americans, and because he was himself so fully acquainted with that gentleman, and knew him to be a person of good understanding, strict honor, conciliating temper, and well inclined to the United States. I gave him the best answer of civility in my power, with assurances of the reciprocal favorable dispositions of the Executive of the United States; and that from the partial acquaintance I had formerly had the pleasure to have with M. de Freire, as well as from the excellent reputation he universally sustained, there was no doubt he would be perfectly well received in, and highly acceptable as a *Diplomatic Character* to the United States; but I observed that the designation of this gentleman *as such* was not known in

America at the time when I left it; that therefore the overtures contained in the letter I had just had the honor of delivering to him, originated spontaneously with the American government in the same friendly sentiments which had influenced her most Faithful Majesty to make this nomination; that this was the first new arrangement of a diplomatic nature which had been proposed since the establishment of the present government; that his Excellency would be pleased to notice that motives of economy and difference in circumstances between our young nation and the old nations of Europe, were the reasons which operated with the Executive of the United States for wishing to keep only a Chargé des affaires at this court; that altho' the President of the United States /with the advice & consent of the Senate/ had the appointment of diplomatic characters, yet the pecuniary provision for their subsistence was made solely by acts of the legislature; and that the existing act of the legislature for this purpose had granted a specific appropriation of monies to the disposal of the President, with a limitation that he might allow to a Minister plenipotentiary & a Chargé des affaires an annual salary not exceeding such a sum for each. The minister of her most Faithful Majesty replied, that he fully comprehended the scope of the observations in Mr. Jefferson's letter, but that he did not perceive any inconvenience could result to the United States on account of the pecuniary appointment, because the salary which would support a Chargé des affaires might also answer for a Minister resident, whose intermediate grade between a Minister plenipoy. & a Chargé des affaires, would certainly give him more respectability than the latter, without subjecting him of necessity to more expence; and he named an instance of a Minister Resident, who being a merchant, did not receive a single farthing of pay from his Court, and yet enjoyed all the privileges & favour annexed to that Grade. But he laid the principal stress of the propriety of the measure of naming a Minister resident from the Court of Lisbon to the United States upon their not being able to select a *sufficiently worthy and dignified character*, who would consent to go such a distance in only the capacity of Chargé des affaires. He finished by saying, that as such good dispositions prevailed on both parts, he flattered himself there could not be a difficulty about names, rather than things; that he was not however enabled to give any conclusive opinion, without first consulting the Queen and her other ministers. Here I took occasion of enlarging as much as I could with decency, upon our situation as a new nation in a manner disseuered from the rest of the world, the system which had been established by us, the policy and propriety there might be for European nations to dispense with forms in regard to us, and the conduct of Spain on this subject; together with whatever other topics I judged might without indiscretion be adduced as tending to obtain the object in view. The Chr. de Pinto rejoined much to the same effect he had before, and added that he would also give the sentiments he had now expressed, in writing to you, in answer to your letter, particularly on the impossibility of finding a proper character who would be willing to go to America, merely in the quality of Chargé des affaires. As he appeared to be somewhat unwell, and as the ground of the business had been so much changed from what it was understood to be when I left America, by the actual appointment of the Chr. de Freire as

Minister Resident to the United States, I did not press the conversation so much at that interview as I should otherwise have done; but before I took my leave I added, that as he had been pleased to mention that whatever had fallen from him in the course of this conversation was not to be considered as conclusive, and as perhaps something farther would occur to make some alteration of opinion in consequence of the observations that had been or might be made, it was my desire to know at what time I might have the honor of seeing him again on the subject of this conference. He assigned this day at twelve O'Clock.

I attended at the time appointed, and the Chr. de Pinto informed me, that having considered attentively the subject of your letter, he was still fully confirmed in the sentiments he had expressed to me in our first conversation; that he greatly applauded the system of severe economy in which we were laying the foundations of our new Government; that attention to this economy (as he had before observed) need however occasion no objection against our naming a Minister Resident rather than a Chargé des affaires, because there need be no difference of expence in the grades; and that altho' the etiquette which had formerly been observed by the Court of Lisbon in not admitting Chargés des affaires to equal privileges with Ministers might be dispensed with, yet the policy of keeping a person of respectable character from that Court in the United States had made it absolutely necessary to appoint a Minister Resident; for he repeated the assertion to me upon his word of honor and with the greatest appearance of earnestness, that they could not find a person who was proper to be employed in a public character in America, and who would accept the appointment as Chargé des Affaires. He also mentioned that it was impossible for the Queen to receive a Diplomatic character of a different denomination from that which she sent. I observed in reply, that the embarrassment of the government of the United States would not probably be occasioned so much by the article of expence in the present instance, as by a deviation from the system to which they had wished to adhere; that it would be peculiarly unfortunate & much to be regretted, if the systems of the two nations should be so incompatible, as to prevent an exchange of diplomatic characters, when the mutual interests & inclinations of both seemed to render it so expedient; and after recapitulating, under different points of view, several observations which had been before suggested, I remarked that altho' his Excellency might have noticed it was hinted in your letter, that whatever should be agreed with me as to the grade of diplomatic characters to be exchanged, should be considered as settled, yet as I was not authorized to agree upon the exchange of any but in the capacity of Chargés des affaires, and as in the mean time a Minister Resident had been appointed by this Court, I did not perceive what could be done at present farther than to state the circumstances to the Executive of the United States. He said if I would give him leave, he would read to me the draft of a letter he was preparing for you, which he did, and which as well as I could comprehend from a single reading, I believe, in addition to what I have already had the the honor to report, will bring you sufficiently well acquainted with the purport of what passed in the conferences I was directed to hold with the Chr. de Pinto on the subject of your letter to him. The polite attention of that minister merits all my acknowledgments. Having made arrangements for hiring Mules, I propose to set out for Spain immediately, and to return here before it will be possible for your answer to this letter to arrive in this place.

An ambassador extraordinary from Vienna has just come to Lisbon to announce to this Court the election of the Emperor of Germany. A Portuguese frigate destined to carry an ambassador to the new Emperor of Morocco, went down the river yesterday. Nothing farther is known here respecting the terms of the Convention between Spain and England, than when I wrote to you on the 19th. of this month.

With sentiments of perfect esteem & consideration

> I have the Honor to be
>> Sir
>>> Your most obedient
>>>> & most humble Servt.
>>>> (signed)   D. HUMPHREYS[1]

---

[1] A copy of the letter, in the hand of Henry Remsen, Jr., is in President's Messages on Foreign Relations, Executive Proceedings, SR, DNA. It is related to George Washington's message journalized February 18, 1791.

Nominations of Militia Officers for Territory South of the Ohio River

Report of the Secretary of War to the President, with Enclosures

The Secretary for the Department of War, to whom was referred the Letter from Governor Blount, to the Secretary of State, dated the 26th. of November 1790.

REPORTS,

That by the eighth section of the Act, intituled, "An Act to accept a cession of the claims of the State of North-Carolina to a certain district of Western territory"—it is provided "that the laws in force and use in the State of North-Carolina, at the time of passing this Act, shall be, and continue in full force within the territory hereby ceded, until the same shall be repealed, or otherwise altered by the legislative authority of the said State."

That the Act, intituled, "An Act for the Government of the territory of the United States, South of the River Ohio"—Provides, "that the inhabitants of the said territory shall enjoy all the privileges, benefits and advantages, set forth in the Ordinance of the late Congress, for the Government of the territory of the United States, North-West of the Ohio."

That the said Ordinance of the late Congress—Provides, that all General Officers of the Militia in the territory North-west of the Ohio, shall be appointed and Commissioned by Congress.

That the said Governor Blount, and Hugh Williamson Esqr., representative for North-Carolina, by their Letters hereunto annexed, alledge that by the laws of the said State, at the time the United States accepted of the Cession before mentioned, provided for two Brigadiers General, within the territory ceded to the United States—the one for Washington district, and the other for Miro district.

That at the time of the aforesaid Cession, John Sevier was Brigadier General of the Militia for Washington district, and Daniel Smith for that of Miro— but that the latter is now Secretary of the said Government.

On this statement the Secretary of War is of opinion, That in conformity to the usage before established by the laws of North-Carolina, with respect to a Brigadier of Militia for each of the said districts of Washington and Miro, as well as in regard to the propriety of the measure, that it would be highly neces-

475

sary for the general Government, to appoint a Brigadier for each of the said districts.

That from the Letters of the said Governor Blount and Hugh Williamson, and other information, it would appear, that the following Characters would be proper for the said Offices, to wit:

John Sevier, Brigadier General
of Militia for
Washington District
James Robertson, Brigadier General
of Militia for
Miro District.

All which is humbly submitted to the President of the United States.

War Department   )   H. KNOX
February 22d. 1791)   Secy. of War.[1]

[1] The report, in the hand of Benjamin Bankson and signed by Henry Knox, and the following enclosures are in Executive Nominations, third session, Executive Proceedings, SR, DNA. They are related to George Washington's message journalized February 22, 1791.

(1)
Extract of a Letter from Governor William Blount to the Secretary of State

26t. November 1790

By the eighth article of the act of cession of the state of North Carolina the laws in force and use at the time of passing that act are to continue so until they are repealed or altered by the legislative authority of the territory; and by the militia law of North Carolina there is a brigadier general to each district. At the time that act passed John Sevier was the brigadier for the district of Washington and Daniel Smith for Mero. By the ordinance for the government of the territory the appointment of all officers above the rank of field officers is in Congress. It is my duty to inform you that in my opinion John Sevier is the most proper man again to fill that station in the district of Washington, he has spirit judgment, experience and as a general the confidence of the people in general, and James Robertson now the Colonel of Davidson county is the most proper for the district of Mero; he is cool, brave and prudent and has the confidence of the people. Daniel Smith is now secretary and if there was a propriety in again appointing him, I know he would not accept.[1]

[1] The extract is in the hand of William Jackson.

(2)
Hugh Williamson to the Secretary of War

5th. February 1791

SIR,

I waited on the secretary of State who proposes to attend to the necessary measures towards a legislative representation of the inhabitants south of the Ohio.

Whatever respects the militia must belong to your department, for this reason I take the liberty of submitting to your consideration, that in the government south of the Ohio the laws of N. Carolina are in force, That according to the laws of N. Carolina the militia of each district are commanded by a brigadier general. The ceded territory includes two districts, vizt., Washington and Mero. The late brigadiers were Sevier and Smith. The gentleman last named is now secretary and may contingently have the powers of governor. This will probably operate against his reappointment. I submit to your consideration whether Col. James Robertson might not with propriety be appointed: He is the oldest Colonel in the district; is an excellent soldier and has decidedly the confidence of the people in preference to other officers. He formerly declined the appointment in favor of Mr. Smith. With respect to Mr. Sevier the late brigadier of Washington I shall only observe that he has not only the plenary confidence of the people but is certainly better qualified to command the militia in a frontier settlement than most other officers.

I have the honor to be
with the utmost respect
Sir
Your most obedient
and very humble servant

(signed)   HU. WILLIAMSON[1]

---

[1] The extract is in the hand of William Jackson.

Resignation of William S. Johnson

William Samuel Johnson to the Vice President

Philadelphia 4 March 1791

SR,

The state of my health, the situation of my affairs, & my time of Life render it very inconvenient for me longer to attend Congress. I therefore resign my seat as a Senator from the State of Connecticut, & request that proper Notice thereof may be given to the Legislature of sd. State that they may supply the Vacancy. I have the Honor to be with the greatest respect & esteem.

Sr.

Your most obedient
& most humble
Servant
WM. SAML. JOHNSON[1]

[1] The letter, in the hand of William Samuel Johnson, is in Executive Nominations (Second Congress), special session, Executive Proceedings, SR, DNA.

APPENDIX

Biographies of Nominees
in the
First Congress

Connecticut

BISSELL, RUSSELL (1755–Dec. 18, 1807). Appointed lieutenant in U.S. infantry (1791); soldier; born in Vernon, Conn.; resided (1790) in East Hartford, Conn.; son of Ozias and Mabel Roberts Bissell; married Eunice Rockwell (c. 1782); ensign in the Revolution, lieutenant in infantry (1791) until promoted to captain (1793), major in 2nd infantry (1807).
Source: William Cutter, *Genealogical History of Connecticut,* 4 vols. (New York, 1911), vol. 2.

BRADLEY, DANIEL (Feb. 13, 1757–Dec. 8, 1837). Appointed lieutenant in U.S. infantry (1791); soldier; son of Daniel and Mary Banks Bradley; married Elizabeth Stratton; lieutenant in the Revolution (1776–83), lieutenant in infantry (1791) until promoted to captain (1791), major (1797), honorably discharged (1802); member of Society of the Cincinnati.
Sources: Samuel Hart et al., eds., *Encyclopedia of Connecticut Biography,* 10 vols. (New York, 1917–23), vol. 8; Frazer Wilson, *Journal of Captain Daniel Bradley* (Greenville, Ohio, 1935).

BRADLEY, PHILIP B. (Mar. 26, 1738–Jan. 4, 1821). Appointed U.S. marshal (1789–1802); merchant and farmer; born in Ridgefield, Conn.; resided (1790) in Ridgefield; son of Daniel and Esther Burr Bradley, Jr.; B.A. Yale (1758); married (1) Mary Bostwick (1762), (2) Ruth Smith (1770); lieutenant-colonel in Conn. militia (1771), colonel of 5th Conn. (1776–81); member of Conn. General Assembly (1769–91); justice of the peace (1793–1801); member of Conn. ratifying convention (1788), and voted for Constitution.
Source: Franklin B. Dexter, *Biographical Sketches of the Graduates of Yale College,* 6 vols. (New York, 1885–1912), vol. 2.

BUELL, JOHN H. (1753–1813). Appointed captain in U.S. infantry (1791); soldier; son of Benjamin and Mary Sprague Buell; married (1) Phebe Hubbell, (2) Sarah Taylor Metcalf; entered Revolutionary service as sergeant (1775), ensign (1776), lieutenant (1777), captain in infantry (1791), promoted to major (1793), honorably discharged (1802); member of Society of the Cincinnati.
Sources: DAR *Lineage Books,* 166 vols. (Washington, D.C., 1890–1939), vols. 13, 14, 33; Albert Wells, *History of the Buell Family* (New York, 1881).

CHESTER, JOHN (Jan. 29, 1749–Nov. 4, 1809). Appointed supervisor of distilled spirits (1791–1801); farmer; born in Wethersfield, Conn.; son of John and Sarah Noyes Chester; B.A. Yale (1766); married Elizabeth Huntington (1773); captain at Bunker Hill, promoted to major (1775), colonel (1776), resigned (1777); justice of the peace for Hartford County (1793–1801); in Conn. General Assembly for many years, and Speaker of the General Assembly (1801); member of Conn. ratifying convention (1788), and voted for Constitu-

tion; member of Society of the Cincinnati. He held $7.30 in loan certificates in
1786.

Sources: Robert E. Chester-Waters, *Genealogical Notes of the Families of
Chester of Blaby, Leicestershire and Chester of Wethersfield, Connecticut, New
England* (Leicester, Conn., 1886); Henry Johnston, *Yale and Her Honor Roll
in the American Revolution* (New York, 1888).

EDWARDS, PIERREPONT (Apr. 8, 1750–Apr. 5, 1826). Appointed U.S. district
attorney (1789); lawyer; born in Northampton, Mass.; resided (1790) in New
Haven, Conn.; son of Jonathan and Sarah Pierrepont Edwards, Jr.; grandson of
Jonathan Edwards; B.A. Princeton (1768); married Frances Ogden (1769);
served in Continental Congress (1787–88); speaker of Conn. General Assembly
(1789–90); member of Conn. ratifying convention (1788), and voted for Constitution; U.S. district judge (1806–26); a Republican.

Source: Dwight Loomis and J. Gilbert Calhoun, eds., *The Judicial and Civil
History of Connecticut* (Boston, 1895).

FITCH, JONATHAN (Apr. 12, 1727–Sept. 22, 1793). Appointed collector at
Middletown (1789–93); steward; born in Norwalk, Conn.; resided (1790) in
New Haven, Conn.; son of Thomas and Hannah Hall Fitch; B.A. Yale (1748);
married (1) Sarah Saltonstall (1751), (2) Elizabeth Mix (1766); colonel in
Conn. militia, commissary for Conn. troops; member of Conn. General Assembly
(1776); sheriff of New Haven (1758–93); naval officer of New Haven (1783–
89). He held $18.67 in loan certificates in 1786.

Sources: Dexter, *Biographical Sketches of the Graduates of Yale College*,
vol. 2; Roscoe C. Fitch, *History of the Fitch Family*, 2 vols. (Haverhill, Mass.,
1930), vol. 1.

FROTHINGHAM, EBENEZER (d. Oct. 22, 1790). Appointed lieutenant in U.S.
infantry (1789); soldier; son of Rev. Ebenezer Frothingham; married Joanna
Langdon (1779); lieutenant in continental infantry (1779–83); killed in action
with Miami Indians near Chillicothe, Ohio.

Source: Thomas B. Wyman, *The Frothingham Genealogy* (Boston, 1916).

HEART [HART], JONATHAN (1748–Nov. 4, 1791). Appointed captain in U.S.
infantry (1789); soldier and teacher; son of Ebenezer and Elizabeth Lawrence
Hart; B.A. Yale (1768); married Abigail Riley (1777); lieutenant in 3rd Conn.
(1776), captain (1780), promoted to brigade major (1781–83), captain under
Confederation (1784–85), captain in army (1789), major (1791); killed in
action with Indians in St. Clair's defeat at Fort Recovery, Ohio; member of
Society of the Cincinnati. His observations of the Ohio country and Indian
ethnology were published in the *Transactions of the American Philosophical
Society*.

Sources: Consul Willshire Butterfield, *Journal of Capt. Jonathan Heart* (Albany, 1885); Dexter, *Biographical Sketches of the Graduates of Yale College*,
vol. 3.

HEARTSHORN[E], ASA (d. June 30, 1794). Ensign in Conn. troops during the Revolution; appointed ensign in infantry (1789), lieutenant (1791), promoted to captain in 1st sub-legion (1792); killed in action with Indians at Fort Recovery, Ohio; witness to Treaty of Fort Harmar (1789).

HUMPHREYS, DAVID (July 10, 1752–Feb. 21, 1818). Appointed commissioner to Southern Indians (1789); minister to Portugal (1790–97); merchant and poet; born in Derby, Conn.; son of Daniel and Sarah Riggs Humphreys; B.A. Yale (1771); married Ann Frances Bulkley (c. 1795); captain in 2nd Conn. (1776), later lieutenant-colonel and aide-de-camp to George Washington, brigadier general in Conn. militia (1812); secretary to Benjamin Franklin and Thomas Jefferson in Paris (1784–86); member of Conn. General Assembly (1786); minister to Spain (1797–1802); a Federalist; close friend of Washington, and a member of his household for many years. He was known as one of the "Hartford Wits."
Sources: Hollis Campbell, William Sharpe, and Frank Basset, *Seymour, Past and Present* (Seymour, Conn., 1902); Charles E. Perry, ed., *Founders and Leaders of Connecticut, 1633–1783* (Boston, 1934).

HUNTINGTON, JEDEDIAH (Aug. 4, 1743–Sept. 25, 1818). Appointed collector at New London (1790–1818); merchant; born in Norwich, Conn.; resided (1790) in New London County, Conn.; son of Jabez and Elizabeth Backus Huntington; B.A. Harvard (1763); M.A. Yale (1770); married (1) Faith Trumbull (1766), (2) Anne Moore; colonel in 8th Conn. (1775); brigadier general in continental army (1777–83); member of Sons of Liberty; sheriff of New London County (1788–89); member of Conn. ratifying convention (1788), and voted for Constitution; treasurer of Conn. (1789–90); a Federalist; member of Society of the Cincinnati; member of the court martial which tried and sentenced Major André. He held $94.84 in loan certificates in 1786.
Sources: Abel McEwen, *A Sermon Preached at the Funeral of General Jedediah Huntington* (New York, 1818); Perry, *Founders and Leaders of Connecticut, 1633–1783*.

IMLAY, WILLIAM (Nov. 12, 1742–Aug. 5, 1807). Appointed commissioner of loans (1790–1807); merchant; born in Bordentown, N.J.; resided (1790) in Hartford, Conn.; son of John and Elizabeth Wright Imlay; married Mary Nevins Church (1778); commissioner of continental loan office for Conn. (1780–90); justice of the peace for Hartford County (1792–1801); an incorporator of Hartford Library Co. (1799).
Source: William H. P. Oliver, *A Brief Account of the American Ancestors and of Some of the Descendents of William Henry Imlay* (n.p., n.d.).

JEFFERS, JOHN. Private during the Revolution, appointed ensign in U.S. army (1789), lieutenant (1790), promoted to captain (1792), resigned (1794).

KINGSBURY, JACOB (July 6, 1756–July 1, 1837). Appointed lieutenant in U.S.

infantry (1789); soldier; born in Franklin, Conn.; son of Nathaniel and Sarah Hill Kingsbury; married Sarah Palmer Ellis (1799); entered continental army (1775), sergeant (1776), commissioned ensign (1780) and served with Lafayette, lieutenant (1789), captain (1791), promoted to major (1797), lieutenant-colonel (1803), colonel (1808), colonel inspector general (1813), honorably discharged (1815); member of Society of the Cincinnati.

Source: States Historical Company, Inc., *Kingsbury, Scovill, Davies and Allied Families* (Hartford, 1937).

LAW, RICHARD (Mar. 7, 1733–Jan. 26, 1806). Appointed U.S. district judge (1789–1806); lawyer; born in Milford, Conn.; resided (1790) in New London County, Conn.; son of Jonathan and Eunice Hall Law; B.A. Yale (1751); married Anne Prentice (1760); member of Conn. General Assembly (1765); member of Governor's Council (1776–86); member of Continental Congress (1778, 1783–84); chief judge of county court (1773–84); chief judge of Conn. Superior Court (1786); mayor of New London (1784–1806); member of Conn. ratifying convention (1788), and voted for Constitution; a Federalist. Working with Roger Sherman, he revised the statutes of the state in 1784.

Sources: Dexter, *Biographical Sketches of the Graduates of Yale College,* vol. 2; Loomis and Calhoun, *The Judicial and Civil History of Connecticut.*

MILLER, ASHER (Nov. 24, 1753–Dec. 24, 1821). Appointed surveyor at Middletown (1789–90); lawyer; born in Middletown, Conn.; resided (1790) in Middletown; son of Giles and Elizabeth Parsons Miller; B.A. Yale (1778); married Sarah Lord Ward (1781); member of Conn. General Assembly (1785, 1788–93, 1798, 1803–4); state attorney (1785–94); member of Conn. ratifying convention (1788), and voted for Constitution; judge of Conn. Superior Court (1793–95); mayor of Middletown (1791–1821); member of Conn. Senate (1806–17); judge of Middlesex county court (1807–21); a Federalist.

Sources: Dexter, *Biographical Sketches of the Graduates of Yale College,* vol. 4; Loomis and Calhoun, *The Judicial and Civil History of Connecticut.*

MILLER, EDWARD (June 30, 1756–July 6, 1823). Appointed ensign in U.S. infantry (1791); soldier; born in Middlesex County, Conn.; son of Jared and Elizabeth Carter Miller; married Elizabeth Rockwell (1783); promoted to lieutenant (1791) and to captain of 2nd sub-legion (1793), resigned (1800).

Source: Robert R. Jones, *Fort Washington at Cincinnati, Ohio* (Cincinnati, 1902).

PALMER, JONATHAN (May 5, 1746–Jan. 2, 1810). Appointed surveyor at Stonington (1790); born in Stonington; son of Jonathan and Prudence Holmes Palmer; married Lucinda Smith (1782); 1st lieutenant in 4th Conn. (1776), lieutenant (1780); justice of the peace (1777–88, 1793–96); member of Conn. General Assembly (1785–92).

Source: Emily W. Leavitt, *John Melvin of Charlestown and Concord, Massachusetts and His Descendants* (Boston, 1901).

PARSONS, SAMUEL H. (May 14, 1737–Nov. 17, 1789). Appointed judge of Western Territory (1789); lawyer; born in Lyme, Conn.; son of Jonathan and Phebe Griswold Parsons; B.A. Harvard (1756); read law with Matthew Griswold; married Mehetable Mather (1761); colonel in 6th Conn. (1775), brigadier general (1776), major general (1780–83); member of Conn. General Assembly (1762–74, 1784–85); appointed by Continental Congress to treat with northwest Indians (1785); member of Conn. ratifying convention (1788), and voted for Constitution; member of Society of the Cincinnati.

Sources: Charles S. Hall, *Hall Ancestry* (New York, 1896); idem, *Life and Letters of Samuel Holden Parsons* (Binghamton, N.Y., 1905); George B. Loring, *A Vindication of General Samuel H. Parsons* (Salem, Mass., 1888).

PRATT, JOHN (1753–Dec. 27, 1824). Appointed lieutenant in U.S. infantry (1789); soldier; married Elizabeth Cooper; lieutenant quartermaster in continental army (1780), lieutenant in army (1789) until promoted to captain (1791), resigned (1793); member of Conn. General Assembly (1799, 1806–9).

Source: Henry Whittemore, *History of Middlesex County, Connecticut* (New York, 1884).

RICHARDS, NATHANIEL (May 25, 1756–June 1, 1832). Appointed surveyor at New London (1790); merchant; resided (1790) in New London County, Conn.; son of Guy and Elizabeth Harris Richards; married (1) Elizabeth Coit (1784), (2) Ann Thompson (1819); entered service as corporal (1775), appointed ensign in militia (1776).

Source: Abner Morse, *Genealogical Register of Descendants of Several Ancient Puritans*, 4 vols. (Boston, 1857–64), vol. 3.

ROGERS, HEZEKIAH (1753–Nov. 3, 1811). Appointed surveyor at New Haven (1790); son of Dr. Uriah and Hannah Lockwood Rogers; married Esther Raymond (1781); captain in 2nd Conn., aide-de-camp to General Huntington (1781–83); member of Conn. General Assembly (1786–88).

Sources: James S. Rogers, *James Rogers of New London, Connecticut and His Descendants* (Boston, 1902); Charles M. Selleck, *Norwalk* (Norwalk, Conn., 1896).

SAGE, COMFORT (Aug. 22, 1731–Mar. 14, 1799). Appointed surveyor at Middletown (1790); merchant; born in Upper Houses, Conn.; resided (1790) in Middletown, Conn.; son of Ebenezer and Hannah Coleman Sage; married Sarah Hamlin (1752); lieutenant in Conn. militia (1761), lieutenant-colonel in 23rd Conn. (1775), colonel (1776), brigadier general (1784–92); member of Conn. General Assembly (1777–86); justice of the peace (1793–98). In his letter of application, Sage told of his financial problems.

Source: Charles C. Adams, *Middletown Upper Houses* (New York, 1908).

SHAYLOR, JOSEPH (1737–Mar. 4, 1816). Appointed captain in U.S. infantry (1791); soldier; ensign and later lieutenant in the Revolution, captain in army

(1791) until promoted to major (1793), resigned (1797); member of Society of the Cincinnati.

Source: Frank D. Henderson, ed., *The Official Roster of the Soldiers of the American Revolution Buried in the State of Ohio* (Columbus, Ohio, 1929).

SMEDLEY, SAMUEL (Mar. 5, 1753–June 13, 1812). Appointed collector at Fairfield (1789–1812); mariner and merchant; born in Fairfield, Conn.; resided (1790) in Fairfield; son of James and Mary Burr Smedley; married Esther Rowland (1771); captain of the privateer *Defence* (1777–82). He owned $3,100 worth of property in 1790.

Source: Louis F. Middlebrook, *Exploits of the Connecticut Ship "Defence"* (Hartford, 1922).

STRONG, DAVID (1744–Aug. 19, 1801). Appointed captain in U.S. infantry (1789); soldier; born in Litchfield County, Conn.; married Chloe Richmond; lieutenant in 5th Conn. (1777), captain in 2nd Conn. (1781–83), captain in army (1789), major (1791), promoted to lieutenant-colonel (1793), and served until his death; member of Society of the Cincinnati.

Source: Ohio Adjutant General's Department, *Soldiers of the American Revolution Who Lived in the State of Ohio* (Columbus, Ohio, 1959).

SUMNER, JOSHUA (Oct. 11, 1761–Jan. 4, 1829). Appointed surgeon's mate in U.S. infantry (1789–90); physician; born in Middletown, Conn.; son of John and Elizabeth Kent Sumner; married (1) Hannah Marsh (1778), (2) Isabella McNeil (1816).

Source: William S. Appleton, *Descendants of William Sumner of Dorchester, Massachusetts* (Boston, 1879).

WOLCOTT, OLIVER, JR. (Jan. 11, 1760–June 11, 1833). Appointed auditor of U.S. Treasury (1789–91); lawyer and manufacturer; born in Litchfield, Conn.; son of Oliver and Laura Collins Wolcott; B.A. Yale (1778); married Elizabeth Stoughton (1785); aide-de-camp to his father in Conn. militia; member of Conn. ratifying convention (1788), and voted for Constitution; comptroller of U.S. Treasury (1791–95); secretary of U.S. Treasury (1795–1800); U.S. district judge (1800–1812); a Federalist, later a Democratic governor of Conn. (1817); founder and first president of the Bank of North America (1812–14).

Source: George Gibbs, ed., *Memoirs of the Administrations of Washington and John Adams, Edited from the Papers of Oliver Wolcott,* 2 vols. (New York, 1846); Anson P. Stokes, *Memorials of Eminent Yale Men,* 2 vols. (New Haven, 1914), vol. 2.

WYLLYS, JOHN P. (Aug. 11, 1754–Oct. 22, 1790). Appointed major in U.S. infantry (1789); soldier; born in Hartford, Conn.; son of George and Mary Woodbridge Wyllys; B.A. Yale (1773); married Jerusha Talcott; major in continental army (1776); killed in action with Miami Indians near Chillicothe, Ohio (1790); member of Society of the Cincinnati.

Source: George D. Seymour, *Captain Nathan Hale, 1755–1776: Yale College 1773; Major John Palsgrave Wyllys, 1754–1790: Yale College 1773, Friends and Yale Classmates, Who Died in Their Country's Service, One Hanged as a Spy by the British, the Other Killed in an Indian Ambuscade on the Far Frontier* (New Haven, 1933).

Delaware

ANDERSON, JOSEPH (Nov. 15, 1757–Apr. 17, 1837). Appointed U.S. judge in Southern Territory (1791–97); lawyer; born in White Marsh, Pa.; son of William and Elizabeth Inslee Anderson; married Only Patience Outlaw (1797); entered service as ensign in 3rd N.J. (1776), lieutenant (1776), captain (1777), brevet major (1783); practiced law in Del. (1783–90); member of first constitutional convention in Tenn. (1796); U.S. senator from Tenn. (1797–1815); comptroller of U.S. Treasury (1815–36); member of Society of the Cincinnati.

Source: Mrs. Charles F. Henley, "The Hon. Joseph Anderson and Some of His Distinguished Relatives and Descendants," *American Historical Magazine and Tennessee Historical Society Quarterly* 3 (1898): 240–59.

BEDFORD, GUNNING, JR. (1747–Mar. 30, 1812). Appointed U.S. district judge (1789–1812); lawyer; born in Philadelphia; son of Gunning and Susannah Jacquett Bedford; B.A. Princeton (1771); married Jane Ballareau Parker (c. 1771); member of Continental Congress (1783–85); Del. attorney general (1784–89); delegate to Philadelphia Convention (1787), and signed Constitution; member of Del. ratifying convention (1787), and voted for Constitution despite suspicions of strong central government; state senator (1788); an anti-slavery advocate.

Sources: Max Farrand, ed., *Notes of Debates in the Federal Convention of 1787, Reported by James Madison* (Columbus, Ohio, 1966); James A. Munroe, *Federalist Delaware, 1775–1815* (Binghamton, N.Y., 1954).

BUSH, GEORGE (d. 1796). Appointed collector at Wilmington (1790–96); merchant; son of David and Ann Bush; lieutenant (1776) and captain (1777–83) in Del. militia; collector at Wilmington (1781–90).

Source: J. M. McCarter and B. F. Jackson, eds., *Historical and Biographical Encyclopedia of Delaware* (Wilmington, Del., 1882).

DUFF, THOMAS, JR. (Sept. 27, 1766–Mar. 1830). Appointed ensign in U.S. infantry (1789). This Thomas Duff was probably the son of Thomas and Jane Williams Duff who was admitted to the Del. bar in 1791; served as clerk of the U.S. district court of Del. (1794–96); and was later a member of the Ohio bar (1804). It is likely that he declined his ensign's commission because of ill health.

Source: J. M. Runk, *Biographical and Genealogical History of the State of Delaware* (Chambersburg, Pa., 1899).

KIRKWOOD, ROBERT (1756–Nov. 4, 1791). Appointed captain in U.S. infantry (1791); soldier; born in England; 1st lieutenant in Del. regiment (1776), captain (1776–83); killed in action in St. Clair's defeat near Fort Recovery, Ohio (1791); member of Society of the Cincinnati.

LATIMER, HENRY (Apr. 24, 1752–Dec. 19, 1819). Appointed supervisor of distilled spirits (1790–91); physician; born in Newport, Del.; son of James Latimer; B.A. Univ. of Pa. (1773); Edinburgh Medical College (1775); surgeon in Revolutionary War (1780–83); member of Del. General Assembly (1787–90); Federalist member of U.S. House of Representatives (1794–95); U.S. senator (1795–1801). He received $10,950 at the time of the funding of the debt (1790).
Sources: Munroe, *Federalist Delaware, 1775–1815*; John T. Scharf, *History of Delaware, 1609–1888*, 2 vols. (Philadelphia, 1888).

McLANE, ALLAN (Aug. 8, 1746–May 22, 1829). Appointed U.S. marshal (1789–97); soldier and farmer; born in Philadelphia; married Rebecca Wells (1769); captain in continental army (1777), retired (1782); member of Del. General Assembly (1785, 1791); delegate to Del. ratifying convention (1787), and voted for Constitution; collector at Wilmington (1797–1829); a Federalist; member of Society of the Cincinnati.
Sources: Munroe, *Federalist Delaware, 1775–1815*; Scharf, *History of Delaware, 1609–1888*, vol. 1.

PEERY, WILLIAM (1732–Dec. 17, 1800). Declined appointment as U.S. judge in Southern Territory (1789); lawyer; son of James and Mary Reeves Peery; married (1) Mary ———, (2) Margaret Wilson (c. 1787); captain in Del. militia (1777–82); member of Del. General Assembly (1782, 1784, 1787, 1793–94); member of Continental Congress (1785–86); treasurer of Sussex County (1786–96); a Democrat.
Source: Lynn Perry, *Some Letters of and Concerning Major William Peery* (Strasburg, Va., 1935).

PLATT, JOHN. Appointed lieutenant in U.S. infantry (1791), promoted to captain (1791); cashiered (1792).

READ, GEORGE, JR. (Aug. 17, 1765–Sept. 3, 1836). Appointed U.S. district attorney (1790–c. 1820); lawyer; born in New Castle, Del.; son of George and Gertrude Ross Read; married Mary Thompson (1786); member of Del. General Assembly (1811–13); a Democrat. After 1790, he owned a cotton plantation in Mississippi.
Source: Henry C. Conrad, *History of the State of Delaware,* 3 vols. (Wilmington, Del., 1908), vol. 3.

TILTON, JAMES (June 1, 1745–May 14, 1822). Appointed commissioner of loans (1789–1801); physician; born in Kent County, Del.; B.M. (1768), M.D. (1771), Univ. of Pa.; surgeon in the Revolution (1776–83); surgeon general of U.S. army (1813–15); member of Del. General Assembly; member of Continental Congress (1783–85); commissioner of loans (1785–89); a Democrat; member of Society of the Cincinnati; first president of Medical Society of Del. (1789–1822).

Sources: R. O. Bausman and J. A. Munroe, eds., "James Tilton's Notes on the Agriculture of Delaware in 1788," *Agricultural History* 20 (1946): 176–87; Munroe, *Federalist Delaware, 1775–1815.*

Georgia

BERRIEN, JOHN (1759–Nov. 6, 1815). Appointed surveyor at Savannah (1789); farmer; born near Princeton, N.J.; son of John and Margarette Eaton Berrien; married (1) Margaret McPherson, (2) Williamenia Moore (1788); 2nd lieutenant in 1st Ga. (1776), brigade major (1778–83); collector at Savannah (1786–87); state treasurer (1798); a Federalist; member of Society of the Cincinnati. He received at least 600 acres of land for service in the Revolution.

Sources: Lucian L. Knight, *Georgian Landmarks, Memorials and Legends* (Atlanta, 1913); Horace Montgomery, ed., *Georgians in Profile* (Athens, Ga., 1958).

CLAY, JAMES (d. Apr. 28, 1798). Appointed ensign in U.S. infantry (1789); son of Joseph and Ann Legardiere Clay.

COLLINS, CORNELIUS (d. Dec. 22, 1791). Appointed collector at Sunbury (1790–91); 1st lieutenant in 2nd Ga. (1777–82); member of Society of the Cincinnati. He received a bounty of 400 acres of land in 1783 for service in the Revolution.

Source: DAR, *Collections of the John Habersham Chapter* (Dalton, Ga., 1902).

FISHBOURN[E], BENJAMIN (d. Nov. 1790). Nominated naval officer at Savannah (1789), but not approved by Senate; married (1) Nancy Wereat (1783), (2) Ann ———; paymaster in 2nd Pa. (1776), captain in 4th Pa. (1777), aide-de-camp to General Wayne (1779–83); naval officer at Savannah under state government prior to 1789; member of Society of the Cincinnati. He owned at least 1,100 acres of land in 1789.

Source: Thomas Gamble, *Savannah Duels and Duellists* (Savannah, Ga., 1923).

FORSYTH, ROBERT (1754–Jan. 11, 1794). Appointed U.S. marshal (1789–94); born in Ireland; married Fanny Johnston; captain in Lee's Battalion of

Light Dragoons (1778), major in Va. regiment (1779–83); killed in line of duty as marshal (1794); member of Society of the Cincinnati. He owned at least 6,000 acres of land in 1792.

Source: Knight, *Georgian Landmarks, Memorials and Legends.*

HABERSHAM, JOHN (Dec. 23, 1754–Nov. 19, 1799). Appointed collector at Savannah (1789–99); merchant; born near Savannah; son of James and Mary Bolten Habersham; attended Princeton; married Nancy Camber (1783); 1st lieutenant in 1st Ga. (1776), captain (1777), major (1778); member of Continental Congress (1785–86); appointed Indian agent by General Washington in late 1780's; member of Society of the Cincinnati. He received 800 acres of land in 1784 for service in the Revolution.

Source: Mrs. Howard H. [Ettie] McCall, *Roster of Revolutionary Soldiers in Georgia,* 2 vols. (Atlanta, 1941–68), vol. 1.

HANDLEY, GEORGE (Feb. 9, 1752–Sept. 17, 1793). Appointed collector at Brunswick (1789); planter; born in England; resided (1790) in Glynn, Ga.; son of Thomas Handley; married Sarah Howe (1789); 1st lieutenant in 1st Ga. (1787); 1st lieutenant in 1st Ga. (1778); member of Ga. Executive Council; Richmond County (1784–86); member of Ga. ratifying convention (1788), and voted for Constitution; governor of Ga. (1788–89); member of Society of the Cincinnati. He owned at least 3,700 acres of land in 1787.

Source: Folks Huxford, *Pioneers of Wiregrass Georgia,* 6 vols. (Homerville, Ga., 1951–71). vol. 5.

HILLARY, CHRISTOPHER (1735–Feb. 18, 1796). Appointed collector at Brunswick (1790); planter; resided (1790) in Glynn, Ga.; married Agnes Hightower (1787); 1st lieutenant in 1st Ga. (1778); member of Ga. Executive Council; member of Ga. ratifying convention (1788), and voted for Constitution; member of Society of the Cincinnati. In 1790, Hillary paid over £2 in taxes on 3 slaves and 1,000 acres of land.

Source: McCall, *Roster of Revolutionary Soldiers in Georgia,* vol. 1.

MCALLISTER, MATTHEW (1758–1823). Appointed U.S. district attorney (1789–96); lawyer; son of Richard and Mary Dill McAllister; B.A. Princeton (1779); married Hannah Gibbons (c. 1787); member of Ga. General Assembly; state attorney general (1787–89); judge of Ga. Superior Court (1796–1801); a Federalist. He was a leading member of the Georgia Company, which purchased the Yazoo tract in 1795.

Source: Warren Grice, "Georgia Appointments By President Washington," *Georgia Historical Quarterly* 7 (1923): 181–212.

MCINTOSH, LACHLAN (Mar. 1725–Feb. 20, 1806). Appointed naval officer at Savannah (1789–91); surveyor and planter; born in Scotland; son of John and Margaret Fraser McIntosh; married Sarah Threadcraft (1756); colonel in 1st Ga. (1776), brigadier general in continental army (1776–83); member of Con-

tinental Congress (1784); Ga. commissioner at Treaty of Hopewell with Cherokee Indians (1785); member of Ga. General Assembly (1789); commissioner
to southern Indians (1789); sheriff of Liberty County (1791); a Federalist;
first president of Ga. Society of the Cincinnati. Though a substantial landowner,
McIntosh was financially ruined by the war. Later he was a leading member of
the Georgia Company, which bought the Yazoo tract in 1795.

Source: Lilla M. Hewes, ed., *Lachlan McIntosh Papers in the University of
Georgia Libraries* (Athens, Ga., 1968).

MARTIN, THOMAS (1748–1819). Appointed lieutenant in U.S. infantry (1789).

MATHEWS, JOHN (c. 1762–1806). Appointed supervisor of distilled spirits
(1790); lawyer; son of George and Anne Paul Mathews; married a cousin,
Elizabeth Mathews; supervisor of revenue under John Adams. His father, George
Mathews, was a member of the First Congress.

Source: John R. Boots, Jr., *The Mat[t]hews Family* (Ocala, Fla.: 1970).

PENDLETON, NATHANIEL (1756–Oct. 20, 1821). Appointed U.S. district judge
(1789–96); lawyer; born in Virginia; son of Nathaniel and Elizabeth Clayton
Pendleton; married Susan Bard (1785); ensign in 10th continental (1776),
1st lieutenant in 11th Va. (1776), captain (1777), aide-de-camp to General
Nathaniel Greene (1780–83); attorney general of Ga.; elected delegate to, but
did not attend, Constitutional Convention in Philadelphia (1787); member of
Continental Congress (1789); chief justice of Ga. Superior Court (1789); a
Federalist and a close friend of Alexander Hamilton. He owned at least 1,000
acres in 1787, and later was a member of the Georgia Company, which purchased the Yazoo tract in 1795.

Sources: Grice, "Georgia Appointments By President Washington"; Lisle A.
Rose, *Prologue to Democracy: The Federalists in the South* (Lexington, Ky.,
1968).

RUDOLPH, MICHAEL (Jan. 5, 1758–1795). Appointed captain in U.S. infantry
(1790); born in Maryland; married Sarah Baker (1783); sergeant major in
Lee's Battalion of Light Dragoons (1778), lieutenant (1779), captain (1779–
83), captain in army (1790), promoted to major (1792), inspector of army
(1793), resigned (1793); member of Ga. General Assembly (1783); collector
at Sunbury (1787).

Source: Marilou Alston Rudulph, "The Legend of Michael Rudulph," *Georgia
Historical Quarterly* 45 (1961): 309–28.

SEAGROVE, JAMES. Appointed collector at St. Mary's (1789–91); farmer and
merchant; member of Ga. General Assembly (1787); delegate to Ga. ratifying
convention (1788), and voted for Constitution; federal agent to Creek Indians
(1791–96); justice of Inferior Court of Camden County (1799–1810). In his
application for office, Seagrove mentioned his financial straits. However, in 1794
he paid £14 in taxes for 9 slaves and 28,620 acres of land.

Source: Daniel M. Smith, "James Seagrove and the Mission to Tuckaubatchee," *Georgia Historical Quarterly* 44 (1960): 41–55.

WYLLY, RICHARD (1744–Oct. 11, 1801). Appointed commissioner of loans (1789); soldier and public servant; born in Ireland; married Mary Bryan Morel (1784); colonel and quartermaster general in continental army under General Lincoln; member of Ga. Provincial Congress; member of Ga. Committee of Safety; member of Society of the Cincinnati. In 1782, Wylly purchased the confiscated estates of three Tories.

Sources: Grice, "Georgia Appointments by President Washington"; McCall, *Roster of Revolutionary Soldiers in Georgia*, vol. 1.

Kentucky

BROWN, JAMES (Sept. 11, 1766–Apr. 7, 1835). Declined appointment as U.S. district attorney (1790); lawyer; born in Virginia; resided (1790) in Lexington, Ky.; son of John and Margaret Preston Brown; graduate of William and Mary; married Ann Hart; commanded a company of sharpshooters against the Indians (1789–91); Ky. secretary of state (1792); secretary of Louisiana Territory (1804) and later district attorney; member of La. constitutional convention (1812); member of U.S. Senate (1813–17, 1819–23); minister to France (1823–29); a Democrat.

Source: Bayless Hardin, "The Brown Family of Liberty Hall," *Filson Club Historical Quarterly* 16 (1942): 75–87.

INNES, HARRY (Jan. 4, 1752–Sept. 20, 1816). Appointed U.S. district judge (1789–1816); lawyer and manufacturer; born in Virginia; resided (1790) in Ky.; son of Robert and Catherine Richards Innes; married (1) Elizabeth Calloway, (2) Mrs. Anne Shields; attorney general for western district of Va. (1784); opposed adoption of Constitution; was suspected of being involved in Wilkinson Plot, but Congress refused to impeach him; a Republican.

Sources: H. Levin, ed., *The Lawyers and Lawmakers of Kentucky* (Chicago, 1897); Patricia Watlington, *The Partisan Spirit: Kentucky Politics, 1779–1792* (New York, 1972).

McDOWELL, SAMUEL, JR. (Feb. 8, 1764–Aug. 1834). Appointed U.S. marshal (1789–98); born in Rockbridge, Va.; son of Samuel and Mary McClung McDowell; married Anna Irvine (c. 1786); private in Revolutionary War under Lafayette; a Federalist.

Sources: John M. Gresham, *The Biographical Cyclopedia of the Commonwealth of Kentucky* (Chicago, 1896); Thomas M. Green, *Historic Families of Kentucky* (Baltimore, 1964).

MURRAY, WILLIAM. Appointed U.S. district attorney (1790–92); lawyer and merchant; attorney general of Ky. (1792); member of Ky. General Assembly (1798), where he opposed Kentucky Resolutions; a Federalist. He was involved in secret negotiations with the Spanish governor of New Orleans to separate Kentucky from the Union.

Sources: John M. Brown, *Town of Frankfort, Kentucky* (Louisville, Ky., 1886); Thomas D. Clark, *A History of Kentucky* (Lexington, Ky., 1960).

NICHOLAS, GEORGE (1753–June, 1799). Appointed U.S. district attorney (1790); lawyer and manufacturer; born in Hanover, Va.; resided (1790) in Lexington, Ky.; son of Robert and Anne Cary Nicholas; attended William and Mary (1772–75); married Mary Smith (1778); captain in 2nd Va. (1775), major (1776), lieutenant-colonel (1777); member of Va. General Assembly (1781, 1784); delegate to Va. ratifying convention (1788), and voted for Constitution; member of Ky. constitutional convention (1792); first attorney general of Ky.; a Republican; took part in the framing of the Kentucky Resolutions. Between 1785 and 1797, Nicholas purchased 69,000 acres of land.

Source: Richard H. Caldemeyer, "The Career of George Nicholas" (Ph.D. diss., University of Indiana, 1951).

TAYLOR, RICHARD (Mar. 22, 1744–Feb. 19, 1826). Appointed collector at Louisville (1790); resided (1790) in Louisville, Ky.; son of Zachary and Elizabeth Lee Taylor; father of President Zachary Taylor; graduate of William and Mary; married Sarah Dabney Strother (1779); 1st lieutenant in 1st Va. (1775), captain (1776), major in 13th Va. (1778), lieutenant-colonel (1779–81); member of Ky. constitutional convention (1792); Ky. General Assembly (1792 and after); presidential elector (1812–24); a Republican. He owned 7 slaves and 6,000 acres of land in 1790.

Source: Brainerd Dyer, *Zachary Taylor* (Baton Rouge, 1946).

Maryland

BALLARD, ROBERT. Appointed surveyor at Baltimore (1790); resided (1790) in Baltimore; married ―――― Plowman; colonel in the Revolution. In his application for office, Ballard said that because of speculation he was destitute and in need of a position in order to provide for his wife and children.

BANNING, JEREMIAH (Mar. 25, 1733–Dec. 23, 1798). Appointed collector at Oxford (1789–91); merchant and planter; born in Talbot, Md.; resided (1790) in Talbot County; son of James and Jane Banning; married Mary Gossage; 1st lieutenant in Md. militia (1775), captain and later major (1776), colonel (1777–83); Md. naval officer at Oxford; judge of Oxford County Court; member of Md. ratifying convention (1788), and voted for Constitution; inspector of revenue (1791). He owned 29 slaves in 1790.

Sources: Jeremiah Banning, *Log and Will of Jeremiah Banning, 1733–1798*

(New York, 1922); Oswald Tilghman, *History of Talbot County, Maryland, 1661–1861,* 2 vols. (Baltimore, 1915).

BISCOE, GEORGE. Appointed collector at Nottingham (1790); resided (1790) in St. Mary's County, Md.; naval officer and deputy collector at Patuxent before 1789. He owned 50 slaves in 1790.

CARMICHAEL, WILLIAM (c. 1738–Feb. 9, 1795). Appointed chargé des affaires at Madrid (1790–95); lawyer and diplomat; born in Queen Anne's County, Md.; son of William and Anne Brooke Carmichael; married (1) ——— Stirling, (2) Antonia Reynon; assistant to Silas Deane and agent of Congress in Paris (1776); in Berlin (1776–78); member of Continental Congress (1778–79); secretary to John Jay in Madrid (1779); chargé at Madrid (1782–90); a Federalist.
Sources: "The Brooke Family," *Maryland Historical Magazine* 1 (1906): 188; Charles Clark, *The Eastern Shore of Maryland and Virginia* (New York, 1950).

CHESLEY, ROBERT. Appointed surveyor at St. Mary's (1790); son of Robert Chesley; lieutenant and captain in Md. militia during the Revolution.

CHILTON, CHARLES (b. 1741). Appointed surveyor at Town Creek (1790); born in Virginia; resided (1790) in St. Mary's County, Md.; son of Thomas Chilton; married Elizabeth Blackwell; member of Md. ratifying convention (1788), and voted for Constitution. He owned 6 slaves in 1790.
Source: George MacKenzie, *Colonial Families of the United States of America,* 7 vols. (1907–20; reprint ed., Baltimore, 1966), vol. 1.

DAVIDSON, JOHN. Appointed collector at Annapolis (1790); resided (1790) in Anne Arundel County, Md.; major in 5th Md., naval officer at Annapolis under state government prior to 1789; member of Society of the Cincinnati. He received 400 acres of land in 1789 for service in the Revolution.

FENWICK, JOSEPH (d. 1823). Appointed U.S. consul to Bordeaux, France (1790); merchant in Bordeaux; son of Ignatius and Sarah Taney Fenwick; married Henritta Maria Lancaster.
Sources: MacKenzie, *Colonial Families of the United States of America,* vol. 1; Hester Richardson, *Side-lights on Maryland History,* 2 vols. (Baltimore, 1967), vol. 2.

GALE, GEORGE (June 3, 1756–Jan. 2, 1815). Appointed supervisor of distilled spirits (1791); planter; born in Somerset County, Md.; married Anna Maria Hollyday; member of Md. ratifying convention (1788), and voted for Constitution; U.S. representative in First Congress (1789–91).
Source: James Bordley, *The Hollyday and Related Families* (Baltimore, 1962).

GUNBY, JOHN (Mar. 10, 1745–May, 1807). Appointed collector at Snow Hill (1789); planter; born in Somerset County, Md.; resided (1790) in Worchester County, Md.; son of John and Sarah Gunby; married Amelia Somers; lieutenant in 7th Md. (1776), colonel (1777), brigadier general by brevet (1783); member of Society of the Cincinnati. He owned a substantial amount of land in Worchester County.

Source: Andrew Gunby, *Colonel John Gunby of the Maryland Line* (Cincinnati, 1902).

HARRISON, ROBERT H. (1745–Apr. 2, 1790). Declined appointment as associate judge of Supreme Court (1789); lawyer; born in Md.; resided (1790) in St. Mary's County, Md.; son of Richard and Dorothy Hanson Harrison; married Grace Dent; lieutenant in 3rd Va. (1775), military secretary to Washington (1776–81); chief judge of General Court of Md. (1781); elected to Philadelphia Constitutional Convention (1787), but did not attend.

Source: Richardson, *Side-lights on Maryland History*, vol. 2.

HARWOOD, THOMAS. Appointed commissioner of loans (1790); son of Richard and Anne Watkins Harwood; married Ann Mayhew (1794); treasurer of Western Shore of Md. (1775–76); commissioner of loans under Confederation.

Source: J. D. Warfield, *Founders of Anne Arundel and Howard Counties* (Baltimore, 1905).

JOHNSON, JOSHUA (June 25, 1742–1802). Appointed U.S. consul to London (1790–97); merchant; son of Thomas and Dorcas Sedgwick Johnson; married Catherine Nuth; brother of Thomas Johnson; father-in-law of John Quincy Adams; while a tobacco merchant in France, became the American agent at Nantes during the Revolution.

Sources: Edward S. Delaplaine, "The Life of Thomas Johnson," *Maryland Historical Magazine* 14 (1919): 46–48; MacKenzie, *Colonial Families of the United States of America*, vol. 1.

JOHNSON, THOMAS (Nov. 4, 1732–Oct. 26, 1819). Declined appointment as U.S. district judge (1789); lawyer and planter; born in Calvert County, Md.; son of Thomas and Dorcas Sedgwick Johnson; married Anne Jennings (1766); brigadier general in Md. militia (1766); member of Md. Provisional Assembly (1762); member of Continental Congress (1774–77); governor of Md. (1777–79); member of Md. General Assembly (1780, 1786–87); member of Md. ratifying convention (1788), and voted for Constitution; chief judge of General Court of Md. (1790–91); associate judge of U.S. Supreme Court (1791–93); chief judge of Territory of Columbia (1801). He owned 38 slaves in 1790.

Source: Edward S. Delaplaine, *The Life of Thomas Johnson* (New York, 1927).

JONES, JOHN C. (Sept. 11, 1754–May 20, 1802). Appointed collector at Nanjemoy (1789); captain in 4th Md.; naval officer under state government prior to 1789.

JORDAN, JEREMIAH. Appointed surveyor at Lewellensburg (1789); resided (1790) in St. Mary's County, Md.; married Elizabeth Lewis; colonel in St. Mary's County militia; member of Md. state convention (1774); member of Md. constitutional convention (1776).
Source: DAR, *Lineage Books,* vol. 4.

LINGAN, JAMES MACCUBBIN (May 31, 1751–July 28, 1812). Appointed collector at Georgetown (1789); merchant; son of Dr. Thomas and Ann Maccubbin Lingan; married Janet Henderson; entered service as lieutenant (1776), captain (1778–83), general in militia after the war; naval officer at Georgetown under state government prior to 1789; a Federalist; member of Society of the Cincinnati. He was killed by a mob because he opposed the War of 1812.
Source: Ella Dorsey, "Biographical Sketch of James M. Lingan, One of the Original Proprietors," *Record of the Columbia Historical Society* 13 (1910): 1–48.

McPHERSON, MARK. Appointed lieutenant in U.S. infantry (1790); lieutenant in 2nd Md. in the Revolution, lieutenant in army (1790), captain (1792), resigned (1792); member of Society of the Cincinnati.

MUIR, JOHN. Appointed collector at Vienna (1789); deputy naval officer at Vienna under state government prior to 1789.

NICOLS, JEREMIAH (July 28, 1748–1806). Appointed collector at Chester (1790); resided (1790) in Kent County, Md.; son of Jeremiah and Deborah Lloyd Nichols; married Anna Maria Lloyd; quartermaster in 13th Md. militia (1777); justice of the orphans court of Kent County (1777–88).
Source: Katherine N. Grove, *The Nicols Family of Maryland* (n.p., 1939).

PACA, WILLIAM (Oct. 31, 1740–Oct. 1799). Appointed U.S. district judge (1789–99); lawyer; born in Abingdon, Md.; resided (1790) in Queen Anne County, Md.; son of John and Elizabeth Smith Paca; B.A. College of Philadelphia (1759); studied law at Middle Temple, London; married (1) Mary Chew (1763), (2) Anne Harrison (1777); member of Md. Provincial Assembly (1771–74); member of Continental Congress (1774–79); signer of Declaration of Independence (1776); chief judge of Md. Superior Court (1778–80); chief justice of court of appeals in prize and admiralty cases (1780–82); governor of Md. (1782–85); member of Md. ratifying convention (1788), and voted for Constitution. He owned 92 slaves in 1790.
Source: Heinrich Buchholz, *Governors of Maryland* (Baltimore, 1908).

POTTS, RICHARD (July 19, 1753–Nov. 25, 1808). Appointed U.S. district attorney (1789–91); lawyer; born in Upper Marlboro, Md.; resided (1790) in Frederick County, Md.; son of William and Sarah Lee Potts; read law with Samuel Chase; married (1) Elizabeth Hughes (1779), (2) Eleanor Murdoch (1799); aide to Brigadier General Thomas Johnson of Md. militia (1777);

member of Md. General Assembly (1779–80, 1787–88); member of Continental Congress (1781–82); member of Md. ratifying convention (1788), and voted for Constitution; chief judge of Md. circuit court (1791–93, 1796–1801); elected as Federalist to U.S. Senate (1793–96); associate judge of Md. court of appeals (1801–4). He owned 22 slaves in 1790.

Source: Morris Radoff, ed., *The Old Line State*, 3 vols. (Hopkinsville, Ky., 1957).

PURVIANCE, ROBERT (1733–1806). Appointed naval officer at Baltimore (1789–94); merchant; born in Ireland; resided (1790) in Baltimore; son of Samuel Purviance; married Frances Young; engaged in privateering during the Revolution; collector at Baltimore (1794); owned 4 slaves in 1790. In his application for office in 1789, Purviance mentioned that he was in debt and in need of a position in order to support his family.

Sources: *The Biographical Cyclopedia of Representative Men of Maryland and District of Columbia* (Baltimore, 1879); Brantz Mayer, *Baltimore Past and Present* (Baltimore, 1871).

RAMSAY, NATHANIEL (May 1, 1741–Oct. 23, 1817). Appointed U.S. marshal (1790–98); lawyer; born in Pa.; resided (1790) in Cecil County, Md.; son of James and Jane Montgomery Ramsay; B.A. Princeton (1767); married (1) Margaret Peale, (2) Charlotte Hall (1792); captain in Smallwood's Md. regiment (1776), lieutenant-colonel in continental army (1776–81); member of Continental Congress (1785–87); naval officer at Baltimore (1794–1817); a Federalist; member of Society of the Cincinnati. In 1790 he owned at least £2,330 worth of land.

Source: W. F. Brand, *A Sketch of the Life and Character of Nathaniel Ramsay* (Baltimore, 1887).

SCOTT, JOHN (d. 1790). Appointed collector at Chester (1789–90); physician; naval officer under state government (1787).

TRUEMAN, ALEXANDER (d. Apr. 20, 1792). Appointed captain in U.S. infantry (1790); ensign in 3rd Md. battalion (1776), captain (1776), retired (1783), captain in army (1790), major (1792), killed by Indians (1792); member of Society of the Cincinnati.

WILLIAMS, OTHO H. (Mar. 1749–July 15, 1794). Appointed collector at Baltimore (1789–94); born in Md.; resided (1790) in Baltimore; son of Joseph and Prudence Holland Williams; married Mary Smith (1786); 1st lieutenant in Md. rifle company (1775), major in Stephenson's regiment (1776), colonel in 6th Md. (1776), brigadier general in continental army (1782–83); naval officer at Baltimore (1783–89); member of Society of the Cincinnati. He received 850 acres of land in 1789 for service in the Revolution.

Source: Osmond Tiffany, "A Sketch of the Life and Services of Gen. Otho H. Williams," *Maryland Historical Society* 2 (1851): 3–31.

Massachusetts

APPLETON, NATHANIEL (Oct. 5, 1731–June 1798). Appointed commissioner of loans (1789–98); merchant; resided (1790) in Boston; son of Rev. Nathaniel and Margaret Gibbs Appleton; B.A. Harvard (1749); married (1) Mary Walker (1755), (2) Rachel Henderson (1756); paid £50 to avoid military service in the continental army; a Son of Liberty; member of Committee of Correspondence (1772); member of Mass. Provincial Congress (1774); representative in Mass. General Court (1783); commissioner of loans (1775–89). Appleton, along with James Swan, wrote in opposition to slave trade from 1766 to 1773.

Sources: William S. Appleton, *A Genealogy of the Appleton Family* (Boston, 1874); Isaac A. Jewett, *Memorial of Samuel Appleton* (Boston, 1850); Clifford K. Shipton, ed., *Biographical Sketches of Those Who Attended Harvard College*, 16 vols. [vols. 1–3 edited by John L. Sibley] (Boston, 1873–85, 1933–), vol. 12.

BARRETT, NATHANIEL (Mar. 27, 1743–Dec. 18, 1793). Appointed U.S. consul at Rouen, France (1789); merchant; son of John and Sarah Gerrish Barrett; married (1) Mary Hunt, (2) widow of General McDougal.

Source: Joseph H. Barrett, "Thomas Barrett of Braintree," *New England Historical and Genealogical Register* 42 (1888): 263.

BATCHELDER, JOSIAH (Sept. 25, 1736–Dec. 10, 1809). Appointed surveyor at Beverly (1789–1809); mariner and shipowner; born in Beverly, Mass.; resided (1790) in Beverly; son of Josiah and Mary Leach Batchelder; married Hannah Dodge (1760); owned and commanded privateers from Beverly during the Revolution; elected six times to Mass. General Court; member of Committee of Correspondence; member of Mass. Provincial Congress (1775–77, 1779).

Sources: Samuel E. Morison, "Beverley Privateers in the American Revolution," *Publications of the Colonial Society of Massachusetts* 24 (1922): 319–32; Frederick C. Pierce, *Batchelder, Batchellor Genealogy* (Chicago, 1898).

BAYLIES, HODIJAH (Sept. 17, 1756–Apr. 26, 1843). Appointed collector at Dighton (1789–1810); soldier and public servant; born in Uxbridge, Mass.; resided (1790) in Dighton, Mass.; son of Nicholas and Elizabeth Park Baylies; B.A. Harvard (1777); married Elizabeth Lincoln (1784); entered service as 1st lieutenant (1777), major and aide-de-camp to General Lincoln (1777), aide-de-camp to General Washington (1782–83); judge of probate in Bristol County (1810–34); member of Society of the Cincinnati.

Sources: Mary R. Allen, *Reminiscences of the Baylies and Richmond Families* (Boston, 1875); Frank Smith, ed., *Memorials of the Massachusetts Society of the Cincinnati* (Boston, 1931).

BOURNE, SYLVANUS (c. 1756–1817). Appointed consul to the island of Hispaniola (1789–92); merchant; born in Barnstable, Mass.; son of Meletiah and Mary Bayard Bourne; B.A. Harvard (1779); vice consul at Amsterdam

(1794–97); consul general to Batavian Republic (1797); consul general at Amsterdam (1815–17).

Sources: Hannah Dykes, *History of Richard Bourne and Some of His Descendants* (Cleveland, 1919); Helen B. J. Lee, *The Bourne Genealogy* (Chester, Conn., 1972).

BURBECK, HENRY (June 8, 1754–Oct. 2, 1848). Appointed captain in U.S. artillery (1789); born in Boston; son of William and Jerusha Glover Burbeck; married Lucy Rudd; lieutenant in Mass. artillery (1775), captain-lieutenant in 3rd continental artillery (1777), captain (1777), brevet major (1783), captain in army (1789), major (1791), lieutenant-colonel in artillery and engineers (1798), colonel (1802–14), brevet brigadier general (1814), honorably discharged (1815); member of Society of the Cincinnati. He is regarded as the founder of the U.S. Military Academy and the Corps of Engineers.

Sources: Asa B. Gardner, "Henry Burbeck," *The Magazine of American History* 9 (1883): 252–62; Smith, *Memorials of the Massachusetts Society of the Cincinnati*.

BURNHAM [BURNAM], JOHN (Dec. 10, 1749–June 8, 1843). Appointed major in U.S. infantry (1791); born in Ipswich, Mass.; son of Samuel and Martha Story Burnham; married Abigail Collins; entered service as lieutenant in Little's Mass. regiment (1775), 1st lieutenant in 12th continental infantry (1776), major in 5th Mass. (1777–83), major in army (1791), resigned (1791); member of Society of the Cincinnati. He was one of the founders of Marietta, Ohio.

Sources: Walter J. Burnham, *Burnham Family Lineage Charts* (Pittsburgh, 1966); Smith, *Memorials of the Massachusetts Society of the Cincinnati*.

CARNES, BURRILL (d. 1805). Appointed consul to Nantes, France (1789–90); merchant; American agent to Nantes (1786–89).

Source: Julian Boyd, ed., *The Papers of Thomas Jefferson*, 19 vols. (Princeton, 1950–), vol. 9.

CHURCH, EDWARD (Sept. 12, 1740–1816). Appointed U.S. consul to Bilboa, Spain (1790); merchant; born in Azores; son of Benjamin and Hannah Dyer Church; B.A. Harvard (1759); married (1) Elizabeth Furness (1763), (2) Hannah Skinner; member of Mass. Provincial Congress (1774); served on Boston Committee of Correspondence (1776); appointed consul to Lisbon (1792). In his application for office, Church told of his poor financial condition due to the Revolution.

Source: John A. Church, *Descendants of Richard Church of Plymouth, Mass.* (Rutland, Vt., 1913).

COBB, DAVID, JR. (Feb. 10, 1773–Nov. 4, 1791). Appointed ensign in U.S. infantry (1791); soldier; son of General David and Eleanor Bradish Cobb; ensign in army (1791); killed in action with Indians on the Miami River, Ohio (1791).

COOK, FRANCIS (c. 1755–1832). Appointed collector at Wiscasset (1789–1829); merchant; resided (1790) in Pownalborough, Maine; member of Mass. General Court (1787–89). He is said to have been a friend of George Washington.
Source: Fannie Chase, *Wiscasset in Pownalborough* (Wiscasset, Me., 1941).

CROSS, STEPHEN (1731–Mar. 30, 1809). Appointed collector at Newburyport (1789); shipbuilder and merchant; resided (1790) in Newburyport, Mass.; son of Ralph and Sarah Johnson Cross; married Hannah Beck (1759); built ships on Lake Ontario, and taken prisoner in French and Indian War; delegate to Mass. Provincial Congress (1774). He served for many years in local offices at Newburyport, where he was a leading Jeffersonian.
Sources: D. Hamilton Hurd, *History of Essex County, Massachusetts,* 2 vols. (Philadelphia, 1888); Benjamin W. Labaree, *Patriots and Partisans* (Cambridge. Mass., 1962).

CUSHING, THOMAS H. (Dec. 1755–Oct. 19, 1822). Appointed captain in U.S. infantry (1791); soldier; born in Pembroke, Mass.; son of Nehemiah and Sarah Humphreys Cushing; sergeant in 6th continental (1776), 2nd lieutenant in 1st Mass. (1777), captain in army (1791), promoted to major in 1st sub-legion (1793), inspector of the army (1797–98), lieutenant-colonel (1802), colonel (1805), brigadier general (1812), honorably discharged (1815); collector at New London, Conn. (1815–22); member of Society of the Cincinnati.
Source: Smith, *Memorials of the Massachusetts Society of the Cincinnati.*

CUSHING, WILLIAM (Mar. 1, 1732–Sept. 13, 1810). Appointed associate justice of Supreme Court (1789–1810); lawyer; born in Scituate, Mass.; resided (1790) in Scituate; son of John and Mary Cotton Cushing; B.A. Harvard (1751); judge of probate for Lincoln County, Maine (1760–72); judge of Mass. superior court (1772–77); chief judge of superior court (1777–89); member of Mass. constitutional convention (1779); delegate and vice president of Mass ratifying convention (1788), and voted for Constitution; a Federalist.
Source: Shipton, *Biographical Sketches of Those Who Attended Harvard College,* vol. 13.

DEARBORN, HENRY (Feb. 23, 1751–June 6, 1829). Appointed U.S. marshal for Maine (1789–93); physician and soldier; born in Hampton, N.H.; resided (1790) in Pittston, Maine; son of Simon and Sarah Marston Dearborn; married (1) Mary Bartlett (1771), (2) Dorcas Osgood Marble (1780), (3) Sarah Bowdoin (1813); captain at Bunker Hill (1775), major in Scammell's 3rd N.H. (1776), colonel and deputy quartermaster general (1781), brigadier general in Maine militia (1787), major general (1789), major general in U.S. army (1812–13); elected as Democrat to U.S. House of Representatives (1793–97); secretary of war (1801–9); collector at Boston (1809–12); minister to Portugal (1822–24).
Source: Lloyd A. Brown and Howard H. Peckham, eds., *Revolutionary War Journals of Henry Dearborn, 1775–1783* (New York, 1939).

DELESDERNIER, LEWIS F. (1752–Feb. 2, 1837). Appointed collector at Passamaquody (1789–1811); born in Halifax, Nova Scotia; resided (1790) in Machias, Maine; married Mrs. Sophia Clark (1817); 2nd lieutenant (1776), later lieutenant in continental army (1783); naval officer at Passamaquody (1785–88); first postmaster of Passamaquody (1794–1805); representative to Mass. General Court (1811–12).
Source: William Kilby, *Eastport and Passamaquoddy* (Eastport, Me., 1888).

EDWARDS, RICHARD. Appointed ensign in U.S. infantry (1791); resigned (July 1791).

EUSTIS, WILLIAM (June 10, 1753–Feb. 6, 1825). Declined appointment as surgeon in U.S. infantry (1791); physician; born in Boston; resided (1790) in Newburyport, Mass.; son of Benjamin and Elizabeth Hill Eustis; B.A. Harvard (1772); married Caroline Langdon (1810); surgeon in the Revolution (1775–83); surgeon under General Lincoln during Shays's Rebellion (1786–87); member of Mass. General Court (1788–94); elected as Democrat to U.S. House of Representatives (1801–5, 1820–23); secretary of war (1809–13); minister to Netherlands (1814–18); governor of Mass. (1823–25); member of Society of the Cincinnati.
Source: Smith, *Memorials of the Massachusetts Society of the Cincinnati.*

FOSDICK, NATHANIEL F. (1760–1819). Appointed collector at Portland and Falmouth (1789–1801); merchant; born in Marblehead, Mass.; resided (1790) in Portland, Maine; son of Thomas and Frances Hitchborn Fosdick; B.A. Harvard (1779); married Abigail Jones (1784); collector at Portland under state government (1787–89). A Federalist, he was removed from his position by Jefferson in 1801.
Source: Raymond Fosdick, *Annals of the Fosdick Family* (New York, 1953).

FOWLE, EBENEZER SMITH (Mar. 25, 1754–Feb. 13, 1791). Appointed lieutenant in U.S. artillery (1789); soldier; born in Watertown, Mass.; son of Edmund and Abigail Whitney Fowle; B.A. Harvard (1776); married Susanna Jackson (1780); 2nd lieutenant in Jackson's continental regiment (1777–78), lieutenant in army (1786), lieutenant in U.S. artillery (1789–91).
Source: Gertrude Graves, *A New England Family and their French Connections* (Boston, 1930).

FREEMAN, CONSTANT (Feb. 1757–Feb. 27, 1824). Declined appointment as captain in U.S. infantry (1791); soldier; born in Charlestown, Mass.; son of Constant and Lois Cobb Freeman, Jr.; lieutenant in Knox's artillery (1776), commissioned major (1795), lieutenant-colonel of 1st artillery (1802), brevet colonel (1812); mustered out (1815); accountant in navy dept. (1816–24); member of Society of the Cincinnati.
Source: Smith, *Memorials of the Massachusetts Society of the Cincinnati.*

GERRY, SAMUEL R. (July 27, 1750–Feb. 1, 1807). Appointed collector at Marblehead (1790); merchant; born in Marblehead, Mass.; resided (1790) in Marblehead; son of Thomas and Elizabeth Greenleaf Gerry; brother of Elbridge Gerry; married (1) Hannah Glover (1773), (2) Sarah Thompson (1783); commissary of military forces (1776), served in local militia; naval officer at Marblehead (1786); appointed collector upon death of Richard Harris (1790).

Source: Samuel Roads, Jr., *The History and Traditions of Marblehead* (Boston, 1880).

GORE, CHRISTOPHER (Sept. 21, 1758–Mar. 1, 1827). Appointed U.S. district attorney (1789–96); lawyer; born in Boston; resided (1790) in Boston; son of John and Frances Pinckney Gore; B.A. Harvard (1776); married Rebecca Payne (1783); delegate to Mass. ratifying convention (1788), and voted for Constitution; member of Mass. General Court (1788–89, 1808); commissioner to England (1796–1803); chargé des affaires at London (1803–4); state senator (1806–7); governor of Mass. (1809–10); U.S. senator (1813–16); presidential elector for Federalist ticket (1816).

Source: Samuel Ripley, *Memoir of the Late Hon. Christopher Gore of Waltham, Massachusetts* (Boston, 1833).

GORHAM, NATHANIEL (May 27, 1738–June 11, 1796). Appointed supervisor of distilled spirits (1790); merchant; born in Charlestown, Mass.; resided (1790) in Charlestown; son of Nathaniel and Mary Soley Gorham; married Rebecca Call (1763); member of Provincial Assembly (1771–75); member of Provincial Congress (1774–75); sat on Mass. Board of War (1778–81); delegate to Mass. state convention (1779); state senator (1780–81); member of Continental Congress (1782–83, 1785–87); judge of court of common pleas (1785–96); delegate to Philadelphia Constitutional Convention (1787), and signed Constitution (1787); member of Mass. ratifying convention (1788), and voted for Constitution. Gorham was an unsuccessful land speculator. In his application for office, he asked for a position in order to support his family.

Source: Amos Otis and C. F. Swift, *Genealogical Notes of Barnstable Families*, 2 vols. (Barnstable, Mass., 1888–90), vol. 1.

GREATON, RICHARD (Aug. 8, 1765–July 1815). Appointed lieutenant in U.S. infantry (1791); soldier; born in Boston; son of General John and Sarah Humphreys Greaton; married Sarah Bourn (1787); ensign in 3rd regiment (1781), lieutenant in army (1791), captain (1793–1802); member of Society of the Cincinnati.

Source: Smith, *Memorials of the Massachusetts Society of the Cincinnati.*

HARRIS, RICHARD (Sept. 1738–July 14, 1790). Appointed collector at Marblehead (1789–90); merchant; son of Samuel and Hannah Goodwin Harris; married (1) Anne Bradstreet (1764), (2) Lucy Bradstreet (1771); collector at Marblehead under the state government. Harris wrote Washington saying he needed a position in order to support his family.

Source: Walter G. Davis, *The Ancestry of Bethia Harris* (Portland, Me., 1934).

HAYWARD, NATHAN (1763–1848). Appointed surgeon's mate (1789); physician; son of Nathan and Susanna Latham Hayward; B.A. Harvard (1785); married Joanna Winslow (1795); surgeon's mate in army (1789), surgeon in army (1792), resigned (1796). He was a noted physician of Plymouth, Mass.
Sources: Maria W. Bryant, *Genealogy of Edward Winslow of the Mayflower* (New Bedford, Mass., 1915); William T. Davis, *History of the Town of Plymouth* (Philadelphia, 1885).

HIGGINSON, JOHN (Jan. 15, 1765–1818). Appointed lieutenant in U.S. infantry (1791); son of Stephen and Susan Cleveland Higginson; married (1) Josephine de la Porte (c. 1796), (2) Elizabeth ———; ensign and recruiting officer during Shays's Rebellion (1786), lieutenant in army (1791), left army and went to Paris (1792).
Source: Thomas Wentworth Higginson, *Life and Times of Stephen Higginson* (Boston, 1907).

HILL, JEREMIAH (Apr. 30, 1747–June 11, 1820). Appointed collector at Biddeford and Pepperellborough (1789–1809); resided (1790) in Biddeford, Maine; son of Jeremiah and Mary Smith Hill; attended Harvard (1770); married Mrs. Sarah Smith Emery (1772); served in Scammon's Mass. regiment (1775), captain in 1st Mass. (1777), resigned (1777); representative to the Mass. General Court from Maine; participated as Federalist in conventions for Maine's separation from Mass.
Sources: Ronald Banks, *Maine Becomes a State* (Middletown, Conn., 1970); Nathan Goold, "Col. Edmund Phinney's 18th Continental Regiment," *Maine Historical Society,* series 2, 9 (1897): 88–89.

HILLER, JOSEPH (1748–Feb. 9, 1814). Appointed collector at Salem (1789–1802); jeweller; born in Boston; resided (1790) in Salem, Mass.; son of Joseph and Hannah Welch Hiller; married Margaret Cleveland; major in Mass. militia during the Revolution; collector of customs under state government (1784–89); removed from office by Jefferson (1802).
Sources: Robert S. Rantoul, "The Port of Salem," *Essex Institute Historical Collections* 10 (1869): 65–66; Thomas B. Wyman, *The Genealogies and Estates of Charlestown* (Boston, 1879).

HODGE, MICHAEL (Sept. 3, 1743–June 24, 1816). Appointed surveyor at Newburyport (1789–92); merchant; born in Newburyport, Mass.; resided (1790) in Newburyport; son of Charles and Elizabeth Titcomb Hodge; married Sarah Sewall; captain in merchant marine (1776); collector and naval officer at various times under state government; town clerk (1780–89); town selectman (1783–85). He was secretary of the first insurance company in Newburyport.
Source: Hurd, *History of Essex County, Massachusetts.*

HOWE, RICHARD S. (c. 1760–Jan. 22, 1793). Appointed lieutenant in U.S. infantry (1791); soldier; born in Boston; son of Thomas and Rebecca Surcomb Howe; ensign in 10th Mass. (1782), lieutenant in army (1791), appointed captain (1792); member of Society of the Cincinnati.

Sources: Daniel W. Howe, *Howe Genealogies* (Boston, 1929); Smith, *Memorials of the Massachusetts Society of the Cincinnati.*

HUNT, THOMAS (Sept. 17, 1754–Aug. 18, 1808). Appointed captain in U.S. infantry (1791); soldier; born in Watertown, Mass.; son of John and Ruth Fessenden Hunt; married Eunice Wellington (1788); sergeant at Lexington (1775), raised to ensign (1775), captain (1777), captain in army (1791), colonel (1803), commanding officer at Fort Wayne, Fort Defiance, and Fort Industry; member of Society of the Cincinnati.

Sources: Henry Bond, *Genealogies of the Families and Descendants of the Early Settlers of Watertown* (Boston, 1860); Smith, *Memorials of the Massachusetts Society of the Cincinnati.*

HUSSEY, STEPHEN (June 2, 1735–Jan. 24, 1805). Appointed collector at Nantucket and Sherbourn (1791); resided (1790) in Sherbourn, Mass.; son of Daniel and Sarah Gorham Hussey; married Rose Barnard (1756); representative to Mass. General Court (1766, 1769–74, 1783); member of Nantucket Committee of Correspondence (1775); judge of superior court of common pleas.

Sources: Emil F. Guba, *Nantucket Odyssey* (Waltham, Mass., 1965); Alexander Starbuck, *The History of Nantucket* (Boston, 1924).

INGERSOLL, GEORGE (Apr. 2, 1754–July 11, 1805). Appointed lieutenant in U.S. artillery (1791); born in Boston; son of Daniel and Bethiah Haskell Ingersoll; married Martha Goldthwaite (1795); private and sergeant in Gridley's regiment (1775), 2nd lieutenant in Steven's artillery (1776), 1st lieutenant in 3rd continental (1779–83), lieutenant in army (1791); captain (1792), major in corps of artillery and engineers (1802), resigned (1804); member of Society of the Cincinnati.

Source: Lillian D. Avery, *A Genealogy of the Ingersoll Family in America, 1629–1925* (New York, 1926).

JACKSON, JONATHAN (June 4, 1743–Mar. 5, 1810). Appointed U.S. marshal (1789–91); merchant; born in Boston; resided (1790) in Newburyport, Mass.; son of Edward and Dorothy Quincy Jackson; B.A. Harvard (1761); married (1) Sarah Barnard (1767), (2) Hannah Tracy (1772); member of Mass. Provincial Congress (1775); member of Mass. General Court (1777); member of Mass. constitutional convention (1779); delegate to Continental Congress (1782); justice of the peace for Essex County (1783); state senator (1789); inspector of the revenue (1791–96); treasurer of Mass. (1802–06); favored adoption of Constitution; a Federalist. In his letter of application, Jackson said that he needed an office in order to support his family.

Sources: Frances Morse, *Henry and Mary Lee* (Boston, 1926); Shipton, *Biographical Sketches of Those Who Attended Harvard College,* vol. 15.

JORDAN, MELATIAH (Dec. 2, 1753–Dec. 22, 1818). Appointed collector at Frenchman's Bay (1789–1818); lumberer and merchant; born in Biddeford, Maine; resided (1790) in Trenton, Maine; son of Samuel and Mercy Bourn Jordan; married Elizabeth Jellison (1776); major in Mass. militia (1791) and later a colonel (1802). A prominent citizen, Jordan held numerous local offices. He owned 150 acres of land in 1792.
Sources: Albert H. Davis, *History of Ellsworth, Maine* (Lewiston, Me., 1927); William M. Pierce, *Old Hancock County Families* (Ellsworth, Me., 1933).

KNOX, HENRY (July 25, 1750–Oct. 25, 1806). Appointed secretary of war (1789–94); born in Boston; son of William and Mary Campbell Knox; married Lucy Flucker (1774); in Mass. militia (1768), colonel in continental artillery (1775), brigadier general (1776), major general (1781), commander of West Point (1782–85); secretary of war under Confederation (1785–89); supported adoption of Constitution; a Federalist; organized the Society of the Cincinnati (1783). In 1790, Knox and his wife owned over 100,000 acres of land in Maine.
Source: North Callahan, *Henry Knox* (New York, 1958).

KNOX, WILLIAM (c. 1756–1795). Appointed consul to Dublin (1790–92); merchant; son of William and Mary Campbell Knox; military secretary to his brother, General Henry Knox (1776); engaged in privateering (1777); made visits to the Netherlands, France, and England to promote U.S. trade (1781–85); clerk in War Department (1789); later committed to Penn Hospital in Philadelphia (1793–95).

LEE, JOHN (May 12, 1751–Oct. 20, 1812). Appointed collector at Penobscot (1789–1801); merchant; born in Concord, Mass.; resided (1790) in Penobscot, Maine; son of Dr. Joseph and Lucy Jones Lee; married Sarah Howard (c. 1785). Lee was a staunch Federalist, almost to the verge of disloyalty, in the War of 1812.
Sources: William Lee, *John Leigh of Agawam (Ipswich), Massachusetts* (Albany, 1888); Grindall Reynolds, *The Story of a Concord Farm and Its Owners* (Concord, Mass., 1883).

LINCOLN, BENJAMIN (Jan. 24, 1733–May 9, 1810). Appointed collector at Boston and Charlestown (1789–1809); soldier and farmer; born in Hingham, Mass.; resided (1790) in Hingham; son of Benjamin and Elizabeth Thaxter Lincoln; married Mary Cushing (1756); adjutant in 3rd Mass. (1755), major in Mass. militia (1763), lieutenant-colonel (1772), brigadier general (1776), major general in continental army (1777), commander of American army in the South (1778), led state troops against Shays's Rebellion (1787); justice of the peace (1762); member of Mass. General Court (1772–73, 1788); member of Mass. Provincial Congress (1774–75); secretary of war (1781–83); delegate to Mass. ratifying convention (1788), and voted for Constitution; commissioner to treat with Creek Indians (1789) and with northwest Indians (1793).

Source: John T. Kirkland, *Notices of the Life of Major General Benjamin Lincoln* (Boston, 1815).

LITHGOW, WILLIAM (1750–Feb. 17, 1796). Appointed U.S. district attorney (1789–94); lawyer; resided (1790) in Georgetown, Maine; son of William and Sarah Noble Lithgow; read law with James Sullivan; captain in Mass. militia (1776), major in 11th Mass. (1777), resigned (1779), major-general in militia (1789); twice senator to Mass. General Court; ran unsuccessfully for Congress (1791); a Federalist.

Sources: William D. Bridge, *Genealogy of the John Bridge Family in America* (Cambridge, Mass., 1924); Paul Goodman, *The Democratic-Republicans of Massachusetts* (Cambridge, Mass., 1964).

LOVELL, JAMES (Oct. 31, 1737–July 14, 1814). Appointed naval officer at Boston and Charlestown (1789–1814); teacher; born in Boston; resided (1790) in Boston; son of John and Abigail Green Lovell; B.A. Harvard (1756); married Mary Middletown (1760); member of Continental Congress (1776–82); receiver of continental taxes (1784–88); collector of customs at Boston (1788–89); supported adoption of Constitution.

Source: Shipton, *Biographical Sketches of Those Who Attended Harvard College,* vol. 14.

LOWELL, JOHN (June 17, 1743–May 6, 1802). Appointed U.S. district judge (1789–1801); lawyer and merchant; born in Newburyport, Mass.; resided (1790) in Boston; son of John and Sarah Champney Lowell; B.A. Harvard (1760); read law with Oxenbridge Thacher; married (1) Sarah Higginson (1767), (2) Susanna Cabot (1774), (3) Rebecca Russell Tyng; member of Mass. General Court (1778, 1780–82); delegate to Mass. constitutional convention (1780); member of Continental Congress (1782–83); state senator (1784–85); judge of Mass. Court of Appeals (1784–89); judge of U.S. circuit court (1801–02); a Federalist.

Source: Shipton, *Biographical Sketches of Those Who Attended Harvard College,* vol. 14.

LUNT, JAMES (1750–Aug. 21, 1800). Appointed surveyor at Portland and Falmouth; resided (1790) in Portland, Maine; son of James and Hannah Noyes Lunt; married Eunice Noyes (1782); captain in Little's Mass. regiment and 12th continental infantry (1775–79); collector of excise for Cumberland County under state government (1783–84).

Source: Thomas S. Lunt, *Lunt, A History of the Lunt Family in America* (Salem, Mass., 1914).

MELVILL[E], THOMAS (Jan. 27, 1751–Sept. 16, 1832). Appointed surveyor at Boston and Charlestown (1789–1824); merchant; resided (1790) in Boston;

son of Allan and Jane Cargill Melvill; grandfather of Herman Melville; close friend of Samuel Adams and Paul Revere; B.A. Princeton (1769); married Priscilla Scollay; major in Mass. artillery (1776); participated in the Boston Tea Party; naval officer under state government (1787–89).

Sources: John Cargill and Helen Cargill, "Capt. David Cargill of Londonderry, N.H. and Some of His Descendants," *New England Historical and Genealogical Register* 117 (1963): 249; Massachusetts Historical Society, *Proceedings* 60 (1927): 177.

MILLS, JOHN (d. July 8, 1796). Appointed captain in U.S. infantry (1791); soldier; born in Boston; entered service as lieutenant in Paterson's regiment (1777), captain (1779), captain in army (1791), major (1793), promoted to adjutant and inspector of the army (1794), distinguished himself in General Wayne's victory over the Miami Indians (1794); member of Society of the Cincinnati.

Source: Smith, *Memorials of the Massachusetts Society of the Cincinnati.*

MOORE, WILLIAM (d. Sept. 10, 1790). Appointed lieutenant in U.S. artillery (1789), sergeant major in 3rd continental artillery (1777), 2nd lieutenant (1778), 1st lieutenant (1783), lieutenant in army (1789).

NEWMAN, SAMUEL (Dec. 1, 1758–Nov. 4, 1791). Appointed lieutenant in U.S. infantry (1791); soldier; born in Boston; son of Henry and Margaret Fletcher Newman; served in navy and lieutenant in artillery regiment during the Revolution, lieutenant in army (1791); killed in St. Clair's battle with Miami Indians (1791); member of Society of the Cincinnati.

Source: Smith, *Memorials of the Massachusetts Society of the Cincinnati.*

OSGOOD, SAMUEL (Feb. 3, 1748–Aug. 12, 1813). Appointed postmaster general (1789–91); merchant; born in Andover, Mass.; son of Peter and Sarah Johnson Osgood; B.A. Harvard (1770); married (1) Martha Brandon (1775), (2) Maria Bowne Franklin (1786); captain at Lexington alarm (1775), major and aide-de-camp to General Ward (1775–76); member of Mass. Provincial Congress; delegate to Continental Congress (1780–84); member of Mass. General Court (1784); commissioner of U.S. Treasury (1785–89); member of N.Y. General Assembly (1800–1803); supervisor of New York State (1801); naval officer at New York City (1803–13). Osgood and his brother were hurt financially by the Revolution.

Source: Ira Osgood and Eben Putnam, *A Genealogy of the Descendants of John, Christopher and William Osgood* (Salem, Mass., 1894).

OTIS, JOSEPH (Mar. 5, 1726–Sept. 23, 1810). Appointed collector at Barnstable (1789); merchant; resided (1790) in Barnstable, Mass.; son of James and Mary Alleyne Otis; brother of James and Samuel Otis and Mercy Otis Warren; married (1) Rebecca Sturgis, (2) Maria Walter (1770); brigadier

general in Mass. militia (1776); representative to Mass. General Court; collector
of customs at Barnstable (1776–89); clerk of the inferior court (1777). Otis was
hurt financially by the war.
    Sources: William A. Otis, *A Genealogical and Historical Memoir of the Otis
Family in America* (Chicago, 1924); John J. Waters, Jr., *The Otis family in
Provincial and Revolutionary Massachusetts* (Chapel Hill, 1968).

    PEASE, JOHN (1731–Dec. 3, 1813). Appointed collector at Edgartown (1791–
1809); resided (1790) in Edgartown, Mass.; son of John and Hepsibah Ripley
Pease; married Jerusha Norton (1756); collector of customs at Edgartown under
state government (1789–91).
    Source: Charles E. Banks, *The History of Martha's Vineyard*, 3 vols. (1921–
25; reprint ed., Edgartown, Mass., 1966), vols. 2, 3.

    PEIRCE, JOHN (Sept. 28, 1750–July 22, 1798). Appointed lieutenant in U.S.
artillery (1789); soldier; born in Boston; son of Isaac and Mary Hardy Peirce;
lieutenant in Knox's artillery (1776), captain-lieutenant (1778), lieutenant under
Confederation (1787), lieutenant in artillery (1789), captain (1791); member
of Society of the Cincinnati.
    Sources: Smith, *Memorials of the Massachusetts Society of the Cincinnati*;
E. W. West, *The Peirce Family Record, 1687–1893* (New York, 1894).

    PHELON [PHELAN], PATRICK (d. Nov. 4, 1791). Appointed captain in U.S.
infantry (1791); soldier; born in Ireland; commissioned 1st lieutenant in Henley's continental regiment (1777), brevet captain (1783), captain in army
(1791); killed in action against Miami Indians (1791); member of Society of
the Cincinnati.
    Source: Smith, *Memorials of the Massachusetts Society of the Cincinnati.*

    PICKMAN, WILLIAM (Mar. 12, 1748–Nov. 3, 1815). Appointed naval officer
at Salem (1789–1803); merchant; resided (1790) in Salem, Mass.; son of
Benjamin and Love Rawlins Pickman; B.A. Harvard (1766); married Elizabeth
Leavitt (1776); representative to Mass. General Court (1785–89); a Federalist.
Pickman suffered losses in privateering during the Revolution.
    Sources: George F. Dow, *The Diary and Letters of Benjamin Pickman*
(Newport, R.I., 1928); Shipton, *Biographical Sketches of Those Who Attended
Harvard College,* vol. 16.

    POPE, EDWARD (Feb. 15, 1740–June 10, 1818). Appointed collector at New
Bedford (1789); lawyer; resided (1790) in New Bedford, Mass.; son of
Thomas and Thankful Dillingham Pope; attended Harvard (1765); married
(1) Elizabeth Ballard (1768), (2) Mrs. Elizabeth Greenleaf Eliot; colonel in
Mass. militia (1776–78), major in War of 1812; for many years collector at
New Bedford and judge of Court of Common Pleas for Bristol County; a
Federalist.
    Source: Dora Pope Worden, *Genealogy of Thomas Pope and His Descendants*
(Hamilton, N.Y., 1917).

PORTER, MOSES (Mar. 26, 1756–Apr. 14, 1822). Appointed lieutenant in U.S. artillery (1789); born in Danvers, Mass.; son of Benjamin and ———— Rea Porter; ensign in 6th Mass. (1777), 2nd lieutenant in 3rd continental artillery (1779), lieutenant in army (1789), captain (1791), major in 1st artillerists and engineers (1800), colonel (1812), brevet brigadier general (1813).

Source: Alfred P. Putman, "General Moses Porter, An Unrecognized Hero of American History," *New England Historical and Genealogical Register* 44 (1890): 120–25.

PRAY, JOHN (d. Sept. 1812). Appointed captain in U.S. infantry; born in Portsmouth, N.H.; son of Samuel and Alice Pray; married Jane Mesier; sergeant in Scammon's regiment (1775), ensign in 18th continental (1776), 1st lieutenant in 12th Mass. (1777), captain (1779–83); member of Society of the Cincinnati.

Source: Smith, *Memorials of the Massachusetts Society of the Cincinnati.*

PUTNAM, BARTHOLOMEW (Feb. 2, 1738–Apr. 17, 1815). Appointed surveyor at Salem (1789–1809); mariner and shipowner; born in Salem, Mass.; resided (1790) in Salem; son of Bartholomew and Ruth Gardner Putnam; married Sarah Hodges (1760); served in a Salem company of volunteers in Rhode Island (1778–79).

Source: Eben Putnam, *A History of the Putnam Family in England and America* (Salem, Mass., 1891).

PUTNAM, RUFUS (Apr. 9, 1738–May 4, 1824). Appointed judge in the Western Territory (1790–96); soldier and surveyor; born in Sutton, Mass.; resided (1790) in Rutland, Mass.; son of Elisha and Susanna Fuller Putnam; married (1) Elizabeth Ayres (1761), (2) Persis Rice (1765); lieutenant-colonel (1775), colonel and chief of army engineers (1776), brigadier general (1783), later brigadier general in U.S. army (1792); surveyor of western lands (1785); surveyor general of U.S. (1796–1803); delegate to Ohio constitutional convention (1802). He was founder of Marietta, Ohio (1788).

Source: Eben Putnam, *The Putnam Lineage* (Salem, Mass., 1907).

RICKARD, WILLIAM (d. Jan. 9, 1813). Appointed lieutenant in U.S. infantry (1792); soldier; entered service as sergeant (1777), ensign (1779), lieutenant (1782), lieutenant in army (1792), captain in 3rd sub-legion (1794), resigned (1800); member of Society of the Cincinnati.

Source: Smith, *Memorials of the Massachusetts Society of the Cincinnati.*

SARGENT, EPES (Nov. 2, 1748–Apr. 18, 1822). Appointed collector at Gloucester (1789–95); merchant; born in Gloucester, Mass.; resided (1790) in Gloucester; son of Epes and Catherine Osborne Sargent; B.A. Harvard (1766); married Dorcas Babson (1772); delegate to Mass. constitutional convention (1779); later president of the Suffolk Insurance Co. Sargent made a fortune as captain of a privateer during the Revolution.

Sources: Emma Sargent, *Epes Sargent of Gloucester and His Descendants*

(Boston, 1923); Shipton, *Biographical Sketches of Those Who Attended Harvard College*, vol. 16.

SARGENT, WINTHROP (May 1, 1753–June 3, 1820). Appointed secretary of the Western Territory (1789–98); born in Gloucester, Mass.; resided (1790) in Beverly, Mass.; son of Winthrop and Judith Sanders Sargent; B.A. Harvard (1771); married (1) Rowena Tupper (1789), (2) Mary McIntosh Williams (1798); lieutenant in artillery (1775), brevet major (1783), adjutant general under St. Clair (1791); surveyor of Northwest Territory (1786); secretary of Western Territory (1787–89); governor of Mississippi Territory (1798–1801); a Federalist; member of Society of the Cincinnati.
Source: Sargent, *Epes Sargent of Gloucester and His Descendants*.

SAVAGE, JOSEPH (June 13, 1756–Jan. 20, 1814). Appointed captain in U.S. artillery (1789); soldier and merchant; born in Boston; son of Samuel Phillips and Sarah Tyler Savage; married Catherine Hubbard (1793); entered army (1775), 2nd lieutenant in Knox's artillery (1776), captain (1779), captain in army (1789), resigned (1791); moved to Berwick, Maine, in 1793 and was postmaster at Doughty's Falls, Maine (1796–1808); member of Society of the Cincinnati.
Sources: Lawrence Park, *Major Thomas Savage of Boston* (Boston, 1914); Smith, *Memorials of the Massachusetts Society of the Cincinnati*.

SEDGWICK, THEODORE III (Oct. 30, 1768–July 20, 1843). Appointed ensign in U.S. infantry (1791); soldier; born in Litchfield County, Conn.; son of Benjamin and Mary Tuttle Sedgwick, Jr.; nephew of Representative Theodore Sedgwick of Mass.; married Abigail Couch (1806); ensign in army (1791), lieutenant in 2nd sub-legion (1792), captain (1793), honorable discharge (1802), appointed captain in artillery (1812).
Source: Hubert M. Sedgwick, *A Sedgwick Genealogy* (Hamden, Conn., 1961).

SEWALL, DAVID (Oct. 7, 1735–Oct. 12, 1825). Appointed U.S. district judge (1789–1818); lawyer and jurist; born in York, Maine; resided (1790) in York; son of Samuel and Sarah Batchelder Titcomb Sewall; B.A. Harvard (1755); married Mary Parker (1762); appointed register of probate (1766); associate justice of Mass. Supreme Court (1777); a staunch Federalist.
Sources: William T. Davis, *Bench and Bar of the Commonwealth of Massachusetts*, 2 vols. (Boston, 1895), vol. 1; William Willis, *A History of the Law, the Courts and the Lawyers of Maine* (Portland, Me., 1863).

SHAW, SAMUEL (Oct. 2, 1754–May 30, 1794). Appointed consul to Canton (1790–94); merchant; born in Boston; son of Francis and Sarah Burt Shaw; married Hannah Phillips (1792); 2nd lieutenant (1775), 1st lieutenant in 3rd continental artillery (1777), captain and aide-de-camp to General Knox (1780); consul to Canton under Confederation (1786–89); member of Society of the Cincinnati.
Source: Smith, *Memorials of the Massachusetts Society of the Cincinnati*.

SMITH, STEPHEN (May 30, 1739–Sept. 29, 1806). Appointed collector at Machias (1790); mill owner; born in Sandwich, Mass.; resided (1790) in Machias, Maine; son of Samuel and Bethia Chipman Smith; married Deborah Ellis (1762); captain in Machias militia (1777); member of Committee of Safety and Correspondence (1781); naval officer at Machias (1782, 1785–86); selectman of Machias (1784).
Source: George T. Little, *Genealogical and Family History of the State of Maine,* 4 vols. (New York, 1909), vol. 1.

SOHIER, MARTIN BRIMMER (d. July 12, 1792). Appointed ensign in U.S. infantry (1791); soldier; ensign in army (1791), promoted to lieutenant (1791–92).

STANIFORD, JEREMIAH. Appointed surveyor at Ipswich (1789); resided (1790) in Ipswich, Mass. This was probably the Jeremiah Staniford (Sept. 28, 1751–Feb. 29, 1816) born to Jeremiah and Mary Potter Staniford and married to Mary Fowler (1774).

TITCOMB, JONATHAN (Sept. 12, 1727–Mar. 10, 1817). Appointed naval officer at Newburyport (1789–1812); merchant; born in Newbury, Mass.; resided (1790) in Newburyport; son of Josiah and Martha Rolf Titcomb; married (1) Mary Dole (1751), (2) Sarah Stedman; colonel and brigadier general of Essex County troops during the Revolution; representative to Mass. Provincial Congress (1774–75); member of Mass. constitutional convention (1780); naval officer at Newburyport during the Confederation; delegate to Mass. ratifying convention (1788), and voted for Constitution; a Federalist.
Sources: Labaree, *Patriots and Partisans*; Gilbert M. Titcomb, *Descendants of William Titcomb of Newbury, Massachusetts* (Ann Arbor, Mich., 1969).

TRESCOTT, LEMUEL (May 23, 1751–Aug. 10, 1826). Appointed major in U.S. infantry (1791); merchant and carpenter; born in Dorchester, Mass.; resided (1790) in Machias, Maine; son of John and Sarah Davenport Trescott; married (1) Susannah ———, (2) Rebecca Larrabee Edes; captain at Bunker Hill, major (1778), major in army (1791), resigned (1791); treasurer of Eastport, Maine (1798); town moderator (1803–7); collector of customs at Machias (1808–11); collector at Passamaquoddy (1811); member of Society of the Cincinnati.
Sources: Kilby, *Eastport and Passamaquoddy*; Paul Trescott, *An Account of the Ventures, Adventures and Misadventures of William Trescott* (Charleston, S.C., 1970).

TREVETT, RICHARD (d. July 12, 1793). Appointed collector at York (1791–93); mariner; resided (1790) in York, Maine; married Hannah Sewall (1749); commander of a privateer during the Revolution; member of York Committee of Safety and Correspondence (1782–84); naval officer under state government (1776, 1780–91).
Source: Charles E. Banks, *History of York, Maine,* 2 vols. (Baltimore, 1967).

TURNER, EDWARD. Appointed ensign in U.S. infantry (1791); lieutenant (1792), captain in 2nd sub-legion (1793), brigadier inspector (1799–1802), resigned (1805).

WARREN, WINSLOW (1759–1791). Appointed lieutenant in U.S. infantry (1791); son of James and Mercy Otis Warren; lieutenant in army (1791); killed in St. Clair's defeat by the Miami Indians (1791). Previous to his commission, Warren was imprisoned for debt in Massachusetts.
Source: John C. Warren, *Genealogy of Warren* (Boston, 1854).

WATSON, WILLIAM (May 7, 1730–Apr. 21, 1815). Appointed collector at Plymouth (1789–1803); merchant; resided (1790) in Plymouth, Mass.; son of John and Priscilla Thomas Watson; B.A. Harvard (1751); married Elizabeth Marston (1756); justice of the peace (1762); member of Committee of Correspondence (1774); naval officer at Plymouth (1782); judge on Plymouth bench (1783–1810); a Federalist.
Source: Shipton, *Biographical Sketches of Those Who Attended Harvard College,* Vol. 13.

WEBB, WILLIAM (c. 1764–May 1822). Appointed collector at Bath (1789–1804); resided (1790) in Bath, Maine; married Hannah ————; collector at Bath under state government (1779–89).
Source: Patrick M. Reed, *History of Bath and Environs* (Portland, Me., 1894).

WHITTEMORE, SAMUEL (June 13, 1733–July 15, 1806). Appointed surveyor at Gloucester (1790–1803); schoolmaster; resided (1790) in Gloucester, Mass.; son of Samuel and Margaret Hicks Whittemore; B.A. Harvard (1751); married (1) Margaret Gee (1757), (2) Sarah Parsons (1774); member of three Provincial Congresses; representative to Mass. General Court (1776, 1783–84); delegate to Mass. constitutional convention (1780); justice of the peace (1776–95); naval officer at Gloucester (1776); inspector of the port (1792–1803); a Federalist.
Sources: Shipton, *Biographical Sketches of Those Who Attended Harvard College,* vol. 13; Bernard B. Whittemore, *A Genealogy of Four Branches of the Whittemore Family* (Nashua, N.H., 1880).

WYATT, LEMUEL. Appointed collector at Rehoboth (1789); resided (1790) in Rehoboth, Mass. He purchased some land in Ohio in 1787.
Source: Albion M. Dyer, "First Ownership of Ohio Lands," *New England Historical and Genealogical Register* 65 (1911): 228.

New Hampshire

CASS, JONATHAN (Oct. 9, 1752–Aug. 14, 1830). Appointed captain in U.S. infantry (1791); blacksmith; born in East Kingston, N.H.; married Mary

Gilman (1781); private at Bunker Hill (1775), ensign in 3rd N.H. (1776), 2nd lieutenant in 3rd N.H. (1777), captain in 2nd N.H. (1782–83), captain in army (1791), major (1793), resigned (1801); member of Society of the Cincinnati.

Source: Ohio Adjutant General's Office, *The Official Roster of the Soldiers of the American Revolution Buried in the State of Ohio.*

GARDNER, WILLIAM (1751–Apr. 29, 1834). Appointed commissioner of loans (1791–96); merchant; born in Portsmouth, N.H.; son of John Gardner; married the daughter of Captain Purcell; ensign in Captain John Langdon's cavalry company (1778) and later major; commissary for U.S. army; a Republican. He went into debt while purchasing supplies for the army during the Revolution.

Sources: Charles W. Brewster, *Rambles About Portsmouth* (Portsmouth, N.H., 1859); Joseph Foster, *Records of the Soldiers, Sailors and Marines who Served the United States of America Buried in the City of Portsmouth, New Hampshire* (Portsmouth, N.H., 1893).

GILMAN, JOHN TAYLOR (Dec. 19, 1753–Sept. 1, 1828). Declined appointment as commissioner for settling accounts between the U.S. and the states (1790); shipbuilder and merchant; born in Exeter, N.H.; son of Nicholas and Ann Taylor Gilman; married (1) Deborah Folsom (1775), (2) Mrs. Mary Adams, (3) Mrs. Charlotte Hamilton; sergeant in Exeter militia (1775), commissary to N.H. troops; member of N.H. General Court (1779, 1781, 1810–11); member of Continental Congress (1782–83); treasurer of N.H. (1783–87, 1791–94); commissioner for settling accounts (1786–89); delegate to N.H. ratifying convention (1788), and voted for Constitution; governor of N.H. (1794–1805, 1813–16); a Federalist; trustee of Phillips Exeter Academy (1796–1827).

Sources: Alexander W. Gillman, *Searches into the History of the Gillman or Gilman Family* (London, 1895); Willard A. Nichols, *Nichols Genealogy* (Redlands, Calif., 1911).

GILMAN, JOSEPH SMITH (c. 1761–Sept. 27, 1826). Appointed ensign in U.S. infantry (1790); son of Israel and Hannah Smith Gilman; married Elizabeth Gilman.

Source: Arthur Gilman, *The Gilman Family* (Albany, 1869).

GILMAN, NATHANIEL (Nov. 10, 1759–Jan. 26, 1847). Declined appointment as commissioner of loans (1790); son of Nicholas and Ann Taylor Gilman; brother of John T. Gilman, a Washington appointee; married (1) Abigail Odlin (1785), (2) Dorothy Folsom (1796); colonel in N.H. militia; continental loan officer in N.H. (1783–89); member of N.H. General Court (1792, 1795, 1802).

Source: Charles H. Bell, *History of the Town of Exeter, New Hampshire* (Exeter, N.H., 1888).

HOWE, BEZALAEL (Nov. 28, 1750–Sept. 16, 1825). Appointed lieutenant in

U.S. infantry (1791); merchant; born in Marlborough, Mass.; son of Bezalael and Anna Howe; married (1) Hannah Merritt (1787), (2) Catharine Moffat (1800); private in Reed's N.H. regiment (1775), 2nd lieutenant in 1st N.H. (1776), 1st lieutenant (1779), captain (1783), lieutenant in army (1791), captain in 4th sub-legion (1791), major (1794), discharged (1796); served in N.Y. custom house (1796); inspector of revenue for N.Y. City (1799); member of New York Society of the Cincinnati.

Source: Herbert B. Howe, *Major Bezalael Howe, 1750–1825: An Officer in the Continental & Regular Armies* (Mount Kisco, N.Y., 1950).

LANGDON, WOODBURY (1739–Jan. 13, 1805). Appointed commissioner for settling accounts between the U.S. and the states (1791); merchant; born in Portsmouth, N.H.; son of John and Mary Hall Langdon; married Sarah Sherbourne (1765); member of N.H. General Court (1774–75, 1778–79); member of Continental Congress (1779–80); judge of N.H. Superior Court (1782, 1786–90); member of N.H. Senate (1784–85); unsuccessful Republican candidate for Congress (1796).

Sources: Nathaniel Adams, *Annals of Portsmouth* (Portsmouth, N.H., 1825); Charles H. Bell, *The Bench and Bar of New Hampshire* (Boston, 1894).

MARTIN, THOMAS (c. 1732–Feb. 4, 1805). Appointed surveyor at Portsmouth (1790–98); merchant; married Ann Peirce; member of N.H. General Court (1777); collector at Portsmouth (1798–1801).

Source: Brewster, *Rambles About Portsmouth*.

PARKER, JOHN (Nov. 16, 1732–Oct. 4, 1791). Appointed U.S. marshal (1790–91); mariner and head of insurance house; born in Portsmouth, N.H.; son of William Parker; captain in Bedel's N.H. Rangers (1775–76); sheriff of Rockingham County (1771–76).

Source: Adams, *Annals of Portsmouth*.

PEIRCE, JOSEPH, JR. (Mar. 8, 1773–1832). Declined appointment as ensign in U.S. infantry (1791); born in Boston; son of Joseph and Ann Dawes Peirce; married (1) Frances Temple Cordis (1791), (2) Abby Robinson (1819).

Source: E. W. West, *The Peirce Family Record, 1687–1893*.

RUSSELL, ELEAZER (c. 1720–Sept. 18, 1798). Appointed naval officer at Portsmouth (1790–98); resided (1790) in Portsmouth, N.H.; son of ――― and Margaret Waldron Russell; naval officer at Portsmouth (1776–89); collector of imposts for N.H.

Sources: Brewster, *Rambles About Portsmouth*; Arthur H. Locke, *Portsmouth and New Castle, N.H., Cemetery Inscriptions* (Portsmouth, N.H., 1907).

SHERBURNE, SAMUEL J. (1757–Aug. 2, 1830). Appointed U.S. district attorney (1789–93); lawyer; born in Portsmouth, N.H.; son of John and Elizabeth Moffat Sherburne; M.A. Dartmouth (1776); married Submit Boyd; major in General Whipple's brigade of N.H. militia (1776–78); lost a leg at battle of

Quaker Hill (1778); member of N.H. General Court (1776, 1790–93, 1799, 1801); justice of the peace (1788); member of U.S. House of Representatives (1793–97); U.S. district attorney (1801–4); U.S. district judge (1804–30); testified against Judge Timothy Pickering and replaced him after his removal in 1804. In 1789, after the death of his father John, Samuel Sherburne changed his first name to John. The Senate Executive Journal cites him as Samuel, Junr., but it is unlikely that he was referred to as junior before he changed his name.

Source: Bell, *The Bench and Bar of New Hampshire.*

SULLIVAN, JOHN (Feb. 17, 1740–Jan. 23, 1795). Appointed U.S. District Judge (1789–95); lawyer; born in Berwick, Maine; son of John and Margery Browne Sullivan; studied law with Samuel Livermore; married Lydia Worcester (1760); major in N.H. militia (1772), brigadier general in continental army (1775), major general (1776), resigned (1779); member of Continental Congress (1774–75, 1780–81); attorney general of N.H. (1782–86); Speaker of N.H. General Court (1785, 1788); president of N.H. (1786–87, 1789); delegate to N.H. ratifying convention (1788), and voted for Constitution; president of N.H. Society of the Cincinnati.

Sources: Bell, *The Bench and Bar of New Hampshire*; Brewster, *Rambles About Portsmouth.*

WENTWORTH, JOSHUA (1742–1809). Appointed supervisor of distilled spirits (1791–98); merchant; son of Daniel Wentworth; married Sarah Peirce (1774); lieutenant-colonel in 1st N.H. (1776), colonel (1781); naval officer at Portsmouth (1776); member of N.H. Board of War (1778); elected but declined to attend Continental Congress (1779); N.H. senator (1779–83).

Source: Brewster, *Rambles About Portsmouth.*

WHIPPLE, JOSEPH (c. 1738–Feb. 26, 1816). Appointed collector at Portsmouth (1789–98); merchant; born in Kittery Point, Maine; son of William and Mary Cutt Whipple; married Hannah Billings (1763); colonel in 25th N.H. militia (1784); member of N.H. General Court (1776–78, 1782–83, 1785); justice of the peace (1779); state collector of impost at Portsmouth (1786–89); collector at Portsmouth (1801–16); a Republican. He was a substantial landowner in Dartmouth, N.H.

Sources: Joseph Foster, *The Soldiers' Memorial, Portsmouth, N.H.* (Portsmouth, N.H., 1922); Dorothy M. Vaughn, *This Was a Man: A Biography of William Whipple* (Lunenberg, Vt., 1964).

New Jersey

BENEZET, DANIEL, JR. (Feb. 18, 1760–1798). Appointed collector at Great Egg Harbor (1790); born in Philadelphia; son of Daniel and Elizabeth Benezet; married Roxanna ———; commissioned 2nd lieutenant in Pa. militia (1780).

Source: Samuel Small, *Genealogical Records* (Philadelphia, 1905).

BREARLY, DAVID (June 11, 1745–Aug. 16, 1790). Appointed U.S. district judge (1789–90); lawyer; son of David and Mary Clark Brearly; married (1) Elizabeth Mullen (1767), (2) Elizabeth Higbee (1783); lieutenant-colonel in 4th N.J. (1776–79); chief justice of N.J. Supreme Court (1779–89); delegate to Federal Convention at Philadelphia (1787), and signed the Constitution; presided over N.J. ratifying convention (1787), and voted for Constitution; member of Society of the Cincinnati. In 1788, Brearly was a member of the N.J. Land Company, which was seeking land in Northwest Territory. He also held public securities.
Source: W. H. Brearly, *Genealogy of the Brearly Family* (Detroit, 1886).

CARMICHAEL, JOHN F. (d. Oct. 21, 1837). Appointed surgeon's mate in U.S. infantry (1789), honorably discharged (1790), surgeon in army (1792–1801), post surgeon (1802), resigned (1804).

DOUGHTY, JOHN (1754–Sept. 16, 1826). Appointed major in U.S. artillery (1789); soldier; born in New York City; son of Joseph and Siche Wiltsie Doughty; B.A. King's College (1770); captain and aide-de-camp to General Schuyler (1777), major in continental army (1784), major in army (1789), resigned (1791), reentered as lieutenant-colonel (1798), retired (1800); member of N.J. Legislature; member of Society of the Cincinnati. Doughty built and commanded Fort Harmar (1785) and Fort Washington (1800).
Source: Jones, *Fort Washington at Cincinnati, Ohio.*

DUNHAM, AARON. Appointed supervisor of distilled spirits (1791); a Federalist; member of the N.J. Land Company, which was interested in the Northwest Territory.

ELMER, ELI (d. 1806). Appointed collector at Bridgetown (1789); physician; son of Theophilus and Theodosia Sayre Elmer; married Jane Thompson (1781); 2nd lieutenant in artillery and paymaster during the Revolution; state collector of customs (1786–89); delegate to N.J. ratifying convention (1787), and voted for Constitution; judge in court of common pleas (1787); member of N.J. Legislature (1788); member of Governor's Council (1795); member of Society of the Cincinnati.
Source: H. Stanley Craig, *Cumberland County Genealogical Data* (Merchantville, N.J., 1938).

EWING, JAMES (July 12, 1744–1824). Appointed commissioner of loans (1790); son of Thomas and Mary Maskell Ewing; married Martha Boyd (1778); paymaster, 2nd lieutenant, and captain in N.J. militia during the Revolution; member of N.J. Legislature (1774, 1778); county collector (1777–79); commissioner of loans under Continental Congress (1786–1789); mayor of Trenton (1797–1803); judge for Hunterdon County.
Sources: Eli F. Cooley, *Genealogy of Early Settlers in Trenton and Ewing* (Trenton, N.J., 1883); Joseph L. Ewing, *Sketches of the Families of Ewing* (Stratford, N.J., 1910).

FORD, MAHLON (July 22, 1756–June 14, 1820). Appointed lieutenant in U.S. artillery (1789); soldier; born in Morristown, N.J.; son of John and Martha Rayhnor Ford; married Sophia B. Spencer (1793); ensign in 3rd N.J. (1777), 1st lieutenant (1780), brevet captain (1783), lieutenant in army (1789), promoted to captain (1791), major in 1st artillery (1798), honorably discharged (1802); member of Society of the Cincinnati; a witness at the Treaty of Fort Stanwix (1784).

Source: Elizabeth C. Stewart, *The Descendants of Andrew Ford of Weymouth, Massachusetts* (Montpelier, Vt., 1968).

HALSTEAD [HALSTED], JOHN (c. 1732–1813). Appointed collector at Perth Amboy (1789–1800); son of John and Susannah Blanchard Halstead; married (1) Elizabeth DeHart, (2) Alleta W. Waters; commissary for the army under Benedict Arnold (1776–77). At the time of his appointment, Halstead was in financial difficulty, having lost all of his property in Canada as a result of the Revolution.

Sources: William L. Halstead, *The Story of the Halsteads of the United States* (n.p., 1934); Laura A. Shoptaugh, *Some Descendants of Jonas Halsted* (Oakland, Calif., 1954).

KERSEY, WILLIAM (d. Mar. 21, 1800). Appointed lieutenant in U.S. infantry (1789); soldier; entered service as private in 3rd N.J. (1776), ensign (1777), 1st lieutenant (1780), lieutenant in army (1789), promoted to captain (1791), major in 4th sub-legion (1794); member of Society of the Cincinnati.

LOWREY, THOMAS (Sept. 3, 1737–Nov. 10, 1806). Appointed U.S. marshal (1789–1803); merchant; born in Ireland; married Esther Fleming; lieutenant-colonel in N.J. militia (1776), however never active in the service; member of N.J. Provincial Congress (1775); member of N.J. Legislature (1791–92).

Source: Henry Race, *Historico-Genealogical Sketch of Col. Thomas Lowrey* (Flemington, N.J., 1892).

LUSE [LUCE], FRANCIS. Appointed ensign in U.S. infantry (1789); private, corporal, and sergeant (1775–80), ensign (1780), ensign in army (1789), resigned (1790); member of Society of the Cincinnati; a witness at the Treaty of Fort Harmar (1789).

MERCER, JOHN. Appointed captain in U.S. infantry (1789); son of Dr. William and Lucy Tyson Mercer; ensign in 1st N.J. (1775), 1st lieutenant (1776), captain (1777), captain in army (1789), resigned (1790); after resignation, stayed in Ohio and was justice of the peace (1793) and judge of the Court of Common Pleas of Hamilton County (1799); member of Society of the Cincinnati; a witness at the Treaty of Fort Stanwix (1784).

Source: Francis B. Lee, *Genealogical and Memorial History of the State of New Jersey*, 4 vols. (New York, 1910), vols. 2, 4.

MORGAN, JOHN. Appointed ensign in U.S. infantry (1790); married Elizabeth

Ward (1781); promoted to lieutenant (1791), cashiered (1793). After his service, Morgan settled in Hamilton County, Ohio.

MORRIS, ROBERT (c. 1745–June 2, 1815). Appointed U.S. district judge (1789–1815); lawyer; born in New Brunswick, N.J.; son of Robert Hunter Morris; chief justice of N.J. Supreme Court (1777–79); a Federalist.
Source: E. Q. Keasbey, *The Courts and Lawyers of New Jersey, 1661–1912*, 2 vols. (New York, 1912), vol. 2.

OGDEN, ABRAHAM (Dec. 30, 1743–Jan. 31, 1798). Appointed U.S. district attorney (1791–98); lawyer; son of David and Gertrude Gouverneur Ogden; married Sarah F. Ludlow (1767); captain, major, and lieutenant-colonel in N.J. militia (1776–79); member of N.J. Legislature (1790). He held a large tract of land in northern New York, and Ogdensburg is named after him.
Source: William O. Wheeler, *The Ogden Family* (Philadelphia, 1907).

ROSS, JOHN (Mar. 2, 1752–Sept. 7, 1796). Appointed collector at Burlington (1789); physician; born in Mount Holly, N.J.; son of Dr. Alexander Ross; married Mary Brainerd (1778); captain in 3rd N.J. (1776), major in 2nd N.J. (1779), lieutenant-colonel of militia (1782); naval officer under state government (1781–89); member of Society of the Cincinnati.
Sources: "Necrology," New Jersey Historical Society *Proceedings*, series 2, 1 (1896): 100; E. M. Woodward and John Hageman, *History of Burlington and Mercer Counties* (Philadelphia, 1883).

SCOTT, JOHN M. (1760–July 9, 1851). Appointed surgeon's mate in U.S. infantry (1789); born in Burlington County, N.J.; private in the Revolution, surgeon's mate in army (1789), surgeon (1792), resigned (1797).

SEDAM, CORNELIUS R. (1759–May 10, 1823). Appointed ensign in U.S. infantry (1789); soldier; born in N.J.; married (1) ——— Winton (1799), (2) Nancy Haynes (1815); private, corporal, and ensign during the Revolution, ensign in army (1789), lieutenant (1790), promoted to captain (1792), honorably discharged (1796); pioneer of Cincinnati, Ohio; member of Society of the Cincinnati.
Source: Emma Backus, "Cornelius Sedam and His Friends in Washington's Time," *Ohio Archaeological and Historical Quarterly* 41 (1932): 28–50.

STOCKTON, RICHARD (Apr. 17, 1764–Mar. 7, 1828). Appointed U.S. district attorney (1790–91); lawyer; born near Princeton, N.J.; son of Richard and Annis Boudinot Stockton; B.A. Princeton (1779); studied law with Elias Boudinot; married Mary Field; Federalist in U.S. Senate (1796–99); unsuccessful candidate for N.J. governor (1801–4); member of U.S. House of Representatives (1813–15). Stockton was a member of the N.J. Land Company (1788), and he owned 5,000 acres of land in Oneida County, N.Y.

Source: Lucius Q. C. Elmer, *The Constitution and Government of the Province and State of New Jersey* (Trenton, N.J., 1872).

SYMMES, JOHN CLEVES (July 21, 1742–Feb. 26, 1814). Appointed judge of the Northwest Territory (1789–1803); pioneer and speculator; born in Long Island, N.Y.; son of Timothy and Mary Cleves Symmes; married (1) Anna Tuttle, (2) Mrs. Mary Halsey, (3) Susanna Livingston; colonel in N.J. militia; member of N.J. Legislature (1776, 1778, 1780, 1785); chief justice of N.J. Supreme Court (1777–87); member of Continental Congress (1785–86). A founder of Cincinnati, Ohio, Symmes was a prominent speculator in Ohio lands at the time of his appointment.

Sources: Beverley Bond, ed., *Correspondence of John Cleves Symmes* (New York, 1926); Charles Winfield, "John Cleves Symmes," New Jersey Historical Society *Proceedings*, series 2, 5 (1879): 22–43.

TUCKER, EBENEZER (Nov. 15, 1758–Sept. 5, 1845). Appointed surveyor at Little Egg Harbor (1789); merchant; son of Reuben and Ruth Sulse Tucker; married (1) Catherine Buck, (2) Phebe Ridgeway (1802); justice of the peace and judge of the Court of Common Pleas of Burlington County; postmaster of Tuckerton (1806–25, 1831–45); collector of customs at Tuckerton; member of U.S. House of Representatives (1825–29). The founder of Tuckerton, N.J., Tucker was a wealthy landowner in Little Egg Harbor as well as a merchant.

Sources: Leah Blackman, *History of Little Egg Harbor Township* (Trenton, N.J., 1963); Edwin Salter, *History of Monmouth and Ocean Counties* (Bayonne, N.J., 1890).

New York

BOGART, HENRY. Appointed surveyor at Albany (1790); 2nd lieutenant in continental artillery (1777–78); member of Albany Committee of Safety and Correspondence (1775).

BRADFORD, JAMES (d. Nov. 4, 1791). Appointed captain in U.S. artillery (1789); born in Pa.; 1st lieutenant in continental artillery during the Revolution, captain in army (1789), killed in action with the Indians on the Maumee River (1791).

BRUSH, EBENEZER (Mar. 18, 1763–May 1814). Appointed consul to Surinam (1790–92); merchant; born in Huntington, N.Y.; son of John and Hannah Wickes Brush; married Sally Shattuck (1796).

Source: Conklin Mann, "Thomas and Richard Brush," *New York Genealogical and Biographical Record* 67 (1936): 21.

COCHRAN, JOHN (Sept. 1, 1730–Apr. 6, 1807). Appointed commissioner of loans (1790); physician; born in Sudsbury, Pa.; son of James and Isabella Cochran; married Mrs. Gertrude Schuyler (1760); surgeon's mate in Seven Years' War; surgeon general of continental army (1777); director general of army hospitals (1781); commissioner of loans under Confederation government (1786–89); member of Society of the Cincinnati; founder of the New Jersey Medical Society (1769). In his application for office, Cochran commented on his poor financial condition.

Source: Walter L. C. Biddle, "Doctor John Cochran," *Pennsylvania Magazine of History and Biography* 3 (1879): 241–49.

DERING, HENRY P. (July 3, 1763–Apr. 30, 1822). Appointed collector at Sag Harbor (1790–1822); son of Thomas and Mary Sylvester Dering; B.A. Yale (1784); married Anna Fosdick (1793); postmaster at Sag Harbor (1790–1822). He owned a considerable landed estate on Shelter Island.

Source: Dexter, *Biographical Sketches of Graduates of Yale College*, vol. 4.

DUANE, JAMES (Feb. 6, 1733–Feb. 1, 1797). Appointed U.S. district judge (1789–94); lawyer; born in New York City; son of Anthony and Althea Kettletas Duane; studied law under James Alexander; married Mary Livingston (1759); N.Y. attorney general (1767); member of New York City Committee of Correspondence (1774); member of Continental Congress (1774–84); state senator (1782–85, 1788–90); mayor of New York (1784–89); delegate to N.Y. ratifying convention (1788), and voted for Constitution; a Federalist. At the time of his appointment, Duane owned an estate of 40,000 acres. He was also an unsuccessful speculator in Vermont.

Source: Edward P. Alexander, *A Revolutionary Conservative: James Duane of New York* (New York, 1938).

ELLIOT, JOHN (d. Mar. 26, 1809). Appointed surgeon's mate in U.S. infantry (1789); born in New York State; surgeon's mate in 3rd N.Y. (1776–83), surgeon's mate in army (1789–91), surgeon in army (1791–1802).

ERNEST, MATTHEW (d. 1805). Appointed lieutenant in U.S. artillery (1789); son of John and Sarah Ernest; private in 5th N.Y. (1779–81), lieutenant (1786), lieutenant in army (1789), battalion paymaster (1790), resigned (1791).

GELSTON, JOHN (Aug. 1, 1750–1831). Appointed collector at Sag Harbor (1789), resigned (1790); storekeeper; resided (1790) in Southampton, N.Y.; son of Maltby and Mary Jones Gelston; married (1) Phebe Foster Morehouse (c. 1778), (2) Phebe Herrick; served as adjutant in Suffolk County troops; member of the N.Y. Legislature (1791–95).

Source: Frederic Gregory Mather, *The Refugees of 1776 from Long Island to Connecticut* (Albany, 1913).

HAMILTON, ALEXANDER (1755–July 12, 1804). Appointed secretary of the treasury (1789–95); statesman and lawyer; born on Nevis Island, West Indies; son of James Hamilton and Rachael Faucett Lavien; attended King's College; married Elizabeth Schuyler (1780); captain in N.Y. artillery company (1776), lieutenant-colonel and aide-de-camp to General Washington (1777–81), appointed inspector general of the army (1798–1800); collector of revenue for New York City (1782); member of Continental Congress (1782–83); attended Constitutional Convention (1787), and signed Constitution; member of N.Y. Legislature (1787); attended N.Y. ratifying convention (1788); member of Society of the Cincinnati; collaborated with Madison and Jay in writing *The Federalist*; a founder of the Bank of N.Y.; owned $800 worth of public securities in 1789; fatally wounded in duel with Aaron Burr.

Sources: Broadus Mitchell, *Alexander Hamilton: Youth to Maturity, 1755– 1788* (New York, 1957); idem, *Alexander Hamilton: The National Adventure, 1788–1804* (New York, 1962).

HAMTRAMCK, JOHN F. (Aug. 16, 1756–Apr. 11, 1803). Appointed major in U.S. infantry (1789); soldier; born in Quebec, Canada; son of Charles D. and Marie Anne Berton Hamtramck; married (1) Marie E. Perrot (1790), (2) Rebecca MacKenzie (1797); captain in 5th and 2nd N.Y. (1776–83), major in army (1789), lieutenant-colonel and commandant of 1st sub-legion (1793), colonel in 1st infantry (1802); oversaw construction of Fort Dearborn, the eventual site of Chicago.

Sources: F. Clever Bald, "Colonel John Francis Hamtramck," *Indiana Magazine of History* 44 (1948): 335–54; George B. Catlin, "Colonel John Francis Hamtramck," *Indiana Magazine of History* 26 (1930): 237–52.

HARRISON, RICHARD (c. 1748–Dec. 6, 1829). Appointed U.S. district attorney (1789–1801); lawyer; son of Francis Harrison; member of N.Y. Legislature (1788–89); recorder of N.Y. City (1798–1801); a Federalist. In his application for office, Harrison stated that his financial situation forced him to request a position in the new government.

Source: E. B. O'Callaghan, "Biographical Sketch of Francis Harrison," *New York Genealogical and Biographical Record* 9 (1878): 49–51.

JAY, JOHN (Dec. 12, 1745–May 17, 1829). Appointed chief justice of the Supreme Court (1789–95); jurist and statesman; born in New York City; son of Peter and Mary Anna Van Cortlandt Jay; graduated King's College (1764); married Sarah Livingston (1774); member of New York Committee of Correspondence; member of Continental Congress (1774–77, 1778, 1779); chief justice of N.Y. (1777–78); minister plenipotentiary to Spain (1779); minister to negotiate peace with Great Britain (1781), and signed Treaty of Paris (1783); secretary of foreign affairs (1784–89); delegate to N.Y. ratifying convention (1788), and voted for Constitution; minister plenipotentiary to Great

Britain (1794–95), and negotiated Jay Treaty (1794); governor of N.Y. (1795–1801); a Federalist. In 1790, Jay owned at least 500 acres of land and received $8,747.45 for loan certificates.

Source: Frank Monaghan, *John Jay* (New York, 1935).

LAMB, JOHN (Jan. 1, 1735–May 31, 1800). Appointed collector at New York (1789–97); merchant; born in New York City; son of Anthony and ——— Ham Lamb; married Catherine Jandine (1755); captain in N.Y. artillery (1775), major-commandant (1776), colonel in continental artillery (1777–83), brigadier general by brevet (1783); a Son of Liberty (1765); member of N.Y. Legislature (1784); collector at New York City (1784–89); opposed ratification of Constitution; resigned in 1797 after a shortage of funds was discovered. Lamb was a speculator in the syndicate which purchased 48,000 acres of land in New York (1791).

Source: Isaac Q. Leake, *Memoir of the Life and Times of Gen. John Lamb* (Albany, 1850).

LANSING, JEREMIAH (Apr. 14, 1754–Oct. 7, 1817). Appointed surveyor at Albany (1789–90); son of Peter and Elizabeth Wendell Lansing; married Helena Wendell (1780); member of N.Y. Legislature (1798–99).

Source: Claude G. Munsell, *The Lansing Family* (n.p., 1916).

LASHER, JOHN (Mar. 4, 1724–Feb. 29, 1806). Appointed surveyor at New York City (1789); merchant; son of John and Eva Binder Lasher; married (1) Helena Pears (1753), (2) Catherine Ernest (1763); colonel in N.Y. militia (1775–83); member of N.Y. Committee of Safety (1775); surveyor at New York (1784–89). In his application for office, Lasher wrote that he was financially hurt by the war and in need of a position in order to support his wife and children.

Source: A. P. Lasher, *Lasher Genealogy* (New York, 1904).

PETERS, WILLIAM (b. May 13, 1764). Appointed lieutenant in U.S. infantry (1789); son of Valentine and Ruth Smith Peters; married Ann Hamilton (c. 1783); ensign in 2nd N.Y. (1781–83), lieutenant in army (1789), raised to captain (1791), major in 4th sub-legion (1794), honorably discharged (1802).

Source: Charles Peters, *A Peters Lineage* (Poughkeepsie, N.Y., 1896).

PINTARD, JOHN M. Appointed consul to Madeira (1789–99); merchant; married Betsey Bayard; American agent at Madeira (1783–89).

PRIOR, ABNER (d. Dec. 5, 1800). Appointed ensign in U.S. infantry (1789); physician; surgeon's mate in 4th N.Y. (1780–83), ensign in army (1789), promoted to lieutenant (1790), captain in 3rd sub-legion (1792), served at least until 1796.

SCHUYLER, DIRCK (Nov. 29, 1761–June, 1811). Appointed lieutenant in U.S. artillery (1789); born in Albany; son of Harmanus and Christina Ten Broeck Schuyler; ensign in 2nd N.Y. (1782–83), lieutenant (1786), lieutenant in army (1789), resigned (1792).
Source: Emma Ten Broeck Runk, *The Ten Broeck Genealogy* (New York, 1897).

SMITH, JOHN (d. June 6, 1811). Appointed captain in U.S. infantry (1789), 2nd lieutenant in continental artillery (1781–83), captain in infantry (1786), captain in army (1789), promoted to major (1791), resigned (1793), later lieutenant-colonel in 5th U.S. infantry (1799), honorably discharged (1800), lieutenant-colonel in 3rd U.S. infantry (1809).

SMITH, WILLIAM S. (Nov. 8, 1755–June 10, 1816). Appointed U.S. marshal (1789–1800); lawyer; born in New York; son of John and Margaret Stephens Smith; B.A. Princeton (1774); married Abigail Adams, daughter of John Adams (1786); major and aide-de-camp to General Sullivan (1776), lieutenant-colonel (1777), aide-de-camp to General Lafayette (1780–81), aide-de-camp to General Washington (1781–83); secretary to American legation in London (1785–88); surveyor of N.Y. (1800–1807); elected as Federalist to House of Representatives (1813–15); a founder of Society of the Cincinnati. In 1786, Smith held continental debt certificates worth $3,800.
Source: Marcius D. Raymond, "Colonel William Stephens Smith," *New York Genealogical and Biographical Record* 25 (1894): 153–61.

TEN BROECK, JOHN C. (Mar. 15, 1755–Aug. 10, 1835). Appointed surveyor at Hudson (1789); son of Cornelius and Maria Bodyn Ten Broeck; married Antje Ten Broeck (1784); 2nd lieutenant in 4th N.Y. (1775), 1st lieutenant (1776), captain (1781–83); member of Society of the Cincinnati.
Source: Runk, *The Ten Broeck Genealogy.*

WALKER, BENJAMIN (1753–Jan. 13, 1818). Appointed naval officer at New York (1791–98); born in London, England; lieutenant (1775), captain (1776), major and aide-de-camp to General Von Steuben (1778), lieutenant-colonel and aide-de-camp to General Washington (1782–83); Democrat in U.S. House of Representatives (1801–3).
Source: Dixon Ryan Fox, *The Decline of Aristocracy in the Politics of New York* (New York, 1919).

North Carolina

ALBERTSON, ELIAS (b. Sept. 24, 1763). Appointed surveyor at Newbiggen Creek (1790); resided (1790) in Pasquotank County, N.C.; son of Elias and Elizabeth Albertson. He owned 3 slaves in 1790.

Source: Mrs. Watson [Ellen] Winslow, *History of Perquimans County* (Raleigh, 1931).

BAKER, JOHN. Appointed surveyor at Bennits Creek (1790); son of Henry and Ruth Chancey Baker; married Martha Cherry (1790); lieutenant in 7th N.C. (1776), captain (1777), colonel in militia (1778); member of N.C. General Assembly (1787); delegate to second N.C. ratifying convention (1789), and voted for Constitution; a Federalist. He owned 32 slaves and 650 acres of land in 1790.
Source: Winslow, *History of Perquimans County.*

BENBURY, THOMAS. Appointed collector at Edenton (1790); resided (1790) in Chowan County, N.C.; paymaster of 5th N.C. (1776); member of Committee of Safety (1774–75); member of N.C. General Assembly (1774–82); favored adoption of Constitution. He owned 88 slaves in 1790.
Source: John H. Wheeler, *Reminiscences and Memoirs of North Carolina* (Columbus, Ohio, 1884).

BENSON, WILLIAM (d. 1802). Appointed surveyor at Windsor (1790); resided (1790) in Dobbs County, N.C.; justice of Bertie County (1777–85); postmaster of Windsor (1795–1800). He owned 15 slaves in 1790.
Source: *Bertie County Records: Wills, 1762–1844*, North Carolina Dept. of Archives and History, Raleigh.

BLOUNT, LEVI. Appointed surveyor at Plymouth (1790); resided (1790) in Tyrrell County, N.C.; representative to N.C. General Assembly (1794–95); collector of state revenue (1797–98). He owned 23 slaves in 1790.
Source: *North Carolina General Assembly Records: Legislative Papers, 1794–1795*, North Carolina Dept. of Archives and History, Raleigh.

BLOUNT, WILLIAM (Mar. 26, 1749–Mar. 21, 1800). Appointed governor of Southern Territory (1790–96); merchant and planter; born in Bertie County, N.C.; son of Jacob and Barbara Gray Blount; married Mary Grainger (1778); paymaster of N.C. troops (1777); member of N.C. General Assembly (1780–84); Continental Congress (1782–83, 1786–87); delegate to Philadelphia Convention (1787), and signed Constitution; member of second N.C. ratifying convention (1789), and voted for Constitution; state senator (1788–90); superintendent of Indian affairs (1790–96); chairman of Tenn. constitutional convention (1796); U.S. senator from Tenn. (1796–97); Tenn. state senator (1797–1800); at first a Federalist, later a Republican. He owned 30 slaves and 5,000 acres of land in 1790.
Source: William H. Masterson, *William Blount* (Baton Rouge, 1954).

CALLENDER, THOMAS (d. 1828). Appointed surveyor at Wilmington (1790); merchant; resided (1790) in Wilmington, N.C.; ensign in 1st N.C. (1776), lieutenant (1777–80), captain (1780–83); inspector of naval stores at Wilmington (1785–91); treasurer of Wilmington (1828); member of Society of the Cincinnati. He received 3,800 acres of land in Tenn. in 1786 for service in the Revolution, and he owned 8 slaves in 1790.

Source: *New Hanover County Records: Estates Records, 1741–1939*, North Carolina Dept. of Archives and History, Raleigh.

DAVES, JOHN (1748–Oct. 12, 1804). Appointed collector at New Bern (1790); planter; born in Mecklenburg County, Va.; resided (1790) in New Bern, N.C.; married (1) Sally Bryan (c. 1776), (2) Mary Haynes (1782); ensign in 2nd N.C. (1776), 1st lieutenant (1777), captain (1781–83); state collector at Beaufort (1784); member of Society of the Cincinnati. He received 3,800 acres of land in Tenn. for service in the Revolution, and he owned 23 slaves in 1790.

Source: Graham Daves, *A Sketch of the Military Career of Captain John Daves* (Baltimore, 1892).

DAVIE, WILLIAM R. (June 20, 1756–Nov. 29, 1820). Declined appointment as U.S. district judge (1790); lawyer and planter; born in England; son of Archibald and Mary Richardson Davie; B.A. Princeton (1776); married Sarah Jones (1782); lieutenant (1779), colonel (1780), commissary general (1781); member of N.C. General Assembly (1786–98); delegate to Philadelphia Convention (1787), and favored adoption of Constitution; governor of N.C. (1798); peace commissioner to France (1799); appointed by Jefferson to treat with Tuscarora Indians (1802); a Federalist; founder of University of N.C. (1789). He owned 36 slaves in 1790.

Source: Blackwell P. Robinson, *William Davie* (Chapel Hill, 1957).

EASTON, JOHN (d. 1802). Appointed surveyor at Beaufort (1790–1802); merchant; resided (1790) in New Bern, N.C.; colonel of Carteret County Militia (1781–89); member of New Bern Committee of Safety (1774–75); delegate to N.C. Provincial Congress (1775–76); justice of Carteret County (1776–90); member of N.C. General Assembly (1778–81, 1784); state senator (1783, 1785–87). He owned 21 slaves in 1790.

Source: *Carteret County Records: Wills, 1741–1887*, North Carolina Dept. of Archives and History, Raleigh.

FREEMAN, THOMAS D. (d. Nov. 8, 1821). Appointed surveyor at Plymouth (1790); born in Ireland; resided (1790) in Tyrrell County, N.C.; married Mary ————.

Source: *Gazette of North Carolina*, November 25, 1790.

GREGORY, ISAAC (1740–1800). Appointed collector at Plankbridge (1790); soldier and planter; born in Camden County, N.C.; resided (1790) in Edenton, N.C.; son of William and Judith Morgan Gregory; married (1) Elizabeth Whedbee, (2) Sarah Lamb; lieutenant-colonel and brigadier general of militia in the Revolution; member of Edenton Committee of Safety (1776); member of

N.C. Provincial Congress (1776); state senator intermittently (1778–96); a Federalist. He owned 23 slaves and 623 acres of land in 1790.

Source: Jesse F. Pugh, *Three Hundred Years Along the Pasquotank: A Biographical History of Camden County* (Camden, N.C., 1957).

HILL, WILLIAM H. (May 1, 1767–1809). Appointed U.S. district attorney (1790–94); lawyer and planter; born in Brunswick, N.C.; resided (1790) in Wilmington, N.C.; son of William and Margaret Moore Hill; married (1) Elizabeth Moore, (2) Alice Starkey, (3) Eliza Ashe; favored adoption of Constitution; member of N.C. Senate (1794); Federalist in U.S. House of Representatives (1799–1803); a midnight appointment by John Adams as district judge, withdrawn by Thomas Jefferson (1801). He owned 45 slaves in 1790.

Source: Samuel A. Ashe, *Biographical History of North Carolina*, 8 vols. (Greensboro, N.C., 1905–17), vol. 4.

HUNTER, HENRY (Aug. 11, 1751–May 17, 1837). Appointed surveyor at Skewarkey (1790); married Asia Blount (1783); private in the Revolution.

IREDELL, JAMES (Oct. 5, 1751–Oct. 20, 1799). Appointed associate justice of Supreme Court (1790–99); lawyer; born in England; son of Francis and Margaret McCulloh Iredell; married Hannah Johnston (1773); comptroller of customs at Edenton, N.C. (1768–74); collector at Edenton (1774–76); superior court judge (1777); state attorney general (1779–81); member of N.C. General Assembly (1787–88); delegate to first N.C. ratifying convention (1788), and voted for Constitution; a Federalist; noted for his opinion, in *Calder vs. Bull* (1792), that the Supreme Court had the power of judicial review. He owned 8 slaves and 4,530 acres of land in 1787.

Sources: H. G. Connor, *James Iredell, 1751–1799, Lawyer, Statesman, Judge* (Raleigh, 1912); Griffith J. McRee, *Life and Correspondence of James Iredell*, 2 vols. (New York, 1857–58).

JASPER, SAMUEL (d. 1801). Appointed surveyor at Currituck Inlet (1790); merchant; resided (1790) in Edenton, N.C.; son of Samuel and Ann Jasper; justice of Currituck County, N.C. (1789–90). He owned 5 slaves in 1790.

Source: *Governor's Office Records: Appointments of Justices and Militia Officers, 1782–1806*, North Carolina Dept. of Archives and History, Raleigh.

KEAIS, NATHAN (Oct. 12, 1740–Oct. 15, 1795). Appointed collector at Washington (1790–95); merchant; married Barbara Low; captain in 2nd N.C. regiment (1775–78); member of N.C. General Assembly (1777); commissioner of navigation at Bath (1777, 1783); justice of Beaufort County (1784–86); state collector of customs at Bath (1784–90); member of first N.C. ratifying convention (1788), and voted for Constitution. He owned 2,000 acres of land in 1790.

Sources: William C. Pool, "An Economic Interpretation of the Ratification of the Federal Constitution in North Carolina," *North Carolina Historical Review* 27 (1950): 127; Marilu B. Smallwood, *Some Colonial and Revolutionary Families of North Carolina*, 2 vols. (n.p., 1964–69), vol. 2.

KNOX, HUGH (d. Dec. 22, 1817). Appointed surveyor at Nixinton (1790); merchant; resided (1790) in Edenton, N.C.

Source: *Pasquotank County Records: Estates Records, 1757–1866*, North Carolina Dept. of Archives and History, Raleigh.

MCCULLOUGH, JOHN (d. 1799). Appointed surveyor at Swansborough (1790–95); master carpenter; collector of customs at Swansborough (1788–90).

Source: *Treasurer's and Comptroller's Records: Ports*, North Carolina Dept. of Archives and History, Raleigh.

MONFORT, JOSEPH (d. Apr. 27, 1792). Appointed captain in U.S. infantry (1790); soldier; son of Joseph Monfort; commissioned as ensign (1776), 1st lieutenant in 3rd N.C. (1776), captain-lieutenant (1777), captain (1779–83), captain in army (1790); killed in action (1792); member of Society of the Cincinnati.

MURFREE, HARDY (June 5, 1752–July 6, 1809). Appointed surveyor at Murfreesboro (1790); planter; born in Hertford County, N.C.; son of William and Mary Moore Murfree; married Sallie Brickell; appointed captain in 2nd N.C. (1775), major (1776), ended service as lieutenant-colonel; member of second N.C. ratifying convention (1789), and voted for Constitution; member of Society of the Cincinnati. He owned 45 slaves and 4,000 acres of land in N.C. and Tenn. in 1790.

Source: John H. Wheeler, *Historical Sketches of North Carolina* (Philadelphia, 1851).

PASTEUR, THOMAS (d. July 29, 1806). Appointed lieutenant in U.S. infantry (1790); soldier; ensign in 4th N.C. (1777), lieutenant (1778), regimental adjutant (1779–83), lieutenant in army (1790), captain in infantry (1792), promoted to major (1803); member of Society of the Cincinnati.

POLK, WILLIAM (July 9, 1758–Jan. 14, 1834). Appointed supervisor of distilled spirits (1791–1808); soldier and public servant; born in Mecklenburg County, N.C.; resided (1790) in Salisbury, N.C.; son of Thomas and Susan Spratt Polk; attended Queen's College at Charlotte (1775); married (1) Grizelda Gilchrist (1789), (2) Sarah Hawkins (1801); commissioned 2nd lieutenant in 3rd S.C. (1775), major in 9th N.C. (1776), later lieutenant-colonel in 4th S.C.; surveyor general of N.C. (1783); member of N.C. General Assembly (1785–87, 1790); a Federalist; member of Society of the Cincinnati; first president of State Bank of N.C. (1811–19). He received 1,888 acres of land in Tenn. for service in the Revolution, and he owned 21 slaves in 1790.

Source: Worth S. Ray, *The Mecklenburg Signers and Their Neighbors* (Baltimore, 1966).

POLK[E], EZEKIEL (d. 1791). Appointed ensign in U.S. infantry (1790).

READ, JAMES (d. 1803). Appointed collector at Wilmington (1790); resided

(1790) in Wilmington, N.C.; ensign in 1st N.C. (1776), captain (1777), colonel in N.C. militia (1778), lieutenant-colonel (1799–1800); opposed adoption of Constitution; dismissed from office in 1798 for embezzlement; member of Society of the Cincinnati. He owned 32 slaves in 1790.

Sources: Archibald Henderson, *North Carolina: the Old North State and the New*, 2 vols. (Chicago, 1941), vol. 1; John Steele, *The Papers of John Steele* (Raleigh, 1924).

ROBERTSON, JAMES (June 28, 1742–Sept. 1, 1814). Appointed brigadier general of Southern Territory (1790–94); soldier and pioneer; born in Brunswick County, Va.; son of John and Mary Gower Robertson; married Charlotte Reeves (1768); captain and colonel in the Revolution; member of N.C. General Assembly (1785, 1787); member of Tenn. constitutional convention (1796); Tenn. state senator (1798); served as Indian agent (1807–14).

Source: A. W. Putnam, *History of Middle Tennessee, or the Life and Times of Gen. James Robertson* (Nashville, 1859).

SAWYER, EDMUND. Appointed surveyor at Pasquotank (1790); merchant; resided (1790) in Camden County, N.C.; son of Lemuel and Susannah Sawyer; justice of Camden County (1788–90). He owned 11 slaves in 1790.

Source: Pugh, *Three Hundred Years Along the Pasquotank, A Biographical History of Camden County.*

SEVIER, JOHN (Sept. 23, 1745–Sept. 24, 1815). Appointed brigadier general of Southern Territory (1791–96); politician and pioneer; born in New Market, Va.; son of Valentine and Joanna Goade Sevier; married (1) Sarah Hawkins (1761), (2) Catherine Sherrill (1780); captain in N.C. militia against the Indians (1773–74); governor of State of Franklin (1785–88); delegate to second N.C. ratifying convention (1789), and voted for Constitution; elected as Democrat to U.S. House of Representatives (1789–91, 1811–15); governor of Tenn. (1796–1801, 1803–9); Tenn. state senator (1809–11).

Source: Carl S. Driver, *John Sevier, Pioneer of the Old Southwest* (Chapel Hill, 1932).

SITGREAVES, JOHN (1757–Mar. 4, 1802). Appointed U.S. district attorney (June 1790); U.S. district judge (December 1790–1802); lawyer; born in England; resided (1790) in New Bern, N.C.; married Mrs. Martha Jones Green; lieutenant and aide-de-camp to General Caswell (1776–80); member of Continental Congress (1784–85); member of N.C. General Assembly (1784, 1786–89); favored adoption of Constitution; a Federalist. He received 640 acres of land in Tenn. for service in the Revolution.

Source· Wheeler, *Historical Sketches of North Carolina.*

SKINNER, JOHN. Appointed U.S. marshal (1790); resided (1790) in Edenton,

N.C.; member of N.C. General Assembly (1783); state senator (1784–88); delegate to first N.C. ratifying convention (1788), and voted for Constitution. He owned 38 slaves and 850 acres of land in 1790.

Source: Pool, "An Economic Interpretation of the Ratification of the Federal Constitution in North Carolina," p. 137.

SKINNER, JOSHUA (d. 1798). Appointed surveyor at Hartford (1790); planter; resided (1790) in Edenton, N.C.; married Martha ———; delegate to first N.C. ratifying convention (1788), and voted for Constitution; state senator (1790–94); U.S. commissioner of loans (1798). He owned 20 slaves and 830 acres of land in 1790.

Source: Pool, "An Economic Interpretation of the Ratification of the Federal Constitution in North Carolina," p. 137.

SKINNER, WILLIAM (d. 1798). Appointed commissioner of loans (1790–98); planter; resided (1790) in Edenton, N.C.; son of Richard Skinner; married twice; lieutenant-colonel in N.C. militia (1776), brigadier general (1777–79); member of N.C. Provincial Congress (1775–76); state treasurer (1779); delegate to first N.C. ratifying convention (1788), and voted for Constitution. He owned 47 slaves and 1,399 acres of land in 1790.

Sources: Ashe, *Biographical History of North Carolina*, vol. 5; Pool, "An Economic Interpretation of the Ratification of the Federal Constitution in North Carolina," p. 137.

STOKES, JOHN (Mar. 20, 1756–Oct. 12, 1790). Appointed U.S. district judge (1790); lawyer; born in Va.; son of David and Sarah Montfort Stokes; married Elizabeth Pearson; commissioned ensign in 6th Va. (1776), 1st lieutenant (1776), captain (1778–83); attended second N.C. ratifying convention (1789), and voted for Constitution. He owned 275 acres of land in 1789.

Source: Ashe, *Biographical History of North Carolina*, vol. 5.

WALKER, JOHN (1755–1841). Appointed naval officer at Wilmington (1790); born in Va.; son of John and Elizabeth Watson Walker; lieutenant and captain in the Revolution.

Source: Clarence Griffen, *Revolutionary Service of Col. John Walker and Family* (Forest City, N.C., 1930).

WILLIAMS, THOMAS. Appointed surveyor at Indiantown (1790); member of N.C. Provincial Congress (1776); delegate to first N.C. ratifying convention (1788), and voted for Constitution; member of N.C. General Assembly (1788–89). He owned 12 slaves in 1790.

Source: Pool, "An Economic Interpretation of the Ratification of the Federal Constitution in North Carolina," pp. 443–44.

WYNNS, WILLIAM. Appointed surveyor at Winton (1790); resided (1790) in Hertford County, N.C.; member of N. C. General Assembly (1779–80, 1782); sheriff of Hertford County (1790–94). He owned 29 slaves in 1790.

Source: Benjamin B. Winborne, *The Colonial and State Political History of Hertford County, N.C.* (n.p., 1906).

Pennsylvania

ALLISON, RICHARD (1757–Mar. 22, 1816). Appointed surgeon in U.S. infantry (1789); physician; born in Goshen, N.Y.; graduate of Jefferson Medical College (1776); married Rebecca Strong (1794); surgeon's mate in 5th Pa. and 1st Pa. (1778–83), surgeon's mate in U.S. infantry (1784–88), surgeon in army (1789), surgeon of the legion (1792–96); after discharge, practiced medicine; member of Society of the Cincinnati. He was the first physician in Cincinnati, Ohio.

Sources: Louis C. Duncan, *Medical Men in the American Revolution, 1775–1783* (Carlisle, Pa., 1931); Ohio Adjutant General's Office, *The Official Roster of the Soldiers of the American Revolution Buried in the State of Ohio*; idem, *Official Roster, III, Soldiers of the American Revolution Who Lived in the State of Ohio* (Columbus, Ohio, 1959).

ARMSTRONG, HAMILTON (d. May 22, 1801). Appointed ensign in U.S. infantry (1791), promoted to lieutenant (1792), captain (1794), resigned (1797).

ARMSTRONG, JOHN (Apr. 20, 1755–Feb. 4, 1816). Appointed lieutenant in U.S. infantry (1789); born in New Jersey; son of Thomas and Jane Hamilton Armstrong; sergeant (1776–77), ensign (1777), lieutenant in 3rd Pa. (1779), lieutenant in army (1789), promoted to captain (1790), major (1792), resigned (1793); treasurer of Northwest Territory (1796–1816); judge of Hamilton county court; member of Society of the Cincinnati.

Source: "Notes and Queries," *Pennsylvania Magazine of History and Biography* 29 (1905): 483–86.

ASHTON, JOSEPH. Appointed captain in U.S. infantry (1789), sergeant and later lieutenant in 4th continental artillery during the Revolution, captain in army (1789), promoted to major (1791), resigned (1792); member of Society of the Cincinnati.

BEATTY, ERKURIES (Oct. 9, 1759–Feb. 23, 1823). Appointed captain in U.S. infantry (1789); soldier and public servant; son of Charles and Ann Reading Beatty; married Susanna Ewing Ferguson (1799); enlisted as private in continental army (1775), ensign (1777), 1st lieutenant (1777–78), regimental paymaster (1779–83), lieutenant in U.S. infantry (1784), captain (1789), major (1792), resigned (1792); after retirement, moved to Princeton, N.J., where he was justice of the peace and justice of county court; member of N.J. Legislature; member of Society of the Cincinnati.

Source: J. M. Beatty, "Letters of the Four Beatty Brothers of the Continental Congress," *Pennsylvania Magazine of History and Biography* 44 (1920): 193–98.

BIDDLE, CLEMENT (May 10, 1740–July 14, 1814). Appointed U.S. marshal (1789–93); merchant; born in Philadelphia; resided (1790) in Philadelphia; son of John and Sarah Owen Biddle; married (1) Mary Richardson, (2) Rebekah Cornell (1774); deputy quartermaster general and aide-de-camp to General Nathaniel Greene (1776), commissary general (1777–80), quarter-master general (1781); justice of Pa. Court of Common Pleas (1788). A close friend of George Washington, Biddle handled Washington's business affairs in Philadelphia. In 1786, Biddle held almost $3,000 in continental loan certificates.

Source: "Correspondence of Clement Biddle," *Pennsylvania Magazine of History and Biography* 42 (1918): 310–43.

BIRD, ROSS. Appointed ensign in U.S. infantry (1791), lieutenant (1792), captain in 1st sub-legion (1794), honorable discharge (1796), reentered as captain of 3rd infantry (1808), major (1813), resigned (1813).

BRITT, DANIEL (d. Oct. 23, 1799). Served as Pa. paymaster (1790); appointed ensign in U.S. infantry (1791), lieutenant (1791), promoted to captain in 1st sub-legion (1793).

CLYMER, GEORGE (Mar. 16, 1739–Jan. 24, 1813). Appointed supervisor of distilled spirits (1791–94); merchant; born in Philadelphia; son of Christopher and Deborah Fitzwater Clymer; attended the College of Philadelphia; married Elizabeth Meredith (1765); captain in 3rd Pa. (1775); signer of Declaration of Independence (1776); member of Continental Congress (1776–78, 1780–83); member of Pa. General Assembly (1785–88); signed Constitution (1787); elected to First Congress as Federalist (1789–91); treaty commissioner to Cherokees and Creeks (1796); first president of the Philadelphia Bank. Both Clymer and his wife had considerable fortunes, and at one time he and his brother-in-law, Samuel Meredith, owned about 1,000,000 acres of western lands.

Sources: Wharton Dickenson, "George Clymer, The Signer," *Magazine of American History* 5 (1880): 196–203; James R. Macfarlane, *George Clymer, Signer of the Declaration of Independence* (Sewickley, Pa., 1927).

DENNY, EBENEZER (Mar. 11, 1761–July 21, 1822). Appointed lieutenant in U.S. infantry (1789); public servant and businessman; born in Carlisle, Pa.; son of William and Agnes Parker Denny; married Nancy Wilkins (1793); ensign and lieutenant during the Revolution, lieutenant in army (1789), captain (1791), resigned (1793), served in Pa. militia as captain (1794) and as major (1795); unsuccessful Federalist candidate for Pa. General Assembly; treasurer of Allegheny County (1803, 1808); first mayor of Pittsburgh (1816); member of Society of the Cincinnati; director of the Bank of Pittsburgh; a witness to the Treaty of Fort Harmar (1789).

Sources: William H. Denny, *Military Journal of Major Ebenezer Denny with an Introductory Memoir* (Philadelphia, 1860); Jones, *Fort Washington at Cincinnati, Ohio.*

DOYLE, THOMAS (d. Feb. 15, 1805). Appointed lieutenant in U.S. infantry (1789); lieutenant in continental infantry (1779–83), lieutenant (1784), lieutenant in army (1789), captain (1790), promoted to major in 1st sub-legion (1792), honorably discharged (1796); member of Society of the Cincinnati; a witness to the Treaty of the Great Miami (1786).
Source: Jones, *Fort Washington at Cincinnati, Ohio.*

DULANY, SHARPE. Appointed collector at Philadelphia (1789). He served as collector of customs at Philadelphia during the Confederation.

FERGUSON, WILLIAM (d. Nov. 4, 1791). Appointed captain in U.S. artillery (1789); soldier; born in Armagh, Ireland; son of Usher and Mary Ferguson; married Susanna Ewing (1789); lieutenant and captain in continental army, captain of artillery (1789), raised to major (1791), killed in action in St. Clair's defeat; a principal builder of Fort Washington at Cincinnati.
Source: Charles B. Alexander, *Major William Ferguson* (New York, 1908).

HARMAR, JOSIAH (Nov. 10, 1753–Aug. 20, 1813). Appointed brigadier general in U.S. army (1789); born in Philadelphia; son of Rachel Harmar; married Sarah Jenkins (1784); captain in 1st Pa. (1776), lieutenant-colonel (1777–83), Indian agent in Northwest Territory, a witness to the Treaty of Fort McIntosh (1785) and the Treaties of Fort Harmar (1789), brigadier general (1787), resigned (1792), adjutant general of Pa. (1792–99); carried ratified peace treaty to France (1784); member of Society of the Cincinnati.
Source: Howard H. Peckham, "Josiah Harmar and His Indian Expedition," *Ohio State Archaeological and Historical Quarterly* 55 (1946): 227–41.

HODGDON, SAMUEL. Appointed quartermaster in U.S. army (1791); commissary for military stores (1777), deputy commissary general (1778), commissary general (1781), quartermaster in army (1791–92); member of Society of the Cincinnati.

HOPKINSON, FRANCIS (1737–May 9, 1791). Appointed U.S. district judge (1789–91); lawyer and musician; born in Philadelphia; son of Thomas and Mary Johnson Hopkinson; B.A. College of Philadelphia (1757); married Ann Borden (1768); collector of customs at Salem, N.J. (1763) and New Castle, Del. (1772); member of Governor's Council of N.J. (1774–76); member of Continental Congress (1776); signer of Declaration of Independence (1776); judge of admiralty court of Pa. (1779–89); supported ratification of the Constitution. Hopkinson was a founder of the American Philosophical Society. He also published numerous poems and musical compositions.
Source: Charles R. Hildeburn, "Francis Hopkinson," *Pennsylvania Magazine of History and Biography* 2 (1878): 314–24.

IRVINE, WILLIAM (Nov. 3, 1741–July 29, 1804). Appointed commissioner for settling accounts between U.S. and the states (1790); physician; born in Ireland;

graduate of Trinity College, Dublin; married Anne Callender; colonel in 6th Pa. (1776), brigadier general (1779–83), led state troops against Whiskey Rebellion (1794); member of Pa. Provincial Congress (1774); delegate to Continental Congress (1786–1788); member of Pa. ratifying convention (1787), and voted for Constitution; U.S. representative (1793–95); presidential elector for Jefferson (1796); a Republican; member of Society of the Cincinnati. In 1791, Irvine received $11,000 in certificates of the funded debt.

Sources: L. Boyd, *The Irvines and Their Kin* (Chicago, 1908); John W. Jordan, ed., *Genealogical and Personal History of Northern Pennsylvania*, 3 vols. (New York, 1913), vol. 1.

LEWIS, WILLIAM (Feb. 2, 1751–Aug. 15, 1819). Appointed U.S. district attorney (1789–91); lawyer; born near Edgemont, Pa.; son of Josiah and Martha Allen Lewis; married (1) Rosanna Lort, (2) Frances Durdin; member of Pa. General Assembly (1787, 1789); delegate to Pa. constitutional convention (1789), where he objected to extension of franchise; judge of U.S. district court (1791–92); ardent Federalist; counsel for petitioners against the election of Albert Gallatin to U.S. Senate (1794); advocate for the abolition of slavery in the 1780's.

Source: William Primrose, "Biography of William Lewis," *Pennsylvania Magazine of History and Biography* 20 (1896): 30–40.

McCURDY, WILLIAM. Captain of 1st Pa. infantry in the Revolution; appointed captain in U.S. infantry (1789); resigned (1791); member of Society of the Cincinnati; a witness at the Treaty of Fort Harmar (1789).

McDOWELL, NATHAN. Ensign in 1st continental infantry; appointed ensign in U.S. infantry (1789), resigned (1790); a witness to the Treaty of the Great Miami (1786).

McNAIRY, JOHN (Mar. 30, 1762–Nov. 10, 1837). Appointed judge of Southeast Territory (1790–96); lawyer; born in Lancaster County, Pa.; studied law in N.C. and went to Tenn. in 1788; member of Tenn. constitutional convention (1796); judge of Tenn. Superior Court (1796); U.S. district judge (1797–1834).

Sources: Joseph R. McNary, *The Clan McNary* (Pittsburgh, 1914); John T. Moore, *Tennessee, The Volunteer State*, 4 vols. (Chicago, 1923), vol. 2.

McPHERSON, WILLIAM (d. Nov. 18, 1813). Appointed surveyor at Philadelphia (1789–92); professional soldier; married (1) Margaret Stout, (2) Elizabeth White (1803); major in Revolutionary army (1779), aide-de-camp to Generals St. Clair, Lafayette, and Lincoln (1781–83), commanded a battalion against Whiskey Rebellion (1794), appointed brigadier general by President Adams (1799) to suppress Fries's Rebellion; member of Pa. General Assembly (1788–89); attended Pa. ratifying convention (1787), and voted for Constitution; inspector of revenue (1792); naval officer at Philadelphia (1793–1813);

founder of Pa. Society of the Cincinnati. When McPherson applied for his appointment, he told Washington he had no means of support for his large family.

Source: "Notes, Queries and Corrections," *Publications of the Genealogical Society of Pennsylvania* 7 (1919): 199–200.

MELCHER, JACOB. Cadet in continental infantry; appointed ensign in U.S. infantry (1789), lieutenant in infantry (1791), promoted to captain in 1st sublegion (1792), resigned (1793).

MEREDITH, SAMUEL (1741–Feb. 10, 1817). Appointed treasurer of the United States (1789–1801); merchant; born in Philadelphia; son of Reese and Martha Carpenter Meredith; married Margaret Cadwalader (1772); major and lieutenant-colonel in the Revolution, brigadier general (1777–78); member of Pa. General Assembly (1778–79, 1781–83); member of Continental Congress (1786–88); surveyor of Philadelphia (1789). He lent the government $100,000 during the war. He and his brother-in-law, George Clymer, owned about 1,000,000 acres in western lands.

Source: Wharton Dickenson, "Brigadier-General Samuel Meredith," *Magazine of American History* 4 (1879): 555–63.

PHILE, FREDERICK (d. Oct. 19, 1793). Appointed naval officer at Philadelphia (1789–93); physician; married Elizabeth Parrish; surgeon in 5th Pa. (1776–77); naval officer at Philadelphia under state government (1777–89). He owned 335 acres in Westmoreland County, Pa., as well as various lots in Philadelphia.

Source: J. Granville Leach, "The Record of Some Resident in the Vicinity of Middle Ferry, Philadelphia, During the Latter Half of the Eighteenth Century," *Publications of the Genealogical Society of Pennsylvania* 9 (1924): 69–70.

ST. CLAIR, ARTHUR (Mar. 23, 1734–Aug. 31, 1818). Appointed governor of the Northwest Territory (1789–1802); soldier and public servant; born in Scotland; probably the son of William and Elizabeth Balfour Sinclair; attended the University of Edinburgh; married Phoebe Bayard (1760); ensign and lieutenant in British army in North America (1757–62), colonel in Pa. militia (1775), brigadier general in continental army (1776), major general (1777–83), major general and commandant of U.S. army (1791–92); justice of Westmoreland County Court (1773); member of Westmoreland County Committee of Safety (1774); member of Council of Pennsylvania (1783); delegate to Continental Congress (1785–87); president of Continental Congress (1787); negotiated Treaties of Fort Harmar (1789); suffered a disastrous defeat at the hands of the Miami Indians (Nov. 4, 1791); unsuccessful candidate for governor of Pa. (1790); a Federalist. He owned 4,000 acres of land in 1790.

Sources: Ellis Beals, "Arthur St. Clair: Western Pennsylvania's Leading Citizen, 1764–1818," *Western Pennsylvania Historical Magazine* 12 (1929): 75–94, 175–92; Albert Douglas, "Major-General Arthur St. Clair," *Ohio Archaeological and Historical Quarterly* 16 (1907): 455–76; William Henry Smith, *The Life and Public Services of Arthur St. Clair*, 2 vols. (Cincinnati, 1882).

SMITH, THOMAS (1745–Mar. 31, 1809). Appointed commissioner of loans (1789); lawyer; born in Scotland; son of Thomas and Elizabeth Duncan Smith; attended University of Edinburgh; married Letitia Van Deren (1781); colonel in Pa. militia; member of Committee of Correspondence (1775); delegate to state constitutional convention (1776); member of Pa. General Assembly (1776–80); delegate to Continental Congress (1780–82); commissioner of loans under Confederation; judge of Pa. Court of Common Pleas (1791); judge of Pa. Supreme Court (1794–1809).

Source: Burton A. Konkle, *The Life and Times of Thomas Smith, 1745–1809* (Philadelphia, 1904).

SPEAR, EDWARD (d. Nov. 4, 1791). Appointed lieutenant in U.S. artillery (1789); married Jane Holliday; lieutenant in 1st Pa. during the Revolution; lieutenant in artillery (1789), killed in action in St. Clair's defeat.

Source: Ohio Adjutant General's Office, *The Official Roster, II, of the Soldiers of the American Revolution Who Lived in the State of Ohio* (Columbus, Ohio, 1938).

THOMPSON, ROBERT (d. 1809). Appointed ensign in U.S. infantry (1789), lieutenant (1791), resigned (1792), reenlisted as lieutenant (1792), promoted to captain (1793), resigned (1799); a witness at the Treaty of Fort Harmar (1789).

WADE, JOHN. Appointed ensign in U.S. infantry (1791), lieutenant (1792), promoted to captain (1794), resigned (1802).

WILSON, JAMES (Sept. 14, 1742–Aug. 21, 1798). Appointed associate justice of Supreme Court (1789–98); lawyer; born in Scotland; son of William and Aleson Landale Wilson; attended St. Andrews, Glasgow, and Edinburgh universities; married (1) Rachel Bird (1771), (2) Hannah Gray (1793); colonel and brigadier general in Pa. militia; member of Committee of Correspondence (1774); signer of Declaration of Independence (1776); member of Continental Congress (1775–76, 1782–83, 1785–87); played a prominent role in Constitutional Convention (1787), and signed Constitution; member of Pa. ratifying convention (1787), and voted for Constitution. He was an inveterate and largely unsuccessful speculator in western lands.

Source: Burton A. Konkle, *James Wilson and the Constitution* (Philadelphia, 1907).

YARD, JAMES. Appointed consul to island of Santa Cruz (1789); merchant.

ZIEGLER, DAVID (July 1748–Sept. 24, 1811). Appointed captain in U.S. infantry (1789); soldier and public servant; born in Heidelberg, Germany; son of Johann and Louise Kern Ziegler; married Lucy Sheffield (1789); served in Seven Years War under Frederick the Great, enlisted in Russian army of Catherine II (1768), came to America in 1775, 2nd lieutenant (1776), 1st lieutenant (1777), promoted to captain (1778–83), captain in Pa. militia (1785), captain in army (1789), major (1790), resigned (1792), later adjutant general of Ohio (1807); a Republican; supported Jefferson in 1800; first chief magistrate of Cincinnati (1802–3); appointed U.S. marshal (1804); collector at Cincinnati (1809–11); member of Society of the Cincinnati.

Sources: Henry Howe, *Historical Collections of Ohio*, 2 vols. (1902), vol. 1; George A. Katzenburger, "Major David Ziegler," *Ohio Archaeological and Historical Quarterly* 21 (1912): 127–74.

Rhode Island

ABORN, JOHN ANTHONY. Declined appointment as surveyor at Patuxet (1790); resided (1790) in Warwick, R.I.; married Sally Rhodes. He owned at least 140 acres of land in 1792.

ARNOLD, THOMAS (d. May 8, 1821). Appointed surveyor at East Greenwich (1790); son of Benjamin Arnold; M.A. Brown University; married Mary Brown (c. 1771); lieutenant (1776), captain in 1st R.I. (1777–83); opposed ratification; collector of excise in Kent County; justice of the peace in Newport (1789–91); member of R.I. General Assembly (1792). He was a Quaker and an outspoken critic of slavery.

Sources: Joseph J. Smith, *Civil and Military List of Rhode Island* (Providence, 1901); Mack Thompson, *Moses Brown, Reluctant Reformer* (Chapel Hill, 1962).

BARTON, WILLIAM (May 26, 1748–Oct. 22, 1831). Declined appointment as judge of the Western Territory, but later appointed surveyor at Providence (1790); lawyer and merchant; resided (1790) in Providence, R.I.; son of Benjamin Barton; married Rhoda Carver (1770); captain-lieutenant in 2nd R.I. (1775), major (1776), lieutenant-colonel and later colonel in 1st R.I. (1777), adjutant general of militia (1788); justice of the peace (1775–91); collector of impost for Bristol County (1784–86); member of R.I. ratifying convention (1790), and voted for Constitution; member of R.I. General Assembly (1782, 1788); justice of Bristol County Inferior Court (1790–92); a Federalist; owned 1 slave in 1790. In his letter of application, Barton requested an office because war wounds had incapacitated him for business pursuits.

Source: L. E. Rogers, ed., *The Biographical Cyclopedia of Representative Men of Rhode Island* (Providence, 1881).

BOSWORTH, SAMUEL (May 19, 1744–May 4, 1824). Appointed surveyor at Bristol (1790–1824); cooper; resided (1790) in Bristol, R.I.; son of Joseph and Anne Low Bosworth, Jr.; married (1) Elizabeth Joy, (2) Tabitha Wardwalt (1782); ensign (1770–74), lieutenant in Barrington Co. (1775); collector of excise in Bristol County (1787).

Source: Thomas W. Bicknell, *A History of Barrington, Rhode Island* (Providence, 1898).

BOWEN, JABEZ (June 2, 1739–May 7, 1815). Appointed commissioner of loans (1790); physician and jurist; resided (1790) in Providence, R.I.; son of Ephraim and Mary Fenner Bowen; B.A. Yale (1757); LL.M. Brown University (1769); married (1) Sarah Brown (1762), (2) ———— Leonard; colonel in 1st R.I. (1778–79); justice of R.I. Superior Court (1776–77); deputy governor of R.I. (1778–86); member of R.I. ratifying conventions (1790), and voted for Constitution; a Federalist; chancellor of Brown University (1785–1815); member of board of directors of First Bank of R.I. (1791). Bowen was a wealthy speculator in land and paper money and an active member of the Masons.
Sources: "The Adjustment of Rhode Island into the Union in 1790," Rhode Island Historical Society *Publications* 8 (1900): 104–35; David H. Fischer, *The Revolution of American Conservatism* (New York, 1965).

CHANNING, WILLIAM (May 31, 1751–Sept. 21, 1793). Appointed U.S. district attorney (1790); lawyer; resided (1790) in Newport, R.I.; son of John Channing; B.A. Princeton (1769); married Lucy Ellery (1773); major in Newport County regiment (1775); justice of the peace in Newport (1775); R.I. attorney general (1777–87, 1791); favored adoption of Constitution; a Federalist. He owned 2 slaves in 1790.
Source: Wilkins Updike, *Memoirs of the Rhode Island Bar* (Boston, 1842).

COMSTOCK, JOB. Declined appointment as surveyor at East Greenwich (1790); farmer; resided (1790) in East Greenwich, R.I.; served on R.I. Council of War (1777–78); collector of imposts for Bristol County (1787–89); justice of the peace (1787–88); state surveyor at East Greenwich (1789–90); member of R.I. ratifying convention (1790), and voted against Constitution; a Republican; member of R.I. Abolition Society.
Source: Irwin H. Polishook, *Rhode Island and the Union* (Evanston, Ill., 1969).

CROOKE, ROBERT. Appointed naval officer at Newport (1790); lawyer; resided (1790) in Newport, R.I.; collector of impost for Newport (1783–87); opposed adoption of Constitution. He owned 1 slave in 1790.
Sources: "The Adjustment of Rhode Island into the Union in 1790"; *U.S. Gazette* (Providence), June 24, 1790.

DEXTER, JOHN S. Appointed supervisor of distilled spirits (1791); resided (1790) in Cumberland, R.I.; lieutenant (1775), captain (1776), major (1781); justice of the peace (1785–91); member of R.I. General Assembly (1782); member of R.I. ratifying convention (1790), and voted for Constitution; member of R.I. Abolition Society.
Source: W. R. Staples, *Rhode Island in the Continental Congress* (Providence, 1870).

ELLERY, WILLIAM (Dec. 22, 1727–Feb. 15, 1820). Appointed collector at Newport (1790–1820); lawyer and merchant; born in Newport, R.I.; son of William and Elizabeth Almy Ellery; B.A. Harvard (1747); married (1) Ann Demington (1750), (2) Abigail Cary (1767); signer of Declaration of Independence (1776); delegate to Continental Congress (1776–79, 1781, 1783–86); elected chief justice of R.I. Superior Court (1785); commissioner of loans (1786–90); a Federalist.

Source: H. R. Palmer, "William Ellery," in *Rhode Island Signers of the Declaration of Independence*, ed. Robert P. Brown (Providence, 1913).

FOSTER, THEODORE (Apr. 29, 1752–Jan. 13, 1828). Declined appointment as naval officer at Providence (1790); lawyer and merchant; born in Brookfield, Mass.; B.A. Brown University (1770); married (1) Lydia Fenner (1771), (2) Esther Millard (1803); town clerk of Providence (1775–87); member of R.I. General Assembly (1776–82, 1812–16); judge of court of admiralty (1785); favored adoption of Constitution (1790); U.S. senator (1790–1803); a Federalist. He was a prominent merchant in Providence and a trustee of Brown University (1794–1822).

Sources: Fischer, *The Revolution of American Conservatism*; Polishook, *Rhode Island and the Union*.

LYMAN, DANIEL (Apr. 10, 1756–1830). Appointed surveyor at Newport (1790–1802); lawyer and manufacturer; resided (1790) in Newport, R.I.; son of Thomas Lyman; B.A. Yale (1776); married Mary Wanton (1782); colonel in continental army and aide-de-camp to General Heath; justice of the peace in Newport (1790); chief justice of R.I. Supreme Court (1812–16); delegate to Hartford Convention (1814); a Federalist; member of Society of the Cincinnati. He owned 1 slave in 1790.

Sources: Fischer, *The Revolution of American Conservatism*; Rogers, *The Biographical Cyclopedia of Representative Men of Rhode Island*.

MARCHANT, HENRY (Apr. 19, 1741–Aug. 30, 1796). Appointed U.S. district judge (1790–96); lawyer; born in Martha's Vineyard, Mass.; son of Hexford and ——— Butler Marchant; M.A. College of Philadelphia (1762); married Rebecca Cooke (1765); R.I. attorney general (1771–76); delegate to Continental Congress (1777–79); member of R.I. General Assembly (1784–90); delegate to R.I. ratifying convention (1790), and voted for Constitution; a Federalist.

Source: Updike, *Memoirs of the Rhode Island Bar*.

OLNEY, JEREMIAH (Dec. 7, 1749–Nov. 10, 1812). Appointed collector at Providence (1790–1809); born in Providence, R.I.; resided (1790) in Smithfield, R.I.; son of Joseph and Elizabeth Mawney Olney; married Sally Cooke (1780); captain (1775), lieutenant-colonel in 2nd R.I. (1776), lieutenant-colonel in continental army (1781); member of R.I. General Assembly (1785–86); a Federalist; resigned his post as collector (1809) in protest to Jefferson's Embargo Act; member of Society of the Cincinnati.

Source: Sidney S. Rider, *An Historical Inquiry Concerning an Attempt to Raise a Regiment of Slaves* (Providence, 1880).

PECK, WILLIAM (d. May 19, 1832). Appointed U.S. marshal (1790); resided (1790) in Providence, R.I.; brigade major (1776), major and aide-de-camp (1776–78), colonel and deputy adjutant general (1777–81). In his recommendation of Peck, Jabez Bowen says Peck suffered financially from the war.
Source: "The Adjustment of Rhode Island into the Union in 1790."

PHILLIPS, NATHANIEL (1756–1832). Appointed surveyor at Warren and Barrington (1790); resided (1790) in Warren, R.I.; entered army in July 1777 and left in 1783 after attaining the rank of sergeant.

RHODES, ZACHARIAH (b. March 1755). Appointed surveyor at Patuxet (1789–90); resided (1790) in Cranston, R.I.; son of James Rhodes; privateer commander (1778); lieutenant in U.S. Navy (1798); justice of the peace (1789–90); inspector of customs (1792).

SAYLES, DAVID (d. Jan. 9, 1820). Appointed captain in U.S. infantry (1790); ensign in 7th R.I. (1775), ensign in Smithfield 1st co. (1780), promoted to captain (1782); member of R.I. General Assembly.
Sources: J. N. Arnold, *Vital Records of Rhode Island 1636–1850* (Providence, 1907); Smith, *Civil and Military List of Rhode Island.*

SHERMAN, HENRY, JR. (d. Apr. 8, 1829). Appointed lieutenant in U.S. infantry (1790); resided (1790) in North Kingstown, R.I.; ensign in Sherburn's continental regiment (1777), promoted to lieutenant (1779), lieutenant in Olney battalion (1781–83).

STILLMAN, GEORGE. Appointed surveyor at Pawcatuck River (1790); resided (1790) in Westerly, R.I.; captain in R.I. militia (1779–84), major (1785–90); justice of the peace (1787, 1789–91); delegate to R.I. ratifying convention (1790), and voted for Constitution.

THOMPSON, EBENEZER. Appointed naval officer at Providence (1790); resided (1790) in Providence, R.I.; ensign in Providence co. (1774–75), major in Providence County regiment (1776); served in R.I. General Assembly (1783–84); member of Providence town council (1783–92); justice of Providence County Inferior Court (1786–89). He owned 2 slaves in 1790.
Source: W. R. Staples, *Annals of the Town of Providence* (Providence, 1843).

TILLINGHAST, GEORGE. Appointed ensign in U.S. infantry (1790); ensign in army (1786), captain in 16th R.I. (1799–1800).

UPDIKE, DANIEL E. (1761–June 15, 1842). Appointed surveyor at North Kingstown (1790); lawyer; resided (1790) in Kingstown, R.I.; son of Lodowick and Abigail Gardiner Updike; married ———— Arnold (1799); member of R.I. General Assembly (1789–90, 1792); secretary of R.I. ratifying convention (1790); R.I. attorney general (1791); presidential elector (1796).

Source: Rogers, *The Biographical Cyclopedia of Representative Men of Rhode Island.*

South Carolina

AGNEW, ANDREW. Appointed collector at Beaufort (1790); resided (1790) in Beaufort, S.C.; married (1) Mary Albergotti (1752), (2) Mary Williams (1762), (3) Mary Nelson (1777). He owned 8 slaves in 1790.

Source: Joseph W. Barnwell and Mabel L. Webber, "St. Helena's Parish Register," *South Carolina Historical Magazine* 23 (1922): 10–11.

BEE, THOMAS (1740–Feb. 18, 1812). Appointed U.S. district judge (1790–1812); lawyer and planter; born in Charleston, S.C.; resided (1790) in Charleston; son of John and Susannah Simmons Bee; educated at Oxford; married (1) Susannah Holmes (1761), (2) Mrs. Sarah Smith McKenzie (1773), (3) Mrs. Susannah Bulline Shubuck (1786); served in the S.C. Commons House of Assembly (1762–65, 1772–75); member of S.C. Provincial Congress (1775–76); member of S.C. General Assembly (1776–79, 1782); lieutenant-governor of S.C. (1779–80); delegate to Continental Congress (1780–82); delegate to S.C. ratifying convention (1788), and voted for the Constitution. He owned 184 slaves in 1790.

Sources: Emily B. Reynolds and Joan R. Faunt, eds., *Biographical Directory of the Senate of the State of South Carolina, 1776–1964* (Columbia, S.C., 1964); "Historical Notes," *South Carolina Historical Magazine* 7 (1906): 104; "Records Kept By Colonel Isaac Hayne," *South Carolina Historical Magazine* 10 (1909): 234; "Records Kept By Colonel Isaac Hayne," *South Carolina Historical Magazine* 11 (1910): 99.

COGDELL, JOHN (Sept. 19, 1729–Nov. 16, 1807). Appointed collector at Georgetown (1790); merchant; born in N.C.; resided (1790) in Georgetown, S.C.; married Esther ————. He owned 41 slaves in 1790.

Source: Louise R. Johnson and Julia Rosa, "Inscriptions from the Churchyard of Prince George Winyah, Georgetown, South Carolina," *South Carolina Historical Magazine* 31 (1930): 293.

DICKINSON, JOSEPH (July 4, 1765–Mar. 1807). Appointed ensign in U.S. infantry (1791); son of David and Avis Dickinson; married Catherine Cudworth (1793); private in the Revolution, ensign in army (1791), commissioned lieutenant (1791), promoted to captain (1793), honorably discharged (1800).

Sources: Elizabeth H. Jervey, "Marriage and Death Notices from the City-Gazett and Daily Advertiser," *South Carolina Historical Magazine* 30 (1929):

249–50; "Register of the Independent Congregational (Circular) Church of Charleston, S.C.," *South Carolina Historical Magazine* 33 (1932): 31.

DRAYTON, WILLIAM (Mar. 21, 1732–May 18, 1790). Appointed U.S. district judge (1789–90); lawyer; born in S.C.; son of Thomas and Elizabeth Bull Drayton; studied law at Middle Temple in London; married (1) Mary Martin, (2) Mary Gates (c. 1780); chief justice of the province of East Florida (1767–76); resided in England during the Revolution (1777–80); judge of admiralty court; associate justice of S.C. Supreme Court (1789).

Source: E. A. Jones, *American Members of the Inns of Court* (London, 1924).

EVELEIGH, NICHOLAS (c. 1748–Apr. 16, 1791). Appointed comptroller of U.S. Treasury (1789–91); farmer; born in Charleston, S.C.; son of Samuel Eveleigh; educated in England; married Mary Shubrick (1774); captain in 2nd S.C. regiment (1775), colonel and deputy adjutant general (1777), resigned (1778); member of General Assembly (1781); delegate to Continental Congress (1781–82); served on state legislative council (1783).

Sources: Joseph W. Barnwell, "Correspondence of Hon. Arthur Middleton," *South Carolina Historical Magazine* 27 (1926): 3; "Records Kept By Colonel Isaac Hayne," *South Carolina Historical Magazine* 11 (1910): 103; Lothrop Withington, "South Carolina Gleanings in England," *South Carolina Historical Magazine* 11 (1910): 131.

HALL, GEORGE A. (d. Aug. 1, 1791). Appointed collector at Charleston (1789–91); merchant; son of John Hall; married Lois Mathews (1764); officer in a S.C. regiment; member of Charleston Committee of Correspondence (1774); member of S.C. Provincial Congress (1775–76); collector under state government (1776–89); a Federalist. He owned 19 slaves in 1790.

Sources: "Historical Notes," p. 103; Mabel L. Webber, "Marriage and Death Notices from the South Carolina Weekly Gazette," *South Carolina Historical Magazine* 19 (1918): 137; idem, "Josiah Smith's Diary, 1780–1781," *South Carolina Historical Magazine* 33 (1932): 198.

HUGER, FRANCIS (b. July 26, 1769). Appointed lieutenant in U.S. infantry (1791). Probably the son of Isaac and Elizabeth Chalmers Huger, he may have attained the rank of captain before resigning in 1801.

HUGER, ISAAC (Mar. 19, 1743–Oct. 17, 1797). Appointed U.S. marshal (1790); son of Daniel and Mary Cordes Huger; married Elizabeth Chalmers (1762); lieutenant-colonel in 1st S.C. (1775), colonel in 5th S.C. (1776), brigadier general in continental army (1779–83); member of S.C. Provincial Congress (1775, 1778); member of S.C. General Assembly (1782); member of Society of the Cincinnati.

Source: Reynolds and Faunt, *Biographical Directory of the Senate of the State of South Carolina, 1776–1964*.

KEAN, JOHN (1756–May 4, 1795). Appointed commissioner for settling accounts between U.S. and the states (1789); planter and merchant; born in Charleston, S.C.; resided (1790) in Beaufort, S.C.; married Susan Livingston (1786); officer in S.C. militia; member of S.C. General Assembly (1781); member of Continental Congress (1785–87); delegate to S.C. ratifying convention (1788), and voted for Constitution; appointed cashier of the Bank of the United States (1791–95); owned 50 slaves in 1790. In 1791, Kean wrote Washington that, because of his financial problems, he would like a more permanent government office.

Source: C. S. Williams, *John Kean of the Continental Congress from South Carolina* (New York, 1911).

MOTTE, ISAAC (Dec. 8, 1738–May 8, 1795). Appointed naval officer at Charleston (1789–95); planter; born in Charleston, S.C.; resided (1790) in Charleston; son of Jacob and Elizabeth Martin Motte; married (1) Anne Smith (1763), (2) Catherine Deas (1776), (3) Mary Broughton (1777); lieutenant in Seven Years' War, lieutenant-colonel in 2nd S.C. (1775), colonel (1776), brevet brigadier general (1783); member of S.C. General Assembly (1772, 1778–80); served in S.C. Provincial Congress (1774–76); S.C. Privy Council (1779–80); delegate to Continental Congress (1780–82); member of S.C. ratifying convention (1788), and voted for Constitution. He owned 12 slaves in 1790.

Source: Reynolds and Faunt, *Biographical Directory of the Senate of the State of South Carolina, 1776–1964.*

NEUFVILLE, JOHN (Oct. 31, 1727–July 29, 1804). Appointed commissioner of loans (1790–93); merchant; born in Charleston, S.C.; resided (1790) in Charleston; son of John and Elizabeth Marston Neufville; married Elizabeth Moore (1750); member of S.C. General Assembly (1776–78); served on S.C. Privy Council (1779); owned 11 slaves in 1790. He suffered financial setbacks as a result of the Revolution.

Source: Reynolds and Faunt, *Biographical Directory of the Senate of the State of South Carolina, 1776–1964.*

PINCKNEY, THOMAS (Oct. 23, 1750–Nov. 2, 1828). Declined appointment as U.S. district judge (1789); lawyer, diplomat, and planter; born in Charleston, S.C.; resided (1790) in Charleston; son of Charles and Elizabeth Lucas Pinckney; attended Oxford (1768); studied law at Middle Temple, London; married (1) Elizabeth Motte (1779), (2) Mrs. Frances Motte Middleton (1797); captain in 1st S.C. (1775), major (1778–81); governor of S.C. (1787–88); presided over S.C. ratifying convention (1788); member of S.C. General Assembly (1791); minister to England (1792–96); envoy to Spain to negotiate boundary treaty (1794–95); Federalist vice presidential candidate (1796); Federalist member of U.S. House of Representatives (1797–1801); president of S.C. Society of the Cincinnati (1806–26). He owned 118 slaves in 1790.

Source: John B. O'Neall, *Biographical Sketches of the Bench and Bar of South Carolina,* 2 vols. (Charleston, S.C., 1859), vol. 2.

PRINGLE, JOHN J. (July 22, 1753–Mar. 17, 1843). Appointed U.S. district attorney (1789–92); lawyer; born in Charleston, S.C.; resided (1790) in Charleston; son of Robert and Judith Mayrant Pringle; studied law at Middle Temple, London; married Susannah Reid (1784); secretary to Ralph Izard in France (1778–79); member of S.C. General Assembly (1785–88); delegate to S.C. ratifying convention (1788), and voted for Constitution; S.C. attorney general (1792–1808); declined position as U.S. attorney general (1805); president of board of trustees of College of Charleston (1811–15). He owned 22 slaves in 1790.
Source: O'Neall, *Biographical Sketches of the Bench and Bar of South Carolina*, vol. 2.

ROBERTS, RICHARD BROOKE (Dec. 15, 1757–Jan. 18, 1797). Appointed captain in U.S. infantry (1791); soldier; son of Owen and Anne Frazer Cattell Roberts; married Van Braam Hongheest (1785); captain in 4th S.C. (1779), aide-de-camp to General Lincoln (1782), captain in army (1791), promoted to major in 3rd sub-legion (1793).
Source: "Order Book of John Faucheraud Grimké," *South Carolina Historical Magazine* 16 (1915): 124–25.

RUTLEDGE, JOHN (Sept. 1739–July 23, 1800). Appointed associate justice of Supreme Court (1789–91); lawyer and planter; born in Charleston, S.C.; resided (1790) in Charleston; son of John and Sarah Hext Rutledge; studied law at Middle Temple, London; married Elizabeth Grimké (1763); member of S.C. General Assembly (1762, 1784–89); S.C. attorney general (1764–65); delegate to Stamp Act Congress (1765); member of Continental Congress (1774–76, 1782–83); president of S.C. (1776–78); governor of S.C. (1779–82); delegate to Constitutional Convention (1787); chief justice of S.C. (1791–95); appointed chief justice of U.S. Supreme Court (1795), but nomination rejected by Senate; a Federalist. He owned at least 243 slaves in 1790.
Sources: Richard Barry, *Mr. Rutledge of South Carolina* (New York, 1942); O'Neall, *Biographical Sketches of the Bench and Bar of South Carolina*, vol. 1.

STEVENS, DANIEL (Nov. 7, 1746–Mar. 20, 1835). Appointed supervisor of distilled spirits (1791–1801); merchant and planter; born in Charleston, S.C.; resided (1790) in Charleston; son of Samuel and Catherine Willard Stevens; educated under Rev. George Whitefield; married (1) Patience Norton (1767), (2) Sarah Sprocole (1770), (3) Mrs. Mary Adams (1779); 1st sergeant in Charleston artillery (1776), 2nd lieutenant, 1st lieutenant (1781), later a captain; member of S.C. House of Representatives (1781–82, 1784–90); sheriff of Charleston (1782–84); member of S.C. Senate (1790–91); delegate to S.C. ratifying convention (1788), and voted for Constitution. He owned 6 slaves in 1790.
Source: Reynolds and Faunt, *Biographical Directory of the Senate of the State of South Carolina, 1776–1964.*

WEYMAN, EDWARD (c. 1730–Jan. 6, 1793). Appointed surveyor at Charleston (1789–93); mechanic; resided (1790) in Charleston; married Rebecca ———;

captain in S.C. artillery (1779–81); member of Charleston Committee of Correspondence (1774); member of S.C. Provincial Congress (1775–76); served in S.C. General Assembly (1782). He owned 8 slaves in 1790.

Sources: "Papers of the Second Council of Safety of the Revolutionary Party in South Carolina, November 1775–March 1776," *South Carolina Historical Magazine* 4 (1903): 13; "Historical Notes," p. 104; Mabel L. Webber, "Marriage and Death Notices from the City Gazette," *South Carolina Historical Magazine* 21 (1920): 153; Richard Walsh, *The Writings of Christopher Gadsden, 1746–1805* (Columbia, S.C., 1966).

Vermont

CHIPMAN, NATHANIEL (Nov. 15, 1752–Feb. 15, 1843). Appointed U.S. district judge (1791–93); lawyer and jurist; born in Salisbury, Conn.; resided (1790) in Rutland, Vt.; son of Samuel and Hannah Austin Chipman; B.A. Yale (1777); married Sarah Hill (1781); ensign (1777), later commissioned 1st lieutenant, resigned (1778); member of Vt. General Assembly (1784–85, 1806–9, 1811); assistant justice of Vt. Supreme Court (1787); chief justice (1790, 1796, 1813–15); delegate to Vt. ratifying convention (1791), and supported ratification; member of U.S. Senate (1797–1803); a Federalist; professor of law at Middlebury College (1816–43). He published *Sketches of the Principles of Government* (Rutland, Vt., 1793).

Sources: Daniel Chipman, *Life of the Honorable Nathaniel Chipman* (Boston, 1846); Dexter, *Biographical Sketches of Graduates of Yale College*, vol. 3; Chilton Williamson, *Vermont in Quandary: 1763–1825* (Montpelier, Vt., 1949).

JACOB, STEPHEN (Dec. 7, 1755–Jan. 27, 1817). Appointed U.S. district attorney (1791); lawyer; born in Sheffield, Mass.; resided (1790) in Windsor, Vt.; son of Richard and Thankful Jacob; B.A. Yale (1778); read law with Theodore Sedgwick; married Pamela Farrand (1779); member of Vt. General Assembly (1781, 1788, 1794); state attorney (1786); member of Vt. constitutional convention (1793); member of Governor's Council (1796–1801); judge of Vt. Supreme Court (1801–3); a Federalist; trustee of Dartmouth College (1802–17). Jacob owned a large amount of land and several slaves.

Sources: Walter H. Crockett, *Vermont, The Green Mountain State*, 5 vols. (New York, 1921) vol. 5; Dexter, *Biographical Sketches of Graduates of Yale College*, vol. 4.

KEYES, STEPHEN (Dec. 6, 1753–c. 1804). Appointed collector at Allburg (1791); merchant; born in Pomfret, Conn.; resided (1790) in Burlington, Vt.; son of Stephen and Abigail Peabody Keyes; married Elizabeth Sheldon; 1st lieutenant in 10th continental infantry (Conn.) (1776); town selectman of Burlington (1793–96). He sought the position of collector because of business losses in the Canadian market.

Sources: Abby M. Hemenway, *Vermont Historical Gazeteer*, 5 vols. (Brandon, Vt., 1868–91), vol. 1; Asa Keyes, *Genealogy of Keyes* (Brattleboro, Vt., 1880); Williamson, *Vermont in Quandary: 1763–1825*.

MORRIS, LEWIS R. (Nov. 2, 1760–Dec. 29, 1825). Appointed U.S. marshal (1791–1801); politician, businessman, and landowner; born in Scarsdale, N.Y.; resided (1790) in Springfield, Vt.; son of Richard and Sarah Ludlow Morris; married (1) Mary Dwight (1786), (2) Theodotia Olcott, (3) Ellen Hunt; aide to Generals Schuyler and Clinton, later brigadier and major general in Vt. militia; a commissioner for Vt. statehood (1791); attended Vt. ratifying convention (1791), and voted for Constitution; member of Vt. constitutional convention (1793); Representative to Vt. General Assembly (1795–96, 1803, 1805–6, 1808); elected to U.S. House of Representatives as Federalist (1797–1803). His abstention in the 1800 House vote gave Jefferson the Presidency.
Sources: Crockett, *Vermont, The Green Mountain State*, vol. 2; Fischer, *The Revolution of American Conservatism*; John A. Williams, ed., *The Public Papers of Governor Thomas Chittenden* (Barre, Vt., 1969).

SMITH, NOAH (Jan. 27, 1756–Dec. 23, 1812). Appointed supervisor of distilled spirits (1791); lawyer; born in Suffield, Conn.; resided (1790) in Bennington, Vt.; B.A. Yale (1778); married Chloe Burrall (1779); state attorney (1779, 1781); representative to Vt. General Assembly (1789); elected judge of Vt. Supreme Court (1791, 1798–1801); member of Governor's Council (1798–1801). Imprisoned early in the nineteenth century for debt, he was later released because of "mental derangement."
Sources: Crockett, *Vermont, The Green Mountain State*, vol. 5; Dexter, *Biographical Sketches of Graduates of Yale College*, vol. 4.

Virginia

ARCHER, ABRAHAM. Appointed collector at York (1789); married ———— Lypscomb; collector and naval officer at York (1781–87); member of York Common Council (1787); mayor of York (1790); collector at Portsmouth (1794). In 1786, Archer had $657 in continental loan certificates.
Source: Mary Newman, "The Borough of York," *Tyler's Quarterly Historical and Genealogical Magazine* 9 (1927): 95–96.

ARCHER, RICHARD. Declined appointment as ensign in U.S. infantry (1791); married Mary C. Cocke (1794); ensign in 3rd Va. (1780–83).
Source: "Marriage Bonds in Amelia County," *William and Mary Quarterly*, series 1, 15 (1907): 255–64.

BARTLETT, BENJAMIN. Appointed surveyor at Suffolk; married Alec Evans (1782); captain in the Revolution.

BEDINGER, DANIEL (1766–1818). Appointed surveyor at Norfolk and Portsmouth (1790–97); merchant; born in Pa.; son of Henry and Magdelene von Schlegal Bedinger; married Sarah Rutherford (1791); 1st lieutenant in 11th Va. (1776–77); naval officer and deputy collector at Norfolk (1783–89); superintendent of Norfolk Navy Yard (1802–8); a Republican. In 1786, Bedinger had $139 in continental loan certificates.
Source: Mrs. Danske B. [Caroline] Dandridge, *George Michael Bedinger: A Kentucky Pioneer* (Charlottesville, Va., 1909).

BLAIR, JOHN (1732–Aug. 31, 1800). Appointed associate justice of Supreme Court (1789–96); lawyer; born in Williamsburg, Va.; son of John and Mary Munro Blair; attended William and Mary; studied law at Middle Temple in London; married Jean Balfour; member of Va. General Assembly (1766–70); member of Va. Privy Council (1776–77); judge and later chief judge of court of appeals (1778–80); judge of high court of chancery (1780); delegate to Constitutional Convention (1787), and signed Constitution; member of Va. ratifying convention (1788), and voted for Constitution.
Source: Hugh B. Grigsby, *Convention of 1776* (Richmond, 1853).

BOWNE, THOMAS. Appointed collector at South Quay (1790); 2nd lieutenant in 10th Va. (1777), captain (1778–83).

BRAXTON, CORBIN. Appointed surveyor at Richmond (1789–90); son of Carter and ——— Corbin Braxton; attended William and Mary (c. 1777); member of Va. General Assembly (1784); searcher at West Point (1788).
Source: T. M. Robinson, "Robinson Family," *William and Mary Quarterly*, Series 1, 18 (1910): 182.

CALL, RICHARD (d. Sept. 28, 1792). Appointed major in U.S. infantry (1791); 1st lieutenant in 1st continental dragoons (1776), captain (1776), major (1782–83), major in army (1791); member of Society of the Cincinnati.

CAMPBELL, DAVID H. R. (1750–1812). Appointed judge of Southeast Territory (1790–96); lawyer; born in Va.; son of David and Mary Hamilton Campbell; married Elizabeth Outlaw; major in Va. militia (1776–80); chief judge of state of Franklin; member of Tenn. constitutional convention (1796); judge of Tenn. Supreme Court (1797–1807); judge of Mississippi Territory (1810–12).
Sources: Moore, *Tennessee, The Volunteer State*, vol. 2; Margaret C. Pilcher, *Historical Sketches of the Campbell, Pilcher and Kindred Families* (Nashville, 1911).

CARRINGTON, EDWARD (Feb. 11, 1748–Oct. 28, 1810). Appointed U.S. marshal (1789) and supervisor of distilled spirits (1791–94); lawyer; born in Cumberland County, Va.; son of George and Anne Mayo Carrington; married Mrs. Elizabeth Ambler Brent (1790); lieutenant-colonel in 1st continental artillery

(1776); deputy quartermaster general (1780–83); member of Va. General Assembly (1784–85, 1788–89); member of Continental Congress (1785–86); favored adoption of Constitution; mayor of Richmond (1806, 1809); a Federalist; member of Society of the Cincinnati; foreman of jury during trial of Aaron Burr (1807).

Source: Garland E. Hopkins, *Colonel Carrington of Cumberland* (Winchester, Va., 1942).

CATLETT, GEORGE (May 6, 1743–Sept. 13, 1814). Appointed surveyor at Port Royal (1790); son of William and Sarah Garnett Catlett; married (1) Eleanor Johnson (1798), (2) Lucy Beverley Buckner; lieutenant in navy (1776–81); searcher of vessels at Port Royal (1788).

Source: William C. Stubbs and Mrs. William C. [Elizabeth] Stubbs, *A History of Two Virginia Families* (New Orleans, 1918).

DAVIS, STAIGE (d. 1815). Declined appointment as surveyor at Urbanna (1789); son of Andrew and Lucia Staige Davis; married Elizabeth Minor Gardner (1791).

Source: Charles B. Heinemann, *Davis Families of the Southern States*, 2 vols. (Chicago, 1938).

GAINES, BERNARD. Appointed ensign in U.S. infantry (1791), lieutenant (1792), captain in 1st sub-legion (1794), resigned (1799).

GATEWOOD, PHILEMON. Appointed naval officer at Norfolk (1789); son of Thomas and Ann Cunningham Gatewood; married (1) Dorothy Edmundson (1778), (2) Dorothy Dix; deputy naval officer at Norfolk before 1789.

Source: "Edmundson Family," *Tyler's Quarterly Historical and Genealogical Magazine* 7 (1926): 188.

GIBBONS, JAMES. Appointed surveyor at Petersburgh (1789); son of Thomas and Anne Eppes Gibbons; served in Va. militia during the Revolution. In 1792, Gibbons wrote Washington requesting another position in order to better support his family.

Source: E. T. C., "Gibbons Family," *William and Mary Quarterly*, series 2, 2 (1922): 136.

GIBBS, WILLIAM. Appointed collector at Folly Landing (1789); naval officer at Accomack (1787–89).

GRIFFIN, CYRUS (July 16, 1748–Dec. 14, 1810). Appointed commissioner to Creek Indians (1789) and U.S. district judge (1789–1810); lawyer; born in Richmond County, Va.; son of Leroy and Mary Ann Bertrand Griffin; studied law at University of Edinburgh (c. 1770) and at Middle Temple, London (c. 1773); married Lady Christiana Stuart (1770); member of Va. General Assembly (1777–78, 1786–87); member of Continental Congress (1778–81,

1787); president of Continental Congress (1788); judge of admiralty court (1780–87); a Federalist; presided over trial of Aaron Burr in 1807.

Source: Lyon G. Tyler, ed., *Encyclopedia of Va. Biography*, 5 vols. (New York, 1915), vol. 2.

HANSON, SAMUEL. Appointed surveyor at Alexandria (1789); B.A. University of Pennsylvania (1771); dismissed as purser in Navy Yard (1811).

HARRISON, RICHARD (1750–July 10, 1841). Appointed consul to Cadiz, Spain (1789–91); son of Daniel Harrison; married (1) Dolly ———, (2) Anne Smith; American agent in Spain under John Jay (1784–89); auditor of the U.S. Treasury (1791–1836).

Sources: Mrs. J. O. James, "Greensville Co. Marriage Bonds," *Virginia Magazine of History and Biography* 24 (1916): 305; "Notes from the Records of Brunswick County," *Virginia Magazine of History and Biography* 28 (1920): 165.

HETH, JOHN (d. Nov. 20, 1810). Appointed ensign in U.S. infantry (1790); ensign in 11th Va. (1777), 2nd lieutenant in 1st Va. (1781–83), ensign in army (1790), lieutenant (1791), captain in 3rd sub-legion (1792), honorably discharged (1802); member of Society of the Cincinnati.

HETH, WILLIAM (1735–Apr. 15, 1808). Appointed collector at Bermuda Hundred (1789–1802); farmer; born in Va.; son of John and Mary Mackey Heth; married (1) Rebecca Young, (2) Eliza Briggs; officer during French and Indian War, lieutenant (1775), major in 11th Va. (1776), lieutenant-colonel in 3rd Va. (1777), colonel (1778–83); a Federalist; member of Society of the Cincinnati. In 1786, Heth had $684.36 in continental loan certificates.

Source: B. Floyd Flickinger, ed., *The Diary of Lt. William Heth* (Winchester, Va., 1931).

HOPKINS, JOHN (c. 1757–Oct. 23, 1827). Appointed commissioner of loans (1789); merchant; married (1) Lucy Lyons, (2) Cornelia Lee (1806); colonel in Va. militia; commissioner of loans (1780–89).

Source: Walter L. Hopkins, *Hopkins of Virginia and Related Families* (Richmond, 1931).

HURT, JOHN (1752–1824). Appointed chaplain in U.S. army (1791); minister; born in Va.; married Sallie Franklin (1788); chaplain in 6th Va. (1776), brigade chaplain (1778–83), chaplain in army (1791), resigned (1794); member of Society of the Cincinnati.

Source: Dorothy F. Wulfeck, *Marriages of Some Virginia Residents, 1607–1800*, 6 vols. (Naugatuck, Conn., 1961–67), vol. 3.

JEFFERSON, THOMAS (Apr. 13, 1743–July 4, 1826). Appointed secretary of state (1789–93); statesman and politician; born at Shadwell, Albemarle County,

Va.; son of Peter and Jane Randolph Jefferson; graduate of William and Mary (1762); studied law under George Wythe (1762–67); married Mrs. Martha Wayles Skelton (1772); member of Va. General Assembly (1769–74, 1776–79, 1782); member of Continental Congress (1775–76, 1783–85); governor of Va. (1779–81); minister to France (1784–88); vice president of the U.S. (1797–1801); president of the U.S. (1801–9); a founder of the Democratic-Republican party; author of the Declaration of Independence; founder of the University of Virginia; author of Va. bill for religious freedom. In 1794, Jefferson owned 155 slaves and 60,647 acres of land.

Sources: Dumas Malone, *Jefferson the Virginian* (Boston, 1948); idem, *Jefferson and the Rights of Man* (Boston, 1951); idem, *Jefferson and the Ordeal of Liberty* (Boston, 1962).

KEMP, PETER (c. 1763–Aug. 1819). Appointed surveyor at Rappahannock (1790); married Hannah ——— (1784); captain in Va. state regiment (1779–81).

Source: "Marriage Bonds in Middlesex County," *William and Mary Quarterly*, series 1, 7 (1899): 193.

LAMBERT, DAVID (born c. 1754). Appointed surveyor at Richmond (1789); merchant; son of Josias Lambert; married (1) Sarah Stevens, (2) Nancy ———; lieutenant-colonel in Va. militia (1798); alderman of Richmond (1788); a Republican. In 1786 Lambert had $497.77 in continental loan certificates.

Source: Joseph S. Watson and David Watson, "Letters from William and Mary College, 1798–1801," *Virginia Magazine of History and Biography* 29 (1921): 178.

LEE, CHARLES (1758–June 24, 1815). Appointed collector at Alexandria (1789–93); lawyer; son of Henry and Lucy Grymes Lee; B.A. Princeton (1775); married (1) Anne Lee (1789), (2) Mrs. Margaret Scott Peyton; naval officer at Alexandria (1777–89); supported adoption of Constitution (1788); member of Va. General Assembly (1793–95); U.S. attorney general (1795–1801); a Federalist; a defense lawyer for Aaron Burr in 1807. In 1786, Lee had $499.92 in continental loan certificates.

Source: E. J. Lee, *Lee of Virginia, 1642–1892* (Richmond, 1895).

LINDSAY, WILLIAM (d. Sept. 1, 1797). Appointed collector at Norfolk and Portsmouth (1789–97); merchant; son of Robert and Susanna Lindsay; married Ann Calvert (1766); 2nd lieutenant in 1st continental dragoons (1777), captain in Lee's Battalion of Light Dragoons (1778). Joseph Jones recommended Lindsay to Washington and said that Lindsay needed a position in order to support his large family.

Source: Margaret I. Lindsay, *The Lindsays of America* (Albany, 1889).

MARSHALL, JOHN (Sept. 24, 1755–July 6, 1835). Declined appointment as U.S. district attorney (1789); lawyer and jurist; born in Germantown, Va.; son of Thomas and Mary Randolph Marshall; married Mary Ambler (1783); lieutenant in 3rd Va. (1776), captain (1777–81); member of Va. General Assembly (1780, 1782–88); member of Va. Executive Council (1782–95); delegate to Va. ratifying convention (1788), and voted for Constitution; commissioner to France (1797–98); member of U.S. House of Representatives (1799–1800); secretary of state (1800–1801); chief justice of U.S. Supreme Court (1801–35); a Federalist.

Source: A. J. Beveridge, *The Life of John Marshall*, 4 vols. (Boston, 1916–19).

MAURY, JAMES (b. before 1769). Appointed consul to Liverpool, England (1789–1831); son of James Maury; attended William and Mary; married (1) Catharine Armistead, (2) Emily Rutger; consul to Liverpool under Confederation government (1786–89). He owned $327 in continental loan certificates in 1786.

Source: William A. Maury, *John Walker Maury: His Lineage and Life* (Washington, D.C., 1916).

MOORE, JOHN SPOTSWOOD. Appointed surveyor at West Point (1789); married Mary Murry; searcher at West Point under state government before 1789. In his application, Moore said he was relatively poor and had a growing family.

Source: "Historical and Genealogical Notes," *William and Mary Quarterly*, series 1, 22 (1913): 69.

MUSE, HUDSON (d. July 5, 1799). Appointed collector at Tappahannock (1790); merchant; son of Daniel Muse; member of Va. constitutional convention (1776); naval officer on Rappahannock River (1782–89).

Source: "Memoranda from the Fredericksburg, Va., Gazette, 1787–1803," *Virginia Magazine of History and Biography* 13 (1906): 430.

NELSON, WILLIAM, JR. (d. Mar. 8, 1813). Appointed U.S. district attorney (1789); lawyer; son of William and Elizabeth Burwell Nelson; educated at William and Mary; married (1) Mary Taliaferro (c. 1779), (2) Abby Byrd; private in a Va. regiment (1775), major in 7th Va. (1776), lieutenant-colonel (1776–77); member of Va. Executive Council (1783); judge of General Court of Commonwealth; professor of law at William and Mary.

Sources: "The Will of Mrs. Mary Willing Byrd, of Westover, 1813, with a List of the Westover Portraits," *Virginia Magazine of History and Biography* 6 (1899): 357; "Will of Colonel William Byrd, III," *Virginia Magazine of History and Biography* 9 (1901): 81.

NOURSE, JOSEPH (July 16, 1754–Sept. 1, 1841). Appointed register of the Treasury (1789–1829); born in London, England; son of James and Sarah Fouace Nourse; married ———— Bull; military secretary to General Charles Lee

(1776); clerk and paymaster of the Board of War (1777–81); auditor of the U.S. Treasury (1781–89); vice president of American Bible Society for 25 years. He received $5,144 in certificates of the funded debt in 1790.

Sources: Maria Cook Nourse Lyle, "James Nourse of Virginia," *Virginia Magazine of History and Biography* 8 (1900): 200; Leonard D. White, *The Federalists* (New York, 1948).

PARKER, ALEXANDER (died c. 1820). Declined appointment as major in U.S. infantry (1789); soldier and planter; son of Richard Parker; married ———— Redman; ensign in 2nd Va. (1775), 1st lieutenant (1776), captain (1777–83), colonel in 5th U.S. infantry (1808), resigned (1809), major general in Va. militia (1812); member of Society of the Cincinnati.

Source: D. Parker, "The Parker Family," *Virginia Magazine of History and Biography* 6 (1899): 302.

PENDLETON, EDMUND (Sept. 9, 1721–Oct. 23, 1803). Declined appointment as U.S. district judge (1789); lawyer; born in Caroline County, Va.; son of Henry and Mary Taylor Pendleton; married (1) Elizabeth Roy (1742), (2) Sarah Pollard (1743); justice of the peace for Caroline County (1751); member of Va. General Assembly (1752–74); member of Committee of Correspondence (1773); delegate to Continental Congress (1774–75); president of Committee of Safety (1775); delegate to Va. constitutional convention (1776); speaker of Va. General Assembly (1776–77); chief judge of Va. Supreme Court of Appeals (1779–1803); presided over Va. ratifying convention (1788), and supported adoption of Constitution; a Republican.

Source: Robert L. Hilldrup, *The Life and Times of Edmund Pendleton* (Chapel Hill, 1939).

RANDOLPH, EDMUND J. (Aug. 10, 1753–Sept. 12, 1813). Appointed U.S. attorney general (1789–94); lawyer; born in Williamsburg, Va.; son of John and Ariana Jenings Randolph; graduate of William and Mary; married Elizabeth Nicholas (1776); aide-de-camp to General Washington (1776); member of Continental Congress (1779–82); governor of Va. (1786–88); delegate to Philadelphia Convention (1787), but did not sign Constitution; delegate to Va. ratifying convention (1788), and supported adoption of Constitution; member of Va. General Assembly (1788–89); secretary of state (1794–95); a Republican; chief counsel for Aaron Burr.

Source: D. R. Anderson, "Edmund Randolph," in *The American Secretaries of State and Their Diplomacy*, ed. S. F. Bemis, 10 vols. (New York, 1927–29), vol. 2.

RICHARDSON, ARCHIBALD (1756–Feb. 17, 1804). Appointed surveyor at Suffolk (1789–90); married Christiana Reddick (1780). He owned $58.82 in continental loan certificates in 1786.

Source: Wulfeck, *Marriages of Some Virginia Residents, 1607–1800*, vol. 6.

ROANE, CHRISTOPHER (1756–1828). Appointed surveyor at Bermuda Hundred (1789); married Elizabeth Temple Royal; captain in Va. militia (1777–82); searcher under state government before 1789.
Source: Wulfeck, *Marriages of Some Virginia Residents, 1607–1800*, vol. 6.

ROWLAND, ZACHARIAH (1745–May 28, 1802). Appointed surveyor at Richmond (1790); merchant.
Source: "Personal Notes," *William and Mary Quarterly*, series 1, 18 (1909): 115.

SAVAGE, GEORGE (d. June 4, 1824). Appointed collector at Cherry Stone (1789–90); naval officer and commissioner of wrecks under state government (1782–89).

SCOTT, RICHARD M. Appointed collector at Dumfries (1789); lawyer; naval officer under state government prior to 1789; delegate to Va. General Assembly.

SEAYRES, THOMAS. Appointed ensign in U.S. infantry (1790); lieutenant (1791); resigned (1791); son of Colonel John Seayres.

SHORT, PEYTON (Dec. 17, 1761–Sept. 1, 1815). Declined appointment as collector at Louisville (1789); pioneer; born in Surry County, Va.; son of William and Elizabeth Skipwith Short; brother of William Short; graduate of William and Mary; married (1) Maria Symmes (1787), (2) Mrs. Jane Churchill; member of Ky. Senate (1792–96).
Source: L. Belle Hamlin, ed., "Brief Accounts of Journeys in the Western Country 1809–1812," *Historical and Philosophical Society of Ohio Quarterly* 5 (1910): 3.

SHORT, WILLIAM (Sept. 30, 1759–Dec. 5, 1849). Appointed chargé des affaires to France (1789–92); diplomat and lawyer; born in Surry County, Va.; son of William and Elizabeth Skipwith Short; B.A. William and Mary (1779); major in Va. militia (1780–81); secretary to Jefferson in France (1785–89); minister to the Hague (1792–93); minister to Spain (1793–95); appointed minister to Russia (1808) but rejected by the Senate; one of the founders of Phi Beta Kappa; president of American Colonization Society.
Source: George G. Shackelford, "William Short: Jefferson's Adopted Son" (Ph.D. diss., University of Virginia, 1955).

SKIPWITH, FULWAR (1765–1839). Appointed consul to Martinique (1790–99); merchant; son of Fulwar and Marie Skipwith; cousin of William Short; married Evalina Barlie van den Cloaster; with Jefferson in Paris (1786); commercial agent in Paris (1800–1805); governor of West Florida (1810); a Republican.
Source: Henry B. Cox, *The Parisian American: Fulwar Skipwith of Virginia* (Washington, D.C., 1964).

SMITH, BALLARD (d. Mar. 20, 1794). Appointed captain in U.S. infantry (1790); soldier; ensign in 1st Va. (1776), 1st lieutenant (1777), captain-lieutenant (1779–83), captain in army (1790), promoted to major (1792).

SMITH, DANIEL (Oct. 1748–June 16, 1818). Appointed secretary of the Southern Territory (1790–96); surveyor and planter; born in Stafford County, Va.; son of Henry and Sarah Crosby Smith; attended William and Mary; married Sarah Ann Michie (1773); major (1777) and colonel (1781) in Va. militia, general in Tenn. state militia; member of N.C. ratifying convention (1789); member of first Tenn. constitutional convention (1796); member of U.S. Senate (1798–99, 1805–9); a Republican. He made the first map of Tennessee.
Source: St. George L. Sioussat, ed., *The Journal of Daniel Smith* (Nashville, 1915).

STEEL, JOHN. Appointed lieutenant in U.S. infantry (1790); ensign in 9th Va. (1777), 2nd lieutenant (1778), 1st lieutenant in 1st Va. (1781).

WELLS, JAMES. Appointed surveyor at Smithfield (1789); commander of Va. militia co. in 1794.

WILKINS, NATHANIEL. Appointed collector at Cherry Stone (1790); married Susanna Wilkins (1779); 2nd lieutenant in 9th Va. (1776), 1st lieutenant (1777–78). He lost his hand during the war and was in indigent circumstances in 1790.

WRAY, GEORGE, JR. (died c. 1810). Appointed collector at Hampton (1790); son of Jacob and Mary Ashton Wray; colonel in Va. militia (1807); commissioner for supervising presidential election of 1800; a Republican.

WRAY, JACOB (died c. 1797). Appointed collector at Hampton (1789–90); merchant; son of George and Helen Walker Wray; married Mary Ashton (1761); member of Committee of Safety (1774–75); naval officer and customs collector at Hampton under state government (1781–89).
Sources: Charles W. Coleman, "The County Committees of 1774–'75 in Virginia," *William and Mary Quarterly*, series 1, 5 (1896): 103; "Old Kecoughtan; or, Elizabeth City County," *William and Mary Quarterly*, series 1, 9 (1900): 128.

Miscellaneous

AULDJO, THOMAS. Appointed consul to Cowes (1790); a merchant and native of Cowes. The British objected to the commission of consul at the port of Cowes.
Source: Boyd, *The Papers of Thomas Jefferson*, vols. 17, 18.

CATHALAN, ETIENNE, JR. Appointed vice consul to Marseilles (1790); native of France and merchant at Marseilles, where he and his father, Etienne Cathalan, Sr., served as American agents during the Revolution. He was an acquaintance of Thomas Jefferson during Jefferson's service as American Minister to France, and his appointment was recommended by Jefferson.
Source: Boyd, *The Papers of Thomas Jefferson*, vols. 14, 16.

LA MOTTE, ———. Appointed vice consul to Havre (1790); native of France and merchant at Havre. He was an acquaintance of Thomas Jefferson during Jefferson's service as American Minister to France.
Source: Boyd, *The Papers of Thomas Jefferson*, vol. 15.

McLANE, DANIEL. Appointed lieutenant in U.S. artillery (1791); 2nd lieutenant in 3rd continental artillery (1776), 1st lieutenant (1778–83), lieutenant in army (1791), captain (1791), resigned (1793); member of Society of the Cincinnati.

PARISH, JOHN. Declined appointment as vice consul to Hamburg (1790); consul to Hamburg (1793–96).

POIREY, JOSEPH-LÉONARD. Appointed brevet captain (1790); member of King's Guard in France (1770); came to America in 1780 and served as military secretary to Lafayette; took part in battles of Petersburg, Jamestown, and Yorktown; returned to France with Lafayette (1788) and served as lieutenant in 1st battalion at Rohan; captain secretary general of Paris National Guard and staff officer to Lafayette (1789); secretary general of Paris troops (1792); honorary member of Society of the Cincinnati in France.
Source: Ludovic de Contenson, *La Societe des Cincinnati de France* (Paris, 1934).

SARMENTO, FRANCISCO. Nominated vice consul to Teneriffe (1790), but not approved by Senate; merchant; a Spaniard; married ——— Craig of Philadelphia; settled at Teneriffe in the Canary Islands.
Source: Boyd, *The Papers of Thomas Jefferson*, vol. 17.

STREET, JOHN (d. May 1, 1807). Appointed vice consul to island of Fayal (1790).

TURNER, GEORGE. Appointed judge of Western Territory (1790); a native of England and friend of George Washington; collaborated with Arthur St. Clair and John C. Symmes to overhaul territorial laws in 1795. In 1790, Turner had an interest in land speculation in the Northwest Territory.
Source: Beverley W. Bond, Jr., *The Foundations of Ohio* (Columbus, Ohio, 1941).

General Bibliography

MANUSCRIPTS

The George Washington Papers. Manuscript Division, DLC.

Letters of Application and Recommendation During the Administration of John Adams, 1797–1801. RG 59, M406, DNA.

Letters of Application and Recommendation During the Administration of Thomas Jefferson, 1801–1809. RG 59, M418, DNA.

Letters of Application and Recommendation During the Administration of James Madison, 1809–1817. RG 59, M438, DNA.

Miscellaneous Letters of the Department of State, 1789–1906. RG 59, M179, DNA.

Records of the Bureau of the Public Debt. RG 53, DNA.

Records of the Continental and Confederation Congresses and the Constitutional Convention. RG 360, M247, DNA.

Records of the Veterans Administration. RG 15, DNA.

PRIMARY SOURCES

Boyd, Julian P., ed. *The Papers of Thomas Jefferson.* 19 vols. Princeton, 1950–.

Burnett, E. C., ed. *Letters of Members of the Continental Congress.* 8 vols. Washington, D.C., 1921–38.

Fitzpatrick, John C., ed. *The Writings of George Washington from the Original Manuscript Sources, 1745–1799.* 39 vols. Washington, D.C., 1931–44.

SECONDARY SOURCES

Dexter, Franklin B. *Biographical Sketches of the Graduates of Yale College.* 6 vols. New York, 1896–1912.

Heitman, Francis B. *Historical Register and Dictionary of the United States Army.* Washington, D.C., 1903.

————. *Historical Register of Officers of the Continental Army.* Washington, D.C., 1914.

Johnson, Allen, and Malone, Dumas, eds. *Dictionary of American Biography.* 22 vols. New York, 1928–44.

Shipton, Clifford K., ed. *Biographical Sketches of Those Who Attended Harvard College.* 16 vols. [vols. 1–3 edited by John L. Sibley]. Boston, 1873–85, 1933–.

U.S. Congress, *Biographical Directory of the American Congress, 1774–1971.* Washington, D.C., 1971.

White, Leonard D. *The Federalists.* New York, 1948.

Wilson, James G., and Fiske, John, eds. *Appleton's Cyclopedia of American Biography.* 6 vols. New York, 1887–89.

State Bibliographies

CONNECTICUT

Connecticut Historical Society. *Collections.* 31 vols. 1860–1967.

Hoadly, C. J., and Labaree, L. W., eds. *Public Records of the State of Connecticut, 1776–1796.* 8 vols. Hartford, 1894–1951.

Hollister, Gideon H. *The History of Connecticut.* 2 vols. New Haven, 1855.

Purcell, Richard. *Connecticut in Transition, 1775–1818.* Washington, D.C., 1918.

DELAWARE

Cooch, Edward. *Delaware Historic Events.* Cooch's Bridge, Del., 1946.

Delaware Archives. 5 vols. Wilmington, Del., 1911.

Hancock, Harold B. "Loaves and Fishes: Applications for Office from Delaware to George Washington." *Delaware History* 14 (1970): 135–58.

Reed, Henry C., ed. *Delaware: A History of the First State.* 3 vols. New York, 1947.

Rodney, Caesar. *Letters To and From Caesar Rodney, 1756–1784.* Edited by G. H. Ryden. Philadelphia, 1933.

GEORGIA

Blair, Ruth, ed. *Some Early Tax Digests of Georgia.* Atlanta, 1926.

Candler, A. D., ed. *Revolutionary Records of the State of Georgia, 1769–1784.* 3 vols. Atlanta, 1908.

Davidson, Grace G., ed. *Early Records of Georgia, Wilkes County.* 2 vols. Macon, Ga., 1932.

Warren, Mary B. *Marriages and Deaths, 1763–1820.* Danielsville, Ga., 1968.

Wilson, Caroline P., ed. *Annals of Georgia: Important Early Records of the State.* New York, 1928.

KENTUCKY

Connelly, W. E., and Coulter, E. M. *History of Kentucky.* 5 vols. Chicago, 1922.

Filson Club. *Publications.* 21 vols. 1884–1906.

Gresham, John M., ed. *The Biographical Cyclopedia of the Commonwealth of Kentucky.* Chicago, 1896.

MARYLAND

Brumbaugh, Gaius. *Maryland Records: Colonial, Revolutionary, County and Church from Original Sources.* Baltimore, 1915.

Clark, Charles B. *The Eastern Shore of Maryland and Virginia.* New York, 1950.

Richardson, Hester D. *Side-lights on Maryland History.* 2 vols. Baltimore, 1967.

Scharf, J. T. *History of Maryland from the Earliest Period to the Present Day.* 3 vols. Baltimore, 1879.

Tilghman, Oswald. *History of Talbot County, Maryland, 1661–1861.* 2 vols. Baltimore, 1915.

MASSACHUSETTS

Colonial Society of Massachusetts. *Publications.* 1895–.

Davis, William T. *Bench and Bar of the Commonwealth of Massachusetts.* 2 vols. Boston, 1895.

Essex Institute. *Historical Collections.* 1859–.

Hatch, Louis C. *Maine: A History.* 3 vols. New York, 1919.

Hurd, D. Hamilton. *History of Essex County, Massachusetts.* 2 vols. Philadelphia, 1888.

Massachusetts Historical Society. *Proceedings.* 1791–.

New England Historic Genealogical Society. *New England Historical and Genealogical Register.* 1847–.

Smith, Frank, ed. *Memorials of the Massachusetts Society of the Cincinnati.* Boston, 1931.

Willis, William. *A History of the Law, the Courts and the Lawyers of Maine.* Portland, Me., 1863.

NEW HAMPSHIRE

Batchellor, Albert S., ed. *Early State Papers of New Hampshire.* Manchester, N.H., 1891.

Bouton, Nathaniel, ed. *Documents and Records Relating to the State of New Hampshire During the Period of the American Revolution, 1776–83.* Concord, N.H., 1874.

New Hampshire Historical Society. *Collections.* 15 vols. 1824–1939.

Tibbets, Charles W., ed. *The New Hampshire Genealogical Record.* 6 vols. Dover, N.H., 1904–9.

NEW JERSEY

American Historical Society. *Cyclopedia of New Jersey Biography.* Newark, N.J., 1916.

Craig, H. Stanley. *Cumberland County Genealogical Data.* Merchantville, N.J., 1938.

New Jersey Historical Society. *Proceedings.* 1847–.

Society of the Cincinnati in the State of New Jersey. Trenton, N.J., 1898.

NEW YORK

Flick, Alexander C., ed. *History of the State of New York.* 10 vols. New York, 1933–37.

New York Genealogical and Biographical Record. 1870–.

O'Callaghan, E. B., ed. *Documentary History of the State of New York.* 4 vols. Albany, 1849–51.

Werner, Edgar A. *Civil List and Constitutional History of New York.* Albany, 1889.

NORTH CAROLINA

Ashe, Samuel A. *History of North Carolina.* 2 vols. Greensboro, N.C., 1908.
Clark, Walter, ed. *State Records of North Carolina, 1777–1790.* 16 vols. Winston and Goldsboro, N.C., 1895–1905.
Davis, Charles L. *North Carolina Society of the Cincinnati.* Boston, 1907.
North Carolina Historical Review. 1924–.
Wheeler, John H. *Reminiscences and Memoirs of North Carolina.* Columbus, Ohio, 1884.

PENNSYLVANIA

Godcharles, Frederic A., ed. *Encyclopedia of Pennsylvania Biography.* 20 vols. New York, 1914–32.
Martin, J. H. *Martin's Bench and Bar of Philadelphia.* Philadelphia, 1883.
Pennsylvania Magazine of History and Biography. 1877–.
Reed, George I., ed. *Century Cyclopedia of History and Biography of Pennsylvania.* Chicago, 1904.

RHODE ISLAND

Arnold, James N. *Vital Records of Rhode Island, 1636–1850.* Providence, 1907.
Polishook, Irwin H. *Rhode Island and the Union.* Evanston, Ill., 1969.
Rhode Island Historical Society. *Collections.* 34 vols. 1827–1941.
Rogers, L. E., ed. *The Biographical Cyclopedia of Representative Men of Rhode Island.* Providence, 1881.
Smith, Joseph J., ed. *Civil and Military List of Rhode Island.* 3 vols. Providence, 1900–1907.
Staples, W. R. *Rhode Island in the Continental Congress.* Providence, 1870.

SOUTH CAROLINA

O'Neall, John B. *Bench and Bar of South Carolina.* 2 vols. Charleston, S.C., 1859.
Reynolds, Emily B., and Faunt, Joan R., eds. *Biographical Directory of the Senate of the State of South Carolina, 1776–1964.* Columbia, S.C., 1964.
South Carolina Historical and Genealogical Magazine. 1900–.

VERMONT

Crockett, Walter H. *Vermont, The Green Mountain State.* 5 vols. New York, 1921.
Deming, Leonard. *Catalogue of the Principal Officers of Vermont, 1778–1850.* Middlebury, Vt., 1851.
Williamson, Chilton. *Vermont in Quandary: 1763–1825.* Montpelier, Vt., 1949.

Virginia

Palmer, W. P., et al., eds. *Calendar of Virginia State Papers and Other Manuscripts . . . Preserved . . . at Richmond.* 11 vols. Richmond, 1875–93.

Tyler, Lyon G., ed. *Encyclopedia of Virginia Biography.* 5 vols. New York, 1915.

————. *Tyler's Quarterly Historical and Genealogical Magazine.* 33 vols. 1919–52.

Virginia Magazine of History and Biography. Richmond, 1893–.

William and Mary Quarterly. 1944–.

U

United Indian Nations, speech of, 146–48
Updike, Daniel, E., 83, 86, 541–42
Urbanna, Virginia, port officer of, 16, 21
U.S. prisoners in Algiers. *See* Algiers, U.S. prisoners in

V

Varick, Richard, 247, 250
Vergennes, Gravier de, 328, 340, 341, 346
Vermont: biographies of nominees from, 546–47; judicial officers of, 127, 129; port officers of, 127, 129; supervisor of distilled spirits of, 128, 130
Vermont Statehood Bill [S–19], 127
Vice president, 134
—letters to on
  Algiers, U.S. prisoners in, 436
  militia, nominations for, 479
  tonnage on French vessels, 419
Vienna, Maryland, port officer of, 15, 20
Virginia: biographies of nominees from, 547–55; commissioner of loans of, 89; governor of (*see* Randolph, Beverley, letter from); judicial officers of, 44, 47, 59, 62; militia officers from, 72, 73, 99, 132; port officers of, 15–16, 21–22, 22, 23, 28, 38, 40, 68, 69, 70, 99, 100; supervisor of distilled spirits of, 129, 130; troops from, 237

W

Wabash Confederates, speech of, 146–48
Wade, John, 132, 537
Walker, Benjamin, 14, 18, 525
Walker, John (N.C.), 57, 60, 531
Walker, John (Va.), vote recorded, 97
Walton, George. *See* Georgia, governor of
Walton, Jess, 174
Ward, Artemas, 383, 384
Warren, Rhode Island, port officer of, 83
Warren, Winslow, 132, 514
Washington, George, 248, 250, 455, 485, 492, 497, 500, 502, 523, 525, 533, 553, 56. *See also* President
Washington, North Carolina, port officer of, 58, 60
Washington district, militia officers of, 119, 475–77
Watson, William, 13, 19, 514
Webb, William, 14, 19, 514
Wells, James, 15, 21, 555
Wells, Nathaniel, letter to, 368–73

Wentworth, Joshua, 128, 129, 517
Western Territory. *See* Northwest territory
West Point, Virginia, port officer of, 16, 21
Weyman, Edward, 16, 22, 545–46
Whale oil, acts of France on, 354–55, 416–19
Whipple, Joseph, 13, 19, 517
White, Colonel James, 191
White, Dr. James, 202
White, ———, 196
Whittemore, Samuel, 13, 18, 514
Wilkins, Nathaniel, 69, 70, 555
Willett, Marinus, 247, 250
Williams, Isaac, Jr., 159
Williams, Otho H., 15, 20, 499
Williams, Thomas, 58, 61, 531
Williamson, Hugh, 475; letter from, 477
Wilmington, Delaware, port officer of, 15, 20
Wilmington, North Carolina, 68; port officers of, 57, 60
Wilmot, Montague, 385, 386
Wilson, James, 44, 45, 537
Wilson, William, 159
Wilucot, Montague. *See* Wilmot, Montague
Windsor, North Carolina, 58; port officer of, 68
Wingate, Paine: attendance, 126; vote recorded, 92, 93, 112 n
Winn, Richard, 202
Winton, North Carolina, port officer of, 58, 61
Wiscassett, Massachusetts, port officer of, 14, 19
Wolcott, Oliver, Jr., 4, 38, 39, 137, 139, 160, 488
Wolf[e], John, 440
Woods, John, 177
Wray, George, Jr., 68, 555
Wray, Jacob, 15, 21, 68, 555
Wyandots, 41, 144, 151; treaties with, 4, 6, 37, 38, 42, 43, 140–43, 152–60
Wyatt, Lemuel, 40, 514
Wylly, Richard, 89, 494
Wyllys, John P., 51, 72, 131, 488–89
Wynns, William, 58, 61, 531–32

Y

Yard, James, 120, 121, 537
Yeocomico River, Virginia, port officer of, 16, 21
York, Massachusetts, port officer of, 14, 19
Yorktown, Virginia, port officer of, 16, 21
Young, Robert, 15, 21, 38

Z

Ziegler, David, 51, 72, 131, 537–38